A SOCIAL HISTORY
OF MUSIC
FROM THE
MIDDLE AGES TO BEETHOVEN

HENRY RAYNOR

A Social History of Music

FROM THE
MIDDLE AGES TO BEETHOVEN

A CRESCENDO BOOK

TAPLINGER PUBLISHING COMPANY

NEW YORK

This edition first published in 1978 by
TAPLINGER PUBLISHING CO., INC.
New York, New York

Copyright © 1972, 1976 by Henry Raynor
All rights reserved. Printed in the U.S.A.

Published by arrangement with Schocken Books, Inc.,
200 Madison Avenue, New York, N.Y. 10016

Library of Congress Catalog Number: 78-58318
ISBN 0-8008-7238-X

Contents

Preface

This book is an attempt to fill some part of the gap between the normal and necessary history of music which deals with the development of musical styles and the general history of the world in which composers carried out their function. It does not attempt the highly speculative task of linking the work which composers produced to the general currents of thought to which their age exposed them. Its more humble duty is to follow the course of music along its developing relationships to the patrons or audiences for whom it was originally written, the singers or instrumentalists who were first expected to perform it and the means at the composer's disposal for placing his work before the public. There are, of course, points at which the composer's submission to the general current of thought is explicit and of importance to his position as a member of society empowered to act as its mouthpiece, but I have made no effort to go beyond these into any fascinating conjectures about the place of a Mozart, a Beethoven or a Wagner in the thought of their days. There are, too, points at which the social function of music has a clear bearing on questions of style which would otherwise remain obscure. I have not tried to follow stylistic questions beyond their obvious bearings on the theme of a history which is primarily concerned with the composers' efforts to perform a social function; other questions are approached only from the point of their bearing on this neglected dimension of the history of music.

Haydn died in 1809, having lived within a system unchanged since music had first been recognised as a social necessity: Beethoven, who died eighteen years later, lived as a modern composer lives, on the earnings of his work in a free market. That is the development which this book sets out to trace, from the establishment within the Christian Church of the first musical organisations to have a clearly recorded history. It considers the changing functions of church musicians, the place of music in the courts of the Renaissance and of eighteenth-century Germany and Austria, noting the expansion of the composer's work brought about by the invention of printing and the growth of amateur music-making organisations, the consequent development of music publishing and the gradual creation of an international audience. It attempts to follow these developments until, combined with the social and political results of the Napoleonic War, they turned the composer from a humble functionary whose one advantage was his close contact with an audience which found his work socially necessary into a freelance whose life was one of inevitable insecurity.

My indebtedness to very many people is extremely great. All my friends have borne with me throughout this book's elephantine gestatory period, listening patiently, commenting aptly, criticising constructively and encouraging judiciously. I am specially grateful to many, some of them unknown to me except by correspondence, who have put their own work aside at my request to clarify problems, suggest solutions or guide me to sources of information within their own fields of specialist knowledge:

Dr. Peter Burke (University of Sussex)
Dr. Otfried Büthe (Stadt-und Universitäts Bibliothek, Frankfurt)
Mr. A. E. F. Dickinson, Mr. Julian Herbage, Mr. H. C. Robbins Landon, Dr. Eric Mackerness (Sheffield University)
Mr. Stephen Pratt (Headmaster, King Edward VI School, Stratford-upon-Avon)
Mr. Christopher Raeburn, the late Dr. Ernst Roth, Dr. Stanley Sadie, Mr. Fritz Spiegl, Professor Denis Stevens (Columbia University, New York)
Mr. Harry Vickers (House Governor, Chetham's Hospital School, Manchester)
Mr. John S. Weissmann, Mr. W. S. Wright (Librarian, Dulwich College). Frau Hildegard Dubrau, of Munich, has hunted for difficult or inaccessible sources of information.

The exemplary patience, co-operation and encouragement of Mr. John M. Thomson, Mr. David Sharp and Mr. John G. Pattisson, who have been very closely and professionally concerned with seeing that this book actually got written, and of Messrs. Barrie and Jenkins in general, are things for which my gratitude cannot end with the completion of my task.

HENRY RAYNOR

I Musical History—Problems and Sources

History is probably the most complex of studies. For ease of digestion we break it down into various constituents and plan to study political history or social history, economic or military history; we think of the history of art or of science, of literature or of music. As soon as the student approaches any of these nicely departmentalised sections of the subject, however, he finds that he cannot completely apprehend it without reference at least to some of the others. Can we, for example, understand the development of trade and industry after the Reformation without getting to know something about the revolutionary attitude to money which grew from the reformation and made the advance of capitalism possible by removing a good deal of the stigma from usury? We cannot understand the history of Napoleon's rise and fall if we are not able to refer, amongst other things, to Britain's industrial, and therefore financial, power.

History, however much we departmentalise it, tends always to become a single study, its boundaries extremely vague because of its vast comprehensiveness. It is after all the record of human activities in general, and human activities are necessarily interdependent; because they overlap, the unavoidable departmentalisations inevitably falsify.

The history of music is, first of all, part of the vast, unwieldy complex that is history; we can break it into its own departments of harmony, form and textures. The history of instruments is obviously and inextricably bound to this, for a history of forms involves the way in which the various instruments were used at different times both alone and in ensemble. The history of various musical organisations—orchestras, choirs, opera houses—and the history of their patrons, from emperors, archdukes and electors down to the general public of today, who buy or refuse to buy tickets, all contribute to the history of music. Music can come to life only in society; it cannot exist, any more than a play can exist, merely as print on a page, for it presupposes both players and listeners. It is, therefore, open to all influences that society and the changes in social beliefs, habits and customs, can exert.

What we tend to call 'musical history' is the story of musical styles and their development. On the most elementary level this is traced through the sham history which can be deduced from the biographies of composers, which show how A is linked to D, F and H through his influence on B, who influenced D, and on both C and E, who in their turn influenced both F and G, whose influence was the decisive factor in the development of H.

This is only sham history because it simplifies a vast, complex development

until it becomes no more than an evolutionary chain prolonging itself through a
series of personal relationships and personal decisions. It creates a succession, if
not a hierarchy, of composers upon whose individual activities the entire structure of western music is made to depend. Composers of the second rank whose
work was of enormous importance and therefore of enormous influence in the
past, those whom Tovey dismissed rather patronisingly as 'Interesting Historical
Figures', do not appear. The hierarchy of such Victorian musicians as, for
example, the Reverend W. H. Haweis, who wrote historically, makes little or
no room for them. The pattern which has established itself in the historians'
minds needs no Bachs other than Johann Sebastian, so that Carl Philipp Emanuel
Bach, who did as much as anyone to establish sonata form, and Johann Christian
Bach, one of the formative influences on the development of Mozart, seem to
have no importance to them.

The limitations of such an approach to the development of music are obvious
enough. The variety of the influences exerted on Mozart's music, many of them
from comparative nonentities, do nothing to explain a style which develops its
own personality through so vast a synthesis as that which Mozart achieved; it
creates its own inaccuracies, suggesting that a genius as great as Schütz must have
meant something to Bach simply because he lived before Bach, although the only
possible contact between Bach and the music of Schütz was limited to the
possibility that as a chorister of Lüneburg he may have sung some of the small
number of works by Schütz collected in the library of the *Michaeliskirche*, and it
neglects the obvious and quite audible fact that nothing Bach wrote sounds in
the least like Schütz's music.

To look for the influence of major composers on the work of all other major
composers is to see Berlioz as a unique megalomaniac. His own writings make it
clear that he worshipped Beethoven's symphonies and was enthusiastic about the
operas of Mozart and Weber as well as those of composers like Spontini—an idol
whose clay feet we probably take for granted without listening to his music. But
the 'Babylonian, Ninevitish', fantastic Berlioz of the *Symphonie Fantastique*, the
Messe des Mortès, the *Symphonie Funbre et Triomphale* and the *Te Deum* has
nothing to do with any of his musical gods so far as the demand for vast forces and
sensational effects is concerned. Such music is within a definite but disregarded
French tradition, inherited from the public and ceremonial music of the French
Revolution, which itself descended from the ceremonial court music of the age
of Louis XIV.

For that matter it is possible to doubt whether any composer ever exerted a
more powerful influence on the history of music than Muzio Clementi, who to
all intents and purposes created the piano style which Beethoven developed.

If then we cannot create a history of music from the biography of composers
alone, we cannot do so simply by enlarging the field of study until all composers
whose works have survived are included. The difference between the piano style
of Haydn and Mozart and that of Beethoven is not simply that Clementi inter-
vened and, for example, wrote a piano sonata which provided a ground plan for

Beethoven's *Sonata Pathétique*. Beethoven's piano style, which descends from Clementi, is far richer than that of Mozart and Haydn in *sostenuto* and *legato* effects which would have been impossible on the instruments with which Haydn and Mozart were familiar. The development of valved brass instruments in the early nineteenth century, no less than Beethoven's transfer of the trombone from the church to the concert hall, had an important influence upon the way in which composers handled the orchestra. Without an iron-framed piano and double escapement the technique which made possible Liszt's stylistic developments would not have happened.

Nevertheless a consistent stylistic history of music is not only possible but has come to be the accepted way of tracing and explaining the development of the art. Such histories proliferate: stylistic history is necessarily critical history, for it is our way of explaining our present concerns through uncovering their relationship to the music of the past. Its emphasis, the intellectual pattern it proposes to establish, changes with developments in taste. In the late nineteenth century its purpose was first to accommodate the music of Wagner and then to resolve the battle between the followers of Brahms and those of Wagner. Since then the historians of music have investigated the places to be allotted within the tradition of music to Bruckner and Mahler; more recently, they have shown that Schoenberg and Webern stand in direct relationship to the music of the past. Stylistically, the next historical step is that which relates the work of Boulez, Stockhausen and their contemporaries to the past.

The mutability of stylistic history does not invalidate what it has to say. A history of histories of music—a task which some scholar may one day find it worth while to undertake—would demonstrate quite clearly the function of historians as, indirectly, historians of taste. To trace the way in which certain composers have been treated in the type of history books to which we are most indebted and with which we are most familiar is to see how the historian is involved in the movement of taste. To read of Brahms as a stalwart, restrained and classical composer is to be surprised, and to examine the evidence, drawn chiefly from orchestral works, is not to be convinced, because we are conscious throughout the symphonies and concertos of extreme and exciting tensions between the form and the themes and melodies it contains or at times circumscribes.

If we wonder how the writers of the past, who treated other and earlier composers so much more sensitively and acutely, seemed to hear Brahms's work so insensitively (whether they approved of his 'classicism' as a bulwark against chromatic excess and formal chaos, or disliked it as a stumbling block in the way of a richer and more emotionally responsive art), we need to remember that the judgements involved were made by authorities not really aware of the work of Brahms as a *Lieder* composer or a writer of lyrical piano pieces. Before the 1880s songs were entirely domestic music, and the reputation of Brahms remained partial and biased until his *Lieder* were well known by the public. Whether or not the historians whose view of the composer we have mentioned were aware of them, that is to say had read them in score and played or sung them in order to grasp this great and important aspect of his work, they had little opportunity to hear them in the concert hall.

It is easy to find a number of other cases in which the natural bias of stylistic history clearly shows itself. Consider Burney's treatment of sixteenth- and seventeenth-century music, especially of the work of Purcell, and the sublime self-confidence with which, in the name of correctitude, he alters the examples he prints, removing things in which we today find disturbing acerbities and stabbing poignancy. For centuries Dufay was an academic bogeyman strangling the art of at least a generation in the multitudinous tentacles of a wantonly elaborated technique; any recent history of music, however, will allow him an extremely high place amongst the composers of the past.

The treatment of eighteenth-century music by the authorities of the nineteenth demonstrates the attitudes of one age to the works of another. Schumann found in Mozart's G minor Symphony, to us one of the most desperate and forceful of works, 'a flowing, soaring grace'. Berlioz dismissed the symphonies and concertos of Mozart as the necessary hack work of a great musical dramatist. Wagner could find nothing more in the symphonies of Haydn than a childish playing with notes. Even the reactionary Hanslick, writing of *Parsifal* in 1882, suggested that what the opera needed was 'a naïve composer, possibly a kind of Mozart';[1] the adjective baffles the modern reader.

A composer is always the severest critic of those composers of no particular use to him as a stimulus, so that what the literary-minded romantic composers said of their predecessors puts the case at its most extreme. If Burney and Hawkins represent the eighteenth-century conviction that the art of the Enlightenment is the peak of perfection towards which all the work of the past had struggled, the critic-composers of the nineteenth century expressed the equally deep conviction that there is an essential dichotomy between energy and passion of expression on the one hand, and balance and perfection of form on the other. A readable, factually accurate and liberal-minded English historian, not given to the wholesale dismissal of major works, illustrates in a more generous way the same nineteenth-century doctrine: 'In dramatic power he [Joseph Haydn] was deficient; it was in fact, foreign to that easy cheerfulness of his character which makes itself felt in all his works.' The same author, James E. Matthew,[2] writes eulogistically not only of Mendelssohn but also of Spohr, accepts Wagner as a great but difficult composer, and refers to Berlioz as 'a master of orchestration . . . these works [Berlioz's symphonies] contain many beautiful passages; but his writing frequently degenerates into a noisy vulgarity which it is difficult to qualify with the name of music. In addition to the works mentioned, he wrote an oratorio, *L'Enfance du Christ*, a comparatively sane work.'

Stylistic history is necessarily critical history. The historian who sets out to prove a historical point, or to use history to demonstrate or prove his general

[1] Eduard Hanslick: *Music Criticism, 1846–99*, translated and edited by Henry Pleasants. Penguin Books, 1963.
[2] James E. Matthew: *A Manual of Music History*. London, 1892.

musical beliefs, must select and organise his material, and distribute the necessary emphasis in the way that most clearly demonstrates his doctrine. History is not merely a chronological record of events; it is an explanation of the past through the present and of the present through the past. Therefore stylistic history does not become less necessary though it is written to show what its author wishes to show, an aspect of truth which he may take to be the whole truth. It manifests the past as the past stands in relation to certain later activities; the past it shows may not be our past but it is as real a past as ours. Once history sets out to interpret the past, it may not select the facts it uses—any deliberate selection of the convenient and disregard of the awkward is obvious enough to rule it at once out of court—but by laying its own emphases where it thinks they should go, it creates its own pattern of causes, events and consequences. We read it not to be told the final unassailable truth but in order that, knowing what it has to say we may establish from it and from the other interpretations at our disposal our own truth.

Unfortunately, music is not written and does not exist in a vaccum. The composer, whether or not he likes to recognise the fact, lives in some relationship to his age and a community, for even the most inaccessible of ivory towers is only a negative relationship to his age and his community. He is also, whether he accepts or rejects the music of his predecessors, influenced by all the music that is accessible to him. To be sufficiently aware of a type of music to detest it is to be influenced by it. This network of relationships and the extensions and developments of style and technique which it brings about are sufficiently tangled to permit all the legitimate interpretations which have been provided for us, but interpretations only reshuffle the kaleidoscope; they do not fix it in any pattern we can accept as the final truth.

It is obvious, however, that when we trace the way in which the vocabulary, grammar and syntax of music have developed, we reveal more clearly a variety of problems which stylistic history is not equipped to answer. Music, unless it is no more than a purposeless doodling in sounds, has its place in the general history of ideas, for it is, if it is in any sense intellectual and expressive, influenced by what is going on in the world, by political and religious beliefs, by habits and customs or by their overthrow; it has its influence, perhaps veiled and subtle, on the development of ideas outside music.

In one sense this is the most stimulating aspect of musical history.

We like to consider the actual changes to music itself which can be linked with, for example, the movement of its centre of gravity from the church to the court, with the intellectual excitements of the Reformation, with the rise of liberalism, with the nationalist politics of the second half of the nineteenth century. A Schütz or a Bach, for example, differs from a Perotin or a Palestrina in that he feels himself to be not merely a messenger delivering in his own way and his own language a text which he has received but an interpreter privileged to offer his gloss upon words which it is his duty to explain. *Eli, Eli, lama sabachthani*, in the *St. Matthew Passion*, is a moment of exegesis in which Bach offers a heretical explanation of Christ's words 'My God, my God, why hast thou forsaken me?' The accompanying strings, which have added sweetness and intensity to Christ's words, give way startlingly to the naked continuo; the Godhead has departed. It is the liberal Beethoven who cries out to embrace the millions, having, according to Goethe, ploughed his way hat on head past the emperor; it is the unorthodox socialist Wagner who analyses the morality of power and the free-thinker Berlioz who creates in sound the eschatological terrors of judgement and the incredible simplicities of the birth of Christ, just as the freemason Mozart found a wit and a morality amongst servants superior to that of their masters and a Turk more magnanimous than the Christians. It is not necessary to subject *The Marriage of Figaro* to intense analysis almost bar by bar, as Sigmund Levarie did,[1] to realise that if da Ponte's libretto won acceptance by emasculating the inflammatory derision of Beaumarchais' play, the opera exists in the atmosphere which, only five years after its first performance, was to precipitate the French Revolution and turn Europe upside-down. The work is no less a revolutionary manifesto than, on the level of Shaw's *The Perfect Wagnerite*, is *Der Ring der Nibelungen*.

There are a vast number of necessary questions to which stylistic history provides no answer. The romantic movement created a new alliance between music and literature; the German *Lied* became an important art form long before the song recital made it a useful way of popularising its composer's outlook and abilities; the programme symphony and the symphonic poem can be seen—and the view seems to be completely valid—as a device to enable the listener to make contact with the composer's mind, as do the landscape symphonies of Mendelssohn. Such questions are crucial to our understanding of musical history. How far they can be answered, or how far they are invitations to speculation, it is hard to say.

A history which attempts to account for music as an aspect of European thought is so obviously a desirable addition to our stock of musical knowledge that various writers have attempted it. Their materials however are usually suspect; the most direct approach to their task is the creation and listing of analogies with the other and more explicit arts, to see to what extent truths proved in their discussion of literary, political, philosophical, religious and social history are equally true of music. There is singularly little material available which could be described as purely musical; Mozart's letters explain how he will contrive effects that will delight his audience, Haydn's and Beethoven's show how publishers should be dealt with; their successors are equally business-like and equally concerned not with aims but with practicalities. Even Berlioz drops into mere practicality when he talks about his own music or his conducting of other people's. Beethoven explained that he introduced trombones into the orchestra because 'they make a better sound'. 'Better' is a useless word until we know for what purpose 'a better sound' is required; 'a better sound' in a Prince's

[1] Sigmund Levarie: *Le Nozze di Figaro, a Critical Analysis*. University of Chicago Press, 1952.

music room is not necessarily 'a better sound' in a large concert hall; 'a better sound' for an oratorio is not 'a better sound' for a comic opera. The trouble with composers' *dicta* is that they regard their purposes as self-evident or simply inexpressible.

We have little firm internal evidence, that is evidence which comes directly from the music itself or from a composer's exegesis of his work, to enable us to show how the work fits into the world of ideas. Bach's religious thought can be deduced from cantatas, passions, chorale preludes and church music in general in so far as it is possible to deduce further from this body of work a system of imagery which relates his work in general to the ideas of his church music. We know that Mozart intended the reconciliation at the end of *The Marriage of Figaro* to be taken completely seriously; Count Almaviva's 'Contessa, perdono' is a sublimely religious solemn chorale-type melody. If *The Magic Flute* seems, as an unallegorically minded past believed it to be, a rather absurd pantomime its overture insists that it be viewed as an earnest and rather solemn affair, and yet nobody seriously believes that the tone of the overture denies that of the opera. The point of the four semibreves—C, D, F, E—which are the pivot of the last movement of the *Jupiter Symphony* is not easy to discover although they are obviously very important to the composer. They have a similar function in the development section of the first movement of the B flat Symphony (K.319), and the same phrase recurs at each repetition of the word *Credo* in the *Missa Brevis* in F (K.116). It appeared in the first symphony he wrote (K.16) as no more than a useful polyphonic formula. At the heart of Mozart's musical creed was a belief in tonality, and from that point onwards, anything we have to say about this key phrase, as about Beethoven's triumphant or consolatory themes climbing up a major triad, is simply speculation; it may be stimulating; it may even be revealing, but it is simply an individual's interpretation, in the light of his knowledge of the bulk of the composer's work, his general musical experience and his sensitivity, of what the composer has placed before him.

At the same time, however, music must exist socially. It is written down so that people other than its composer can play it. The bulk of it presupposes the creative and the interpretative efforts of two, three or as many as a hundred performers; there are some works which demand the services of vastly more musicians. Most music presupposes, too, the attention of the audience. When and to what extent a composer is consciously communicating, consciously transmuting experience or ideas into music for the delight of others, or to share with them whatever occupies or even obsesses his mind, is often obscure. A study of audiences and attitudes presupposed by the music created for them is of some importance. The Catholic Church approved of music which did not obtrude itself too forcefully upon its hearers; the authorities of the Counter-Reformation approved of the work of Palestrina not because of its perfection of style and its suavely fine richness of melody but because it is reasonably possible for the relatively unmusical to regard it as an undistracting and emotionally pleasing way of treating the text of the Mass. Congregations, however, like singers, are rather likely to prefer something more square, more symmetrical, a parodied version of *L'Homme Armé* or *O Westron Wynd* or something far more sentimental, like the pseudo-plainchant *Missa de Angelis* or Gounod's *Messe Solennelle*; they can even put the turbulent imagination of Byrd into the same pigeon hole as the serenity of Palestrina. Protestant audiences listened to church music from quite a different point of view; the impassioned rhetoric of Schütz—and it has its equivalents in Catholic music—would irritate any audience which did not take it for granted that a composer's version of Holy Writ is not only admissible but also interestingly important.

The court audience, too, is interesting. At Salzburg both Leopold and Wolfgang Mozart were apparently expected to produce entertainment music. Frederick the Great was obviously uninterested in a large number of types of music; it was not simply that he wanted to play the flute but also that he wanted to listen to a sort of music which is formal, mannered, civilised and restrained; the greatest composer in his service, the almost extravagantly expressive C. P. E. Bach, was given very little encouragement. There is no evidence that Haydn was actually encouraged to conduct expressive experiments at Eszterhaza, and it is possible to believe that he stopped writing *Sturm und Drang* symphonies rather suddenly because his princely employer did not wish to be disturbed; but he was still free to take liberties, like the use of folk song and gypsy-type melodies in symphonic and chamber works. Such behaviour would have been unthinkable at Versailles, Potsdam or Stuttgart. Consciousness of the wishes of his audience, the chief member of which was his employer, was one of the composer's essential duties.

Mozart, who for the last passionately active ten years of his life had no real employer except the public, was quite clear about the necessity to surprise and delight those who listened to him. There is no suggestion that he worked away in a state of lonely abstraction. Amongst the multitude of precise calculations which went into the composition of his works was, his letters suggest, an accurate estimation of the taste of its recipient and its intended audience.

To judge by his letters, the basis of Mozart's aesthetic was 'effectiveness', a complex idea in which were subsumed the quality of musical ideas, the skill with which they were treated to exploit both their intrinsic qualities and the special abilities of the performers, and the impact of all these upon the audience. The creator's personal satisfaction and highest reward was to achieve this complex, and a work's failure to hold an audience's attention was one of the very many things about which he wrote scathingly. A composer, in Mozart's view, wrote for an audience which it was his business to 'please'; the notion of a retreat into an ivory tower seems never to have entered his head even at his most desperate when he might have considered himself rejected by those to whom he had offered delight.

Beethoven was left to appeal to a general public whose tastes were unpredictable and whose reactions to novelty could not be accounted for. Nevertheless, although he was inclined to treat his friends amongst the aristocracy with far less ceremony than Haydn, and had no anxious authority to whom he felt in any way bound to describe his musical activities as Mozart described his compositions to his father, his ceaseless attack on the widest possible range of the public is something which no one who considers his relations with publishers can fail to notice. From the time of his migration to Vienna he almost bombarded publishers with works—not only the tremendous outpouring of masterpieces for piano, string quartet and orchestra, but also slighter, immediately accessible works addressed to the amateur player.

The ivory tower, in brief, was built in the nineteenth century. It was never leased by Berlioz, Wagner, Brahms or Mahler, who explained to his wife shortly after their marriage that his opponents were 'the philistine and the immature',[1] and described with delight the success of his Second Symphony in Lvov. It is not until Schoenberg that we find a major composer rejecting the audience as a more or less distasteful necessity. 'I also hold the view that a work doesn't have to live, i.e., be performed, at all costs, either, if it means losing parts of it that may even be ugly or faulty but which it was born with. The second question is that of consideration for the listener. I have exactly as little of this as he has for me. All I know is that he exists, and in so far as he isn't indispensable for acoustic reasons (since music doesn't sound well in an empty hall), he's only a nuisance.'[2] It is, of course, fair to point out that in 1918 Schoenberg was a completely neglected composer struggling with unforgettable courage and integrity against total neglect; whether his attitude to audiences would have been the same had his struggles been less terrible is a nicely interesting point of speculation. This letter is, perhaps, the utterance of a composer despairing of his music's power to do what we have always understood as its duty of creating some sort of communication or fellowship in experience between composer, players and audience. Beethoven seems to have realised that it would take some time for popular taste to catch up with his later quartets, but he presupposed that they existed to be heard by all and sundry; and it is worth mentioning that, if only for economic reasons, Schoenberg took all the steps he could to see that his works were heard whenever possible.

Music arises in part at any rate from the attitudes of mind which the composer shares with, or which he opposes to, his contemporaries. He writes for player or singers, often for specific individuals of particular talents and attainments. He addresses what he writes to an audience, even if only to what we sometimes feel to be half-imagined, ideal audience with special sympathies and responses. He reaches his audience in particular ways: by means of performance if possible, through publication if not. The way in which he approaches this audience can be, and must almost necessarily be, influenced by these social considerations.

Until the nineteenth century the musician had a definite if not exalted place in society and a clearly defined social function, writing and playing the music he was paid to write and play. So long as he was competent to do the work expected

[1] Alma Mahler: *Gustav Mahler, Memories and Letters.* John Murray, 1946. Letter of December 14, 1901.
[2] Letter to Alexander von Zemlinsky, February 23, 1918.

of him, his livelihood was assured and his audience, except in very unusual circumstances, was known to him. The nineteenth century deprived him of both place and function, and it is still through nineteenth-century eyes that we see the whole course of musical history. If we are less inclined than our grandparents and their fathers to pay much attention to the idea of the artist as prophet or as 'unacknowledged legislator of the world', we still fail to take into account the economic and social pressures upon him. His social rejection in the nineteenth century—he could be above or beneath society but not part of it—can be interpreted as a freedom beyond that of the ordinary man who makes money by regular work, for the composer was under no obligation to any work other than that which his nature overridingly compelled him to do. He pays—or so we are traditionally taught to believe—for his freedom not only by the nervous agonies of creation but also by the uncertainty and probably poverty of his life and the loneliness of his endless effort to create or to find the audience he needs, which in reality is the community of which he is by nature a member.

If this is a romantic simplification of the composer's life in the nineteenth century and a complete misstatement of his career in any earlier period, it still presupposes that music is a social art in that it requires a community of players to address it to a community of listeners. It takes for granted that the musician is by the nature of his art dependent for the real existence of his work upon the efforts of a society to play and or sing his work. Even the apparently abstract *Die Kunst der Fuge*—in Bach's manuscript merely notes with no directions as to even the instrument or instruments which were to play them—sounds compelling, exciting and beautiful in almost any instrumental arrangement.

No less than anyone else the composer has to earn his living. When he lived in an age which was socially organised in such a way that it offered him the possibility of regular employment as a composer, it automatically created the conditions with which he was expected to comply. Not only was he writing for performance by a permanent orchestra and chorus whose collective and individual capacities he knew; he was also writing to please a patron whose tastes were equally clear to him. A composer at Potsdam in the reign of Frederick the Great would hardly, whatever the quality of his work, have won a hearing for a series of Mannheim-type symphonies: C. P. E. Bach's works were rejected by Frederick not in spite of but because of their brilliant originality; Frederick's intense but narrow love for opera was formed in his youth on the works of such composers as Handel, Telemann and Hasse, so that he never came to terms with Gluck. Similarly, if the patron were himself a player, like Frederick or Prince Nikolaus Eszterhazy, there would be no point in composing for him music that passed beyond his power. Music to accompany a banquet cannot be the same thing as music for possibly concentrated listening after dinner. A court orchestra, augmented when necessary by the trumpeters and drummers of its employer's troops, occupied its *Kapellmeister's* attention also as an ensemble without brass. The nature of a man's employment necessarily creates the conditions which he must observe.

A social system like our own—where a composer cannot simply as a composer achieve secure, regular employment—creates conditions no less binding upon the composer who has to earn a living. The unestablished composer—there seems to be no better term for him—has to win an audience from the general body of music lovers, and their tastes are not necessarily less limiting than the prejudices of an employer. In an age like ours, with music perhaps too widely available, he is in the unenviable position of having to be noticeably and externally 'original' in every work if he is to win the detailed consideration of critics, although he knows that public taste is by and large conservative. What he cannot do economically is to reject this audience (which necessarily includes those who buy copies of, say, his piano works to play to themselves for their own pleasure) even though, like Schoenberg, he may wish to reject it spiritually.

Thus it is not possible, except when we need to study some particular aspect or aspects of the art in isolation, really to separate the works a composer writes and the style in which he writes them from the facilities available for their performance and promulgation even when the composer is a freelance whose money is earned by the performance of his work. In one way or another society creates conditions in which he functions as best he can. Our musical thinking has been so completely dominated by the nineteenth-century conceptions of art as pure activity, occupying only the higher strata of its creator's consciousness and unaffected by such lower strata as those which reckon up the bills and consider the possibility of paying them, that we do not consider the composer's relationship to the musical world in which he must, as employee no less than as freelance, secure performance and publication.

One aspect of the composer's problem—and it seems unnecessary to try to estimate its precise weight in the composer's mind or the extent of its influence upon his products—is to find the way to create, and at the same time to communicate within the framework of what is not totally unintelligible to his audience, what it is his concern or compulsion to create. If he wishes or is under some sort of spiritual compulsion to create work which entirely transcends a musically trained audience's musical experience—and not even Beethoven in the later quartets, or Wagner when *Tristan* grew beyond his first partial conception of its nature as something closely akin to a pot-boiler, did this—he does so at considerable risk. If like Haydn he admits into court music elements which seem to belong elsewhere—the plainsong themes of, for example, the *Lamentation Symphony*, the rustic folk music and gypsy tunes which were never far from his mind, or the tragic expressiveness of the *Trauer*, *Abschieds* or *Passione* Symphonies—he is courting rebuke. If, like Schoenberg or Webern, he develops a style and technique foreign to almost all his potential audience, he is not really in a position to grumble if he has to develop heroic qualities of fortitude and patience while he waits for listeners to discover how, by mastering a new musical syntax, to listen to his work. It is not only composers but singers and instrumentalists too who must earn their livings, and concert-giving organisations, justifying their work even when they do not want to finance it by the size of the audience they draw, have to depend upon the performance of works which will not intimidate or repel potential patrons.

Nevertheless the relationship between composer and audience is not necessarily one which leaves the creator fettered to the task of satisfying a static taste and a musical appetite altogether inferior to his own. Every important body of work—the symphonies and string quartets of Haydn and Beethoven, for example, and the operas of Wagner—shows great development of style through the way in which it tackles the task of communicating matters of growing profundity and intensity. Such a series of works carries with it an audience ready to grow as the composer grows; the story of Wagner's career is not the story of a heroically prophetic voice crying in the wilderness and heard only by an awed posterity; the heroism was that of a leader on a battleground over which adherents and opponents—a vigorous insurgent opposition led by the composer confronting an embattled establishment convinced of its musical rectitude—fought with considerable ferocity. Some of the money with which the *Festspielhaus* in Bayreuth was built came from public subscription.

On the other hand the story of the composer who despite genius is a complete failure as a money-maker—that of Schubert, for instance—does not tell us about the world's inability to recognise greatness, but only about Schubert's inability, because of the class into which he was born and the musical and social organisation of the Austria of his day, to take command of the limited means at his disposal for the propagation of his music. Without any public triumphs in his youth to create an appetite for more mature masterpieces as they arrived, devoting a good deal of his time to the new, intimate form of *Lieder* which could not make a living for him in spite of the unfailing stream of great songs he produced during the last dozen years of his life, Schubert suffered the inevitable fate of a composer not great enough as a performer to subsidise his creative work. In addition, while he belonged to a class which had little access to the spheres which could influence upon Viennese musical organisations on his behalf, he was at the same time a composer enlarging the concepts of instrumental and orchestral forms in a manner revolutionary enough to antagonise the musical establishment in a city notoriously conservative. He was not simply writing, or even prepared to write, music which gently tickled the ears of his easy-going contemporaries.

When we grant that a composer has to earn his living even when the economics of the musical world compel him, as they compelled Berlioz, to do so for much of the time through activities only on the fringe of his art, and the corollary that the necessity of earning a living imposes its own conditions upon him, the account of his actual, practical life becomes a matter of considerable musical importance. It is an aspect of an element of musical history which we tend to overlook. In so far as the conditions are imposed by the musical organisations—using the term in its widest legitimate sense to denote orchestras and choirs often linked to such extra-musical organisations as church, court or municipality, amateur players and singers and the whole structure of the musical printing or publishing mechanisms—through which he had to work, the study of such organisations, their influence on him and the way in which his work modified them, becomes historically important. This dimension of history may affect style no more than obliquely, but it demonstrates the conditions out of which styles and traditions arise.

To study the historical development of the practicalities of music making, the evolution of musical organisations and the conditions they have imposed upon composers, together with the means at the composer's disposal for answering them, is to study, from a historical point of view, the place of music in society. Music cannot exist in isolation from the normal course of history and the evolution of social life, for art in part rises—in whatever mysterious ways we are unable satisfactorily to analyse—from the life its creator lives and the thoughts he thinks. It exists to be played and to be heard, not as sound in its creator's head or as symbols written or printed on paper but as actual physical sound made by and for those who wish to gain satisfaction from what the composer offers them. Through the attempt to trace the actual, analysable, creative relationship between the musician and society, not through speculations which try to find the relationship between the composer's extra-musical religious, political or social ideas—all the fascinating imponderables which have their unanalysable effect on his work—but through the interplay between the composers and the means at their disposal for promulgating and popularising their music, we find light cast upon the development of styles. Such quite factual concerns as the actual instruments at his disposal, the nature of the audience for which the work was intended and the length of time for which its attention could be taken for granted naturally affect the way in which he writes, they are musically as well as socially important.

This adds several dimensions to the conventional idea of the history of music. It casts out communicating lines to the general course of life and it places the historian in a similar position to that of Charles Burney: 'The prospect widens as I advance. 'Tis a chaos to which God knows whether I shall have life, leisure, or abilities to give order. I find it connected with Religion, Philosophy, History, Poetry, Painting, public exhibitions and private life. It is, like gold, to be found though but in small particles, even in lead ore, and in the coal mine; which are equivalent to heavy authors and the dust and rubbish of antiquity.'[1]

We could, without great difficulty, widen the field of enquiry which perturbed Burney by its extensiveness; politics and the rise and fall of states have influenced the course of music, for any art requiring the services of a large number of skilled performers needs the support of considerable wealth, and for this reason the economic triumphs and vicissitudes of nations, rulers and their cities also affects the work of musicians. Music has even been decisively influenced by the buildings for which it was written; the music of the baroque age owed an incalculable amount to the domes of the nave and transepts of St. Mark's in Venice, and to the cathedral's use of antiphonal choirs and organs. Virgilio Mazzocchi's compositions for St. Peter's Rome exploit the acoustic properties of the dome and the

---

[1] Quoted in Lonsdale: *The Life of Charles Burney*. Letter William Mason: May, 1770.

tower above it when choirs were positioned in each of them as well as in the
choir stalls. Orazio Benevoli's Mass for the consecration of Salzburg Cathedral is,
in score, a work of singular harmonic naïvety which may well, under the conditions of the performance for which the composer planned, be greatly modified by
the way in which the resonance of the building influenced the performance. There
is nothing intrinsically startling in a great fanfare in E flat which eventually
subsides with a crash on D, but played by four groups of brass instruments
widely separated from each other in an extremely resonant building they make
the opening of the *Tuba mirum* of Berlioz's *Requiem* into a thing of resplendently
awesome majesty. Similarly, Berlioz calculated the antiphony of organ in the
Te Deum to suit the precise acoustic conditions of the church of St. Eustace in
Paris, so that only a building of the same size, with the organ at the same distance
from the orchestra and, ideally, with as many people sitting in the space between
them, can provide a performance which precisely fulfils the composer's intention.

The whole social, political and practical background to musical history is
necessary knowledge if we are clearly to understand not only what was done by a
large number of composers in a large number of cases, but also why it was done.
No more than stylistic history can such an account of music explain the incidence
of genius among musicians; it would take a genius no less great than Mozart to
tell us why the Statue Music in *Don Giovanni*—which can easily be analysed—is
for all its simplicity perhaps the most terrifying music yet written, or why the
tenor's cry '*Et homo factus est*', in the *Credo* of Beethoven's Mass in D, is a
radiant shout of triumph in the major after the minor forebodings of the humilia-
tion of coming down from heaven and the tragedy of betrayal, suffering and
death. In the earlier Mass in C, eleven years before, being made man had not
been a triumph but a descent into tragedy. No sort of history explains the vision
of genius; it can only show the conditions which gave genius its direction and to
which it reacted.

Musical history, even when it has been written for 'the general reader' who
has no wish for specialised information, hastens to neglect these considerations.
The historian, where he finds a convenient practical explanation for some purely
musical development, naturally uses it; he does not look for a coherent and
developing background to the history of music. The nineteenth-century historian
was chiefly concerned with the underlying 'meaning' and 'message' of art; the
twentieth-century historian is puritanically concerned with the arts as things in
themselves, so that stylistic developments in music seem, to him, to tell all the
essential story. To discover a more rounded account of music, so that its history
becomes part of the general human experience, it is necessary to go back to the
eighteenth century; amongst the vast mass of material which Hawkins gathered
into unwieldy heaps and which Burney deployed with a delightful elegance of
both thought and style, is as much as could be easily gathered about the essential
background to musical activity. Hawkins's insatiable appetite for documentation
provides his *History* with all the evidence of medieval practice which he came
across and his first-hand account of early court life, racy, sardonic and amusing,

is invaluable because it explains the music which was played. Burney too cannot imagine music in isolation from the course of common life; he points out the connection between economic strength and artistic development; music, in his history as in Hawkins's, is made by and for people.

To attempt to relate the development of music to the world in which it exists and to consider the relationship of the composer to the economic and social world in which he lived is to answer a variety of questions which, although they are crucial, are not answered by the stylistic historian. Though Britten found in chamber opera a means of deepening and intensifying his style why, after the great success of the full-scale *Peter Grimes*, did he first turn to the smaller, more esoteric form? Why, in the mid-twentieth century, did the 'conservative' musical establishment vanish as a force which tended to block the 'progressive' composer's way? Why did the international style of the first half of the nineteenth century break down into a variety of nationalist schools? Why was Beethoven a reasonably successful freelance composer while Mozart, a mere quarter of a century before him, died in extreme poverty although his music was phenomenally popular? There are a vast number of such questions, important as well as interesting to the musician, which may be answered by a social history of music but which do not come into the field of enquiry cultivated by the stylistic historian.

2 The Medieval Church

Any history of music in the early days of Christian Europe necessarily begins with the church, for only the church provides any information which can be verified from precise records. Music as an element in worship, filling a necessary place in the ritual, has to be correctly sung. A mistake in the music of worship, like a mistake in word, gesture or movement, was held to have invalidated the celebration which had therefore to be repeated. For this reason music had to be taught and its correct forms memorised; methods of notation had to be devised and developed to assist the musicians' memory, so that the history of the development of western notation is a history of the attempts of ecclesiastical musicians to ensure the accuracy of the rite.

At the same time it was only the church which possessed the intellectual resources and the facilities for scholarship which made possible not only the notation of melodies but also the codification of techniques and any rationale of styles. What is on record, available for our study, comes from the church because outside the church written records, even of things of more immediate practical importance than music, hardly exist. It is for example at least very probable that by the year 1000 secular music-making was beginning to exert a powerful influence on the development of church music; the new interest of church musicians in instruments which belonged to secular music, and in light dancing measured rhythms both seemed to suggest a breach in the wall which had kept secular music away from the purposes of worship. But the supposition remains a supposition, and anything we want to say about the techniques and styles of secular music at the end of the Dark Ages can only be found by inference from developments in the codified, recorded music of the church.

Originally music was a utility to establish the rhythms to which men could work, to embellish the rhythms of dances which were ritual observances rather than mere social pleasures. The Christian church used it, as pagan worship had done, for the sake of the other-worldly atmosphere which it could create and to remove worship from the realm of subjective personal experience and emotion. The chant of the Catholic church was meant to be the voice of the church, not that of any individual worshipper; the monotone of prayers, lessons, epistles and gospels, with its formulae of intonation to mark points of punctuation, like the chants of psalms or austere settings of the congregation's share of the Mass, were meant to give objectivity to words which could too easily be bogged down in subjective personal feeling. The simple reading of a text permits the intrusion of far more individual interpretation, dangerous and possibly even heretical, than

16

does its singing or its recitation in monotone. Music was meant to be the voice of a universal church; individual devotion could of course find expression within the order of worship as well as in hymns, poems and religious songs outside the liturgy, but in the liturgy it remained subordinate to the work of the church itself.

As soon as music has been admitted as a utility it begins to make claims for independence. Naturally enough the plainchant of the church developed its own subjectivities, its romantic devotionalism. The pattern of the breviary offices, the lesser services which punctuated the monastic day, goes back traceably to the time of St. Benedict. It is a pattern of psalms, a reading, a hymn and a prayer; the psalms are introduced by an antiphon which summarises, in music more elaborate than that of the psalm, the teaching of the Psalm itself. The hymn, a metrical poem, could not but invite its poet to express himself lyrically and to stimulate lyrical music from the composer whose task was to set it. The magnificent Passiontide *Vexilla regis prodeunt*, the melody of which streams out like the banners it describes, dates from the latter part of the sixth century, the time at which Pope Gregory the Great was organising and rationalising the official music of the church.

If legitimate additions to the liturgy made possible expansions of its music, these expansions in turn led to the elaboration of simple chants, particularly in the music of the Mass, with tropes, elaborately decorative melismata which extended them sometimes to more than twice their original length. Eventually the tropes gained words of their own which fitted like parentheses into the text, perhaps to help singers to maintain unanimity in performances.

The process of expansion was accelerated by the stabilisation of the liturgy throughout Europe after the creation of a central authority by Charlemagne. The authority of the Holy Roman Empire, though it was always a convenient myth, half-political and half-religious in nature, emphasised the central position of the Papacy and things Roman in European religious life. Various local deviations from the Roman rite continued to exist, and some of them differed considerably. The pattern of the Roman Mass became virtually the standard for Europe. The invariable 'Ordinary' of the Mass, repeated at every celebration, henceforth consisted for the musician of the *Kyrie Eleison*, the *Gloria in Excelsis*, the Creed, the *Sanctus* and *Benedictus* and the *Agnus Dei*; on lesser days and during Lent and Advent, the *Gloria* and the Creed were omitted. Musically, the 'Proper' of the Mass, chosen to celebrate the particular ecclesiastical season or Saint's Day, consisted of the Introit—an antiphon, a psalm which came to be represented by a single verse, the *Gloria Patris* and a repetition of the antiphon—the Gradual, an antiphon and psalm verse sung between the Epistle and the Gospel, the Offertory, an antiphon sung while the bread and wine were prepared for consecration, and the Communion, sung as the celebrant (and, perhaps, the people) received the consecrated Elements.

Perhaps it is possible to explain the growth of the trope by something more tangible than the obvious fact that musicians are never easily restrained from making the fullest use of the materials at their disposal. It was possible that early untroped chants left occasional gaps in the celebration of the liturgy. The Introit and *Kyrie* are sung by the choir while the celebrant and his assistants say their preparatory prayers at the foot of the altar steps. The Gradual occupies the time in which the celebrant reads the Gospel to himself, the Deacon's procession is formed and blessed and the length of time occupied by procession and attendant ceremonies to the place, properly at the head of the nave, at which the Gospel is read. At the Communion, too, there has always been the possibility of expanding music without delaying the completion of the rite.

The development of words interpolated into the ritual text of the *Kyrie Eleison* for example, as though to mop up the notes of the trope, are still remembered but only as a means of identifying the various alternate plainchant settings: the *Kyrie* chant for Easter Day is called '*Fons et origo*', the words interpolated between '*Kyrie*' and '*Eleison*'; the traditional mass for solemn feast is either '*Fons bonitatis*' or '*Deus Sempiterne*'; these provide easier ways of identifying a chant than a mere number. The Creed, ideally speaking, was everyone's declaration of faith, so it was never troped.

It was at the Gradual that tropes grew most elaborate; often they extended into a hymn, the Sequence, and liturgical literature is crowded with discarded Sequences many of which had only local currency. The Sequence very often became a metrical hymn in a set verse form, offering all the opportunities for modernism provided by the hymns in the breviary services. Of the vast number at one time in use, those of the Requiem Mass (the *Dies Irae*), the Easter Mass (*Victimae Paschali Laudi*), the Whitsun Mass (*Veni Sancte Spiritus*) and the Mass of Corpus Christi (*Lauda Sion*), still survive in the liturgy.

As trope texts in general were not part of the Rite in any strict sense they were always associated with music less austere than that which was given to the Rite itself; and the Sequence, because it was a metrical hymn within the Mass and therefore familiar to every worshipper (relatively few were familiar with the breviary hymns), was the most powerful agent for musical development. The discarded Epiphany Sequence (*Corde Natus ex Parentis*) is an almost dance-like trochaic tune which suggests that some monastic musician had allowed himself to be too deeply influenced by the music of the outside world.

It was from the Introit trope that the dramatisations which modern authorities call 'Liturgical Operas' originally arose. The Introit on Easter Day, for example, provided what was originally a brief interlude which permitted a deacon to represent the angel at Christ's empty sepulchre and three others to represent the women making their way to complete His burial. The *Visitatio Sepulchri*, or '*Quem Quaeretis*' trope (so-called from its first words, '*Quem quaeretis in sepulchro, Christicolae?*') began as a tiny elaboration of the Introit chant and, between the tenth and thirteenth centuries, turned into a dramatic representation of the events round the empty tomb lasting in some places for as much as half an hour and taking its music from a variety of liturgical sources. It was not difficult to control the music for strictly liturgical texts; the music of interpolations offered the composer his opportunity for self-expression.

Our relatively modern notion of 'the composer' hardly matches the conditions and methods of the musician of the middle ages and has no parallel in the way in which the people of that time thought about their art. Nevertheless we sense the creative mind and personality operating in anonymity. A masterpiece like the *Dies Irae*, even though the methods used to notate and to diffuse music did not prevent its undergoing a number of modifications as it travelled about Europe, remains the work of a single formidable mind. Whose mind that was is not even a problem; it does not matter in the way that a proper ascription of the *Jena* Symphony matters, or in the way that the authentication of Haydn's symphonies matter. The once-common ascription of the *Jena* Symphony to Beethoven meant a rethinking of our attitude to the whole body of Beethoven's early work in our attempt to find room within it for a not characteristic example; the music of Beethoven is a separate body of work, each piece relating by personality to each other, valued for its personal, unique qualities as the expression of a special personal insight into experience and a special power of transmuting that experience into music. Any of the masterpieces of plainchant is too deeply embedded in a tradition and too concentrated on the task of expressing a specially Christian insight for the question of individual authorship, and the related idea of a special personal insight, to affect our understanding of what it says.

It was the materials available to the men who were responsible for the decent singing of the liturgy which made possible everything from the development of the trope, its application to the music of such special books and liturgical events as those which were codified in the *Processionale* and other occasional services. The same materials made the development of some form of harmony inevitable and the beginnings of polyphony possible. These things depended on a musical organisation which had developed by the seventh century in Christian centres and which was common throughout Europe by the end of the tenth century.

The Mass and the daily office in monastic churches, collegiate churches and cathedrals, were invariably sung. In cathedrals and collegiate churches it was the duty of the canons or their vicars—the clerical substitutes then employed to attend to the canons' functions in the choir whilst they occupied themselves with other work which ranged from the care of a parish to administrative or political duties at the court of a feudal lord or even of a king. Each canon was obliged to serve his cathedral, to be 'in residence', for some period of each year, and at such times the vicar was his domestic servant. Although the vicars had originally to be in priests' orders, eventually deacons and subdeacons were allowed to join the College of Vicars in any cathedral, and by the end of the middle ages, when the singing of the services was a task for specialist musicians, 'lay vicars' or 'singing men' were accepted.

The earliest musical body for which we can find a continuous history is the Papal Choir, staffed by singers trained in the Roman *Schola Cantorum* which took its final form under Pope Gregory the Great, who reigned from 590 to 604. Its history goes by tradition to the pontificate of St. Sylvester, between 314 and 335, but it certainly existed and was apparently re-organised under St. Hilarius, who was Pope from 461 to 468. After the destruction of St. Benedict's abbey of Monte Cassino the Benedictine community fled to Rome in 580 and opened seminaries near the church of St. John Lateran. Gregory the Great, having reformed and codified the Christian chant, entrusted the running of the *Schola Cantorum* to them, and their duty was to preserve and teach the authentic chant as Gregory had established it. The *Schola Cantorum* provided the whole of Europe with tutors whose duty was to see not only that high standards of performance were maintained, but also to ensure that the reformed chant and not some local traditional music or some local variant of the new music was sung. Authenticity away from Rome, however, lasted as long as the instructions of some authority from Rome remained clear in the memory, for the vagueness of notation by neumes meant that music could not be written with sufficient clarity for it to be preserved accurately, and memorised music is often modified by the tastes and traditions of individual singers.

The prestige of the Roman choir and of the *Schola Cantorum* from which it was recruited was such that in 650 Abbot Benedict of Wearmouth sent to Rome for a singer who could 'teach in his monastery the system of singing throughout the year as it is practised at St. Peter's in Rome'. Less than a century later, at the Council of Cloveshoe, the Church in England made the use of the Roman chant compulsory throughout the country.

Naturally, charged with the duty of preserving the absolute purity of Roman plainchant, the Papal choir became the most conservative of bodies to which all innovations for a long time remained anathema. But the monasteries first of all, and then the cathedrals, created the organisation which made new developments inevitable. The monasteries were centres of education from their foundation. They had the duty of teaching their own recruits, many of them young boys with unbroken voices who were in duty bound to take their part in the singing of Mass and the daily office. The elaborate music of the tropes often extended over a range which made unison octave singing by boys and men impossible, so that those whose voices could not tackle the higher or the lower notes would be driven to alight almost haphazardly on some concord—haphazardly because the notes out of range of certain singers were not necessarily part of any cadence at which some degree of harmonisation is logical to our ears. But it seems to have been the arbitrary effect of mixed voice choirs of boys and men forced to cope with elaborate music that created the appetite for harmony which grew into organum, faux bourdon and the other early forms of harmony.

The enrichment of liturgical music in the monasteries spread to cathedrals and collegiate churches to many of which song schools had been attached for a considerable time. A song school was founded to serve York Minster in 627; Salzburg Cathedral School dates from 774. Christianity came later to Northern Germany, but St. Michael's monastery church in Lüneburg was founded in 995. Lübeck Cathedral was founded in 1270 with its song school, the chief church of Darmstadt, St. Mary's, with its school in 1369. Schools of various sorts were attached to similar churches, as they were to the Augustinian collegiate churches like St. Thomas's in Leipzig (an institution of breath-taking consequence for the history of music, founded in 1212) and the church which in the nineteenth century became Manchester Cathedral. Such schools found themselves with the duty of teaching. This itself involved the teaching of music, for in 1003 the *Patrologia Latina* declared 'in what-so-ever school shall be found boys to sing, they are to be taken out and brought up in the song school'.

The song school existed to train boys in music before it needed to consider to what extent and in what way it should provide them with a general education. The Leipzig *Thomasschule* provided teaching for poor boys with good voices who could be trained to take part in the music of the liturgy. Its boys assisted at funerals and in fund-raising processions in the city; they were boarders and their own buildings were begun in 1254, though their schoolrooms continued to be in the canon's buildings. As the city of Leipzig expanded, the *Thomasschule* was forced into a double role as song school for poor boys, who remained boarders, and grammar school for the sons of the city merchants, who were day boys.

Thus by the tenth century the musical assistance of boys had become a liturgical necessity and the song schools had become a form of education which was usually the first step towards eventual training for the priesthood. When Norwich Cathedral and Priory were created at the end of the eleventh century, the first bishop of the See, Hubert de Losinga, wrote orders determining the place and behaviour of boys in the Cloister. The music of the Notre Dame composers presupposes the presence of unbroken voices in the choir, as do the Worcester choir book and the choir books of several of the Spanish cathedrals. Cathedral schools existed all over Austria—at Passau, Steyr and Linz, for example—by the thirteenth century, and where they did not work parallel to already existing song schools they provided a nucleus for one.

Most of the teaching of music was still done largely through memory, for though the improvements in notation achieved by Hucbald, Guido d'Arezzo and Nolker Balbulus had provided accurate means of getting plainchant on to paper, books were still expensive and rare so that a choir book was more often a book of reference for the cantor who trained the choir; pictures of medieval choirs show the singers gathered round a lectern holding a gigantic choir book to which the cantor is pointing, apparently leading his forces through a work note by note.

Most song schools remained small specialist institutions where little besides music was taught. Their organisation and methods hardly varied through Europe. A precentor took charge of the music for the liturgy, a cantor trained the musicians; the cathedral chancellor, originally the head of the school, normally appointed a Rector or Headmaster as disciplinary and organising head. Originally, the boys had boarded with the canons and had acted as their servants, as did the adult vicars, but the more or less universal adoption of the collegiate system rescued them from that and they moved into their own colleges or boarding houses under the control of the cantor. Throughout the middle ages the extra-musical education provided for them improved until they reached the point at which they could matriculate and enter university.

In the middle ages there was no intention to create what any musician of the last three hundred years would regard as a balanced choir. Examples from England can be taken as typical of choral establishments throughout Europe. York had, by statute, thirty-six canons and seven boys; Wells had fifty-four canons and sometimes as many as twelve boys; there were thirty-four canons at Exeter, and statutes of 1337 demanded twelve boys. Lichfield with twenty-one canons had twelve boys; even under Colet at the end of the fifteenth century St. Paul's, with thirty vicars-choral, had only eight boys in the song school as distinct from Colet's grammar school. The primary function of the choir was the singing of the plainchant; as the presence of trained singers stimulated composers to create more polyphonic works for festivals and for special services, the occasional polyphonic music was given to small, picked groups of singers with perhaps only one voice to each part.

By the end of the twelfth century, as the works of the Notre Dame composers like Pérotin and his predecessor Léonin show, instrumental accompaniment had become more or less customary. Organs had been becoming increasingly common for a couple of hundred years. The 'great' organ only gradually became the indispensible church instrument; though it was available, its activities were restricted by its clumsy, stiff mechanism, which made any but long sustained notes impracticable. As it improved it became more adaptable, but three hundred years of rather dubious existence passed before it became sufficiently versatile to be frequently used. The development of smaller instruments, the positive and portative organs which could be more easily played, were not too noisy, and on which relatively quick music was possible, followed. Even a positive organ could be moved with little trouble and expense to any part of a building in which it would be useful; during the fourteenth and fifteenth centuries, the organ became a feature, it seems, of almost every church, and the smallness of the instrument of the day meant that organs could be installed in cathedrals wherever they might be useful—a nave organ, an organ in the choir, or an organ on each side of the choir as liturgical singing was largely antiphonal, and a portative to be used wherever no fixed organ was installed, became quite frequent parts of the cathedral furniture. A Lady Chapel, in which services would be almost as frequent as those in the choir, would have its own organ; the growth of extra-liturgical devotional services took the performance away from the choir stalls, which were kept mainly for the liturgical offices which concerned the canons of the Chapter. So we find that for some unspecified service at Norwich Cathedral in 1381, both great and small organs were moved to the Lady Chapel; the cost of the removal was twenty shillings, probably about £15 of our money, and this shows that the organs were neither so small nor so easily portable as readers have sometimes been led to believe.

The entry of the organ into liturgical music cannot be precisely dated by anything that we may call musical evidence—that is to say, evidence from the survival of any distinct references to its taking any precise part in services—until long after their existence had been recorded. The fact that we know when they began to be built into cathedrals and large churches implies nothing definite about how they were used or the points at which they played, and no information of this sort seems to exist before the fourteenth century. In 1365 the Chapter of St. Stephen's Cathedral, Vienna, made statutes that on all major festivals both the Mass and the Office should be sung, with organ accompaniment, by the professors and students of the university. In 1384 Margrave William of Saxony ordered that regular votive masses of Our Lady should be sung in Leipzig with organ accompaniment. At about this time service books began to include instruction about the use of the organ; something is to be sung '*cum organis modulis*', something else is '*cantare organice*', and there are demands that '*organa dulcia sunt resonanda*' and for '*melliflua organa*'.

The organ had been in some way associated with worship for a considerable time, but the use of other instruments in worship from the twelfth century onward marked the beginning of a great revolution in church music. From its earliest days the western church had outlawed musical instruments because they were associated with pagan worship and with the lax morality of social life outside the early church. 'We use only one instrument,' declared St. Clement of Alexandria, 'that is, the word of peace with which we honour God; we no longer need the old psaltery, trumpet, drum and trumpet.' St. John Chrysostom said, 'David formerly sang in psalms and we today sing with him; he played a lyre with lifeless strings, but we need no lyre; our tongues are living strings, with a different tone—that of a more responsive piety.' St. Jerome, more extreme, hoped that no decently brought up Christian girl would ever discover what a lute or harp could be. It was not simply that the Roman church was hostile to the use of instruments in church; it was simply hostile to musical instruments; it attempted to put down the entire breed of wandering entertainers and did its utmost to prescribe public secular music and dancing. It was attempting to impose a new way of life on a pagan world and could not relax its efforts to destroy whatever remained from the past.

Christian champions like Charlemagne and Alfred the Great hardly helped, for Charlemagne loved and collected the old heathen songs and legends, while Alfred's ability as a harpist enabled him to spy on his Danish enemies before the Battle of Edington in 878; because the church had forbidden Christians to play the harp the king's disguise as a wandering musician was convincing. The common people were treated to stories enough to frighten them away from any love of secular music. The church authorities complained almost interminably about peasants, and often priests, who sang 'wicked songs with a chorus of dancing women' or performed 'ballads and dancings and evil songs and such-like lures of the devil'. To make matters worse, the place and time of these profane jollifications was in the churchyard after Mass on Sundays because there and then the whole community was together and without work to do. Repeated attempts to stop them failed, and in many places Sunday merry-making went on until after the Reformation in spite of the terrible fate of the dancers of Kolbeck, a village near Cologne. Sometime in the eleventh century the story grew up (it is told in the English of the day by Robert Manning of Bowne, at the end of the thirteenth century, in the poem *Handlyng Synne*) of the profane villagers of Kolbeck who danced in the churchyard on Christmas Eve. Either they were turned into trees and remained rooted to the spot for a year, or they were unable to stop dancing for a year, until the Archbishop of Cologne took the curse from them: two versions are told. Giraldus Cambrensis tells the sad story of the Worcestershire priest who was kept awake at night by the villagers singing and dancing in his churchyard; their favourite song had the refrain '*Swete Lamman dhinore*' (Sweetheart, pity me). Next morning at Mass he could not concentrate on his duties through weariness, and instead of turning to the congregation and saying '*Dominus vobiscum*', he said '*Swete Lamman dhinore*' and there was a dreadful scandal.

In the eyes of other Christians, worldly music could be sanctified. It was a vision of Christ himself who taught Caedmon to sing the stories of the Old Testament and the Gospel to tunes of a frankly popular sort, while St. Adhelm (*c.* 640–709) who was Bishop of Sherborne, apparently attracted congregations by playing the harp, having discovered that his flock would listen to sermons only if they were prefaced by music. The Celtic Church, in Ireland, Wales and England, had no objection whatsoever to the introduction of worldly music into the services. In the same way areas on the eastern fringe of Roman authority did not share the extreme puritan distaste for music, but as the central authority of the Pope became exerted over the entire western church—it gained control of the English church at the Synod of Whitby in 664—the same puritanical rejection of music affected Christians everywhere.

Even teachers otherwise as attractively liberal as Alcuin (735–804) who went from York to teach at the court of Charlemagne and whose writing is lyrical, eloquent and Virgilian both in style and at times in theme, could see nothing of value in any music but that of the church; in one of his letters, written in 791, he told a friend that by admitting jongleurs and dancers to his house he had 'admitted a mass of evil spirits'. The opposition of the puritanical element in the church went on throughout the middle ages, even after instrumental music was accepted in church. John Cotton, writing shortly before 1100, says that 'only the tuneful music of voices can be called music' and grows sarcastic about 'idiots stupid enough to believe that any sound could be called music'; later writers did not all accept the enrichment of church music with enthusiasm or equanimity.

For all that, pictures and carvings begin to show what was happening to church music. The choirs of angels seen to be accompanied by varieties of harps, fiddles, viols, rotas, flutes, psalteries, dulcimers, organistra (the keyed hurdy-gurdies), shawms, trumpets and trombones, as though the instruments of Nebuchadnezzar's decree ordering the worship of his golden idol had been added to the more sanctified list of instruments in Psalm 150: King David on his throne, the choir of angels worshipping the Lamb of the Apocalypse and adoring angels praising the Blessed Virgin all, in medieval illustrations, use instruments as though heaven regards them as completely acceptable.

The middle ages had no conception of a balanced instrumental ensemble. The idea of a balanced choir seems to have arrived in the works of the St. Martial composers and those of Compostela in Spain at the beginning of the eleventh century. But what instruments were used in such music, and what precisely they played, depended less on a composer's wish to create particular qualities of sound than upon local conditions and the instruments available. It was a considerable time before any sort of unanimity was established. Only in the fourteenth century did the statutes of Canterbury Cathedral establish a group of instrumentalists who were to play cornetts and sackbutts in the services. Manuscripts of the 'Liturgical Operas', dating from after the tenth century, have references not only to the use of the organ but also to the use of harps, bells and other instruments in solo music, while apparently taking for granted that the musicians who used the manuscript had some traditional principles governing the employment of instruments. The Winchester Troper, which dates from about 980, provides a very early version of the most famous of these very beautiful works with a very limited musical notation to represent what is sung but practically no rubrics or stage directions. A document of about the same date, the *Regularis Concordia*, describes the performance in detail, puts it at the end of Lauds (the epilogue to Breviary mattins) and ends the play with the singing of the *Te Deum* (which is the liturgical conclusion of Lauds) by actors, choir and congregation accompanied by bells.

Thus, between the twelfth and fourteenth century, the monasteries, cathedrals and larger churches achieved a considerable and varied musical life; the choir, with a preponderance of men, sang the Mass and the Daily Office with its group of specialists trained to sing whatever was required in 'figural' polyphonic style; there was a group of instrumentalists, an organist and others unspecified, to accompany at any rate the figural music.

Naturally they found themselves involved in the perennial struggle about the nature of church music: to what extent should it simply be a vehicle for the text, endowing it with a certain solemn dignity, and to what extent could it legitimately convey the personal devotion, joy or lamentation of the individual; what place has subjective religious feeling within what is essentially the act of worship of the church itself? The quarrels which we have always heard about church music are really about this, though they are always expressed in terms of the admirableness or otherwise of innovation, the suitability or otherwise of particular styles for employment in the liturgy. The argument goes back to the elaboration of church music by the gorgeous melismata of the tropes, with their demand for trained singers and their consequent silencing of the congregation. In the years from about 1000 to 1200 it raged over the new style pioneered at St. Martial near Limoges, and the monastery of Santiago at Compostela, developed by the composers at Notre Dame in Paris.

Polyphony seems to have been a north-European art and its development at Compostela to have been a sort of sport. The earliest collection of works from Compostela, the *Codex Calixtinus*, is a very modern-looking volume for the twelfth century, using a four-line plainchant notation before its use was universal; but the vast majority of the works it contains are plainchant, and the most famous of the polyphonic works in it, *Congaudeant Catholici*, is attributed to 'Master Albert of Paris'. English manuscripts of the period contain works imported from France which served as models for English composers, but polyphonic music does not appear until later in Italy and Germany.

The importance of the Notre Dame development can be estimated from the fact that its two leaders, Léonin and Pérotin, were the first composers to escape from the anonymity which was the natural lot of the medieval musician and are known to posterity by pet names; each name is a diminutive, 'Little Leo' and 'Little Pierre'. Léonin was active between about 1150 and 1180, and Pérotin probably continued his work, apparently after starting as one of Léonin's choir-boys, until about 1230. They both worked in what was a new cathedral, for the building of the choir of Notre Dame was not completed until 1183. Little is known about either of them but it seems that Pérotin was succentor, or first bass, of the Cathedral choir.

The sudden revolutionary activity of musicians in France and Spain during the twelfth century is only part of a much bigger development of European intellectual life. Trade and municipal organisation show both the influence of new ideas and progressive ways of thought; the heaviness and solidity of the architectural style known in Britain as Norman gave way to the greater richness and elaboration of Gothic; literature and the arts outside the church flowered; the foundation stones of Scholastic philosophy were laid, not only by Peter Abelard, whose revolutionary ideas no less than his tragically scandalous life were a cause for his persecution by the traditionalists, but by European philosophers far more daring in speculation than later masters of the school. The universities were founded in response to the new appetite for knowledge, and by their existence encouraged speculative thought and new ideas, not only in theology and philosophy but also in music which was part of the standard university course because of its alliance with theology, as a practical subject, and philosophy, as a mathematical illustration of philosophical ideas.

In many ways the rise of the cities had quite as much effect as the new prestige of music and academic study of its theory. In the cities music was becoming a social and ceremonial necessity with the formation of the town bands of waits, *Stadtpfeifer* and *pifferi*, who made instrumental music popular and more respectable. At the same time, the wealthy citizens were giving more wealth to the church to make developments possible.

Inevitably the sort of music which was heard outside the church began to influence the music heard inside it. The intrusion of instruments into worship threw the church composer back on the established techniques employed in secular music, just as the rhythms and melodic styles of secular music seem to have influenced the church composer; as little of the secular music of the twelfth and thirteenth centuries remains, we are guessing when we suggest that the dancing rhythms and melodic idioms of the Limoges and Notre Dame composers brought the idioms as well as the instruments of the secular world into church; but it is impossible to believe that the new style leapt fully developed into the liturgy.

Possibly *Sumer is icumen in*, the Reading Rota, throws some light on the question of popular influences on the early days of church polyphony. The contrapuntal complexity of a four-part canon over a repeating groundbass was not merely the music of a spring song but also of a Christian hymn, *Perspice Christicola*, sung in the Abbey Church; Manfred Bukofzer dated the work to the period between 1280 and 1310. Latin directions appended to the religious text explain how the round is to be sung, suggesting that the singers of Reading Abbey were unfamiliar with counterpoint so highly developed. But counterpoint at that degree of sophistication cannot appear fully grown from nowhere; it seems that outside Reading Abbey such feats of technique were not uncommon and that some people could deal with them, and the song's springy twelve-eight rhythm is no vast distance from the lively upper parts written in St. Martial and Notre Dame.

The early move towards freedom in church music had been through the *Conductus*, which had a metrical text and was, as its title declares, processional music, influential in that it demanded music in measured notation and voices moving together homophonically, and through the *Clausula*, in which a prose text was set with a plainsong melody in the tenor and two or three other voices which moved, not homophonically to the same rhythm but polyphonically and freely against it. A *Clausula* was an integral part of the liturgy, but the *Conductus* and its successor, the motet, were additions to the text of the rite and could therefore be treated with greater freedom by the composer. The motet, which became the most influential of those early musical forms, apparently entered the Mass as a musical addition which followed the Gradual. The Gradual had been sung, as plainsong was always sung, by the entire body of singers, while the motet had been the task of whatever group of singers was trained to perform polyphony.

Naturally the motet took advantage of the freedoms implicit in its being an extra-liturgical, devotional, emotional intrusion into the service. It often enough had, or at least referred to, a text used in the liturgy in other contexts, so that it too had a plainchant in its tenor as its musical foundation, but it developed a variety of strange and to the traditionalist objectionable features; it accepted instrumental accompaniment and coupled different texts together in the different voices; there were motets in which four or five notes of a plainchant melody were all the composer needed; it was, in other words, the most fruitful and influential form which the medieval church had evolved, and the challenges it offered led to considerable development of technique. That is why in a short space of time it moved into the nobleman's banqueting hall and became a secular as well as a church form—often it seems as a song for a solo voice with its other polyphonic parts given to instruments.

This did not set the composer free to touch the essential words of the liturgy.

The composer was allowed to glorify the service only by treating additions to its texts. Tropes provided the writer of *Clausulae* with his opportunities but left him bound by a predetermined plainsong melody and the text which had grown on it, so that in the long run the freer *Conductus* and motet allowed more hope of musical development.

Although their work was extra-liturgical the composers were faced with the invariable arguments about the use of over-elaborate music in worship. When the chant of the Mass and the Offices had, comparatively early in their history, grown so elaborate that only trained singers could do them justice, the more austere authorities had protested not only on the grounds that the magnificence of the music distracted attention from the words of the Rite; they had also pointed out that the movements, gestures and facial expressions of the singers engaged in difficult music were themselves unedifying and distracting. The victory of music over its detractors is shown by the simple fact that the elaborations of the chant became its customary form throughout Europe. When the more revolutionary musical styles erupted into the music of the church in the eleventh and twelfth centuries, matching in sound the vigour and unconventionality of the buildings in which it was sung and the richness of visual decoration they admitted, the re-actionary mind expressed itself vigorously.

The situation is hard to clarify; whilst harmony, rhythmic, measured music and instrumental accompaniment became increasingly common, even a religious order as strict as the Cistercians—an offshoot of the Benedictines created as a protest against what its creator, St. Bernard, felt to be the ease and luxury of the older order—noted in 1217 that in some of its houses the monks were singing part music, and in the fourteenth century it permitted the building of organs in its churches. Nevertheless as late as 1526 the head of the Order in England insisted that the Abbey at Thame gave up the singing of polyphonic music. No general edict of the sort which was issued later controlled the music sung during the liturgy, not, perhaps, because the authorities were prepared to tolerate anything but because the range and variety of practices employed were never totally appreciated by those who might have considered control necessary. Therefore, whilst the various developments were in progress, Aeldred, who was Abbot of Rivaulx in the middle of the twelfth century, protested against elaborated church music in terms which delighted the Puritan William Prynne, who translated his objections five hundred years after they were made into Puritan pamphleteer's vigorous, robust and admirable English:

> Whence hath the church so many Organs and Musical Instruments? To what purpose, I pray you, is that terrible blowing of Bellows, expressing rather the cracks of thunder than the sweetness of a Voyce? To what purpose serves that contraction and inflection of the Voyce ... In the meantime, the common people standing by, trembling and astonished, admire the sound of Organs, the noise of the Cymballs and Musical Instruments, the Harmony of Pipes and Cornetts.[1]

[1] Quoted in H. Davey: *History of English Music* (second edition, 1921).

John of Salisbury, a scholar of international reputation in the twelfth century was equally vigorous in his opposition to 'ennervating performances executed with all the devices of the art. You might think it a song of sirens, but not of men, and you would be astonished at the singers' facility with which, indeed, neither that of the nightingale nor of the parrot, nor whatever else there may be that is more remarkable in this kind, can compare. . . . In all this, the high or even the highest notes of the scale are so mingled with the low and the lowest that ears are almost deprived of their power to distinguish.'[1] John de Muris, Canon of Paris and Master of the Sorbonne, who died in 1370, was even more passionate in denouncing the excesses of a couple of centuries later, protesting with what seems excessive violence against the scandal of what he called, in contemporary terminology, 'coloured' music:

> O Magnus abuses! Magna ruditas! Nam inducere cum deberent delecta-
> tionem adducunt tristitiam . . . Mihi non congruis, mihi adversaris, scandalum
> tu mihi es; utinam taceres; sed deliras et discordus.[2]

For all that, the intrusion of music other than plainchant into the treatment of liturgical words themselves, as distinct from extra-liturgical additions to the text of the Rite, does not seem to have followed any strict rule and it was not auto-matically subject to complaints from the authorities. The complainants whose words have been used to represent the conservative attitude were not, after all, musical or administrative authorities; they were merely voicing the objection of individual, though influential, churchmen to something new which they felt to be a degradation of the real purpose of worship. In most places polyphonic music, like the motet, slid into the service between the sections of the liturgy, but the great works of the Notre Dame composers were not only liturgical, they were apparently demanded by ecclesiastical authorities. The *Liber Organi*, from which we know their works, contains settings of liturgical texts for the Mass and the Offices. We can trace the origin of some of them. Bishop Eude de Sully, in 1198, issued an edict at the command of the Pope instituting the celebration of the Feast of the Circumcision on January 1st, in place of the dubious students' celebration, the 'Donkey's Feast', which had previously occupied the day, and his edict refers specifically to the music that should be sung:

> The responsory and *Benedicamus* [at Vespers], can be sung as a triplum,
> a quadruplum, or in organum . . . The third and sixth responsories [at
> Mattins] will be sung in organum, in triplum or in quadruplum . . . The
> responsory and *Alleluia* [at Mass] will be sung in triplum, in quadruplum
> or in organum.

Triplum and Quadruplum signify three or four part music, here to be sung, like the organum, to specifically liturgical texts. The passage suggests that Pérotin's enormous quadruplum *Viderunt* was written—as its text is appropriate to the Christmas season—for the celebration of the Feast of the Circumcision in Notre

---

[1] Quoted in H. E. Wooldridge: *Oxford History of Music*, Vol. I.
[2] Quoted in Ernst Tittel: *Oesterreichische Kirchenmusik*, Verlag Herder, Vienna, 1961.

Dame. A year later the bishop issued another edict demanding that 'in the Mass, the responsory and *Alleluia* will be sung in triplum, in quadruplum or as organum'. It may be that Pérotin's other masterpiece, the quadruplum *Sederunt Principes* (the text is that of the Introit at Mass on St. Stephen's day) was composed for December 26, 1199, in response to Bishop Eude de Sully's wishes.

But apart from these occasional irruptions of music into the liturgy itself, the general custom in most places seems to have been that all the liturgical text was sung to its traditional plainchant and that polyphonic pieces wedged themselves into the Rite, as the motet had done, or clustered round the extra-liturgical devotions which became increasingly popular as the middle ages progressed. A great deal of extra-liturgical devotion was paid to the Virgin Mary; her Mass was sung daily in addition to the proper Mass of the day, and hymns or an antiphon in her honour were sung each evening before her statue. These extra-liturgical practices gave a greater freedom to the musician than the fixed daily worship, and it is quite likely that the works in her honour, which outnumber any other religious works surviving from the later middle ages, are due not only to the composers' personal devotion to her but also to the fact that her cult permitted him a greater degree of freedom of action than he could otherwise obtain. Thus the new style of music gradually took possession of words which once had been sacrosanct.

Actually, however, the *Liber Organi* of Léonin and Pérotin, which includes a great deal of music known to be by others, contains music for the 'Proper' of the Mass, the texts for which, belonging to specific occasions, vary from day to day, and these are what the edicts of Bishop Eude allowed the composer freedom to elaborate. An audience listening to a Mass by Victoria, Palestrina or any of their successors, is listening to music for the invariable 'Ordinary' of the Rite and not to the variable insertions which depend upon the actual day of the celebration. The setting of the 'Ordinary', the portions of the Mass traditionally sung by the congregation, was in reality a victory for music over the natural conservatism of the churchmen, and the first Mass to which we can ascribe a composer's name—that of Machaut—was probably composed for the coronation of the French king Charles V at Rheims in 1364, the solemnity and pomp of the occasion explaining and excusing its revolutionary audacity; but it was more than a century before the words of the liturgical text began to be regularly treated by composers in spite of the frequent bitter attacks on 'progressive' church music.

Guillaume de Machaut himself symbolises the beginning of a change in the status of musicians. Born in 1300 near Rheims, he took Holy Orders after studying apparently in Paris. For the rest of his life he was not a musician working in the choir of a monastery or cathedral but, like his younger contemporary Geoffrey Chaucer, spent his life as a civil servant. In 1323 he took service under the King of Bohemia, John of Luxembourg, with whom he travelled to Lithuania and Italy and on various campaigns as well as living at court in Prague. He rose in the service, being successively almoner, notary, legal secretary and secretary.

John of Luxembourg was killed at the battle of Crécy and Machaut took service under his daughter, Boune, the wife of Jean Duke of Normandy who later succeeded to the throne of France. When his patroness died three years later Machaut went to the court of the King of Navarre until strained relations between Navarre and France persuaded him that it would be wise to return to his native country. He became an official at the French court and then entered the service of the Duke of Berry until he retired and was given a canonry at Rheims Cathedral.

Machaut, therefore, wrote music not for a choir in which he sang or which he trained, but for aristocratic patrons; he was not a specialist musician but a composer of church music and of secular music in a variety of styles, adapting the motet to secular words with a solo voice accompanied, it seems, by instruments which took the place of the lower voices. He composed songs, too, in all the fashionable troubadour forms. His works were sung wherever he travelled with any of his royal masters, and his works are preserved in thirty-two manuscripts dating from his own lifetime, some of them apparently written under his supervision and all probably made for the pleasure of monarchs and noblemen with whom he had come into contact. He is, so to speak, the first composer expected to be an all-rounder and write whatever music, religious or secular, was required for any occasion.

By the fourteenth century written records are available to make clear the conditions under which church musicians worked and the duties allotted to them. In Vienna for example the regulations of St. Stephen's Cathedral in 1365 demanded that both the daily office and the votive office of Our Lady should be sung each day, but left no regulations as to the type of music which should be used. The choirmaster in a cathedral, always one of the vicars, had strictly defined duties which enable us to discover what the musical life of the institution which employed him actually was, while our notion of the medieval choirboy comes from Chaucer's *Prioress' Tale:*

> A litel scole of Cristen folk ther stood
> Doun at the further ende, in which there were
> Children an heep, ycomen of Cristen blood,
> That lerned in that scole year by year
> Swich maner doctrine as men used there,
> This is to seyn, to singen and to rede,
> As smale children doon in hir childhede.
>
> Among thise children was a widwes sonne,
> A litel clergeon, seven yeers of age,
> That day by day to scole as was his wone
> And eek also, wher-as he saugh th'image
> of Cristes moder, hadde he in usage
> As him was taught, to knele adoun and seye
> His *Ave Marie* as he goth by the way
>
> Thus had this widwe hir litel sone ytought
> Our blissful lady, Cristes moder dere
> To worshipe ay, and he forgat it naught,

For sely child wol alday sone lere;
But ay, when I remembre on this matere,
Saint Nicholas stant ever in my prescence,
For he so young to Crist did revence.

This litel child, his litel book lerninge,
As he sat in the scole at his prymer,
He *Alma redemptoris* herde sings,
As children learned hir antiphoner
And, as he droste, he drough him ner and ner,
And herkened ay the wordes and the note,
Til he the first vers coude all by rote.

Chaucer's 'litel clergeon' did not know enough to have been admitted to the choir itself; that would have come a year or so later had he not been the chosen victim in a ritual murder. The story, of course, comes from a sentimental lady vowed to chastity and fond of the pets her rule really forbade her to keep, so he is an angel in disguise. What is musically interesting is that at the turn of the fourteenth century the music the little boy is aware of is dedicated to Our Lady; it would be interesting to know whether the boys learning their antiphoner were singing the *Alma redemptoris Mater* in plainchant or to some later and more intricate polyphonic setting.

The *Schottenschule* in Vienna, the house of a community of Scottish monks of the brotherhood of St. James, decreed in its statutes of 1310 that 'the boys would normally take their part in the priestly song', that is in the chanting of the daily Office, and that as well as music they should be taught grammar, rhetoric and dialectic. At St. Stephen's twenty-four boys were to sing at the daily High Mass, and the statutes of 1363 demand that on Festivals they sing Vespers and High Mass with the organ. Foundations in the Tyrol appointed a *Scholasticus* to supervise the boys' general studies and to take care of them outside school, while a *Chorallehrer* and the Cantor were to teach them choral singing and the chanting of psalms and lessons. Education in subjects other than music was generally considered to be important enough anywhere to warrant the appointment of a master for its supervision, but the master of the boys in most cathedrals was not only the musician who taught them their job but also the authority who was responsible for their discipline and general behaviour, standing in the place of a parent. It is not surprising that from the beginnings of cathedral and song school education until now many choirboys profited by their comprehensive musical education to make a career in the art.

There was an almost immediate alliance between the universities and the church, which meant also between the music of the cathedrals and larger churches and of the king's and noblemen's chapels, and the actual teaching carried on was the same in all these institutions. Music, after all, was in medieval opinion an important branch of practical mathematics. In Paris many of the lecturers were musicians influential at Notre Dame, and many of the singers and the teachers of the boy choristers were either lecturers or students at the university. The choir school itself acted as preparatory school to the university, regularly sending its broken-voiced ex-choristers to study there and providing quite a considerable number of them with scholarships. It was, of course, the University of Paris which provided Europe with an invaluable model, so that when Prague University was founded in 1348, it imported the Parisian system completely and in detail.

In England the development of the collegiate system in fourteenth-century Oxford and Cambridge had a more immediately practical effect upon musical styles. The colleges were religious houses which, like the monasteries, stood quite a way outside the normal system of diocesan authority. From their foundations each was equipped with the staff of men and boys necessary for what had become the normal manner of singing the Mass and the Offices. Unlike the monasteries they were not by outlook and organisation conservative bodies bound to the preservation of tradition—changes in monastery worship had to be won from the traditionalists with far more difficulty than in cathedrals and collegiate churches —but their atmosphere of intellectual exploration made them natural centres of musical development. The same is true of the great non-monastic and non-cathedral schools, like that founded at Winchester by William of Wykeham, or like Henry VI's foundation at Eton.

Later collegiate churches and the chapels of the Oxford and Cambridge colleges like the chapels of kings and noblemen, seem to have advanced the cause of polyphony. The collegiate church of Ottery St. Mary, which was given its foundation statutes by Bishop Grandison of Exeter late in the fourteenth century, provides an example; it was established with eight vicars, eight *Secondarii* from whom the successors to the vicars would be chosen, and eight choirboys. The precentor and chaplain of the Ottery St. Mary Lady Chapel were bound by statute to teach such boys as were sufficiently musical to sing *in cantu organico* (that is to say, polyphonic part music) and to play the organ. The creation of a more balanced choir is itself an indication of development in style.

Similarly the statutes of the Queen's College, Oxford, of 1340 decreed that there should be half as many choristers as there were students; New College was established with sixteen choirboys as well as the necessary number of men; the sixteen boys of Magdelen College, Oxford, were to be taught 'plainsong and other song'. All this suggests that the founders of these institutions were beginning to see the need for balanced choirs in place of the small groups of higher voices which were all that was needed in the eleventh and twelfth centuries when polyphonic intrusions into the music of the church were entrusted to small groups of soloists. As the new style of choral singing became more familiar, first the cathedrals and then the monasteries came, with no written declarations on the subject, to accept and employ it.

We can see the spread of the new style in the regulations governing the appointment of choirmasters. Statutes for the *Thomaskirche* in Leipzig, drawn up in 1450, describe the work of the Cantor, who had to be a man of honest life and respectability, to exercise control over the boys of the *Thomasschule*, to arrange the music to be sung in the church, and to train the boys to sing it; he is, so to speak, becoming the musical authority over the head of the precentor simply by virtue of his expert knowledge. The composer Richard Hygons, who was appointed choirmaster at Wells Cathedral in 1479, was chosen from among the vicars choral. His duties were to instruct the boys in plainchant, descant and mensural singing as well as to teach the organ to any boys who showed sufficient musical ability. He had to sing the daily votive Mass of Our Lady in the Lady Chapel (ten of the vicars were to form his choir for this), and on the days and at the times when he was ordered to do so to sing the antiphon of Our Lady before her image by the choir screen door; the choir sang the necessary responses to this and was specially paid for this extra duty. Hygons also had to be present to sing in the choir at Matins, Vespers and High Mass on Sundays and Festivals.

Alonso d'Alva, who became *maestro di capilla* at Seville Cathedral in 1503, not only taught the boys of the choir school but also was provided by the chapter with a large house by the cathedral in which he boarded the boys and was allowed extra payment to provide for their upkeep, so that he was directly responsible for their upbringing. Martin de Rivafrecha, *maestro di capilla* at Palencia Cathedral from 1503 to 1521, had an assistant from the choirmen to look after the boys' welfare; he himself had to train them to sing antiphonally—half singing plainchant answered by the other half singing polyphony; he was to teach all the twenty boys of the choir to improvise melodies above a plainchant *cantus firmus*, to direct the music on Sundays, Festivals and all days when processions were ordered, to take complete control of musical performances, to choose the necessary soloists, to decide the accompaniment, and to exercise discipline over the entire choir; for the purposes of music, everyone with a seat in the choir stalls, clerical or lay, even the canons who were members of the cathedral chapter, was under his authority and bound to obey his instructions.

The cantor, who became the choirmaster, was specially responsible for extra-liturgical worship, for the hymns and chants sung during processions, for the music of votive services and devotions, while the precentor remained the authority over the musical performance of the liturgy. The cantor became, so to speak, the musical liaison officer between the church and congregational worship. The regulations binding upon the precentor demanded that he acted, whether or not he felt like one, as a conservative musician, while the cantor's increasing and fruitful contact with the laity and, through them, with the world of secular music, not only permitted him greater freedom of action but also stimulated his development of new ideas and his investigation of new styles which demanded the increasing admission of specialist singers not in holy orders into the choir as lay vicars.

Thus, right up to the time of the Reformation, the various types of church music co-existed; many of the churches which employed choirs, probably the vast majority, sang plainsong on most days of the year and saved musical elaborations for great festivals and for extra-liturgical worship. The spread of polyphony, however, was rapid enough to lead to complaint and, at one time, to restriction, but the catholic church was a body international not only in its doctrines and its worship, but also in the music which ennobled its services; through the church, and sometimes in spite of it, polyphony spread to every country where it was established.

3   The Spread of Northern Polyphony

In the fourteenth century a disputed Papal election caused the Great Schism, leaving a Pope in Rome and his rival, actually the true Pope, in Avignon. The results for the French city, and especially for its architecture, were splendid. Its musical results were not at first so noticeable; but by the end of the century and in the years that followed, the history not only of Italian music but of the European music in general was directed by a process of internationalisation which was the immediate consequence of the Pope's 'Babylonian Captivity' in the south of France.

When Clement V removed his throne to Avignon, leaving not only his choir but also its directors behind him in Rome, the prestige of providing music for the Papal ceremonies and services passed to a choir recruited locally from musicians who belonged to any part of Europe west of the Rhine and included what later times would call Flemish and Belgian singers, as well as musicians from southern France. They were singers, not only in touch with the developments which had been achieved at Saint Martial and Notre Dame, and aware of the music of troubadours and trouvères, but many of them were also composers in the new forms and in the new styles. Clement's problems left him little time for the personal supervision of liturgical music, so that the Avignon choir became a centre for musicians of and entirely in sympathy with the new style. The elaborations and effects which had been growing increasingly common in Northern Europe received if not official sanction at least tacit consent in the Papal Court, and the prestige they thus gained hastened their spread.

The extent of their new style's progress is indicated by the Bull *Docta Sanctorum*, which Clement's successor, John XXII, issued in 1323, the seventh year of his pontificate:

> Certain disciples of the new school, much occupying themselves with the measured dividing of the *tempora*, display their prolation in notes that are new to us, preferring to devise new methods of their own rather than to continue singing in the old way. Therefore the music of the Divine Office is disturbed with notes of these small values. Moreover, they hinder the melody with hoquets, they deprave them with descants, and sometimes they pad them out with upper parts made out of secular songs. The result is that they often seem to be losing sight of the fundamental sources of our melodies in the Antiphoner and Gradual, and forget what it is that they are burying under their superstructures. They may become entirely ignorant of the ecclesiastical modes, which they have already ceased to distinguish and the limits of which they abuse in the prolixity

of their notes. The modest rise and temperate descents of plainsong, by
which the modes themselves are recognised, are entirely obscured. The
voices incessantly to and fro, intoxicating rather than soothing the ear,
while the singers themselves try to convey the emotion of the music by
their gestures. The consequence of all this is that devotion, the true aim
of all worship, is neglected, and wantonness, which ought to be eschewed,
increases.

   This state of things, which has become the common one, we and our
brethren have come to regard as needing correction. Therefore we hasten
to forbid these methods, or rather to drive them more effectively out of
the house of God than has been done in the past. For this reason, having
taken counsel with our brethren, we strictly command that no one shall
henceforth consider himself at liberty to use these methods, or methods
like them, in the singing of the canonical Office or in solemn celebrations
of the Mass. . . .

   Nevertheless, it is not our wish to forbid the occasional use—especially
on feast days or in solemn celebration of the Mass and the Divine Office—
the use of some consonances, for example, the octave, the fifth and the
fourth, which heighten the beauty of the melody. Such intervals, therefore, may be sung above the ecclesiastical chant, but in such a way that
the integrity of the chant remains intact and that nothing in the pre-
scribed music be changed. Used thus, the consonances would, more than
any other music is able to do, both soothe the hearer and inspire his
devotion without destroying religious feeling in the minds of the singers.

   The Bull deserves to be quoted at length because it perfectly illustrates the
conservative attitude to innovations in church music. John XXII was prepared
in 1323 to accept a style regarded as offensive two hundred years before while
forbidding a later, musically more autonomous style. The point is, of course, that
anything which seems new is therefore disturbing; by its novelty it calls attention
to itself, and therefore is regarded as a distraction in the worship of the church.
The idea of music as a means of expressing some sort of Christian truth or some
specifically Christian attitude was obviously not in the Pope's mind.

   In 1377, when Pope Gregory XI returned with his choir to Rome, the old and
new Papal choirs, the northerners who had functioned at Avignon and the traditional Roman choir which had sung through the interregnum amalgamated, not
into the old *Schola Cantorum* but into a new *Collegio dei Cappellani Cantori*, under
a 'Master of the Pontifical chapel'. From that date onwards the choir was an
international body composed not only of native Italians but also of singers drawn
mainly from France and Flanders. During the pontificates of Martin V (1417–31)
and Eugenius IV (1431–47), in the fifty years which followed the Great Schism,
seventeen musicians from the north served in the Papal choir; the majority of
them came from the area around Cambrai, Tournai and Arras.[1]

   Singers were recruited from the north not simply for the beauty of their voices,
for Italy has always been amply supplied with voices of exceptional quality. The
development of urban civilisation in the north had brought into being large and

---

[1] Manfred Schuler: *Zur Geschichte der Kapelle Papst Eugens IV. Acta Musi-
cologica*; 1968, Fasc. IV.

well-trained choirs entirely familiar with the new polyphonic style which continued in spite of John XXII's objections to it. Both boys and adults in the growing choirs, which increased in size because they were endowed by men who were making great fortunes out of trade, could not only sing polyphony but were capable of reading it fluently even in the difficult notation of the late middle ages; amongst them was an impressive number of composers, for it seems that to absorb a child's mind in music from the age of eight or nine onwards, and to base his education upon music and its practice, is not only to equip him with secure technical foundations but also to stimulate any creative instincts he possesses. Therefore, because the Papal choir, like almost every other, was admitting polyphonic music into its repertoire and was dependent upon its own members for compositions to sing, it required experts to assist it to do so. Its adoption of the new style and its patronage of northern composers advanced the prestige of the new style throughout Europe.

Freedom of experiment in music originally had depended upon the unchronicled development of secular song and dance, upon the availability of sufficient trained and unbroken voices to stimulate the composer's imagination and upon the difficulty of maintaining papal discipline in a world of limited communications, so that the most exciting developments in church music took place away from Rome. By the end of the fourteenth century other factors had entered. The gradual conquest of Italian music by musicians from France and Flanders shows not only that the style they had developed and which was flourishing in England was attractive to countries in which it was not indigenous, but also that trained musicians were being produced in the north in such numbers that the new style could not only be spread across Italy but that standards of composition, teaching and performance could be maintained at home. On the whole it was the greatest who left their native country and spent years, if not their entire professional lifetime, in the south. They did so because the wealth and prestige, not only of the Papacy but also of the great Italian noblemen and the great Italian cities, could offer richer rewards than were available in the area from which the composers and singers migrated.

The region later to be known as the Netherlands was unique in the middle ages because it stood outside the normal process of political development. By the thirteenth century practically every trace of the feudal system had vanished from the region now divided into Belgium and Holland, leaving a land in which the greater landowners employed paid workers because serfdom was extinct. In the eastern Netherlands there was an independent peasantry which had democratic powers in the choice of its leaders. As the towns developed a similar semi-democratic system developed within them, so that instead of depending upon privileges granted to them by a feudal lord, the citizens controlled their own destinies and were free to expand their trade as rapidly and as profitably as they could. Holland itself had an hereditary prince and the regions bordering on France had their aristocratic rulers, but these, in countries which depended not on natural wealth but on the volume of trade, made it their business to leave merchants and tradesmen as free as possible. Originally the feudal authorities had encouraged the development of cities within their territories as a means of increasing their own wealth, and consequently their power against their neighbours. Businessmen, however, rapidly discovered that their interests did not come to an end at some arbitrary division drawn on the map and separating them from the next town, but depended on the progress of their colleagues in neighbouring states, so that the initial partnership between feudal aristocracy and the mercantile system was only short-lived. It existed just long enough to establish the towns firmly.

The medieval city, it may be as well to remember, was a place in which a collection of more or less equal and equally responsible merchants and tradesmen lived for their convenience. It was not a place rising from the need of employers to create housing for the mass of poorer people who did the less-skilled work which they had to offer. The result was a beauty which eighteenth- and nineteenth-century cities failed to recapture. The centres of the wool trade in England can stand as examples—Cotswold towns like Chipping Camden, Northleach and Painswick, East Anglian towns like Bury St. Edmunds, Thaxted and Lavenham —to show the sense of style and dignity which went into the creation of cities, in which all the amenities were to be shared by more or less equal and equally wealthy citizens. The churches of such towns and the splendid elaboration of many chantry chapels show how much middle-class money flowed into the service of religion.

In England the creation of guild chapels, such as that at Stratford on Avon, where services were sung, tended to increase the employment of musicians and probably allowed entry to a freer style of church music than would normally be heard in parish churches or cathedrals. On the continent music often benefited more directly from the wealth which grew from commerce. In many north-European cities bequests were made to replace the clerical vicars of the choir with professional singers who were laymen. The wealthy businessmen not only made bequests to cathedrals and churches; they founded religious fraternities which had among their rules the duty of supporting daily services with choir and full musical accompaniment. In the fifteenth century it may well have been the example of the laity which moved Antwerp Cathedral Chapter to apply some of the income from its prebends to the payment of professional singers and to increasing the size of the choir; in 1443, when Ockeghem joined it as a treble, Antwerp Cathedral had twenty-five singers of polyphonic music on its *cantoris* side, and twenty-six on the *decani* side to sing plainchant; by 1480 it had some sixty singers in its choir. If, as it is reasonable to claim, the great things not only in religious art and architecture but also in church music depended upon the wealth of the new middle class, this applied more specifically to the highly urbanised area of Flanders and the Netherlands than to any other part of Europe.

The connection between prosperity and the state of the arts is something that occurred to Charles Burney when he considered the history of music in the Netherlands; 'As the polite arts are the children of affluence and dependent upon

superfluity for support,' he wrote,[1] 'it is natural to suppose that they would thrive
well at this time.' The great developments in urban life in the twelfth and thirteenth century created not only an appetite for music but also developed the
institutions which could supply it. The large choirs of the northern cities trained
not only the superfluity of singers who could travel across Europe carrying the
Flemish style with them, but also sufficient highly skilled and highly gifted
musicians to maintain high standards at home. Economic developments may
not have an immediate effect on the arts, but they create conditions which the
arts can use as a springboard.

   Trade was necessarily international. The English wool merchants of the
Staple traded from a centre which was sometimes at Bruges, sometimes at
Antwerp, and sometimes at Calais, where it eventually settled early in the
fifteenth century; it was sometimes in England, leading merchants from the
continent from Dover through Canterbury to London in considerable numbers.
Merchants from Spain and Italy, no less than from the Netherlands, France and
Germany, thronged the markets, and there was a regular service of packet ships
from the Netherlands to Italy as early as the thirteenth century. What was worked
out in one country's art or industry could travel the length and breadth of Europe:
music heard by travellers at Mass in Bruges, Ghent, Antwerp, Mechlin, Cambrai
or any of the important northern trade and musical centres could create among
travellers an appetite for some particular style of music only to be satisfied by the
sponsoring of similar developments in their own countries. Continental merchants
making their way to London and taking the opportunity of their journey to visit
the shrine of St. Thomas of Canterbury, might hear, for example, the works of
Leonel Power, who seems to have been one of the monks at Canterbury Cathedral
and whose music, regarded as both revolutionary and exquisitely expressed,
approached that of Dunstable in power. They would carry with them, in their
heads if not on paper, a memory of the rich textures, the idiosyncratically English
techniques and melodic outlines of Power's music. At home they would use
whatever influence they had to stimulate the adoption of whatever in the new
music that they found attractive.

   The increasing diffusion of music can be placed beyond conjecture by considering the important collections of manuscripts built up in the fourteenth and
fifteenth centuries, and their increasingly cosmopolitan contents. A manuscript
collection of music made for the Augustinian Priory of St. Alban's contains a good
deal of music by the Notre Dame composers, but, because it was apparently
intended for the choir offices of a community church, it contains nothing which
is extra-liturgical like the motet. Copies of French music were made for St. Paul's
Cathedral, and for Worcester Cathedral, where Pérotin's music was among the
works sung. The Old Hall Manuscript, kept in the Old Hall at Ware which
became St. Edmund's College, was apparently made for the Chapel Royal, for it
consists of works by composers known to be associated with the King's court in
Lancastrian days; it contains a hundred and forty pieces, four of which can be

---

[1] Charles Burney: *General History of Music.*

found in collections made at about the same time at Aosta, three in Bologna, three in Munich, four in Modena and two in the rather later collection known as the Trent Codices, made for the cathedral at Trent in the southern Tyrol. This collection has works by two French, four Italian, eight English, twelve Flemish and four German composers as well as a large number of anonymous, unidentifiable works.

The sources of the works of two English composers show how music had begun to travel. John Dunstable died and was buried in London in 1453, after spending some years abroad in the service of the Duke of Bedford, the English Regent in France after the death of Henry V. Most of his music is preserved not in English or French manuscripts but in manuscript copies in Modena, Bologna, Trent and Aosta. Dunstable was the inspiration of musicians in the north, not of Italian composers, and there is no record of his ever having visited Italy. Walter Frye, his almost unknown contemporary, was it seems cantor at Ely in 1443—a fact which suggests that he had risen in the service of Ely Cathedral over a number of years—but he is named in the roll of a London Guild of Musicians in 1447. Only one of his works—and he wrote secular songs as well as masses and motets—is found complete in an English collection; three of his masses are known only from copies in the Bibliothèque Royale de Belgique, some of his motets are in manuscript collections in the library of the Escorial, and in the Trent Codices. His chansons and motets are found in the Mellon and Schedel *Liederbücher*. An *Ave Maria* appears in thirteen manuscripts, and Obrecht used it as the basis for a motet of his own with the same text, as well as for the *cantus firmus* of a mass. His song *Tant a pour moy* was used as a *cantus firmus* by Josquin, Agricola and Tinctoris, which means that it had travelled widely round Europe although the Walter Frye who served at Ely and was known in London remains a mysterious figure with nothing to link him to music on the continent.[1]

The growth of the northern choirs, and the number of highly skilled musicians whom they trained, meant an overflow from the north which carried with it the new more intricate style which had developed there. Until the northern style had become internationally accepted and similar methods of training to those available in northern France, Flanders and the western Netherlands had been adopted elsewhere, highly trained singers, men and boys, were naturally in demand for their musicianship as well as the quality of their voices, throughout the south of Europe as soon as the style of singing they exploited won the prestige of Papal approval at Avignon.

The centre of early experiment and development had been Paris. The Hundred Years' War pushed the centre of gravity further north, to Flanders, where the commercial wealth of such cities as Cambrai (not part of France until it was

[1] Sylvia W. Kenney: *Walter Frye and the Contenance Angloise*, Yale University Press, 1964, establishes the identity of a Walter Frye who was cantor at Ely. Grove (fifth edition, 1956) suggests that the English-sounding surname is an anglicisation of the old German word *Frai*, which would indicate that the composer was a free-lance, not in official service to any institution. Grove, however, antedates Miss Kenney's detective work.

annexed in the wars of Louis XIV), Arras, Mons, Liège, Ghent, Lille, Bruges, Antwerp and Ypres had an effect on music which can be seen from the number of composers whom their choirs produced or who spent at least some part of their lives serving in their choirs.

The peripatetic nature of court employment, which from the fourteenth century onwards became an alternative to the church service for the trained musician, helps to explain the popularisation of northern style. The Dukes of Burgundy, although they regarded Dijon as their capital, were almost perpetually on the move between the Franche-Comté and the North Sea, taking with them their private chapels of musicians. A ruler's musicians accompanied him on diplomatic missions, not only picking up new musical interests but also diffusing the styles and techniques of his own court; the process of internationalisation was, on the whole, remarkably swift once the Great Schism healed, and it helps to explain the international dominance of the northern composers whom the text books refer to as the Burgundian, or Flemish school. Rome, Milan, Florence, Mantua, Ferrara, Naples and Venice all came, directly or indirectly, under the northern influence. Furthermore secular music had a more honoured social place in the Italian cities and was therefore more highly developed. As a composer was a salaried functionary providing music for the entertainment of the court, the new style applied itself no less powerfully to secular music than to church works.

Furthermore Italian approval began to be regarded as the necessary indication of excellence long before the Italian style which developed in the seventeenth and eighteenth centuries from the fusion of what was naturally Latin with the scholarly and technically polished music of the North. The appearance of the northerners created an appetite for a new and complex style in which they were skilled and Italians were not; hence the presence in their court records not only of the masters from Flanders and Burgundy whose names are well known, but of a multitude of singers and instrumentalists who appear with such surnames as 'Francesi', 'Alemanni' or 'Oltramontani'. The influx of the foreigners was supported by political and economic developments. The prosperity of the Italian towns— Florence, Milan and Venice in particular—created a demand for music of the type which the northern cities had developed to satisfy similar demands for civic and religious dignity. If there was an element of snobbery in the concerted rush to appropriate the best foreign talent—as there must be in any concerted rush to be quite up to date—the mere fact that northerners could not only sing elaborate polyphonic music but could read it even when they were small boys made them for a time indispensable members of any ensemble; and as it was singers and not instrumentalists who were in demand, the choir schools of the northern cities, enlarged to satisfy the cities' own taste for music, could supply the need; they produced more good musicians than northern music making could absorb.

Furthermore, the influence was not one-sided, for Italy had its own effect upon the immigrants. Before the musical commerce with Italy started, the composers who had inherited the elaborations of *Ars Nova* were technically superior to their southern contemporaries. Dufay and the generations which followed him—and Dufay was a member of the Papal Choir from 1428 to 1437—brought back to northern music the profundity of technique which had been its gift to the south, but into it had been injected an Italianate love of rich melody, and the style which developed as the musical *lingua franca* was not purely northern, but the fusion of two traditions and two attitudes. The benefits of the northerners' invasion were not all Italy's.

4 The Domestication of the Minstrels

Though all the evidence seems to show that the church continually borrowed from secular music, consecrating, so to speak, the efforts of composers outside, what was done inside the church was organised, co-ordinated and recorded whilst secular activities were undertaken without any sense that their method or purpose should be written down. If we do not know with any certainty what was played by the instruments which were used in church in the middle ages, we do at least know how the music was organised, what singers and what players were available for its performance and enough of the music itself to be able to follow the development of styles.

Musical resources grew both inside and outside the church, but secular music, however much it influenced what was heard in the services, remains a less easily recorded growth. It is reasonable enough to guess that much which we can now relate only to its employment in church was adopted from secular practice; did the secular words 'Sumer is i-cumen in' for example follow or precede the Latin hymn *Perspice Christicola* as a text for the 'Reading Rota'? It is only later in history that we can find records of secular music sufficiently coherent to show how the art developed. Whatever was done inside the church was given scholarly treatment and noted in the archives; the isorhythmic structures of the *Ars Nova*, an almost preciously self-conscious art form appealing to the musically educated connoisseur and based upon plainsong melodies, entered secular music, so far as we can tell, only after isorhythmic structures had been developed by secular musicians. The church musician had the facilities and the trained musicians available to deal academically with new ideas and new methods. Nevertheless, we have no sure way of knowing what innovations before the period of the *Ars Nova* originated outside the church; the irruption of a wide variety of instruments into liturgical music, for example, suggests the adoption by church musicians of what was done—apparently with a good deal of certainty as to its technique and effect—outside. At any rate, though a Latin rubric explains to the monastic choir of Reading how the rota should be sung, the music which demands the use of instruments appears without such directions, as though the work they had to do was familiar enough to be taken for granted; and the instruments shown in the pictures to be taking part in the church services were not 'church' instruments, that is, unassociated with music elsewhere, but those which, on the same evidence of pictures, were equally familiar outside it.

The musical centre of gravity did not, however, pass from the church until the beginning of the Renaissance, when it settled in the royal and aristocratic courts.

44

Nevertheless music had been part of aristocratic life throughout history, closely bound up not only with worship but with every sort of entertainment, as it is in modern 'show business', with which early secular music seems to have much in common. It had originally been part of the duty of court entertainers, who were also jugglers, acrobats, dancers, trainers of performing animals and comic cross-talk men; our word 'juggler' has the same root as the medieval term 'jongleur', which is the name often given to the minstrel of the early middle ages whether he was an inferior domestic in some aristocratic household or a member of what, nowadays, we should call a variety troupe. Regulations drawn up by and for the guidance of wandering entertainer musicians in medieval Germany have survived; the minstrel has 'to know how to invent, to make rhymes, to acquit himself well as a swordsman; to know how to play drums, cymbals and the *Bauernleier* (hurdy-gurdy) well; to know how to throw up little apples and to catch them on the point of a knife; to imitate the songs of birds, perform tricks with cards and jump through hoops; to play the cittern and the mandoline, to handle the clavichord and the guitar, to string the seven-stringed rotte, to accompany well with the fiddle, and to speak and sing pleasantly'. A jongleur in aristocratic service was expected to entertain his master and his master's guests in whatever way they wished, just as an itinerant performer, to earn his living, had to be story-teller, singer, instrumentalist, acrobat, juggler and anything else he could convincingly manage to be.

While it is only sensible to suppose that some aristocrats developed a taste for music which made their entertainers into specialist musicians before the eleventh century, the greatest factor in the development of aristocratic music seems to have been the rise of the Troubadours of southern France and the Trouvères of northern France in the eleventh and twelfth centuries and the emergence of the *Minnesänger* in Germany nearly a century later. Music, like goods and new ideas of all sorts, had flowed along the main trade routes; goods and manners came to France across Germany from Italy; the secular music of troubadours and trouvères went in the opposite direction, slowly acclimatising itself to German customs. The crusaders' routes, too, carried the new style: after all, an optimistic aristocrat with a thirst for glory would, like the English Richard I, consider himself well repaid by the services of an attendant minstrel who could not only entertain him and probably his friends but who was also qualified to immortalise his glorious deeds in song. Such an attendant would take with him, and propagate along the line of the march, the songs and music of his normal repertory. The song movement, as it spread across Europe, was primarily aristocratic, concerned with courtly and high-minded themes, expressed in measured, metrical music (unlike much of the text with which church composers were occupied) in one of a small number of closed, strictly observed lyric and musical forms which persisted into the Renaissance. It was accompanied, though precisely how we can only guess, by any portable instrument the attendant minstrel or the knightly singer himself could play. Whether the aristocratic singers provided the music for their own lyrics as a matter of course, or who provided it for them, is an unanswerable question; but they introduced the word 'minstrel' into the European languages as the accurate term for a musician who was singer and performer simply because they took with them one who was originally a member of the jongleur fraternity to 'minister' to them musically and as a servant, to accompany their singing and to act probably as batman-valet; in medieval illustrations, troubadour and minstrel appear together, the latter carrying a vielle, the primitive violin-type instrument which became so common that its name often applied to its player, so that in later times the words 'vielle' and 'jongleur' became interchangeable.

Because troubadours, trouvères and Minnesingers were usually aristocrats, they could afford to have their compositions and the other songs they sang collected into chansonnières, some of which survive, though it was not until the thirteenth and fourteenth centuries that the task of collecting and copying out the songs was taken seriously, and by that time many of them had become subject to the inevitable variation and corruption of oral transmission; and, of course, the idea of appending the name or names of poet and composer, even if it had chimed in with medieval custom, would have been impossible for very many songs. Nevertheless the itinerant, unattached jongleurs adopted the new songs and the new styles into their repertoires, and it is more likely than improbable that the jongleurs themselves composed quite extensively in trouvère style.

There were always commoners who were ranked amongst the troubadours and their equivalents, so that aristocratic birth, though it was commonplace among members, was never a condition of entry. Adam de la Halle—who was born in the middle of the thirteenth century, probably about 1240, and according to a contemporary, Jean Bodin, died in 1285 or the following year—was the son of a middle-class official somehow employed by the Sheriff of Arras. Adam, designed for holy orders by his parents, was sent to the Abbey of Vauxcelles near Cambrai, from which he escaped in order to marry a girl with whom he had fallen in love. Then, apparently deserting his wife, he ran away to Paris to continue his studies and it seems re-entered the monastic life; Prud'homme's *Dictionnaire Historique* has him dying as a monk at Vauxcelles. In 1283, however, he was in the service of Comte Robert of Artois, in the expedition sent to Naples to avenge the slaughter of the Sicilian Vespers. De la Halle is classed among the trouvères, although his background is bourgeois and he was merely a minstrel in aristocratic service. Because he came late in the movement and achieved fame, his authorship of a number of chansons, motets and music dramas was remembered when the song books were collected—this is itself enough to prove his eminence—and the collectors showed that his interests extended a long way beyond the typical trouvères' song with instrumental accompaniment.

The new lyric forms and the types of music they stimulated were quickly taken up into religious service. There was at first no place for them in the music of the liturgy, but in the hands of the Franciscans they became a vehicle for popular devotion. One of the names for the Franciscan Friars was '*joculatores Dei*': 'joculator' is the Latin original from which the word '*Jongleur*' was derived, and the Franciscans were itinerant religious minstrels in so far as they developed a style of popular religious song which followed the pattern of the songs of the minstrels; perhaps the most famous example is St. Francis's own 'Canticle of the Sun'. It was not long before this new rhythmic, popularly melodious style found its way, as the basis of polyphonic motets and later of passages from the Mass, into church worship. Henry of Pisa, one of the early Franciscans, was one of the first of the many evangelists who have wondered why the devil should be allowed all the best tunes; he heard a servant girl singing a love song one morning; the tune appealed to him, so he gave it new words, '*Christe Deus, Christe meus, Christe Rex et Domine.*'

The itinerant musicians—probably on the whole the less efficient, for a post in an aristocratic household ensured its holder's livelihood—were not socially acceptable or given more than the coldest tolerance by the church. 'Can a minstrel be saved?' asked a theologian, Honorius of Autun, and answered himself categorically: 'No; minstrels are ministers of Satan. They laugh now, but God shall laugh at them on the last day.' They were condemned more or less out of hand by the church authorities, although there are monastic accounts which show that in some places travelling entertainers earned a good deal of money from performances in monasteries; nevertheless they probably lived poorly enough until, in the fourteenth century, a new and wider possibility of employment opened for them as civic watchmen and ceremonial musicians. In the fourteenth century, all over Europe, town minstrels became, in England, 'waits', in Germany '*Türmer*' ('tower men'). Both words refer to their duties as watchmen who could, by means of their instruments, give warning of any danger approaching or arising in the town. Elsewhere in Germany they became '*Stadtpfeifer*', in Italy they became '*Pifferi*'. Organised into guilds and jealous of their professional status and privileges, they did not absorb the entire number of wandering entertainers who lived as best they could off the proceeds of their oddly assorted skills; the wanderers remained homeless 'rogues and vagabonds', legislated against as were actors until the actors settled down in regularly organised companies with permanent theatres and, more often than not, aristocratic patronage. If the legislation was acted upon only half-heartedly, the lack of any deliberate and purposeful persecution of the itinerants was only due to the difficulty, in the late-medieval world, of enforcing laws across countries where communications were slow and inefficient.

As poetry and music came increasingly under aristocratic and royal patronage, and as music won a definite place in the middle-class society of the medieval towns, the wandering minstrels became increasingly disliked by their more fortunate colleagues who held assured positions. The regularly employed rapidly developed the ambition—natural enough in our eyes but apparently new to the fourteenth century—to be known as the creators of songs or poems. A contemporary of Chaucer in England, in a poem *Winnour and Wastour*, complains bitterly of the use made by itinerants of the works of others and, although the notion of music or poetry as its creator's intellectual property was new, describes the piracy of the travelling entertainers as a new and ominous sign of a decadent age.

> But now a child upon a chair, without chin-weeds,
> That never wrought through wit three words together,
> For he can jangle as a jay and japes tell,
> He shall be believed and loved and let of a while
> Well more than the man who made it himselven.

It is in these circumstances that the career of Machaut[1] sets what becomes something of a pattern for the careers of later composers. Music and poetry, to both of which arts he made splendid contributions, were not his full-time occupations; unlike the other composers whose names have survived for us from the age in which he worked, he was not primarily concerned with the composition and performance of music; he was neither a monk nor a cathedral dignitary contributing naturally what his special talent could offer in the Divine Service, but an administrator and functionary the importance of whose music to his employers cannot be estimated because all his official posts were in the nature of civil service employment rather than in the musical establishments of his masters. So far as we can tell, music and poetry—and most of his biography is compiled from information given in his verse—occupied his leisure. Although it was written to be heard in court circles, to what extent his livelihood may have depended upon it is something we cannot tell. Wherever his royal masters went, his duty led him to follow, and in whatever he wrote for their pleasure he followed the secular style of the trouvères and the religious motet style of the *Ars Nova*; he was amongst those who developed the relatively short-lived form of the secular motet, employing *Ars Nova* polyphonic principles to court entertainment music. The fact that he moved about continually in exalted circles and was brought into contact with the mighty enabled his works to survive with greater authenticity than those of many others of his contemporaries. For the first time, we encounter a musician whose secular music and whose church music take equal rank.

Machaut's work presupposes that not only a group of singers and instrumentalists will be available to perform Latin motets in church but that also, when secular songs are required, instrumentalists will be available to accompany the singing voice or voices. Just as the motet had become a secular form as well as a type of work suitable for filling otherwise silent moments of the liturgy, in Machaut's *Ballades Notées* it provides the stylistic foundation for solo songs or duets—the singing voice or voices being the highest part or parts, accompanied by a couple of instruments, or in duets by a solo instrument treated in a way as freely polyphonic as the voice. Machaut, although he composed the earliest setting of the Ordinary of the Mass which can be ascribed to a composer, actually wrote more secular music than works for the church. As a courtier, he was interested in the entertainment and pleasure of his employers, so that his division of interest is easy to understand.

The development of such courtly entertainment into the duty of a more or less

[1] See Chapter 2, pp. 30–31.

consistent group of singers and instrumentalists, more or less balanced in voices and tonal weight, seems to have been at least in part another result of the Papal exile at Avignon. At any rate, in emulation of the performers who provided not only the music for the Papal services but also such entertainment music as the Pope might require, noblemen became to call the groups of musicians whom they maintained a 'chapel' and to follow the style of music and music making which had Papal prestige to glorify it as well as the most modern and attractive musical style. The word 'chapel' turns up, in this connection, from the early fifteenth century in every European language, and the various musical establishments began if not to take a stereotyped form, at least to follow a similar pattern of development, with choirs, usually quite small, and a heterogeneous group of instruments which could be used either as an accompaniment or to make music independently.

The word 'chapel' is derived from the 'Cappella' (or cloak) of St. Martin, the holiest relic of the Frankish kings, on which oaths were sworn and which was carried before their troops in battle. Its guardians were 'cappellani' and the sanctuary in which it was kept was the 'cappella', so that 'cappella' became the word for a religious building, its furnishings and its personnel, that is to say, for the entire establishment required for worship by a king or nobleman.

The English kings, for example, kept such an establishment at least from early in the twelfth century. By the end of the fourteenth century the Chapel Royal had become the centre of a school of composers, and remained so until the seventeenth century. The Old Hall Manuscript, one of the best sources for English medieval music, is the choir book of the Chapel Royal composers of the reigns of Henry IV and Henry V, both of whom were keen musicians. Henry IV was regarded as brilliant by his contemporaries, and authorities disagree as to whether he, or his eldest son, was composer of the *Gloria in Excelsis* and the *Sanctus* preserved in the Old Hall Manuscript as the work of 'Roy Henry'.

The English Chapel Royal under Edward I, in 1292, consisted of thirteen priest-chaplains, thirteen clerks in priest's orders and six singing boys. It was smaller than the choirs immovably stationed in the Palace of Westminster and in St. George's Chapel Windsor, each of which was ruled by a Dean and twelve canons in addition to being served by choirs of the same size as that of the peripatetic Chapel Royal. This English organisation was the model for the *Sainte Chapelle* of the French kings.

The three royal foundations were enlarged by the Yorkist Kings Edward IV and Richard III in the later fifteenth century, but such establishments parallel not only the Sainte Chapelle in Paris but also the Imperial *Kapelle* set up in Vienna, Prague and Innsbruck. Although permanently organised and permanently active, they became second in importance and influence to the chapels set up in and attached to royal households to accompany the monarch wherever he went and to remain permanently under his control as the providers of music for his private devotions and his special ceremonies. Henry III, early in the thirteenth century, had regularly three and sometimes four clerks whom he paid for

singing the music required by his private services. In the account book of the
Royal Wardrobe for 1393, some hundred and fifty years later, Richard II's household chapel had grown to eleven chaplains and clerks, one of whom was William
Excestre, some of whose compositions are found in the Old Hall Manuscript. A
body of instrumentalists had also been in attendance on the king at least since the
reign of Edward III, who had nineteen players—five trumpeters, one cyteler,
five pipers, one tabret player, one mabrer, two clarions, one fiddler and three
waits playing oboes—in his service. Singers and instrumentalists constituting a
'chapel' were not simply the choir and accompaniment of church services, they
were also the royal entertainers.

The Lancastrian kings developed these bodies into an organisation similar to
those growing up at the same time at all the major European courts. We discover
that boys had joined the household musicians when, early in his reign, Henry IV
appointed an extra chaplain to the boys of his private chapel which in 1402, when
he had been king for three years, contained eighteen chaplains and clerks. In
1413, almost immediately after his accession, Henry V raised the number to
twenty-seven, four of whom were composers of importance: John Burrell, John
Cooke, Thomas Damett and Nicholas Sturgeon. By 1420, Henry had authorised
the composer John Pyamour to 'impress' boys into royal service, taking them by
royal authority and if necessary without their parents' consent; these new
recruits were sent to join the king's private chapel in Normandy, where it had
been in attendance on him since 1417. In 1421 and 1422 the private chapel in
France had sixteen boys; a year later, after Henry V's death, only six. The international prestige which Henry's chapel won—the French and Burgundian
courtiers and rulers came into contact with it—together with the work of such
English composers as John Dunstable had an international effect. Foreign rulers
became eager to employ English singers. Alonso V of Portugal in 1438, the
Emperor Frederick in 1442 and Galeazzo Maria Sforza of Milan in 1471, all sent
agents to England to collect English musicians.

By 1436 Henry VI's chapel had seven members, and in 1440 he again ordered
boys to be impressed, raising the number of members of the household chapel
to twenty-six. In 1444 he paid forty marks a year to the composer John Plummer
for the 'exhibition' of eight boys of the chapel, indicating that the boys had been
placed under Plummer's control. In 1455 there were ten boys, and the priests
and clerks were complaining about the weight of work which had fallen to them
'because their number was less than formerly'; they asked the Privy Council to
authorise that there should be at least twenty-four singing men, the number the
members themselves considered necessary.

When, in 1483, Edward IV gave his 'Royal Free Chapel of the Household' the
endowment of St. Peter's Chapel in the Tower of London (thus maintaining his
private musicians without needing to dip into his privy purse to do so), he
organised it with a dean and three canons, who were sub-dean, treasurer and
precentor, and twenty-four chaplains and gentlemen clerks, thus officially employing laymen as singers for the first time. At the same time, the king's household

book—the *Liber Regis Nigrorum*—gives an account of the duties of his thirteen minstrels, 'some with trumpets, some with shawms and small pipes, and some strange men coming to court at the five feasts of the year' (Christmas, Easter, Ascension, Whitsun and Corpus Christi) to augment the domestic minstrels when special celebrations would be held. The minstrels were, amongst other things, the court time-keepers; one had to do the duty of a wait, as night watch-man, and they were all ordered on festival days to warn everyone 'by their blowing and piping' to prepare 'the King's meat and soupers'.

Edward's regulations attempt to provide for the future of the boys who had been in his service: if, by the time they were eighteen (an age which suggests that they lost their boys' voices singularly late), no position at court was open to them, 'the King assigneth such child to a college at Oxford or Cambridge of the King's foundation'. They were to continue with their studies at university until the king found occasion to employ them.

By Tudor times the Household Chapel was more or less stabilised, even though stabilisation meant the frequent impressment of boys. In the first half of the sixteenth century the Gentlemen of the Chapel Royal numbered between eighteen and twenty-one. Henry VIII increased the number of the boys to twelve and their master was almost always an extremely distinguished musician—Gilbert Banister, William Newark, Robert Jones and Thomas Tallis, as well as a number of other composers less remarkably gifted, held the post. The Chapel Royal, by this time a body of specialist musicians, offered members a reasonable certainty of tenure and reasonable pay as well as enormous prestige, and Henry VIII, whose consideration of the difficulties of others was not always one of his most notable qualities, took a good deal of trouble to try to match the rise in prices during his reign with a compensating increase in salaries.

The nobleman's chapel goes back to the middle ages. John of Gaunt, the uncle of Richard II, had four chaplains and two clerks in his service in 1371, and the records which explain its existence add that ten years later he added three boys to his establishment. John, Duke of Bedford, his grandson and younger brother of King Henry V, was regent in France under the Treaty of Troyes after his brother's death in 1422, and John Pyamour, who had been responsible for taking Henry V's household musicians to Normandy in 1420, turns up again as chief of Bedford's musicians whilst the Duke tried to maintain English power in France, first from Paris between 1423 and 1429, and then until 1436 from Rouen. Apparently the mysterious John Dunstable, the greatest composer of the age, was not one of the chapel, for though an inscription in an astronomical text book is said to have been written for the Duke by Dunstable, he is not listed among the Duke's musicians.

If the nobleman's chapel was set up in emulation of that of the King, it seems that originally the purposes it fulfilled were more restricted than those of the royal musicians. The constitution and regulations of the Earl of Northumber-land's chapel in 1512 were quoted by Hawkins: the earl employed eight singing men, four boys, an Epistoler, an organist and a master for the boys.

The singers, Hawkins makes it clear,[1] were engaged simply for worship in the earl's chapel; whatever instrumentalists he kept in service—if he kept any— seemed to have had no part in religious music, just as the regulations indicate that the chapel choir had no share in the secular music, such as it might have been.

The number recorded as members of the Royal Chapels in England and elsewhere can be held to indicate a variety of things; the late medieval and early renaissance delight in pomp and splendour and the growing social importance of music. But they also indicate the gradual triumph of polyphony as it spread from the art of ensemble of solo singers into choral music. Six boys and twice as many men are a good number for plainsong, and the intrusion of ensemble passages of polyphony—like a royal *Gloria* and *Sanctus*—need not create any anxious problems of balance if they are sung by ensembles of one voice to each vocal part; but Henry VIII's twelve boys to four or five voices for each of the lower parts creates a choir which is capable of balanced polyphonic singing.

The custom of 'impressment' was not purely an English way of finding good unbroken voices and musical ability. During the fifteenth and sixteenth centuries, boys whose beauty of voice was in any way matched by their skill in reading music were not uncommonly whisked from one end of Europe to the other, more frequently, of course, from the musically developed, urban north to Italy. The demand for singers trained in the Netherlands schools meant that Roland Lassus, or Orlando di Lasso, for example, was three times abducted from Mons, where he was a treble in the choir of St. Nicholas' Church. Lassus was born in 1532, and the third abduction, when he was nine years old, succeeded, for his parents agreed to allow Ferdinand Gonzaga, regent of Sicily and commander of the emperor's forces at the siege of Saint-Dizier, to keep the boy and eventually to take him first to Palermo and then to Milan. In 1518 it seems that Cardinal Wolsey was annoyed by Henry VIII's demand that he hand over the solo boy of his chapel to the king's establishment, for the Dean of the Chapel Royal, Richard Pace, wrote to the cardinal:

> My Lord, if it were not for the personal love that the King's Highness doth bear Your Grace, surely he would have out of your chapel not children only, but men also; for His Grace hath plainly shown unto Cornishe that Your Grace's Chapel is better than his.

William Cornyshe, the composer, had been 'master of the singing boys' at Westminster Abbey from 1480 to 1491, and had entered the Chapel Royal in about 1492 (his name first appears among its members in 1496), becoming 'master of the children' in 1509. He took the Chapel Royal to France during Henry's French campaign of 1513 and 1514, and again for the ceremonial splendour of the Field of the Cloth of Gold. Cornyshe was an impressive composer of both church and secular music, but Henry VIII was a skilled musician who would not relish the superiority of an underling's musicians. Wolsey's boy— a star performer, it seems—was handed over, and Pace wrote a second letter a

---

[1] Sir John Hawkins: *A General History of the Science and Practice of Music.* 1776.

mere day after his first (March 26, 1518), explaining that the king insisted upon the boy's being handed over without troubling Cornyshe to apply the normal machinery for procuring choirboys, and on April 1 he wrote to Wolsey again:

> Cornyshe doth greatly laud and praise the child of your chapel sent hither, not only for his sure and cleanly singing but also for his good and and crafty descant, and doth in like manner extol Mr. Pygotte [the master of Wolsey's choirboys] for the teaching of him.

The official machinery, incidentally, did not always work: in the reign of Henry VI there was one case where the king's agents were paid six shillings and eightpence not to take away three choirboys.

Perhaps it is as well that we have the choirboy's account of all this. Thomas Tusser, the sixteenth-century author of the long didactic poem, *The Five Points of Good Husbandry*, was born in the reign of Henry VIII, sent by his father to Wallingford College as a singing boy, and impressed from there into the choir of St. Paul's, for the 'placards' permitting the impressment of boys did not apply only to the royal establishments; other institutions could seek authority to use them. Tusser's experiences found their way into the naïvely amiable jog-trot of his poem.

> It came to pass that born I was
> Of lineage good and gentle blood,
> In Essex lair, in village fair
>   That Rivenhall hight;
> Which village did by Banktree side.
> There did I spend my infancy;
> There then my name in honest fame
>   Remained in sight.
>
> I yet was young, no speech of tongue,
> No tears withal that often fall
> From mother's eyes when child outcries
>   To part her from
> Could pity make my father take,
> But out I must to song be thrust;
> Say what I would, do what I could,
>   His mind was so.
>
> Oh painful time! For every crime
> What toosed ears, like baited bears!
> What bobbed lips, what jerks, what nips,
>   What hellish toys!
> What robes! How bare! What college fare,
> What bread how stale, what penny ale,
> Then Wallingford, wert thou abhorred
>   Of silly boys!
>
> Then for my voice, I must (no choice
> Away by force, like posting horse,
> For sundry men had placards then
>   Such child to take;

> The better breast, the little rest
> To serve the choir, now there, now here
> For time so spent may I repent
>   And sorrow make.
>
> But mark the change, myself to range,
> By friendship's lot to Paul's I got,
> So found I grace a certain space
>   Still to remain
> With Redford there, the like nowhere
> For cunning much and virtue much,
> By whom some part of music art
>   So did I gain.

John Redford, one of the six vicars-choral of St. Paul's who signed the Act of Supremacy by which Henry VIII in 1534 declared himself to be Head of the Church in England, became organist to the cathedral and, probably in 1534, was made Master of the Choristers. It seems from the poem that St. Paul's, after Colet's educational reforms there, was a more humane place for a choirboy's education than was Wallingford College or the Eton of Nicholas Udall, where Tusser next found himself.

5 Municipal Musicians— the Professionals

The development of the towns in the later middle ages was not only a spur to revolutionary music-making inside the church. It created a way of life which required music to express its dignity and enhance its ceremonies. Just as the nobility felt that their position and prestige demanded the salutes of trumpets and drums and their social diversions the pleasure of strings and woodwind, the middle classes demanded that music added its symbolic and active glories to their own proceedings. While the continental cities made it their business to glorify the churches and enlarge the church choirs as well as to employ the best available singer-composers for the service of religion, they wanted music socially, to enhance the dignity and civilisation of their lives.

Originally, music had been a civic utility provided by the members of the guild of waits, *Stadtpfeifer* or *pifferi* who still were civic watchmen, one of whom was the *Türmer*, given a room in the tower from which he could best observe the city and its approaches so that with the assistance of a musical instrument he could give warning of the outbreak of fire or any other catastrophe and warn the citizens of the approach of any group of travellers. As a necessary civic official, he had apprentices to share the watch with him. He played a shawm—a type of primitive oboe—simply because it was the loudest instrument available. Trumpets were pre-empted by the nobility and became symbolic of aristocracy for this reason. Sackbuts, the primitive medieval trombones, were not so loud as shawm and were church instruments, so that their connotations would be no more accurate than those of trumpets.

The *Stadtpfeifer* or wait was on duty whenever he was needed. In Frankfurt, he was allowed a trumpet to herald the approach of ships along the River Main. He rang the church bells before service, or if the church had no bell, summoned the congregation with appropriate music: if the town clock had no chimes he sounded the hours. His function was to begin with almost depressingly utilitarian, and it was the desire of the citizens themselves to adapt something like courtly pomp to their proceedings which encouraged the town musicians to make themselves more important. Caspar Bach, one of the second generation of that most fantastically gifted family, became *Stadtpfeifer* in Gotha in the late sixteenth century. He lived in the tower of the town hall, had to strike the hours on the town hall bell, keep watch day and night for travellers approaching the city, give warning when any two or more came in company, and report any fire he saw, whether near or at a distance. At the same time he was the head of a tiny musicians' guild in the town, consisting of himself and a handful of qualified musicians

55

who were journeymen and each of whom had his own apprentice or apprentices who were expected to qualify as musicians through a system of training not essentially different in nature from that by which an apprentice tailor qualified for mastery.

The town musicians were sometimes players of considerable ability, capable of satisfactory performance on several instruments and in requirement for all civic functions and for the musical accompaniment to church services. So many of the Bach family became town musicians in seventeenth- and early eighteenth-century Thuringia that a protocol of the Erfurt town council in December, 1716, referred to 'the local privileged band of town musicians, or Bachs', and a certain Tobias Sabelitzky, one of the citizens, was threatened with a fine of 5 talers if he engaged any musicians not members of 'the Bachs' to play at his daughter's wedding. Johann Sebastian's father, Johann Ambrosius Bach, began his career in the Erfurt town band but became leader of the town musicians at Eisenach in 1671, with an additional post as chamber musician to Prince Johann Georg Eisenach, a double career which left him in the happy position of being able to employ a deputy to do his civic work for him, so that he was no longer required to ring the warning bell when there was an outbreak of fire, to ring the bell which summoned the citizens to pay their taxes or to make an annual inspection of fireplaces.

In the first place town musicians were domesticated minstrels who found an opportunity to settle down in a town, having probably failed to find a place in the household of some nobleman. It became their duty to supply the townsfolk with whatever music was required whilst acting as city watchmen. Naturally enough, in the middle ages they adopted the standard form of craftsmen's organisation and banded themselves together in musicians' guilds. They were responsible to the town council, which appointed a leader—a 'wait' in England, a '*Stadtmusikus*' in Germany—and the leader organised a small band of three or four musicians who were fully qualified to play all the 'wait' instruments—a qualification which began with oboes, cornetts and bassoons and, by the end of the middle ages, had come to include trumpets and trombones as well as, occasionally, horns. In the late Renaissance they found it advantageous to adopt violins and cellos as well, so that the necessary qualifications for an eighteenth-century town musician were not easily obtained. Qualified musicians were, in guild terminology, 'masters' of their craft; each trained as many apprentices as was practicable or as guild regulations in their area allowed. The apprentices boarded with them and worked as servants in their houses until they were qualified as journeymen and left free to find work elsewhere if the town had no vacancy for them. The wait or *Stadtmusikus* was chosen by the council from among the masters, journeymen who had been given positions in the city as vacancies occurred, or who had migrated from some other city, and the training of apprentices was strictly regulated by the rules of the guild, which were imposed nationally rather than locally. The guild rules maintained standards, expelled the inefficient or the dishonest, who were thus deprived of any regular means of earning their living, and drew up the tests which governed promotion from grade to grade. The surviving rules very often refer to periods when the guilds were already old-established bodies of players; thus those of the governing body of the Saxon guilds—the *Instrumental-Musikalisches Collegium*—which was responsible for the conduct of the musicians' guilds throughout the entire kingdom of Saxony—come to us from the seventeenth century when the town band was a long-established and traditional body. Amongst other ordinances it lays down 'In order that he may be adequately trained and fully experienced in his art, and be master of many instruments, some wind and some strings, no apprentice shall be set free until he had undergone at least five years' training.' There were traditional short cuts: either Handel or his friend Johann Mattheson might have settled down as town organist in Lübeck if he had agreed to marry the daughter of the city organist Buxtehude, who had obtained his post by marrying the daughter of his predecessor, Franz Tunder. Marrying the master's daughter was a recognised route to preferment and abbreviating the uncertain years otherwise spent as a journeyman.

Like the members of other guilds the town musicians wore the uniform and badge of their craft but, unlike the members of other guilds, their official work was not extensive enough to provide them with a sufficient salary. In addition to their spasmodic civic work—for their duties as watchmen became increasingly light until they disappeared in the sixteenth or early seventeenth centuries—they had the monopoly of all the town's music-making; in practice this meant that they provided all the music needed at weddings and funerals, and their monopoly was jealously defended. The fees for their services were laid down by the guild, which found itself involved in an interminable struggle—it continued until the second half of the eighteenth century—to preserve their privileges against the encroachments of amateurs, of wandering players or of unofficially organised bands which were prepared to undercut their prices.

Nevertheless, despite what seems a hazardous way of life, civic employment in a prosperous city came to bring its holder almost as much prestige as employment at a nobleman's court. In the Hansa towns and in Frankfurt, Augsburg, Nuremberg or Leipzig, for example, there was a large, affluent population eager to make the most of its social life and therefore automatically allowing the musicians whose services were a social necessity to win a position a great deal more independent than that of a musician in service to some comparatively minor aristocrat. A civic appointment lasted for the appointee's lifetime, but a court appointment depended on the pleasure and financial well-being of a single patron; the town musician who behaved himself was secure for life—a fact which gave Johann Sebastian Bach something to grumble about when he drew up a memorandum of suggested improvements for the consideration of the Leipzig town council in 1730: some of the musicians had been in service for many years under his predecessor, who had already been dead for nearly ten years, and were, he declared, 'fit only for superannuation'.

Musicians' guilds began to proliferate during the fourteenth century. St. Gallen, in Switzerland, had a Town Musician in 1272, the records of a London guild begin in 1334, and those of the guild in Basle go back to 1350. In 1391 the fee of the four Bristol waits for playing a civic function is fixed at five marks (and the same sum, incidentally, was the Lord Mayor's allowance for wine). Nuremberg appointed a *Stadtpfeifer* and his assistant in 1377; Lincoln records first mention a wait in 1399. Throughout the next century such municipal guilds of the musicians were formed not only in the important towns but wherever there was a population which needed a public watchman and could pay for music at the great social occasions of its citizens' private lives. In 1479 the city of Leipzig appointed Hans Nagel to be *Stadtmusikus*, with his two sons as his journeyman and his apprentice; their joint wage was 40 gulden a year, and they were provided with their uniforms. In Canterbury, in 1498, each of the waits was paid £1 per year.

Their duties were substantially the same throughout Europe, except in Italy where membership of the musicians' guild did not automatically preclude membership of another craftsman's guild; the *pifferi* of several of the Italian cities—Florence for example—were not dependent on their spasmodic civic duties and their occasional employment by the citizens but were occupied in other trades with music as a secondary employment. Benvenuto Cellini, who was born in 1500, was a good flautist and cornett player, taught by his father who, according to Benvenuto's *Memoirs*, sang well, played the flute and made 'wonderful organs with wooden pipes, the best clavicembalos, viols, lutes and harps' although he was by profession a carver of ivory. Benvenuto explains how his father joined the town band of *pifferi* at the invitation of the other members, who belonged to the exclusive and rather snobbish guild of wool and silk weavers, but was dismissed from the band by Piero de Medici, who was afraid that if he spent too much time on music Cellini senior might do less well in his own art. He was reinstated when he assured Piero that his official employment would not suffer. Father Cellini's frustrated ambition was to make his son into a musician, and when the boy had made it clear that music meant comparatively little to him—the *Memoirs* gave their reader the impression that any natural musicality Benvenuto possessed was obliterated by too much early training reluctantly received —the goldsmith to whom he was eventually apprenticed was himself a member of the *pifferi* of Bologna.

In spite of this looser organisation the *pifferi* undertook more or less the same duties as the town musicians of the rest of Europe; they played at performances of miracle plays, to honour visiting royalty or other notabilities, and to give dignity to such civic and religious occasions as processions. The city records of Urbino and Udine, for example, detail the part the town musicians had to play in the Corpus Christi procession and on the feast of St. Bernard. At Ferrara, in 1472, they announced the marriage of Duke Ercole d'Este from the balcony of his palace. In Venice—where the town musicians were people of enormous social prestige—they took part in the endless civic ceremonial, like the marriage of the Doge to the sea every Ascension Day, and in the shows put on on the slightest pretext by that pioneer resort of tourism: for example the signing of the alliance between Milan and Venice in 1495 was an excuse for civic festivities in which the town musicians played a prominent part. In Florence the *pifferi* were expected to play in procession through the streets on St. John's Day—St. John was the city's patron saint—'with such a storm of trumpets and pipes that the whole earth resounded with it'. In 1475 they were ordered to play to the people from the balcony of the town hall at eleven o'clock every Saturday night to honour the government for having administered justice during the past week, and it was to the sound of the music of the town band that Savonarola's bonfire of objectionable books was lighted during his heyday in Florence, between 1494 and 1497.

Despite this greater freedom and the naturally spasmodic nature of their municipal duties, the functions of the Italian bands were as closely regulated by the authorities as those of any English, German or French body of civic musicians. A detailed list of the duties of the musicians of Perugia was drawn up in 1342. The Signoria of Florence organised the work of its musicians in 1361, providing them with lodgings in the district of San Michele in Palchetto. (The provision of municipal housing for the town band was a commonplace; the Leipzig musicians were housed in the *Stadtpfeifergasse*: other towns had their *Stadtpfeifergassen* or their *Stadtpfeiferalleen*.) A statute passed in 1472 gives the Signoria the duties of appointing the musicians and providing the instruments they were to play. A list of salaries survives from Venice, where it was drawn up in 1501: the trombonist was paid 20 lire a month, one of the *pifferi* was paid 10 lire, and each of the others received a ducat (six lire four sous). Their problems were those which bedevilled the life of civic musicians everywhere, notably the preservation of their monopoly against the competition of freelance musicians who undercut their prices. The instrumentalists of St. Mark's Venice, for example, were not members of the Guild of St. Sylvester which was the city's musicians' guild, and therefore the city musicians objected to the members of the St. Mark's body of instrumentalists taking any part in weddings. This gave rise to an almost interminable dispute between two monopolies which managed quite ingeniously to be both overlapping and mutually exclusive, for no one but the St. Mark's musicians had any right to play at St. Mark's, while no one but the Guild of St. Sylvester had a right to play at weddings; playing at weddings, furthermore, was a monopoly too casually defined; did it mean at the church ceremony or the subsequent social celebration, or did it mean both? Monteverdi, in the anomalous position of belonging to both sides and neither—for as *maestro di cappella* of St. Mark's he was also the doge's chief musician and therefore responsible for any ceremonial music in which the doge was concerned—was drawn physically into the quarrel and had his beard pulled by some of the angry city musicians before the authorities settled the dispute with a clearer demarcation of privileges which really acted in favour of the guild.

The Italian city musicians were woodwind and brass players amongst whom, by the fifteenth century, trumpeters were the most important. Trumpets, however, were only slowly domesticated into the German town bands because of their traditional association with the aristocracy and with warfare. A nobleman would raise a band of trumpeters to announce his presence and provide the ceremonial music he needed; outside Italy, as the trumpet became a more widely used instrument, trumpeters were granted privileges beyond those of the ordinary musicians; in negotiations for the exchange of prisoners of war, for example, they ranked as officers, and commoners required special permission before they were allowed trumpet music at their weddings. Trumpeters were normally less versatile in the range of instruments they played than the other town musicians, but were exceptionally highly skilled at their single instrument, masters of the high, clarino style of playing which J. S. Bach was the last of the great composers to exploit and which died with the death of the musicians' guilds; they therefore, in many places, formed special guilds with special privileges and higher rates of pay than the other musicians. In Germany the early town bands consisted of shawms (oboes), cornetts, bassoons and sackbuts (trombones); the trombone, however, was as essentially a church instrument as a trumpet was a court instrument, and won its place outside the church only gradually; the players were usually capable of interchanging instruments.

It was in the fifteenth century that trumpets began to join them. Despite the wealth and importance of Nuremberg as a free city with the right to raise a regiment of troops for its own defence, its town music was not allowed to include trumpeters until 1440, close on seventy years after the first group of *Stadtpfeifer* had been organised. The three original *Stadtpfeifer* of Leipzig, in 1479, played trumpet, cornett and trombone. Salzburg added a corps of trumpeters to its *Stadtmusik* under Archbishop Wolf Dietrich, who created the city more or less as we know it today, at the end of the sixteenth century: they were to play in the Archbishop's *Tafelmusik*, to greet important visitors, to rouse the citizens at the beginning of the day and to send them home at its end. The whole body, trumpeters and all, were given homes in the *Stadtpfeiferallee*, and amongst them were four *Türmer*, with oboe, bassoon, cornett and horn, who played hymns thrice daily—at sunrise, midday and sunset—on feast days and for the birthdays and name-days of important citizens.

English bands of waits—usually four, five or six musicians, though there were nine in London—did not normally play brass instruments, except the sackbut. English players were also slower than their European counterparts to adopt string instruments as an addition to their traditional attractions. It is, however, possible to assume from the indirect evidence of music printed for small, homogeneous consort groups towards the end of the reign of Elizabeth I that in England string playing was a relatively common domestic pleasure among the class that on the continent normally paid to hear it. At any rate, though the waits did what they could to extend their range of attractions, there is little evidence that they much impressed as players of the viol or the violin.

Morley's *Consort Lessons*, published in 1599, is the first printed music book to mention the London waits, who play 'a Double Curtall (bassoon), a Lyserden (tenor cornett), a treble oboe, a cornett and a set (one to each of the four voices) of recorders'. The records of the London Court of Aldermen make notes of various purchases; in 1559 a sackbut, in 1569 a set of recorders, and in 1597 a sackbut, a double sackbut (bass trombone) and a curtal, all for the use of the waits. In 1590 the Chester musicians are noted as having oboes, recorders, cornetts and violins, while in 1602 the Exeter waits bought a 'set'—again a complete consort—of viols.

In England, as in Italy and Germany, the musicians' guilds were involved in an often desperate struggle to preserve their monopoly of all the music-making, ceremonial and social, which went on in their towns. Apart from the municipal duties in which they were unchallenged but which were simply not worth the payment of a living wage by the authorities, they had the right not only to make all the music required at weddings—the official scale of charges was drawn up to allow for the difference in social status between the various types of weddings at which they would be required—but they could be engaged, again according to a fixed scale of charges, by private citizens for their own domestic or social celebrations.

In the 'Induction' of Beaumont and Fletcher's *The Knight of the Burning Pestle*, the 'Citizen' who interrupts the 'Speaker of the Prologue' demands 'stately music' to accompany the action, and when he discovers that the company of players has no shawms, he demands that they send, at his expense, for 'the waits of Southwark—as rare fellows as any are in England', and is prepared to pay two shillings as a sufficient fee for the part he wished them to play in the entertainment. The mere fact that the Citizen expected to have a particular sort of music provided by the theatre company itself indicated the difficulty of maintaining the official waits' monopoly.

Not only in London but in any British or continental city the demand for music worked, paradoxically enough, against the interests of the official musicians, waits, *Stadtpfeifer*, *pifferi* or whatever name they were called. By training they could hardly avoid conservatism; the whole system of guild tuition, from apprenticeship through *Wanderjahre* to mastery, was a training in tradition. In most towns they usually remained faithful to their traditional instruments while public tastes were changing, and the music they played was that traditionally associated with its particular occasion. For example the monopoly of the Leipzig *Stadtpfeifer* was first challenged by the city's *Feldpfeifer* and *Trommelschläger*, who worked in two pairs, a fife and a drum each, as town criers; they had also been used to call together those citizens required for military training and service. In 1550 the town council gave them permission to play at weddings—after all, no less than the *Stadtpfeifer* they required sufficient work to subsidise their lowly paid official existence—and the resulting quarrel between them and the *Stadtpfeifer* was not settled until, in 1587, the four *Stadtpfeifer* and the two pairs of town criers were officially reorganised, by the council, into four groups to perform in alternation. But manners and housing conditions were changing, and whilst the *Stadtpfeifer* remained faithful to their old instruments, their new colleagues began to profit from the citizens' desire for music in their homes by taking up the violin, more acceptable in small rooms than old-fashioned oboe, cornett, trumpet and trombone. In 1595 the town council accepted the new situation by licensing two fiddlers to play at weddings; eight years later, they started calling the official fiddlers 'Town Fiddlers', as though they were to some extent a body separate from the *Stadtpfeifer*, who were still treated as the senior musicians of the city: in 1602, and in 1607 the records refer to them as 'Town Fiddlers'. By 1626 they had become *Kunstgeiger*—'violin artists'. They did not, however, restrict themselves to string instruments but adopted, in addition, the woodwind and brass which were the prerogative of the *Stadtpfeifer*, to whom, as a sort of cadet branch, they were affiliated.

The *Stadtpfeifer* retained all their old privileges; they had the higher salary, on account of their twice-daily fanfares from the *Rathaus* tower, were exclusively employed by the university at the ceremonies marking the graduation of masters and doctors, were engaged at the theatre during the three annual fairs, played at Whitsun shooting matches, made money by playing New Year serenades for prosperous townsmen, and were treated preferentially in the matter of weddings: they alone were able to provide music for weddings in the city, while the new-comers were allowed to make music at 'poor weddings outside the gates' or at the less profitable of any two marriages being celebrated on the same day. The official classification of weddings makes it clear that the privilege was carefully guarded. A *Brautmesse*, with music by both *Stadtpfeifer* and *Kunstgeiger*, took place in the afternoon; a *Halb-Brautmesse*, with music by the *Kunstgeiger* alone was solemnised in the morning; a *Schlechten Hochzeit* without music was a poor man's way out of paying the musicians' fees and must be solemnised in one of the minor churches of the city. In spite of that it was not always easy for the town musicians to collect the fees that were theirs by statute, so that Johann Christoph Bach, the uncle of Johann Sebastian, who was town organist of Arnstadt from 1665 until his death in 1693 and lived in a state of continual acrimony with the town council and his senior colleague the *Stadtmusikus*, tried without success to arrange that the fees for the music at the wedding should be paid in advance, when the banns were confirmed. In Leipzig, however, the two bodies coalesced for a number of purposes, and as the *Kunstgeiger* had learned to make themselves masters of the *Stadtpfeifer* instruments, vacancies amongst the *Stadtpfeifer* were automatically filled by recruits from amongst the *Kunstgeiger*.

German town musicians had the duty of assisting in the music sung and played in church. In pre-Reformation days the example of the nobility and their court musicians had made the instrumental accompaniment of the services normal procedure. The musicians' guild of Vienna, the *Nicolaibrüder* founded in the thirteenth century, had accompanied the services in St. Stephen's Cathedral since very early in its history, before the church had achieved the status of a cathedral. Church music seems to have been so much a matter of course amongst the town musicians' duties that it seems to have been a long time before it was considered necessary that they should be mentioned in the civic records.

At Amberg, in Bavaria, for example, the earliest mention in the city archives of the *Stadttürmer* who provided the city's music is not made until as late as 1708. It is, however, a petition from one of the journeymen-*Türmer*, Andrea Schwärz of Auerbach, who wanted a promotion after completing his six years as a journeyman and had proved his ability as a trumpeter and a faithful watchman. This indicates that the Amberg town musicians had been in existence for some time before Schwärz asked for a move up the ladder. There is no statement of their duties—the duties would be understood—but the importance of their contribution to church music is made clear by the record of their quarrel with the Cantor, a certain Sicca, in 1715. The Cantor, they complained, had not only stolen a *Te Deum* which he claimed to have composed, but also was abusive to the *Türmeister* Jonas Leutenroth at rehearsals in the choir. Sicca's reply was a mere counter-accusation which made no mention of the alleged plagiarism; the complaint, he said, was a great insult to him. Leutenroth came drunk to rehearsals, and the rest of his band were always chattering; therefore, as Cantor, Sicca claimed the right to censure their bad behaviour.

The next reference in the Amberg archives to the town musicians is their plea for official protection against outside competition. Citizens, they protest, have frequently employed 'soldiers and foreigners' to provide the music at weddings, and the official *Türmusiker* seem to have given up hope of recovering their privileges for all they beg is that no foreigner should be employed as a musician at fairs and carnivals.

Regulations by town councils did not however solve the problems of subordinate bodies of musicians or prevent outsiders earning their livings, or at any rate useful sums of money, at the expense of the official musicians. The two Leipzig bodies, for example, did not really settle down in peaceful co-existence until 1725, when the *Kunstgeiger* were allowed lodgings, like the *Stadtpfeifer*, in the *Stadtpfeifergässlein*. Finally, thirty years later, they succeeded in winning the same privileges as were allowed for the widow of a *Stadtpfeifer*—six months' freedom to remain in official lodgings, with a continuation during that period of the dead husband's official salary and half the fees his successor earned from weddings and other *Accidenten*.

But if the subordinate bodies of musicians under the council's control could be a nuisance to the older guilds, particularly when they specialised in indoor music rather than the outdoor music of the traditional *Stadtpfeifer* instruments, the *modus vivendi* was reached in time for the now official bodies to face yet another challenge, which continued from the late sixteenth century onwards. There were amateur or semi-professional musicians, who were not guildsmen, and would undercut the official rates of pay or make money as buskers in the streets and who could find loopholes in the legislation which protected the official musicians. Such 'beer fiddlers', as they came to be known, were dismissed as disgustingly incompetent by their rivals, but were engaged in interminable feuds with the official players. Johann Bach, the brother of Johann Sebastian's grandfather, was faced with their competition throughout his work as *Stadtmusikus* at Erfurt from 1635 until his death in 1673. Erfurt, a town of considerable size at the beginning of the seventeenth century, suffered severely during the Thirty Years' War; the city had always been an important musical and educational centre; its church had one of the first organs in Germany, built during the eleventh century, and its university had been founded in 1392. That is to say, it was the type of town in which there was a longstanding tradition of musical activity and a trained appetite for music. As the rival armies of the Thirty Years' War swept backwards and forwards across North Germany, Erfurt found itself taxed year by year beyond its capacity to pay; between 1622 and 1630 the war had cost the citizens 367,000 florins, and these extortions were followed in 1631 by five years of Swedish occupation. It was to this, actually, that Johannes Bach owed his appointment; a Swedish captain had been invited, in 1635, to the house of one of the Erfurt citizens, a merchant named Hans Rothlander, who had engaged the town musicians to play at his party. The Swedish guest drank too much, fell asleep and, waking suddenly, imagined that he was being attacked, drew his sword and killed everyone within reach, including the town musician and several of his band.

The citizens of a town so impoverished by war would naturally do their best to get their music at the cheapest price, so the rise of the 'beer fiddlers' is not surprising in these circumstances. It is to a play that we owe the liveliest account of the feud between the unofficial and the official players. *Musicus Curiosus*, or *Battalus, the Inquisitive Musician; the Struggle for Precedence between the Kunst Pfeifer and the Common Players* was published in Freiburg in 1691. This dramatisation of the perpetual struggle is ascribed to Johann Kuhnau, Bach's predecessor and the author of another, but undramatic, musical satire, *Der Musikalische Quacksalber*.

Musicus Curiosus is a parody of the sort of folk play which Shakespeare mocks in the 'Pyramus and Thisbe' episodes of *A Midsummer Night's Dream*. Its scenes are set in the streets of the town and in the inn where the two sorts of musicians pass their leisure time. The beer fiddlers wrangle amongst themselves about the next round of beer and whose responsibility it is to pay for it, mentioning their rivals from time to time with a noticeable contempt; after all, they themselves can play anything they hear as soon as they have committed it to memory; the *Stadtpfeifer* are helpless unless they have the notes printed in front of them. Two of the *Stadtpfeifer* apprentices take it upon themselves to beat up the beer fiddlers while they are optimistically engaged in a serenade which its recipient has never ordered. The injured buskers take their case to law, amusing the authorities by the style of their supplication—a slangily modern account of what had occurred. Each side of the dispute defends itself by acting a comedy to attempt to put its claims in the correct light.

The quality of *Stadtpfeifer* performance is something we cannot know. A modern reader is inclined to believe the praise lavished on the Leipzig players at the beginning of the eighteenth century and—noting how J. S. Bach wrote extremely difficult orchestral parts in spite of his official strictures on the players —is prepared to believe that their quality was at least equally high during the next generation. But a hundred years before there had been the quarrelling between Cantor and *Stadtpfeiferei* at Amberg, and at about the same time, the town musicians in Nuremberg were ordered to rehearse in the Town Hall and in the presence of a musically educated alderman; this was the only way of ensuring that they ever bothered to rehearse. Like any other musical body they seem to have had their inevitable ups and downs.

The story of the musicians' guilds is not, however, entirely one of quaint and often hilarious side issues which distract attention from the actual course of music. Just as in towns like Arnstadt, where music was served for several generations by one or other member of the Bach family and which was the seat of a small not particularly wealthy court, the town musician and his men were co-opted into the ducal orchestra, other towns themselves employed their musicians to give public performances. Erfurt, for example, added a balcony to the Town Hall in 1687 as a stage from which the town musicians could give public performances on Saturday and Wednesday afternoons, and Kuhnau wrote enthusiastically of the performances of the Leipzig players. At the lowest evaluation of their contribution to music, the town bands created an appetite for public performance.

In England the waits never reached a comparable importance. Their problems, and the steps taken to solve them, were largely the same as those which arose in Germany and Italy. When Richard II's officials investigated the activities of the various guilds in 1389, they included an account of the Ordinances of a Fellowship of Musicians drawn up in 1350; the Fellowship was properly constituted, with its own livery, but although it called itself the Guild of the City of London Minstrels, it was an association formed only for social and charitable purposes. No genuine guild, such as existed in York, Beverley, Bristol and elsewhere in the country, is mentioned in London until 1500.

English musicians faced the same problems and were organised to deal with them in much the same way as the guild musicians of the continent. Every town of any size had its waits, which it protected by the granting of a monopoly of local music-making and whom it found various ways to pay; in some places, the waits had rent-free land to cultivate; in some they were paid directly by the town council; in others the townspeople were assessed for the contribution they must make towards the upkeep of their musicians. By the middle of the fifteenth century, all these waits were occupied with duties in which their function as a town watch had almost completely given way to their duties as musicians. By Elizabethan times, they were permitted to go on tour and seem, sometimes, to have been away from their cities for as much as three months at a time; in 1579, the York waits were paid by the city of Nottingham for performances given in Nottingham on June 7 and on September 13, suggesting that they called at Nottingham on the outward leg of a tour of the south, and returned through Nottingham on the homeward journey. Several guilds were taken under the protection of the nobility; the Norwich waits were the Earl of Essex's musicians, which suggests that they must, at certain times in the year, have done some work

for him in addition to the duties they undertook at home; the Norwich waits
went with Sir Walter Ralegh on his expedition against Cadiz in 1596, taking with
them 'three new howboyes, and one treble recorder and one saquebut' but also,
it seems likely, the strings which had become necessary to them since the growth
of domestic music. William Kemp, the comedian who in 1600 danced a morris
from London to Norwich, was greeted, at his journey's end, by the city waits,
'such Waytes . . . fewe Citties in our Realme have the like, none better. Who,
besides their excellency in wind instruments, their rare cunning on the Vyoll,
and Violin: theyr voices be admirable, euerie one of them able to serue in any
Cathedrall Church in Christendoome for Quiristers.'[1] How many waits were
able to appear not only as instrumentalists but as singers—apprentices would
serve as trebles and altos—is not recorded. The London waits sang, if not
regularly, by 1555, when the diarist Henry Machyn noted, 'A goodly procession
from St. Peter's in Cornhill with the fishmongers and my lord mayor, with a
hundred copes, unto Paul's, and there they offered, with the waits playing and
singing.'

The history of the London waits and of the City minstrels who, with them,
eventually constituted the London guild, is a good deal more complex. The size
and wealth of London and the density of its population made London a magnet
for the wandering entertainers who were usually not qualified to perform in
public because they were not members of any guild. In addition, the frequent
presence of the King's musicians in the capital, together with those of the
members of the aristocracy who were needed at court or in parliament, all of
whom were in a position to exercise certain limited rights in the city, made the
organisation of London musicians a difficult task.

Henry VI, made aware of the activities of unofficial performers, some of whom
wore his livery and impersonated his own musicians, set up a commission of
enquiry which, in 1469, under Edward IV, led to the granting of a musicians'
charter by which the king's musicians were empowered to control the organisation
of music throughout the country; the charter accepted the guild system, although
no London guild of musicians existed at the time, as the only feasible way of
organising the country's musicians. The London musicians, who were both city
minstrels under the authority of the Lord Mayor and waits, formed themselves
into a guild and began a career of litigation against the royal musicians to clarify
the position of two exclusive musical authorities operating on each other's door-
steps. The litigation did not end when the Marshal of the King's Musicians—by
charter the foremost musical authority in the land, applied for and was granted
membership of the city guild to show that he accepted its authority. The city
musicians, however, were granted some special privileges, like the right of each
member to train two apprentices while other musicians were allowed only one.

A certain amount of musical activity outside the control of the London
authorities could not be avoided; there was, for example, the music of the theatres
in the latter part of Elizabeth I's reign, and new charters, under James I in 1604

[1] William Kemp: *Kemp's Nine Daies Wonder*. London, 1600.

and James II in 1688, did not solve the problem of the co-existence of the two authorities, and although the activity of musicians outside the guild grew to unmanageable proportions—in 1737 the London guild prosecuted singers from the opera for taking part in a concert in the city itself—the guilds each struggled to maintain their theoretical rights, and the problems which agitated them had not really been solved when the coming of the Napoleonic Wars began to bring an end to the waits and their organisations all over the country. They continued their official existence until the Municipal Reform Act of 1835.

Their greatest days, apparently, were those of the latter part of Elizabeth I's reign and the early part of James II's. Morley, Rosseter and others, with their collections of consort works brought to publication, had only the waits and the theatre musicians for their market, and those seemed to be enough for them to write a fair amount of music of high standard for them. But whilst in Germany the town players were involved in all the music-making that went on, as *ex-officio* members of a local *Collegium Musicum*, paid for their services at what was primarily an amateur function, and were busily occupied as church orchestras, even in London their English counterparts remained bogged down in a medieval routine which had little to do with the practice or pleasure of the seventeenth and eighteenth centuries. According to Hawkins,[1] the waits 'consisted of fiddlers and others, such as in the night season were wont to parade the city and suburbs. . . . The music of these men could hardly be called a concert, for it had no variety of parts or commixture of different instruments; half a dozen of fiddlers would scrape . . . till they and their audience were tired, after which as many players on the hautboy would in the most harsh and discordant tones grate forth.' It was a matter of quite outstanding interest to Hawkins that two notable musicians rose from amongst the waits. 'Thomas Farmer, one of the waits in London, was nevertheless admitted to the degree of bachelor-in-music in the University of Cambridge. He composed many songs printed in the collections of this time.' (Farmer, who died round about 1690, did not graduate until 1684, and from 1671 to 1680 he had been a member of the King's Band of Musicke; the earliest of his compositions can be dated to 1672.) 'John Ravenscroft,' Hawkins continues, 'was one of the waits of the Tower Hamlets, and in the band of Goodman's Fields playhouse was a *ripieno* violinist, notwithstanding which . . . he was able to do justice to a concerto of Corelli or an overture of Handel.' Ravenscroft died in about 1745 and was a notable composer of hornpipes, two of which Hawkins quotes as examples of the form.[2]

The number of *Stadtpfeifer* who were reasonably efficient composers was a great deal higher, and because of their extensive duties their works were a good deal more ambitious than Farmer's songs or Ravenscroft's hornpipes. Some of them—at least five of the early Bachs, for example, who served as town musicians here and there in Thuringia—were composers of real merit who had gained their training through the guild routine but who all their lives had been involved in lively and up-to-date music-making. The rise of the public concert left the waits

---

[1] *Op. cit.*   [2] *Ibid.*

on one side as humble functionaries of no particular account. Their history, like that of their continental counterparts, is the history of an attempt to organise the musical profession to fit in with requirements satisfactory to the members of other guilds in the late middle ages but which were never easy to apply to so amorphous a profession as music, which is not an economic necessity of life and which was, as education spread and tastes widened, inevitably faced with amateur, and cheaper, competition.

There never was a period in their history when the town musicians were not engaged in a bitter struggle to preserve their monopoly. In church, at any rate, the *Stadtmusikanten* of those cities which were not the residence of some local aristocrat had taken over the playing of the trumpet in spite of the monopoly of the German *Trompeterkameradschaft*, an organisation not technically a guild because its methods of enrolment and training were different. Outside church, all town bands tried to circumvent the need for trumpets by playing the slide trumpet—not a court or military instrument—and the high-pitched horn in C, which produced a trumpet-like tone.

The rival guild monopolies were, of course, archaic. The *Stadtpfeifer* learned to play the trumpet with his other traditional instruments. Johann Joachim Quantz, remembered as flute teacher and flute maker to Frederick the Great, for whom he wrote an enormous amount of music, was trained as apprentice by his uncle the *Stadtmusikus* at Merseburg in 1708. 'The first instrument I had to learn,' he wrote in his *Autobiography*, 'was the violin. After that followed the trumpet and the oboe.' As a journeyman-musician in the *Stadtpfeiferei* of Dresden, he was told in 1717 that he could not play the trumpet in the annual service commemorating the Reformation unless he would apply for membership of the Trumpeters' Fellowship and thus officially become a court trumpeter and paid on a higher scale than a *Stadtpfeifer*; Quantz refused, but joined the court orchestra as an oboist a year later.

In Munich the battle of the *Trompeterkameradschaft* and the *Stadtmusikanten* went on into the nineteenth century. During the course of the quarrel, in 1792, the trumpeters reminded the king that their pay was an equal share of the 300 gulden which had been allotted to the Fellowship 14 years earlier, when it consisted of four trumpeters and two drummers; by 1792 it had to be divided among ten players. Therefore they insisted that it was necessary for them to hold strictly to their statutory privileges. In 1782 the choirmaster of the church of Our Lady had attempted to prevent the trumpeters playing in the services he controlled because he himself could provide all the necessary players and thus save the high fees they charged. As the trumpeters were court officials they won the king's backing, as they did in their attempts to find a corner in as many of the *Stadtpfeifer* activities as they could; in spite of the regular and lengthy complaints of the town players, they continued to play regularly in church and in religious processions.

The quarrel was never settled. The *Trompeterkameradschaft* was dissolved in 1810 and its members, few of whom were unable to play other instruments, were co-opted into the court orchestras. The Munich Town Musicians—the other party to the quarrel—cut down their members, and turned themselves into an up-to-date ensemble playing thoroughly rehearsed and popular music.[1] They continued their operations on the continent until they became integral parts of the late eighteenth-century and nineteenth-century orchestras. The Leipzig *Stadtmusiker* became *ex-officio* members of the Gewandhaus Orchestra; whenever Liszt required a specially large orchestra for his concerts at the Weimar Court after 1842, he automatically co-opted the Weimar *Stadtpfeiferei*.

[1] Christoph Helmut Mahling: *Münchener Hoftrompeter und Stadtmusikanten im späten 18. Jahrhundert.* In *Zeitschrift für Bayerische Landesgeschichte.* 1968, Band 31, Heft 2.

6 Municipal Musicians—
   the Amateurs

It might be possible to see in the rise of the Mastersinger Fellowships in fifteenth-century German-speaking Europe a determination on the part of the ambitious, newly wealthy middle classes of the towns to emulate the manners and pastimes of the aristocracy, just as the town bands of municipal *Stadtpfeifer* and waits were the application to city life and ceremonial of the sort of music which accompanied the public activities of the great. The Mastersingers were medieval and Renaissance tradesmen who met to sing their own songs and to listen to the songs of their fellow members. They offered no unseemly competition to the official town players, were not in any sense prepared to put themselves forward as public entertainers and did not form a musical guild of their own (except in the loose sense that any fellowship imposing tests for admission upon would-be members could be regarded as a guild). To them, music was a good, moral, social relaxation, and they took the art extremely seriously. Their approach was academic, and they deduced the rules of composition by which they considered themselves to be bound from the songs of the *Minnesänger* of an earlier period.

A misreading of history led the Mastersingers to claim, as the founders of their movement, a group of twelve singer-composers who they believed had been active in the reign of the Emperor Otto (962–73), and who, they believed, had sung for the Emperor and for Pope Leo VIII. The twelve 'founders' however were a group of twelve *Minnesänger*, including Walther von der Vogelweide, who was probably born in 1170 and died in 1230; von der Vogelweide's poems have survived, but very little of his music has come down to us although his reputation amongst his contemporaries for the beauty of his melodies as well as for the width and profundity of his learning was very high; his reputation for scholarship was based partly on the fact that he did not merely dictate his songs to a scribe but actually wrote them down himself. Another of the 'founders' was Wolfram von Eschenbach, who in Wagner's *Tannhäuser* is hopelessly and unsuccessfully devoted to the heroine Elisabeth; Wolfram, who was a precise contemporary of Walther von der Vogelweide, wrote the original epic poem upon which Wagner based *Parsifal*. Incidentally, Tannhäuser himself was a historical personage and not a mere invention of Wagner's imagination, and he actually competed with von Eschenbach at a tournament of song in 1207, thus giving Wagner a great curtain scene for the second act of his opera. A third of the Mastersingers' 'founders' was Heinrich von Meissen, who died in 1318 and who was nicknamed '*Frauenlob*' ('Praiser of ladies') because he insisted on addressing the recipients of his songs as 'Frau' rather than as merely 'Weib', or 'woman'.

The nine other Mastersinger founders were equally genuine composers of the *Minnesänger* period, flourishing more than two hundred years after the dates the Mastersingers assigned to them.

Against this background, the Mastersingers take their place as a typical but belated group of wealthy middle-class citizens adopting the ideas of the aristocracy; the odd thing about them is the time-lag between them and the artists who were their models and inspiration. By the time their class had reached the level of education which permitted them to utilise a leisure which was a fairly new aspect of artisan life, music had travelled a good distance in the church and the courts; the old minstrel traditions, however, remained alive in the work of wandering entertainers, and the Mastersingers worked back through these to the self-conscious artistry of the originals. In another sense, however, the Mastersingers were simply one of the confraternities of singers with aims and principles primarily religious which sprang up in fifteenth-century Europe—the *Laudesi* in Italy, the *Confrères* or *Puys* in France, the *Consistori del quy Saber* in Spain, and the *Dezidares* in Portugal. The difference between the German brotherhoods and the others was the fact that the Germans devoted themselves to a highly skilled and scholastic, if extremely out-of-date, art. And they persisted long after the other, parallel fellowships had died away. It was their claim to a special inheritance which marked them out; while the *Laudesi* were applying the Franciscan or Salvation Army principle of impounding attractive popular songs for the purposes of religion, and by doing so had some influence on the future of music, particularly in the creation of oratorios, the Mastersingers refused to shift the roots which they had laid down in the musical past; their songs were monodic, disdaining accompaniment and rejecting anything that could not be justified by reference to the precise, extremely formalist art of the thirteenth century, Wagner's affectionate account of Nuremberg Mastersingers tends to under-emphasise the conservatism which in the long run—for actually the movement persisted in many places until the eighteenth century—stultified the products of musicians who succeeded in domesticating music as an art with stringent rules and a firm academic basis in all the important Central European cities, with results for the future of German music which were probably incalculable. It is easy to mock a pedantic insistence on academic rules, but even though it can stifle inspiration pedantry never cheapens art by accepting what is too easy, too formless and too derivative to be really achieved.

Legends notwithstanding, the first notable Mastersinger was Michael Beheim, a soldier and singer from Heidelberg who was born in 1416 and died in 1474. Beheim's services as a mercenary in the service of various German princes, the Danes and the Hungarians, covered most of Central Europe and are traditionally accepted as influential in spreading the ideals which the Mastersingers fostered.

Though they owed their inspiration to the professional, aristocratic *Minnesänger* and to wandering musicians, professional and amateur, the Mastersingers remained local associations—rules varied in particulars from city to city, from brotherhood to brotherhood—which, although they were communities of

amateurs banded together for a pleasure which was also at least a semi-religious
exercise, adopted the guild system for purposes of training and admitting
applicants to membership. A member-to-be stood in relation to an acknowledged
Master as the apprentice David and Walther von Stolzing stood to Wagner's
Hans Sachs: he became a musical apprentice of a master who would teach him
the rules and show him how to apply them. The movement began in towns along
the Rhine Valley—the *Gesangmeisterschaft* of Mainz is the earliest of which
records survive—spread during the fourteenth and fifteenth centuries, and by the
sixteenth had reached those towns of what is now Czechoslovakia where the
population was predominantly German; it did not apparently attract the Slav
population with which the Germans mingled.

Thirteenth-century song had itself been extremely formal art and, like all the
art which compresses expression within extremely rigid rules, much of its vigour
was won from the tensions between the creator's determination to express himself and the formal regulations, limitations and inhibitions which he accepted.
These tensions, however, are not evident in the songs of the Mastersingers, who
regarded both poetry and music as no more than the result of the punctilious
observation of rules. Because, like the singing brotherhoods elsewhere in the
Europe of their day, they were primarily religious brotherhoods, their poetry was
normally didactic, much of it versifying the Bible and often including in its
opening stanza precise reference to the book, chapter and verse which was to be
treated in song. Each line had to be sung in a single breath, so that no line of more
than thirteen syllables was permitted; there was no restriction on the number of
lines in a stanza so long as the lines were laid out in proper form. Adam Pusch-
mann, the last of the important Mastersingers to exercise influence over a widespread European movement—he lived from 1532 to 1600 and was a pupil of
Hans Sachs—wrote in his *Gründlichen Bericht des deutschen Meistergesangs* that a
stanza of a hundred lines was long enough.

A would-be Mastersinger joined the local Mastersinger School as a *Schüler*;
when he had learned the *Tablatur*, the small rule-book dealing with the ceremonies
of the local brotherhood (for each local association had its own book of rules,
containing its regulation for the members' behaviour and the principles of composition and versification which were acceptable to it), he rose to the rank of
Schulfreund, becoming a *Sänger* when he thoroughly knew four or six *Töne*; if
he wrote new words, strictly following the rules and precedents, for an existing
Ton, he was accepted as a *Dichter*; if he invented a *Ton*, he became a *Meister*.
Then, according to the number of acceptable compositions for which he was
responsible—and these included both words and music—the Nuremberg Fellowship classed him first as *Singermeister*, than as *Singermeistermeister* and finally, if
his invention proved unflagging, as *Singermeistermeistermeister*.

The Mastersingers' terminology, however, is not always clear. When, in
Wagner's opera, Hans Sachs heard the song by Walther which was going to win
the competition and become the *Preislied*, he accepted it as though officially; '*Es
ist ein Meisterlied*,' he declared. He christened its tune, or '*Weise*' the '*Selige-*

morgentraumdeutweise' or 'melody of the interpretation of blessed morning dream'—in what was the customary way of giving descriptive names to the members' inventions. These names, however, were usually given to the *Ton*, which meant the style of versification and the rhyme scheme (the two together, of course, governed the song's melodic shape) rather than the mere *Weise*. But sometimes *Ton* means versification and music together, and sometimes *Ton* and *Weise* are used as though they are interchangeable. A large number of *Töne* were available, many of them accurately taken over from the songs of the Minnesingers; they were mostly named, some of them as floridly as Walther's, after some element in the song which they embodied, like the '*Ton* of the Proud Miller's Daughter'. The four most honoured and important were the four 'crowned tones' found in works by four of the founders—Frauenlob, Mügling, Regenbogen and Marker. The setting of new works to an existing *Ton*—that is, metre and rhyme-scheme—was the way in which a *Dichter* won his rank, but there was only a limited number of old tunes to which the setting of new words was permissible. In Nuremberg only four were available for such modernisation, and in Colmar, where the Mastersinger records survive from the early days of the movement, seven old songs could be fitted with new words. At Donaueschingen twenty-one traditional tones were preserved for the members' use. Despite the stringently conservative rules governing the versification, rhyme-scheme and melodic form to be imposed upon the Mastersingers' work, no contribution could be accepted as a Mastersong if its melody reminded any hearer of that of an existing *Meister-ton*. Thus an attempt at originality at all costs accompanied a stringent conventionalism of forms, style and even phrasings.

Satisfactory songs in the convention could only be created by strict observance of the rules contained in the *Tablatur* for, as the Colmar rules put it, 'Song at all times teaches modesty and discipline; song is the origin of good things,' and the modesty and discipline arose from the careful observance of the rules: this, therefore, was the beginning of the 'good things'. No popular song, which meant largely any song written in an up-to-date style, could by rule be sung in the Mastersingers' schools, and no unpublished mastersong could be sung outside them. The works of the Mastersingers reached the public only in the public plays which they began to perform in the sixteenth century and of which Hans Sachs was a prolific author. Originality, perhaps, is responsible for the sometimes jerky melismata which interrupted the melodies of the songs and may also have been a means of compensating for the absence of any instrumental accompaniment. The validity of all these things, their consonance with tradition and the *Tablatur*, were carefully checked as a song was performed. Wagner's Beckmesser, the *Merker* who chalked up Walther von Stolzing's mistakes on his blackboard, may seem to us to be a grotesque champion of tradition, but all Mastersingers won acceptance through such a contest as that which Walther endured. It would, however, have been held in grave privacy, and Beckmesser would, had it suited Wagner's purposes to adopt a slavish correctness to Mastersingers' procedure, have been joined by three other *Merker* who would have penalised faults of versification and rhyme as energetically as Beckmesser noted down unconventionalities of musical style.

It seems, paradoxically, that the force which kept the Mastersinger brotherhoods active and influential for a long time was this hide-bound and illiberal insistence on tradition. While the *Laudesi*, who were even more strictly religious bodies than the Mastersingers, took whatever was new and made use of it, refusing to depend upon precedents, the Mastersingers regarded music as a craft to be learned, and honoured it as they honoured any other skilful occupation, adding to the strictness of their rules a firm insistence on unaccompanied song. Any musical importance the *Laudesi* might have had worked itself out in the marriage between secular and religious styles which was consummated in the seventeenth and eighteenth centuries, so that when Charles Burney visited Florence in 1770 and heard a company of *Laudesi* singing in procession, the music they used came, he was told, from a new compilation recently made for them; it was indistinguishable from any other music, and members were those who wanted to sing in honour of God; they were not men who had undergone a rigorous if rather irrelevant training in prosody and composition according to the styles of an earlier age; they had not erected their fellowship into a mystery.

The *Laudesi* were a public and reasonably undemanding body primarily concerned with propaganda. Their readiness to adopt whatever was new made them at first a progressive body, for it meant that they associated religion with the new styles of secular music, but eventually it made them entirely neutral as a musical force once their original musical object was achieved. To be a Mastersinger meant that one had undergone strict tests, had shown a specially and strictly applied knowledge and was, in a real sense, a master if not of an art, at least of a highly skilled craft; it gave one authority and status. Musically, it meant that throughout central Europe there were large numbers of middle-class, reasonably well-to-do tradesmen who regarded music not as an easy-going, undemanding social pleasure but as a strict and valuable intellectual discipline which offered its own rewards to those who would face its rigours. If it took its pleasures with an almost frightening earnestness—for Wagner's pompous Teutonic jollification at the end of act three of *The Mastersingers* is a misinterpretation of their attitude —at any rate it bred generations of music lovers whose attitude to music accepted the fact that art is a firm intellectual and spiritual discipline.

7   Renaissance Court Music

The Renaissance court was a powerfully creative force in music. If, in its beginnings, it was merely an attempt to ape the grandeurs of royalty, by the middle of the fifteenth century and for a considerable time afterwards, the rulers who patronised music were men of fine taste and educated outlook who knew what was good and tended to admire what was up-to-date. It was a generally accepted doctrine that an understanding of music was both necessary socially and advantageous educationally, for music was part of the world of the Universal Man who was the Renaissance ideal. In 1528, in *The Book of the Courtier*, Baldassare Castiglione defined the place of music in aristocratic life; he was however merely rationalising something that existed and was powerful before his book was written:

> I am not pleased with the courtier if he be not also a musician, and beside his cunning and understanding upon the book, have skill in like manner upon sundry instruments. For, if we weigh it well, there is no ease of the labours and medicine of feeble minds to be found more honest and praiseworthy than it. And principally in courts, where (beside the refreshing of vexations that music bringeth to each man) many things are taken in hand to please women, whose tender and soft breasts are soon pierced with melody and filled with sweetness. Therefore it is no marvel that in the old days and nowadays they have been inclined to musicians and counted this a most acceptable food of the mind.

Music naturally assisted ostentation. Just as it added pomp and splendour to the ceremonies of a king's court, the nobility glorified their lives by surrounding themselves with a similar magnificence. From the functional use of music as an adjunct of the stately life to the acceptance of the art as a necessary activity of civilised man was a step which took a good deal of time; in the intellectual excitement of the Renaissance music came into its own as one of the necessary and more laudable accomplishments of civilised man. Castiglione's doctrine is expounded over and over again, gradually climbing down from the ranks of the Italian nobility until it became a commonplace middle-class teaching and, in the 1590s, Shakespeare's Lorenzo lectures the Jewish Jessica on the spiritual and moral value of music, taking it for granted that a heterogeneous Elizabethan audience will accept the point while taking it for granted that a wealthy heiress like Portia will employ the consort of viol players whose music inspires Lorenzo's discourse.

The musical inspiration of the early Renaissance was the work of John Dunstable, whose decisive achievement was his success in breaking away from the melodic and rhythmic conventions of the *Ars Nova*, so that Martin le Franc, writing a poem in praise of Dufay and Binchois in 1437, sixteen years before Dunstable's death, found it necessary to explain the achievement of the English composer to do justice to his successors:

> The English guise they wear with grace,
> They follow Dunstable aright,
> And thereby they have learned apace
> To make their music gay and bright.[1]

The careers of the composers of the period show how the world of the musician had expanded. Léonin and Pérotin, so far as we know, spent their lives in Paris working at and for Notre Dame. That, with putative records of their birth and death, is all we know about them that is not conjecture. We know nothing of Leonel Power except that in 1438 he was connected with Canterbury Cathedral; in what precise capacity remains a mystery. Richard Hygons is known to us through his connection with Wells Cathedral, which he served at any rate from 1459 when he became one of the Vicars; in 1474 he became 'Master of the Choristers' and in 1507 he undertook to pay a deputy for teaching the choristers; if he became a vicar at the time of his ordination, he must have been in his seventies when the deputy was appointed. So far as we know, he died in 1509. The musicians of the middle ages, and neither Hygons nor Power was a negligible composer, lived for the most part in almost complete obscurity. Their successors at the close of the middle ages are people of far greater worldly consequence. It is not merely that their names turn up in places as far apart as, say, Mons, Florence, Antwerp and Venice; it is also that, as educated and, by virtue of their skills, travelled men they had spheres of usefulness beyond their official occupation. The generation of composers born in the first fifty years of the fifteenth century had careers far more lively and varied than those of any of their predecessors except the courtier Machaut.

The life of Arnold de Lantins, for example, is a mystery until he appears in the records of the Papal Chapel as a singer from 1431 to 1432; before that he had made his way to Italy from the Netherlands; he seems to have been in Venice in 1428. Pierre de Fontaine, who seems to have been a choirboy at Rouen Cathedral, was a court musician in Burgundy until 1420, when he made his way to Florence, where the Papal choir was stationed at the time, with Nicolas Grenon. Grenon's life seems to have been quite eventful. He appears in the Burgundian records in 1385, but he succeeded his brother Jean as a canon of Saint-Sepulchre in Paris from 1399 to 1405, when he became choirmaster at Cambrai and, incidentally, Dufay's teacher. In 1425 he made his journey to Italy, where he was Master of the boys in the Papal choir until 1427. Then he went back to Burgundy, was in charge of the music at Bruges Cathedral in 1437 but reappears in Cambrai in 1440.

Dufay was born in about 1400 and apparently joined the choir of Cambrai

---

[1] Translated in Gustave Reese: *Music in the Renaissance.*

Cathedral when he was nine years old. The Bishop of Cambrai was an important delegate to the Council of Constance between 1414 and 1418; he was attended by thirty-four of the clergy of his diocese and by at least some of his cathedral musicians, the boy Dufay amongst them. It was probably here that Dufay met Carlo Malatesta, Duke of Rimini, with whom he seems to have spent some years, for a group of his compositions written between 1419 and 1426 celebrate events at the Malatesta court and in the Malatesta family history. In 1427 he was at the University of Bologna, with leave of absence from Cambrai, apparently as a student. A year later he was in the Papal choir with which he remained until 1437, during which time he developed a valuable connection with the Duke of Savoy at whose court he seems to have spent his leaves, and at the same time he gathered an impressive collection of benefices and prebends, which he held as an absentee but which rewarded him handsomely.

Apparently his experience of the Council of Constance had been sufficiently active to warrant his nomination as one of the delegates from Cambrai to the Council of Basle in 1438, but he spent only a year at the lengthy series of meetings which expanded the Pope's power over the church in an attempt to deal with heresy and disaffection in Europe. From 1440 until his death thirty-seven years later, ecclesiastical politics seem not to have mixed themselves with music in his life; Cambrai seems to have been his home, but the Marquis of Ferrara commissioned works from him and paid him well for them; he was paid by the Chapter of his own cathedral for new works—earlier composers in an ecclesiastical institution had produced new music as a matter of course—was given the task of supervising the copying of his music so that what we know of it comes mostly from authentic texts, and was given charge of the choirboys. His experience of affairs caused him to be sent on a mission to the Duke of Burgundy. Another lump sum as a reward for the music with which he had enriched the cathedral services came in the closing years of his life, and his musical reputation at the time of his death was international in a sense which cannot be used of any of his predecessors. At the same time, the degree of Bachelor of Laws conferred upon him was not, it seems, a tribute to his music but a recognition of his quality as a man of affairs.

If the life of his contemporary, Gilles Binchois, seems rather humdrum after so much movement across Europe, at any rate it is far wider than that of the earlier composers whose music we remember. Binchois was brought up in the choir at Mons, spent a period in Paris and then worked for more than thirty-five years at the Burgundian court.

Ockeghem, of the next generation, was born in about 1420. He was trained in Antwerp Cathedral Choir, served the Duke of Bourbon for two years, from 1446 to 1448, and in the early 1450s entered the service of Charles VII of France, at whose death he headed the list of the royal musicians; he remained at the French court for the rest of his life, was made Treasurer of the Abbey of St. Martin, at Tours—a very rich and rewarding preferment which provided him with a satisfactory livelihood apart from his official salary—and in 1469 was sent on a diplomatic mission to Spain. Obrecht, born in 1453, studied at Louvain University, was ordained priest and became Master of the boys at Cambrai, but was dismissed in little more than a year, in 1485, for neglecting the welfare of the boys. He became succentor of the Church of Saint-Donatien in Bruges, but found time to spend six months at the d'Este court in Ferrara and lived the rest of his life between Antwerp and Bruges.

Josquin des Prés, born about 1451, was equally widely travelled although he seems to have been anything but the influential personality we gather Dufay to have been. He was a choirboy under Ockeghem at Saint Quentin, was a member of the Papal choir from 1486 to 1494—though he seems to have spent some time in Italy at the Sforza court in Milan as much as fourteen years before he took service in Rome—and seems to have moved from Milan to Ferrara. After his time in Rome he was choirmaster at Cambrai and then went to the court of Louis XII of France. In 1501 he toured the Netherlands recruiting choirboys for Paris and was back in Italy in 1503. He seems to have spent some time in the Netherlands, at Saint Quentin, but round about 1516 he became a canon of the collegiate church of Condé, though his connection with the French court continued, for Charles V paid him for some songs in 1520, about a year before his death.

Not even Dufay, however, lived so colourful a life as Heinrich Isaac, who appears in history as a musician in the court of Lorenzo de Medici soon after Lorenzo's accession in 1469; he succeeded the great Antonio Squarcialupi as court organist in 1475 and became the music master of Lorenzo's children. At the same time he held church posts—at San Giovanni, Santa Maria del Fiore and the church of the Annunciation—posts in which he was expected to supply new music for the services in addition to his court duties—and he set to music his patron's religious drama *San Giovanni e San Paolo* as well as Lorenzo's carnival songs. During his work in Florence, however, he found time to appear at the Ferrara court and to spend some time at Innsbruck in the service of Archduke Sigismund of Tyrol.

Isaac's life in Florence was cut short by the rise of Savonarola and the brief period of puritan stringency inaugurated by Savonarola's revolution after the fall of Piero II de Medici in 1494. The fact that the Emperor Maximilian was in Italy, at Pisa, preparing his siege of Leghorn, and the fact that Isaac had sent some works to him five years before through the Imperial Ambassador in Milan, smoothed the composer's way into a new post. Maximilian was occupied at the time with the reorganisation of his *Kapelle* which he was moving from Augsburg to Vienna. He had an active *Kapelle* on campaign with him, and the services of a composer who had won a high reputation in Italy was too good to be rejected, so that Isaac was enrolled and despatched to Vienna. His appointment as imperial court composer came in 1497, bringing him a salary of 150 Rhenish florins a year and guaranteeing his widow a pension of 50 florins.

Isaac's duties for Maximilian were not executive; he was neither *Kapellmeister* nor court organist but purely and simply a composer, so that all he had to do was to supply the *Kapelle* with new compositions as and when they were required. Therefore he was not compelled to live in court nor precluded from making money elsewhere. He lived at Torgau and in Augsburg, but seems to have made Innsbruck his base until, after the downfall and execution of Savonarola, he returned to Florence in 1502. His greatest work, the *Choralis Constantinus*, a setting in four parts of all the Mass propers for the ecclesiastical year, seems to take its name from Isaac's attendance on the emperor at Constance—Maximilian's headquarters for his attack on Venice—in 1508, for until the Medicis regained power in Florence in 1512 his ties with the city were very loose. He was offered a court post at Ferrara—to be held in conjunction with his service to the emperor—with a salary of 120 ducats a year, but seems to have procrastinated over the offer until after the death of his prospective patron, Duke Ercole I. This suggests that his presence in Italy was not simply due to his preference for living there but was already tied up with his value to Maximilian as a diplomat or secret agent. In 1515 when he asked to be allowed permission to live permanently in Italy, Maximilian granted the petition with the endorsement that Isaac was of more value in Italy than when actually present at court, and allowed his salary to continue with the deduction of only 30 ducats, as long as his services, which are unspecified in the document, warrant the payment.

The rest of Isaac's life was apparently spent in combined music and diplomacy in Florence, in conditions which must have been extremely comfortable. His old pupil Giovanni de Medici had become Pope Leo X in 1513 and was a devoted musician, so that from a distance he enjoyed papal protection and encouragement. He had his Imperial salary and had recovered both his Florentine position and its pay.

The pattern of music-making set up by kings and their nobility, and the sort of regulations by which it was controlled, can stand as well as any to indicate the pattern of what, during the two centuries between 1350 and 1550, became normal European practice. In France, the Dukes of Anjou, Bar, Berry, Beaune, Brittany and Orleans, amongst others, were active supporters of music with considerable musical establishments of their own. Gilles de Rais, the soldier-courtier-politician executed in 1440 for perversion and murder, kept between fifteen and twenty singers in his household. Two of the chapels stand out both for the excellence and variety of their music and for their influences on musical style: the first is that of Burgundy, between 1360 and 1477; the second is the *Kapelle* of the Imperial Court as it was reorganised by the Emperor Maximilian in Vienna after 1488.

Burgundian music—a matter which authorities like Gustave Reese attempt to define at great length and with exemplary thoroughness—developed the style which had been growing in France ever since the revolutionary days of the composers of the Abbey of St. Martial and of Léonin and Pérotin and which, since the Hundred Years' War, had become most active in the north-east of the country and across its frontiers, in the Netherlands. There the large choirs and effective choir schools made possible a style of polyphony which became the business of an entire choir and not of a solo ensemble of specialists. The large choirs of Antwerp, Arras, Mons, Ghent, Lille, Liège, Bruges and Ypres produced a large number of career musicians, men who differed from their predecessors because they functioned entirely as musicians. They and their work expanded beyond their native land because there was insufficient work for them at home and because they were experts in a new style which other countries, Italy in particular, had not mastered. They in their turn were influenced by their up-bringing in the cosmopolitan Netherlands. The long English presence in northern France had brought the style of Dunstable; from the eastern rim of the Nether-lands came a more sombrely intense, emotional style, and the music-loving Burgundian rulers were the catalyst which gave these different elements a unity which provided the northern music with the attractions not only of a more exciting and elaborate technique but also a wider range of emotional expression.

Burgundy is a name which has meant a number of different things at different times. The original Duchy of Burgundy was more or less the Franche-Comté, and during the middle ages came to include Lyonnais, Dauphiné, Savoy and Provence and grew further through dynastic marriages before the original line of dukes died out in the fourteenth century and the Duchy reverted to the French throne. King John II gave it, with hereditary rights, to his son Philip the Bold in 1363. Philip's marriage to Margaret, the heiress of Flanders, Artois and Brabant, expanded it considerably. Philip's son and grandson, John the Fearless and Charles the Good, who succeeded in 1404 and 1419, by judicious marriages, war and purchase added to their territories the rest of Belgium, Zeeland, Friesland and North Holland, with other possessions held in fief from France. Politically, Greater Burgundy in the fifteenth century was an anomalous sort of dukedom, some of it held from the French king, who was the duke's feudal lord, the rest of it free from feudal claims.

Burgundian policy became an attempt to gain complete freedom from French overlordship and to establish an independent state which would control the entire course of the navigable Rhine from Switzerland to the North Sea, and thus gain a highly profitable stranglehold on Europe's main north to south trade route. The voltes-face of Burgundy's alliance with England during the reign of Henry V and the first half of Henry VI's, until the coronation of the Dauphin as Charles VII —the stroke of policy by which Joan of Arc reawakened French enthusiasm for the French cause—and then with France until the English were driven out, were caused by the pursuit of an aim which demanded that Burgundian interests could best be served by siding with those on the winning side in the struggle.

The foundations of Burgundian music—which is a style, or a conflation of the various European styles which grew up in Burgundian dominions or in lands with which Burgundian musicians came into contact rather than a national 'school'— were laid in the reign of Philip the Bold; it exploited the musical traditions of the Netherlands cities from which it drew many of its finest players and singers as well as its composers. Philip, like his son and grandson, was himself a musician, and as a son of the King of France it was natural that he recruited the upper personnel of his Chapel from amongst Parisian musicians and occupied it chiefly with Parisian music. John the Fearless, apparently impressed by the size and accomplishment of Henry V's musicians when the English king and the Burgundian duke were occupied in the negotiations which led to the Treaty of Troyes, built up a choir and body of instrumentalists of equivalent size, so that in the reign of Charles the Good Burgundy became the centre from which the new-style polyphony radiated out all over Europe. The chapel grew from an original fifteen to twenty-six musicians, the later arrivals all coming from the Netherlands; they were augmented by the duke's minstrels—a cosmopolitan body of trumpeters, viellists, harpists, lutenists and organists. From the start the Burgundians employed or patronised important composers and supported those who were ready to innovate. Amongst the musicians of Philip the Bold was Pierre de Fontaine, a composer of attractive songs. Jean Tapissier, whose church music has survived in copies at Bologna and in the Bodleian Library, was *valet de chambre* to John the Fearless, a title which means that he was employed not only as a musician but needed an official non-musical post so that the records could explain his salary. The painter Jan van Eyck and the sculptor Claus Sluter were given the same title, as were the composers Jacques Vide and Haym van Gyseghem during the reign of Charles the Good.

Tastes did not change, although they developed, as the Burgundian dukes succeeded each other. John the Fearless employed the composers Guillaume Ruby and Richard de Belleagues amongst his musicians. He took over the more famous Nicolas Grenon from his uncle the Duke of Berry in 1412. Charles the Good maintained all three of them in his service, was a patron, if not for a time the actual employer, of Dufay, and kept Gilles Binchois at the Burgundian court for over thirty years. Robert Morton, the English composer, spent most of his life in Burgundian service, and Charles' son Charles the Bold, who ruled from 1467 to 1477, was taught to play the harp by the time he was seven and in later life both sang and composed songs, kept on his father's musicians and added to them Antoine Busnois, another composer with a European reputation.

In 1477 Margaret, the daughter of Charles the Bold, married the Austrian Archduke Maximilian who was eighteen at the time and who never recovered from the impression made upon him by the ostentatious culture of his father-in-law's court. As his succession to the imperial throne drew nearer Maximilian began to collect a similar chapel, mainly from Netherlandish musicians; the task occupied him from 1486 to 1496; in the meantime, in 1488, he was declared King of the Romans to undergo a sort of probationary period before the imperial election, was declared Emperor-Elect in 1493 and was crowned Holy Roman Emperor in 1496. He had already founded his imperial court musical establishment in 1490, amalgamating his father's household and court musicians with his own *Kapelle*, so that his father's collection of Austrian, German, Slavonic and Burgundian musicians, a not very distinguished body, became part of a large establishment in which the Burgundian influence entirely predominated. The imperial residences were at Prague, Augsburg, Linz and Vienna, and in each of these cities an imperial *Kapelle* existed. Maximilian's father Frederick III had already begun the administrative reorganisation on the basis of which Maximilian increased imperial power and influence. In 1469 Frederick had separated Vienna from the diocese of Passau, creating bishoprics at Vienna and at the south-eastern stronghold Wiener Neustadt, where he set up his summer palace. His enhancement of the position of Vienna was the beginning of the rise to glory of a city which the Pope of the day, Pius II, had described only a little time before as a cultural desert.

Maximilian's life as emperor was spent in ceaseless movement round his dominions; Cologne and Mechlin in the north-west, Prague, Innsbruck, Linz, Augsburg, Vienna and Wiener-Neustadt were the towns in which political necessity demanded that he set up court regularly, and war took him into Italy. At Innsbruck, Prague and Vienna he maintained permanent *Kapellen*, and kept with him a small ensemble of players and singers who accompanied him on all his journeys; they provided not only his church music but also such *Tafel* and chamber music as he might desire; the ensemble consisted of twelve singers of different voices, a 'Praeceptor' to teach singing and grammar to the boys among them, and a group of instrumentalists.

It was in Vienna that his ambitions spread their wings most widely. By 1509, under Georg von Slatkonia—who was both Bishop of Vienna and choirmaster of St. Stephen's Cathedral, an unusual combination of offices—he had about fifty singers, including twenty *Sängerknaben* and twenty-nine boy probationers.

Paul Hofhaimer, the greatest organist of the day, who had been in the service of Archduke Sigismund of Tyrol and refused the offer of a post at the Bohemian Court, seems to have been in the service of Maximilian, stationed at Innsbruck from 1450 until Maximilian's death in 1519. Isaac joined his establishment in 1496. Ludwig Senfl was apparently brought up in the imperial court and chosen to succeed Isaac as court composer. The presence of such famous musicians is enough in itself to show the importance which Maximilian placed upon music, but the famous series of woodcuts, for which he himself wrote captions, known as *Maximilian's Triumph-zug* (or 'triumphal procession') shows the whole body of his musicians together, notwithstanding the distance between the establishments he maintained.

The woodcuts, by Hans Burgmair and a number of other artists, who probably include Albrecht Dürer, show the members of the emperor's *Kapelle* in procession, riding in wagons from which they play and sing, following a horseman with a *Waldhorn* and a mounted company of three flautists and five drummers. The first cart carries three lutenists and three viola da gamba players. A second cart carries a trombonist, two oboists and two crumhorn players; following them comes Hofhaimer playing a portable organ. A mixed band, which Maximilian's caption describes as '*Musica süess Meledey*', follows in the next cart; its members are a violist, a harpist, a fiddler, a lutenist, a quintern, a pipe and tabor player and two *Rauschpfeifen* (the combination looks odd, probably sounded no less odd, and shows more clearly than any amount of verbal explanation the mixed tonal ensembles which Renaissance ears enjoyed). The final wagon is captioned *Hofkapelle*; a huge choir book on a lectern faces six choirboys, behind whom are seven men, with a cornettist and a trombonist on their left, and at the back of the wagon the Bishop-choirmaster Georg von Slatkonia.

Court musicians, no less than their masters, were peripatetic. The dukes of Burgundy regarded Dijon as their capital but were in almost continual movement round their domains or on campaign, as was Maximilian, who took his musicians with him not only round his normal government circuit but also on campaign across Switzerland into Italy. This in itself, as visits were made to other courts or to towns where church and municipal music flourished, was a powerful way of accelerating the spread of new works and the internationalisation of the new style. It helps to explain, as does the internationalisation of the Papal choir, the domination of northern composers—of what text books call 'Flemish' or 'Burgundian' music—over Italy. The Papal choir, the cathedral and the court of the Sforzas at Milan, the court of the d'Estes at Ferrara, the Gonzaga court at Mantua, the cathedral and city of Venice and Bavarian Munich all became centres of the new style. Even where few northerners were employed, as in Mantua, the choir books at the beginning of the sixteenth century, when Francesco Gonzaga began to reform the court church music, contain a large number of works by northern composers.

It was natural since the days of Dufay that acceptance in Italy should be an enormous feather in a composer's hat. As late as the eighteenth century, when Italian music dominated Europe no less powerfully than Burgundian music had done a couple of centuries before, an extensive knowledge of Italy and Italian styles gained from residence in the country, was a necessary sign of excellence, so that, even while Italian authorities were eager to find musicians trained in the north, Italian approval was the best testimonial that any composer could take with him in his search for a satisfactory court or church post.

The result was the influential presence in Milan, Ferrara, Florence, Naples and Venice of musicians from the north. Milan had been a historic musical centre since St. Ambrose had stabilised and organised Christian chant there in the second half of the fourth century, and is reputed to have had its *Schola Cantorum* since before 400. Before the influx of northern musicians reached the city Milan cathedral was served by organist-choirmasters famous throughout Italy, but in 1460, when it employed less than four singers, membership of the choir was thrown open to French and Flemish musicians and it began to expand.

It was, however, after the conquest of the dukedom by Francesco Sforza in 1450, and in the reign of the second Sforza duke, Galeazzo Maria, that music grew in the city. Galeazzo Maria established his own *capella* in 1470; of his forty musicians, eighteen were kept for chamber music and the other twenty-two for the chapel services; he appointed as his *maestro de cappella* Gaspard van Weerbecke, a native of Oudenarde and a pupil of Ockeghem. Weerbecke had risen from the ranks of the town musicians; in the year before his appointment to court, he appears in the Milanese records in 1469 as 'Keeper of the City Watch'. In 1472 and again in 1474 he is described as *maestro di cappella* at the Cathedral, but he seems to have had no close connection with the music of the ducal chapel which was under the control of the Italian Abbate Guinati; Galeazzo Maria may have had a traditional attitude to church music. Josquin des Prés, Compère and Jacques Godebrie visited and worked at the Sforza court, while Cardinal Ascanio, Galeazzo Maria's brother, worked to bring the cathedral music up to a standard comparable with that of the court.

Ludovico Sforza, whom people nicknamed '*Il Moro*', inheriting the excellent establishment which had been created, instituted a chair of music at the university, installing in it Franchino Gafori, who had been connected with the cathedral since 1484 and was one of the first generation of Italians thoroughly to have assimilated the new musical style. His own prestige as one of the foremost scholars of the day gave importance to the new professorship, and this remained after the Sforzas had been driven from their dukedom in 1499 by the combined forces of Venice and Spain in the series of small and less small wars which, among other changes, brought the Papal states into existence as a political reality after they had been for generations a theological speculation. The status of the cathedral with all it owed to the Sforzas was maintained throughout the sixteenth century, preserved by the work of a succession of good composers, some Italian and some Flemish.

Florentine music could not claim so long a recorded history as could music in Milan, but since the middle ages Florence had been the more active centre. Dante, the most renowned of all Florentines, continually shows in his writings an educated enthusiast's knowledge of music, not only of the forms current in his day but also of the technical premises on which they were based. The libraries of the city preserve medieval treatises: the Florentine *Laudario* shows that popular religious music was accepted from its earliest days, the thirteenth-century *Antiphonario Medicium* is a choir book which contains examples of all the varieties of early religious polyphony including works by the Notre Dame composers. Florentine composers themselves were writing effectively in early polyphonic styles by the thirteenth century.

At the same time secular music, tied to civic ceremonies and the annual carnival, was perhaps more consciously cultivated in Florence than in any other European city of the time; at least its functions and developments were more consciously recorded. As a city which owed its eminence to commerce it was in touch with all the European developments, and it rapidly became the Italian centre of the mannered style of the *Ars Nova*, where composers, both natives of the city and those who took advantage of its wealth and atmosphere to settle there, developed the secular, melodic and metrically regular forms of the *ballata*, the *canzone* and the *rondello* rather than any of the specifically religious styles. The works collected in the Squarcialupi Codex show the city's unusual interest in secular music, and the composers who worked there in the fifteenth and sixteenth century did little to enrich its store of religious works. Antonio Squarcialupi, whose property the Codex originally was, was a butcher's son who, in 1467, became organist of the church of Santa Maria. His influence extended a long way beyond Florence: Ludovico Sforza asked his opinion of a German lutenist before offering the player a port at court, and Squarcialupi corresponded regularly with Dufay. His codex preserves, among much other old music vital for understanding of early secular style, the work of the blind organist Francesco Landini who died in 1397 at the age of seventy-two and who, significantly enough, survives as composer of secular vocal works. Dufay's connection with Florence, where he does not seem to have spent any considerable time, was strong enough to cause him to write the motet *Nuper rosarum flores* for the consecration of the church of Santa Maria del Fiore in 1436. It may be significant that the special work commissioned for this great occasion came from an international master and was not obtained from a local musician, whose preoccupations were always at that time with secular music.

Florence perhaps more forcefully than any other city of the period shows the changed atmosphere into which the northern musicians entered when they made their way to Italy. Outside Florence, Isaac was primarily concerned with religious music; as an employee of the Medicis he taught music, played the organ in church and composed a great deal more secular than religious work. He composed the music for example for Lorenzo de Medici's carnival songs, setting them in three or four parts, and apparently composing instrumental music for court and civic occasions as well as for the carnival itself. In most of the other Italian cities secular music was cultivated as a delightful and valuable art whilst throughout northern Europe it remained a ceremonial utility, but Florence was the busiest producer of all the styles used outside the church. Two things had probably achieved this result; Italy was closer to the conservative centre of religious life, in close contact with conservative traditions. The nearer one was to Rome the more powerful were the disciplinary obligations which the Papacy demanded, for the effectiveness of law depended to a great extent on communications. Furthermore, the ancient sense of civic community stretching back to the great days of the Roman Empire enhanced the importance of town music. The atmosphere in which a family like the Medici—who were themselves amateur singers and players—was brought up accepted the importance of civic ceremony and its music, the special significance of the Florentine carnival and the propriety of a conservative musical tradition in the liturgy; and the Medici were the quintessential Italian nobility of the time. What they inherited they developed, and it was not that other rulers in Italy so much followed their lead as that the Italian nobility in general had been exposed to much the same influence without, in most cases, anything quite comparable to Medici wealth.

That almost all the secular music of Isaac, like almost all Florentine carnival music, should have failed to survive, while his church music and that of others in no way so outstanding should be accessible, is not surprising and does not invalidate the importance that should be attached to the Renaissance Italian's appetite for music outside the church. The church, whether or not it wished to create a repertory of works for continued use, had not only facilities for preserving manuscripts but also an appetite for manuscripts to preserve; what was written for the church, and what the church had therefore purchased, was not individual property to be casually disposed of; it was stored whether or not it was wanted. Secular music was written simply for a specific occasion, usually in the latest style, and then forgotten; it was the property of a Sforza, a Gonzaga, a Medici, a d'Este, men whose wealth existed to be squandered in the cause of impressing the world and maintaining a reputation for grandeur. Thus what was written for secular use was enjoyed and discarded, and what we know of the Florence carnival and its music in the days of Heinrich Isaac and Lorenzo the Magnificent comes to us from accounts such as that which the architect Antonio di San Gallo wrote in his diary:

> The Carnival procession set out after dinner and continued sometimes till three or four a.m. A body of over three hundred masked horsemen in rich costumes took part. As many followed on foot, carrying lighted torches, that made the night lighter than the day and delighted all beholders. In this manner they passed through the city, singing harmoniously in four, eight, twelve and as many as fifteen parts, accompanied by all sorts of instruments, their songs, *ballate*, madrigals and *barzelette* illustrating the subjects represented by the groups of pageantry.[1]

The other Italian courts were equally enthusiastic in their support of secular music. The d'Este chapel at Ferrara, which numbered twenty-five under Duke Hercules who for some time had Josquin des Prés in his service, and had risen to thirty-five under his grandson Alphonsus II at the end of the fifteenth century, was the largest musical establishment in northern Italy. Like that of Florence, it spent time and trouble on its church music but employed its musicians to write secular works. The Mantua *cappella* where Monteverdi served for many years became more important than Florence itself as a centre for early opera, but it added little of value to the store of church music.

Thus we come to understand the influence of Italy on the foreign musicians who worked there. If their work became more lyrical, more openly melodious, lighter in style and texture while preserving its technical mastery and strength, we notice that they were working in conditions where such lyrical freedom and lightness were not merely encouraged but actually expected of them. Whilst a great deal of the secular music of the early and middle Renaissance is a matter of verbal record and discussion rather than of scores available for performance or study the fact was that the Burgundians and Flemings—whatever name we like to apply generally to them—were taking their technical revolution into a musical culture which was developing along quite different lines from those in which they had grown up, and that most of them were stimulated by the new atmosphere. Secular music depended not on the prose rhythms of the Mass and the Bible but on regular verse forms, on the balance of line against line and strophe against

---

[1] Quoted in Grace O'Brien: *The Golden Age of Italian Music*. Jarrolds, London.

strophe; it presented a new sort of expressive freedom and a new sort of technical discipline.

The consequences can be seen in the development of music for the Mass. Settings of the Ordinary come from the period of Machaut but are not common until the fifteenth century. The dominance of plainsong demanded that their foundation be an accepted traditional chant in the tenor; hence the title of masses such as, for example, the *Iste Confessor*, *Assumpta est Maria* and *Ecce Sacerdos Magnus* of Palestrina, which spread their polyphonic textures round the chant with which these Latin texts, as antiphons or motets, were associated. In the fifteenth century plainchant melodies became 'parodied', that is to say converted into mensural, regularly rhythmic music. Already, in the Bull of 1323, Pope John XXII had protested against the intrusion of secular song into the music of the liturgy, but the technique of parodying a plainchant melody began to obliterate the differences between the traditional music of the church and the songs which musicians created outside it. It was not long before parody technique began to pervert the old modes of plainsong into modern tonalities. In addition to that, concentration upon secular music and the attractiveness of regular rhythm and tonality not only added melodic simplicity and a rhythmic sense of direction to plainsong; they modernised it in the sense that they gave it the qualities which were most admired in the music of the world outside.

From this to the use of secular songs as the basis of liturgical compositions was only a step. The technique of taking a mere song as tenor and weaving a polyphonic texture around it was forbidden by the church, but a technique which depended enormously upon points of imitation between the voices was a good disguise of profanity even if the original worldly tune was not sufficiently dismembered by the treatment to have lost its objectionable character. Left to itself, it does not seem very likely that the song *L'Homme Armé* would have survived for us with more vitality than perhaps a hundred popular songs of the Renaissance. It is a pleasantly jaunty tune, perhaps a folk song, with enough rhythmic variety to catch the memory; but it became the basis of a Mass by nearly every composer of its period, from Dufay beyond Palestrina to Carissimi, as well as of a vast number of settings by composers whose names have been lost. The tune perhaps invites polyphonic treatment not only through its rhythmic variety but also through its punctuating insistence upon falls of a fifth in the melody. Of course *L'Homme Armé* was not the only tune used in this way; another popular melody was that of the mysterious Walter Frye's *Si la Face ay Pale*, and in England, where secular songs were rarely used as theme of a Mass, John Taverner wrote a beautiful setting of the liturgy using the love song *Westron Wynde* as his foundation.

If this was to some extent a secularisation of church music—and probably the composer, and those with sharper ears, were delighted to recognise forbidden and even scandalous melodies when their treatment was so elaborate that the less musical never noticed it—it was no less a sanctification of secular music. It is the result, more than anything else, of the ambitious attitude of Italian patrons, singers and composers to work outside the church.

Germany was the last country to feel the full effect of the northern revolution. The Emperor Maximilian's employment of Flemish and Netherlands musicians in his establishments at Augsburg, Graz, Vienna and Innsbruck, however, inevitably influenced the German courts. The enthusiasm for music of the Fuggers, the great banking family in Augsburg with its enormously ramifying interests stretching from Central Italy to the Baltic, became another powerful force for carrying the products of the new school. Judicious loans to Maximilian had enormously increased not only their wealth but also their authority; they had enormous concessions in the mining rights of minerals throughout the Empire, controlled the receipts from a large portion of the Spanish crown property, held silver and quicksilver mines in Spain as security for loans to the crown, and largely controlled Italian banking and the banks of Antwerp. Their relations with Maximilian's successor Charles V were equally close and dubiously squalid, as they made it possible for Charles to outbid all competitors in what is the most venal Imperial Election on record, and they used his inability to repay them to advance themselves socially and politically. Church building and charities, as did music, occupied the Fuggers though the firm paid a dividend of fifty-four per cent every year from 1536 to 1552; its head became a Count of the Holy Roman Empire and, by virtue of his devotion to charity, was regarded as a noble and high-minded pillar of religion.

The family interests demanded the supervision of a Fugger wherever they arose, so that the great commercial towns of the continent became not only seats of the family's commercial interests but also places where their wealth enabled them to live as they wished. It was the Fuggers of Nuremberg who brought the advanced instrumental and choral style of the Gabrielis from Venice into Germany, and their relations took to it no less affectionately, so that it was heard wherever they were in residence. This became possible because an Italianised Fugger, Gian Giacomo, was Intendant of the choir of St. Mark's during the time that Andrea Gabrieli was organist there, between 1566 and his death in 1586. In 1578 Jacob Fugger, the head of the family in Augsburg, took Johann Eccard, a pupil of Lassus, from Munich, into his household music, a fact we know from Eccard's dedication of his *Neue deutsche Lieder*, published in 1578, to Jacob and his two brothers. The Fuggers used their wealth to live like noblemen, and if there was something of the middle-class upstart about their determination to do everything the nobility did their enthusiasm for music, and particularly for the new styles of their day, hastened the spread of the new works across the continent.

The first German court to rise to glory as a musical centre was that of Bavaria. Munich had been the ducal capital since 1255 when Duke Ludwig of Bavaria surrounded the city with walls and a moat. Bavarian musical traditions go back to Duke Albrecht II, who reigned from 1397 to 1439 and spent most of his time at Ingolstadt, where he established a corps of trombonists. In 1523 Ludwig Senfl was at the Bavarian court *Kapelle*, his service with Maximilian having ended with the Emperor's death in 1519. Senfl was one of a distinguished line of Bavarian court musicians which had included the blind organist Paumann, who from 1467 until his death six years later had been organist to Duke Albrecht IV and who was perhaps the first German musician—he had been born in Nuremberg—to become internationally famous.

Senfl's position in Munich is not clear, for if he became officially *Kapellmeister* he must have retired by 1552 when Ludwig Daser was appointed to the post. During Senfl's time, although court music in Munich was almost entirely staffed by Germans, works by Josquin and Isaac were in the *Kapelle* repertoire, as was music by Gombert, Willaert and Clemens. Senfl's own work itself was known well beyond the borders of Bavaria, prompting an enthusiastic letter from Martin Luther, whose enthusiasm for music was always capable of overcoming any doctrinal scruples about publicising the works of catholic composers for their church.

Roland Lassus had been brought to Munich in 1556 by Duke Albrecht V, who was building up his *Kapelle* and eager to recruit musicians trained in the Netherlands. He was twenty-four years old and already had a notable reputation. After his years with the Gonzaga family[1] he had worked in Naples and had been made choirmaster of St. John Lateran in Rome in 1553. He had travelled perhaps in England and certainly in France, worked for two years in Antwerp and found himself, apparently, able to mix on easy terms with the wealthy and the musically minded nobility. Before he reached Munich he had a long and varied musical experience and a considerable knowledge of the world.

He reached the Bavarian court nominally as a singer, and it was not until 1563 that he appears in the records as *Kapellmeister*. Nevertheless, from the start he held a privileged position, with a higher salary than any of the other singers and even than Daser, the *Kapellmeister* under whom he at first served, and after a year in Bavarian service he was already paid 200 florins a year.

Daser and Zauner, his immediate predecessors, were both musicians of considerable importance. Daser seems to have suited the taste of Albrecht V perfectly. He was made *Kapellmeister* in 1552, and was granted a patent of nobility a year later. In 1563, he was granted his dismissal on the grounds of 'protracted ill health'. The reality behind what seems to have been an excuse devised to allow the duke to pay him a pension after his services had ended seems to have been that Daser had become a Protestant at a Catholic court. At the time Protestant services were permitted in Bavaria, but a court composer was responsible for the music and performance of Catholic rites. If his *Kapellmeister* had been discharged on religious grounds the archduke might have found it difficult to make any gesture in his favour, and Daser's ill-health, if it kept him in Munich as a private citizen until Protestant services were forbidden throughout the country in 1572 (they had been permitted by the Diet of Ingolstadt in 1563), did not prevent his becoming *Kapellmeister* to the Lutheran court at Stuttgart where

See Chapter 4, p. 52.

he remained until his death in 1589; the Bavarian pension was paid to his widow for at least twelve years after his death. He remained in correspondence with Lassus whose music he introduced to Stuttgart.

Zauner, who was considerably senior to Lassus when the composer entered the *Kapelle* as a tenor, lived until 1577 as a subordinate of the newcomer. Lassus himself was not the first foreigner to find employment at the Bavarian court. The tide of Flemish and Netherlands singers and musicians seems to have begun its advance into Bavaria with a certain Matthias the Netherlander (who appears in the court account books as 'Matthes Nidlender') in 1552, at about the time that his fellow countryman Arnold von Bruck (whose surname may indicate that he came from Bruges) with the brothers Vaet and Philip de Monte arrived in Vienna, and Johann Walther reached Dresden. Lassus started early in his Munich career to collect a number of his compatriots round him; this is one of the consequences of a great expansion of the Munich *Kapelle*. In 1514 there were eighteen musicians in the archduke's service and the number had risen by 1551 to twenty-six; a decree of 1552 laid down thirty-three as the greatest number the court *Kapelle* would need but, notwithstanding that, by 1579 the number had risen to sixty-one, a figure which included not only the singers and instrumentalists but also the choirboys and the trumpeters and drummers of the duke's guard. Between 1556 and 1567 the account books list a variety of new members —Joachim von Scheveningen, Petrus von Edam, Martinus de Hove, Wilhelmus de Diest (who is also called 'Wilhelmus Niderland') and Johannes Martini, all of whom were Netherlanders and most of whose names amply indicate their birthplaces—as well as Cornelius de Burgos, whose surname is equally revelatory; Cornelius, apparently, did not make his way directly from Spain but had spent some time as a member of the cathedral choir in Antwerp.

On taking office in Munich Lassus found himself committed to a programme of work rather startling in its range. Every morning he was in charge of the music for High Mass in the court church of St. Lawrence, and there was daily *Tafelmusik* to entertain the archduke in the evening; the extent of the demands this later item made on him is indicated by the number of his settings of the Grace before meals, *Agimus tibi gratias*. He was in charge of the teaching of instruments to gifted boys, for a decree of 1560 instructs the treasury authorities to pay him an extra sum for teaching the *Zink* to one of the boys. Instrumentalists and singers are listed separately in the account books; of the former there are organists, violinists, cornettists, trombonists and lutenists. The violinists and organists were Italians, the first signs of Italy's future dominance over string playing. The register of the singers keeps the boys separate from the men, listing them as trebles. In 1572 the thirty-three members of the *Kapelle* cost, in salaries and occasional bonuses, 10,000 florins. A year later with additional members the *Kapelle* uniforms are noted as costing 748 florins. Singers and instrumentalists were paid from 144 to 180 florins each, the organ maker and attendants 50 florins or less; the boys' board cost 28 florins per head. The eleven members of the trumpeter corps, one of whom was a drummer, earned 34 florins each. Lassus himself was paid 400 florins and allowed 40 florins for his servant's board, and another allowance was made for fodder for his horse.

Throughout Lassus's period in Munich church music was instrumentally accompanied. In addition to the church and *Tafel* music which he had to supply, ceremonial music for the trumpeters was needed. He was the choirboys' house-master, supervising their education and their home life in the *Kantoreihaus* (the motets he wrote for them to sing at the beginnings of holidays seem to suggest that relations between him and the children were unusually friendly), handling the money for their food and clothing and an extra allowance for whatever educational materials were needed. He himself was their music teacher, but in 1561 a choir 'schoolmaster' was appointed to teach Latin, Bible history, classical history and mythology, and rhetoric; these subjects, with music, comprised their school curriculum as it had comprised the curriculum which Lassus had followed as a boy in the choir at Mons. As in the towns where no court dominated music-making, Lassus's choirboys had the duty of singing in procession through the city on special occasions, and the music, as well as the actual teaching it involved, was again the choirmaster's responsibility. As Lassus had no assistant *Kapell-meister* until Johann a Fossa joined the *Kapelle* in 1569 (at a salary of 180 florins, which indicated the distance between his position and Lassus's) the composer's industriousness and organising ability must have been outstanding.

The public processions, as a means of spreading advanced music further than the court as well as occasions of some quaint antiquarian interest, deserve mention. A full instruction for the organisation of the Corpus Christi procession of 1584 survives,[1] and this indicated the extent of the celebration and the involve-ment in it of the court musicians. The boys of the Jesuit school and of the cathedral all took part, as did the *Stadtpfeifer* and the members of the various trade guilds in the city. The performers were costumed to take part in tableaux; some of the boys were to join the Barbers' Guild and, all in appropriate costumes, sing and play '*antiqua Musica Hebraeorum*'. King David was to be represented by a harpist, leading thirty-six boys 'big and small' who would be angels; the adult angels would be five basses and as many tenors. Twenty-four big boys from the charity school would be pilgrims, six or seven of them playing instruments, fiddles, lutes, cornetts, trombones and whatever other instruments they could manage. Seven small angels would sing before the Virgin Mary; their music would be in parts, and they could learn it in the school one day. Nine angels would sing round the Crib, 'for their *Kapellmeister* Orlando has composed a special song about the Nativity of Christ'. Then each strophe of the Pilgrim's hymn sung by the charity schoolboys would be followed by the 'little angels' singing '*choraliter*' *Sancta Maria, ora pro nobis*. The rehearsals for the court choirboys' part in this would not be held in the *Kantoreihaus* but in the ballroom of the Archducal Palace. The supervision of all the music was to be undertaken by Lassus; the master of ceremonies was a court chamberlain, Caesare Bandelli.

Until 1579, when the *Kapelle* reached its largest, Lassus collected singers and

[1] Wolfgang Boetticher: *Aus Orlando di Lassus Wirkungskreis*. Bärenreiter, 1963.

players, especially gifted boys with good voices, from all over Europe. In 1560 Margaret of Parma offered the Munich establishment 'some singers and choir boys', and her offer was accepted. In 1574 Lassus was in Italy collecting musicians, buying instruments and reporting back regularly to the archduke by letter. The court lists note the expansion of the *Kapelle* through the importation of foreign talent. In 1557 the arrival of 'four boys' from the Netherlands is announced. 'Three Spanish choirboys' arrived in 1582. In the 1580s the court began to employ *castrati*, and found castrated boys in the Netherlands and Germany. The rise of the Jesuit order after the revocation of tolerance to Protestants apparently brought some reorganisation of the court *Kapelle*. In 1571 the choir accounts mention that 726 gulden were paid to the Jesuits for boarding twelve boys, and in addition to the court comedies which were among their normal duties the choirboys began to act in the religious plays which were among the Jesuits' many educational innovations.

The period of expansion came to an end after 1579, when the *Kapelle* was costing Archduke Wilhelm 2,000,000 gulden a year and he reluctantly undertook to economise, cutting the number of musicians from forty-four to twenty-two adult, salaried members. It never regained its old strength although in 1591, three years before Lassus's death, it had climbed again to thirty-eight. Nevertheless, the Munich establishment and its *Kapellmeister* remained internationally famous. The Pope had accepted the dedication of Lassus's book of Masses, *Patrocinium Musices*, when the composer had been in Italy.

The creative force of the Renaissance court as a musical centre is clear enough. It needed secular music no less than it needed music for the church, and this gave to music outside the liturgy a range and social importance it had never previously attained. It fostered the use of instruments no less than that of voices, and found it necessary on many occasions, particularly in national and civic ceremonies, to make instruments independent of voices. It created well-disciplined ensembles of singers and players to perform works written usually in the most advanced and striking styles of the time. It did not standardise the orchestra it used, but employed whatever instruments were available to the best advantage; standardisation did not effectively begin for another century or more but the value of instrumental music was something about which the Renaissance court had no doubt, so that Praetorius's *Syntagma Musicum*, printed in 1615, details fourteen ways in which a madrigal by Lassus could be treated by a choir and a variety of instrumental groups.

Court music enhanced the prestige of the composer even though it did not always provide him with the material surroundings and conditions most advantageous to creative work. His salary might be quite reasonably high; it might be parsimonious. In Milan, Galeazzo Maria Sforza paid Josquin des Prés, during the two years (1474 to 1476) which Josquin spent in Milan, a monthly salary of 10 ducats while the obscure and unimportant Abbate who controlled the court's church music was paid 40. In 1470 the singers of the Papal choir never received more than 2 or 3 ducats a month, and three-quarters of a century later, the *maestro di cappella* at Bologna was paid between a third and a quarter of the salary allotted to the professor of humanities at the university. Gafori, the theorist teacher-composer, who joined the staff of Milan Cathedral in 1484, lamented that any book he might require cost him the better part of a month's salary.

Pay rose comparatively little in a time of rising prices. In Venice in 1488, although a sumptuary decree forbade the spending of more than half a ducat on a single meal, citizens spent between 400 and 500 ducats a month on food; the legal half-ducat was, however, a tenth of the average singer's monthly salary, and Josquin, for example, never earned more than 60 ducats *per annum* (not per month) although he held positions which provided him with what the educational papers used to call 'residential emoluments'. It is significant that Willaert, who managed to leave his widow 10,000 ducats invested in Fugger's bank, was a city and not a court musician.

The vicissitudes which might overtake a court composer are perhaps most clearly demonstrated by the relationship of Monteverdi to successive dukes of Mantua, a city which owed its wealth, influence and final collapse to its position as the gateway to the Alpine passes and therefore a place of key importance in the rivalry between France and Spain for power in north Italy. Monteverdi was certainly in Mantua as a musician in the service of Duke Vincenzo I by 1591. Possibly by that date he had already spent two years there as a violist among the ducal players. Mantuan greatness and pomp were at their height; for a hundred years the Gonzaga family had been vigorous patrons in whose court Italian musicians had held their own against northern invaders, surrendering traditional music to the new Netherlands style but maintaining their positions undisturbed. Palestrina had written a Mass and a number of motets for Vincenzo's father Guglielmo I, whose compositions he corrected and with whom he carried on a voluminous correspondence. During his reign from 1550 to 1587 Guglielmo did his best to induce musicians as important as Marenzio and Orazio Vecchi to his court, and appointed Giaches de Wert, a northerner and the exception to customary Mantuan appointments, as his *maestro di cappella*.

Vincenzo I, whose appetite for magnificence, range of interests and energetic career as a lover played havoc with Mantuan finances, was a patron of Rubens and Pourbus, protector of Galileo and creator of a theatre company which travelled to the Louvre and Fontainebleau in 1608. In some ways he treated Monteverdi with unusual indulgence; he gave the composer special permission to marry, conferred Mantuan citizenship upon him and eventually granted him a settled annual pension. Nevertheless, even when Monteverdi was at the height of his powers and had proved himself to be the first great music dramatist, Vincenzo preferred the work of senior but undistinguished members of his *cappella* whom Monteverdi described in his letters with a bitterness that is sometimes humorous, sometimes irritated and always picturesque. When Vincenzo went on campaign against the Turks in 1595 he took the composer with him as temporary *maestro di cappella*—although Monteverdi's official position at the time was merely that of *cantore*, or leading singer—in charge of a travelling musical staff of five.

The death of Giaches de Wert in 1596 raised Monteverdi's hopes of the succession to the post of *maestro di cappella*, and in the light of the works he had written by then, such hopes were not unreasonable; the appointment of Benedetto Pallavicino to the vacant post struck him as a deliberate insult. Nevertheless he accompanied Vincenzo to Florence—the terms of his employment did not permit him the pleasure of walking out on the post he had held for some years— so that it almost seems that Vincenzo preferred Monteverdi's company to his music. The retirement of Pallavicino in 1601 did not immediately bring the composer the promotion to which he felt he was entitled after his ten years' service and the reputation his music had won him beyond Italy through his travels with the duke, so that the delay in appointing a new *maestro di cappella* prompted him to petition for the post with a sarcasm he hardly bothered to veil:

> If, on the occasion of Benedetto Pallavicino's death,[1] I myself made no haste to request from Your Serene Highness's great favour the rank Signor Giaches once held as a musician, it might perhaps fall out to my regret that envy of the endeavours of my colleagues (by means of rhetoric rather than music) would be urged against me publicly in such a fashion as would cloud the good opinion Your Serene Highness holds of me, and would make it appear that my envy originated in anxiety as to my own capacity, or in overweening conceit of my own person, so that therewithal my ambition betrayed me into expecting what an unimportant servant such as I am should seek to obtain without especial humility and earnest entreaty. If, likewise, I no longer cultivated opportunities of serving Your Highness, even though Your Grace offered them to me, there would be cause indeed of deploring my lack of zeal in serving you if, when I could make my motets and Masses acceptable to your exquisitely sensitive ear, it would surely be a matter for justifiable complaint. And if, when the world at large had been aware of the continuance of my zeal in your service, as well as of Your Grace's favour towards me . . . if, indeed, I were still to fail in aspiring to secure appointment to the ecclesiastical post now vacant (not as a recompense for exceptional talent but as a reward for faithful and especial devotion such as I have always displayed in Your Highness's service) and if, when all is said and done, I were to fail to beseech you ardently and with deep humility for the aforesaid post, my default of zeal would then give rise to scandal. Considering all this, and taking into account such things as are vital to my career and such as would be fulfilled by the instrument of your favour; and considering, also, that Your Highness has never disdained to hear my modest compositions, I do most earnestly pray you to grant me the post of *maestro di cappella* of chamber music.

Vincenzo granted Monteverdi the position and at the same time made him a Mantuan citizen. It is interesting to speculate upon the slowness of the composer's rise to authority when, of the various efficient mediocrities who were his colleagues and seniors, there is not a single one whose abilities can stand more

---

[1] According to H. F. Redlich (*Claudio Monteverdi*), the composer was mistaken in believing Pallavicino dead when the post of *maestro di cappella* became vacant, as the *ex-maestro*, after leaving Mantua, became a friar of the Order of Camaldoli, continuing to publish new works for more than eleven years.

than the remotest comparison with his. According to the composer's letter Vincenzo approved of his work; Vincenzo's choice of Monteverdi as companion on his travels suggests that the duke, whose extravagance did not stretch towards the payment of luxurious salaries to his artists, has some personal regard for him. Monteverdi's famous controversy with Giovanni Maria Artusi, the canon of Bologna who defended the reactionary aesthetic against Monteverdi's modernising tendencies, did not begin until after his appointment, so that there seems to have been no reason whatever for Vincenzo's neglect of Monteverdi's obvious claims to promotion—not that any Italian duke of the period would have been likely to allow external criticism of a musician he favoured to influence his judgement. Furthermore, from 1602 onwards—only a short time after his promotion —Monteverdi's salary seems to have been permanently in arrears, as the letter he wrote to the Court Chamberlain, Annibale Chieppo, on December 2, 1608, shows:

> The fortune that I have enjoyed throughout nineteen years in Mantua has caused me to feel ill-disposed rather than friendly. . . . When at last, fortune seems to favour me and I allowed myself to believe that by His Highness's favour I should receive a pension of 100 scudi of Mantuan currency from the City Governor, His Highness withdrew his favour from me once again. And then, after my marriage, it was no longer 100 scudi, but only 70; and in addition I was deprived of the facilities I had requested and of the payment due for the months gone by. And then it seemed as if 100 scudi might have been considered too much. If the 20 scudi I drew as salary had been added to it, it would have amounted to as much as 22 golden ducats a month. . . . Up to the present time, I have lost about 200 scudi, and I lose more as each day passes. . . . It was also decreed that I should be given 25 scudi, and to my grief 5 scudi were withdrawn from me.

The volume which contains the great Vespers of 1610—not a liturgical setting but the psalms for Vespers of the Blessed Virgin Mary (which remain the same for all her feasts) introduced by antiphons which come from the rites not of a single feast day but from a variety of them, together with two settings of the *Magnificat* and a variety of religious pieces all in Monteverdi's modern style, seems to have been compiled simply to attract the attention of aristocratic households with large musical resources. It suggests that discontent with Mantua was beginning to persuade him to look for a position in which he might financially better himself. The work is designed, according to its composer's description, not for church use but for 'the palaces of princes', and is intended to demonstrate his mastery of both new and traditional styles. 1610 also saw him making important but fruitless contacts in Rome, and then others, which eventually proved splendidly fruitful, in Venice. It was however the sudden death of Vincenzo in 1612 which released him from bondage before any of these schemes for obtaining fresh employment—if that is what they actually were—had become in the least effective. Francesco IV, the new duke, immediately dismissed Monteverdi so that the composer left Mantuan service with precisely 25 scudi as the result of twenty-one years' service in which he had composed madrigals, church music and operas of the greatest importance and of remarkable, expressive beauty which had won the leadership of the new world of opera away from its birthplace in Florence. Francesco IV was not long in thinking better of his action and inviting Monteverdi to return to Mantua, and his efforts to recover his father's *maestro di cappella* were followed by those of his two brothers, but Monteverdi found that his position in Venice was more satisfying both socially and financially than the life he had lived in Mantua.

This account of a great composer's experience of court patronage shows as clearly as anything can the weakness of a musician's position under court patronage and in court employment. The apparently friendly relations with his Prince did not appear to be a compensation to Monteverdi for cuts in his salary imposed quite arbitrarily as Vincenzo II thought fit, nor for pay held long in arrears and dismissal unceremoniously imposed on him after the duke's death.

The ups and downs of the Papal Chapel, of the Pope's private musicians as distinct from the choir which attended his personal services, demonstrates the composer's insecurity. Whilst a family tradition inevitably spelled some sort of security of tenure for the musician at court—so long as there were Gonzagas in Mantua, they maintained some musicians even though they treated their greatest composer shabbily—the election of a new Pope meant that such a traditional security of office could not be taken for granted. The newcomer might dislike music altogether or might have strong tastes which could not be satisfied by his predecessor's musicians. The Renaissance produced Popes who were passionately devoted to scholarship and the arts, just as, particularly in its later stages, it produced others who were passionately involved in the struggle for political and international power. The Papal musicians were a fluctuating and more or less disregarded body until the coronation of Leo X, the Medici Pope, who was himself a composer of songs which he sang agreeably to his own accompaniment, so that the Venetian ambassador reported with some amazement after the coronation that the new Pope played the lute. He appointed the French composer Elzéar Genet, often referred to as 'Carpentras' after his birthplace, to take charge of his domestic music and formed round him a body of musicians greater than any of his predecessors had bothered to maintain. Genet he rewarded with a splendid collection of canonries, prebends and priories, so that the greater part of the cost of maintaining first-class music did not fall on the Papal exchequer. This was not an unusual way for the Popes to finance their music. The Spanish Juan de Encina, who divided his time between court and church employment—he wrote most of his music for Ferdinand and Isabella, whose marriage united Spain—attracted the attention of the Spanish Pope Alexander VI who granted him a benefice in the diocese of Salamanca although he was not in Holy Orders. The Italian Julius II made him Archdeacon of Malaga despite his being a layman, and Leo X sent for him to Italy. The Bull which demanded his services in Rome, which reached Malaga in October 1514, contained the following instructions to the Malaga Chapter: 'During the attendance of the Archdeacon of Malaga at the Pontifical Court he is in no wise to be disturbed nor molested in the enjoyment of his full income no matter what statutes of Malaga Cathedral may conflict with this provision.'[1]

The death of Leo X in 1521 and the coronation of Adrian VI, who was committed to the reform of the church and its institutions, ended the line of art-loving Popes. Court music in Rome came more or less to an end and Encina, like a number of other musicians, found Rome no longer a profitable place in which to live; those who were borrowed from other establishments and had been favoured by other authorities were in a not unhappy position; the others were simply left to find what employment they could.

This was the special vulnerability of the court musician. He held office at the pleasure of his patron, and if he did nothing to annoy his employer he was safe until the employer's death. Then his contract was automatically ended—this explains Monteverdi's unceremonious dismissal from Mantua—but probably he was reinstated by the next ruler. Musicians were less important than civil servants and administrators, so that they were the first to suffer from the shortages of money which frequently attacked the various noble and royal treasuries. At such times they would be paid only a fraction of their official salaries and what was owed was allowed to mount up over a period of years. Monteverdi was only one of many who suffered in this way, and the probability was that a composer trapped into this situation would never be paid in full.

At the same time the court musician, having accepted his post, was not free to leave it in order to better himself; if he broke his contract to do so, he was liable to imprisonment. Alfonso d'Este, Duke of Ferrara, pointed out to Antoine Brumel when he offered employment to the composer that if Brumel accepted the post he could not be allowed to leave Ferrara without the duke's permission. Similar provisions were written into musicians' contracts until the end of the eighteenth century. The way for a composer to leave court employment was to receive an invitation to a new post and then petition for his discharge from the position he held; the petition might or might not be granted.

At a wealthy court a composer could make a good deal of money; early in the period, and throughout it in Spain, where the Renaissance was the greatest creative period through which the country had passed, this depended on the number of ecclesiastical benefices which he might hold. By the second half of the sixteenth century, however, the greatest masters outside Spain were not in Holy Orders, and their material success had come to depend upon the popularity of their work. If the conditions of the contracts which bound them to their posts were stringent—so that, for instance, their work belonged to the employers for whom they wrote it—a composer whose patron valued him, and whose work began to reach publication, might find himself rewarded by half a dozen or more other aristocrats who received copies of his works, or he might, by publishing

[1] Translated in Robert Stevenson: *Spanish Music in the Age of Columbus.* Martinus Nijhoff, The Hague, 1960.

them or by distributing copies to well-wishers, augment his often meagre salary considerably.

In other words, the Renaissance established music as a profession; where in the towns musicians had banded together in guilds, the relative paucity of work open to them, and the difficulty of maintaining a monopoly, had made the professional organisation of their craft little more than a convenient fiction, in the courts a musician became a professional, not merely a chaplain or a secretary with a useful talent to be exploited but a man employed simply for his skill in organising performances, performing himself and providing the music which was to be performed. Dufay's success depended on the fact that he was a clergyman with, apparently, a valuable secondary talent for negotiation, as well as brilliant musical gifts. A hundred years later, Lassus and Monteverdi, one in court and the other in a church and municipal post, were as much or more preoccupied with secular music as with religious works. Each disseminated his work in print and neither was a clergyman or employed for any extra-musical talents he may have possessed (though each seems to have been a gifted organiser and a man capable of exerting a great deal of influence over subordinates, blessed with gifts of leadership), but simply as a composer-musical director.

The shift of the musical centre of gravity from the church to the court established music as a real profession even though the numbers who could be employed in it were necessarily limited. At the same time, it made secular music not only the equal in importance but also the more adventurous branch of the art, and so indispensable to social life in general that no composer of the period found it possible to restrict his output to work for the church. Virgilio Mazzochi, who was *maestro di Cappella* at St. John Lateran in 1629 and then at St. Peter from 1630 until his death in 1646, collaborated in the composition of the first comic opera. Ludovico Grossi, normally called 'Viadana' after his birthplace, who was *maestro di Cappella* at the cathedral in Mantua in 1590, while Monteverdi was at the Gonzaga court, composed not only a considerable amount of church music which employed the new style of declamatory music and the figured bass for the first time in church, but also canzonets and madrigals.

8   Music in Print

Considering the difficulties involved in mere physical movement about the continent, the distances which music travelled during the middle ages are surprising. Often they can be explained by judicious guess-work: the travels of Machaut with his royal patrons created, we may justifiably feel, a market for his works at the courts they visited, and these would spread along the usual diplomatic channels. For instance, English contacts with France, diplomatic or military, suggest how the works of the Notre Dame composers may have reached this country while they were still fairly new.

The mysteries, however, vastly outnumber the explicable facts. If the choir of Worcester Cathedral in the thirteenth century sang music from Notre Dame composers, we can tell ourselves that we know why and admire the skill of genius in making its presence felt in spite of heavily restricting conditions. Why, on the other hand, is there no English trace of the work of Dunstable or, for that matter, of Walter Frye? How did music of Ockeghem, for example, find its way into the choir books of Spanish cathedrals at a time when Spanish musicians had little direct contact with the music of the north?

The coming of printed music at the end of the fifteenth century removes most of the mysteries of that sort. The printing of music became a technical possibility in the last quarter of the century, but the difficulty of reproducing in print the complexities of contemporary notation, and the uncertainty of any worth-while market for music composed on what we may call the principle of expendability which demanded a work's almost immediate replacement after it had been heard once or twice, made its publication a hazardous commercial operation. As soon as a printer or publisher committed himself to the creation of an edition of any musical work, he was committing himself to the idea of a musical repertory in which certain works would have, if not a continual, at any rate a lengthy existence, and at the end of the fifteenth century such a repertory did not exist even in the musician's mind. To some extent the availability of printed music created both the idea of a repertory and its actual existence.

In these circumstances it was natural that printers of music began their work by issuing liturgical books which, preserving the authority of ecclesiastical chants, could be reasonably sure of a fairly extensive sale. A Gradual, with the year's music for the Proper of the Mass, appeared in 1473. This was followed three years later by the production—its printer was Ulrich Hans, of Ingolstadt—of a missal which gave the chants of the Ordinary, and before 1501 nearly two hundred and seventy liturgical books, and the appropriate music, were published.[1] The limitation of the musical compass involved—all the notes fit a four-line stave except on very rare occasions, when a change of clef can avoid the use of ledger lines—and the few varieties of note shapes required to indicate rhythmic and time values made it possible to print such books with movable types like those used for the letters of the alphabet.

Even liturgies seem for a time to have been projects too ambitious for the exiguous book market of the day. The numerous local versions of the chant which existed along with the authorised Roman music restricted the use of any volume that could be published, and for a time the more profitable way of printing them was to print only the staves and leave them blank, so that the actual music in use wherever they were bought could be written into them by hand above the words which the printer, of course, supplied. Nevertheless, a missal with music according to the Sarum rite—that is, with the musical and textual variants accepted at Salisbury and more or less throughout the greater part of England—was issued in 1500.

Musical text books and treatises were a different matter. A brief musical illustration of anything that was current practice round about the turn of the fifteenth century posed the printer a variety of problems of layout, synchronisation and varieties of type face required by the various notes in use, and these could best be answered by engraving the illustration on metal and using it as a block for printing, or by making a woodcut which could be used in the same way. This, usually, involved printing by double impression, the first printing the staves and the second fitting on to them the notes, clef signs, key signatures if necessary and anything else that was required. Therefore printing from engraved blocks was slow and complicated; it was also more expensive than printing with movable types in a single impression, for the types used naturally contained the necessary portion of stave and not merely the head and tail of the note itself.

The greatest music printer of the period, Ottaviano de Petrucci, received an exclusive licence to print music in Venice in 1498 and his first book *Odhecaton* appeared in 1501. The three years' gap between the granting of the licence and the issue of its first fruits suggests that Petrucci was occupied during the interval in technical experiments, improving his methods and considering effective layouts. The result is printed music of a clarity and elegance which has not been surpassed. Petrucci's method, unfortunately, needed three impressions, and was both slow and costly; a first printing set the staves on the paper; the second positioned the notes on the staves and the third printed the words beneath the notes, added page numbers, ornamental initials, titles and signatures. Between 1501 and 1509 he printed forty-three books of vocal music and four of music in lute tablature. In 1511 he returned to Fossombrone, his birthplace, and in the next ten years produced another fourteen volumes of vocal music.

---

[1] A. Hyatt King: *400 Years of Music Printing*. British Museum, 1964.

Small editions of beautifully printed and bound music, whether produced by two- or three-impression systems, were necessarily expensive. London, Nuremberg and several other German and Italian cities had printers who apparently found the effort and the expense worth while, but the possibilities of cheaper music depended on the development of single-impression printing with movable types; this, again, meant the cutting of a vast number of varieties of note types, of accidentals, clef signs, rests, ledger lines and so on, and the storing of them ready for use. The extension of movable types from the printing of plainchant to the music of the time may have been the invention of a certain Pierre Haultin, of Paris, who is traditionally supposed to have printed a book by this method in 1525; the book, however, has been lost for something like a couple of centuries. A London printer, Thomas Rastelle, brought out two pieces of music printed by this means at about the same time, but the first publisher to use it extensively and to have left a considerable number of samples of his work behind was Pierre Attaignant whose *Trente et quatre Chansons musicales a quatre parties* was published in Paris in 1528. A great deal of work appeared in the first half of the sixteenth century printed in this way, and the method, with various improvements, has continued in use ever since.

Petrucci and his followers did not print music in score, but printed each part separately one under the other, with the soprano at the top if the works were in three parts, or across two pages, with soprano and tenor on the left, alto and bass on the right, if it were in four parts. In addition, they printed a large number of separate part books, a number of works anthologised with each voice part contained in a separate book. It seems from the careful way in which the surviving books have been handled that they were not often used in actual performances but apparently kept as reference books, the works inside them being copied for performance. The church music issued this way, of course, would not be easy to read from a large lectern by small boys whose parts are printed at the top of each page.

The music made available by the early printers showed how far a work might travel. The first two of Petrucci's publications were books of secular *chansons*, in three or four parts, by Isaac, Josquin, Obrecht, Ockeghem and several of their contemporaries. Attaignant not only printed more lute music than Petrucci, but issued thirty-five volumes of four-part songs which altogether provide text and music for nearly a thousand works by French and Flemish composers, as well as seven books of Masses and thirteen books of motets. Thirty-four of Petrucci's sixty-one publications are of church works, however, so that it seems that the Italian churches were more ready to buy music than the French, and that Attaignant's patrons seem to have had more opportunity than their Italian coevals for the performance of secular music.

The effect of printing on the spread of music is easy to see from the works which appeared and the places in which they were published. Anthologies, like Petrucci's *Odhecaton*, were for a long time more popular than volumes devoted to a single composer, which Petrucci used only for church works; he brought out volumes of Isaac, Josquin, Obrecht, Brumel and three or four other composers, only one of whom, incidentally, was Italian. He ranged across Europe for materials, not always succeeding in ascribing works to their actual composers, for a motet by the Spanish Juan de Anchieta appears in the third book of Petrucci's *Motetti de la Corona* as the work of the French Loyset Compère. It was not only the Flemish composers whose work he issued, but also, apart from Anchieta's motet, he includes several secular Spanish motets in his anthologies, and within a few years the whole music-publishing business had become remarkably international. Robert Stephenson[1] traces the early publications of music by Spanish composers. Morales's works were anthologised in Antwerp, Augsburg, Lyons, Milan, Nuremberg, Rome, Salamanca, Valladolid, Venice and Wittenberg. Doctrinal differences did nothing to impede the popularity of his works in Protestant Germany; five of his *Magnificats* appeared in a volume published in Wittenberg by Luther's own publisher, Georg Rhau in 1544, and in 1545 Rhau published one of his motets in a book of Christmas music.

The works of Guerrero, the next in the great line of Spanish cathedral composers, began to appear in print in 1555 when the composer was only twenty-eight years old. They demonstrate a new aspect of the value of publication: anthologised works, like the posthumous collections which Petrucci had brought out, are useful to the historian whom they provide with a great deal of information about the tastes of the public, the extent of musical education and the extent to which music was diffused about the continent; if they meant anything to the composer, it was only that his work had somewhat increased in international status; they brought him no material advantage. Before Guerrero's works reached the customary anthologies, however, they had appeared in volumes printed at the composer's own expense, organised as he wished them to be organised and presented by him to potential patrons and to the directors of choirs, hoping—and apparently with some success—that such presentations would result in gifts capable of reimbursing him for his expenditure; before this, he had distributed his works to the same people in splendid manuscript copies which seemed to have paid their way. His *Sacrae Cantiones* came from Martin a Montes d'Oca, a Sevillian printer. In 1563 he chose Pierre Phalèse of Louvain, an expert on the printing of polyphonic works whose products were highly esteemed on the international music market, to bring out his settings of the *Magnificat* in all eight modes. In 1566 he turned to Nicolas du Chemin of Paris for the printing of a book of Masses, and a volume of motets came from the press of the Venetian Francisco Gordano, prefaced with an attack, apparently intended for the eyes of the authorities meeting at the Council of Trent, on those churchmen who wanted to see a simplification of church music. Gordano brought out Guerrero's music for Vespers in 1584, and in 1588 Guerrero was granted permission by the Chapter of Seville Cathedral, where he was choirmaster, to go to Venice to arrange for the printing of his second book of motets, which Gordano issued in 1589. A final book of motets was printed in 1597. In

---

[1] *Spanish Cathedral Music in the Golden Age.*

the meantime his work had begun to make its way into the anthologies, especially those printed in protestant Nuremberg where a *Magnificat* appeared in 1591 and other works by Guerrero were included in a volume with the up-to-date and (for Guerrero's work) less than strictly accurate title *Sacrae Symphoniae* issued by Paul Kaufmann in 1600.

Privately sponsored publication by a composer—a method of publication which eventually grew into publication by subscription, the composer obtaining in advance undertakings from a sufficient number of well-wishers ready to buy the completed work—seems in Guerrero's case to have been profitable. It is unlikely that, on his salary from Seville Cathedral, he could have afforded to persist in unprofitable efforts to spread his work. In 1552 Elzéar Genet or Carpentras, the *maestro di cappella* to Pope Leo X, had sponsored two volumes of his own work, and these have the historical distinction of being the first books to use round-headed, instead of lozenge-shaped, notes. Hernando di Cabezon, who worked at the court of Philip II, had arranged for the printing of his *Obras Musica para Tecla Harpa y Vihuela* in 1576, and had paid 5,000 reales for twelve hundred copies of a book of a hundred and twenty-seven leaves each, printed in tablature on pages of less than foolscap size; his printer, Francisco Sanchez of Madrid, agreed in their contract to provide matrices and types. Alfonso Lobo, the *maestro di cappella* at Toledo Cathedral, contracted in 1605 with a printer Juan Flamenco ('John the Fleming') for the printing of nine books of his vocal music and one of its organ accompaniment; he demanded a hundred and thirty copies of each, each volume containing a hundred and thirty-seven leaves; for this he paid more than 5936 reales, more than twice as much as the same printer had demanded two years before for a hundred and thirty copies of Victoria's *Missae, Magnificat, Moctecta, Psalmi et alia*. As the loss or gain in these cases would be the composer's, and as the point of arranging an edition was to present potential patrons with one's work in the most elegantly enticing format, the vast difference between the price demanded from Victoria and that charged to Lobo is an unexplained puzzle. The salary of a Spanish *maestro di cappella* varied a good deal, of course; at Avila in 1526 Morales was paid 100 ducats; at Plasencia in 1530 his salary was 60,000 maravedis. At Toledo, in 1545, he was granted an increase of 6,000 maravedis on the normal salary of 100 ducats. As a real was the equivalent of 34 maravedis, Lobo's volume of 1603 cost him the equivalent of about five years' salary.[1] We do not know what sponsorship may have been available to assist him in financing the publication.

Victoria at any rate had the help of wealthy friends and patrons in the task of publishing his works, and Victoria, the greatest master of the Spanish Renaissance, became a wealthy man. The stipends of the benefices he collected and the salary of his post as Chaplain to the Dowager Empress after 1587 came to 1227 ducats; to this the Empress added a yearly endowment of 120 ducats (the composer sold his interest in this to pay for his first publications), and from the

[1] See Appendix: Tables of Currency.

sale of his works he received varying sums—82 ducats in 1598, 50 ducats in 1602, 100 ducats in 1604 and 14 ducats in 1606, for example. These sums came from the Spanish cathedrals, from Flanders and from Lima.

Victoria's work was handled by printers all over Europe. His first volume appeared in 1572, when he was twenty-four years old, and his music appeared in volumes from printers in Rome, Dillingen, Milan and Madrid. That a German printer, in 1589, should reprint a book of motets originally printed in Rome six years before indicated the spread of his music north of the Alps.

All the successful composers of the time succeeded to some extent in capturing an international audience. Claude de Sermisy, who was a canon of the Sainte-Chapelle in Paris and *Maistre de Chapelle* of Louis XII's private chapel, published his first book, *Trente et huyt Chansons Musicales a quatre Parties*, through Attaignant in 1529 and continued to bring out his works, first with Attaignant and then with Nicolas du Chemin, in Paris. Adrian le Roy and Robert Ballard, in Paris, anthologised his works, as did Moderne in Lyons, and both Scotto and Susato in Venice, showing how far his Parisian volumes travelled.

Ludwig Senfl brought out three volumes of his own music through printers in Nuremberg, the centre of German printing, between 1526 and 1537. The Nuremberg publishers included nearly a hundred and fifty of his works in anthologies, and his music appeared in a variety of books issued throughout Europe. Jacobus van Kerle, whose career took him from the choir school at Ypres to Orvieto, Augsburg, Vienna and Prague, and whose settings of the prayers for the Council of Trent, composed in 1561, were directed to the defence of polyphony against authorities in the Council who were demanding a simplification of church music,[1] published his work in Rome, Venice, Antwerp, Nuremberg, Munich and Prague. Lassus, the great popular composer of the end of the sixteenth century, naturally arranged for the printing of his works himself, but they were brought out by printers, both as items in anthologies and in one-man volumes the flood of which did not abate until fifty years after the composer's death, and it seemed to wash over the entire continent.

The value to a composer of this new means of publicising his work can be estimated from the Dedicatory Letter to Pope Sixtus V with which Palestrina prefaced his *Lamentations* of 1588:

> Worldly cares of any kind are adverse to the muses, and particularly so are those which result from a lack of private means. When there is enough money to provide a sufficiency (and only a greedy man would ask for more), the mind can more easily dissociate itself from worldly cares; if it cannot, it is itself to blame. Those who have had to work to provide a sufficiency know how the lack of it distracts them from learning and the study of the arts.
>
> I have known this lack all my life, and do so especially at present, but I think God's goodness, first, that my course is almost finished and my goal nearly in sight; secondly, that in spite of great difficulties, I have

[1] See p. 126–7.

never had to interrupt my study of music. As I have been dedicated to music since my boyhood, what other interest could I have had? I wish that I could believe my achievements to equal my labour and diligence.

I have composed and published a good deal. I have much more music in my possession, but this I cannot publish because of the lack of money which I have already described. To publish this work would need the spending of sums which I cannot afford, especially of the large print which music naturally requires were used for it.

The result was that in spite of his enormous reputation and the prestige of his position in Rome—possibly the highest musical office which the Catholic church had to offer—and his authority as the chief editor of the liturgical chant, much of Palestrina's music appeared only posthumously. Amongst other works, four books of motets had been published. He was engaged in preparing the seventh book of Masses for the press when he died in 1594, and after his death the Papal treasury made a small grant towards the expense of bringing out the volume. Palestrina was not badly paid as church musicians and their salaries went in the sixteenth century. When in 1551 he had gone to direct the Julian choir, the body which Pope Julius II had set up in 1513 to train singers for the Papal choir and for the choirs of the Roman basilicas, the official salary attached to the post had been raised as an inducement to him to accept it, and his salary at Santa Maria Maggiore was raised in 1578 to induce him not to accept an appointment away from there. Nevertheless the cost of publishing his entire works eluded him although his authority throughout Europe would almost indubitably have made the publication of his works a very profitable speculation.

Unlike their great European contemporaries the English composers published comparatively little until the closing years of the sixteenth century. Nothing of Christopher Tye's, for example, reached print until, in 1641, John Barnard included his motet *I will exalt Thee* in his anthology of *Selected English Church Music*. In 1575 Queen Elizabeth I granted Tallis and Byrd a monopoly of the right to print music and music paper in England. Five of Tallis's anthems had already appeared in anthologies of English church music published between 1560 and 1565, and in partnership they published their *Cantiones Sacrae*, each contributing seven motets to the volume.

In addition to this collaboration, Byrd published five further volumes of *Cantiones Sacrae* without any collaborator (Tallis had died in 1585) between 1588 and 1593. *Psalmes, Sonets and Songs of Sadnes and Pietie* appeared in 1588, the two volumes of Byrd's *Gradualia* in 1605 and 1607, and his *Psalms, Songs and Sonets* in 1611. Morley, Byrd's successor in the monopoly, published *Canzonets for Three Voices* in 1593; the second edition of this, with three additional pieces, came out in 1606 and gave rise to German versions published in translation in Cassel in 1612 and in Rostock in 1624. The *Madrigals to Foure Voyces* appeared in 1594, and the *First Book of Ballets to Five Voyces* in 1595: an Italian edition was printed in London in the same year, a second English edition was printed in London in 1600, and a German version emerged in Nuremberg in 1609. The *First Book of Canzonets to Two Voyces* came in 1595, and it reached a second

edition in 1619. The *Canzonets or Little Short Songs to Foure Voyces* of 1597 was a
selection of Italian pieces to which Morley added two works of his own; another
collection of Italian music, *Madrigals to Five Voyces*, and the *Canzonets or
Little Short Aers to Five or Six Voyces* both came in the same year. The *First
Booke of Consort Lessons*, an anthology, went through two editions in 1599 and
1611, and *The First Book of Ayres or Little Short Songs* was printed in 1600.
Morley published *The Triumphs of Oriana*, to which he contributed two madrigals, in 1601. *A Plaine and Easie Introduction to Practicall Musicke*, published in
1597, reached a second edition in nine years. Morley, of course, undertook none
of the practical business of printing himself; he simply 'assigned' these publications to various printers, notably to William Barley whose printing shop was in
Little St. Helens, and they were sold from Barley's own house, or the house of
whatever printer Morley used. The volumes which Morley saw into print were
not all of his own work, and some of them contained nothing by him; as mono-
polist, he acted as editor in their production.

The idea of Elizabethan England as a nest of singing birds rushing to their
part books to sing elaborate madrigals by Byrd, Morley, Gibbons and others, as
well as by Palestrina, Lassus and Monteverdi is a little discouraged by the relative paucity of music which came into print during the second half of Elizabeth's
life, and even more by the fact that in the first two years of the monopoly Byrd
and Tallis petitioned the queen for an allowance of money (which they received)
on the grounds that they had lost 200 marks from their sale of music. After
Tallis's death, however, the demand for their products seemed to increase and
the monopoly began to become profitable as the queen had intended it to be.
Both Byrd and Morley imported music from the continent to add to the English
work which they handled.

The names of the volumes, both English and continental, mentioned here—
and these are roughly representative of all the music printed in the late sixteenth
and early seventeenth centuries—indicate two things. The bulk of it is no longer
church music produced in 'de luxe' editions intended as library copies for reference or to dignify the library of the wealthy connoisseur; most of it is music in
parts intended for use in the homes of musical amateurs; it indicates more
clearly than anything else the spread of music amongst a comfortably off and
artistically lively middle class of business men and merchants. It is, as a matter of
fact, the only direct and incontrovertible evidence that exists for our traditional
belief in the intense musicality of the Elizabethan English, and it also indicates
that the same appetite for vocal music existed over most of Europe, together
with sufficient skill in music to make use of printed parts.

Secondly, it demonstrates the growing appetite for instrumental works. Much
of the instrumental music originally published was vocal music, often church
works, adapted for the lute and printed in tablature or in vocal parts and simply
handed over to whatever collection of instruments was available. At the beginning of the period Petrucci's catalogue includes four books in the lute tablature
printed in 1507 and 1508. Attaignant published a text book for lutenists and

two books of dances, containing between them a large collection of both country dances and newly composed tunes, in 1529 and 1530; the lute song spread across Europe, reaching perhaps its highest point of development in England at the end of the century. Ballard of Paris, Janssen of Amsterdam and a variety of other publishers all over the continent brought out considerable quantities of lute music, while as early as 1577 Gordano printed the madrigals of Cipriano de Rore in score instead of in separate parts, and mentioned on their title page their value as possible additions to the string repertory. Byrd's issue of his various volumes of Ayres and solo vocal music with an accompaniment not for lute but for string consort presupposes a profitable market amongst those able to play the viol or some other instrument than the lute.

The appearance in late 1611 or early 1612 of *Parthenia*, a collection of keyboard works by Byrd, Bull and Orlando Gibbons printed by William Hole, who claimed that his volume was 'the first musicke that was ever printed for the Virginals', and, for example, the issue of Frescobaldi's organ music by Nicolo Barbone in a series of volumes which began to appear in 1615, make the importance of the amateur player even more obvious, and indicate that sufficient people could afford to buy virginals to make the publication of works for them more than a rash venture or an attempt to win prestige. As for strings, Morley's *Consort Lessons* had appeared in the same year (1599) as Anthony Holborne's *Pavans, Galliards, Almains and other short Aers both grave and light*. The spread of music in practical, performing editions can only mean that it was matched by the number of players able to take advantage of it, and the movement of music about the continent shows how completely international the art had become by the beginning of the seventeenth century.

Printing techniques, however, had developed. The engraving of music—an entire work, staves, clefs, titles, notes, words and all, on copper plates—had been attempted in the mid-sixteenth century; devotional prints, for example, show works of music, or portions of works of music, which were produced by engraving well before any musical edition itself was produced in this way, and publishers quickly found that illustrations in text books, for example, could be given a sharper and cleaner appearance if printed by copper-plate engraving than from woodcuts. In 1586 Simon Verovius, a native of Hertogenbosch who had settled in Rome, brought out two books of four-part canzonetti in a totally engraved edition. Engraved music became quite common, so that amongst the editions it has been necessary to quote to demonstrate the international spread of music, many are engraved prints while others were printed from movable types. Engraving slowly became the more normal method of producing printed music, neater, clearer and cleaner in appearance than music printed from types, much of which, in the sixteenth and seventeenth centuries, was clumsily made with ugly, jagged broken stave lines. It was possible, as the rise of opera and oratorio demanded the regular creation of complex printed scores, to produce these by type-setting, but elaborate works could be more swiftly and safely made, despite the expensiveness of the copper plates needed, by engraving. *Parthenia*, with all

the problems of spacing keyboard music and finding the correct vertical align-
ment of chords, was an engraved book because engraving made accuracy easier
and no more expensive than alternative methods of printing. Barbone's edition
of Frescobaldi's organ works, for the same reasons, was engraved, but until the
second or third decades of the seventeenth century engraved music remained
much less common than music printed by the hand-setting of movable types.

9   The Reformation and the Counter-Reformation

'Luther was a German, national, a man of the people. It is startling to find that he could play the lute and sang with a tenor voice.'[1] If there is a specific type of north-German music lover, high-spirited, hot-tempered but intensely serious, Luther entirely represented it. As a small boy, before he took religious vows or Holy Orders, Luther had the usual thorough training of a German choirboy and like all other choirboys sang in the frequent *Kurrende* processions for alms through the town and at the weddings and funerals of local dignitaries. His complete devotion to music had its influence on everything he touched, not only his German liturgy but also German education, and his life was almost as important for the future of music as it was for the future of religion.

> The noble art of music [he wrote when as a successful revolutionary he was establishing and organising his own church] is, as God's word declares, the highest of earthly treasures. It rules all thoughts and senses, the heart and the temperament. Do you want to comfort the troubled, to tame the impudent and wild into mildness, to soften the arrogant, and so on? What could be better for such purposes than this high, dear, worthy, noble art? The Holy Spirit Himself values it highly, for He drove the evil spirit from Saul when David made music on his harp. Again, when Elisha wished to prophesy, he asked that a musician be brought in to him to play the harp. Therefore it was not without reason that the Fathers of the Church, and the Prophets, have always wished the Church and Music to remain close together: that is why we have so many hymns and psalms. It is through this precious gift, bestowed only on mankind, that any man remembers his duty always to praise and glorify God.

Though it is possible to see Luther as history's greatest rebel—greatest because he was born and made himself effective at the earliest moment when it was possible to divide the Christian Church in Europe—he was in most respects intensely conservative. Every Christian reformer, Catholic or Protestant, has declared his aim to be the cleansing of the Church from corrupt recent accretions and a return to the simplicity of a truly Apostolic tradition. The changes which Luther made allowed him to preserve not only the popular externals of Catholicism—the ceremonies and the music which, richly colourful in themselves, bred in the worshipper a sense of awe and mystery—but also a great deal of the doctrinal foundation of the Catholic faith. He knew that the celebration of the Mass,

[1] Owen Chadwick: *The Reformation* (Pelican History of the Church, Volume 3). Penguin Books, Harmondsworth.

its dialogues between celebrant and people, its ritual gestures and drama as well as its music, were in themselves an enormous reservoir of popular devotion which it would be almost impossible to replace, so that while he insisted on a lively and positive teaching of the Faith as he saw it through preaching, with sermons regularly delivered at both morning and evening services, he set this emphasis on teaching within the traditional liturgical framework of the Mass, which kept almost all its musical structure.

It was typical of his attitude to the past that when, in 1523, he drew up his *Formula Missae*, the liturgy remained in Latin. It offered alternative services for cathedrals and great city churches on one side and, on the other, for churches in small towns and villages. The former were encouraged, but not compelled, to sing the services in Latin; the latter were offered a German translation. The traditional liturgy, in either language, was simplified, as were the ceremonies which were traditionally a part of it.

From the start Luther gave as much care to the musical structure of the new Rite as he did to its liturgical bases and its verbal accuracy. He sent for Johann Walther, a bass singer and composer from the *Kapelle* in Torgau who was later to become *Kapellmeister* to the Elector of Saxony. Walther was a convinced Lutheran, and it was apparently he, rather than the amateur Luther, who provided the detailed organisation of Lutheran music. It was the retention of Latin in some churches, continuing in some places for special services into the middle of the eighteenth century, which explains the settings of the *Magnificat* and of the *Missa Brevis* in Latin by composers as late as J. S. Bach and his son Carl Philipp Emanuel.

A good deal of the traditional chant survived particularly in such portions of the Rite as passages of dialogue between the celebrant and the people and the celebrant's Preface before the *Sanctus*. So did polyphonic motets which Luther himself loved and preserved except when there was anything in their texts which suggested the Catholic doctrine of the Mass as a sacrifice or some other un-Lutheran dogma.

The traditional liturgical Introit survived in the 'Great Service', though this replaced the Gradual, the Offertory and the Communion chants of the Catholic past with chorales, hymns in German, while additional hymns were sung before and after the sermon; these hymns could, however, be replaced with motets or other polyphonic works; a motet was sung between the Introit and the *Kyrie*, which was still retained in its traditional form.

This careful preservation of links with the Catholic past accounts for the way in which the works of the great pre-Reformation polyphonic composers remained popular in Lutheran Germany and for the survival in the libraries of Lutheran church choirs of copies of their works. It explains, too, the undoctrinal alacrity with which the great German churches after the Reformation added works by new Catholic composers to the repertory of their choirs. The library of the *Thomaskirche* in Leipzig, when it was catalogued in 1564, contained all the latest collections of Lutheran chorales, but the bulk of the music it housed at that time was originally written for the Latin rite. It had comparatively few printed music books (a fact which suggests that J. S. Bach's predecessors in the years after the Reformation were quite happy to use the music which had been familiar to the choir in the old Catholic days), but an anthology entitled *Missae sex Vocum* included Mass settings by such post-Reformation masters as Willaert and Morales. Earlier composers like Heinrich Isaac were represented both by service music and by motets. As late as 1696, four years before Johann Sebastian Bach joined its choir as a fourteen-year-old treble, the *Michaeliskirche* in Lüneburg had its library recatalogued; it contained volumes by the Catholic Lassus and the *Selve Morale e Spirituale* of Monteverdi; this latter was still a comparatively *avant-garde* collection of settings many of which require instrumental accompaniment by viols, violins or trombones. Of course, it had copies of volumes by Protestant composers—Praetorius, Scheidt, Hammerschmidt, Selle, Schein and both A. and Johann Krieger; Schütz, the greatest Protestant master before Bach, was represented only by some of his *Kleine Geistliche Konzerte*, the *Musikalische Exequien* and the *Psalmen Davids*. There was, too, a great deal of music by lesser Lutheran composers, but it is plain that in musical centres like the *Thomaskirche* in Leipzig, the *Michaeliskirche* in Lüneburg and the *Kreuzkirche* in Dresden, musical quality rather than doctrinal beliefs or sectarian loyalties governed the choice of music because of the way in which Luther, from the beginning of the revolt, had made musical quality an important adjunct to his liturgy.

The political division of the Lutheran states, however, led to a certain variation of details in the treatment of the standard liturgy. A few more or less haphazard examples show how, in the German north where Lutheranism was strongest, variations in the precise celebration of the Lutheran Mass were taken for granted. The Lübeck 'Church Order', for example, was drawn up in 1531 to strike a typically Lutheran balance between evangelical zeal and conservative traditionalism. The Introit was to be sung on Feast Days in its original Latin. The *Kyrie* and *Gloria* were to be sung always in German, *Herr erbarme dich* and *Ehre sei Gott in der Höhe*. In Schleswig-Holstein, however, the *Kyrie* was sung to its traditional chants taken from the *de tempore* plainchant settings and varying according to the season. In Lübeck the *Gloria* was omitted, as it is in the Catholic Mass, during Passiontide. In Osnabrück the salutation *Dominus Vobiscum* remained in Latin, while in Lauenburg, in orders drawn up in 1585, either Latin or German was permitted. In Lübeck the Collect for the day had to be said in German, but in Osnabrück either Latin or German was permitted.

The *Alleluia* of the Latin Mass, which follows the Gradual on festal days, was generally preserved, but in place of the Sequence which follows it on the greatest feasts, the Lübeck order insisted that on Christmas Day, Easter Day and Whit Sunday a 'German song', that is, a chorale, should be sung. In Lübeck the Creed was to follow the sermon and was to be sung in Luther's version as a German hymn, *Wir glauben all' an einen Gott*. The Preface remained in Latin, but the *Agnus Dei* was sung in its German hymn form, as *Christe, du Lamm*

Gottes. Naturally so much variety led to a demand for a good deal of music of varying types.

It was the 'German songs', the hymns which for some reason are always known to English people as chorales, which became the distinctive musical feature of Lutheran music. The German Mass, as Luther designed it for churches where Latin would be meaningless to the congregation, was given simplified music as well as a German text. The Gradual and Communion texts became hymns, arranged according to the day and the Proper of the service, while the Communion chorale *'Jesus Christus unser Heiland'* was an invariable part of the liturgy. The chorale tune, with direct, homophonic four-part harmonies, written in the modern major or minor mode and not in the medieval church modes, thus became an integral (and musically modernising) part of the service, written to replace some of the variable Proper of the Mass. 'Much music in the Mass,' wrote Luther in the *Vermahnung zum Sakrament,* 'is excellent, for it is an expression of thankfulness and it is dearly loved. In such pieces as the *Gloria in excelsis,* the Creed, the *Preface,* the *Sanctus* and *Benedictus* and the *Agnus Dei* there is nothing but thankfulness and praise, and for this reason we keep them in the Mass. Of all the Mass music, the *Agnus Dei* most truly serves the sacrament, because it praises Christ, who has borne our sins; in simple words it enhances our reverence for Christ's Passion.' The *Agnus Dei* therefore became, as did the *Gloria* and Creed of the German Mass, a metrical chorale with German words which all could understand. In this way, *Allein Gott in der Höh sei Ehr, Wir Glauben all' an einen Gott* and *Christe du Lamm Gottes* were sacrificed by the musician Luther to Luther the reformer, for the musician Luther had no particular love for the congregational singing in unison and permitted it, or invited it, only to allow the congregation to make a declaration of faith with complete understanding of what they were singing.

In the *Vermahnung an die Geistlichen auf dem Augsburger Reichstag,* Luther wrote about the variable music of the Mass: 'It is best of all that the finest music of the Latin *de tempore* remains to us, though it is overshadowed by our new hymns.' What concerned him was that the hymns, which at first in the simplified German Mass and only later in the *Hauptgottesdienst* of great churches, which included sermon and motets and culminated in the German Mass, should be liturgically appropriate and refer to the Epistle or the Gospel which had to be read, so that the chorales sung at the Gradual and the Communion became a new German Proper referring to a particular Sunday or feast day; such chorales provided the first section of all the successive chorale books which were issued in and after Luther's lifetime, and they were supplemented by a wealth of miscellaneous hymns from which the variable pre- and post-sermon chorales could be selected, although even these had to be liturgically appropriate.

Luther's first intention in the substitution of hymns for sections of the liturgy, and their admission into other parts of the rite when no choir was available to sing the Renaissance motets which were his great delight, seems to have been no more than pedagogical; the congregation would profit from listening to them as the choir sang them, and could even join in singing the hymns at the Creed and the *Gloria* more effectively than they could in the singing of a polyphonic Mass or even the traditional plainchant. Apart from these two necessary declarations by which the congregation affirmed its faith, he was not specially interested in congregational singing though he conceded that it might be a profitable spiritual exercise. The suggestion appears in the *Table Talk* piously collected by his disciples: 'I wish we had more hymns which the people could sing during Mass or to accompany the *Gradual*, *Sanctus* and *Agnus Dei*,' he said on one occasion; and on another, 'We have decided to follow the example of the prophets and the fathers of the church and write German hymns for the German people.' For all that, he was not enthusiastic about hearty community singing in unison, and the 'more hymns' for which he wished were all to be liturgical and to call in the congregation to participate in the rite, not simply to sing for the good of their souls. He looked back always to the glories of Renaissance music with which he had grown up. In the chorale book published by Rhau and Forster in 1538 he wrote: 'When natural music is sharpened and polished by art, then one begins to see the great and perfect wisdom of God in His wonderful work of music, where one voice takes a simple part, and round it sing three, four or five other voices, leaping, springing round about, marvellously gracing the simple part, like a dance in heaven.' The reference is obviously to the old-fashioned *cantus firmus* type Mass and motet; congregational unison singing is 'natural music', and Luther has no words to say in its praise; the function of all but the liturgically necessary chorales was to be sung in well-balanced harmony by the choir for the instruction and edification of the listeners; the trouble was that their musical structure and the type of melody they adopted encouraged the participation of the congregation. The first chorale collection to be published harked back to the music which Luther regarded as the ideal of church music, for it produced five-part settings of thirty-five chorales, each of which is given its melody *cantus-firmus*-wise, in the tenor.

Some of the chorales were Latin hymns translated into German; these were chiefly traditional office hymns. Others, less integral to the Liturgy, could be sung either in Latin or in German. There were, too, German devotional songs dating from before the Reformation, and together with these came the setting of religious words to old and new popular tunes: the 'Passion Chorale', familiar to everyone who has heard Bach's *St. Matthew Passion* began its career as a love song by Hans Leo Hassler, *Mein G'mut ist mir verwirret das macht ein Jungfrau zart* (My brain is topsy-turvey because of a pretty girl).

Perhaps the greatest of all the chorales is the group of hymns by or attributed to Luther himself, and for which the music, too, is, traditionally ascribed to the reformer. His paraphrase of Psalm 46, *Ein feste Burg ist unser Gott*, with its defiantly challenging melody, became the hymn of embattled protestantism everywhere. Psalm 130, the *De Profundis*, he paraphrased into *Aus tiefer Not*. Other hymns by Luther, like *Christ lag in Todesbanden*, were original poems.

The growth of Lutheran hymnody was rapid and did not stop with Luther, who refused either to draw or to allow his followers to draw any hard and fast distinction between religious and secular music. A good tune has its place in worship no matter where it came from; if the authorities a century before had seen in the use of *L'Homme armé* as a Mass *cantus firmus* a secularisation of church music, Luther believed that the adoption of such tunes for chorales was a sanctification of the secular, and he had no objection to the use of popular songs, *Minnesänger* melodies or anything of which he could musically approve, as a vehicle for religious words. For this reason, for two hundred years Lutheran music moved with the times and thus kept the general church-going public, that is everybody, in touch with the latest musical developments.

The position of the chorale in the Liturgy, however, was never completely regulated. As Lutheranism accepted the idea of state religion and the organisation of the church through the machinery of political government, practice varied widely in different parts of Germany; the quasi-liturgical *de tempore* chorales were more or less assured of their place in every Lutheran church, but the precise form in which they did so varied enormously. The order for *Hauptgottesdienst* in Halle in the seventeenth century, for example, demanded that the congregation participated in singing the hymns before and after the sermon and in the invariable Communion hymn, *Jesus Christus unser Heiland*; for the rest, the Gradual and the Latin Creed might be replaced by a hymn, and a postcommunion hymn might replace the motet, in which case the congregation would sing with the choir. At Vespers, when hymns were sung, only one was ordered to be sung congregationally; the hymn liturgically proper to the day (in Catholic parlance, the Office Hymn) could be sung in Latin by the choir alone or in German by both choir and congregation. That before the sermon, the choir's exclusive property, could have an aria added to it.

Nevertheless, the chorale normally became an opportunity for congregational singing more or less in spite of Luther. To expect the congregation to remain silently attentive during the singing of familiar popular melodies was perhaps expecting a more than natural degree of self-control from it, and Luther's educational theories, put into practice by his disciples all over Protestant Germany, had led to a great expansion of musical culture. 'A schoolmaster ought to be able to sing,' declared Luther with characteristic dogmatic vigour, according to his *Table Talk*. 'If he can't sing, I shall have nothing to do with him. If young men haven't studied and practised music, I would never admit them to the ministry.' Therefore teachers in general were trained to teach singing and the elements of music even where a school was not wealthy enough to have the services of a specialist music master in the person of the town Cantor. The grounding which children received led in many small cities as well as many large ones to the founding of choral societies such as that on which J. S. Bach called for his *Ratswahl* cantata (*Gott ist mein König*, Number 51) composed for the service at which the new Town Council in Mühlhausen took office in 1708. The Mühlhausen *Musikalische Societät* had existed as an amateur choir and a predominantly amateur group of instrumentalists (its professional members were the town organist and the *Stadtpfeiferei*) since 1617. With so much more or less trained, entirely enthusiastic, singing from members of the congregation, it was natural that the chorale should be taken over by the congregation as its own particular contribution to the service.

Even before the Reformation the citizens of many German towns had begun to organise schools for the children where there were no already established church schools, so that their sons might receive as much education as was necessary for success in business. As in the church schools, music was enthusiastically taught both as a valuable intellectual discipline, a religious duty and a social pleasure. There is a multitude of surviving German text books designed, in the Reformation and immediate post-Reformation periods, for the teaching of music, dealing not only with singing but with the theory of music and with composition. Many of them presuppose a remarkably high degree of technical skill in their users; for instance Georg Rhau's anthology *Newe Geistliche Gesenge fuer die gemeinem Schulen*, published in 1544, is a collection of motet-type pieces, mostly based on chorale melodies and using chorale texts, written by the best German composers of the time. The result is that in 1620, Michael Altenburg described musical life and activity in Germany: 'There is scarcely a village, especially in Thuringia, in which both vocal and instrumental music does not thrive and prosper. If there is no organ, then vocal music is adorned with at least five or six strings, something hardly known before even in the cities.'[1]

A few years later, when a collection of settings of Psalm 116 was published, its Preface by Burckhart Grossman looks back to a golden age of music from the first agonies of the Thirty Years' War; the 'Spear of Saul', wielded by the enemies of religion, was equally determined to kill German music. The devil had put a spear into the old king's hands so that he could slay the harpist David, who played for him when the evil spirit possessed him.

> Saul's spear is not only in the hands of court finance ministers who lock their doors when they hear musicians approach; it is also wielded by teachers and cantors who study the *Vass*[2] rather than the bass, and are among the enemies of music. Thus on all sides we hear the complaint that there is a shortage of sopranos, for which there is no other reason than that they use the Spear of Saul rather than the baton. Today in Thuringia, where the peasant servants and youths take their places at the choir desks after following the plough through the entire week, they both sing and play, surpassing many in skill if not in pronunciation.[3]

Grossman, of course, refers to Thuringia as an area not (when he was writing in 1623) yet ravaged by war.

Musically, the effect of the chorales cannot be over-estimated. Though Luther was not particularly enthusiastic about the organ, its use was not forbidden as a substitute for or addition to the use of *Stadtpfeifer* and string instruments, so that

[1] Quoted in H. J. Moser and Carl Pfatteicher: *Heinrich Schütz, His Life and Works*. Concordia, St. Louis, 1959.
[2] *Vass*—barrel.
[3] *Ibid*.

from the start chorale melodies were subject to organ accompaniment and polyphonic elaboration. Those which were integral to the service—the *de tempore*
hymns—gave rise even before the time of J. S. Bach to annual cycles of chorale
preludes in which the familiar melodies were elaborated, varied and subjected
to all appropriate manners of polyphonic treatment. Their melodies were for the
most part strongly tonal, and those which had survived from the modal past
evolved, as did many popular melodies, into tonality. Thus German composers
were given popular modern melodies with which to work for the church at a
time when French composers eager to follow a modern style were still shackled
by the modality of plainchant, which for the sake of modernity they corrupted
into tonality and called *plainchant musical*. Not only Luther's attitude to music
but the actual materials musicians were given to work on became powerful
modernising agents.

The popularity of the chorales provided composers with a handy, readily
intelligible symbolism; the chorales and their words were ingrained in the minds
of the congregation, so that doctrinal cross reference, so to speak, was another
tool in the composer's chest. It was, like most of the German Protestant techniques, used most powerfully by J. S. Bach. On the Feast of Epiphany, 1734, the
congregation in the Leipzig *Thomaskirche* heard the sixth cantata, in what we
have come to call the Christmas Oratorio, end with the Passion chorale melody
(that of *O Haupt voll Blut und Wunden*) set to words celebrating the Incarnation,
so that Bach had musically telescoped the doctrine of the Atonement for his
congregation.

If these were the facts about Lutheran music, there were, too, imponderables
of enormous significance. To Lutherans as well as to the more radical reformers,
authority in religion was vested in the Bible, the Word of God, rather than in the
living tradition of the church. Whatever was said in church which drew its
text from the Bible, and to an almost equal extent prayers like the *Kyrie* and
instructive texts like that of the Creed, needed to be heard and understood;
words should not, as they had become in the bulk of the works of the Renaissance
masters, be merely the raw materials of music used to give a structure and design
to something autonomously musical. If they were set to music it was the composer's duty to see that they were delivered with complete clarity. Such an attitude to music was not, of course, specifically Protestant; it was merely a revival
in a new situation of traditional Catholic objections to over-elaborate church
music and marks a point at which the wheel came full circle and the extreme
Protestants found themselves using the same arguments as extreme conserva-
tives in the Catholic church.

The importance of the text was, too, an encouragement to the composer, who
felt the words of the liturgy or the Bible subjectively. It would be utterly
ridiculous to suggest that Catholic music is always in some mysterious way more
'objective' than that composed for the Lutheran church, or that what was created
for medieval and Renaissance choirs to sing was always impersonal; only a pitifully limited awareness of medieval church music would assert anything so far

from reality. Nevertheless, the Catholic church had exalted an ideal of musical impersonality and was from time to time moved to condemn the works which deliberately or obtrusively neglected to approach it. The Protestant idea of the Bible as the Revealed Word of God made available to all believers, so that they might study it for themselves and meditate upon it to gain personal and individual insights into the divine will and purpose, was an open invitation to subjective interpretation and a home-made religion created by every man for himself. Thus a composer was expected to interpret the words of the Bible and the liturgy for the instruction, delight and edification of the worshippers.

The musical result of this attitude can be seen at its most marvellously developed in the church music of J. S. Bach. Any consideration of the works which he wrote for the Lutheran Liturgy points out the wealth of doctrinal references which is fed into them; some of these can easily be read as statements of Bach's own other than entirely orthodox beliefs. Whilst the Catholic composer's duty was to write music which would act as the hand-maiden of the liturgy, to express the humility of the faithful and to speak not for himself but for the church, Bach and the great Protestant composers used music to express for others certain personal insights into Christianity regardless of whether they would be regarded as entirely acceptable by the authorities.

It is impossible to measure as musical fact the effect of this freedom of interpretation; but though the results of such changes in attitude cannot be measured, the composer's freedom to expand, to write elaborate works which, in the hundred years which followed Luther's creation of the German Liturgy, had made the musical aspects of the rite the most extended and elaborate feature of Lutheran worship. In other words, the Protestant composer's right to express himself freely was not any longer subject to dogmatic or even strict liturgical control.

Whilst this freedom of approach was granted to composers, and the Lutheran church was presenting to its musicians a new range of duties and new materials, the organisation itself influenced their social life and conditions of work. Lutheran organisation emphasised the importance of the political authority in both state and city, and therefore decided the form of municipal organisations. In 1548 the Diet of Augsburg permitted what might be described as the minimum degree of reform satisfactory to Lutherans, and therefore drove into exile the left wing of extremists like Martin Bucer. The Catholic right wing, and the Imperial authority itself, found the provisions of what was meant as an interim settlement interpreted in a far more radical spirit than they had originally intended. Charles V was compelled to accept the various Protestant glosses on a formula which he had accepted as a means of controlling Protestantism while allowing what the obdurate regarded as absolutely necessary to their conscience if they were to live in peace within the Empire. To oppose the entire Protestant movement, moderates as well as extremists, would have made it impossible for Charles to maintain order within the Empire at a time when the Catholic south-east was under pressure from Turkey and the Protestant south had entered into an alliance with Catholic France. So long as doctrinal differences could be exploited in the interest of national policies and national ambitions, the final settlement (which both sides regarded as a necessity if future violence was to be avoided) had to be delayed by compromise. The Peace of Augsburg, in 1555, stabilised the compromise through its formula *Cuius regio, eius religio*, bound the German people to accept the religion of the State they inhabited, Catholic or Lutheran, as the issues were decided by its ruler in accordance with his conscience or with the demands of expediency. The ruin of the German extremists in 1548 prevented the development of Calvinist forms of worship, though not of Calvinist teaching inside the Lutheran framework, for a couple of generations. Then the compromise collapsed in the Thirty Years' War and it was left to the rival armies to draw the boundaries between the different confessions of faith and forms of Christian worship.

The years between 1555 and 1618, when the war began, permitted Lutheran organisation to work itself smoothly into a running order which survived the war and the exhaustion that followed it. In 1577, eighty-six German states or Free Cities, the bulk of them in the north and the whole of them comprising roughly half of the German-speaking Europe, accepted the Formula of Concord, which prevented any official acceptance of Calvinism. The rejection of Papal authority in those areas left a gap into which the temporal rulers of the various states willingly stepped. Luther's belief in the essential unity of church and State, inherited from the middle ages, made it natural for him to approve of the prince as the leader of reform in his dominions. The prince, recognising in this a way of securing the enthusiastic support of the commercially progressive middle class, stood to gain immeasurably from Luther's teaching; he appointed a consistory of influential churchmen and lawyers, over which he presided or which was controlled by his appointed deputy, as the central government of the church in his realm, responsible for its administration.

In the towns the magistrates and the town council controlled parochial administration. Like the consistories they had no power to decide doctrine, but as they appointed the clergy their indirect power over matters of doctrine was extremely powerful. In the same way they controlled the schools, and all civic musical appointments, except that of the *Stadtpfeifer* band, existed within the framework of church and school. Thus, not only the *Stadtmusikus*, who controlled the town band, but also the town Cantor, who was the principal musical authority of the city and its *Hauptkirche* and the senior music master in the most important town school, and the town organist, were all municipal appointments awarded as the results of open competitions. J. S. Bach became Cantor at the *Thomasschule* in Leipzig, which made him the senior musical authority in the town, the third in rank in the school hierarchy and its senior Latin as well as its senior music master, as the result of competition with Graupner when it was discovered that Telemann, the city council's first choice, did not want the post. Bach was the least acceptable of the applicants, given the post by default when Graupner withdrew, because he was not a university graduate and his teaching ability was therefore in doubt; German musicians who were in a position to attend university normally graduated in order to qualify for a Cantor's post should one come their way.

The *Thomasschule* was one of the old church schools which had for centuries been the centre of advanced education leading to a university career; they had musical lives stretching back three or four centuries. The passing of control from the church to the city council had meant no noticeable change in their characters. St. Katherine's, the medieval monastery school in Lübeck, came under municipal control in 1531. The Lübeck Cantor was its principal music teacher and third in rank amongst the staff after the Rector and Conrector, with four pedagogi beneath him; the number of junior masters depended on the size of the school. Leipzig corporation bought the *Thomasschule* in 1543; its organisation, like that of the *Johannischule*, in Hamburg, followed the standard represented by the *Katherinenschule* in Lübeck.

As in the past a number of foundation scholars, all boarders and all at least meant to be poor boys who could not afford to pay for their education, were taken in for the quality of their voices. They received specialist training in singing and in instrumental music, filling up (at least in theory) all the places made available by the school's endowments and providing the music of the main city churches—the pupils of the *Thomasschule* were responsible for the music at St. Thomas's, St. Nicholas's, the New Church and St. Peter's. The Hamburg Cantor and his choir were responsible for the services at St. Peter's, St. Nicholas's, St. Katherine's and St. James's, while the Lübeck choir was responsible for the music of St. Mary's, St. Peter's, St. James's and St. Aegidius's. This did not mean, however, that each of these churches celebrated *Hauptgottesdienst*, with orchestra and motets or cantatas every Sunday. In Leipzig, for example, *Hauptgottesdienst* was celebrated on alternate Sundays in St. Thomas's and St. Nicholas's; a few boys, under a prefect, led the singing at St. Peter's, where there was no organ, and another small group of boys with an organist led the congregational singing in the New Church.

The *alumni*, the boys of the choir, joined the fee-paying city boys for other lessons but their primary function was musical, they were the core of the school, and its curriculum was based on their needs as specialist music pupils. The nearest modern parallel to their position and to the choirs they formed—for they were the tenors and basses as well as the trebles and altos of the choir—would be those of Oxford and Cambridge colleges in which the broken voices are those of undergraduates, so that style and precision had to compensate for the immaturity of the adult voices. To what extent they did so and what the standard at Leipzig, Lübeck or Hamburg the choirmaster could attain, is something we cannot possibly know except by deduction from the demands made upon them by composers like Selle, Kuhnau, Telemann or Bach.

The municipal schools did not improve the conditions of the scholars in the old foundations which were taken over. The boys were subject to a discipline based on vigorous corporal punishment and were usually badly fed and housed.

The money provided for their subsistence, as for that of the cantor and the rest of their teachers, was so meagre that it had to be supplemented by *Accidenten*— the fees they earned for singing at weddings, funerals and occasional private or municipal functions, and from the *Kurrende* processions in which the choir, split into groups, sang in different places throughout the city to gain alms. For boys to grumble about school food is one of the inevitable consequences of boarding-school education; in the German schools their complaints were joined by those of the Cantor and the other masters.

The teaching itself remained old-fashioned until the spread of the eighteenth-century Enlightenment. It was based on the needs of the choir and paid more attention to Latin and music than to any of the other studies which business men wanted for their sons. As late as in the year of Bach's death in 1750, *Thomas-schule* boys were not allowed to speak to each other in German, even in their spare time, but were restricted to Latin.

The Cantor had not only to choose the music, to train the singers and to rehearse each Sunday's performances. The paucity of printed music, and its high cost, put it beyond the reach of most German churches; therefore the Cantor had himself to supply what was not easily available from elsewhere. For this reason he had to compose a vast amount of music simply for church use whether or not he felt inspired to do so. The vast eighteenth-century collections of yearly cycles of cantatas by Bach and Telemann, for example, though they are the result of a later development, are typical of the demands made on the Cantor by the principal duty he took up. Added to this were his duties as the municipal director of music whose functions demanded that he controlled all municipal music-making.

The organisation of city music, however, meant that until the catastrophe of the Thirty Years' War the centre of gravity of German music-making was in the cities rather than the courts, few of which could finance music so lavishly as busy commercial centres like Hamburg, Lübeck, Leipzig, Nuremberg, Frankfurt and so on. The great developments after the war came chiefly from the northern towns who escaped the worst of its furies. Until 1618 however the situation at a court like that of Cassel, where Heinrich Schütz had his education and early musical training and from where he was sent to Venice in 1609 to study under Giovanni Gabrieli, was rare among German courts. Shortly before this the town council of Nuremberg had sent the brothers Hans Leo and Jacob Hassler to Venice as pupils of Andrea and Giovanni Gabrieli. The wealth of the important cities made it possible for them to support and encourage music in this way although civic authorities were always prepared to employ musicians at rates of pay long out of date and expect them to augment their earnings by *Accidenten*: as the rates for the funeral and wedding music which were the most frequent sources of pay were unchanged from pre-Reformation times, the lot of the town musician was never financially easy.

The radical reformers, however, distrusted music because it reminded them of the rites of the Catholic church and because it seemed to them to be primarily a sensual indulgence which had nothing to do with religion; good music elaborately composed and well sung distracted the worshipper's attention from the real business of prayer and worship. Everything which was not scriptural was banished from their services, so that hymns and motets were outlawed and for a time Zwingli, in Switzerland, forbade the use of any music whatever in churches. Taking the text from the Epistle to the Colossians, chapter three, verse six, which had traditionally been held to justify church music—'Let the word of Christ dwell in your hearts with wisdom; teaching and admonishing one another in psalms and hymns and spiritual songs, singing with grace in your hearts to the Lord'—as a condemnation of actual music, Zwingli not only outlawed the art but tried to guard against its re-emergence by smashing organs; that of Zürich Cathedral was hacked to pieces while the organist stood by in tears. According to Zwingli's *Commentary on the Bible*, the Pauline injunction stands against actual music because it speaks of singing 'in your hearts' and makes no mention of voices.

Calvin, however, reprieved music. He approved of the singing of the Psalms in metrical translation, unaccompanied and in unison, and for a time this remained the only music in Puritan services; even the chanted dialogue of versicle and response between clergyman and congregation vanished, and only in Holland did any instrumental music continue. Holland had a tradition of organ-building and playing which not even the religious revolution could destroy. The metrical psalter gave rise to many fine, sturdy tunes, like those of the Huguenot psalter, but there was no way in which these could gather a musical influence comparable to that of the Lutheran Chorale.

Despite the demonstration of force by Zwingli in Zürich, the majority of the fine organs which vanished were not destroyed but dismantled and sold or left to decay. Calvin did not object to the playing of appropriate music before and after the services though he did not wish to encourage it. When in 1544 the Calvinists of Rive, near Geneva, decided that the church organ there was a bulky inconvenience too big and too splendid to be erected in any smaller building, they suggested that it be rebuilt in St. Peter's Church in the city. Calvin, however, decided that the erection of an organ in any church under his control would give rise to scandal and forbade the move. The council therefore decided to sell the instrument by auction, replaced a missing stop and mended the bellows to bring it into prime condition; as no buyer could be found, the instrument, in spite of Calvin, was stored in St. Peter's until, in 1562, the council ordered its pipes to be melted down and allowed whatever was of use from its materials and mechanism to be taken away by the authorities of the local hospital.

The English Reformation in its early stages gave rise to no definite anti-musical policy in the church services. Both Henry VIII and Archbishop Cranmer regarded some simplification of the more elaborate, uncongregational type of music to be necessary, and began to introduce English texts into the services—the Litany in English was the only notable liturgical change brought about in Henry VIII's days—but even in England, in the reign of Edward VI, some

organs disappeared from parish churches and that of Worcester Cathedral had
its pipes taken to make plate for the prebendaries while its case was converted
into a bed. The dissolution of the monasteries threw out of employment a large
number of musicians only a minority of whom were able to find new employment
in the cathedrals of Henry VIII's new foundation.

Nevertheless, the conservatism of the Anglican Liturgy as it was formulated
by Cranmer in 1549 and revised under Elizabeth I ten years later demanded
settings of the canticles at Matins and Evensong, and of the traditionally choral
parts of the Communion service, which were identical with those of the Mass.
This was a musical richness reserved for the cathedrals, for the medieval colleges of canons attached to many parish churches had been dissolved and the
parish churches, however well-to-do their parishioners or lavish their endowments, had been left without any musical organisation; the schools originally
attached to such functions were not wiped out but secularised—many of the
grammar schools which seem from their titles to be foundations of Henry VIII
and his son Edward VI were, like that at Stratford on Avon, medieval schools
converted into the new model under the instructions of, or at least in the reigns
of, the two kings.

The Henrician cathedrals of the 'new foundation', however, were created
entirely upon the medieval pattern, with chapters of canons presided over by a
dean, with music under the control of a precentor and a choir school for the boy
singers attached. The choirmen were now lay vicars or lay clerks, not the clerical
substitutes of canons who had parochial or other duties outside the cathedral.

The first purely Anglican service book was that of Marbeck, *The Booke of
Common Praier noted*, published in 1550 when the new liturgy was only a
year old. Marbeck was organist of St. George's Chapel, Windsor, apparently
appointed by Henry VIII—he was known to have been in office in 1531—and
remaining in office until his death, apparently in 1585. His period of service was
interrupted in 1544 by his trial for heresy and imprisonment. His other compositions, a Mass, two motets and a carol, all seem to have preceded the Reformation and his own conversion to Protestantism.

The Booke of Common Praier noted is a strictly austere setting, in semi-
plainchant style, with one note to a syllable and suitable for congregational
singing; the notation Marbeck adopted, with notes of four lengths ambiguously
explained in his preface, presents problems which have never been solved but it
accords not only with his own Protestantism but also with the ideas of Archbishop Cranmer, who had pleaded for such a simplification of church music
during the reign of Henry VIII when the Latin Liturgy and traditions prevailed,
and also with those of a great number of Catholic reformers on the continent.

The Anglican 'Service', comprising the Canticles and Versicles and responses
of Matins and Evensong together with the congregational portions of the Mass or
Holy Communion, were the specifically Anglican contributions to church music,
and Marbeck's first setting, which should be seen as a conservative rather than a
revolutionary treatment of the problems of music in the liturgy, was followed

in the reign of Elizabeth by settings from composers such as Tallis (who had remained a church composer throughout the Reformation period, writing his earliest works for the Latin rite and his later for the English Prayer Book) and Byrd. In the Bodleian Library, the Wanley Manuscript contains settings of the Matins and Evensong canticles together with ten settings of the Anglican Communion, dating from the first half of the reign of Elizabeth I and showing how, from its inception, the Church of England had been open (to say the least) to an entirely traditional musical treatment of its English words. By the latter part of the reign of Elizabeth I, Byrd and others were contributing settings of great elaboration and beauty, and adding them to the motet-type 'anthems', apparently a corruption of the word 'antiphon', for which time was provided in both Matins and Evensong. It is typical of the English Reformation that Byrd, an unconverted though unobtrusive Roman Catholic, wrote services and anthems for the Church of England and held an honoured place in the Chapel Royal while still composing Masses and the Latin service music of his *Gradualia* with no practical hope of its ever being put to use. By the time of Elizabeth the 'anthem' often took an instrumental accompaniment to itself, and employed viols as well as or instead of accompaniment by the organ.

Parish churches, however, achieved an almost Calvinist austerity more by accident than by intention. With the organ in most places silent or destroyed and no established choir, the psalms and canticles were read to the congregation by the parish clerk, and the musical portion of the service was simply the singing of the metrical translations of the psalms (which in the cathedrals were sung in the Prayer Book translation to the new style of 'Anglican Chant'—that is, in its early days, a plainchant melody in the tenor surrounded by harmonies from the soprano, alto and bass) in the verse translations of Sternhold and Hopkins. Thus another collection of melodies like those of the Lutherans and the Calvinists, with a similar strength and dignity, came into existence; the tune we know as the 'Old Hundredth', still sung to the verse translation of the hundredth psalm, is typical of them. Soon after the Restoration Thomas Mace wrote lamenting the decay of psalm singing in the Churches and pointing out that for £30 any church could buy an organ and thus improve its singing beyond measure.

But because the Anglican Liturgy remained conservative in its use of music and did not admit the old psalm tunes as part of the essential liturgy itself, the psalm tunes had little musical influence. Their modern style did not weave itself into the essentially liturgical music of the rite.

It would be possible to argue that in spite of Luther's devotion to the polyphonic motet and the innate conservatism of the Church of England the tendency of the Reformers was towards a complication of the music used in the services. Even the Lutheran chorales, though their relationship to the congregation was not at first clear, brought a good deal of the liturgy into the language of the worshippers in square-cut, popular, striding tunes and brought about what many historians of music like to call, perhaps optimistically as well as barbarously, a 'democratisation' of music; but the German *Hauptgottesdienst* demanded, even more than the Anglican service, a vast amount of elaborate music meant for highly trained singers and treating the congregation simply as an audience. It took less than a hundred years for the Lutheran churches to involve themselves in works like those of Schütz with their fantastic interplay of soloists, two or three separated choral bodies, and instruments. Church music was made 'democratic' only in Calvinist churches, for even the Anglican simplicities of Marbeck were overwhelmed by the number of elaborate choral settings produced by composers from Tallis to Tomkins, who continued to work until the Civil War in 1642, producing works for the Church of England which if not 'conservative' in treatment or substance were conservative in their attitude to the place of music in worship. The music of the English parish church was usually too exiguous to be described as 'democratic' or, indeed, as anything else.

This however was not a purely Protestant simplification; the same determination to prevent the Liturgy from being regarded as an occasion for passive listening by the bulk of worshippers motivated the authorities of the Counter-Reformation. The Council of Trent, called to reform whatever in the Catholic church needed reformation and to modernise such of its practices as needed modernisation, was first convened in 1545. Its meetings continued spasmodically until 1563. The regulation of church music was not a task it regarded as being of the greatest urgency, but there was widespread feeling that during the previous century the 'secularisation' of church music had continued almost unopposed, that the elaborate vocal and instrumental compositions allowed to be heard in churches had permitted performance to take the place of worship and that a return to simplicity was necessary.

Bishop Cirillo Franco of Loretto, for example, in the third book of his *Lettere volgare di diverso nobilissima Huomini* published in Venice in 1567, used one of his letters (dated February 16, 1549) to Ugolino Guateruzzi, to complain about 'the impropriety of modern choral music in the Mass and ecclesiastical chant'. The Bishop's immediate target was the 'Hercules' Mass, by Josquin des Prés, composed for the Duke of Ferrara. In conservative Spain, where music was beginning the 'Golden Age' which stretched from Morales to Victoria and produced some of the most richly sombre choral music we have, an anonymous writer early in the seventeenth century produced a pamphlet called 'Ynconvenientes y gravissimos danos se siguende las Religiones tengan Musica de canto de Organo'.

> Although the use of plainchant is a laudable custom, [he explained] polyphony should never in any circumstances be allowed in religious houses. *First*, the singing of polyphony requires special talents which do not necessarily accompany a religious vocation. Where part music is sung, novices are all too often enrolled solely for the sake of good voices. Furthermore, they often rise to positions of authority. . . . The better the singer, the more unlikely he is to be a satisfactory preacher, teacher or exhorter. *Secondly*, the sort of polyphony sung nowadays contravenes the objects for which music was first introduced into the church services, to convert rather than to entertain. St. Augustine and St. Bernard

believed that it was sinful to listen to church music for its beauty rather than for its call to penitence ... singers who care for the beauty of sound never pay much attention to the sense of a text and hardly ever care whether its words can be understood or not. ... What should we say of the cornetts, sackbuts and other wind instruments that some religious houses permit? Their use ought to be extirpated. Monks who allow the glossing, embellishing and disfiguration that these and similar instruments frequently add, should blush for shame. To add to the abuses which polyphony engenders, the majority of the monks sit as mute as statues while a select few gargle their runs.[1]

A certain Dr. Navarro who lived from 1491 to 1586 told the story of an old monk who, moved by the liturgy and its music, began to sing during the complex polyphony of the service for one of the greater feasts: the choir was struck into horrified silence by the ugliness of his voice, but the silence was broken by the sound of words from heaven, '*Solus raucus auditur*'.[2] The anonymous author of the *Ynconvenientes* pointed out that, while the secular clergy should be allowed polyphony if they considered it essential, 'the strictest orders, like the Carthusians, the Recollects and the Discalced Friars should know no such things as polyphony. Several Franciscan Generals have proposed its abolition. At the recent Friars Minor meeting in Segovia, its use was utterly condemned. The Dominicans gave it up long ago.'

The demand for simplicity among the Spanish clergy led in 1565 to the promulgation in Toledo of an *Actio di Reformatio* which declared that 'whatever is sung in churches must resound to the glory of God and be understood by the people. Words must not be obscured. Polyphonic singing may be retained but the text must be clearly intelligible. Above all, theatrical music, and any music which arouses venereal or warlike passions ... must be rigorously excluded.'

The demand for musical simplicity did, of course, affect Protestants and Catholics alike. Puritanism was, in fact, an inter-denominational reaction against the worldly laxity and permissiveness of the pre-Reformation age. In 1555 Pope Paul IV ordered Daniel de Volterra to paint clothes on the naked figures of Michelangelo's frescos in the Sistine Chapel. He dismissed all married singers from the Papal choir, insisting that it become an entirely celibate body, and thus compelled Palestrina to resign. Naturally church musicians began to fear for their livelihood when the Council of Trent came to consider liturgical reform, especially as in 1555 an attack on the secular styles used in church music was repeated by Pope Marcellus II in vigorous admonishment of his own choir. He referred to Masses based on secular *cantus firmi*, the technical complications which made it impossible for the congregation to understand the words of the rite, the use of noisy instruments, bad pronunciation, carelessness and irreverence.

A venerable legend attributes the salvation of church polyphony to Palestrina, who it is said composed the *Missa Papae Marcelli* to prove that a six-part

[1] Quoted in Robert Stephenson: *Spanish Cathedral Music in the Golden Age.*
[2] *Ibid.*

polyphonic Mass could meet all the requirements, musical, devotional and
liturgical, of the reformers and still be intelligible to the congregation. Pope
Marcellus, however, died in 1555, and no mention is made in the Papal choir
books of the Mass bearing his name until 1560; it was printed at its composer's
expense in 1567. There is however evidence that Palestrina was impressed by and
sympathetic to Paul IV's regulations, and he later claimed that it was listening
to his music which persuaded Pope Paul not to outlaw polyphonic music.

On the other hand, the regulations of the Council of Trent which deal with
music date from September 1562; they speak in generalities, and are more concerned with laying down principles than enforcing practicalities.

> All things should be so ordered, [the Council decided] that Masses,
> whether they be celebrated with or without music, may reach tranquilly
> into the hearts and ears of those who hear them, when everything is
> executed clearly and at the right speed, in the case of those Masses which
> are celebrated with singing and with organ, let nothing profane be inter-
> mingled, but only hymns and divine praises. The whole plan of singing
> in musical modes should be constituted not to give empty pleasure to the
> ear but in such a way that the words may be clearly understood by all,
> and thus the hearts of listeners may be drawn to the desire of heavenly
> harmonies, in the contemplation of the joy of the blessed. . . . They
> should also banish from the church all music that contains, whether in
> the singing or the organ playing, things that are lascivious and impure.

The onus of reform is thus firmly laid not on regulations and a system of law
but on the taste and devotion of individual authorities, and in addition to this the
canon only insists that church music must be 'purged of all seductive and impure
melodies, all vain and worldly texts, all outcries and uproars'.

As the Council met day by day it heard the special prayers composed to open
its sessions sung to a setting which Jacobus van Kerle had dedicated to the
cardinals of the commission specially appointed to examine church music.
Kerle, who was born in Ypres in about 1531, was *maestro di cappella* at Orvieto
Cathedral in 1555. When the setting of the *Preces Speciales* was commissioned he
visited Trent to direct their performance and was taken into the service of the
Bishop of Augsburg, having contrived a polyphonic setting which, like the music
of Palestrina's Mass, was intended to show that polyphony did not necessarily
clash with the devotional and liturgical ideals of the counter-Reformation.
When the prayers were published in 1562 Kerle tactfully made no mention of
their function as propaganda for the style of music he wrote.

> These ten forms of prayer, [he explained in the Preface] under the title of
> 'Responses', by Pietro Solo, a member of the Dominican Order and a man
> of apostolic life and doctrine, and accomodated to the figures and modes
> of music by me at the command of my best and most distinguished
> Prince, the Cardinal Archbishop of Augsburg, my patron, I have thought
> best to send to you, most wise and illustrious fathers who preside over
> the public councils of the Christian church. . . . I have hoped that these
> prayers, not unrelated either to the praises of God or the time of the
> Church, would not be displeasing to you. You will not, I think, reject

the idea of joining musical numbers to these prayers, a plan by which that most holy man David, a man after God's heart, employed. If you less approve my skill in the matter, you will surely not disapprove of my purpose, for I what I can I contribute to the glory of God and in the sight of all. For if God judges the services and works of men not by the weight of the matter but by their minds, then the nearer to God you approach than other men, the more you are wishing to imitate His benignity.

Kerle's *Preces Speciales* might well have done without this special pleading as a model of liturgical propriety for the authorities of the Council. Its part-writing is entirely transparent and frequently homophonic, so that the words are carried along with complete clarity; it is, too, a gentle and devout work showing what a composer can do for the church services without transgressing the bounds of liturgical decorum. Possibly it was Kerle more than Palestrina who saved polyphonic church music (and thus left the door open for less decorous styles) at the time of danger.

Nevertheless in March 1563 the Liturgical Commission decided to advocate monophonic music in spite of Kerle's demonstration of correct liturgical polyphony and the example of Palestrina. In doing so it ran into opposition from the Emperor, Ferdinand I. Since the Sack of Rome by Imperial troops in 1527, Imperial opposition was not something the Papal authorities could face without anxiety. In addition, the aims of the Council of Trent were to purge the Catholic church of abuses, to redefine Catholic doctrine and to restore as much as possible of the ground lost to the Protestants. In this programme music was only a minor matter, on the periphery of their great design and not, in the opinion of the members, sufficiently important to be worth the creation of another controversy.

When Palestrina returned to St. Peter's as choirmaster in 1570 he was employed by Pope Gregory XIII to join Annibale Zoilo, the *maestro di cappella* at St. John Lateran, in the task of revising the traditional chant to match the revision of the text which had already been carried out. Both verbally and musically, the revision was intended for the use of the entire church, to replace local variants with an authoritatively approved correct version which, incidentally, Philip II of Spain, the Catholic monarch most devoted to the ideals of the counter-Reformation, refused to accept.

'Antiphoners, Graduals and Psalters that have been provided with music for the celebration of the Divine Praises and Offices in plainchant (as it was called) since the publication of the Breviary and Missal ordered by the Council of Trent have been filled to overflowing with barbarisms, obscurities, contrarieties and superfluities. . . .' ran the Pope's charge to Palestrina and Zoilo. 'Therefore we charge you with the business of purging, correcting and reforming these Antiphoners, Graduals and Psalters.' The two were empowered to co-opt other musicians to assist in what would have been an almost impossible task even to specialist musicians with unlimited time and freedom to travel. Neither Palestrina nor Zoilo was a medievalist—medievalists did not exist in the sixteenth century—but their work on the revision occupied them until they were allowed to abandon it in the 1580s.

The more important matter of a polyphonic style based on the practice of Palestrina and Kerle came to mean little outside Spain and the City of Rome itself. While the more intensely expressive sonorities of Byrd, who was working so to speak in an Anglican vacuum, could hardly be affected by decisions taken in Rome, composers even as near to the centre as those in Venice were developing the antiphonal style which soon developed into the polychoral style, to the vocal *concertato* of the baroque period, worlds away in spirit from the requirements of the Council of Trent. Willaert who was *maestro di cappella* at St. Mark's Venice, was in office during most of the period of the attack on elaborate church music— he died in 1562—but he continued to work with two choirs, each supported by its own organ, and to exploit the fascinating sonorities created by the domes, arches and transepts of the Cathedral. The rise of the Jesuit Order in the 1580s provided powerful impetus to the new, colourful and dramatic style of music which was to spread across Europe and dominate not only Catholic music but the music of the Lutheran Church. The Jesuits, for all their organisation as an entirely Papal Order, were primarily missionaries who saw in the excitements of the new style a powerful magnet to draw men back to the old Faith.

The musical centre of gravity had moved from the one-time Burgundy to Italy, so that although in France and parts of the Netherlands Catholicism maintained its hold, church music there was on a relatively unambitious scale and the Tridentine decrees barely affected the work of composers. The Catholic States of the Empire—Austria, Bavaria and so on—continued to use the elaborate condemned style and to cling even to such condemned forms as the parody Mass with a secular *cantus firmus*, although this had been the only type of church music specifically condemned by the Council. Within a few years composition of this kind was to fall under the spell of the glorious sensationalism of the Baroque style and to flower into new glories of its own.

10   Music in a Middle-Class Society

'In the past, music was chiefly maintained by cathedral churches, abbeys, colleges, parish churches, chantries, guilds, fraternities etc. but when the abbeys and colleges without the universities, with guilds and fraternities etc. were suppressed, then went music to decay. To speak of music in houses, you shall understand that divers noblemen and women, in time past, imitating the Prince, would have organists and singing men to serve God after the manner of that time in their private chapels. But that imitation is also left. Then for such as served for private recreation in houses, which were for the nobility and worshipful, were no less esteemed than the others, till time that the rascal and scum of the profession, who be, or ought to be, called minstrels (although nowadays many do call them musicians) these, I say, did and do make it common to every Jack, going about to every place and country for the same purpose.'

Thus Thomas Whythorne, in his *Autobiography*,[1] began his sketch of musical life in England of the 1570s, a few years before the spectacular flowering of the art in the later years of Elizabeth I. 'Now,' he continues, 'I will speak of the use of music in this time present.' What he reported reads gloomily: in the cathedrals, when the players and singers of his day became too old to work, there would be no properly trained musicians left to succeed them. In their place would be half-trained men who claimed to be musicians although they were incapable of composing and had learnt only enough to sing or play their parts, or 'speculators', as Whythorne called them, who claimed to be able to compose by text-book rules but who had never learnt to sing or to play an instrument. There were others who had learnt enough to sing and play efficiently but who made no use of their skills. Others could play or sing by ear and claimed to be musicians; some of these had actually become singing men, minstrels or even schoolmasters.

Whythorne's *Autobiography* was published in 1571, and its lamentations for the decay of music, the lack of science and scholarship which teachers passed on to their unfortunate pupils, was re-echoed by many of the great men of the generation which followed its author. Morley's *Plaine and Easie Introduction to Practicall Musick*, published in 1597, deplores the happy-go-lucky methods of musical education which had grown up and seeks to teach the science of music without tears; to train his middle-class ignoramus to sing, the master teaches him the whole theory of music as Morley understood it, and explains the laws of harmony and composition. The 'Golden Age of English Music' was, to those

[1] Thomas Whythorne: *Autobiography*, edited by James A. Osborn. O.U.P. 1961.

129

who lived during its course, an age of poor teaching and casual, undisciplined composition.

Whythorne, who was born in 1528, was settled in his career when he wrote his *Autobiography*. The book does not suggest that he was consciously helping to create the age of the English madrigal, and readers who could not set him into the context of musical development in the later part of the reign of Elizabeth I would leave his book saddened by the picture he paints of a decaying art. He was educated at New College School, to which he was sent by his uncle, a priest, who died before he had finished his studies at New College. Whythorne was an organist, could play the lute, the citterne and the bass lute; he was determined to become a musician. His curtailed education, however, led him to work in a number of posts as teacher-servant, teaching not only music but all that was considered necessary to a cultured Elizabethan; for a short time he was tutor to the son of William Bromfield, a London merchant who became Lieutenant General to the Ordnance and was sent abroad on the expedition to Le Havre; Whythorne was left in charge not only of the son but of Bromfield's business. Most of his posts were in houses where someone—a widowed mistress, a marriageable daughter or even an unmarried housekeeper—threatened matrimony, and the *Autobiography* (a book in which principles of phonetic spelling are carried to desperately logical extremes) describes his many escapes from wedlock.

Determined to win his right to specialise in music, he published his book of *Songes, for Three, Fower and Fiue Voyces* in 1571 and as a result was engaged by the Archbishop of Canterbury, Matthew Parker, as 'Master of Music in his Chapel'. Parker, like Queen Elizabeth I, was a supporter of traditional church music, and Whythorne, for his part, accepted the post because the archbishop, 'by his place was the most honourable man in the realm after the Queen'. Parker encouraged Whythorne to write church music, and the result was a set of psalm settings in four parts of Parker's own metrical translation of the Psalter, none of which has survived. At this point the *Autobiography* ends. Whythorne subsequently married. In 1590 he published his *Duos, or Songs for Two Voices*, with the typical Elizabethan note that the first group of twenty-two songs was intended for 'young beginners' or for 'a man and a childe to sing, or otherwise for voices or instruments of musicke that be of the lyke compasse or distance in sound. The second [group] are made for two children to sing. Also they be aptly made for two treble cornetts to play or sound; or otherwise for two voices or Musicall Instruments that be of lyke compasse or distance in sound. And the third part which doth begin at the XXXVIII. song (being all canons of two parts in one) be of divers compasses or distances, and are therefore to be used with voices or instruments accordingly.'

Whythorne's career until his death in about 1595 or 1596 allows us to draw some conclusions about the situation of the composer in the first three-quarters of the reign of Elizabeth. For the greater part of his life Whythorne was not able to live simply as a musician. The houses in which he was employed, though some of them were of considerable social eminence, did not want a full-time, specialist music teacher, and Whythorne of necessity undertook to teach the whole curriculum considered necessary to a Tudor gentleman. Before the dissolution of the monasteries and the religious changes in the reign of Edward VI, there would have been ample opportunity for a composer whose favourite instrument was the organ to find employment in church, but Whythorne was employed to teach the children of the well off more often than those of the aristocracy, and to see that they could pass muster as socially acceptable amateurs. He complained of the difficulty of the skilled musician in finding work, but not of any lack of musical enthusiasm or a debasement of taste; what seemed to him to be dangerous was the lack, among professionals no less than the amateurs, of musical learning. The 'Golden Age of English Music' was an age which depended upon domestic, amateur music-making. It was, perhaps, the last age in which it was possible for a great English composer to work in a popular idiom for a large public which included just about every urban music lover and everyone who had gained any musical training.

This was not a world which old-fashioned 'learned' musicians could entirely accept; Whythorne's care in pointing out that the third section of his *Duos* was a set of canons indicates that he was looking back to the past while attempting to suit the taste of the present. 'Learned' music had its roots in the church, and Whythorne grew up during the temporary decay of English church music which was halted, so far as the Chapel Royal and the cathedrals were concerned, by Elizabeth I and the composers she fostered.

The English Reformation went perhaps half the distance which the radical reformers would have wished it to go, and though historians show that advanced opinions were held by a minority, that minority was vigorous, well organised and articulate. The views it advanced about church music were shared, as we have seen, by many Catholics and were really the traditional view of elaborate and over-assertive music in the services; when Erasmus, living in England during the reign of Henry VIII, expressed his opinion—he was anything but impartial, for he remembered his unhappy childhood as a choirboy—he was simply repeating what strict Christian opinion had been saying for more than a thousand years:

'Modern church music,' he declared, 'is so constructed that the congregation cannot hear one distinct word. The choristers themselves do not understand what they are singing, yet according to priests and monks it constitutes the whole of religion. . . . There was no music in St. Paul's time: Words were then pronounced. Words nowadays seem to mean nothing. . . . Money must be raised to buy organs and train boys to squeal and to learn not another thing that is good for them. . . . If they want music, let them sing Psalms like rational beings, and not too many of them.'[1] The words of John Bale, an ex-monk turned Anglican bishop, in a sermon called *The Image of the Church* are not violently dissimilar: 'No longer shall the sweet organs, containing the melodious noise of all manner

---

[1] Erasmus: Commentary on *1 Corinthians XIV*.

of instruments and birds, be played upon, nor the great bells rung after than, not yet the fresh descant, pricksong, counterpoint and fa-bourden be called for in thee, which are the very synagogue of Satan.'[1]

Nevertheless official policy supported tradition except for the brief period of Edward VI's reign. In 1550 the playing of organs in church was forbidden and an official injunction was made 'that the two organists of St. George's Chapel, Windsor, should continue to receive their salaries for life, if they continue in that Colledge, in as large and ample a manner as if organ playing had still continued in church'. After the restoration of Catholicism for the five years of the reign of Mary Tudor, the Elizabethan settlement did not forbid the church organ though it remained silent in those parish churches where the clergy disapproved of its use and had sufficient authority over their congregations to see that their wishes were obeyed. In 1563, five years after Elizabeth's accession, the lower House of Convocation debated a resolution to order the removal of organs from churches but according to Bishop Burnett's *History of the Reformation* the resolution was defeated by one vote.

The destruction of organs was, of course, anything but complete. In 1634, three army officers toured England and wrote an account of their travels. They heard, not merely the organ played in a voluntary—something permissible even in Puritan practice—but the service sung with organ accompaniment in the cathedrals of York, Durham, Carlisle, Hereford, Exeter, Gloucester, Bristol and Wells. One parish church in York, and eighteen in Bristol (a Puritan city) retained their organs. But the congregational singing of the metrical psalter, ordered in the reign of Edward VI, became extremely popular; it spread even to the cathedrals, with psalm-singing services, as distinct from the services of the Prayer Book, attracting great congregations to St. Paul's Cathedral.

The attitude of the authorities to the use of the organ and the style of music permitted in church becomes important to the general history of music because, especially in the bigger towns where the real strength of Puritanism lay, it affected musical education. The bulk of musicians had always received their training in cathedral schools or in song schools because music was primarily an adjunct to worship. The growing neglect of church music, because it influenced the way in which boys were taught and trained, not only affected musical education but explains Whythorne's dispirited account of the situation in the 1570s; proper musical training, not merely to sing or to play an instrument but also to understand the 'science' of music and to be able to create the music one played, had died out; in place of all-rounders there were mere scholars, musicologists, with neither creative nor practical ability, and executants ignorant of the intellectual discipline of music, with whatever creative faculty they possessed left dormant and untended. Whythorne's argument is that a real musician is executant, musicologist and creative composer all in one person trained, that is to say, as musicians had been trained before the Reformation.

Thus when Elizabeth I became queen church music could not be isolated

[1] Quoted in John Stevens: *Music and Poetry in the Early Tudor Court.*

from music in general because the training it gave was necessary to all completely trained musicians. Whythorne's placing of the blame for a decline on the changes in religious practice is supported by a pamphlet published early in the seventeenth century, *The Praise of Musick, ye profite and delight it bringeth to man and the other creatures of God, the necessary use of it in ye service and Christian Church of God.* This, though it appeared during what is rightly regarded as a golden age of English music, not only bemoans the decline of religious music but reflects on the limitation of training that had followed as a consequence:

> And it is to be remembered, [the author writes] that at about the same tyme [that is, 'about the nynthe yeare of Queen Elizabeth', 1567] not so fewe as an 100 paires organs were pulled down (and many of them sold or imploide to make pewter dishes). And commands were given [by the clergy themselves, not by the Queen or archbishops] for short playinge, or none at all, for shorteninge or alteringe their songes and service to give place for preachinge, and castinge service as it were quite out of doores. So as fewe or none of ye people would vouchsafe to come into the Quyres during the singynge service but would stand without, dancynge and sportynge themselves untill the sermons and lectures did begin, scornynge and derydynge both ye service and those which were imployed therein, so as hereby the practize and use of skillful musick and those which exercised the same began to be odious, and the professors to be accounted but rogues, drunkards and idle persons, which was the cause that all indevor for teachynge of musick and the formynge of voyces by good teachers was neglected as well in men as in children, which neglect, (and little better reputation) continueth to this day. . . . A poore singyng man's maintenance in a Churche of a new erection doth not answer the wayes and entertainment that any of them giveth to his housekeeper.[1]

The writer goes on to lament that, of all the boys kept by a college or even the Chapel Royal, only about a quarter can sing a note. Music is in as great demand, he admits, in 'nobleman's and gentleman's private service', but he complains that rich men 'entice both players and singers, men and boys, from the old choirs' and even from those of St. Paul's and Westminster Abbey

About a quarter of a century before, John Case, echoing Whythorne in *The Praise of Musick* in 1586, seeks to revive 'that studie which laie as dead for a time', and Morley, in *A Plaine and Easie Introduction*, in 1597, laments that music, by 'the negligence of its professors is almost fallen into the nature of a mechanicall arte, rather than reckoned among the other sciences'. Each of these authors repeats, in his own words, Whythorne's analysis of the situation which they all take to be the dire consequence of the decline of cathedral music and, therefore, of the musical education which had been necessary in choir and song schools. The golden age was an age of popular and not really of professional music.

Nevertheless it was in the later years of Elizabeth I's reign that the English church, the *via media* in religion, found its own character, practice and devotion.

[1] Quoted in Morrison Comegys Boyd: *Elizabethan Music and Music Criticism.*

Richard Hooker's *Of the Laws of Ecclesiastical Polity*, in 1594, is the first plain statement of the attitude of mind which in a few years was to produce the sermons and *Divine Poems* of John Donne, the poetry of George Herbert, the devotional writings of Lancelot Andrews and the music of, among many others, Orlando Gibbons and Thomas Tomkins. 'Musical harmony,' declared Hooker, 'is a thing which delighteth all ages and becometh all states; a thing as seasonable in grief as in joy; as decent being added unto actions of great weight and solemnitie as being used when men most sequester themselves from action. The reason hereof is an admirable facilitie which musique hath to express and to represent to the mind more inwardly than any other sensible meane the very standing, rising and falling, the very steps and inflections every way, the turns and varieties of all passions whereunto the minde is subject.' Nothing could be more 'pestilential than bad music', but music which inspires the mind with virtues and ideals is good, and has its place in worship. This was, if only temporarily, the beginning of a recovery in church music.

At the same time no Englishman with a thousandth part of Luther's force and authority suggested that education must necessarily make room for music as both an intellectual discipline and a source of pleasure. The choir schools and song schools languished wherever and whenever the musical elements of worship were neglected, but it is hard to believe the anonymous pamphleteer's strictures on the Chapel Royal of Elizabeth, who like her father was a musician herself and who had, moreover, a very conservative attitude to religious change. The complaint of an extremist bishop against the crucifix and candles on the altar of her chapel brought about their removal for as long as it took for his memory of her weakness to fade, and then they were replaced. The records of her musical establishment collected by Lafontaine in *The King's Musick* deal with instrumentalists and not with the Chapel Royal choir in any detail, but in 1560 after only two years as queen she issued commissions allowing all boys except those of St. Paul's Cathedral and her Household Chapel to be impressed into cathedral choirs, and in 1580 a further commission allowed the impressment of boys from St. Paul's. The dazzling list of names in which the men of her Chapel Royal figure suggests that it maintained a high standard, though Sir John Hawkins, writing a couple of hundred years later, pointed out that 'the servants of her Chapel experienced the effects of that parsimony which, it must be confessed, was part of her character'.[1] But he also noted 'an affection which she manifested for the solemn choral service'. Byrd's explanation of the financial plight into which the monopoly of music printing and paper had plunged him and his partner Tallis, also explained that his regular attendance at the Chapel Royal, of which he had been made a Gentleman in 1570, prevented him from 'reaping such commodity by teaching as formerly he did'. Elizabeth, although in 1559 she issued injunctions to the clergy tending to limit music and ceremonial—the forty-ninth of them insisted that the music of cathedral and collegiate churches should not be allowed to obliterate the words—also insisted that the services in

---

[1] Hawkins: *op. cit.*

her Chapel should normally be accompanied by the organ and on feast days by cornetts, sackbutts and other instruments. Membership of her Chapel Royal was not a sinecure though it was obviously awarded to all first-rate musicians as both a necessary honour and a way of subsidising his future work, and this suggests that the boys of the choir could hardly have been inefficiently or carelessly trained. The complaint included in *The Praise of Musick* dates from the early years of the reign of James I, whose prediliction for Puritan doctrine combined with authoritative episcopal church government—a paradoxical attitude perhaps more worthy of a pragmatical Englishman than a hard-headed Scot—may have led to a decline of the Chapel Royal at a time when other choirs were struggling to survive. When Elizabeth I was buried in 1603 mourning livery was provided for twelve boys of the Chapel Royal; the same number took part in the funeral of Prince Henry, in 1612, and in the funeral of Queen Anne, in 1619; in all three ceremonies they were led by the same master, Nathaniel Giles, and twelve boys of the Chapel still took part in James I's funeral in 1625. The pamphleteer's case against the Chapel Royal seems unproven, but there is evidence enough to support him against the cathedrals.

The neglect of cathedral music—no composer of importance worked in the provinces throughout the Tudor period until Thomas Tomkins was appointed organist of Worcester Cathedral in 1598; Weelkes described himself as organist of Winchester College in 1600 and was, we know, appointed organist at Chichester Cathedral round about 1602—was, it seems, one of the consequences of the Tudor monarchs' creation of a Chapel Royal beyond comparison with any other musical establishment in the country; good musicians were always needed in London. The list of Chapel Royal composers from Henry VIII's break with Rome in the 1530s until the death of James I in 1625 is startling in the number of great names it contains, among them Tallis, Byrd, Morley, Bull and Orlando Gibbons; possibly Weelkes, too, was a Gentleman of the Chapel Royal for some time before his appointment to Chichester Cathedral. Other patronage was less important. Campion was a doctor of physic who wrote songs, Farnaby was a free-lance composer and, possibly, a maker of instruments; Rosseter, trained as a boy at Elizabeth's court, was a free-lance; Dowland, a convert to Catholicism, failed because of his religion to secure a place among the queen's musicians and spent much of his life in the service of foreign courts. The brothers Antony and William Holborne, although the title page of their *Cittern School* published in 1598 describes them as 'servants to her Majesty', seem to have been amateurs. Only Wilbye, inferior to none in invention and as a stylist, though his work ranges for less distance than those of most of his great contemporaries, was the only great Elizabethan who passed his life in a gentleman's household, as resident musician in the house of Sir Thomas Kytson of Hengrave Hall. He took up service there when he was twenty-one, in 1595, and remained there until 1628. Wilbye seems to have done reasonably well, for he lived in retirement for another ten years apparently on the proceeds of property which he had bought with his professional earnings.

The position of the English musicians had been complicated by the dissolution of the monasteries between 1536 and 1539, and then by the closing of the
chantry schools in the reign of Edward VI. Exactly how many trained musicians
were left without work is something that cannot exactly be ascertained. Trevelyan's *English Social History* estimates that about 8,600 religious were pushed
out into the world; Bindoff, in *Tudor England*, puts the number at 'nearly
10,000'. Those who actually were professed monks, friars or nuns received the
pension which the government allotted to them; many of those who were in
Holy Orders but prepared to serve the new order were given benefices. Nothing
else in the story of Henry VIII's dealing with the church is less discreditable to
the government. Unfortunately, not all those who lost their means of livelihood
at the dissolution of the monasteries were professed clergymen; the monasteries
employed servants, workmen, labourers of all sorts and professional musicians,
but it would be difficult to discover how many, where and under what conditions; it is equally difficult to discover what became of them.

The case of Osbert Parsley is the best known. Parsley, some of whose compositions have survived, was a lay-clerk at Norwich Cathedral who died in 1585,
at the age of 74. All that is known of his life story is told on his monument in
the north aisle of the cathedral; his epitaph ends with the lines:

> Who here a singing-man did spend his days
> Full fifty years in our church melody.
> His Memory shines bright whom thus we praise.

Before the dissolution, Norwich Cathedral was a priory church, and if Parsley
were a singing man there 'full fifty years', his service began three years before
the dissolution. He was never, so far as we can tell, a novice intending to take
religious vows but a layman singing in a monastic choir before the priory became
a cathedral and he himself was turned into a cathedral lay-clerk. This is clear
because his will leaves his estate, of something like £1000 in modern money,
almost entirely to his wife after bequests were paid to his son and his nephews.
In Norwich, apart from laymen like Parsley, twenty-two of the monks remained
to serve the new order which converted their church into a cathedral; six of these
were prebendaries and sixteen vicars choral who may or may not have been in
Holy Orders. Nevertheless, in spite of figures like these, there is every indication
that in later Tudor times, too many musicians were chasing too little work.

More than anything else it was the neglect of musical education which led to
the situation which distressed Whythorne in the 1570s. There were more than
forty choir schools in which the musically gifted child could receive a free education by virtue of his ability as a singer, several of them providing places for no
more than half a dozen boys—Bangor, Carlisle, Dublin, Gloucester, the collegiate churches in Manchester and Newark, Norwich, Southwell and Wells
were among them. But the best boys were likely to be carried off to sing in the
Chapel Royal and the basis of the education these boys received was musical,
though the choir schools of most cathedrals did not reach such a degree of

musical specialisation that the rest of their educational curriculum suffered. Weelkes's choirboys at Chichester had their musical training between eight and nine o'clock in the morning and between two and three o'clock in the afternoon, while they were juniors, and an hour later if they were seniors, but a number of them were able to go on to university at Cambridge, so that they had not devoted to music the time needed for other studies.

Music as an intellectual discipline generally regarded as valuable ceased to be a part of education. The doctorates awarded at Oxford and Cambridge were granted on the basis of an exercise—an original composition in motet style—and not for what Whythorne would have called 'scientific' knowledge of the subject; thus the actual amount of knowledge and preparation the degree required had sunk to a minimum, and the grammar schools, made increasingly aware of the need for practical education, began to restrict the study of music to the type of singing lessons which the middle-aged and elderly in the second half of the twentieth century remember with some distress. In Scotland this worried educationalists so much that in the 1570s they began to set up new song schools and, in consequence, a hundred years later Thomas Mace began to offer the Scottish song schools as a model of what was missing in English education. By the end of the Elizabethan period, the place of music in the English school curriculum depended, more than on anything else, on the taste and ability of the individual schoolmaster.

Naturally, the queen being a skilled instrumentalist, Queen Elizabeth's wards were given a thorough musical education. Their schoolmaster was to be able to play the lute, the bandora and the cittern; the pupils were to have two hours' musical instruction each day and time for individual practice. Queen Elizabeth's establishment paid its music master £26 per year, while the music master at Christ's Hospital, still in those days a charity school, was paid only £2 13s. 4d. until 1609, when the master, John Farrant, had his salary raised to £4. A private patron raised this meagre sum to £20 on condition that a group of ten or twelve picked boys should be given training in 'prickesong', and three or four of these be taught to play an instrument. The same patron, Robert Dow, provided virginals, viols and music books which cost him £10 6s. 4d. But in 1589, the governors of the school made an order which declared that 'Henceforth none of the children in the Hospital shall be apprenticed to any musyssioner other than such as be blinde, lame and not able to be put to other service.' The governors of a school in the special position of Christ's Hospital, of course, would try to keep children for whom they were responsible out of jobs which offered too limited prospects.

A talented boy trained in a cathedral school or song school should have been trained to play the organ or 'various kinds of musical instruments' as an injunction made in Norwich in 1608 commanded. The Bishop of Norwich in 1570, Bishop Parkhurst, had decreed 'That the choristers should be poor men's children and such as have most need, and not inheritors and rich men's sons.' The purpose of a choir school, in Bishop Parkhurst's view, was not primarily that of seeing that the worship of the church was sung with as much beauty as possible; it was to provide the children of the poor, who might otherwise have some difficulty in gaining the training needed for any profession, with a skill which might be put to professional use when their education was over. Ten years later, however, Norwich Cathedral statutes fixed the number of the boys in the choir school at eight and there is no evidence that before 1608 any of them was given any instrumental training.

Chapel Royal boys were not automatically committed to a musical career. Even a man as eminent as Cornyshe, who was Master of the Boys in Henry VIII's Chapel, was occupied in general administration as well as his musical duties; he was apparently chief organiser of pageants and entertainments, so that a payment to him for 'Lead . . . and other necessaries at Greenwich', in 1516, shows him to have been responsible for the preparation of the Whitsuntide celebrations —jousts and a play. Cornyshe's successor, William Crane, was a water-bailiff, a wool exporter and a wine importer. Intelligent boys who were not primarily musical but who had good trainable voices found that membership of the Chapel Royal was a relatively easy pathway to university or to official employment at court; a couple of hundred years later any boy in the Chapel Royal choir or the choir of any cathedral would have found it difficult to escape from the training he had received into any profession not ancilliary to music except, maybe, the church. The bulk of professional musicians came from the choir schools in which they had been given a thorough musical training.

The extent to which, outside the choir schools, musical education depended on the attitude of the individual schoolmaster can be judged from the writings of educational theorists. Roger Ascham, whose practical concern was the teaching of aristocratic youths to fit their station in life, regarded music as a reasonable course of study provided that not too much time was spent upon it, an opinion which he supported with Galen's dictum that 'Much music marreth man's manners.' William Kempe, the author of *The Education of Children in Learning*, published in 1588, drew up a suggested curriculum for schools without mentioning music at all, while Richard Mulcaster, who wrote his book of educational theory (*Positions wherein those Primitive Circumstances can be examined, which are necessary for the Training up of Children, either for Skill in their Books or Health in their Bodie*) in 1581 after ten years' experience of headmastership at Merchant Taylors' and another ten at St. Paul's, wanted singing taught as a basic necessity, with reading and writing, before real academic studies began. Mulcaster encouraged the teaching of instruments and was creator of the boys' company of actors which earned a sour reference from Shakespeare in *Hamlet*. Christ's Hospital opened its door to poor boys from the London streets, admitting three hundred and eighty of them at its foundation in 1552 and putting them under the care of a specialist music master who taught both singing and instrumental music until they left to become apprenticed. Pupils of Bedford School and Merchant Taylors' who left their Memoirs for our enlightenment refer to the care and the amount of time given in their schools to instruction in music.

This was of course the fag end of medieval educational policy, learning for its own sake and not for the practicalities of earning a living through useful skills. A combination of the power of advancing Puritanism (a phenomenon of the towns and therefore deeply influential on educational policy) with the growing needs of a commercial economy began to demand education without frills. Thus Blackburn Grammar School, an Elizabethan foundation, received an order from its governors in 1590 declaring that 'no English interlude or plays be henceforth used or played in the said school', an injunction which affected music only indirectly and did not prohibit the performance of Latin plays which might be regarded as educationally more advantageous. In 1600 it received new statutes which specified that 'writing, ciphering, singing and such-like' should be outside the normal curriculum of classics, arithmetic, geometry and cosmography.

What an Elizabethan grammar school taught might include not only French and Italian but also music—as an intellectual discipline and not merely as a get-together or sing-song—but whether it did so or not depended upon local conditions, the attitude of the governors and the ability of its headmaster. In most places the governors were members of the local business community obsessed with the necessity of practical, useful, Gradgrindian education. It is almost impossible to discover in detail what precise syllabus most schools followed; when the Guild School at Stratford on Avon, a medieval foundation, became King Edward VI's grammar school, no new statutes or regulations were drawn up for it, and the inference seems to be that for some time its medieval educational policy continued.

If the claims of gentility, which demanded music as a necessary accomplishment, clashed with those of 'practical education' the claims of gentility eventually lost the struggle. A privately educated boy like Thomas Cromwell's son Gregory was taught the use of arms and the playing of instruments as well as the classics, French and arithmetic; but the statutes of Edward Alleyn's 'College of God's Gift', which developed in the nineteenth century into Dulwich College and Alleyn's School, suggests the virtual disappearance of music from the general course of school life simply through its apparent impracticabilty.

Alleyn, having made his fortune on the Elizabethan stage and used his money to buy the manor of Dulwich and a fair amount of land adjacent to it, left its income to endow almshouses and a school for six poor old men, six poor old women and twelve poor boys, who could be joined by fee-paying boys from the neighbourhood of Dulwich. The Statutes of his Foundation show that his models were Westminster School and Winchester College, both old-fashioned medieval foundations. A chapel building was one of the first requirements of his 'college', and it was furnished with 'a paire of orgaines' a year before the statutes became effective in 1619. The entire college—bedesmen, bedeswomen and the poor boys, were to be under the care of four fellows, who were to be warden, schoolmaster, preacher and usher. In addition, there were to be six junior fellows, two of whom were to be organists while the other four were to be competent singers, capable of reading their parts and helping to teach music to

the boys, though they should, at the same time, be qualified tradesmen teaching
unacademic skills to those who were not capable of gaining admission to a university. Every boy was to be present at singing lessons each morning and afternoon, and Matins and Evensong were to be sung daily as they were 'in the
King's Chappell or in the Collegiate Church of St. Peter at Westminster'. In
addition the boys were to be taught instrumental music.

A mere fifteen years later, when Archbishop Laud as Visitor of the Foundation
carried out an official visitation, he found it necessary to draw the attention of
the fellows to these statutes and to remind them that they were expected to be
present in chapel, each wearing his surplice, at every service. The warden's reply
that as a mere layman he felt himself to be unworthy to sit in the choir and to
be surpliced suggests that the statutes were not so much forgotten as puritanically disregarded. The six junior fellows were never appointed, so that all the
music teaching of the foundation fell upon the organist, who rapidly made his
way into the list of fellows. Some of the Dulwich organists—Cosyn, Francis
Forcer and, in the eighteenth century John Reading—were people of importance
in London music, a fact which suggests that they had a good deal of leisure from
their scholastic occupations. According to the account books of the Foundation,
the only music books which seem to have been bought are four-part settings of
the Psalms in the metrical version of Sternhold and Hopkins (before the Commonwealth period, these seem to have been regularly replaced as they suffered
wear and tear), but there are references to sums paid for tuning and repairing
the organ and to expenditure on harpsichords and viols. Alleyn's musical
ambitions never came to full fruition, but there seems to have been regular
instrumental training for at least some of the scholars.

In 1653 a Manchester business man, Humphrey Chetham, whose family
home was the medieval Augustinian Priory originally attached to the collegiate
church which eventually became Manchester Cathedral, founded the 'blue coat
school' now known as Chetham's Hospital to give free education for the children
of 'honest, industrious and painful parents', who were to be taught until 'they
could be put into apprenticeship or some other preferment'. There is, in other
words, an open possibility of their proceeding to university, but nothing in
Chetham's stated intentions mentions the teaching or practice of music.

It might be valid from these facts to argue forward to the century's eclipse of
native English music after the Handelian period; at any rate, English musical
education contrasts sharply with the attention paid to music in German schools
and the Italian discovery that the best way to prepare an orphan to earn his or
her living was to train him as a musician. Mercantile England had already discovered the benefits of utilitarian education for the middle classes and the poor;
the upper classes did not take long to decide that it was socially demeaning to
learn to play musical instruments because the playing of instruments was a
profitable trade or profession. In Italy, with a less developed business life in
most cities, it was natural to train musicians because both inside and outside the
court life of the aristocracy music was a common pleasure and to play in the

orchestra of one of the new opera houses or to take service with a church or a nobleman did not lay the expense of apprenticeship indentures on the benevolence of those who had been responsible for a child's upkeep and training. Thus, in the eighteenth century, Italy was able to supply Europe with skilled musicians. Mulcaster, at St. Paul's in the later part of the reign of Queen Elizabeth, was standing against the age when he advocated that girls as well as boys should be taught in schools and took it for granted that music is a valuable study because it is 'verie comfortable to the wearyed mind, the princesse of delites and the delite of princes'. His suggested curriculum, in *The First Part of the Elementarye which Entreateth Chefely of the right writing of our English Tung*, demands 'five principles, *reading, writing, drawing, singing and playing*, besides exercise'. These 'be the onelie artificial means to make a minde capable of all the best qualities'. But by the time that Thomas Mace published *Musick's Monument* in 1676, he advised parents:

> Wheresoever you send your *children to school*, (I mean to the Grammar School) *indent* so with the *Master*, that your *Children* shall be *taught one hour* every day to *sing*, or one *half day* in every *week at least*, either by *himself*, or by some *Musick Master* whom he should procure And on doubt but (if you will pay for it) the *business* may be effected.
>
> For there are divers who are able to *teach to sing*, and many more would quickly be, if such a general course were followed *throughout the Nation*.
>
> There would scarcely be a *Schoolmaster* but would, or might be easily able himself to do the *business*, once in a quarter or half a year; and in a very short time every *Senior Boy* in the School will be able to do it sufficiently well.

If, within seventy years of the death of Queen Elizabeth, music had so withered away as a school subject that Mace's readers had to take special steps if they wanted their sons taught, throughout the Elizabethan heyday and after it into the reign of James I music remained a very valuable social accomplishment. Nicholas Wotton, ordered to report to Henry VIII on the suitability of Anne of Cleves as a potential wife for the king, drew attention to what he obviously regarded as one of her drawbacks: 'Frenche, Latyn or any other Languige, she hath none, nor yet she canne not synge nor pleye any instrument, for they take it heere in Germany for a rebuke and an occasion of lightnesse that great ladies should be lernyd or have any knowledge of Musike.' But Anne of Cleves came from a Calvinist German state, and the English upper class demanded the proper social accomplishments of those who were expected to be its leaders, just as the middle classes, as soon as they found themselves with money and leisure enough, adopted the pleasures of their social superiors. The middle-class grammar schools neglected these things because their controllers and, it seems, as often as not their masters, had suddenly discovered the virtues of vocational education and jettisoned music rather than the Latin which, in *The Merry Wives of Windsor*, enables Sir Hugh Evans to make life a misery for little William Page.

For all the aristocratic love of music, private patronage did not on the whole play any decisive part in the development of English music. Wilbye apart, musicians employed in wealthy houses in England left behind no important body of compositions. But the decline of music in the church meant its elevation elsewhere, as though the availability of musicians who had lost their church employment rapidly came to feed a growing appetite for social music. The employment of musicians in England was, as it was elsewhere, a demonstration of social position—an English musician in private service was still a liveried retainer—but what was written for such musicians to play, whether it was specially created for them or imported from elsewhere, seems not to have been important in the development of the English composers' style. The music written for the aristocracy is preserved in the titles of, for example, keyboard works by William Byrd rather than in momentous collections of manuscripts from the Tudor period. What has been preserved in great profusion, apparently because of its greater popularity and consequent wider spread, is the vocal, consort and keyboard music meant for amateur players and singers. Despite the rarity of printed keyboard music, we still have *My Ladye Nevill's Book*, the *Fitzwilliam Book* and Benjamin Cosyn's collection of organ pieces to prove the popularity of keyboard music.

When Wilbye, the most refined stylist among the English madrigal composers, was resident musician to the Kytson family at Hengrave Hall, near Bury St. Edmunds (where Robert Johnson and Edward Johnson also worked), the inventory of instruments and music seems to represent the music-loving Elizabethan household on its largest scale:

Item, one borded chest, with lock and key, with vj viols	iiij *li*
Item, one borded chest, with six violinns	iij li
Item, one case of recorders, in number vij	xl s
Item, iiij cornutes, one being a mute cornute	x s
Item, one great base lewte, and a meane lewte, both without cases	xxx s
Item, one trebble lewte and a meane lewte, with cases	xl s
Item, one bandore, and a sitherne with a double case	xxx s
Item, two sackboots wth ther cases	xxx s
Item, two hoboys with a curtall and a lysarden	xx s
Item, two flewtes without cases	ii s vj d
Item, one payer of little virginalls	x s
Item, one wind instrument like a virginall	xx s
Item, two lewting books covered with leather	
Item, two books covered with pchement, cont^g vj setts in a book, with songs of iiij, v, vj, vij, and viii partes	ij s
Item v books covered with pchement cont^g iii setts in a booke of English songs of iiij, v and vj partes	iij s
Item, v bookes covered with pchement, with pavins, galliards, measures and cuntry daunces	v s
Item, V books of levaultoes and corrantos	vj d
Item, V old bookes covered with pchement with songs of v partes	vj d
Item, v books covered with blackelether	ii s

Item, iiij bookes covered with pchement with songes of iiij
    partes   vj d
Item, v books covered with pchement with pavines and
    galliards for the consort   iij s
Item, one greate booke wh came from Cadis covered
    wth redd lether, and gyllt   x s
Item, V books contg one sett of Italyan fa laes   xviij d
Item, one greate payer of dooble virginalls. In the parlor   xxx s
Item, one payer of greate orgaynes. In the church   vL i

This list indicates that the Kytsons kept some sort of domestic band, possibly formed by their own musical employees and the Bury St. Edmunds waits, possibly entirely consisting of their musicians and others in the pay of the family who combined music with other, possibly menial duties as footmen, kitchenmen, cooks and gardeners. What was written for the Kytson family, however, survives only in the works of Wilbye and the Johnsons. Consort music existed in print before 1621, but all that the Kytson inventory contains is dance music. There is no indication that they collected any particular quantity of new instrumental music, let alone of works written for the domestic musicians of the household to play. Wilbye's madrigals were not, apparently, designed for any specific body of professional or semi-professional group of singers but purely as amateur social music, and his own position was not defined, as it would have been on the continent, by any explanatory title. Financially he was a successful man to whom Sir Thomas Kytson leased the best farm on his estate and who owned land at Diss, Bury St. Edmunds and elsewhere in the neighbourhood.

The Petries, of Ingatestone Hall in Essex—a Catholic family which did not scruple to make a good thing out of the dissolution of the monasteries, eventually made peace with the Church of England and rose high in government service— were not only music lovers but friends and patrons of William Byrd, who stayed at Ingatestone in 1586 if not at other times. In his house John Petrie had an organ, virginals, a lute and a cittern as well as viols, the cost of which and of their occasional repair is noted in account books, as is the cost of bringing professional musicians to Ingatestone. When Byrd visited the house, Petrie sent for five musicians from London to provide music at Christmas. In 1559, and then again for his daughter's wedding a year later, he had hired the boys of St. Paul's Cathedral to sing, paying six shillings and eightpence for their services on each occasion. The account books mention payments to waits, welsh harpists and minstrels, but he kept only one professional musician in regular employment: this was 'John the Frenchman', who played upon the instruments and was, apparently, the family music teacher as well as a performer. His wages were ten shillings a year, equal to those of an upper servant. Obviously, music-making at Ingatestone Hall was a matter for family entertainment and only on great occasions for professional performance. Only three fragments from the Petrie music library survive—the bass volume of a collection of English songs, and the alto and the bass books of a collection of continental part-songs; there is no trace of any instrumental music.

During this period, Thomas Sackville, first Earl of Dorset, kept a band of at least ten musicians at Knole, in Kent, a far greater house than Hengrave or Ingatestone. The Knole account books for 1608 include a note of the payment of half a year's wages to nine musicians and a quarter's wages to a tenth at a total cost of £95. One of the Sackville players may have been among the lutenists at the funeral of Queen Elizabeth in 1603, and three later joined the King's Musick. The enthusiasm of the Earl for their work is made clear by his will, which left each of the musicians an annuity of £20, but there is no indication of what music was played or of the provenance of the works performed at any time.[1]

The great concentration of music and musicians at court prevented any widespread diffusion of first-rate talent. The Tudor monarchs followed what was obviously a deliberate policy of attracting all the first-rate composers into their service to the detriment of music elsewhere. From Lancastrian days onwards England had been developing a more strongly centralised government than any of the other European countries of the late middle ages and the Renaissance, and the weakness of the nobility after the barons' 'Wars of the Roses', followed by the deliberately anti-aristocratic policy of Henry VII and Henry VIII, strengthened the central control. It is natural in these circumstances that Henry VIII should be jealous of Cardinal Wolsey's musicians and should demand the transfer of Wolsey's star treble to the Chapel Royal; to be king meant to have the very best of everything that was available. It is equally natural that genuine talented musicians like the Tudor monarchs should be able to create an unrivalled musical organisation.

Monarchs create fashions, and the taste of the Tudor monarchs was sophisticated. It tended to develop from the instrumental forces of the Chapel Royal a body as well equipped for indoor chamber music as for ceremonial occasions and for the church. The Tudors reduced the number of brass players and drummers in their service but balanced the reduction by employing more keyboard, woodwind and string players, many of whom at first were from the continent. At the funeral of King Henry VII, in 1509, according to Lafontaine's list in *The King's Musick*, the musicians involved were two minstrels, three minstrels of the chamber, four sackbuts and shawms, nine trumpets, eleven players who were 'the King's trumpets', eleven 'children of the Chapel', six further trumpeters and eight further minstrels as well as the eighteen 'Gentlemen of the Chapel and singing men'.

At the funeral of Henry VIII, thirty-eight years later, there were twenty 'gentilmen', eighteen trumpeters, five unspecified 'musytians', four sackbuts, six 'vyolls', five 'fluttes', two 'vyalls', a 'fyfer', a drummer, a harper and a bagpiper. In addition, Henry VIII had kept at court four lutenists, a virginalist and three rebec players.

The greatest influx of foreign musicians came during the reign of Henry VIII; all the violists listed, one of the lutenists, two of the trumpeters, two flautists,

[1] Susi Jeans: Seventeenth Century Musicians in *The Sackville Papers. Monthly Musical Record*, Vol. 88, No. 929. September–October, 1958.

three of the 'musicians' and two of the organists were immigrants. The names of the violists—Albertt de Denyce, Zorgi de Cremona, Ambrose de Myllan, Frauncis de Vyzenza and Vicenzo de Venetia, 'who played with Marcke Antoni' —indicate their places of origin. The lutenist Philip van Wylder, a Fleming, was also active as a composer. In the reign of Henry VIII this invasion was, it seems, simply the result of the king's love of music, which made him offer employment to foreign musicians whose skill was in departments of the art which English players had not yet developed. Eleven new Italian players are named in a warrant for new liveries drawn up in 1555 in the reign of Mary I, whose precocious but short-lived brother Edward VI had added another harpist, six violists, two flautists and two virginalists, as well as 'five players of interludes' to the royal band while dismissing three sackbut players and his father's taborists.

The list of those who required liveries for the coronation of Elizabeth I in 1558 has six musicians all surnamed 'Bassany'; later accounts refer to four of them as brothers. It seems that two more members of the same family were active in England for a time. There are three violists; one is Philip van Wylder and the other two are English; six violins whose names had appeared among the violists in the list compiled at Henry VIII's funeral eleven years before. There were seventeen trumpeters and six sackbut players.

A 'List of all the offices in England, with their fees', drawn up in 1593 ten years before the death of Elizabeth I, mentions a 'Sergeant trumpeter' and sixteen other trumpet players, six sackbut players, eight violists, two flautists, three virginalists, four 'musicians straungers'—the same Bassanys—and eight 'players of interludes'. At Elizabeth's funeral, the lists note seven violinists, five of them Italian and two apparently English; the Bassanys have become five Bassanos, who, with an apparently French Lanier and an obviously English Baker appear as 'recorders'. The sixth Bassano, with another Lanier and two possibly French Guys, is a flautist. Two more Laniers are among the six players of hoboies and sackbuts; Antonio Ferrabosco is one of six lutenists. There are twenty-two trumpeters and four drums and fifes. There are twenty-four 'Gentlemen of the Chapple'—the names of Bull, Gyles and Byrd are among them— twelve 'children of the Chapple' and four 'gentlemen of the Chapple extraordinary'.

The influx of foreigners seems, so far as can be discovered, to have remained simply a means of satisfying musical demands. Gustave Reese suggests that some musicians came to England as religious refugees like the Flemish weavers who came to England during the days of Elizabeth I, but the bulk of immigrant musicians were Italians, apparently more concerned with earning a living than with escaping to religious freedom. Their presence naturally influenced the music which was heard at court.

To what extent court music set the fashion for the English Golden Age, and to what extent the monarchy itself was responding to tendencies present in the atmosphere of the time it would be impossible even to guess; nevertheless royal enthusiasm for music not merely as an adjunct to ceremony helped the movement in England towards domestic music, the madrigal, the consort and the keyboard piece.

'With the defeat of the Armada in 1588,' writes Ernest Walker, 'the danger of religious upheaval passed away from England; and musicians turned with a curious suddenness, and with almost complete unanimity, to follow secular ideals.'[1] Perhaps neither the suddenness nor the unanimity were surprising as there was less demand for music in the church and, probably, an uncertain number of musicians still looking about for profitable work. Nevertheless the tendency in the home as well as in the court was towards, first, amateur singing of madrigals, ballets and part songs, then to consort playing and then to the keyboard. The real pleasure, although professional musicians were available for hire, seems to have been amateur music-making. Henry VIII and his children were all skilled keyboard players and *The Compleat Gentleman*, published in 1622, quotes Erasmus as the authority for saying that Henry VIII 'could not only sing his part sure, but of himself compose a Service of foure, five and six parts'. William Camden's *Annales rerum Anglicarum et Hibernicarum regnante Elizabethae*, translated in 1615 by 'R. N. Gent.', declared of Queen Elizabeth that 'neither did she neglect Musicke, so farre forth as might beseeme a Princesse, being able to sing and play the Lute prettily and sweetly'. Sir James Melville, sent by Mary Queen of Scots on a diplomatic mission to the English court, wrote a detailed account of the way in which Elizabeth was determined to convince him that she was a better virginalist than her Scottish cousin.

If the evidence indicates that music in houses like Ingatestone and Hengrave Halls was an amateur activity undertaken as a pleasant hobby by the family and its servants, Morley shows that by 1597 music as a hobby was socially important in London middle-class society. The teacher and the two pupils whose questions, answers and explanations make up his *A Plaine and Easie Introduction to Practicall Musick* are not aristocrats: they would in their case have been brought up, as gentlemen necessarily were, with a private tutor who would insist upon some knowledge of music as a social accomplishment; they want to know about music because it is a social necessity in the circles in which they move. It is only because ignorance of music is socially disgraceful that Philomathes, the new pupil, has decided to take lessons: 'Supper being ended,' he explains, 'and musicke-books, according to the custome, being brought to the table, the mistress of the house presented me with a parte, earnestly requesting me to sing. But when, after manie excuses, I protested unfainedly that I could not, everie one began to wonder. Yea, some whispered to others, demanding how I was brought up. So that upon shame of my ignorance, I go now to seeke mine olde friends Master Gnorimus, to make myself his scholler.'

The middle-class cultivation of music was probably restricted to London. Places like Bristol, Norwich and King's Lynn, large for their period and vitally important to the country's economy, were, according to Trevelyan's *English*

[1] Ernest Walker: *A History of Music in England.*

Social History, towns of only about 20,000 inhabitants, while London had 200,000 at the peak of its Elizabethan greatness and continued to increase rapidly. A. L. Rowse in *The England of Elizabeth* estimated that Norwich had 17,000 people when the population of London was approaching 300,000. The drift to the south-east had begun its still-continuing progress, culturally and economically depriving provincial life. The capital drew into its clutches all the bright young men of the provinces who hurried to London to make their fortunes because London was simply richer than the rest of the country. 'The annual value of its customs,' wrote Rowse[1] in demonstration, 'was over twenty times that of Bristol, which came next.' Whether, therefore, the private music-making which meant so much to Londoners was also a provincial amusement among the middle classes seems to be doubtful. The waits of the more populous and wealthy towns extended their activities and their numbers, adding strings to their traditional instruments, making extra money from private engagements with families like the Petries and the Kytsons; but there is little evidence from the provincial cities of the sort of enthusiastic amateur music-making which is perhaps exaggeratedly held to have delighted Londoners.

The traditional view of Elizabethan music seems, from the number of works available for domestic performance, to apply only to the later years of Elizabeth's reign and the first half of James I's. But the development of amateur domestic music both vocal and instrumental, together with the number of theoretical and teaching books which emerged towards the end of the sixteenth century, shows that the Golden Age had been evolving from the beginning of Tudor times. Whythorne's first *Booke of Songs* in 1571 was the first published collection for over forty years. Yonge's *Musica Transalpina*, in 1588, addressed its collection of European, mainly Italian, madrigals and part-songs to 'gentlemen and merchants of good accompt', because they 'Have taken in good part such entertainment of pleasure'. In the quarter-century that followed, thirty-five books of madrigals by individual English composers were published, apart from imported collections and anthologies. The lute songs followed: Dowland's *First Book of Airs* was published in 1597, and by 1622, when Attey's *Book of Ayres* appeared and ended a wonderful achievement, nineteen composers had produced thirty-one song books. Dowland's Third Book sold over a thousand copies, but this may not represent the average sales of such works for Dowland was a virtuoso lutenist whose accompaniments are so full and rich in texture that many of those who could play the lute part in a Campion song might well have decided that Dowland's work was far beyond them.

Instrumental music had a slower start. Instructions books for would-be lutenists began to appear in 1565; Anthony Holborne's *Citthorne School* in 1597 included thirty-two compositions for solo lute as well as ensemble pieces for cittern and viols, and from then onwards lute music, in tablature or in notation, and transcriptions of vocal works in tablature became common. The lute works of Dowland, whose *Lacrime* became the most popular work of the age (if the

[1] A. L. Rowse: *The England of Elizabeth*. Macmillan, 1950.

number of times it was treated by other composers and the number of references to it in contemporary poetry are a fair guide) were extremely popular in spite of their difficulty. But Dowland was an international celebrity, praised as a performer as well as a composer from Copenhagen to Venice.

The number of transcriptions from church music and from secular vocal music into lute tablature shows that something new was coming into being: the lute was reaching great popularity as an amateur musician's instrument although it had an extremely limited repertory. And just as the lutenist had to take a good deal of his repertory from vocal works, it was not until Morley's *First Booke of Consort Lessons* in 1599 that other instruments in reasonably common use began to gain a repertory of their own. As early as *Romeo and Juliet*, that is 1595 at the latest, Shakespeare refers to the popular repertory, but the clown Peter expects them to play a piece of dance music, 'a dump', which would exist in a multitude of arrangements—the players probably made their own anyhow—to make it available to all who had instruments to play it. Those in reasonably common use, viols, recorders and so on, might be pressed into service for any music. They might replace missing voices in a madrigal, or even turn a madrigal into a solo song with instrumental accompaniment if more players than singers found themselves with time on their hands. Music was written adaptably, so that whoever wanted it could use it irrespective of whether it was set out for the instrument he played. Anthony Holborne published *Pavans, Galliards, Almains and other short Aers* in the same year as Morley's *Consort Lessons*, and described them as being 'for viols, violins, or other musical wind instruments' (a puzzling piece of English usage) while Morley announced that his anthology, 'Made by divers exquisite Authors', was for 'sixe Instruments to play together: viz. the treble lute, the Pandora, the Citterne, the base-viol, the flute and the treble-viol'. This suggests that these were the instruments which could be found most frequently in the hands of the amateurs who could be expected to buy Morley's book, and it also indicates that the composer seems to have anticipated and planned for specific chamber music colours and sonorities. Rosseter's *Lessons for Consort* which appeared in 1609 was equally definite in instrumentation.

But just as composers were prepared to accept instruments into a vocal consort and would write music 'fit for voyce or for vyols', most composers recognised the virtues of adaptability. Tobias Hume's two books of instrumental music are remarkably explicit in explaining the variety of ways in which the music can be played. *The First Part of Airs*, of 1605, often known from its page-headings as *Musical Humour*, completes its remarkably thorough title with the words 'for two Leero Viols [a Lyra Viol is larger than a tenor] or also for the Leero viole, with two treble viols, or two with one treble. Lastly, for the Leero viole to play alone, and some Songes to be sung to the Viole, with the Lute, or better with the Viole alone.' The later *Poeticale Musicke* of 1607 has the gargantuan explanation, 'so contrived that it may be plaied 8. several waies upon sundry instruments with muche facilitie. 1. The first way or musicke is for one Base-viole to play alone in parts, which standeth alwaies on the right side of this Booke. 2. The seconde musicke is for two Basse-viols to play together. 3. The third musicke, for three Basse-Viols to play together. 4. The fourth Musicke, for two Tenor-Viols and a Basse-Viol. 5. The Fifth Musicke, for two Lutes and a Basse-Viole. 6. The sixth Musicke, for two Orpherions and a Basse-Viole. 7. The seventh Musicke, to use the voyce to some of these musicks, but specially to the three Basse Viols, or the two Orpherions with one Basse-Viole to play the ground. The eighth and laste Musicke, is consorting all these instruments together with the Virginals, or rather with a winde instrument and the voyce.'

The deliberate adaptability not only of air and madrigal to a variety of instrumental treatments, but also of the first purely instrumental music, indicates the beginning of a new repertoire and the need to supply a variety of players with whatever music was within the ranges of their instruments. The composer had a market to exploit, and he exploited it to the best of his ability. There was no time for specialised instrumental writing and, obviously, no standard consort group on which the composer could settle his attention.

Keyboard music did not appear in print until *Parthenia* was published in 1611, but *My Ladye Nevell's Booke*, in which forty-two of Byrd's keyboard pieces were collected, was copied by a certain John Baldwin who finished his work on September 11, 1591. The manuscript collection in the much larger *Fitzwilliam Virginals Book* (two hundred and ninety-seven works), and Benjamin Cosyn's *Virginal Book* of ninety pieces, are manuscripts from the early 1620s. The difficulty of printing keyboard music may account in part for the slowness with which music as vivid as that of Byrd, Bull and Farnaby for keyboard instruments reached print; but keyboard instruments, which had to be imported from Italy, Flanders and Germany, were more expensive than recorders, viols, lutes and so on, which were more amply catered for in print. Cosyn's book, like the earlier *Mulliner Book* which seems to date from between 1540 and about 1575, is the work book in which a practising musician kept his repertory and shows how, at that early stage in his instrument's history, he had to fill up his repertoire with transcription of vocal pieces. The other books, it seems significant to note, were the property of wealthy amateurs and show how keyboard music was still restricted in its circulation while other instrumental forms spread quite rapidly.

By the 1590s, at least in London, there was more public music to be heard and it depended not simply upon the waits and minstrels. There were the theatres too. The mystery and miracle plays of the middle ages had shown an instinctive sense of the dramatic value of incidental music and song, and this sense was part of Elizabethan drama from its beginnings. The work accepted by literary historians as the first English tragedy, *Gorboduc* by Thomas Norton and Thomas Sackville, presented in the Inns of Court as part of the Christmas celebrations of 1561-2, makes ambitious musical demands, carefully explained in stage directions—perhaps because it had to codify what, for later authors, became standard practice. Each of the play's five acts is introduced by a dumb show to music. The first is accompanied by a 'musicke of Violenze', though whether the authors meant violins, instruments at that time very new to English music, or viols, is not clear; violins were rare, but a wealthy audience like that to which *Gorboduc* was first acted might well have been able to afford violinists. The second act is introduced by 'the musicke of cornetts', the third by flutes, the fourth by hautboys and the fifth by flutes and drums. These instruments have a symbolic value of which the authors must have believed their audience to be aware; the first dumb show is a mime in which national disunity is exemplified by 'wild men' who try to break but cannot break sticks tied together in a bundle. The cornetts provide appropriate music for a court scene, while the flutes prepare a scene of mourning and 'ill-advised misgovernment'. The oboes introduce a scene in which 'the Furies chastise kings and queens who had unnaturally slain their own children'. The drums and flutes, with the mime they accompany, symbolise 'tumults, rebellions, and arms and civil wars'.

The various boys' companies—from St. George's Chapel, Windsor, the Chapel Royal, St. Paul's, Westminster Abbey and the chapels at Blackfriars and Whitefriars, became extremely popular in the closing years of the sixteenth century. They were all connected with important choirs and naturally exploited the trained voices and musical abilities of their members. 'These boys,' wrote James Gershaw, one of the Duke of Stettin's entourage when the duke visited London in 1602 and saw a performance at the Blackfriars Theatre, 'have special preceptors in the various arts, and in particular excellent instructors in music. . . . For a whole hour preceding the play one listens to delightful entertainment on organs, lutes, pandoras, viols and flutes, as on the present occasion when a boy *cum voce tremula* sang so charmingly to the accompaniment of a base viol.'[1]

The public theatres could not usually provide music on this scale, but their companies were compelled to try to keep up with whatever was offered by the boys' companies because of its popular appeal. From the beginning of the English theatre the public was taught to expect a drama into which music was integrated. This meant not only that stage royalty had to be greeted with trumpets, that trumpets and drums should signal the progress of an offstage battle and that there should be actual music and dancing at the Capulets' ball in *Romeo and Juliet*, but also that there should be songs to point a dramatic situation and that music should be used atmospherically. People like Portia in *The Merchant of Venice* and Orsino in *Twelfth Night* should have domestic musicians available to appear in their livery on the stage to make appropriate music, and some badly played music outside Pontefract Castle should stir the captive Richard II into his fatal attack upon his gaoler. Music is used in this way by all Shakespeare's contemporaries, usually without any detailed stage directions, as though the conventions governing its employment are perfectly clear to everyone concerned. Only Marston, writing for the specially musical boys' companies, gave stage directions which help us to see how the integration was achieved in practical stage terms.

Marlow, for example, took it for granted that a Scythian conqueror like

[1] Charles William Wallace: *The Children of the Chapel in Blackfriars.*

Tamburlaine the Great should take the musicians of his domestic chapel on campaign with him so that they are available to comfort the death of Queen Zenocrate with music. By the time that Shakespeare retired from practical work in the theatre and wrote his final plays, he was using the theatre musicians to rival, as well as they could, fashionable court entertainment, writing into *The Tempest* Prospero's masque of the spirits to celebrate the betrothal of his daughter Miranda to Prince Ferdinand, putting the song and dance of the sheep shearing festival into *A Winter's Tale* and including in *Henry VIII* both the masquerade in which the king chooses Anne Boleyn as his dancing partner and the beatific vision to 'sad and solemn music' of the dying Katharine of Aragon.

The singers required by the company—all except Ophelia play characters somewhat on the periphery of the drama which involves them; in *As You Like It* there are the two page boys who sing 'It was a lover and his lass' and Amiens, whose songs create the atmosphere of the uncertain golden age in the forest of Arden, Feste in *Twelfth Night*, Balthazar in *Much Ado about Nothing*—were acting members of the company, for the Elizabethan actor was trained to the top of his bent in singing and dancing as he was in swordsmanship; several of them were respectable instrumentalists. Augustine Phillips, a member of the Shakespeare–Burbage company who died in 1605, left a bass viol, among other things, to his 'late apprentice' and a cittern, a bandore and a lute to the boy who was his apprentice at the time of his death, to be handed over when the youth's apprenticeship had ended. When Edward Alleyn began to buy land on the south-east fringe of London, a deed of sale (dated April 26, 1595) describes him as 'Edward Alleyn, musitian'.[1] A letter from Alleyn to his wife, written a few years before this, asks for his 'lewte bookes' to be sent after him while he was on tour, suggesting that he played and quite likely sang in some role or roles as an actor, but the deed of sale only seems to indicate that a musician, who might be a qualified member of a guild and therefore a freeman of his city, was socially more acceptable as a landowner than was an actor, whose profession had only recently, in most people's eyes, emerged from vagabondage.

Apart from lutenist actor-singers, the theatre companies needed trumpeters and drummers; they needed the musicians who, at the beginning of *Twelfth Night*, play the music which, according to Orsino, has the properties of an aphrodisiac and the piece which, in *The Merchant of Venice*, prompts Lorenzo's Platonic–Pythagorean discourse; they wanted the players of the mixed consort, 'Sneak's noise', which Falstaff engaged when he invited Doll Tearsheet to supper; the bergomask of the tradesmen—amateur actors of *A Midsummer Night's Dream* suggests another sort of musical accompaniment, perhaps by pipe and tabor; Hamlet sends for a consort of recorder players in the excitement following the scene of the play within the play.

All this suggests a rather small but very versatile group of musicians each

[1] George F. Warner: *Manuscripts and Muniments of Dulwich College*, series I (Muniments 106). London, 1881.
[2] *Ibid.* (Alleyn Papers 13).

capable, as the members of the waits would be, of doubling on a number of instruments, ready to supply a string consort, a recorder consort, a mixed consort of brass, woodwind and strings together with the instruments of the lute family —lute, pandora and cittern. This was the sort of ensemble presupposed by Morley's *Consort Lessons* of 1611, Leighton's *Tears and Lamentations* of 1614 and Rosseter's *Consort Lessons* of 1621, three anthologies which some authorities believe to have been issued to supply theatre musicians with appropriate pieces for all dramatic situations; the same pieces would, of course, have served the musicians of any nobleman's household or the waits of any very prosperous town, for the sort of theatre ensemble suggested by the requirements of the theatres seems to have been a rather conventional group.

The instruments on which they played were apparently the theatre's property. The *Diary* of Philip Henslowe—the father-in-law of Edward Alleyn, owner of the Rose Theatre and the theatre at Newington Butts and partner with his great son-in-law in the Fortune and Hope theatres—is a record of day-to-day theatrical expenses and receipts in the later years of Elizabeth I. On November 10, 1598, Henslowe 'lent unto John and Thomas Downton to bye a sackbute of Mark Antony XXXXs'; Mark Antony was one of the Italian members of the Queen's Musick. On December 22 of the same year, Henslowe lent forty shillings to Richard Jones 'to bye a bass vyall and other instruments for the company'. On February 7, 1599, Robert Shaa signed a receipt for twenty-two shillings which Henslowe had advanced him to buy two trumpets.[1]

Unfortunately, this says nothing about the actual players and their status. The multiple anomalies in the organisation of London music may have made it possible for the theatres to engage guildsmen of the London Company of musicians, though not, apparently, the entire body of them or the Waits of Southwark, in whose area most of the theatres operated. When the music provided by the company acting in Beaumont and Fletcher's *The Knight of the Burning Pestle* were found to be without hautboys to provide 'stately music', the Citizen who interrupts the 'Induction' and almost takes charge of the play suggests that they go to hire the Waits of Southwark and is ready to provide two shillings to pay their fee. This, and the fact that Henslowe had to provide the instruments, seems to indicate that the theatres employed independent musicians from outside the official organisations and counted them among the permanent staff; the theatres were, of course, fined from time to time because they infringed the official musicians' monopoly.

Who the players were and how they were trained is not known; apart from conjecture prompted by the publication of music suitable for a theatre consort, they are things which no Elizabethan authority bothered to explain. Contemporary writers are enthusiastic about the music they heard in the theatres which, if they had their own staff musicians, were in a position not only to offer good training to promising singers among the boy apprentices but also to give

[1] Philip Henslowe: *Diary*; edited by Foakes and Rickert. Cambridge University Press, 1961.

them instrumental teaching if they showed any of the necessary aptitude. Therefore the high opinions of foreign visitors to the theatres are easier to accept than
the severities of Hawkins, writing more than a century and a half after Shakespeare's death and, for once, delivering a personal opinion without any recourse
to contemporary authorities.

> The music was seldom better than that of a few wretched fiddles, haut-
> boys, or cornetts; and to soothe those affections which tragedy is cal-
> culated to excite, that of flutes was also made use of; but the music for
> these several classes of instruments, when associated, being in unison,
> was very different from what we understand by concert and symphony;
> and upon the whole mean and despicable. . . . If at any time a bass
> instrument was added, it was only for the purpose of playing a ground
> bass to those divisions on an old ballad or country dance tune which at
> that time were the only music that pleased the common people.[1]

Probably Hawkins was only guessing from the decadence of the street music
which he heard and described when writing about the performances of the
London theatre musicians and waits as he knew them. The public theatre was
a more or less classless institution at its beginning, and the foreign visitors who
were of some social eminence took a point of view entirely opposed to that of
Hawkins.

In the Elizabethan and Jacobean world of domestic music, the theatre depended upon professional performers whose function grew in scope until, as the
masque became the special aristocrat entertainment, the public theatres followed
the lead of 'society' as they are always bound to do and introduced masque-like
scenes like the masque of the spirits in *The Tempest*, demanding more and more
complex music. It is obvious that the companies must have increased the number
of musicians they employed, if not permanently at least for specific performances,
to keep pace with the demands placed upon them. It would be pleasant but
profitless to speculate about the influence of this professional theatre music
performed to an audience in an age unaccustomed to professional musical
standards, particularly in the light of the great expansion of public music-making
in London after the Commonwealth, a period well within the memory of very
many who had attended the theatre before its post-Shakespearean decline. Such
speculations would not be likely to lead us far, for the theatres were closed by
the Commonwealth to reopen again with the entertainments which ought to
have laid the foundations of a great national English opera but failed to do so.

This sort of professionalism did not crowd out domestic music-making,
which was highly thought-of by authorities which looked askance at the drama
as an essentially irreligious abuse of art. There is no factual ground on which
we can consider whether and in what way theatre music influenced any other
aspect of the art. There was always a sense in which it stood outside the mainstream of the country's musical development; Roger North, for instance,
writing about music as a relaxation from his legal career in the reign of James II,

[1] Hawkins: *op. cit.*

looked back not to the large mixed consort of the theatre but to the democratic social pleasure of domestic consort music. What the English middle-class society of the golden age really developed was the intimate social pleasure of chamber music, both for voices and for instruments.

11   The Beginnings of Opera

We can never really say why one more or less universal style is superseded by another. To look back to the beginnings of Baroque music in the late sixteenth century and say that as one style dies of exhaustion another takes its place would be a dangerously simplified way of looking at the situation. The established polyphonic style continued side by side with the new music, and Monteverdi, the greatest master of the early Baroque, wrote no less well in the old style which he called the *prima prattica*. The change came not from the exhaustion of polyphony but from a real change in European sensibility; its causes are among the imponderables of history which we can know only by their results.

Two principles found expression in Baroque music. One, the dramatic monody which grew into opera, was new and revolutionary: the other, the principle by which extended works were built by contrast, the concertato style which grew into the early concerto, was a development, owing more to Venetian composers than to anyone else, of Renaissance practice. The history of music from about 1600 to 1750 is the story of the interaction and development of these two principles.

A traditional simplification ascribes the creation of opera to the meetings of the *Camerata*—the group of artists who discussed their problems with Giovanni Bardi, Count of Vernio. Vincenzo Galilei, Caccini, Strozzi, Corsi, Peri and Rinuccini, with their patron, were an *accademia*, or artists' club, of remarkable intellectual and artistic distinction. The simplification is excusable because it starts the history of opera at a point from which all its later developments flow with precision and in logical order. Opera, however, developed from a variety of causes, some of which the *Camerata* would have repudiated with contempt. Whatever the age and authenticity of popular drama as it has been preserved by folklorists, its modern survivals as well as the earliest of the miracle plays show that the earliest European playwrights chose a form in which music was expected to add intensity to words which were at times sung and at others recited to a musical accompaniment.

We can trace what we might call 'art drama' back as far as manuscripts of the tenth century from the library at St. Gall. These contain the trope dramas which expanded into short dramas independent of the liturgy. From its beginnings, European drama seems to have accepted the idea of music as an intensification at least, and sometimes as a manifestation, of the drama.

In the sixteenth century, the *mascherata* which had been one of the attractions of the carnival time of the Italian cities developed into the ballet and were copied for court functions in France. Their medley of allegorical mythology and medieval legend was treated, by the French, in courtly poetry instead of the rough and ready folk verse of the carnival. From this grew French *ballet de cour*, which had a definitive influence on the entire future of the French theatre, at least until the rise of the nineteenth century grand opera. French poets, no less than the members of Count Bardi's *Camerata*, were fascinated by the possibility of forms in which music and poetry could be integrated, and began to meet in the *Académie de Poési et de Musique* in 1570 almost thirty years before the Florentine intellectuals began their discussions. They experimented with strongly accented, highly rhythmical poetry which they called *vers mesurés* and in which the rhythmic force of the words predetermined the stresses and rhythmic plan of the music to which they were set by composers such as Claude le Jeune and Jacques Maudut. The rhythm of *vers mesurés* is strong but very variable, and it became the style of passages for solo voice (*récits*) in the music of *ballet de cour* until, in the mid-seventeenth century, Lully transformed it into French recitative.

The aim of the *Académie*, was the recovery of a style which its members believed had been one of the glories of the classic age of Greek literature; it would discover a musical style which would no longer treat verse as mere raw material for a composer's exploitation but a style in which, reinforced by music, verse would be declaimed in such a way that while the music made its own appeal the verbal pattern of rhythm and inflection would be emphasised by their union with the musical values of fixed rhythm and pitch. This was a reflection in specifically French terms of the Renaissance passion for and determination to recover the glories of classical antiquity. Much in the Greek theatre, the Renaissance man of culture was convinced, had been musical. Aristophanes, in *The Frogs*, had derisively referred to the 'plunkety-plunk-plunk-plunk' of lute strings between the strophes of a tragic chorus, for example, and other texts existed to support the view of Greek drama as a type of primitive opera. The music, Renaissance scholars decided, must have been designed not to 'express' the words of a Greek play so much as to convey them with the maximum effectiveness through the control of pitch and rhythm. It was that idea which they fed into the medley of song, dance, chorus and mime which was *ballet de cour*.

Music in France was already under the control of royal statutes as vague as those of the Council of Trent; in other words, regulations existed which attempted to govern attitudes rather than to legislate for precise types of composition. Charles IX had promulgated a statute which declared, quite sensibly enough, that any country's music reflected its social situation. Ronsard, whose influence as a great poet gave weight to any dictum he made, had talked in Platonic terms about the influence of music over the listener's mind, and the king echoed him by declaring that when music was crude and disorganised, manners would be depraved, but that well-ordered music would create the possibility of sane and well-balanced lives; music, in other words, was a powerful social weapon, and we can trace the course of the art in France from this official recognition of its social importance and effect.

Nevertheless, the *Académie de Poésie et de Musique*, when in 1570 it applied for letters patent to register its foundation, was refused them because, according to the Paris *Parlement*, its teachings would corrupt the young. Its official existence started in 1571, when the writer Jean-Antoine de Baïf applied over the head of *Parlement* directly to the king for recognition. The corruption which *Parlement* envisaged was, of course, merely verbal and literary, as though the introduction of classical qualitative metres into French verse, instead of the accentual metres with which every literate Frenchman was familiar, seemed to the *Parlement de Paris* a piece of very doubtful morality. Nevertheless, the publishing firm of Le Roy et Ballard put into circulation a large number of the songs heard at the *Académie*; they are the natural foundation of *ballet de cour*, the Lullian opera which grew from it and, more remotely, the grand opera through which Meyerbeer turned the grand style of the eighteenth century into a splendidly sensational bourgeois entertainment.

In 1581 for the marriage of the Duke of Joyeuse and Mlle de Vaudemont, Baltasar de Beaujoyeulx, a valet-violinist who had left Italy to enter the employment of Catherine de Medici and had served under Mary Stuart, Charles V and Henry III, designed what he claimed, apparently with justification, to be the first dramatic ballet, *Circe*, or the *Ballet comique de la Reine*. The adjective '*comique*', its composer explained, indicated that it is not merely a medley of songs, choruses and dances but a continuous story told in music, dance, mime and all the other materials of the earlier court ballet. 'I have given life and speech to the ballet,' declared Beaujoyeulx, 'I have given song and music to comedy, and I have assisted these with many rich and unusual scenes and decorations, so that I am happy in the creation of a well-proportioned body, satisfying the eye, the ear and the understanding.'[1]

Ballet de cour consisted of a number of *entrées*, danced or mimed, introduced by verses sung as *récités* or spoken. Choral music, songs with lute accompaniment or instrumental ensembles accompanied the dance and mime. The singers and instrumentalists were kept out of sight unless something in the story demanded that they take part in the action. The form was entirely courtly; the dancers were courtiers and the finale, a *grand ballet*, became an opportunity for royalty, if it wished, to show its dignity, grace and technical skill in the dance. Gradually it became more stylised, banished speech and became entirely unified by music. Caccini, the Florentine singer-composer who was one of the most important members of Count Bardi's *Camerata*, went to Paris at the command of the French Queen, Maria de Medici, wife of Henry IV. Caccini's style of singing, which had developed the swift responsiveness to drama of what up-to-date Italian musicians were beginning to call the *stilo rappresentativo*, with its dependence on recitative and dramatic declamation, impressed the French court and in particular Pierre Guédron, who in 1601 had become court composer and was therefore responsible for the creation of a large number of ballets. As it was after Caccini's visit that spoken poetry disappeared from the *ballet de cour* to be

[1] Quoted in Henri Prunière: *Le Ballet de Cour en France*.

replaced by music in a free recitative style, the teachings of the Florentine pioneers had its influence on the extremely different style of dramatic music which arose in France although after 1620 the idea of continuous drama disappeared from the *ballet de cour*, which reverted to presenting a medley of diverting scenes with no particular regard for continuity. The sacrifice of poets to choreographers and composers eventually gave the ballet its own continuity and form; dance became an elaborate interpretation as well as decoration of the scores which motivated it.

It was natural that the English masque, for all the elaboration of its decor and music, should remain closer to spoken drama than the parallel developments in Italy and France. Its subjects were very limited; it could not equal the range of spoken drama from, say, *The Comedy of Errors* to *The Revenger's Tragedy* or from *Gammer Gurton's Needle* to *King Lear*. It began as an off-shoot of a highly developed drama, designed to allow more space than drama could afford for fashionable amusements like song and dance, and for elaboration of decor and setting. The drama continued to dominate because it was at once both extremely popular in its appeal and entirely sophisticated in its technique. The habit of thinking in terms of drama, with proper attention to balance, consistency of characterisation, contrast of scene and the sort of credibility which comes from the successful persuasion of an audience to suspend its disbelief, did more than anything else to stand in the way of the development of a real English opera until the twentieth century.

The result of the experiments in monody carried out by the *Camerata* was, at first, to break with popular traditions as completely as the *ballet de cour* broke with the popular traditions of France. Court drama, in Italy as elsewhere, allowed room for musical insertions called *intermezzi* (or originally *intermedii*); each *intermedio* presented a self-sufficient piece, or self-sufficient pieces, of music— ballets, madrigals, secular motets, solo songs or works for instrumental ensemble, each designed only as a cheerful contrast to the play. They linked the spoken drama to the music of carnivals and public festivities, to become elaborate demonstrations of courtly pomp and ceremony during the sixteenth century. In Florence in 1539 the marriage of Cosimo I de' Medici and Eleonora of Toledo called for an entertainment in which one of the *intermedii* consisted of four solo songs and four madrigals, some for four and some for eight voices, all with a varied orchestral accompaniment, by Francesco Corteccia. Before the end of the century, when Ferdinand de' Medici married Christina of Lorraine, the *intermedii*, which were designed by Bardi himself, had texts by (among others) Ottavio Rinuccini, who was to provide the libretti of the first operas. Marenzio and Cavalieri, madrigalist and opera-composer-to-be, were among the composers who provided madrigals, double choruses, triple choruses, instrumental *sinfonie* and a final madrigal which called for seven unequally voiced groups which made a total of thirty parts each requiring two singers. The work was scored for organs, lutes, viols, lyres, harps, trombones, cornetts and wood-wind instruments, the typical Italian court orchestra of the time which Monteverdi was to use with some additions and dazzling imagination in his *Orfeo*. The Bardi *intermedii*, unlike the vast majority of such things, was considered worthy of publication and reached print in Venice.

Whilst this process of musical elaboration was going on, the staging of *intermedii* became sensationally elaborate too, so that its visual appeal as well as its music turned the drama which it was supposed to lighten into a mere appendage. With the pastoral play, a form which became popular for court entertainment in sixteenth-century Italy and which interspersed its action with songs and choruses, the *intermedii* encouraged forms like the dramatic madrigal-cycle, the best-known example of which is Orazio Vecchi's *L'Amfiparnasso*, in which eleven dialogues and one monologue are all except one set as five-part madrigals; the exception is set for four voices. Dialogues are five-part compositions, the three lower voices singing to and answered by the three higher, so that the middle voice, a tenor, is both questioner and answerer, a member of both groups.

The madrigal cycles took their plots from *commedia del'arte* themes; there is no record of the actual staging of *L'Amfiparnasso*, but later cycles were acted in mime while the singers remained behind the scenes. They were the first works in which music was deliberately linked to comedy, and Vecchi's work, though it is the earliest of which we know, is genuinely comic in its treatment of dialogue, while its monologues are set in an enjoyable but normally serious madrigal style. Like all the early forms from which opera developed, it was in touch with popular musical traditions; its links with the *commedia del' arte* ensured that.

Although Count Bardi, as an aristocratic connoisseur and dilettante was involved in conventional court entertainment, when his *Camerata* began to meet round about the year 1590, he was looking for something far removed from any sort of musical drama which could utilise any of the popular forms of the day. The *Camerata* turned its back on the popular traditions which had already harnessed music to the stage and were to some degree exploited both by the English masque and the *ballet de cour*. Bardi's circle consisted of intellectuals able to determine the sort of entertainment they desired and socially and financially capable of testing its effect in performance.

Two trains of thought converged in their creation of a new style; the first was the Renaissance psychology of 'humours', the doctrine that individual character is determined by a predominating mood or emotion, a doctrine which reverberates loudly through the English drama of Elizabethan and Jacobean days and which gave rise to the Baroque musical doctrine of 'affections', which declared that any single piece of music could only, and should attempt only, to express a single mood or emotion. *L'Amfiparnasso* is subtitled 'the various humours of modern music', and sets out to describe a set of fourteen characters who are Serious, Cheerful, Universal, Mixed, Libertine and so on down to Melancholy.

This was generally accepted doctrine and not the primary concern of the *Camerata*. Like their French counterparts of the *Académie de Poésie et de Musique*, Bardi's circle was enthusiastically determined to recover the glories of ancient Greek tragedy, with its seriousness, elevation and power. If the music heard in the Greek theatre had been worthy of tragic themes—and this belief persisted until the end of the eighteenth century—it must have been music of unparalleled power and beauty. But at the same time it must have conveyed and not obscured the words to which it was set, and must therefore have taken as its foundation the inflections and intonations of the speaking voice of an actor capable of doing justice to the glories of Greek dramatic verse. It must find the musical equivalent of the laws of rhetoric and observe them faithfully.

This was the complaint of the *Camerata* against the music of the age before their own; it devoured words for its own purposes and might convey all sorts of things—the emotions prompted in the composer by the text, the general atmosphere created by the text and the dramatic situation for example—but it could not clearly and distinctly convey words so that they, as well as the music, made their own effect on the listener. Renaissance polyphony was an art they rejected because of its relative independence of words except as an excuse or reason for composition.

The earliest works of the musicians of the *Camerata* to put their ideas into practice were solo compositions for a single voice with a single accompanying instrument. It might be possible to see in such works the natural delight in song asserting itself against the dominance of an art which arose in Northern Europe and for a time submerged what is naturally Italian and southern. But that would be to look almost cross-eyed at the early cantatas which took their texts from the finest available poetry; Galilei's *Il Conte Ugolino* was a setting of words by Dante for voice and theorbo, which has been lost. Some of his pieces, together with music by Peri and Caccini, in which they believed they had recovered the lost secret of dramatic declamation as it had been practised by the ancient Greeks, were published in 1602 in a collection called *Le Nuove Musiche*. In its preface Caccini wrote: 'If we are to speak well in music, we need to have a certain noble disregard of song.' That is to say, if great poetry is to be faithfully delivered in music, the music must sacrifice itself to the pattern of the poet's declamation, and not impose its own rhythmic and melodic patterns on the words. In this, Caccini is only declaring that he has followed the teachings passed on to him in Count Bardi's *Discorso sopra la Musica Moderna*: 'In composing, you will make it your principal aim to arrange the verses well and to declaim the words as intelligibly as possible, not letting yourself be led astray by the counterpoint.'[1] Peri, too, declared his intention of resurrecting the style of Greek music, and in the preface to his *Euridice* explains his score and its almost purely declamatory style by saying that 'the ancient Greeks used a harmony surpassing that of ordinary speech but falling so below melody as to take an intermediate form'.[2] This 'intermediate form', he believed, was the recitative style in which he had composed his opera.

The total rejection of polyphony by these composers even at a time when polyphony was simplifying itself can be seen from the works contained in *Le*

[1] O. Strunk: *Source Readings in Musical History.*
[2] *Ibid.*

Nuove Musiche. The vocal parts almost disdain melody; they do not attempt any consistent, appealing melodic contour but merely set out to give rhetorical force to the words, and their accompaniment was often not merely simple but no more than a bass line of a sort which modern ears find crude. What they did achieve was an almost explosively emotional treatment of exclamatory emotive words; what they had reached was the essential recitative style which music had to achieve before it could put itself completely at the service of drama.

The first operas to emerge from the Florentine *Camerata* round the end of the sixteenth century entirely followed the doctrines the group had evolved. They were almost entirely declamatory works, not often pointed by relevant activities such as expressive dissonance and its resolution in the accompaniment. Dramatically they grew out of the courtly pastoral plays; their stories were taken from classical mythology and were concerned with love, for love either satisfied or frustrated offered the greatest stimulus to passionate verbal—and therefore musical—expression. Like the Greek authors whom they claimed as their masters, the composers preferred that the action should take place off stage and be described by a Messenger. Rinuccini followed this convention because the Messenger's narrative would be a more excited verbal expression than could arise in the course of the action itself and therefore more suitable than action to an art of passionately heightened declamation. Peri's *Dafne*, produced during the Florence carnival of 1597, has been lost, but his *Euridice*, sung in the palace of Duke Corsi for the wedding of Henry IV with Maria de' Medici in 1600 has survived. Duke Corsi himself played the harpsichord in the orchestra, and the only other instruments required, apart from two flutes which are heard in a single *ritornello*, are chittarone, viol de gamba and theorbo. The published copy, which came out very soon after the performance, gives only a figured bass. What is dramatic about the work is dramatic only in a rudimentary sense. Peri knows that drama must vary in pace and intensity, so he makes room—perhaps as a concession to less pure and instructed taste than that of his friends—for occasional songs and choruses.

Early Florentine opera is an almost awesomely intellectual form, an attempt by dedicated scholars to limit the power of music in the service of words. Peri's *Euridice* was something of a sensation at its first performance because it was new and because it was heard by a large number of people to whom the body of doctrine assembled and evolved by the *Camerata*—with which most of them must have been familiar—had not yet been manifested in action. Opera as Peri composed it was too self-abnegatory and puritan a form to survive as it was, eschewing musical expressiveness and binding words to a deliberately formal style of declamation which in the long run hampers the player's ability to make a natural effect. Only seven years lie between Peri's *Euridice* and Monteverdi's *Orfeo*, a *dramma per musica* (according to its composer's subtitle) in which, as in all great opera, the music is the drama no less than the drama is in the text it sets. The gap between Peri's work and Monteverdi's is enormous, for in Monteverdi the born musical dramatist entirely assimilates the drama into his music; but in one sense the bridge across the chasm was already under construction when *Euridice* was first performed.

As the early Florentine operas were designed to recover the practices of the classical Greek theatre they gave a sort of provisional aesthetic to the rebellion of the moderns against polyphony, but they were not intended to be the first powerful, trail-blazing examples of a new form. If they were satisfying to the taste of a highly cultured intelligentsia which happened to live and have influence in Florence at the close of the sixteenth century, it was because the *Camerata* had been led by its antiquarian theories to extremes at which they happily sacrified the claims of music to those of words. True opera was to be a more equal marriage between the rival claims of text and setting.

In 1600, the year of *Euridice*, Cavalieri's *Rappresentazione di Anima e di Corpo* was produced in the Oratory of St. Philip Neri in Rome. The fathers of the oratory had originally collected congregations for devotional, extra-liturgical services at which *Laudi* and other music in popular style had been sung; as their concern was to teach the faith and to inspire devotion they were ready to use anything which might further their aim, so that they had already introduced spoken religious drama into their devotional services with sermons preached and hymns sung between the acts. Cavalieri's work applied the principles of the 'new music' to a morality play of the same style as the English *Everyman*.

Although historically it can be counted as the first oratorio (the form took its name from the type of religious semi-operatic work presented in the oratory), *La Rappresentazione di Anima e di Corpo* needed to be acted and danced, and was fully operatic. It deals with allegorical figures—Soul, Body, Intellect, Pleasure, The World, Time and so on—and uses not merely the declaimed *stilo recitativo* but songs, madrigals and dances; it remembered that it was written not for an assembly of highly cultured connoisseurs but for a 'popular' audience. It developed a more elaborately expressive style of recitative than the Florentine composers had so far evolved—this again seems to have been the result of its venue and its audience—and the age, with its passion for technical nomenclature, called the new departure '*stilo rappresentativo*'—'theatre' or 'acting' style. Cavalieri's work is the source of both oratorio and Roman opera, and his preface indicates not only that the work is meant to be acted but also the precise demands it makes in production. His orchestra—a double-lyre, a chittarone, a clavicembalo, two flutes and two trumpets '*al' antica*', are to play behind the scenes. A madrigal is recommended instead of an instrumental introduction; all the voice parts are to be doubled and accompanied by 'a great number of instruments'. After the prologue has been spoken by two youths, Time enters, and the hidden musicians give him the note on which his music begins. Pleasure is accompanied by two companions; they carry instruments on which they accompany their songs and play the *ritornelli*. Body, when he hears the words '*Si ch' ormai alma mia*' sung, may throw away some of his ornaments, such as his gold collar and the feathers from his hat. The World and Human Life are to appear very gaily dressed and later to be stripped of their trappings so that they look 'very poor and mean' before they die and are seen as corpses. The performance may end with or without a dance. If without, the last chorus is to be doubled in all its parts, vocal and instrumental; but if a ballet is preferred, a verse beginning with the words 'Chiostri altissimi, et stellati' is sung, accompanied 'sedately and reverently by the dance. This shall be followed by other grave steps and figures,' all appropriately solemn. During the *ritornelli*, the four principal dancers are to perform a ballet, *saltato concapriole* (dancing and leaping) without singing. After each stanza, the dance is to be varied, and the four principals are allowed to use the steps of the galliard, the canary and the courant; all the stanzas of the final ballet are to be sung and played by all the musicians and singers.

The keenest members of the oratory congregation were apparently young men from the lower end of the social scale, and while it is possible to imagine (if not readily to share) the pleasure of aristocratic dilettanti at the sound of the un-adorned Florentine *stilo recitativo*, appreciating its scrupulous justice to the words, it is unlikely that an uneducated audience, aware of and probably de-lighted by the natural richness of Italian melody, would have found much appeal in music so unnaturally constrained. Cavalieri had to approach a popular style in his religious opera if he were to win the audience for whom the work was written. There had to be regular melody, vitality of rhythm, colour and point in harmony and orchestration; the singing voice had to flower into something stronger and more appealing than rhetorical declamation, to admit at least the sort of loose melodic construction which came to be known as *arioso* if the music were to move a popular audience. These were the lines along which opera in Rome came to develop parallel to Monteverdi's development between 1607, when he com-posed *Orfeo*, and 1642, when *L'Incoronazione di Poppea* was staged in Venice.

It was not until 1626 that an opera on a secular subject was staged in Rome, Domenico Mazzochi's *La Catena d'Adone*. Thirteen years later Mazzochi and Marazzoli wrote the first comic opera, *Chi Soffre, Speri*, for the great opera house built by the Barberini family—it held over three thousand people—which had opened in 1632 with Landi's *Il Sant' Alessio*, the first biographical opera. Roman opera, like the entire social life of the city, depended on the attitude of the Pope of the day, for the Pope's temporal power over the Papal States was more absolute than that of any Emperor over his realm, as was natural in a small state where the spiritual head was the temporal ruler. His general power over the widely scattered church was minimal in comparison to his hold over his own territories. The Barberini Pope, Urban VIII, who reigned from 1623 to 1644, held a liberal attitude to the arts and had no objection to secular opera, but the form languished in neglect during the reign of Urban's successor, Innocent X, whose quarrel with the Barberini drove them from Rome for the length of his pontificate. The later reign of Clement IV, who as Giulio Rospigliosi had written the libretto of *Il Sant' Alessio* and other religious operas, marked another period of expansion, but the uncertainty of Papal approval made Rome a less than in-fluential centre of opera after the decisive period of Urban VIII, in which Roman composers had followed the example of Cavalieri and had allowed, amongst other things, polyphonic choruses into opera in a way which must have outraged the austere principles of men like Bardi. In Rome, opera came rapidly to distinguish between recitative (which soon developed into *recitativo secco*) and lyrical, emotionally expressive passages.

In one way, throughout its early history, opera in Rome differed decisively from court opera elsewhere in Italy. Court opera was meant to be a manifestation of the greatness and glory of the patron who presented it; opera in Rome was meant to be edifying. Outside Rome sensational production counted for as much as good music; in Rome however neglect of the visual delights of stage work did not mean a concentration on the musical and dramatic quality of opera but left a vacuum into which the integrity of the form disappeared through each department's concentration upon its own speciality.

Elsewhere opera rapidly became a lavishly and spectacularly staged diversion for the aristocratically wealthy. Guido Bentivoglio, who later became a cardinal and papal legate to Flanders, was present at the first performance of Peri's *Euridice* and he described it thus:

> A representation in music was specially successful through the great diversity of exquisite inventions of which it made use, by the singular beauty of its principal scene, which was frequently and almost miraculously transformed into many other scenes, and also by the excellence of the machines, the songs, the music and a thousand other devices which continually swept the audience into admiration. No one could be sure whether all these wonders were fancies or realities, or which was greater, the delight created by such rare and spectacular shows or the delight born through the presence in the theatre of so exalted and majestic an audience.

Cardinal Aldobrandini, too, was present, and the secretary in his entourage noted the event: 'That evening was presented the principal comedy in music, which deserved much praise for its scenic arrangements and *intermezzi*. But the manner of singing it grew easily displeasing, and the moving of the stage machines was not always successful.' To neither of these clerical spectators, the one bursting with enthusiasm and the other less delighted by the entertainment, was music the principal attraction of the show.

Lavishness of production, a passion for ingenuities of ornament and scenic devices, together with the cost of singers and orchestra—for a new style demands that singers be trained in a new way, are therefore scarce and in a commanding position when the question of fees arises—made opera so expensive that it remained for a time the monopoly of wealthy courts. When Peri's lost *Dafne*, the first fruit of the research and experiments of the *Camerata* and more a fascinating experiment than a fully fledged entertainment, had its first performance Marco da Gagliano, one of the composers of the *Camerata* whose own operas were performed in Florence in the first decade of the seventeenth century, noted that 'among the audience were Giovanni de' Medici and other illustrious gentlemen of our city'.

When Peri's *Euridice* and Caccini's lost opera *Il Rapimento de Cefalo* were chosen as suitable entertainments for the marriage of Henry IV and Maria de' Medici in 1600, opera established itself as a form specially suitable to aristocratic celebrations. This adoption was not primarily due to the fact that opera was a new and (despite Bentivoglio and Aldobrandini's secretary) startling form, though this aspect of its existence was not without influence, but rose from the fact that it really satisfied a Baroque ambition. The seventeenth century courts saw opera, as Wagner two hundred years later was to see his music drama, as a *Gesamt-kunstwerk*, a super-art which naturally comprehended and united all the arts—architecture, painting, design, mime, acting, the plastic arts, poetry, dance and song. It chimed sympathetically, for this reason, with the humanist ambition for universality and the conception of the 'complete man', the ideal all-rounder who since the early Renaissance had been the humanist ideal. Monteverdi's first operas were created for aristocratic audiences: *Orfeo* was produced in 1607 at a meeting of the *Academia degli Invaghiti*; the marriage of Francesco Gonzaga, son of the composer's patron, in Mantua the following year was celebrated by a week of opera which culminated in the performance of his *Arianna*, now lost except for the *Lamento* which the composer reworked later. These were produced with a startling sumptuosity and a dizzy refusal to consider expense. They were the pattern for opera production at court for over a century and one of their results was that, where a composer of force and genius did not control the production, someone else, usually the artist-designer responsible for the machinery and setting and concerned with the creation of spectacular effects, took charge; in this latter case the music became secondary to whatever visual excitements could be threaded into the story.

Works designed for ceremonial production in court—and the list of them is enormous, stretching from Peri and Caccini at the beginning of the seventeenth century to the end of the eighteenth—naturally took a dignified, ornate, ceremonially grandiloquent form. Expense was no object, for no nobleman would stint himself and his guests when he had an opportunity to impress his peers and possibly his betters. A nobleman had his own singers, his own choir and his own instrumentalists; he could order operas to be mounted which made extensive use of a chorus, and encourage or insist upon the use of libretti which made a special appeal to an educated audience. Court opera for a long time drew its subject-matter from classical mythology or classical history. A nobleman could also insist on a purer or a more severe style of composition than might be acceptable to a popular audience, giving more authority to the orchestra and exploiting ensemble numbers rather than depending entirely on the appeal of solo singing. Even if a highly cultured aristocrat flattered his guests when he assumed their familiarity with mythological subject-matter set to severe music, a natural refusal to be out of the intellectual swim made a somewhat highbrow style into a court convention.

In this sense opera was the musical form which suited the new political situation of independent nations no longer conscious of their allegiance to a supra-political Catholic church and to the Emperor. Its magnificence was a reflection of their own greatness and their own power; in the age of absolutism which reached its climax in the reigns of Louis XIV and Frederick the Great, when every petty prince was, so far as it was in his power to be, his own *Roi Soleil*, princely grandeur chose opera as its finest and most telling manifestation.

Court opera was financed through the Prince's income, which in the long run meant through taxation, and opera in court, as later in a city, was intended to manifest the grandeur of the authority who sponsored it; therefore it had to be grand. The cost was not counted because the symbolic value of opera was reckoned to be worth whatever exorbitant sums were spent on it.

The elaboration and extravagance of court musical entertainments is recorded in detail in the correspondence, preserved in the State Archives of Ferrara, which Monteverdi received over a commission from Parma, the home of the Marchese Enzio Bentivoglio. Bentivoglio was responsible both for adapting the theatre from a *salon* in the Farnese Palace and organising an entertainment, to regale the Grand Duke (Cosimo de' Medici, during a visit to Parma) 'with all those sorts of grandeur customarily employed by sovereign princes in greeting and fêting crowned heads'. The entertainment was originally planned to be given in 1618, and Bentivoglio for a start looked for the necessary singers in Rome, employing an agent Girolamo Fioretti to look out those who were suitable. Fioretti asked for instructions about the employment of a woman soprano, as the prejudice against the appearance of women on the stage might work against his choice, and suggests, if she is not suitable, two male sopranos, both *castrati*, two contraltos, a tenor and a bass; all these except the contralto (employed by Cardinal Montecelso) were members of the Papal choir. Fioretti plaintively suggested that if he were given a list of the characters who would take part in the entertainment, he could set about finding any others who were necessary.[1]

Pierfrancesco Batisteli, who was responsible for some of the decoration of the Farnese Palace and the vestibule and staircase of its theatre, wrote a report to Bentivoglio in which he mentioned the progress of the building and the construction of the machines for the Gods and for Discord; at the time of writing, he explained, he was designing 'the vans of the Gods that rise'; the Bacchus scenery was complete; a Flemish artist had made the 'scenery of the four parts of the world'. 'The coat of arms,' Batisteli explained, 'has been set up above the stage, and the despatch of its ornaments of cloth and banners is awaited.'

The text of the six *intermedii* is not preserved in the archives which house Bentivoglio's letters, but the progress reports of the librettist, Alfonso Pozzo, are there; the text itself is preserved in the Parma State Archives, recognisable by its references to 'great Cosmo' and 'great Medici', and the statement that the *intermedii* are to be performed 'In His Most Serene Highness' Theatre'. The text shows that each of the *intermedio* except the last was to be followed by a mock battle between companies of knights: the theatre was designed with an open

---

[1] Stuart Reiner: 'Preparations in Parma, 1618, 1627–28', in *Music Review*, vol. 25, no. 4, November, 1964.

space between the boxes and the stage—where, in a modern theatre, the stalls would be—to allow for this type of action, which was very popular in the early Baroque period. The records refer to the composer originally chosen when the entertainment was projected in 1618, but only by his function; his name is not given.

In the event the show did not take place in 1618. The Farnese Theatre, thrown hurriedly into shape to celebrate Cosimo's visit, was not inaugurated in 1618 because the Grand Duke did not reach Parma. Although the entertainment had lost its *raison d'être*, Bentivoglio went on with his plans, apparently so half-heartedly that in the following January (1619), Pozzo was doing his best to recruit his various goddesses and to arrange their modes of transport without any clear directions from his organiser. 'I shall add a couple of machines to it,' he wrote, knowing that from the seventeenth-century point of view, the more spectacular the staging the more the show would please. 'One shall be of Juno, a van drawn by two peacocks; the other, a cloud which shall open, and when open shall reveal Pallas, armed, upon a blazing steed, with Bellona, who shall serve her at the bridle, afoot.'

Thus, completed for a visit which never took place, the Farnese Theatre waited for its inauguration. In 1627 festivities were planned for the marriage of Duke Odoardo II (who succeeded in 1622) to the daughter of the Grand Duke Cosimo. Bentivoglio's scheme, left for nine years in abeyance, was resurrected and Monteverdi was commissioned to provide the music; with not too extensive changes, the *intermedii* previously written and designed could be adapted for a wedding instead of a mere state visit and could be staged to greet the bride's arrival.

Monteverdi by that time was *maestro di cappella* at St. Mark's Venice, and was actually working on a commission from the court at Mantua, to which he offered an earlier opera, *Armida*, instead of the new one for which he was asked. He accepted the Parma commission when he heard that *Armida* would be acceptable to the authorities in Mantua. His preoccupation when Bentivoglio first offered him the commission created a queue of applicants of some importance; among them Bentivoglio favoured Sigismondo d'India, a Sicilian nobleman who had lived in Parma and whose monodies were admired in Florence and Rome. Another of Bentivoglio's agents, Antonio Goretti, poured cold water on the idea of offering the work to him: 'he has in his head certain ideas of wishing to be considered the foremost man in the world, and that no one but he knows anything; and whosoever wishes to be his friend, and to deal with him, has to puff him up with this wind; a thing which one might tolerate and give him this pleasure if he were satisfied with a little of it.' There may have been some professional jealousy about Goretti's letter, for he ended it by reminding Bentivoglio that he had himself composed the music for the original Pozzo libretto which had not been performed in 1618 and suggested that if he were not employed for the marriage celebrations, everybody would believe that he had been passed over because he had provided inferior work. A letter from Monteverdi however suggests that the commission had been offered to him, the Mantuan arrangements made and his terms accepted before Goretti's plea was read.

What Monteverdi had to compose was a set of *intermedii* to be played between the acts of and as a conclusion to Tasso's tragedy *Armida*, and eventually the adaptation of Pozzo's Grand Ducal entertainment had to be far more extensive than was originally expected. What had begun as *La Difesa della Bellezza* in 1617 grew to be 'a dramatic journey' called *Mercurio e Morte*, and five *intermedii*, in which a new poet, Ascanio Pio di Savoia, incorporated a great deal of Pozzo's original work and made use of the 'machines' designed and prepared in 1617. This fitted round and into the tragedy; Monteverdi provided the music for both, but neither score has survived.

The vicissitudes of providing spectacular court entertainment seem to have been endless. Maria Cristina, Cosimo de' Medici's elder daughter, promised to Odoardo II by a wedding contract in 1620, was withdrawn by her father in 1627, very near to the last possible moment, to make a diplomatically more advantageous marriage with the Duke of Orleans, brother and heir presumptive to Louis XIII of France. New negotiations had to be opened and the marriage of Cosimo's second daughter, Margherita, to Odoardo II had to be arranged. Therefore the long-planned festivities and the opening of the theatre took place in 1628, like the long-planned wedding.

Again the unlucky Goretti was involved, for despite the length of time available the final stages of the work had to be hurried and Monteverdi needed musical assistance. Monteverdi accompanied him to Parma in October 1627, but a month later Goretti excused him of responsibility for the slow progress of the score. He made a fair copy of everything Monteverdi composed as soon as it was written, but, he grumbles: 'Signor Claudio composes only in the morning and evening: during the afternoon he does not wish to do anything at all. I urge him, and relieve him of such labour as I can—which means taking his work from under his hands having discussed and arranged it together; and I find it so intricate and tangled that I give Your Illustrious Lordship my word that I labour more than if I were to compose it myself; and that if it had to be left to him to write it, it would take time and plenty of it (and if I were not at his heels so much, he would not have done half that he has done).'

Naturally one wonders if the composer of operas and ballets for Mantua and half the great Italian courts, not far from the composition of the great operas he wrote for the public opera houses in Venice, felt a little bored at the idea of writing old-fashioned *intermedii*, or whether it was his normal way of working which provided Goretti with an excuse for jealous grumbling. What we do not have to wonder about is the status of music in the projected entertainment; the libretto was mythological and decorative, not functionally dramatic, and it was designed to make use of equipment and stage spectacles worked out ten years before. The composer adapted himself to a libretto adapted from someone else's ideas and had no particular say in the matter, so that it seems odd that anybody bothered to bring a composer of Monteverdi's class from Venice to be little more than a musical handyman. Bentivoglio seems to have commissioned him because he was the leader of what then was modern music, whose celebrity would add lustre to the Parmesi celebrations; it is impossible to commission work from the leader of the *avant-garde* without such considerations arising, especially if the work he is commissioned to do makes no demands upon his *avant-garde* ideas and techniques.

'Opera is the delight of Princes,' said Marco da Gagliano. He was *maestro di cappella* at the church of San Lorenzo in Florence, *maestro di cappella* to the Grand Duke of Tuscany and a composer under the patronage of Cardinal Gonzaga. During the great opera festival which was staged in 1608 to celebrate the marriage of Francesco Gonzaga, and which saw the production of Monteverdi's lost *Arianna*, Gagliano was in Mantua, and his opera *Dafne* (a setting of the text which Peri had composed eleven years before) was one of the operas performed. Its recitative is far more openly emotional than Peri's; four of its songs, he explained in the edition published in 1608, were composed by a member of the *Accademia degl' Elevati* of which he himself was a member; he insists that during the performance the instrumentalists should face the singers to ensure that the music moves in perfect harmony; a *sinfonia* should precede the performance in order to capture the audience's attention. Gagliano was paid 200 scudi for his contributions to the festivities.

Court opera remained tied to great events, an extravagantly and often gloriously spectacular affair in which music was often only one of three equal elements; verse and decor were its partners. The form did of course develop musically. In Rome in 1626 Domenico Mazzochi's *La Catena d'Adone* uses the term 'aria' to denote lyrical music, whether for one voice or for more, and shows a fairly clear demarcation between recitative and lyrical expression; it has quite elaborate ensembles, particularly for its act finales. Comic episodes began to appear in serious operas, particularly in those of the Roman composers, and comic operas began to be written as *intermedii* to be played between the acts of serious works.

Court opera defined the essential operatic forms, eventually separating aria from recitative, evolving accompanied recitative for moments of higher intensity than *recitativo secco* was able to reach, exploiting ensemble and chorus, and eventually discovering the importance of tonal relationships between the separate numbers of a work. Because it was tied to occasions of extraordinary ostentation, the extravagance with which it was mounted enabled composers to work with a freedom rarely available to their colleagues writing for less splendid circumstances.

When in 1637 a group of Venetian noblemen formed a company to open a public opera house to be run for profit by offering the new, up-to-date entertainment to anyone who could afford to buy a ticket, they set in train a new musical, as well as a new social, development. The sale of tickets was expected to finance the production, and productions were therefore to be tailored to the revenue which might be reasonably expected to come from the box office. Venice in 1637, like Hamburg half a century later, was as conscious of its own grandeur and of its status as a city attracting vast numbers of tourists as any court might be. Though commercial opera run for a profit could not afford to indulge in costly machinery and great choruses, it won its popularity partly as a manifestation of civic, rather than individual, power; opera meant no less as a symbol to merchant princes than it did in Mantua, Florence, Ferrara or, in a short time, Vienna, where it was a recognised declaration of political authority and wealth.

The first public opera house in Venice was that of San Cassiano—the opera houses were given the names of the parishes in which they stood—and within thirteen years another seven were opened; in 1678 the San Giovanni Crisostomo Theatre, the most magnificent of all the public opera houses of the time, began operations. By the end of the century, there were sixteen public opera houses and more than three hundred and fifty new works had been produced in them. Venice permitted three annual seasons for the theatre—during the Carnival between Epiphany and Ash Wednesday, in the early summer from Ascension Day to the end of June, and from Michaelmas to Advent; a work would be produced and would run as long as it had the power to draw audiences.

Monteverdi, several of whose dramatic works have not survived, composed his last four operas for the public theatres of Venice; two of them, *Adone* and *Le Nozze di Eneo con Lavinia*, are lost; *Il Ritorno d'Ulisse in Patria* and *L'Incoronazione di Poppea*, survive to bear testimony to an old age as glorious as Verdi's, but public opera, and the San Cassiano Theatre, were inaugurated with a lesser work by a lesser composer. Francesco Manelli, a bass singer who had been *maestro di cappella* at Tivoli Cathedral (where, as a boy, he had received his training), had been active with his wife Maddalena, a soprano, and his librettist Benedetto Ferrari, as an opera composer and singer in Rome. He moved to Venice apparently because of the insecurity of an opera composer's life in the Pope's capital. It was his *Andromeda* which was the first opera played to a ticket-buying public. By the time Monteverdi's *Il Ritorno d'Ulisse* was staged in 1641 the essential style of public opera was clear and the puritanism of the *Camerata* had been forgotten, except as an occasional excuse for the idea of opera to be advanced to those who found it an artificial form; public opera was more freely lyrical, readier to use strophic poetry and, therefore, repeating melody, than court opera, and, therefore, automatically widening the distance between recitative and arioso or aria. In the hands of Monteverdi, lyrical melody is, for the first time, really dramatic, a manifestation of character and its response to dramatic situation.

From a purely biographical point of view, it would be completely accurate to see a consistent but surprising progress from the opening trumpet fanfare of *Orfeo* to the blissful duet of Poppea and Nero which ends *L'Incoronazione*, and thus to suggest that Monteverdi was, in his own work, shaping opera into what it must inevitably become. It was not simply the need to win popularity among an unlearned audience which developed the lyrical, expressive, emotional powers of operatic music; those powers were essentially involved in its search to be dramatic.

The Venetian audience consisted of all social classes, for there were seats priced cheaply enough to attract the lower paid, and empty seats were, at least sometimes, given to *gondolieri* to create an enthusiastically grateful *claque*. Whether or not it was the approval of the gondoliers in the pit which was really the guarantee of a work's success, it is a Venetian legend which suggests that a successful work was one which won the approval of a genuinely popular audience. There is however some indication that the Venetian theatres provided a more intelligent and tasteful audience than could usually be found at court, where a noise of trumpets, like that which opens *Orfeo*, was the necessary way to win an audience's attention; the overture, usually in the French style (*Grave, allegro, grave*), became the standard operatic introduction in Venice, where it could lead at once into a prologue in recitative and a consequent plunge into drama, while a court audience apparently wanted some more eye-catching and ear-tickling opening to woo it into the proper receptive mood.

The public theatres were a success during the first hundred years of their life. They made a profit for the noblemen who invested in them, and though success made them increasingly ambitious, they never undertook the vastly spectacular productions customary in court works. Even the chorus was used sparingly, a final chorus in a Venetian opera often being no more than an ensemble for all the members of the cast although it was usually headed *Coro* on the score. Opera for the general public had to make its way through the interest of its story and the appeal of its music, not through the dazzling ingenuity of its setting and production. It was in the public opera houses that the notion of proper material for opera expanded from mythology and ancient history to take in medieval legend and romance, thereby losing some more of the intellectual pretensions which had clung to it since its Florentine beginnings.

The success of the Venetian experiment, however, depended not simply on music but on the genius with which the theatres matched the social conditions of the city. Their chief feature was the horseshoe tiers of boxes—five in San Cassiano, each tier containing thirty-one boxes, each box capable of seating several people. A box was rented by the year and reserved in perpetuity for its lessee and his family until written notice was given of his intention to vacate it. When it was not needed by its owner he had the power to sublet it. He could furnish and decorate it as he pleased; it was in a sense a drawing room in which he could do whatever pleased him. It was as easy to meet his friends in his box and to entertain them there as it would be to meet them in his own home. According to a French traveller in the eighteenth century a box was a place in which to eat, drink and, if its owner felt like it, sleep; it was also, of course, a place in which opera could be enjoyed.

Therefore it became natural to attend the opera for social reasons as well as for musical ones; not to attend the opera was to cut oneself off from society, from the chance of profitable business discussions and the prosecution of personal interests other than music. The San Giovanni e Paulo Theatre, the second of the public opera houses to be built, had a little ante-room immediately behind each

box, between its opening to the auditorium and the passage behind. This was
apparently designed to allow the patron to enjoy himself and be sociable if he
wished without any distraction from the music being performed beyond its door.
How the ante-rooms were used in the late seventeenth century is not recorded,
but about a hundred years later Charles Burney noticed that in La Scala Milan
a similar arrangement existed: 'Across the gallery of communication,' he wrote,
'is a complete room to every box, with a fireplace in it and all convenience for
refreshment and cards.'[1] The box was not only a place in the theatre which
offered comfortable seats for the performance of an opera; it was a social necessity.

> The French ambassador assured a friend that it was necessary for all
> diplomats to attend the opera regularly because there it was possible to
> discover secrets unavailable in the ordinary course of events. The
> English resident was once compelled to complain that the box normally
> given to him by virtue of his position had been overlooked. The note
> adds that 'he did not care for music, esteem poetry or understand the
> stage, but merely desired it for the honour of his office, as his predecessor
> and all the other Residents at present at the Court enjoyed the favour'.[2]

The government itself not only made sure that the theatres were well-conducted
and that order was maintained in them; it saw them as a sign of its prestige and
therefore allotted boxes to all the foreign diplomats. Opera was too important to
be left to look after itself.

The profitable notion of the permanently rented box encouraged a free and
easy attitude to whatever happened on the stage. It was possible to enjoy oneself
at the opera without bothering to listen to a note of music, and quite possible to
stop conversation or cards simply to listen to those parts of an opera which one
happened to enjoy. Nevertheless it is possible to argue that regular attendance at
the opera, even for other than musical reasons, eventually trained the audience in
discrimination. In the 1760s an English visitor reported on the manners and
customs which surprised him at the San Carlo Opera House in Naples.

> The Neapolitan rarely dine or sup with one another, and many of them
> rarely visit but at the Opera; on this account they seldom absent them-
> selves, though the opera be played three nights successively, and it be the
> same Opera, without any change, during ten or twelve weeks. It is
> customary for Gentlemen to run about from box to box, betwixt the acts,
> and even during the midst of the performances; but the Ladies, once
> they are seated, never quit their box for the whole evening. It is the
> fashion to make appointments for such and such nights.[3]

Dr. Burney found the noise during a performance in La Scala 'abominable,
except while two or three airs and a duet were singing'. The casual way in which
Italian audiences treated music in general seemed to him to be rather scandalous:
'Those who are not talking,' he noted in Naples, 'or playing at cards, are usually

[1] Charles Burney: *Present State of Music in France and Italy*. London, 1770.
[2] Simon Townley-Worsthorne: *Venetian Opera in the Seventeenth Century*.
O.U.P., 1954.
[3] S. Sharp: *Letters from Italy, describing the Customs and Manners of that Country*.
London, 1766.

fast asleep. Indeed, music at the theatres, and other public places in Italy, seems but an excuse for people to assemble together, their attention being chiefly placed on play and conversation, even during the performance of a serious opera.'[1]

Such accounts of the conduct of Italian audiences suggest that the social amenities provided for the rich patrons may justify the legend of the gondolier as the expert musical connoisseur. In the pit, to which admission was a mere half-*scudo* (about three shillings of our money), the working classes were offered music without additional amenities, and were left with nothing to distract them from the entertainment being played on the stage.

The Venetian experiment was copied elsewhere: John Evelyn, touring Italy between 1644 and 1646, mentioned Bernini as designer of the baldachino over the High Altar of St. Peter's in Rome, and noted with surprise that 'a little before my Comming to the Citty, [Bernini] gave a Publique Opera . . . where he painted the seanes, cut the Statues, invented the Engines, composed the Musique, writ the Comedy and built the Theater all himself'. In Venice he attended an opera performed by 'the most excellent Musitians vocal and Instrumental, together with a variety of Seanes painted and contrived with no lesse art of Prospective, and Machines, for flying in the aire, and other wonderfull motions'. In Milan he heard an opera 'represented by some *Neapolitans*, and performed all in excellent Musick, and rare Sceanes'.[2]

In 1691 Crema, which was at that time in Venetian territory, opened its opera house, the town council having bought two houses standing side by side and converted them into a theatre. 'Thirty-eight boxes have been built, nineteen in the first row and as many in the second.' One box in each tier was reserved for the civic authorities,

> . . . and the other boxes were distributed by lot, drawn in the presence of his Excellency the Podesta, the *Illustrissimi Proveditori* and of many gentlemen from those who have attempted to have them, by paying ten *filippi* each for those of the first row, and eight for those of the second, on condition that they remain for ever their property and the property of their heirs and successors, and that they are allowed to use them whenever or however they please and to dispose of them even to others, provided that the buyer belongs to the Council or is a Venetian nobleman. . . .
>
> *Lire* 2743·6 were received from those to whom the boxes were allotted. The same sum was devoted to the preparation of the theatre. Front row boxes changed hands for *lire* 92, second row ones for *lire* 73·12. The building of the theatre cost *lire* 2064, 1 scudo.[3]

Gasparo Torelli, the most distinguished architect and theatre designer of the day, was commissioned to build an opera house in Bergamo; his accounts have survived, and show that the entire theatre, complete down to its decorations, cost 7882 *filippi*, the Bergamo *filippo* being equivalent in value to the Venetian *lira*. Accounts of fees and salaries give some indication of the cost of running the

[1] Burney: *op. cit.*
[2] John Evelyn's *Diary*: November 19, 1644; June, 1645; May, 1646.
[3] Minutes of Crema Town Council, September 17, 1681. Quoted in Townley-Worsthorne, *op. cit.*

theatres: at Bergamo, the leading soprano and the leading *castrato* each received 400 *pistole* for the theatre's two-month season; the other singers were paid on a descending scale according to the amount of their work; the *pistola* was a coin with general European validity outside Italy, and was worth about 30 *lire*. At the San Cassiano Theatre in the 1670s the three leading singers—the celebrated castrato Siface was one of them—were paid 1000 *pistole* apiece. The purchase of a box, however, did not admit the patron to the theatre, it simply provided him with the comforts he expected when he had paid his entry fee for the evening's performance.

The spread of opera, first across Italy and then across Europe, had a variety of consequences of the utmost importance to the future of music. As the Venetian theatres became yet another tourist attraction in the most visited of European cities, visitors were induced to press for opera in their own towns and from the imitation of Venice to develop styles of their own. Cosmopolitan audiences made the singers the chief attraction of the entertainment; at court the music was likely to take second place to the splendour of the production, but in the commercial theatres music and story came to be sacrificed to the excitement of listening to a beautiful voice displaying the brilliance of its technique. Neapolitan opera, which had its greatest days in the middle of the eighteenth century, exploited voices and vocal acrobatics to a point which cannot unfairly be described as decadent.

The approval of Venetian audiences, or rather of the great cosmopolitan mixture which was any Venetian audience, took opera in capitals like Naples, Vienna and Milan out of the courts into theatres which, while they were royal institutions and were patronised by the monarchy and the court, admitted the general public. When the monarch wished to attend the opera, the places for him and his retinue were there for them, while on other evenings the theatre continued as a place for the general public without the presence of royalty. In Naples the manners of the royal family were no more restrained and musical than those of their subjects, but Naples was the home of comic opera, and on the whole comic opera was listened to with more attention than was given to serious works; an audience which doesn't listen misses the joke. When Burney described La Scala,[1] his account of the theatre's organisation shows that the Venetian style had simply crossed Italy. 'The opera here,' he wrote, 'is carried on by thirty nobleman who subscribe 60 *sequins* each, for which each subscriber has a box. The rest of the boxes are let by the year at 50 *sequins* for the front row, 40 the second, 30 the third and the rest in proportion. The chance money only arises in the pit and the upper seats.'

It was opera which gave Italy its popular dramatic form. When Thomas Coryate heard with delight the breath-taking music of St. Mark's and the city of Venice, he dismissed the public theatres as entirely inferior to those which he knew in London. 'The house is very beggarly and base in comparison of our stately playhouses in England: neither can their actors compare with us for

[1] Burney: *op. cit.*

apparel, shows and music. Here I observed certain things that I never saw before. For I saw women act . . .'[1] Coryate was writing about Venice in 1608, and the presence of women on the stage is interesting because thirty years later, though Manelli's wife was the Andromeda of the first public opera, the Venus was sung by a *castrato*. The *castrati* found their way into opera to sing the roles of heroines because it was necessary to avoid the Papal ban against actresses. There is no reason however to doubt the accuracy of Coryate's view of the drama in Venice; he was not the sort of traveller to find everything un-English inferior to whatever he had grown up with, and he writes about Venice in general with enormous admiration and a certain degree of surprise at the freedom of behaviour he observed there, some of which he acutely noticed was the result of the upper classes going masked to public entertainment. Italian drama before the rise of opera was neither highly developed nor specially popular. The development of opera involved a development of the text to which it was written, and the libretto, with its directness of plot and characterisation, its musically varied and stimulating types of versification and its strong, uncomplex emotions—complexity in Italian opera is always a quality of the music, not of its words—became the popular classic theatre in Italy; it achieved its Shakespeare (that is, its consummate master who could make the form do everything he wished it to do) in Metastasio, who was born in 1698, wrote the texts of seven oratorios, twenty-seven operas and some forty cantatas and lesser works, and died at the age of eighty-four. His libretti were set over and over again, by Handel and Hasse, by Mozart and Haydn, by every composer until the rise of Verdi and the Verdian development of a tougher, intensely melodramatic opera exploited for the extremity and violence of its emotions. Opera is popular Italian theatre because it developed a dramatic style which, while satisfying a public as well as an artistic need, is designed in metres which invite melodies close enough (as Wagner pointed out in his Italianate youth when he was overwhelmed by the melodic power of Bellini's opera) to Italian folk song never to lose contact with their ancestry.

At the same time, as the influence of opera spread far beyond Italy—it was carried to Mazarin's France by Marco Marazzoli and by Cavalli, the greatest of Monteverdi's immediate successors in Venice. It reached Austria through Pietro Antonio Cesti, the best known of Cavalli's successors whose first opera for the Venetian theatre was composed in 1649 when he was twenty-six; Cesti later became *Kapellmeister* to Archduke Ferdinand of Austria at Innsbruck. In 1667 he had four new operas produced at the Emperor's court theatre in Vienna, where he was *Kapellmeister* from 1666 to 1669. The best remembered of his operas is *Il Pomo d'Oro*, composed for the marriage in 1667 of the Emperor Leopold I to the Spanish Princess Margherita.

Many of Cesti's works were produced in Venice, Vienna and Innsbruck. There were too many opera houses for a sufficiency of works to be composed for each by its own staff musicians and operas had to travel from theatre to theatre and

---

[1] Thomas Coryate: *Coryate's Crudities*. London, 1611.

from court to court; what was seen in a public theatre at one time appeared shortly afterwards, glorified and expanded, in production at court. In this way it helped to stabilise the orchestra; the rich array of instruments assembled by Monteverdi for *Orfeo* were those available to him in Mantua when the work was first performed; they did not constitute a formal early Baroque orchestra, for there was no concept of a fixed, all-purpose instrumental ensemble which contained all that was necessary for every type of colour and expression, and the idea of an invariable group of instruments did not therefore occur to composers early in the seventeenth century. It was the reproduction of operas written for one stage on others far from their birthplace which made it necessary to establish a fixed orchestra on the basis of the quintet of string instruments which could be found anywhere.

From this developed first the concerto grosso of the early eighteenth century and, later, the symphony. The introduction of libretti dramatising heroic, knightly stories from the middle ages made the use of trumpets in the opera orchestra appropriate, and naturally enough these were treated in *concertato* style. Such operatic music, it seems, was the point of departure for the Trumpet Sonatas of the composers who served the church of San Petronio in Bologna and were themselves among the factors out of which grew the concerto grosso. In the theatres, the need to create music which developed according to the tensions of a dramatic situation continually drove the composer towards new styles and new effects which were carried outside the opera house, while the opera overture began to suggest the first movement form of the later symphony and sonata. *Il Pomo d'Oro* has an overture the first section of which is a rudimentary symphonic first movement; the development of the *da capo* aria and its establishment by Alessandro Scarlatti as almost invariable (this form was dramatically valid in terms of the Baroque doctrine that a single piece of music could express only a single emotion and could not develop the situation), had its influence on both the developing concerto and the symphony-sonata style of the future.

On a less speculative plane it was the development of opera in the public theatres which led to the creation of the orchestra pit. Marco da Gagliano had pointed out in the early days of opera that in the interests of real ensemble, orchestra and singers on the stage should be able to see each other, and the effectiveness of this arrangement rapidly ended the court opera idea of placing the orchestra behind the scenes or in some obscure corner so that it would not interfere with the stage picture.

In the same way the spectacular features of opera—the machinery by which witches flew through the air, ships sailed across the stage, gods descended on clouds or in chariots, and all the visual paraphernalia of the baroque musical theatre—seems to have been the decisive factor in putting the stage behind a proscenium arch simply because mechanical wonders are a good deal less wonderful if the machinery is visible and can be seen in operation.

The demand for opera in Italy by the end of the eighteenth century made it possible for the successful composer to live independently of any official appointment. Alessandro Scarlatti was *maestro di cappella* to the King of Naples, Pergolesi, in the next generation—he was born in 1710—was deputy to the city *maestro di cappella* there, but composed works for patrons in Rome and was apparently granted as much freedom as he wished. Paisiello, who was born in 1740, held an official post in St. Petersburg from 1776 to 1784, appointed by Catherine the Great, who introduced Italian opera to Russia, and was briefly Director of Music in Naples after the 1799 revolution.

But Paisiello, like all his important successors, wrote operas for the theatres which needed them, establishing a new career for composers. Early operas by inexperienced composers could find a first performance in an obscure theatre; their fee would not be exciting, the performance would be poor but the experience would be invaluable, and they had the opportunity to make a reputation. If a composer were successful, theatres would begin to commission works from him until, finally established, his commissions came from the great theatres—the San Carlo, La Scala, Turin, Venice and Rome. The official posts remained, but they were alternatives to a more sensational career in the theatre; official posts were safe but they did not make fortunes for their holders; the greater challenge and the greater rewards came to the freelance.

By the end of the seventeenth century opera was an entirely international art, having evolved a form of its own in France, having struggled to evolve one in England, where it achieved the isolated wonder of *Dido and Aeneas*, and being elsewhere Italian almost invariably in both language and style. Outside Italy however only Hamburg has a history of any length and importance as a centre of opera.

In the late seventeenth century Hamburg was the 'Venice of the north'. Like the other Hanseatic towns on the Baltic coast it had suffered little from the Thirty Years' War; it was the greatest centre for the receipt and distribution of goods from England, France and Holland, and its position had made it too important to both sides in the struggle for them to imperil their own supplies by interfering with their source. Therefore, throughout the war, it was a magnet for refugees and by 1650 its population had reached 40,000. Only Danzig and Vienna in the entire German-speaking heart of Europe were larger. It absorbed Flemings, Portuguese, Huguenots and Jews, so that, unlike the other old German cities, it did not force itself into stagnation by refusing to change its medieval customs. It was not hard for a refugee to be granted citizenship but only Lutherans could hold any public office. Its 'patricians', the wealthy burgher class who were its senate, were unlike those of most German cities in refusing to allow the purchase of real estate in the city by any nobleman; having power, they refused to surrender it.

Thus, having escaped the devastation which destroyed so many German cities, in the second half of the seventeenth century Hamburg became a good place for the wealthy. German nobles found that a house in Hamburg and residence there for at least part of every year provided them with something of the pleasure-loving atmosphere of Venice; its increasing financial and commercial importance brought in large numbers of diplomats from the rest of the continent, and the countries which traded with Hamburg established their own offices in the city. It became as cosmopolitan as any seventeenth-century city could be, and cosmopolitanism influenced its own manners; it became customary for wealthy Hamburg merchants to send their sons on the Grand Tour and for the sons to bring back with them the ideas and manners they saw in such romantic cities as Venice.

In 1676 the Danes overran Holstein, driving into exile its ruler the Herzog Albrecht von Gottorp who arrived in Hamburg with his *Kapellmeister* Johann Theile. It was Herzog Albrecht and Theile who seem to have worked out the idea of a public opera house in Hamburg and interested the civic musical authorities in its possibility: when the Opera House in the Gänsemarkt was opened in 1678 it was not the exiles but native Hamburgers—Ratsherr Gerhard Schott, a lesser councillor named Lütkens and Johann Reinicken, the organist of St. Catherine's Church—who were the organisers of the actual theatre. As in Venice, the activities of the Opera House became a matter of civic prestige, but unlike Venetian theatres the Hamburg opera house needed the regular support of the wealthy, whose motives in keeping it alive were both artistic and a matter of patriotic pride. Johann Mattheson, composer, singer, cathedral organist and writer, understood why the opera was a matter of more than artistic importance, and wrote about it in *Der Musikalische Patriot*, in 1728. 'If a state creates a theatre to satisfy the leisure of an increasing population, a prosperous closed society is the best medium to nourish such an organisation. A well-organised and well-administered society makes benefits for itself and through good performances finds itself helped by princes and lords, the sciences, the arts and the crafts are all benefited by the help that comes in, and so it is with good performances of famous operas.'

There was one difficulty in the organisation of a Hamburg opera and that was the attitude of the church authorities, who at first neither encouraged nor opposed the work of the theatre; the evangelical left wing of the Lutheran church, the Pietists, tended to oppose it on principle while encouraging operatic styles in oratorios and cantatas which could be performed outside the church and the liturgy: the more orthodox could see nothing in the ideas of opera which might act against the principles of their religion. Nevertheless, to ingratiate themselves with the church, the theatre authorities inaugurated their first season with a work by Theile which owed more to the Lutheran ritual of Passion Music than to any French or Italian models; *Adam und Eva, oder der erschaffene, gefallene und wieder aufgerichtete Mensch* ('Adam and Eve, or Man created, fallen and at last redeemed') was a sop to a distrustful church. From its production until 1738, the fare provided was more normally operatic. Works were imported from Italy and sung sometimes in their original language, sometimes in a German translation and sometimes with German recitative (so that the audience could follow the story) but with the arias left in their original tongue. Handel's three works for Hamburg were the settings of German libretti adapted by the theatre poet Friedrich Christian Feustking from Italian originals. There were, however, frequent attempts at local German opera of middle-class stories, often humorous or attempting humour. On fare such as this the Hamburg Opera maintained itself as a German company for fifty years, after which opera in Hamburg became Italian, in complete accordance with an almost universal eighteenth-century fashion.

Nicolaus Adam Strungk, who was Vice-*Kapellmeister* to the King of Saxony in Dresden, obtained permission in 1692 to open an opera house in Leipzig. His request was granted because it seemed reasonable that a company in the less important city could act as a nursery for the court company in the capital. The Leipzig Opera, however, operated only for a short season during the yearly trade fair, and though it fell foul of the Cantor, Johann Kuhnau, because it removed from the church orchestra the university students who customarily joined the choir and *Stadtpfeifer* for the Sunday church music at St. Thomas's and provided university singers, traditionally employed by the Cantor, with music they found more exciting and more profitable, it maintained its own company only until 1729. After that it became a stage in the travels of touring opera and drama companies. During the fair, Leipzig was a profitable town for entertainers of any sort to visit. The link with Dresden, an extremely Italianate city where Strungk's official life was a state of permanent war between himself and the Italian members of the *Kapelle*, meant that opera in Leipzig was conventionally Italian.

The touring companies which served the small courts found even more work to occupy them than did their Italian counterparts. There was always the possibility of short seasons for them in wealthy commercial centres like Leipzig and Nuremberg, so that they tended by the middle of the eighteenth century to operate round defined circuits; Weber's father, for example, led his company round Bavarian towns for years without ever needing to look for bookings beyond them.

Thus, court opera and public opera came together not only because the same works were played in public theatres and for the entertainment of rulers but also because the maintenance of an opera company was beyond the ability of all but the richest of kings. In this way Italian opera became a universal musical pleasure, unrivalled anywhere until, in 1791, Mozart's *Die Zauberflöte* was produced. In so far as it sowed the seeds of the music of the future, its influence did not decline even when it was known only in sketchy, hit-or-miss performances by companies trudging round the German provinces.

12   The Baroque Age

A change of style so decisive as that which transformed Renaissance music in the fifty years between 1575 and 1625 did not signal the exhaustion of the polyphonic ideal which had motivated the composers of the Renaissance, for polyphony simply became one of the many possible elements in a more extensive musical language and, for many years, co-existed independently alongside the new style. Monteverdi, beyond all question the greatest composer of the early Baroque, was appointed to St. Mark's Venice to restore the choir's mastery of the old style, in which he was able to write as fluently and as naturally as he did in the Baroque style he helped to pioneer. What changed was the attitudes and sensibilities of a generation, and music changed with them.

To Ernest H. Meyer, 'the harmonic mass effects' made by 'large orchestral groups' in the Baroque period were 'a medium through which the composer and performer harangued their audience'. They were expressing 'the storms which raged in the Italy of the Counter-Reformation', and they showed the way in which Cosmo I [Meyer apparently means Cosimo I, Grand Duke of Tuscany] and Pope Paul V made use of, and in a sense perverted, the progressive traditions of the mercantile towns. 'In every respect,' Meyer concludes, 'music in unsettled early seventeenth-century Italy fulfilled a propagandist function in the desperate struggle of the old social and religious order against the new.'[1]

Meyer's view, that of a writer always, if sometimes tendentiously, conscious of the mutual relevance of music and society, is worthy of consideration. He explains, with formidable conviction, how the intensities and sensationalisms of the Baroque destroyed a finer tradition, that Renaissance vocal and consort music, supplanted the friendly discourse of democratic equals with a new, dictatorial art, hectoring and demogogic in style. The trouble is that unrest in early Baroque Italy was not, in any sense, popular; we cannot find evidence of any popular agitation against the rearrangements of the Counter-Reformation. The warfare of state against state and the French attack on the north were aspects of life with which the early sixteenth century, which had seen Charles V's sack of Rome, was perfectly familiar.

For all that, the decisive factor in the victory of the Baroque was its consonance with the outlook of the age. A purified Catholicism, and a little later an impregnable Protestantism, both looked to music to dramatise their glory and their faith; to the Jesuits, for example, the excitements of the new style were valuable simply because they were wonderful and put their wonder at the disposal of the

[1] Ernest H. Meyer: *English Chamber Music*. Lawrence and Wishart, 1946.

church. The Baroque style dramatised the faith, therefore it was invaluable both to Catholics and to Protestants.

The Baroque composer, by dramatising magnificence, wrote the music of seventeenth- and eighteenth-century absolutism. In a sense, the style manifested the ideas of nationalism and authority which had motivated politicians for more than a hundred years. The system of thought moulded by the Catholic church, which had given Europe its law and its forms of government, had fallen to pieces when Charles V attacked and captured Rome in the interest of the new concept of nationalism. The same concept had motivated Henry VIII's rebellion against the Pope's moral authority and had been held to justify his actions though these, in anyone less than a king, would have been condemned as brutally criminal. Macchiavelli, who had observed the political activities of fifteenth-century Italian rulers at close quarters from the privileged position of a diplomat, had settled down in retirement in 1513 to write the political treatises which codify nationalist practice and provide the textbook of power politics. The great days of Renaissance music were those in which the new world was establishing itself; the age of the Baroque was that in which nationalist power politics had consolidated their grip.

Baroque music exploited not only the principle of monody and its harmonically motivated accompaniment but also a new principle of construction by contrast. These new principles led to musical structures of great strength and power, and they forged a connection with religion, both Catholic and Protestant, because of the status they give to a text. The monodic *stilo recitativo* was developed as a means of declaiming a text, its contours decided by the need to project words clearly to the listeners. The arioso style which grew from recitative was motivated by the same declamatory principle but enriched by the need to intensify the emotional power of the words. Homophonic passages in block harmony were equally considerate to words, and in this respect at least, though its vivid colour and dramatic intensity were not qualities dear to the Catholic authorities, it came closer to the principles of the Catholic reformers than did the old music which, with its homogeneity of texture and its avoidance of drama and sensationalism, was innately devotional.

The deliberate magnificence of the Baroque (and from the polychoral motets of Andrea Gabrieli at the beginning of the period to the *Sanctus* of Bach's B minor Mass and Handel's 'Hallelujah' Chorus at its close, the Baroque age is crowded with deliberate magnificences) seemed to reflect the age of Catholic consolidation just as it reflected the nationalism which was expressed in courtly brilliance and the adulation of monarchy. The music which Heinrich Schütz heard in Venice and carried back with him to Protestant Germany obviously did not convey any specifically Catholic implications, and the entirely Protestant Baroque of Schütz is no less vividly dramatic and sensational than that of Monteverdi. At the same time, the extreme emotionalism of the style formulated musical figures universally accepted as symbolic; Baroque music is made, as often as not, from such symbolic figurations which helped to make the new style easily accessible.

In another respect Baroque music was new. It was music addressed to an audience rather than music primarily addressed to its performers. The singer or the instrumentalist performing Renaissance music is in a position to experience a work at least as fully as any listener: the performer in a big Baroque work experiences little more than his own part.

While monody developed in Florence, the principle of contrast was first exploited in Venice at a time before we can legitimately speak of 'Baroque' music. Venice was fabulously wealthy, having dominated Europe's trade with the Far East ever since Marco Polo, himself a Venetian, had opened a trade route to China in the early thirteenth century. The city and the territories it ruled around it stood outside most of the quarrels of the Italian states in the fifteenth and sixteenth centuries, and its geographical position gave it an almost complete security. It was a republic ruled by a self-perpetuating oligarchy of merchant princes who made a government far more tolerant than most which could be found in the late Renaissance. It welcomed refugees, particularly those who could make some effective contribution to the city's public, intellectual and artistic life, and it took a more broadminded view of unconventional ideas and behaviour than most governments of the day.

The government of Venice, the Council of Ten, had a natural continuity; it did not come to an end at anyone's death, or at an election, to be restarted by someone else. Any employee of the Venetian State could expect to hold his post for his own life time, and not merely for that of his patron. In Venice, Monteverdi pointed out to the Gonzagas when they wanted him to return to Mantua, he was better paid than he had ever been in Mantua, his post there was secure for the rest of his life and he was the social equal of anyone in Venice; he was also, he told them, treated with genuine respect by everyone in the city. He could have reminded Gonzaga that for most of his time in Mantua his salary had been in arrears but that in Venice his salary was sent round to his house on the day it became due.

These conditions had been drawing northern musicians to Venice since the early days of Renaissance music, and it is to Adrian Willaert, a native of Bruges, born about 1490, that we can trace the conscious exploitation of the contrasting weights and dynamics of music for two choirs singing in traditional antiphony. Willaert had travelled a great deal and worked for years in Italy before 1527 when he won the post of *maestro di cappella* at St. Mark's through the public competition which was the normal way to appointment there. He was a law student in Paris, neglecting law for music in 1514. Four years later he was working as a musician in Bologna and in 1522 he was one of the *cappella* of Alfonso I d'Este at Ferrara; in 1525 he was serving another d'Este, Ippolito, the Archbishop of Milan. It seems as though the Sack of Rome by Charles V persuaded him that life in Venice would be more secure.

At St. Mark's, he took charge of a musical organisation which gave him as his subordinates the cathedral's first and second organists, an accomplished band of string and wind players and a large choir famous at the time for its musical standards. The architectural choir of St. Mark's, with choir-stalls occupied by the canons of the cathedral, contained a gallery on each side for the singers, and each gallery had its own organ for use in antiphony. With these conditions to manipulate Willaert developed the idea of the double choir, each half independently accompanied, providing all his singers with beautifully smooth music into which a dramatic, declamatory style sometimes erupts when the words demand it.

One probable influence on Venetian double-choir compositions was the acoustics of St. Mark's itself, just as an obvious influence was the existence of the two organs. St. Mark's great central dome has a smaller dome on each side of it, so that its acoustics are enormously complex and a constant challenge to the composer whose work is to be heard in it. It is a building of multiple echoes and complicated resonances the organisation of which must necessarily have been a delight and a challenge to any composer offered the means to exploit them. To what extent Willaert was stimulated by the St. Mark's acoustics is something at which we can only guess; it was his followers and disciples who made it clear that what they wrote was intended to use St. Mark's as a difficult instrument capable of dazzling brilliance in the hands of a composer who had mastered it.

Willaert died in 1562. His successors included Claudio Merulo, who became first organist in 1566, Andrea Gabrieli, who replaced Merulo at the second organ until 1584, when he was promoted to Merulo's place. After his death, his nephew Giovanni (whose admiration for Andrea's music and affection for its composer seems to be the only reason for his bringing out Andrea's work with his own) included his instrumental *canzone* and *sonate* in a volume which also included some of his own works. The volume appeared as *Concerti di Andrea e di Giovanni Gabrieli . . . continenti Musica di chiesa, Madrigali ed altro, per voci instrumenti musicali*. Giovanni was probably responsible for the new nomenclature; in addition to *concerti* and *sonate*, Giovanni also called his works *symphoniae* and *Dialoghi Musicali*. *Sonate* were simply instrumental, 'sounded' music, as distinct from *Cantate*, or sung music. *Concerti* were music for choir and instruments, while *Symphoniae* usually involved solo voices and orchestra. The Baroque distinction was not between the innately sacred and the innately secular; it was simply a matter of where the music was to be heard, just as a generation or so later there often seems to be little in the nature of many a *sonata da chiesa* to convince us that it would not be perfectly happy to be known as a *sonata da camera*.

Whether or not there was any conscious exploitation of peculiar acoustic conditions in the double-chorus works of the period preceding Giovanni Gabrieli's, once he and his contemporaries created a third or fourth group of performers, the idea of linking a contrast of sonority or dynamics to the exploitation of the vast, resonating echo-chamber which is St. Mark's had to be worked out. He simply had to know how to write for his third or fourth choir and where in the church to place it to ensure that it would make its best effect. We know of Berlioz, about three centuries later, pacing out the nave of St. Eustace in Paris, so that he could organise the antiphonal dialogue of orchestra in the chancel and organ at the west end for the beginning of his *Te Deum*; we have comparatively little information about the methods of Giovanni Gabrieli except that provided by scores which assure us that he never worked casually and was not content with a hit-or-miss method.

For all that, whatever delights there were for a composer who set out to make use of the acoustics of St. Mark's or of any other elaborately resonant building, the contrast principles worked out in Venice in music of so much pomp and magnificence had another pressing influence. The *maestro di cappella* at St. Mark's was not simply the musical director of a wonderful and very rich cathedral; the *cappella* of St. Mark's were the Doge's own musicians, responsible for the music of a state which regarded magnificence as its birthright. The Doge moved on ceremonial occasions behind his official Trumpeters. The Venetian year, as well as its musically exciting carnival season before Lent, was full of ceremonies which demanded music. Apart from state occasions the government officially involved itself, and its music, in the great Christian feasts like Easter, Whitsun and Corpus Christi, just as every Ascension Day, in the most brilliant of all his ceremonies, the Doge symbolically married the sea in recognition of the dependence of the city on the maritime trade which had ended long before the ceremony was discontinued in the late eighteenth century.

By the time that Willaert was in office there, in the middle of the sixteenth century, a visitor's guide book to Venice described its public, ceremonial music as one of its outstanding attractions and, to prove its point, listed the musicians who could be heard there. The back of Venice's commercial supremacy was broken when the Fall of Constantinople in 1453 put a stranglehold on the city's Far Eastern trade, and from then onwards it became more and more consciously a centre of international tourism. People went to Venice then, as they go now, for its strangeness, like the American humorist who on arriving there sent home a telegram saying 'Streets under water. What should I do?' They went for its beauty and its great art collections, for Venice and its conditions of work had attracted painters and sculptors as magnetically as it attracted musicians. They went because of the city's reputation as a place for pleasure-lovers where luxury and freedom reigned. A visit to Venice was necessary to complete a nobleman's education; Venice was an essential port of call on any traveller's itinerary, and any traveller in the late Renaissance period heard new and exciting music there. Travellers who have left accounts of their Venetian experiences seem invariably to have been amazed and impressed by what they heard.

A good deal of the impetus towards the contrast style which the Baroque age called *concertato* came from Venetian ceremonial music. Special occasions were treated with dazzling lavishness. When the Turkish fleet was defeated and driven from the central Mediterranean at the Battle of Lepanto in 1571 (a battle from which Venice benefited enormously but in which Venetian sea power had played a less than decisive role) Veronese was commissioned to paint an allegorical picture of the battle and Zarlino to write and organise the music for victory

celebrations as grandiose as could be devised; Andrea Gabrieli composed music
heard during the jubilations, including a semi-dramatic cantata. The anniversary
of Lepanto became an annual, musically grandiose, celebration. Three years
later Henry III of France paid an official visit of a week in Venice. The city was
decorated by Palladio, Tintoretto and Veronese. The Doge sailed in his state
barge, *The Bucentaur*, to greet him, and the barge also carried a choir and
orchestra to sing the musical welcome composed by Zarlino, who also wrote the
first recorded Venetian opera, an *Orfeo*, to entertain the king. Every evening
musicians entertained Henry III from a floating platform moored outside
the palace in which he stayed, and every night the canals were crowded with
barges full of musicians who sang and played all through the night. Fortunately,
Henry was fanatically devoted to music.

The favourite ending to a Venetian celebration was a mock battle, with
cannons and fireworks; it could be a mock battle of cavalry or, more sensational
still, a sea battle on the lagoon. The sheer brassy flamboyance of much Venetian
music, interspersed with quieter string or woodwind interludes at appropriate
moments, like the *Battaglie* (battle pieces) published by Giovanni Gabrieli and
Annibale Padovano in 1592, suggest (though none of the works can be linked
with any specific occasion) that the mock battle was as accurately planned and
meticulously rehearsed as a ballet.

Delight in vivid contrasts of tone colour and dynamics is perhaps a simple-
minded delight, but for all that it is a musical delight. We shall never know to
what extent it was stimulated either by the sensational nature of Venetian
celebrations or by the particular conditions of performance in St. Mark's; it
probably owes as much to one as to the other, but the secular celebration seems
to have demanded the style before church musicians exploited it; the situation
is that which has occurred with every liberalisation of church music, the importation into the church of what had proved successful in a secular context.

The massiveness of such works, which German musicologists called the
'colossal Baroque', developed into a style for special occasions, just as Monteverdi's *concertato*-style works for St. Mark's seem all to have been written for
great celebrations; for normal occasions he followed the *prima prattica*. The
'colossal Baroque' reached its peak with music by Virgilio Mazzochi, *maestro di
cappella* at St. John Lateran in Rome during 1628 and 1629, who wrote a work
sung in St. Peter's Rome, with one choir in its conventional place, another in the
gallery round the dome and a third in the tower above the dome. Orazio Benevoli
who wrote sometimes for as many as twelve variously accompanied choirs went
even further; for the consecration of Salzburg Cathedral in 1628 he composed a
Mass for two double choirs, each with its own continuo, accompanied by five
orchestras, two of woodwind, two of strings and one of brass, each placed in a
different part of the cathedral. The whole work was set out over a master-figured
bass which reduces the whole work to harmonic naïvety. Like that of the great
E flat fanfares of the four brass groups of the *Tuba Mirum* of Berlioz's *Requiem*,
the effect is due to the exploitation of the space and resonance of the building

in which it was heard; played in different conditions or heard through a single loud-speaker, the work would hardly hold the attention.

Multi-choral writing and the intense expressiveness at which the Baroque style aimed were disastrous to the Liturgy, which evolved into a musical form rather than an expression of the mind and devotion of the church. The *Kyrie* turned its central petitions, *Christi eleison*, into a solo or solo ensemble piece—eventually in the dominant or the relative major of the movement's main key. The *Gloria* and *Credo* each ends with a fugue; often the two fugues have the same subject. The *Sanctus*, like that of Bach's B minor Mass, is usually grandly solemn and direct, leading to a lively *Hosanna* which is foreshortened when it reappears after an extended, lyrical *Benedictus*. The *Dona nobis pacem*, which ends the *Agnus Dei* often, at the beginning of the period, rounded off the work by recapitulating the main ideas of the *Kyrie*; by the end of the period it had become a quick, major-mode coda to a slow minor-mode movement, re-establishing the tonic major of the work. Italy, and Italian composers elsewhere, developed the Cantata Mass which breaks up the text into separate movements, arias, duets and choruses; in other Catholic countries composers were slower to break up the unity of the liturgical text. The sacrifice of liturgy to musical considerations continued with occasional periods of reaction through the nineteenth century.

Catholic Austria rapidly became a centre of Baroque composition. The growing power of the emperor in North Italy made a flow of Italian musicians to Vienna a natural development of the political situation, but the early masters of the new style in Vienna were Austrians. Christoph Strauss was born in 1580; he became *Kapellmeister* at the Imperial Court in 1617 and later director of music at St. Stephen's Cathedral. Often his music suggests an incongruous marriage between the Renaissance and the new age; in his Mass *Veni Sponsa Christi* he bases his music on a traditional plainchant *cantus firmus* but uses big *concertato* effects. His *Requiem*, composed in 1616, is accompanied by strings and brass and is scored for two unequally voiced choirs, a four-part choir of sopranos, altos and first and second tenors opposed to a six-part choir of tenors with basses in five parts; the preponderance of lower voices is used to achieve an emotionally sombre effect. Strauss's *Missa Concertato in Eco*—the echo obtained by the proper positioning of two choirs—exploits a favourite early Baroque device in a colourful way. A generation or so later Heinrich Schmelzer, born in about 1623, Johann Kaspar Kerll, born in 1627, and Heinrich Biber, born in 1644, developed the style. Schmelzer was a court chamber musician in Vienna; Kerll, a pupil of Carissimi, spent three years (1674 to 1677) as a court composer in Vienna before going to Munich as court organist. Biber was high steward and *Kapellmeister* for the Archbishop of Salzburg, and was so renowned as a violinist that the emperor ennobled him for his playing.

For the most part, however, the Baroque style spread across Europe through something like an apostolic succession. Willaert's pupils Cyprian de Rore, Zarlino and Andrea Gabrieli became the next generation at St. Mark's. They were joined in 1557 by Claudio Merulo, who wrote in the Venetian style and in 1574 moved first to Mantua and then to Brescia. De Rore left Venice in 1547 to become *maestro di cappella* to the Duke of Ferrara. Andrea, before settling in Venice as successively second and first organist at St. Mark's under Zarlino, had worked in Munich with Lassus and had been associated in Augsburg with the Fuggers, who transmitted all the music they enjoyed to other members of their internationally powerful family. Andrea Gabrieli taught his nephew Giovanni, who was the leader of the next generation. He also taught Hans Leo Hassler, whose younger brother Jacob was sent to Venice in 1590, so that his teacher was Giovanni Gabrieli.

In 1609 the Landgrave Moritz of Hesse-Cassel sent Heinrich Schütz, one of his ex-choirboys who was at that time a reluctant law student in Darmstadt, to study under Giovanni. Schütz worked in Cassel, in Dresden and in Copenhagen, returning to Venice in 1628 when the Thirty Years' War had temporarily put an end to his work in Germany, so that Schütz thus got to know and was able to study the music of Monteverdi. Alessandro Grandi, the Italian, Pedersön, the Dane and the Flemish Borchgrevinck all went to Venice as Giovanni's pupils, showing the way in which his fame had grown.

The Baroque style's new terminology spread quicky but was not always used consistently. The adjective *'concertato'* indicated, as did the title 'concerto', that orchestra and singers were involved. This, in the early days of the orchestra, implied the use of instruments in contrasting blocks. The usage makes it impossible to decide whether the term 'concerto' is derived from the Latin *Consortio*, 'a fellow-ship or partnership', or from *concertare*, 'to strive or contend'. We are used to the notion of musicians playing together as partners, 'in concert', but the early use of the terms 'concerto' and *concertato* suggest that either Latin source might have prompted the name.

'Concerto', however, was the term Viadana used, apparently for the first time, in 1602 as title of his *Concerti Ecclesiastici*; this is a collection of solo motets and psalms, apparently monodic in style, written over a figured bass which really condenses a traditional polyphonic texture. When the Thirty Years' War left Schütz with only the skeleton of a choir he wrote his *Kleine Geistliche Konzerte* for one, two, three or four voices with an accompaniment for two violins, cello and an organ to play the continuo. But the monumental *Musikalische Exequien*, 'for six, eight and more voices' but with accompaniment for bass and continuo only, is subtitled 'Concerto in the form of a German requiem'. This use of the term 'concerto' as an extended work for soloists, choir and orchestra, using different sized and voiced ensembles for contrast, continued to be applied until the early eighteenth century; J. S. Bach called many of his early church cantatas 'concerto'. Originally, the term seems to have been applied to any church work for a variety of voices and instruments. Such a work, in the early seventeenth century before the orchestra had evolved any homogeneous sonority, would almost inevitably be in *concertato* style, depending on contrast.

'Symphonia', the term Giovanni Gabrieli used for both his and his uncle's choral and orchestral works in *concertato* style, is often indistinguishable from 'concerto'. The great choral works of Gabrieli's *Symphoniae Sacrae* include huge motets like *Buccinate in neomenia*, for three five-part choirs and one four-part choir, with brass, strings and organ, and *In Ecclesiis*, for soprano and baritone soloists, two unequally voiced choirs (the sopranos are in choir one and the basses in choir two), again with brass, strings and organ. In each of these (which are older than Viadana's *Concerti Ecclesiastici*) the choirs and the two bodies of instruments play in concertato style as well as in powerfully massive tutti passages. The Gabrielis' *Symphoniae Sacrae* also include a number of instrumental works like the *Sonata Pian'a Forte*.

Schütz published three volumes of *Symphoniae Sacrae* all with elaborate instrumental accompaniments, the first to Latin texts, the others to German. The second and third are both described as containing '*Deutsche Concerte*'. The only way, perhaps, in which the intensely dramatic *Saul, Saul, warum verfolgst du mich* differs from the Gabrieli works (apart from the fact that it chooses drama rather than monumentalism) is that the instruments are entirely subordinated to the soloists and choir; they are not heard independently. Nor, for that matter, is the continuo of *Musikalische Exequien*. A '*symphonia*' the 'sounding together' of many voices and instruments, could be a 'concerto'.

The inclusion of purely instrumental works in volumes of *Symphoniae Sacrae* and other motet-type pieces included for use in the church service shows that the Baroque age from its beginnings made use of church music for instruments, and the term 'concerto', in the second half of the seventeenth century, came to mean music that would be heard in church; nevertheless, Monteverdi called his Seventh Book of Madrigals, published in 1619, 'Concerto' although they have no instrumental accompaniment. Orchestral preludes and postludes to High Mass, both often quite extended, and a 'sonata' in place of the motet at the Gradual became customary; the 'Epistle Sonata' after the Gradual continued in some places until the late eighteenth century. Mozart wrote fourteen such works for two violins, cello and bass with organ, three in 1767 and the rest between 1772 and 1780 as part of his Salzburg duties.

Mozart's church sonatas were the end of the traditional trio sonata. At the beginning of its history, for composers like Giovanni Gabrieli, 'sonata' was simply music played, as distinct from 'symphonia', which involved instruments and choir, and 'concerto' which might demand voices and instruments or only voices; 'cantata', the direct opposite of 'sonata', simply meant 'music sung', usually by a single voice to a figured bass, and not heard in church.

The development of the sonata was chiefly the result of the development of the violin and its kindred instruments, viola, cello and double bass. The evolution of the violin seems to have been complete by 1550. Philibert Jambe de Fer, in his *Epitome Musical*, published in Lyons in 1556, explains that the viol is the instrument for people of taste while the violin is for 'weddings, dances and mummeries'.[1] The viols were domestic instruments, subdued and mellow; as music moved out to the public the brilliant, more extrovert tone of the violin

---

[1] Grove: fifth edition, article *Violin Family*.

became desirable. The great violin makers of Cremona—Nicolo Amati, Antonio Stradivari and Giuseppe Bartolomeo Guarneri, who came when the instrument had achieved its final form, span the period from 1596 when Amati was born to 1744 when Guarneri died, and by the end of that period the violin had become enormously popular and had an equally enormous influence on instrumental music.

The increasingly homogeneous orchestra, based on a quintet of about a dozen strings, gradually took over the larger instrumental sonata. In establishments like the Church of St. Petronius in Bologna (a church analogous to the university churches of Oxford and Cambridge) where there was one of the best orchestras in Italy, the Baroque sonata style turned into the trumpet sonatas. These were developed by a line of composers from Maurizio Cazzati who was made *maestro di cappella* at St. Petronius in 1657 to 1671 when the San Petronio orchestra, which at that time included Giuseppe Torelli, was disbanded except on the great feasts. It was revived but on a smaller scale in 1701, so that the trumpet sonatas disappear with the original departure of the orchestra. Torelli moved to Ansbach and carried the style with him.

Theatre music—the introductory sinfonia and the intermezzi between opera acts—naturally brought crisper, livelier rhythms and shorter-breathed, more lyrical tunes into the whole of orchestral music. At the same time the status of Louis XIV's France as the home of civilisation brought the influence of the suite, the varied dance forms assembled from French operas and ballets, into general currency and was especially influential in German court music.

All these influences were fed into the *Concerto Grosso*, developed by Corelli and his contemporaries. Corelli was born in 1653 and went to study in Bologna in 1666. Possibly he travelled in Germany, but a visit to France he is traditionally supposed to have made seems to have been no more than a period as a violinist in the French church in Rome. In the *Concerto Grosso* as Corelli wrote it, the *ripieno*, or full orchestra, is contrasted with a solo *concertino* group which plays in more or less trio sonata style. The full orchestra of strings, with the growing popularity of the operatic aria form, became itself more and more responsible for *ritornello* music into which the *concertino* enters as a parallel to the voice.

The concerto and the suite were church music, court music and popular music. The progress of the suite in Central Europe owed a good deal to the *Stadtpfeifer* bands whose speciality was church and dance music. A *Stadtpfeifer* composer like Johann Petzel, who was *Stadtmusikus* in Leipzig during the last quarter of the seventeenth century, was primarily a composer of dance music for brass ensemble which he planned in suites to give a proper sequence of contrasted but complementary pieces.

The orchestral and general instrumental repertory of the seventeenth and eighteenth centuries found enthusiastic players in the Italian *accademia* and in the *collegia musica* of German-speaking Europe which began to spring up in the sixteenth century. The *accademia* of Italy were intellectual organisations whose attitude to the arts were as much scholarly and, in the eighteenth-century sense of the term, 'scientific' or aesthetic. The *collegia musica* and music clubs of Germany, Austria and Switzerland were gatherings of musicians who wanted to play together. 'Right glad I was,' wrote Bishop Fuller in 1662, 'when music was lately shut out of our churches, on what default of hers I may not enquire, it hath since been harboured and welcomed in the halls, parlours and chambers of the primest persons of this nation.'[1] Fuller was thinking, it seems, of organisations like the Oxford music meetings which began in 1656 to meet every week. The College musicians, robbed of their work by the Puritan abolition of the Prayer Book services and the banning of music in the church, met at the house of William Ellis, who, until the beginning of the Commonwealth, had been organist of St. John's College. The meetings continued until early in the eighteenth century and then apparently ended until Handel's visit to Oxford in 1733 reawakened interest in the sort of music which was not normally available in the colleges and the university.

The musicians who gathered at William Ellis's house were primarily church musicians. According to Antony à Wood,

> The meeting was much frequented and many Masters of Musick were there, and such that had belonged to choirs, being out of all employ, and therefore the Meeting, as all other Musick Meetings, did flourish; and music, especially vocal, being discountenanced by the Presbyterians and Independents, because it favoured much the Cathedral and Episcopacy, it was the more used. But when King Charles was restored, and Episcopacy and Cathedrals with him, then did the Meetings decay, especially for this reason, because the Masters of Music were called away to Cathedrals and Collegiate choirs.

Sir John Hawkins, offering a commentary on this, notes that Wood's list of 'Masters of Musick' consists chiefly of the names of members—singers and instrumentalists—from the college choirs and cathedral choir.[2]

Bishop Fuller's note that when music is suppressed in church it makes its presence felt elsewhere could, however, have been prompted by developments in Zwinglian and Calvinist Switzerland. The banishment or extreme restriction of liturgical music led to the formation of musical societies which at first simply performed the music that was no longer heard in church. They performed four-part settings of the psalms, since only unison singing was permitted by the liturgy, as well as older music familiar from the pre-Calvinist Catholic age and new church works which were not doctrinally offensive as often as they found them. Such societies had a considerable number of experienced members—adult musicians formerly connected with the church, the local *Stadtpfeifer* band, and the school choir, which had previously been trained in service music. Others— amateurs and local music-lovers—joined, but whatever was sung or played was exclusively for the members of the society which had no interest in public performance.

[1] Bishop Fuller: *Worthies.* 1662.
[2] Hawkins: *op. cit.*

Originally the place in which such societies met was the church. The earliest Swiss *Collegium Musicum* was formed in Zürich in 1613. In Winterthur as late as 1636 the musicians met in the rood loft of the city's principal church, but in Basle in 1661 it demanded a place in which to make music where an organ could be provided and, its demand being satisfied, it moved out of the church to its own music hall. Some musical societies waited a long time for premises of their own; Cherbuliez notes that the Trogen society continued to meet in the church until 1894.[1]

To move out of the parish church, however, was to widen the society's sphere of activities and to allow it to approach secular instrumental music with an easy conscience. Thus it fell into line with similar societies in Germany. The Swiss *Collegia Musica*—the name was universally adopted in Switzerland—began as a compensation to the musical for the departure of music from the church. In Germany, where music played an even bigger part in the Liturgy than it had done before the Reformation, the spread of amateur musical organisations carried on and expanded the tradition of the Mastersinger Guilds and profited by the concentration on musical education in German schools. In Germany, societies of townsfolk called themselves *Musikkränzlein*, *Convivia Musica* or some less imposing name than *Collegium Musicum*, which until the eighteenth century was usually adopted by a university music society. All these were totally amateur, but the citizens' music clubs co-opted the town *Stadtpfeifer*, and the *Stadtgeiger* and *Rollbrüder* where such official and semi-official subsidiary bodies existed. The Cantor, as the town's principal musical authority, was expected to supervise its activities. This means that when a choir was needed the choir trained by the Cantor who worked with it in the town's chief school and church was available.

A *Musikkränzlein* was formed in Worms in 1561, a similar organisation began in 1568 in Nuremberg, and a *Musikgesellschaft* co-existed with it until 1585. A *Convivia Musica* began in Görlitz in 1570, and another was formed in Wernigerode in 1587. The *Collegium Musicum* in Frankfurt-am-Main was formed in 1588. Mühlhausen formed a *Musikalische Societät* (which was to encourage J. S. Bach in a flight of youthful grandiloquence; his *Ratswahl* Cantata *Gott ist mein König*, No. 71, in 1708, written for the day on which the magistrates and the town council attended the service) in 1617, and the Hamburg *Collegium Musicum* in 1660. Halle's *Collegium Musicum* was founded in 1694.

The academic background of the *Collegia Musica*, like their Latin title, indicates a certain seriousness of outlook. Like the Italian *accademie*, they were meant to take their music seriously and to show a lively interest in music as a theoretical study as well as a pleasure. Most of those which stretched back to the years before 1618 and the Thirty Years' War were forced by the war to suspend their operations until peace was restored, but the German thirst for music revived them as it created others. The *Musikkränzlein*, the *Musikgesellschaften*

---

[1] A. E. Cherbuliez: *Die Schweiz in der Deutschen Musikgeschichte*. Huber, Frauenfeld, 1932.

and the *Conviviae Musicae* tended to take their pleasures seriously. Even the *Collegia Musica*, however, may have been less solemn in their outlook than their earnest title suggests. The students of the *Collegium* at Jena (which was under the direction of Johann Sebastian Bach's second cousin, Johann Nikolaus after 1695) once broke a violin and a horn by beating their director with the instruments.

There was no great degree of uniformity about the organisation of any of these bodies. The Frankfurt lawyer Johann Friedrich Armand von Uffenbach, a devoted amateur musician rich enough to travel for pleasure, left a Travel Diary in which he noted his musical experiences. He was born in 1678, visited London in 1710, and spent the years between 1712 and 1716 travelling in France and Italy. In London he attended 'Academies'—a concert of the Academy of Antient Musick presided over by Pepusch, and the weekly concert given in the Rome Tavern, Gerrard Street, by its landlord Binet. In Oxford he attended a *Musik-kollegium,* by which he meantthe music club which met in Christ's Church. The difference in Uffenbach's terminology is that the London music was available to subscribers or to anyone who bought a ticket while the *Kollegium* in Oxford was exclusively for members and invited guests like Uffenbach himself.

When Uffenbach was an undergraduate at the University of Strasbourg he heard performances by the *Stadtpfeifer,* who had acquired string instruments as well as their traditional woodwind and brass, and who were joined in public performances by the city's military guild of trumpeters and drummers. The concert by the *Stadtpfeifer* which Uffenbach heard on December 12, 1712, his first experience of music in the city, was given in the new church; it lasted from one o'clock in the afternoon until three. Uffenbach was enthusiastic about Beck, a violinist and Tobias Braun, a flautist (the Diary carefully notes that he played a 'traversiaire', not a recorder-type flute). He heard, he wrote, 'a good symphony', and it was well-played, but his use of the term 'symphony' suggests that, like his contemporaries he was less punctilious in naming the works he heard than he was in applying the proper title to the events at which he heard them. As a student he played with the *Collegium Musicum* which had begun to open its meetings to the public.

In Berne, on the way to Italy, he was invited to a meeting of the *Collegium Musicum,* which had its own hall. This had been built 'at the cost of music-loving citizens' and resembled a church; at the far end of the hall was the room in which the musicians played—Uffenbach described it as being 'like the rood-loft of a church'—invisible to the audience. Uffenbach was allowed to sit inside it with the musicians so that he could hear better.[1]

In Italy in 1714 Uffenbach heard opera, church music and occasional oratorio performances, but the few events he described as concerts were *Hauskonzerte,* musical entertainments in private houses to which invitation was a matter of social class and friendship with the householder. In these events amateur and

[1] Eberhard Preussner: *Die musikalischen Reisen des Herrn von Uffenbach.* Bärenreiter, 1949.

professional musicians appeared together. The most memorable of these was in the house of Prince Ruspoli in Rome.

While he was in France a year later he attended what he described in his diary as 'The weekly concert of the Merchants of Lyons'. Forty musicians, all amateurs, performed an act of the opera *Acis*—probably Lully's work although Uffenbach normally gives works their full names and Lully's opera is *Acis and Galatée*— 'Little arias in between' and a Motet 'in the modern French style'.[1] The concert was more enjoyable, he felt, than a complete performance of the opera would have been in the theatre.

By the time Uffenbach settled to professional life in Frankfurt, Georg Philipp Telemann had become the centre of the town's musical life. In 1712, Telemann, already a famous progressive musician, had become Cantor of the *Barfüsserkirche* (the pre-Reformation church of the Capuchin monastery which was also the chief city church) while holding on to his earlier title as *Kapellmeister* to the court at Eisenach. In two or three years he had made his presence felt in every department of Frankfurt's musical life. Because the city was traditionally that in which the Holy Roman Emperor was crowned, Frankfurt had a political prestige which balanced its importance as a trading city with an important annual fair. It had its own aristocracy who stood apart from the activities of the city merchants and who lived their own social life into which the academic and professional society of Frankfurt could gain admission. Uffenbach and Telemann both did so, and between them married the city's *Collegium Musicum* to the aristocratic club which called itself *Hochadeligen Gesellschaft Frauenstein* (the 'Frauenstein Society for the well-born') which took its name from the fact that its premises were the Frauenstein Palace on the Römerberg, the central square in front of the cathedral. Here the *Collegium Musicum*, an assembly of enthusiastic amateurs drawn chiefly from the aristocracy augmented by professional musicians who were teachers, met regularly with the professionals of the *Stadtpfeifer* guild, Telemann's church choir and amateur singers. The weekly 'Frauenstein Concert' was never fully public, but it did not restrict itself entirely to members in spite of the social eminence of its home and foundation. After Telemann had made his way to Hamburg in 1721, Uffenbach, who had become his close friend and ally, continued to be a pillar of Frankfurt music, which after 1739 provided regular public performances, having copied the example of Telemann's Hamburg, and became a 'Grand Concert' until 1808, when the modern concert society, the *Museum Conzertgesellschaft*, was founded.

Hamburg concert life in the earlier years of the eighteenth century was even more adventurous. The city's close contacts with England, which brought a large number of Englishmen with their own ideas of musical organisation to work there, as well as its prosperity and the number of aristocrats from the other German states who found it pleasant or convenient to live there were all inducements towards the setting up of concerts, as opera had been set up, as a promising commercial venture. The Drill Hall of the town militia, used for banquets and

[1] Preussner: *op. cit.*

balls of civic as well as military importance, was already used for concerts by the beginning of the eighteenth century, by which time the Hamburg newspapers had begun to pay attention to them.

Newspaper announcements make it obvious that even at such an early date the city was a good place for the travelling virtuosi who in most parts of Germany could hope for engagements and play only at the courts. On October 18, 1708, the *Relations-Courier* announced the forthcoming visit of John Abell, a somewhat enigmatical Scottish lutenist, counter-tenor and composer whom Evelyn had heard in 1682, when Abell had just returned from Italy where Charles II had sent him to study. 'After supper,' Evelyn wrote, 'came in the famous Trebble, Mr. Abell, newly returned from Italy, and indeed I never heard a more excellent voice, one would have sworn it had been a Woman's it was so high, and so well and skillfully managed.'[1] John Abell sang in the Chapel Royal until the revolution of 1688, when he was dismissed for suspected Popery, and from then on he led an apparently chancy, not over-successful, life touring the continent. By the time he reached Hamburg in 1708 he was fifty-eight years old and probably well past his best.

'To all lovers of good music,' the Hamburg announcement declares, 'we give notice that the world-famous singer Msr. Abell, sometimes singer in the service of his Imperial Roman Majesty and other Royal Courts where his incomparable voice has been admired, will be here during the course of his journey to England, and on the evening before his departure, Thursday, 9th instant, will give a musical concert in the Drill Hall. Tickets can be purchased at the Drill Hall, and the performance will begin at 6 p.m. precisely.'[2] Six years passed before the note of another concert in any of the Hamburg dailies. On October 31, 1714, the *Relations-Courier* announced that 'Celebrated musicians, formerly in the service of Kings, Princes and other Great Gentlemen', whose names are not listed, would give a concert of instrumental music in the *Brauerei-Gesellschaft* in the Hop Market. Six years of newspaper silence does not necessarily mean that six years passed between two consecutive musical events in Hamburg but only that for any one of a variety of reasons, intervening events were not advertised.

The concerts which are announced or commented upon in the eighteenth-century Hamburg press were all those of visiting musicians. In 1716, the *Relations-Courier* announced a concert 'for mixed choir and instruments' the music of which consisted of works by the local masters Keiser and Mattheson; the promoters, however, seemed to find it advisable to announce Keiser not as one of the great composers of the Hamburg opera but by his court title, as '*Kapellmeister* to the Archducal Court at Mecklenburg'. The name Telemann first appears when he directed a Serenade Concert in the Drill Hall in 1723, when the great attraction was not his own music but the playing of Kuhnel, a viola da gambist from the Dutch court.

[1] Grove: after John Evelyn's Diary; 27–i–1682.
[2] Heinz Becker: *Die frühe Hamburgische Tagespresse als musikgeschichtliche Quelle*, in *Beiträge zur Hamburgischen Musikgeschichte*, 1956, 1.

As well as the concerts of visiting musicians the newspapers announce frequent oratorio performances of a sort which became commonplace in the years after Mattheson's appointment in 1715 as Cantor of Hamburg Cathedral, and continued successfully enough to induce Keiser, after his work in Copenhagen and Ludwigsburg, to concentrate on oratorio when he returned to Hamburg. The newspapers' announcement of such events, many of which are listed in Heinz Becker's essay,[1] provide little information about the performers concerned and their musical status. As is the case throughout Germany, the complicated picture of music-making in the first half of the eighteenth century is made vague by the lack of information about details which only become available as later organisations began to function and to draw up statutes which have remained on record. The development of concert life in Hamburg is something on which we have little detailed information about the players concerned, the programmes performed or the balance of amateurs and professionals in the orchestra, although we know that, with its *Stadtpfeifer* and its *Rollbrüder*, Hamburg was better supplied than most cities with performers who could at least claim professional standing.

Similarly the newspapers contain no account of the steps by which Weckmann's *Collegium Musicum* evolved into a public concert giving society before the advent of Telemann in 1721. Telemann's arrival signalled in Hamburg, as it had done when he reached Leipzig as an undergraduate and in Frankfurt as Cantor, a burst of musical activity which it seems incredible to attribute to a single man who also found time to compose a vast amount of music none of which is simply bad or thoughtless, though a good deal of it belongs only to the routine of eighteenth-century musical convention. Telemann was obviously one of the most likeable musicians simply because wherever he went, people seemed only too eager to do what he wanted and to see that his plans worked effectively. As Cantor, he was by tradition director of the *Collegium Musicum*; his directorship of the Hamburg opera was simply a by-product of his endless activity; direction of the *Collegium Musicum* gave him the duty of drawing up its programmes and therefore, indirectly, of composing a great deal that was heard at its meetings.

Gradually in this way the more exclusive *Collegia* began to be heard in public, so that a sort of rudimentary concert life began to exist in most German towns. What the standards of performance were, and how much they varied, are questions which Sir Thomas Browne would have admitted to be 'beyond all conjecture'. There are few accounts in which experienced and travelled musicians like Uffenbach commented on what they heard, and even Uffenbach has little to say about the way in which the musicians played and nothing about the works they performed.

Many of the organisations, of course, grew up before the Baroque age. The *Collegium Musicum* in Prague drawing up its constitution in 1616 declared: 'This Collegium shall exist for the practice of Motets and madrigals.' In 1597 Jan Tollins and Sweelinck both dedicated vocal music—Tollins a book of

[1] *Op. cit.*

madrigals and Sweelinck his second book of Psalms—to the *Collegium* of Amsterdam. But the *Collegia* were dependent on the sort of music currently popular outside the church and, like the Swiss *Collegia*, tended to secularise themselves when they moved out of church though the architecture of the earliest halls designed for music was based on that of churches. Even the 'progressive' *Collegium* in Hamburg met in the cathedral until Telemann moved it into the Drill Hall where the members stayed until 1761 when they were given their own premises, the *Konzertsaale auf dem Kamp*. Naturally they evolved into bodies of singers and instrumentalists. By the end of the seventeenth century even the Swiss *Collegia* were ready to play secular works, some of them even humorous.

Comparatively little music was written for any of these organisations, perhaps because their funds were rarely extensive enough for them to commission any of the music they needed. Arnold Geering lists a handful of cantatas written to celebrate events like the fiftieth anniversary of the *Musikgesellschaft* of the German School in Zürich in 1729, the dedication of a new hall for Bischofszelle *Collegium* in 1756, and a few pieces to commemorate births, marriages and deaths in the families of members.[1] German works for the *Collegia* are equally rare, though Johann Philipp Krieger, a Nuremberger born in 1649 whose career took him to Copenhagen, Vienna and Weissenfels and whose music was very popular in its day, dedicated his *Lustige Feldmusik* to 'the businessmen's *Collegium* in Nuremberg' in recognition of 'so many years of good friendship'.

Probably the *Abendmusiken* organised by Dietrich Buxtehude in St. Mary's Church Lübeck, are the most famous of all the city musical activities in Central Europe round about the last three decades of the seventeenth and the opening years of the eighteenth centuries. They were not only carefully prepared performances of music which was often complex and elaborate; they were also professional performances given to a paying audience and they had a profound effect not only on the music of the Baltic cities close to Lübeck. They were celebrated enough to attract the attention of musicians from far away; J. S. Bach travelled two hundred miles on foot to hear the Buxtehude performances.

The *Abendmusik* performances had their greatest days under Buxtehude, who became organist at St. Mary's in 1668, but were not his invention. The post was one of the best paid in Germany and had already been made famous by the work as composer and player of Franz Tunder, whom Buxtehude succeeded by marrying his daughter. It was Tunder who in 1646 had first given concerts of religious music in the church on certain Sunday evenings. According to Caspar Ruetz, Lübeck Cantor in the mid-eighteenth century who published a history, *Widerlegte Vorurtheile von der Beschaffenheit der Heutigen Kirchenmusik* in 1752, Tunder had been asked by businessmen in Lübeck to give midday concerts of the kind they had heard in Amsterdam and other cities in the Netherlands. They subscribed to the cost of such *Mittagskonzerte* not only sufficient money to make them worthwhile to Tunder himself but enough to make it possible for him to

---

[1] '*Von der Reformation bis zur Romantik*', in *Schweizer Musikbuch*, edited by Willi Schuh. Atlantis Verlag, Zürich, 1939.

include vocal and instrumental soloists in his programmes. Ruetz could find no official records of such concerts but got what information he was able to use from an old man who had been told about them.

The success of the midday church concerts persuaded Tunder that something more ambitious could be done, and in 1646 he was given permission to give concerts after Vespers on Sunday evening. For these he had no financial backing, so that he had to finance his performances out of his own salary, and when he found that he could not raise enough subscribers to face the expenses, sometimes as high as 400 thalers a concert, he let them die quietly.

Buxtehude, almost certainly aware of his father-in-law's experiences, moved with business-like caution towards even more ambitious performances. First he had the choir galleries enlarged to hold about twice as many singers and players as Tunder had used and as were available for the normal choral services. The Council's permission had to be obtained for this, but the work was done by public subscription.

Buxtehude gave his concerts after Vespers on the last Sunday after Trinity and the second, third and fourth Sundays in Advent. As these are not, liturgically or musically, days for jubilation—Advent is a pentitential season—but days on which elaborate service was forbidden in some of the Lutheran liturgies, it would be interesting to know why Buxtehude chose Advent for his special performances—possibly because choir rehearsals were not then busily occupied with elaborate service music—and how he persuaded the church authorities to allow them.

Whatever methods of persuasion he used to arrange *Abendmusiken* in Advent he applied equally or even more effective ones to persuade wealthy citizens to support the expenses of the concerts. He began like Tunder by financing them himself, raising subscriptions as Tunder had done and whipping up interest through sending out to wealthy patrons and potential patrons copies of the programme which included the texts of all the works to be sung. This he expected to bring in larger donations at New Year, when Lübeck citizens traditionally made a donation to their organist. In 1687 he complained that subscriptions had fallen so low that he could barely pay his assistants out of what he received. He pointed out in an appeal to the members of the Merchants' Guild that they had wanted the *Abendmusiken* and that it was therefore up to them to support his work. All his appeals sensibly pointed out that he could not plan concerts unless he knew how much money would be available to pay for them. Eventually Buxtehude succeeded in gaining Council support by writing works to reflect upon and commemorate local and national political events—the Peace of Nijmegen in 1679, the victory over the Turks in 1686, the German victory at the Battle of Mohacz in 1687, the capture of Belgrade in 1688, and so on. If great events were to be celebrated the celebration could come at one of the *Abendmusik* concerts at the end of the year, and a specially gorgeous work could be performed; in this case it would obviously be something in the splendour of which the Council would take a special interest and pay a share of the expenses.

The performances were sometimes on what, for seventeenth-century Germany, was the largest musical scale. In 1679 he listed about forty helpers. His orchestra, though it came to be based on the eventually inevitable quintet of strings, included not only trumpets, trombones, oboes and drums but cornetts and the instruments of the viol family (which, of course, continued in use until the time of Bach). The Latin double-chorus at the end of Buxtehude's cantata *Templum Honoris* expects twenty singers in each choir, and trumpets, drums, waldhorns and oboes with each choir, as well as twenty-five strings, and this is not an isolated example in which Buxtehude for once gives way to the grandiose; many other *Abendmusiken* works are equally ambitious. The players were the *Stadtpfeifer*, the ancilliary musicians' guild of *Rollbrüder* and the amateurs of the *Collegium Musicum*. The schoolboys of the normal choir provided the core of the vocal forces and were the soloists, unless the solo vocal music was beyond their powers in which case adult soloists were imported. Buxtehude organised the concerts not by designing his music to match his resources but by finding the additional musicians he needed to do justice to his ideas.

In other cities the *Collegia* were not taken up into large-scale public music-making. All of them, from the more academic *Collegia* to the social *Conviviae Musicae* and *Musikkränzlein*, had to depend on printed music and the currently fashionable concertos and suites, lacking a Buxtehude with the ambition and the resources to make them part of large-scale, subsidised concerts. At a time when even the lesser courts ordered concertos of one sort and another in sets of six or a dozen, and dramatic *sinfonie* and suites were no less abundant, printed music was naturally becoming more widely available. Since they existed to make music rather than to listen to it or to talk about it, the various organisations became exponents and adherents of the Baroque style. If the local cantors as their musical directors supplied them with music, what they obtained in this way were works like the solo or multiple clavier and violin concertos of Johann Sebastian Bach, all written during his first fourteen years in Leipzig, or the chamber music and concertos which Telemann wrote in Frankfurt and Hamburg; the fact that such composers were officially involved in the work of the *Collegia Musica* of their cities possibly laid them under an obligation to produce works for their instrumentalists though their contracts of employment do not make participation in the meetings of the local *Collegium*, or the composition of works for it, a condition of employment. The point of a seventeenth- or eighteenth-century musician's life is that when music was wanted, he wrote it, and the regular meetings of music societies meant that a vast amount of music was consumed. Not until the mid-eighteenth century could musicians begin to be reasonably sure of finding what they wanted in print. The *Thematic Catalogue* of mainly instrumental works issued by Immanuel Breitkopf from 1762 must have circulated widely among the various musical societies which, unlike the courts, had no facilities for demanding an endless supply of brand new works.

In this way Baroque instrumental and vocal music moved out of the courts which had developed it, just as opera had done when public theatres were built. Because relatively few of the abundant musical societies could regularly get their hands on new works they created a demand for public music which was not answered until the second half of the eighteenth century.

13 Churches, Cantors and Choirs

The pattern of Lutheran church music was created in the first fifty years after the Reformation. It accepted new musical styles as they arose, because the old conservative safeguards built into the Catholic system were not part of Lutheran organisation, so that the only check on the sort of music provided was the civil authority which appointed both the clergy and the musicians of the church. Although the precise form of the liturgy varied from place to place, so that Bach had to note the order of service on the manuscript of a cantata (*Nun Komm der Heiden Heiland*, No. 61), when he first arrived in Leipzig, its demands for music, with an elaborate cantata-style work before and after the sermon at the morning service, and another elaborate work before the sermon at Vespers, remained invariable in the important city churches or wherever there was a musical establishment capable of performing them.

Early Lutheran practice was codified by Michael Praetorius. Praetorius was born in 1571, and became *Kapellmeister* at Lüneburg before 1604 when he was appointed *Kapellmeister* and secretary to the Duke of Brunswick. His own compositions are less important than his *Syntagma Musicum* or 'Musical Treatise', three volumes of which were published between 1613 and 1619; a fourth volume, meant to be a text book of counterpoint, was never completed. The *Syntagma Musicum* deals with every aspect of music as Praetorius knew it, and his advice to cantors and *Kapellmeisters* is neither more nor less than a thorough application of the principles of Venetian Baroque to Lutheran liturgy and practice. He explains the ways in which a traditional unaccompanied choir could be replaced by solo voices with organ accompaniment, by duets and vocal trios. He treats the use of the orchestra as contrasted groups of brass, woodwind, bowed strings and an 'angelic consort' of plucked strings. He suggests rules for the treatment of all the possible solo and ensemble combinations of the available forces and for their use is a powerful *tutti*.

As a demonstration of the possibilities of thoroughly up-to-date church music, Praetorius suggests a treatment of the chorale *Vater unser in Himmelreich* (the Lutheran versification, in nine stanzas, of the Lord's Prayer) for orchestra of strings, bassoon and four trombones, solo sextet and four-part choir; the result will be a work in four movements.

First movement:
Concerto, First verse; two sopranos accompanied by trombones and bassoon.

Second verse: tenor solo with string orchestra, then verse one as *ritornello* for tutti or solo sextet.

Second movement:

Verse three: alto and four trombones, then second soprano and strings.

Verse four: duet for two tenors, and finally the solo sextet.

Ritornello 2, with verse nine for the solo sextet.

Third movement:

Verses five and six: Solo sextet with both instrumental groups (i.e. strings and trombones with bassoon). Then the full choir with the line *Das wir in guten Frieden steh'n* ('that we may live in peace'), as a *cantus firmus*, first in the tenor and then in the soprano.

Fourth movement:

Symphony for both instrumental groups 'in echo'.

Verse seven: bass solo, then the two violins in figuration against the other soloists.

Verse eight: solo trio with strings, then changed to trombones.

Ritornello 2 *da capo.*

Praetorius was one of the authorities who defined the term 'concerto' as derived from 'concertare' or 'contend with', hence his direction that the violins in verse seven should play 'against' (*gegen*) the other soloists, that is, as an effective contrast.

Such an extended treatment of a chorale, he pointed out, would supply the half-hour work needed (before, after or on each side of the sermon) at *Hauptgottesdienst*, the long morning service comprising the equivalent of Matins and the Mass, on Sundays and High Feasts. If such an elaborate musical plan seems reasonable for a ducal court at, for example, Brunswick, and to provide a background for the monumental works of Schütz at the court chapel in Dresden (except that Schütz made comparatively little use of Chorale texts and even less of chorale melodies) it was not simply a piece of early propaganda for a new style. Praetorius's ideas were already in practice by the time the Thirty Years' War began its long torture of Germany.

In Leipzig, for example, the Burgomaster received the dedication of Schütz's *Musicalia ad Chorum Sacrum*, or *Geistlicher Chormusik*, in 1648 as the war came to its end. This, the composer wrote, was 'out of respect for the Choir of the *Thomasschule*, and the music is for five-, six- and seven-part choir with instruments'. Johann Hermann Schein, who had been cantor at the school from 1615 until his death in 1630, had been as ardent a disciple of the new Italian style as Praetorius and had written several books of Italianate secular music for voices and instruments, as well as a collection of *Geistlichen Concerten* 'for three, four and five voices over a figured bass composed in the Italian style', called *Opella Nova* and published in 1618. Many of the works in the collection are based on chorale tunes which are varied, elaborated and decorated to achieve a proper illustration of their texts in the way J. S. Bach was later to treat the same and many other chorale melodies in his Chorale Preludes. Samuel Scheidt's work as *Kapellmeister* at the court church in Halle came to an end in 1625. His patron, the Margrave of Brandenburg, had his capital, Magdeburg, sacked in 1631 and abdicated seven years later, the year after the court church in Magdeburg was burnt down. Scheidt's music, again including elaborate 'sacred concertos' for choir and orchestra, and organ treatments of chorale and other church melodies, was published during the war, between 1620 and 1650.

In Hamburg in 1642 the town council laid down the duties of the town musicians, who were to serve with the cantor, the town organist and the choir whenever 'figural' music was sung.[1] The term 'figural' had begun to be used long before to mean whatever needed to be written out in parts, but had been transferred to whatever music was written in the 'modern' style over a figured bass, and it would be used on all the greater feasts.

The purpose of the new regulations was apparently to restore order to the church music as it began to recover from the war, the indirect effects of which had reduced the subsidiary orchestra of *Rollbrüder* to three; in 1610 there had been fifteen members; by 1651 the number had risen to five. The weakness of the orchestra suggests a reason for co-opting the services of the councillors' domestic musicians.

The cantor himself was 'to provide good, suitable music on feast days as well as for every Sunday, for all the town churches'. This meant that he was the musical authority for the five city churches within the direct jurisdiction of the Hamburg council, expected to apportion singers and players to them in such a way that each would have 'suitable' music, a solemn, musically elaborate *Hauptgottesdienst* at the main city church and straightforward congregational singing, with probably a motet by the choir, at the others. All the other musicians involved—the *Stadtpfeifer* band and the more recently constituted *Rollbrüder* who played the strings and woodwind—were to obey the cantor's orders. 'As usually eight-part music is required in motets, there will always be a demand for a double number of bass voices, and therefore, nine musicians of an honourable councillor will join the choir on Feast Days and Sundays, bringing with them both string and wind instruments. They shall appear before seven a.m. as well as before one p.m. for Vespers. Their instruments must be well-tuned.'

All players had to be punctual at rehearsal, and for the more elaborate music required on certain days, various other musicians would be co-opted. The *Rollbrüder* (so called because their names were registered on a roll of parchment as members of a guild) and the three 'tower musicians' 'shall attend whenever the cantor needs them'. These rules applied also to the singers, and when a specially large choir was needed, a councillor was expected to recruit its extra members. Except when specially difficult music was to be performed schoolboys should be used. The charity boys of the Gymnasium were already under the cantor's

---

[1] Liselotte Krüger: *Verzeichnis der Adjuvanten, Welche zur Music der cantor zu Hamburg alle gemeine Sontage Höchst von Nöthen hat.* In *Beiträge zur Hamburgischen Musikgeschichte*, edited by Heinrich Husmann. Hamburg University, 1956.

authority, as were the boys of the orphanage and the workhouse. Anyone lacking in obedience and industry should be punished.

The cantor was to have a free hand over music as this, the memorandum points out, had proved to be the most effective form of control. Hamburg would not permit the 'slovenly, lazy, bad performances' heard in some towns which cannot do better. Learners were not to be heard in Hamburg churches, but only experienced musicians.

The cantor's instructions are 'to adhere to the modern, fashionable *stilo modulandi*, so that congregations would be able to hear both the old and the new, and both tastes would be pleased. In addition, most people understand the words better in a harmonic rather than a motet setting. The solo singers are to be experienced and good; more mediocre singers can assist by singing in the full choir. The modern style gives endless trouble not only because it is expensive but also because works composed in it have to be adapted to the musicians available in Hamburg.'

A note by Thomas Selle, who became town cantor in 1641 after four years as cantor at St. John's School, reckons that he had only four good singers of each voice, counting his trebles and altos from the church schools and his tenors and basses from the adolescents of the Gymnasium, or pre-university senior school.

The Thirty Years' War obviously affected Hamburg music, but while Hamburg escaped lightly, the story of Schütz, in Dresden, offers a fairly vivid picture of what happened to German cities, and German musicians, during the war. By 1630 Schütz was pointing out that the court *Kapelle* was losing men, that replacements for them had been found but not appointed, and that his own salary was 500 gulden in arrears. There had been a food shortage bad enough to be called famine since 1618; plague raged in 1626 and 341 people died; from 1630 to 1637 the black death was epidemic, and in 1637 foreign soldiers had been billeted in the town. By that date half the population had died. Schütz spent 1628 and 1629 in Venice. Not having received the money due to him for boarding the choirboys before his wife's death in 1626, he was unable to help his singers when, having pressed for payment of arrears of salary, they were told that the Elector had simply cancelled his debt.

When Schütz again asked for leave of absence in 1633, he put his case quite firmly. 'At present I could readily get away, because the times neither demand nor allow music on a big scale, and the more so because the company of singers and instrumentalists has considerably diminished. Some are subject to the infirmities of age; others are occupied with the war or have taken advantage of other opportunities, so that it is now impossible to perform music on a large scale or with many choirs.' The war was 'hampering me in my work', and he wanted to get away 'so that I may industriously and uninterruptedly continue my profession in Lower Saxony [Denmark]'.[1] His practical response to the war

[1] H. J. Moser and M. Pfatteicher: *Heinrich Schütz*. Concordia Press, St. Louis, 1959.

was the composition of the *Kleine Geistliche Konzerte*, for soloists or small ensembles, and these must have become extremely popular, or extremely useful to damaged choirs, as they survive in more manuscript copies than any of his other works.

He stayed in Copenhagen until 1640 because he believed that he could do nothing useful in Dresden, asking for the right to call himself 'Saxon Court *Kapellmeister*' while earning his living and writing large works for the Danish court. He had stayed in Dresden for less than a year, long enough to write forcefully to the Elector about the ruined *Kapelle*, but he was back again in 1641 for the baptism of the Crown Prince's elder son. He had to borrow musicians from Leipzig for the ceremonies, as 'there was no fundamental bass, such as double bass, trombone, bassoon or double-bassoon available in Dresden'.[1]

It was not until 1650 that the rebuilding of the *Kapelle* started, but a year later the court was unable to pay any of its musicians. Schütz again wrote to his patron about the situation of his musicians. 'I testify before God that their misery and lamentation touch my heart, so that I do not know how to comfort them or give them hope of any improvement.' Rather than disgrace the Elector by begging, they were all prepared to leave. He asked for at least half the pay owing to them, explaining that he himself had sold securities, pictures and silver to be able to advance 300 thaler to them. A bitter letter to Reichbrodt, the court marshall and privy secretary, said that he would rather be cantor or organist in some obscure city than remain 'in conditions in which my dear profession disgusts me'.

If this was the situation in a once wealthy and traditionally musical capital, that of other towns was at least as tragic for their musicians. Marburg was occupied eleven times; it lost half its population during the war, and two hundred years later the citizens were still paying interest on a municipal debt which by then had multiplied seven times. Leipzig went bankrupt in 1622. 'From 1623, when the troops first marched across it [Thuringia], every conceivable horror was wreaked by the wild hordes of war at shorter and shorter intervals. . . . Then came the fearful plagues of 1623 and 1635,' wrote Spitta.[2] Veronica Wedgwood, while noting the exaggeration of 'the accounts and figures of contemporaries', points out that such figures as can be proved justify the historical tradition that the war wreaked wholesale destruction in the German cities. The population of Munich numbered 22,000 in 1620, 17,000 in 1650. Augsburg, 48,000 in 1620, 21,000 in 1650. Chemnitz sank from nearly 1000 to under 200. Pirna sank from 876 to 54.[3] 'Population losses for the whole of Germany are estimated at one-third of the city population, two fifths of the rural . . . As a result of the Thirty Years' War, Germany lost her position as the most populous country in

---

[1] H. J. Moser and M. Pfatteicher: *op. cit.*

[2] Philipp Spitta: *Johann Sebastian Bach*, translated by Clara Bell and J. A. Fuller-Maitland. Dover–Novello, 1951.

[3] C. V. Wedgwood: *The Thirty Years' War*. Cape, 1947.

Europe, her population of about twenty million having dropped to between twelve and thirteen million.'[1] The loss of wealth during the Thirty Years' War, notes the same author, 'ruined the foundations of the German standard of living'. The cities almost all lost their cherished independence to the territorial governments which alone could raise sufficient money to wage war on a seventeenth-century scale, so that for the sake of their security the cities were forced into dependence on the Princes, who alone gained from the long horrors of what had set out to be a war of annihilation.

Musical history reflects the social change which the towns felt bitterly. Only Hamburg and Leipzig made an important contribution to music after the second half of the seventeenth century, for the centre of musical gravity in Central Europe slipped from the cities to the nobility.

Hamburg, with 40,000 people, was larger than any German city except Danzig and Vienna, and could afford its opera, its expansion of the *Collegium Musicum* into a public concert society and elaborate church music. Leipzig recovered quickly; with Germany shut away from the main trade routes across the Atlantic, the city adapted itself to the post-war situation, exploiting its position in what in the seventeenth century was the most industrialised area in Germany. It became the central market for Saxon industry, exploiting its connections with, and easy routes to, Frankfurt-am-Main to the west and to Hamburg, Lübeck and Bremen, the old Hansa ports on the Baltic. By the end of the seventeenth century, the Leipzig trade fairs became considerable international events.

But for the most part, while the war changed the political and economic situation of the German cities their institutions remained unchanged. Lutheranism remained a formal, public creed, and in the schools which Lutheranism had remodelled there was no attempt to reshape education to offer a system of education to cope with a changed world.

There was musical development inside the churches because the Lutheran system was created in a way which assimilated musical change. The main musical work, which had at one time been a motet, grew. Praetorius's suggested treatment of the Lord's Prayer showed the way in which the motet could expand into what later authorities called the 'chorale-*concertato*', building an elaborate and impressive work out of a popular hymn and its tune. The work of Schütz, the 'dramatic *concertato*' which depended on scriptural texts and made little or no use of chorale melodies, was a rival style until the two were reconciled by J. S. Bach at the end of the period.

The Praetorius tradition took over Lübeck and Hamburg, for example, when Franz Tunder became organist at St. Mary's, Lübeck, and added to the small orchestra permitted there for a few special services and brought his ensemble of string and trombone players into most of the regular services. His works use chorale words, and take chorale melodies often as *cantus firmi* and often

[1] Hajo Holborn: *A History of Modern Germany, 1648 to 1840*. Eyre and Spottiswoode, 1965.

as themes for variation and elaboration. A similar style of composition emerged
from Matthias Weckmann, who had been court organist at Dresden from 1640
when he was twenty-one, until 1655 when he became organist at St. James
Church in Hamburg. His life was more varied than that of Tunder, and we do
not know why he abandoned the Schütz style when he began to compose for
Hamburg. Selle, who died in 1663, had composed both biblical, or 'dramatic'
concertatos and chorale *concertatos*. It may be that Tunder found congregations
more sympathetic to the musical development of the chorale than to the Schütz
style, which was adopted by Andreas Hammerschmidt, born in 1612 and successively organist at Freiberg and Zittau. Hammerschmidt often used the
'dramatic *concertato*' style in what he called 'dialogues', voices, ensembles or
choirs dramatically responding to each other. 'Dialogue' became an accepted
title, like 'concerto' or 'symphonia sacra', for the major work in the service.

When Dietrich Buxtehude, the outstanding musician of the next generation
(he was born in 1637) inaugurated his *Abendmusiken* performances at St. Mary's
Lübeck in 1673, he seemed instinctively to unite the two traditions, as J. S. Bach
was to do in his Leipzig cantatas after 1722. But the music of Buxtehude which
has come down to us is chiefly music primarily intended for his extra-liturgical
church concerts and conditioned by their freedom rather than by the liturgical
demand that, whatever form the main service music took, it must, like the main
hymns, refer to the text of the Gospel of the day.

The composers' difficulties were the result of social changes after the war. The
new prestige of the aristocracy gave the wealthy businessmen a new pattern to
follow; the aristocrat did not join publicly in church music, so the well-to-do
middle-class followed his example. Those churches which depended on amateur
singers lost those members who felt themselves to be socially superior to the
duties they had previously undertaken, leaving behind the working men and
thus taking away prestige and money as well as singers. In 1655 the *Kantorei* at
Frankenburg was to be told that 'He who has learnt music should not be ashamed
of singing in the choir.' The poor attendance of singers at Bitterfeld led their
cantor to ask them if they considered singing at funerals to be 'a very great
disgrace'.

The answer, as in Hamburg, Dresden, Leipzig, and elsewhere, was to depend
on the schools. In 1664, Pirna, almost depopulated at the end of the war, decided
to form 'a genuine *chorus symphoniacus* of schoolboys' as the old choir barely
existed. The Council of Lunzenau made an ordinance requesting that 'Both
spiritual and secular officials endeavour, by friendly exhortation and practical
means, to persuade parents who have musically gifted children not to deter them
from practising but to encourage them, so that the choir will not be short of
members.' In 1681 the authorities in Glauchau set out to discuss how the *chorus
musicus* could be improved because most of its members were no longer
able to help the singing in church. All but the smallest churches had been
used to elaborate music at weddings, but after the middle 1660s, few could
manage more than hymns with organ accompaniment; this, apparently, was

rather to prevent bad music than an admission of the collapse of choirs, for some choirs, missing the payment, protested against this curtailment of their duties.

Apparently Luther's instructions about the necessity of musically competent teachers had not been obeyed, for at Oschatz in 1683 teachers themselves asked the school authorities to look for teachers with musical qualifications 'as the choir is already seriously denuded of singers, and very few of those who are left have voices, so that the burden of maintaining the church music comes from the teaching faculty, as the other members neglect the choir for the sake of their livelihood'. The Oschatz schoolmasters at least suggest a reason for the breakdown; the real culprit was the war and the poverty which followed it. At any rate the Oschatz teachers pointed out that a hundred years before schoolmasters who did not measure up to the Reformer's musical standards had actually lost their jobs in the Palatinate.

The effectiveness of the remedy is something we cannot now judge. In the *Kreuzschule* in Dresden, the *Thomasschule* in Leipzig and the *Michaelisschule* in Lüneburg, amongst many others, tradition gave a pattern for the creation of school choirs able to tackle the ambitious music which Lutheran congregations expected. St. Michael's in Lüneburg was the only one of the three—there were many similar foundations—which had in any way modified its system after the Thirty Years' War. While its choral scholars had to be 'the offspring of poor people, with nothing to live on, but good voices', the school around them was transformed into a *Ritterakademie*, a boarding school 'for the sons of gentlemen', as a Victorian public school in England might have described itself. It offered lessons in subjects not available in the town schools—French and Italian could be studied—and it treated its choral scholars as a *Mettenchor*, paid for its professional services not only by their education and board but also by a small stipend as they progressed up the school. J. S. Bach, entering the choir as an elderly treble of fourteen in 1700 and probably accepted because he was a good violinist, earned 12 groschen a month and his share of the *Accidenten* earned through weddings, funerals and the *Kurrende* processions through the city organised as a means of collecting money for the choir. Bach also had the advantage of being able to learn French with his social superiors. The *Mettenchor* at St. Michael's was supposed to have a minimum of twenty-five singers. In 1660 it was thirty strong, in 1681 it had more than twenty. The town choir of boys at the *Johannischule*, whose music was vital to the town churches, was short of at least nine Foundation scholars (here as elsewhere poor boys were given their education for the sake of their singing) in 1694. Those whom he had, the cantor complained, were so badly trained that it was impossible for him to do his duty to his own satisfaction.[1]

In 1676 St. Thomas's in Leipzig had a hundred and sixty-seven pupils. Of these, fifty-six were choral scholars who provided a choir of thirteen trebles,

[1] Horst Walter: *Musikgeschichte der Stadt Lüneburg*. Hans Schneiduer, Tutzing, 1967.

twelve altos, eighteen tenors and thirteen basses. Five and a half years later the number of foundation scholars for the choir had gone down to forty-eight.[1]

To create a *Kantorei* or *Chorus Symphoniacus* for *concertato*-style church music within a school meant to draw all the voices required from among boys of between about ten and eighteen years of age. The task is not impossible, but the results in a work like the *St. Matthew Passion*, with the Evangelist and Christus sung by (one hopes) well-trained boys whose voices remained immature, or at best by undergraduates from the university, suggests that Bach tended to outrun the limitations set by practicability. Undergraduates in Leipzig were traditionally paid for assisting in the church music on Sundays and Feast Days; apart from singers, J. S. Bach needed them to augment the strings and for some of the woodwind instruments. In towns like Mühlhausen, where an amateur choir and orchestra had existed almost throughout the seventeenth century, the boys had adult reinforcements for any special service with specially elaborate music, hence the massiveness of *Gott ist mein König*, Bach's *Ratswahl* Cantata (No. 51) for Mühlhausen. But in Leipzig a school choir of about fifty was expected in some way to manage the music of four city churches.

The practical difficulties of dwindling choirs and church orchestras, a long-term result of the Thirty Years' War, was accompanied by the growth of Pietism, a new reforming movement. Lutheranism was stately, formal, impersonal. Its worship followed ancient traditions and left little room for personal devotion. Like the rise of Methodism in England, the rise of Pietism in Germany was a demand for less formal, intensely personal religion.

In 1675 a book *Pia Desideria* by a Lutheran pastor, Spener, appeared at the moment when Lutheranism, with its close ties to secular government, its formalism and its devotion to old traditions, seemed dry enough to many of its adherents to need a powerful injection of enthusiasm. Pietism was not a movement which resisted scholarship or discounted its value in comparison to intense feeling but it voiced a demand for simplicity, spontaneity and the expression of individual feeling in religion. It tended to reject the idea of worship represented by large congregations whose chief function was to listen to long musical works exploiting all the tricks and lures of secular music. It was the sworn enemy of the church orchestra and the slowly evolving church cantata.

Yet this attitude in some ways worked unknowingly for the things it rejected. Though the orchestral semi-operatic form of church music was fundamentally secular and irrelevant to religion, it was still a vehicle for personal expression, for a sense of excitement in religion. The rise of Pietism, which had become a powerful reform movement by 1700, coincided with that of the church cantata which, following the work of Buxtehude, united the two *concertato* traditions and the new excitements and emotionalism of opera in a single work. It was of course anathema to the Pietists, who saw in it the sacrilege of taking into the church the most worldly of all musical forms, but at the same time it suggested

[1] Bernhard Krick: *St. Thomas zu Leipzig; Schule und Chor*. Breitkopf and Härtel, Wiesbaden, 1963.

to composers that the untrammelled expression of their own religious perceptions and beliefs was a valid religious activity.

Intellectual sympathy with Pietism was quickly aroused, but many intellectual sympathisers rejected Pietist ideals once they were put into action. Luther's creation was not merely a church but the one divine church created by Christ and, through Luther's teachings, purged of its pre-Reformation errors. To teach the necessity for deeper personal involvement in religion, for intenser devotion and individual commitment was not offensive. To suggest that the Lutheran church itself was imperfect and in need of change was another matter. In Mühlhausen, for example, Pietist and non-Pietist clergy attached to the town churches were engaged in a holy war with each other, and the musicians— for a time J. S. Bach was town organist there—were open to attack by both sides as well as by old-fashioned music lovers who had been happy enough with the music of the past to resent any changes.

At the same time, while choirs were disintegrating or being rebuilt from the schools, and while a growing body of Pietists were attempting to undermine the liturgical principles which were the justification of the cantor's work, the cost of the music he provided was increasing year by year. At the beginning of the Baroque period the *Stadtpfeifer* band and its auxiliaries, perhaps six or seven players, with perhaps two or three apprentices, had been all the orchestra a cantor needed or could expect. At St. Mary's, Lübeck, Tunder had found a lutenist and a violist engaged for very important days like that on which the council and magistrates officially attended service. He collected strings and trombones and used them as often as possible. Buxtehude's *Abendmusik* depended on a standardised eighteenth-century orchestra of strings, trumpets, trombones, woodwind and drums. As the orchestra became standardised outside the church the cantor was expected to write for a standardised orchestra; the trouble in Munich between the guild of trumpeters and the city musicians who tried to reduce costs by playing trumpet parts on slide trumpets[1] was repeated elsewhere. The cost of church music was increasing and both authorities and the majority of worshippers seem to have approved of the expansion of music. The trouble was to find the money to pay for it, for German town councillors who found that the arts need to be financed were often as nonplussed as those of British cities today when the same need arises.

The vicissitudes of the Leipzig cantor are well chronicled. He taught music and Latin in the school as any cantor was still expected to do. He was responsible for the big *concertato* work at the Sunday morning service and the motet or concerto-style work which, with an often elaborate *Magnificat*, was sung at Vespers. Each of the greater feasts demanded as much music as a Sunday and at least as much rehearsal. He was never expected to build up a regular year's repertory of church music, and was certainly not encouraged to do so. Ideally, in the view of his employers and the congregation which was his audience there was no more point in repeating music, apart from the familiar hymns, than

[1] See Chapter 5, p. 68.

there would have been in repeating sermons. The cantor was under attack if he did not produce new music in an up-to-date style, but he was expected to do so at no real cost to the city authorities.

Johann Kuhnau, a very good musician, a gifted scholar and an amusing writer, has naturally been overshadowed because J. S. Bach was his successor. Kuhnau was a boy at the *Kreuzschule* in Dresden and went to Leipzig in 1682 when he was twenty-two years old. He became organist at St. Thomas's, founded the town *Collegium Musicum* in 1688 and, in 1700, after he had graduated in law to qualify himself for a cantor's post (the cantor's duty of teaching in the school made it more or less necessary that he should be a graduate), he became musical director of the university and a year later cantor at the *Thomaskirche*. It was Kuhnau who introduced the church cantata to Leipzig while engaged in a running battle with the authorities. As he was a more amenable person than his mighty successor he succeeded in getting more of his own way than Bach, and he did so at less cost in anger and bitterness.

In 1709 Kuhnau addressed a memorandum to the council about the needs of both the *Thomasschule* and the church. The school needed a new violin because the one in use there was almost in pieces through over-use. A new regal was needed, for the old one was simply patched up from bits and pieces. The school needed a new colocion (colascione, or Carslute); Kuhnau could get hold of good, cheap instruments from amateurs. The choir gallery in St. Nicholas's needed to be repaired if the *Stadtpfeifer* were not to break their legs or at least their ankles. The St. Nicholas choir gallery was a perpetual bone of contention; it was too small for the choir and orchestra though the *Hauptgottesdienst* was sung on alternate Sundays there and at St. Thomas's.

In his predecessor's time, Kuhnau pointed out, there had always been a few boys, perhaps four or five, more than the minimum needed. Now there were barely enough for the duties that had to be done. The greatest trouble for church music in Leipzig, he explained, was the opera and music in the New Church. The Leipzig Opera had won the allegiance of the students who had in the past been willing auxiliaries of the cantor and the Thomas choir; the cantor had depended on university singers and university instrumentalists, but the singers could earn more by acting as auxiliaries to the opera company. Even those undergraduates who had been *Thomasschule* boys had been seduced from their allegiance. At the New Church, the organist in 1704 had been Georg Philipp Telemann, appointed while still a law student. Telemann was already a popular composer for the Opera and the creator of the university *Collegium Musicum*. Musically he was a modernist, influenced by the lightness and rhythmic vitality of French music, and his prestige drew students to the New Church where the music was lively, operatic and surprising. When Telemann moved on his successors carried on the tradition he had started. With the student's *Collegium* to support its singers—the New Church depended on four solo singers, not a full choir, and the singers were highly trained and active at the Opera—the music there was excellent if unduly and shockingly worldly.

Kuhnau's report went on to discuss his instrumentalists, 'the *Stadtpfeifer*, *Kunstgeiger* and apprentices'. The *Stadtpfeifer* provided him with 'two or more trumpeters, 2 oboists or cornettists, three trombonists or players of similar instruments, and a bassoonist'. The *Kunstgeiger* provided eight players. He wanted to be able to double any viola part, but he had not the players to do it. He wanted stronger bass players to support the voices of his immature bass singers.

Obviously the cantor, for the sakes of his church and its congregation and of his own reputation and prestige, had to keep abreast of the latest developments whether in *Collegia* and music societies or in the performance of well-drilled professional musicians in a nobleman's court or a public opera house. The fact that Leipzig would not allow Kuhnau, or Bach after him, the money to gather performers of equivalent ability to those of the theatre may have been the reason why when Kuhnau died in 1722 the Council made every effort to bring Telemann back to Leipzig as cantor at St. Thomas's. Telemann, however, had accepted the equivalent post at St. John's Hamburg only a year before; his work there spread out into public concert-giving and opera as well as the church services. His reputation enabled him to get rid of those parts of the cantor's work, like the teaching of Latin, which he disliked. So he simply induced the Hamburg town council to raise his salary by pointing out that Leipzig had offered him a post, and made no real effort to move once they had done so.

Kuhnau introduced the Cantata to Leipzig congregations. Unlike many of his contemporaries he went close to secular models; Johann Christoph Bach, Johann Sebastian's brilliant great-cousin, who was town organist at Eisenach ('This is the great expressive Bach,' Johann Sebastian's most revolutionary son, Carl Philipp Emanuel, told the musicologist-biographer, Forkel), was eighteen years older than Kuhnau, and never described a work as a cantata or adopted aria form. Buxtehude, twenty-three years Kuhnau's senior, avoided recitatives and *da capo* arias. Possibly the recitative seemed, to Lutheran congregations, to be the hall-mark of opera, the entirely secular creation which could not be sanctified, because it entered into church music only slowly. Eventually it became the special distinctive feature which turned the church 'concerto' and works in *concertato* style into the cantata.

When Kuhnau's first cantatas were offered to the Leipzig congregations, he presented them with a printed text of the first set, introduced by an essay called *Plan of the Foundations of Cantata Composition*.[1]

> In these compositions, [he wrote] I have tried . . . to give music to the language of the Bible, in its own beauty without the introduction of any foreign matter. This means that they contain no arias or poetical paraphrases. I myself have compiled the texts of the works for Advent Sunday and for Michaelmas, introducing in them one or more verses of our familiar German hymns. I should have continued to work in this way if I had been able to find the time, but I had to find a good friend to take on the labour of collecting the texts.

---

[1] Quoted in Krick, *op. cit.*

I must acknowledge that arias, when they express pathetic words in certain metres and rhythms, give to music a grace which is not easy to find when prose is sung. Nevertheless, I stood firm by my resolution not, in these works, to write arias and recitatives and thus not lay myself open to the accusation of writing in a theatrical style. There are, however, only a few who really understand what the essential difference between church and theatrical music is. . . . In one as in the other, pathetic and emotionally moving words can be found. The essential difference between the two styles is that by the one the hearer is moved to holy devotion, Love, Joy, Sorrow and Pain, while the other offers to the genuine and innocent amateur of music a harmless entertainment while giving the more sensually-minded a pleasure which he may come to need increasingly the more he hears of it. But the Holy Place and the Holy Text demand all the Art, Splendour, Modesty and Honour the composer can give to them. In profane works, delightful passages may be interspersed with others which are weak, trivial, satirical, excessively lively and written against the rules of art.

For the rest, the simple words, in prose, no arias (although the hymns, familiar and belonging to works of this kind, are a similar type of music) . . . call for all possible invention and variation, without which music lacks fineness and delight.

It is difficult to know whether Kuhnau was explaining to a doubtful public that a style new to them could be so tactfully presented, shorn of its distinctive links with opera, that they would like it and cheerfully allow the thin edge of a new wedge to be driven in, or whether he was simply declaring his allegiance to a modified form of cantata. His objections to the use of arias and recitatives are not violent or strongly expressed. Nor is the distinction he draws between church and theatre music one which forcibly ejects the specially theatrical forms from the Church. In a sense the Kuhnau type of cantata—separate numbers or movements setting Biblical texts and commenting upon them in verses from popular chorales—is a type of composition widely used in Lutheran churches from the 1670s onward. The wedge was eventually driven home without any difficulty; the questions of nomenclature and terminology obscure some events, but though Bach clung to the old name 'concerto' for his compositions when he reached Leipzig in 1723 and continued for a time to use it, his church concertos were cantatas, not all of which include arias and recitatives; some of them are lengthy, elaborate and splendid treatments of chorale words and melodies. But those which utilised the essentially theatrical forms, evolving the poetical recitatives which Bach handled with great eloquence and beauty, seem to have been accepted without complaint by a Council which was never able to forget that it appointed him because it could not get either of the musicians it really wanted.

For all that what he called the light-hearted, operatic style of music, which had persisted at the New Church since Telemann had been organist there, annoyed Kuhnau. To some extent his irritation was probably musical; but the existence of a church making music outside his jurisdiction was a blow to both his income and his prestige. If its music were good his reputation would suffer because he did not perform works in the same style and at the same standard. As the chief musical authority in Leipzig his reputation would suffer just as much if the music in the New Church was bad. In 1720 he addressed to the Council *A Proposal whereby Leipzig Church Music might be improved*.[1] In it, he wrote sorely of the state of music at the New Church, where it depended upon students (many of whom, as old boys of the *Thomasschule*, might from gratitude to the school and to him as their ex-teacher, have continued to sing at the two principal churches with the *Thomaschor*) who were eager enough to sing at the opera but were casual in their practice and performance of church music. It should be possible for the council to appoint a permanent organist to be musical director of the New Church, and to pay him between 10 and 25 florins above a normal organist's salary to meet the expenses and trouble he would have to face in finding or providing music, for paper and for copyist's fees. Kuhnau was careful not to suggest that the university might be given a cantor and thus have its music controlled by someone who could claim equal status with him.

Alternatively he, as cantor, could take charge of music in the New Church. This would mean that *Hauptgottesdienst*, with its elaborate orchestral music, instead of moving on alternate Sundays from St. Thomas's to St. Nicholas's, would take in the New Church, so that the choir and orchestra would be heard in each of the three churches on one Sunday in every three. This would be a means of bringing back the defaulting students to the *Thomaschor*, to which Kuhnau felt convinced they owed a duty. They and the other auxiliaries should be willing to rehearse and sing simply for the sake of the church and the honour of God, but it should be possible to exclude them from contributing to the collection; a proportion of the collection could, on the other hand, be reserved as their payment with a share of the *Kantorei* meal which, if they were to be ready for Vespers in the afternoon, was obviously a necessity. On the Sundays when the full choir was not at the New Church he could send a group of singers to it as he sent groups to St. Peter's and St. Matthew's.

Kuhnau's *Proposal* is made in terms of helpful gentleness and was sufficiently effective to put the music in the New Church under the cantor's control, where it lost its glory; from then on its singing became simply congregational and was led by a group of the least accomplished boys from the choir. The modernists transferred themselves to the university church, St. Paul's, which was not under the cantor's control, to clash with Bach in 1723.

Originally the university church had appointed Kuhnau as *Director Chori Musices* at a salary of 12 gulden a year. He had to direct *Gottesdienst* there on certain festivals, like Reformation Sunday, and for certain academic services. In 1710, the university instituted the reformed, shorter and less musical service, the *Neu Gottesdienst* as a regular Sunday service, and appointed its own musical director. Kuhnau protested, not against the provision of regular Sunday services but against the creation of another authority in the town's music. None the less the university appointed a law student, Johann Friedrich Fasch, to

[1] *Akten des Rats der Stadt Leipzig*, VII B. 31 Fol. 7. Quoted in Krick, *op. cit.*

be director of music in the university church. To demonstrate his authority Kuhnau declared that he would direct the old service on the special occasions when it was used, according to his contract, and the new service on Sundays, without any extra pay; he was determined to prove that the town cantor was *ex-officio* musical director of the university.

This was a diminution of the cantor's authority which Bach had to face as soon as he was appointed. When Leipzig had believed that Telemann would accept the cantor's post at St. Thomas's, the university promptly offered him its musical directorship, but three weeks before Bach was appointed it appointed its own director, Johann Gottlieb Görner. Bach was not the man to forgive a slight or to tolerate any diminution of his salary. He asserted his claim to Görner's position by demanding the 12 gulden which had been the cantor's fee for taking care of the university music when Kuhnau had been in control of it before the appointment of Fasch. The university pointed out that it had its own musical director; Bach replied that he was responsible for the old service on those days when it was used, and that any arrangements the university made could not override his authority over that. The council paid him most of the 12 gulden, but kept 12 florins from it towards Görner's pay.

Bach's aim was not simply a necessary augmentation of his salary but the preservation of his office and its authority. What he wanted was a clear statement about his place in the university music, and the squabble continued through several undignified quarrels over works commissioned from him for university occasions but not by the university. Görner could not be expected to work efficiently if the cantor continued to overrule his decisions; his prestige would suffer if every special occasion meant that he was by-passed and the music needed was commissioned from Bach. Eventually, in 1728, the council got Bach's agreement that he would no longer accept commissions for music to be used at the university unless it was commissioned by the council. Bach, in other words, had lost.

It would be easy to dismiss this particular thirty-years' quarrel, in which two successive cantors were involved, as a squalid little row between self-important people whose minds could not rise above trivialities. But in the context of life in the German cities in the fifty or sixty years that followed the Thirty Years' War it shows clearly why neither Kuhnau nor Bach could retreat into an ivory tower and compose, sacrificing the fringes of their jobs—like the control of music in the New Church or the university church—to the important business of writing what they wanted to write.

The cantor's conditions of work, like those of the town organist and the *Stadtmusikus*, and his salary, like their salaries, had been determined before the war. He was still the school's Latin teacher though such musical developments as the stabilisation of the church orchestra had complicated his work. Prices had risen, as prices always do, during the war and, as prices always do, had failed to fall again; but the town musicians, whatever their place in the hierarchy, were paid at rates decided more than a century before and drew part of their pay in kind. The Leipzig cantor's basic salary was 87 thaler 12 groschen a year (at Cöthen, Bach had been paid 400 thaler). He was entitled to an allowance of 13 thaler 3 groschen for firewood and lighting, and to his share of the *Accidenten*, and a quarter—again his fixed share—of the choral scholars' fee for tuition, a matter of about sixpence; when the scholars needed to raise the money for this, they processed singing round the town to win it from the citizens. In a good year for marriages and funerals, he could hope to earn as much as 700 florins.

At the beginning of his career, when he became town organist at Arnstadt in 1703, his salary was 50 florins, and he was allowed an extra 34 florins to pay for board and lodgings. He had to play for the Sunday services at the New Church ('new' because it replaced St. Boniface's, burnt down in 1581) and at extra-liturgical service on Mondays and Thursdays; his choir was a small group of boys from the Latin school, equivalent to an English grammar school, which he had to train because the school did not employ a cantor. The Arnstadt salary was good for a musician of eighteen who was a phenomenal organist but incapable of getting good singing from a choir of adolescent hard cases sent to him because they were not good enough to be used in any of the other churches. Bach, aggressive and quick-tempered—it was in Arnstadt that he fought a town bassoonist—gave up any attempt to work with the choir, took four weeks' leave to hear Buxtehude's *Abendmusik* in Lübeck, stayed for four months and then got into trouble not only for extending his absence but for the complexity of his accompaniments to the chorales; then, after an interval oddly peaceful for Bach, who disliked criticism more than most men, he was in trouble for taking Maria Barbara, whom he was soon to marry, into the organ gallery to sing.

Just thirty years before Johann Sebastian Bach had been appointed in Arnstadt, his uncle Johann Christoph Bach had become a town musician there, and a violinist in the orchestra of Count Ludwig Günther of Schwarzburg-Arnstadt, whose *Kapelle* consisted almost exclusively of such part-time musicians; his work, though less responsible than his nephew's, earned 30 florins with allowance of wood and grain. Johann Christoph Bach, the cousin of Johann Sebastian's father, had become town organist in Eisenach in 1665. Johann Christoph, like Johann Sebastian, was hot-tempered, aggressive and arrogant; Eisenach was not a wealthy town and Johann Christoph, arriving without money, found it hard to collect the quarterly instalments of his salary which had been promised to him to set him on his feet for his first year. He complained that he had been humiliated by the number of times he had been compelled to apply for each instalment. In 1679 he complained that 42 florins 20 groschen (not far from half his salary of 100 florins) was owing to him in unpaid *Accidenten*. Johann Sebastian's father, Johann Ambrosius, earned 40 florins, 4 groschen and 8 pfennige as *Stadtmusikus* of Erfurt. A florin was equal to 1 thaler and 3 groschen, and a thaler amounted to a little more than three shillings of the English money of the period. There were 21 groschen in a florin, and Karl Geiringer[1] quotes a price list printed in the *Bach Journal* of 1927. To sole a pair of men's shoes in the

[1] Karl Geiringer: *The Bach Family.* George Allen and Unwin, 1954.

1680s cost twelve groschen; two pounds of bread cost 1 groschen. Arnstadt considered that 34 florins were enough to pay for a man's board and lodgings; Johann Sebastian's salary there was less than twice his allowance for his keep. The musician employed by a city was not going to be rich, and 12 gulden (about two-thirds of a florin) paid for supervising the university music, if it slipped away into other hands, would leave a gap in the income of a musician with a family as excessive as Johann Sebastian's.

In disgrace at Arnstadt in 1707, Johann Sebastian moved to a similar post at Mühlhausen where he was paid 85 florins and an allowance of grain, wood and fish. After three years he left Mühlhausen to become a court musician first at Weimar, where in five years his salary rose from 150 to 250 thaler, and then at Cöthen.

The Bach who left Calvinist Cöthen to be cantor at Leipzig in order to ensure an orthodox Lutheran education for his sons and in order to organise Lutheran church music in the new age of the Cantata—he gave both reasons for his move—was losing financially by doing so, as well as sacrificing social prestige. He never described himself as cantor, but always more impressively as *Director Musices* or, after his honorary appointment as Court Composer to the Elector of Saxony, as *Kapellmeister*.

The Leipzig council believed that it was making the best of a bad job when it appointed him. Telemann would not come, Graupner from Darmstadt, also better known than Bach, could not obtain his dismissal to take up new work. Therefore Bach, although without a university degree he could not be regarded as properly qualified to teach, was appointed. In addition they discovered that he was not an effective disciplinarian, that he flew into violent rages and that he was apparently incapable of treating municipal authorities with the respect they thought they deserved. The quarrel with the university, which he inherited, was the first of many, in all of which he struggled to keep the cantor's powers and responsibilities as they were laid down by tradition.

In 1728 he insisted on his right as cantor to choose with the preacher all the hymns except those already laid down in the liturgy for the day. His right was contested by a deacon at St. Nicholas's, the church which alternated with St. Thomas's as the one in which the musical *Hauptgottesdienst* was sung. For once he accepted a compromise, agreeing to waive his privilege so long as the hymns were chosen from a collection of which he approved.

His quarrels with the council, his employers, were more bitter. In 1729 there were nine vacancies for choral scholars in the school, and Bach examined twenty-three candidates. The council appointed ten boys—four sopranos and an alto Bach had accepted, four boys whom he had rejected and one who had not attended the examination. He promptly and ostentatiously began to neglect his school duties and this, together with his other failings, caused the council in 1730 to withhold his salary until he had given clear signs of repentance and amendment. The result was a long report on the state of Leipzig church music written in a tone of weary tolerance, as of one compelled to explain the self-evident to the stupid, which must have angered his employers even more than his casual defiance of them had done.

To perform church music as it should be performed, he explained, both singers and instrumentalists are needed. The *Thomasschule* provided all four voices. The music needed soloists and choralists; if the choir was not divided into two choruses, it needed one soloist to each voice, but if it sang in two choruses, as many as eight soloists might be needed and there must be at least two singers to each choral part.

The foundation scholars of the school, he pointed out, provided him with fifty-five singers from whom he had to find the singers for four churches, in which were heard either the 'figural', concerted music performed in alternate weeks at St. Thomas's or St. Nicholas's, or motets or merely hymns at the two others. The music at St. Thomas's, St. Nicholas's and the New Church was sung in parts; at the fourth church, St. Peter's, the choir simply led the singing of hymns in unison. Except at St. Peter's, twelve singers were needed in each choir, so that there would be three singers to each voice, and even if any of the singers was unable to sing, it would still be possible to sing an eight-part motet. Thirty-six boys, therefore, were needed who could sing part music, and the situation would be improved if the choir could be divided into groups of sixteen, four voices to each part.

Instrumentally, he explained, he needed two or even three first violins, two or three second violins, two violas, two cellos and a double-bass, two, if not three, oboes, one or two bassoons, three trumpets and a timpanist, at least eighteen players. He needed flautists (flutes, he kindly explained, 'are of two kinds, *a bec*'— that is, recorders—'or *traversieri*'), adding another two to the necessary total of players. But the council maintained eight—four wind players (the *Stadtpfeifer*), three strings (the *Kunstgeiger*) and an apprentice. Their 'competence and musicianship' were topics he would not discuss. Some of them were ready to be pensioned off and the others were out of practice.

Therefore he needed three trumpeters, a timpanist, a viola player, a cellist, a double-bass player and three oboists; he also wanted two first and two second violins, two violists, two cellists and two flute players. These parts had in the past been supplied by university students and by scholars. The students had played partly because they enjoyed doing so and partly because they used to be paid. 'The occasional *beneficia* which used to find their way into the pockets of the *chorus musicus* have vanished,' he pointed out, 'and the students have vanished with them. Nobody likes to work for nothing.' The shortage of instrumentalists had driven Bach to use boys from the school 'invariably' as violists, cellists and double-bassist, often as second violinists, thus weakening the choir. As these were the requirements of normal Sunday music, he pointed out, the situation at the great festivals, when the shortage of instrumentalists limited his ambitions, was even more serious; he had to rob the choir to provide enough players.

(This throws some light on the first performance of the *St. Matthew Passion*.

This report was written in August, 1730; the *Passion* was written for Good Friday, 1729.)

At the same time, having told the council a number of facts which, as the administrators of the choir and town musicians, they must have known perfectly well, and having done so in a tone of deliberately infuriating patience, he turned gently to the attack. In recent times, he pointed out, so many untrained, incompetent boys had been admitted to the choir that standards had been lowered and would go on falling. It was obviously pointless to take on boys who had neither musical knowledge nor good natural voices. Even boys with some knowledge of music were put into the choir before they were properly trained; when good singers left, bad ones were put into their place. This was a process which had been going on for a long time; his predecessors since Schelle (who had been cantor from 1676 until his death in 1701, when Kuhnau succeeded to the post) had both been compelled to bring in students whenever they had a big work to perform. If the council wanted to restore the standards of music they should make a grant out of which not only the necessary instrumentalists but also three solo singers—an alto, a tenor and a bass—could be paid.

> Modern music [Bach concluded] is quite different from music in the past. Its technique is more complex, and the taste of the public has changed so much that old music sounds quite strange to us. We have to take greater care in obtaining performers who are capable of satisfying modern taste and are instructed in modern technique, to say nothing of the composer's desire to hear his works properly performed. The gratuities, though they were inconsiderable in themselves, were once available for the *chorus musicus* and have now been withdrawn. It is astonishing that everyone expects German musicians to play at sight whatever music is put in front of them, whether it comes from Italy, France, England, or Poland, just as if they were the musicians for whom it was written and who enjoy large salaries as well as leisure in which to learn and master their parts. People do not understand this but leave our players to do the best they can; they have to earn their living, and this gives them little time to perfect their technique and still less to become virtuosi. One example is enough: let anyone go to Dresden and see how the orchestra is paid. The musicians are sure of their livelihood and live without anxiety; each of them is able to develop his talent for his instrument and make himself into an efficient performer to whom it is a pleasure to listen. The lesson is plain; the withdrawing of the *beneficia* which used to be paid to them makes it impossible for me to put the music on a better footing.

What Bach was asking for was a considerably larger annual expenditure on music, which was more than the city could afford. The cost of 'modern' music was too high to be paid by the traditional methods. A decline had set in for example at Lüneburg just as it had in Leipzig. In Darmstadt in 1752 Graupner, the *Kapellmeister*, recommended Albrecht Ludwig Abele to be cantor of the Royal School in charge of the music in the town church. When Abele arrived the catalogue of the school's music and instruments was a series of complaints. 'All the written music is falling apart, a lot of it unusable.' The school owned 'an organ, two violins, two bad violins, two violas, two clarinets in C, a usable double bass and a pair of recorders'.[1] In a year Abele asked for his dismissal and left. His successor, Hertzberger, complained in 1765 about the shortage of good soloists, pointing out that a really good tenor soloist for the *Stadtkirche* would cost 300 florins, and, a few months later, said that the church music went like a four-footed animal with only three legs. Bach, arrogantly aggressive and prepared to stop working if things were not to his liking, would have had the same sort of trouble as that which was his lot in Leipzig in many German cities.

Only a year passed between the withholding of Bach's salary and the appointment of August Ernesti as rector, and thus Bach's superior. Ernesti was a good scholar—a theologian, a philologist and a classicist. He was too a serious educationalist and a man of the Enlightenment; to Ernesti, the *Thomasschule* was a potentially valuable institution hamstrung by its refusal to change with the times. Simply to continue as a choir school, subordinating all other educational purposes to the needs of the church choir was, he believed, wrong; it should offer a wider and more practical system of education. An eighteenth-century commercial centre like Leipzig needed a system of education which taught languages and mathematics for practical purposes. Instead, such cities had schools which spent too much of their time on music and turned out boys who were highly trained in a useless specialization. The poor boys who were the Foundation scholars might be specially equipped by nature for a career in music, but the Foundation scholars were only about one-third of the school's numbers.

Of course any twentieth-century parent imagining himself back in the Leipzig of the 1730s would probably agree with Ernesti's criticisms; the teaching in the *Thomasschule* was slanted towards specialisation in music and had not modified its late medieval view of what was educationally necessary in spite of the vast changes that had taken place in the world. Bach, on the other hand, had sacrificed a better-paid, socially more advanced career to serve the cause of Lutheran church music; or he himself thought that he had done so. He believed in the work he did and was convinced of both its necessity and its value. The council's handling of the school administration was making his work hardly worth the trouble it cost him, for the council refused to finance the improvement of the musical establishment and left him with so ineffective a choir that he had to write solo cantatas instead of the elaborately colourful works he preferred; almost all the solo cantatas seem to have been written in the three years after his Great Expostulation to the council. They were not a cycle but were apparently meant to fill in gaps when on Sundays, the available cantata was beyond the choir's power. Almost everyone of the solo cantatas belongs to a Sunday or a feast day for which Bach had already provided a much more ambitious work; one or two of the solo cantatas are replaced by large-scale later works.

[1] Elisabeth Noack: *Musikgeschichte Darmstadts vom Mittelalter bis zur Goethezeit. Beiträge zur Mittelrheinischen Musikgeschichte.* Schott, Mainz, 1967.

To say that, according to his contemporaries, Bach wrote five complete cycles of some fifty-nine cantatas for the ecclesiastical year does not necessarily mean that he set out to do so. It means that as soon as he could he assembled a cycle of cantatas for the year, probably using in it works composed at Mühlhausen and Weimar, and that having done so, he added to the cycle works which seemed either better or better adapted to the Leipzig situation than some which already existed; and then, because his was the sort of mind which worked in cycles (so that there are two Preludes and Fugues both major and minor for every degree of the chromatic scale, and solo works for violin and for cello exploiting all the keys most natural to them), to have some of an incomplete second cycle, some of an incomplete third cycle and possibly one or two of an incomplete fourth cycle more or less simultaneously in stock would be a constant irritation until he had set all of them in their proper context.

The task of assembling all the cantatas he would need during his reign as cantor—and it was not until 1730, when he realised that his Grand Expostulation was going to have no effect, that he made any serious effort to escape—was a heavy task. Norman Carroll[1] shows how he cannibalised earlier works to provide cantata movements, turning works for solo instruments and, especially, chamber and orchestral works written in Cöthen, into what he needed for cantatas and piecing together large tracts of the *Christmas Oratorio* from mainly secular works; just as he converted a *Siciliano* from the fourth of his Violin and Clavier Sonatas into the piercing duet for alto and violin *Erbarme dich* in the *St. Matthew Passion*.

These were the circumstances in which Ernesti began to set out to reform the school by making music seem a worthless occupation to its pupils. 'Another pot-house fiddler!' he would remark in apparent despair when he saw a boy practising. His campaign was carried out in the way most likely to infuriate Bach who seems to have preferred a stand-up fight to a campaign of ridicule.

Eventually the quarrel became one over the rival authority of rector and cantor. In 1736 Bach appointed a prefect whom Ernesti attempted to punish for over-severity. The prefect ran away and Bach refused to accept the boy appointed in his place by Ernesti. The boy claimed that Bach refused him only to show that it was the cantor's right to make such appointments. Bach's appeal to the council for support, on the grounds that he could not allow the authority of the cantor to be undermined, brought no decision but moved Ernesti to put his own case to the council, and the quarrel, which so far had used the boys as a battle-ground, moved into the official world. Ernesti accused Bach of neglecting his duties and suggested that he was open to bribery in the matter of appointments. Bach made fresh but fruitless efforts to find a new appointment; the title of Court Composer to the Elector of Saxony in November 1736 did not apparently increase his prestige in Leipzig; the council would not commit itself to a decision about the rival claims of rector and cantor. Eventually the Elector was asked for a ruling; he gave it in private, and all we know about it is that it made Bach's

[1] *Bach the Borrower*. George Allen and Unwin, 1967.

position easier. Nevertheless, the burly, hot-tempered genial man of the early portraits had by this time turned into the grim, embittered personality of the later ones; the change in Bach which painters reproduced is explicable only in terms of his Leipzig anxieties, for he was an apparently affectionate father determined to do his best for the unusually gifted sons of whom he was proud.

He published little, only some of his keyboard music. It was more or less customary to publish the libretti of major choral works—that of the Good Friday Passion of 1739 had to be withdrawn after publication because he had not submitted it to the council—but the expense of publishing the music was beyond anything that might be raised from its publication. Apparently some of the cantatas had at least some circulation in manuscript. As an organ specialist, he was highly regarded everywhere within easy reach of his own town. In all his sixty-five years he never moved out of the area in which the Bach family had always made music, from Lüneburg in the north to Leipzig in the south, except for his youthful visit to Lübeck.

Soon after circumstances changed. His son Wilhelm Friedemann, at Halle after 1746, was expected to produce concerted music only on feast days and the third Sunday of every month. Carl Philipp Emanuel Bach became cantor at Hamburg when Telemann died in 1767, administering the complicated musical life of the city, protesting against the limited funds available and, unlike his father, reconciling himself to inevitable mediocrity in the church and concentrating his ambitions on his series of subscription concerts. The type of music to which Johann Sebastian had given his life had grown too big for the methods of finance which existed to care for it.

Ernesti's views of the *Thomasschule* were right, and so were Bach's. Bach saw the institution as its founders had seen it; its equivalent was not a grammar school but a cathedral or college choir school, and if it could not justify itself in Bach's eyes purely by its musical abilities, it should be improved until it did so. In other words, the school was expected to do two jobs and therefore did neither well.

Bach's successor at Leipzig was Gottlob Harrer, who was succeeded by Johann Friedrich Doles, who had been a boy at the *Thomasschule*. Doles, in 1744, wrote a cantata to celebrate the first anniversary of the concert society which had grown out of the *Collegium Musicum* and in which Bach took no interest. As Thomas cantor, Doles had only two churches to serve and, incidentally, it was he who showed Mozart the scores of Bach motets in 1789, the year of his retirement.

Doles had been appointed cantor at Freiberg in 1744, to find himself involved in a struggle with the rector, Johann Gottlieb Biedermann, which echoes the struggle for supremacy between Bach and Ernesti. Biedermann, like Ernesti an impressive scholar, regarded the pre-eminence of music in the school as a danger to educational progress. In 1748, however, he decided that the school should produce a *Singspiel* in the city *Kaufhaus* to celebrate the hundredth

anniversary of the Peace of Westphalia which ended the Hundred Years' War.
Doles wrote the music, scored a great success and, to the annoyance of Biedermann, found his prestige in the school higher than it had ever been. Biedermann's
next public entertainment was an adaptation of the *Mostellaria* by Plautus, the
programme of which set out to show that too much music seduces the young
into luxury and self-indulgence, and refers to Horace's description of musicians
as vagabonds, quacks and beggars. The ancient church had banished them and
permitted them to receive the sacrament only once a year.

   This was a considered public attack on Doles and on the educational policy of
the school fought for the same causes but on even more trivial grounds than the
famous Leipzig quarrel. It involved Bach and Mattheson, who wrote a series of
articles against Biedermann and the Biedermann point of view. The problem
of the schools and therefore of the cantor's authority was not restricted to
Leipzig. It was the result of a general belief that education in Germany should
be modernised, and, together with the increasing and excessive cost of elaborate
church music, it brought about the death of the German cities as great and influential musical centres until some of them, like Leipzig, rose again as the
homes of great orchestras giving important, taste-forming concerts to their
citizens.

14 Music and the French Absolutism

The Baroque was an international style. It stretched out across Europe to acquire, so to speak, a variety of national accents. Only in France was the national accent so strong that it moulded the Baroque language into new shapes and new expressions. French music seeks grandeur of utterance or it seeks charm and elegance; it originates new colours and new forms, but French composers who have originated new intensities of emotional expression have rarely been so highly valued in France as they have been elsewhere. Berlioz, who felt that life anywhere but in Paris would be impossible, lamented that his music was more popular in Germany than in his native land.

The decisive period in the history of French music, as of so much else in French life, was the reign of Louis XIV. The years between 1643, when he came to the throne as a child, and 1715 when he died defeated in his international policies but architect of a way of life from which France has never completely escaped, were those in which French music became its unmistakable self. Louis XIV had not to force his fellow countrymen into a way of life alien to them. They paid enormous sums for his grandeur or sacrificed their hereditary powers to serve him because not so much in his policy as in himself he expressed something essential to the French spirit, and his age encouraged the expression of the same essence in the arts.

In a sense, under Louis XIV the arts became functional. This was not simply because seventeenth-century Paris sucked in every considerable musician, poet and dramatist; London did the same thing, but the artist in London, even if he served the court, was expected to write for another audience or other audiences —in the theatre, the concert rooms, the opera house or the home. Success for any French artist meant acceptance at court, for not only was Louis XIV both the source of patronage, but at the same time his taste was entirely representative of educated French taste. His position at the centre of French culture was the result of a long, painstaking and at times ruthless policy which centralised all the processes of government in the king's hands, his virtue as a representative personality expressing French taste was his fortunate accident.

Not until the Renaissance and the reigns of Francis I and Henry II (1515 to 1559) did the power of the French monarchy become supreme. Taxation enabled the kings to set up a standing army which was large enough to control the feudal nobility; the growing financial power of the middle classes, which enabled the kings to enrich themselves, devalued the fixed incomes of the feudal nobility. They needed, for the first time, to court the king, to seek for positions

at court for the sake of their prestige and their prosperity. Thirty years of religious civil war, which ended in the accession of Henry IV in 1589, destroyed
the commanding position which the monarchy had built for itself and spent
the money on which it depended. Henry IV rebuilt the financial position of
the king, but after his death in 1610, the humbled nobility felt that the time
had come for them to recover their lost independence. Louis XIII came to the
throne at the age of nine, and the nobles set out to exploit his minority not by a
return to feudalism but by demanding pensions and court sinecures as the price
of internal peace, by making themselves rich enough to resist the monarchy.

Thus the thirty-three years of his reign and the rule of Cardinal Richelieu,
from 1624 to 1642, was a time in which royal power was recovered and consolidated, and in which France threaded her way through the complexities of
European politics during the Thirty Years' War. Richelieu's greatest achievement, really, was that he made the France of Louis XIV possible. Political
opposition from the nobility was ruthlessly crushed and, little by little, the local
powers of the aristocracy in the provinces gave way to that of Intendants appointed by the king.

Louis XIII was devoted to music, as was his wife, Anne of Austria. His father
had brought Italian violinists into his own private orchestra and, in 1604, had
arranged for Caccini and his daughter Francesca, herself as celebrated a singer as
her father, to visit France. Thus opera in the Italian style was introduced with
the performance of a *Euridice* which may have been Peri's work of 1597, Caccini's
version of the same text or a work combining parts of each of these two. Rinuccini, the librettist, had accompanied Caccini, and, by way of a cultural exchange,
took back with him to Italy the idea of *ballet de cour*. Caccini was sufficiently
impressed by French music to suggest to the Duke of Mantua that one of the
duke's best singers should be sent to France to study the music there. Henry IV
kept an Italian stage company which threaded music in the Italian style into
performances which exploited the French love of ballet, so thus by 1617, when a
company primarily French produced a work which was almost a complete fusion
of Italian pastoral and ballet, France seemed to be succumbing to the totally
Baroque form of opera.

For all that, Italian-style opera in France remained the perquisite of visiting
companies from Italy, encouraged by Louis XIII. Pastorals like the 1613 *Mad-
delena* became the prototype of the form which the French came to call *Opéra-
Ballet*. The absorption of French music into the international style was slow
partly because of the cultural conservatism of the French and partly because
France lacked any composer of sufficient stature to make the synthesis that was
in the minds of composers and of the king in the creation of works on all the
borderlines of opera. It was not simply that France's operatic genius failed to
put in an appearance but that the other and accustomed music of the composers
of the time—their church music, for example—is remarkably undistinguished.

Therefore the reign of Louis XIII was a great age of French ballet. The king
himself danced, but not with the ease and lack of self-consciousness which had

come naturally to his predecessors. When Louis XIII and Louis XIV stepped into the climax of a ballet, they had to do so with grandeur and unswerving dignity to music which demanded stateliness and slow movement. Almost anyone could attend if he had a hat and a sword to wear, and those without the necessary qualifications crowded up to the windows, climbed up on to the window ledges and watched from there. There was an evening when the hall was so crowded that the king himself could not push his way through to his place.

After 1640, Louis XIII retired as far as he could from public life; after his death, in 1643, Richelieu's successor, Cardinal Mazarin, became the keenest patron of Italian music in France, and during the years of Louis XIV's minority he did everything he could to persuade or coerce the French into adopting Italian opera as it stood. He was Italian, and became a naturalised Frenchman only in 1639. As a boy in the choir of the Oratory of St. Philip Neri, he had taken part in the *rappresentazioni*, the church operas like that of Cavalieri. He had attended operas in the Barberini Palace in Rome. Mazarin's support of opera was due in part to his own love of the form: it was due, too, to his belief that opera, the aristocratic entertainment, the delight of princes, would help to keep the potentially dangerous aristocracy out of mischief, close to the centre of power, where they were under observation.

They found occasional performances of Italian opera interesting; a forced diet of it was more than they enjoyed. Italian singing did not appeal to French taste, recitative seemed unmusical and *castrato* voices had become a bad joke although the first *castrato* to sing in France had been much admired: 'He must find it inconvenient but it makes him sing well,' remarked one lady of Louis XIII's court. The first favourable impressions, however, had evaporated before Mazarin's policy of Italianisation had a chance to become effective. It was not a policy which appealed much to many Italian authorities because it attracted too many Italian artists to Paris. The previous Pope, Urban VIII, had suggested to Louis XIII that France ought to set up a national opera on Italian lines, and his successor, Innocent X, was only deterred from making the same suggestion again by the fact that Louis XIV was only a child.

An Italian opera was produced in the Palais-Royal in February 1645, known only by the survival of its otherwise unexplained libretto, *Nicandro e Felino*. The libretto is printed in Italian and French, like those of later Italian works known to have been performed in Paris, where bilingual copies of libretti were distributed to the audience. Later in 1645, Mazarin had *La Finta Pazza* staged in the Petit-Bourbon Palace; this work had been written by Giulio Strozzi for the opening of the Teatro Novissimo in Venice in 1641, but when it was played in Paris some of its recitative was replaced by spoken dialogue in an attempt to ingratiate to French audiences. Naturally, a ballet had to be added and to appeal to a very young king it consisted of dances of bears, monkeys, eunuchs and parrots. Probably Sacrati wrote the music, but the great success of the entertainment was the machinery, designed by Giacomo Torelli, whose brilliant work in Italy, where among other things he invented a method of changing an entire scene by a single mechanical action, had been enough to bring him to France.

Whatever the artistic success of *La Finta Pazza*, its expensiveness was a weapon which the opposition to Mazarin used with a great deal of vigour. The real cost is not known, but the opposition began by claiming that the production had cost 10,000 livres and ended with the figure of 100,000 livres. Mazarin next set Torelli to design a ballet, with the result that a production of Cavalli's *L'Egisto*, mounted without any scenic elaborations, interested nobody in particular.

The climax both of Mazarin's policy and of the opposition to it—a makeshift collaboration of dissatisfied nobles, conservative devotees to traditional French musical styles and of middle-class people who resented the high level of taxation —came with the production, in March 1647, of *L'Orfeo*, a libretto by Abbé Buti set by Luigi Rossi. The libretto was so complicated that it had to be accompanied by a leaflet explaining its plethora of mythological and allegorical references. The trouble was that it cost more than 300,000 *écus*, pressed out of the people by ruthless taxation; the opposition, of course, suggested that this figure was perhaps no more than half of the real cost. This was money squandered on a foreign art and distributed into foreign pockets. Mazarin became the subject of ribald political songs, and the Fronde, the last struggle of the provincial nobility for independence and the last resistance for more than a century of the tax-paying middle-classes against arbitrary government, found the extravagance of opera an appealing part of their propaganda.

Mazarin next decided to compromise with French taste; when Caprioli's *Nozze di Peleo e di Teti* was staged, he again recruited an Italian company for the work, but he made it palatable by adding to it so many ballets that the French saw it as a triumph for their music. The ballet was not simply added as an inter-mezzo but made as integral to its progress as were the arias and choruses. The work was officially described as a *Comédie Italienne en musique Entremestée d'un ballet sur le mesmes sujet*. Accidentally, it had achieved a form which the French would accept and which they were later to call *Opéra-Ballet*.

For the marriage of Louis XIV in 1660, Mazarin invited Cavalli to provide an opera. Cavalli was the accepted master among Italian opera composers, but was reluctant to undertake the commission and forced up Mazarin's offer, the cardinal apparently regarding this as the decisive moment in his campaign. Cavalli's *Serse* was performed for the festivities before the wedding, with its chorus removed and replaced by ballets which had no relation to the opera's plot, but *Ercole Amante*, which Cavalli composed for the wedding itself was possibly the most splendid of all court opera productions. It lasted for six hours, each act ending with an elaborate ballet—the final one in twenty-one entrées—for which Lully, struggling cleverly towards a commanding position in French music, composed the music.

The defeat of the Fronde had silenced opposition but it had not converted the French to a form of opera which they regarded as both alien and unnatural. In so far as Mazarin had made Italian opera acceptable, he had done so by allowing it to be extended by ballet which at times took over the action. He died before *Ercole Amante* was produced, and without him the pro-Italian party fell to pieces. Colbert, the new finance minister, supported the French party and French musicians began to seize the opportunity created by the cardinal's death.

Louis XIV, as an adult, had no intention of following anyone's lead or of using opera as bait to win support or to subvert the opposition of the nobles. Because he was by nature what the French wanted, admired and were eager to serve, the control of the nobility became simply a matter of his personality and of the system he evolved. Louis XIV made his life into a ceremony, and it became a matter of personal honour as well as of prestige for a nobleman to become involved, even in the smallest way, in the pageant. Sacrificing their traditional political authority in a decentralised France to underlings, they accepted roles in a life which was made as much like a royal entrée in a court ballet as was possible, together with such compensations as freedom from taxation.

The death of Mazarin and the special quality of life which King Louis built around himself demanded a national French opera in which ballet became functional and was set to the service of what Wagner, a couple of centuries later, came to call a *Gesamtkunstwerk*. It thus meant a deepening of artistic expression for it had more seriousness of purpose than the earlier French ballet, which had not concerned itself with homogeneity or even with the use of dance to convey a narrative; it had put together whatever it needed to make an interesting show, disregarding any incongruities that might have arisen even when some sort of narrative or plot was to be conveyed: taken into opera, it became a more serious artistic effort.

French opera, to become an acceptable national form, had to achieve a suave and polished melodic line in which a singer's virtuosity was demonstrated by smoothness of style, sweetness of tone, elegance of phrasing and clarity of diction, rather than by vocal pyrotechnics. Its dialogue had to be given a musical style more elegant and more expressive than Italian recitative, which infuriated French listeners: and in which ballet should be so exploited that a variety of dances should be integral to the action. In one way or another, the adaptation of, or the additions to, the Italian works Mazarin had ordered to be produced had shown the way to a form which would satisfy French taste.

It was *Pastorale*, a work by the dramatist Pierre Perrin and the composer Robert Cambert played before the king in 1659 at Vincennes, to which Louis XIV's mind turned when, after Mazarin's death, he decided to act on the advice of Pope Innocent X and establish national opera. Perrin's libretto was skilfully designed for music, and in an open letter to the Archbishop of Turin, he explained how he had designed it to serve the needs of a style of music which would remedy the 'faults' of standard Italian opera.

Dramatic music had grown inexpressive, he wrote, as though it were copying plainchant, because librettists did not write their poetry with music in mind. *Pastorale* had been so condensed, he claimed, that every scene was an expression of intense emotion and therefore needed intensely expressive music. Unlike other

French works, its music was not simplified to suit the ability of second-class singers. Because it was condensed, its libretto did not run to so many lines that a performance would last for six or seven hours. It did not indulge in recitatives fifty or sixty lines long, which made even the finest singer sound boring. In other operas, there were too many solos for voices of a similar type; Perrin and Cambert had kept each voice to a limit of two recitatives and a duet with one voice of its own type. This was effective and made the work, which lasted about an hour and a half, seem to pass in a mere fifteen minutes. In other operas, the language sung was unknown to the audience but the libretti dealt with metaphors and an elaborate literary style; *Pastorale* was simple, so that everything could be conveyed in music. The huge theatres in which operas had been sung had held audiences so large that not more than half their members had been able to hear anything clearly. *Pastorale* had been successful in a theatre (at Issy) holding only three hundred or four hundred people.[1]

A year or so later, the Paris production of *La Toison d'Or* (a libretto by Corneille the composer of which is unknown) by the Marquis de Sourdeac, who was a gifted stage designer, was another indication of the possibility of French opera. Perrin had petitioned the king for a Privilège granting him the monopoly of operatic productions, and in 1669 Louis granted him what he wanted. He was authorised to create an '*Académie d'Opéra*', which could have branches wherever he wanted to establish them. Anyone else who wanted to stage an opera—though the term had not yet been adopted in France for any work of musical drama— would have to pay heavily for Perrin's permission to do so. To the annoyance of the nobility, nobody had any right of free entry; even courtiers were to pay for their seats.

Perrin was appointed director of music to the new organisation; the king's *maître de ballet*. Beauchamp was in charge of choreography; de Sourdeac was to control the sets, decor and stage machines, while a financier was appointed business manager. The *Académie* leased premises, paying 2400 livres, and in 1671 mounted the first genuine French opera, *Pomone*, with a company recruited by La Grille, the best singer in the company of the *Comédie-Française*. He collected suitable voices wherever he could find them and robbed several of the cathedrals of their best singers. Because there was no free list, this was genuine public opera, but the first audience did not appreciate the new principle of payment by all; the ticket-buyers had no intention of being crowded out of the theatre by noblemen and their attendants; the soldiers on duty to keep order were given a bad time by a stone-throwing mob, and the police had to issue an ordinance to prevent any repetition of the disorder. *Pomone*, however, made 120,000 livres although the king never heard the work. Louis kept away from Paris; it is dangerous to mortal eyes to be exposed to too much sun. Anyhow, every performance was preceded by a disorderly struggle for admission, and it would have been disastrous for Louis to risk his dignity in a public riot.

[1] Norman Demuth: *French Opera, its Development to the Revolution.* Artemis Press, 1963.

Before very long de Sourdeac was working against Perrin, and the Duke of Orleans' musicians had staged an opera at Versailles which pleased the king, who had still not honoured the *Académie* with his presence, so much that he commissioned another work from them. Perrin sold his interest in the *Académie* and joined the duke's musicians, taking with him the Royal Privilège and a heap of debts for which he was imprisoned. Although his colleagues had collaborated with him on the basis of sharing in his monopoly, it was made out in his name, none of them had made any steps to protect their interest in it, and Perrin was able to sell both the document and the rights it represented to Lully, whose new position was ratified by the king. But to indicate the changed constitution, Lully's Academy added the adjective '*royale*' to its title.

The old *Académie* refused to cancel its productions until the king ordered their theatre to be closed by the police. For some months, de Sourdeac's new partner, Guichard, one of the Duke of Orleans' musicians, and Lully spent some time justifying their dislike for each other's machinations by writing scurrilous pamphlets accusing each other of poison—Lully suggested that Guichard had put arsenic into his tobacco—but Lully had won control of French opera and by doing so had made the whole of French court music his empire.

Lully, born in Florence in 1632, was the son of a miller who had been taken to France by the Duc de Mayenne to teach Italian to his sister Mademoiselle de Montpensier. According to Lully himself, his background was aristocratic; according to common legend, he worked in France as a scullion, but both these accounts of him seem to be false. Apparently when he came to France as a child of about twelve he could play the guitar, at least well enough to accompany songs. He studied the violin and the theory of music and resigned from Mademoiselle de Montpensier's service when she supported the Fronde. He found some appointment at court and attracted attention by his wit, his dancing and clowning, and his quality as a violinist. Lully was a good composer who recognised that music could be his way to wealth and authority, and his career was a continuous acquisition of power; the greatest step in his progress, at the top of the tallest tree, was his replacement of Perrin.

Lully first attracted Louis's attention as a dancer, apparently amused and interested him until the two came as close to friendship as was possible with Louis XIV. He used his special relationship to advance his ambitions, writing ballets when ballet kept him under the king's eye. He took French nationality in 1661 and began to share with the court music intendant the duty of administering the king's entire musical establishment, taking over the duties of the four *maistres de musique* who were each responsible for a quarter's performance in each year, leaving them to draw the salaries in happy idleness.

In 1661 he was appointed composer '*de la Musique de la Chambre du Roi*', and in the following year a new post, *Maître de Musique de la Famille Royale*; the two posts brought him a salary of 30,000 livres. He reformed the court music; the French king kept thirty-six musicians who were the *Grande Ecurie*—twelve violinists who also played sackbuts, oboes and cornetts, four other oboists, eight

fife players, tambourine players and musette players; it went wherever the king
went and played for hunting, processions and all outdoor occasions. The Sainte
Chapelle under, Louis XIV, consisted of fourteen adult singers, eight boys and a
player of the serpent. The Chamber Musicians were the string orchestra, the
'Twenty-four Violins' from which Lully moulded a smaller, virtuoso orchestra
of twelve, the *Petits Violons*. Under Lully these forces were combined whenever
the occasion or the music demanded special grandeur.

Lully, when only the theatre music was still beyond his grasp, built up his
position not only through the king's confidence in his abilities but by being a
patriotic Frenchman, persuading Louis to employ only French musicians at
court and appearing as a champion of his adopted nation against interlopers.
With the opera too under his control, he worked first with Molière, turning the
form which Molière called *comédie-ballet* into a new creation, *opéra-ballet*. Submitting his plans in advance to the king, he found a tragic librettist in Philippe
Quinault, with whom he worked on his *Tragédies-Lyriques*, the French equivalent
of *opera seria*. The form was established and in 1673 the *Académie Royale de
Musique* settled in a theatre worthy of its status—the *Salle du Palais-Royal*.

The form was Lully's: it was the Italian careerist who found the recitative
style—eloquent and expressive—which the French language demanded, and the
tone—suave, grand, dignified and glowing with rich but unsensational colour.
But at the same time, it was Louis's. Whether by nature or by application of his
opportunist genius, Lully was able to develop the ideas which Perrin had expressed in music far more powerful and inventive than Cambert could achieve.
But the concept of the *Académie* came from Louis XIV's acceptance of the
ideas on which Perrin and Cambert had worked. In an important sense, Lully
was the voice of Louis XIV.

French opera, from the foundation of Perrin's *Académie d'Opéra*, had never
been a purely court entertainment. It was designed from the first to be sure of the
best of both worlds, not only to please but to express the ideals of the king and
his courtiers through its elegance, its glorification of grace and courage and the
almost obligatary reflections of royal grandeur in its prologues. At the same time
it had to pay its way in the public theatre. Its success in both its objects only helps
to show the extent to which Louis XIV represented a national ideal and set
himself to become the embodiment of what, in his people's eyes, a King of
France should be.

Nevertheless, working from the premises established by Perrin and Cambert,
Lully and Philippe Quinault, the librettist of the classical, heroic works of the
type which French terminology described as '*tragédie lyrique*', did not simply
follow either the Italian pattern for serious opera or the French dramatic form
developed by Corneille and Racine. The necessity in music of contrasted key
structures, tempi and moods meant that tension could be heightened in a basically
tragic work by the suspension of the main action for a scene of gaiety, of reflection or of sheer easy-going charm. Such scenes usually found their way into
the ballet, so that while in one sense it could be suggested that Lully no less

than Cambert could be accused of submitting to the tyranny of an old-fashioned form of entertainment, the ballet was integrated into the opera with a real eye to dramatic effect.

Lully's melodic ideal was simplicity, grace and dignity; the popular musical taste of audiences in his day was simplicity and grace. French audiences, as Addison noted, liked an opportunity to sing themselves and did not share the Italian taste for spectacularly florid bravura arias. 'The chorus, in which this opera abounds,' wrote Addison in 1711, 'gives the parterre frequent opportunities of joining in concert with the stage. This inclination of the audience to sing along with actors so prevails with them, that I have sometimes known the performer on the stage do no more, in a celebrated song, than the clerk of the parish church, who serves only to raise the psalm and is afterwards drowned in the music of the congregation.'[1] When the custom of audience participation arose, and whether or not it was already a feature of French opera before Lully died, is not known, but the directness and simplicity of Lully's melodies must have encouraged it, and the success of his work can be gauged from the fact that his *Académie Royale de Musique* existed as an entirely self-supporting body, with no subsidy to reinforce its takings at the box office.

Financially, too, its arrangements were more satisfactory to its composers than those of any other opera house outside Italy. Lully, a clever business man who invested his money very profitably outside the theatre, mostly in property, earned a regular salary only as Superintendent of the *Académie*. But like everyone who wrote for it he did not sell his works outright for a set sum: the composers whose works were mounted at the *Académie* were paid a fee for each of the first ten performances of an opera. The successful musician in Louis XIV's France was treated better than his equal anywhere else.

Lully created and maintained a superbly efficient organisation. His orchestra was famous for its discipline and unanimity of attack, tone and style; to gain these qualities, he was prepared to smash a violin over its player's head, but he got what he wanted. Only in his attempt to move courtiers from their traditional place in the wings did he make a false move: by charging offenders exorbitant prices for their traditional place, he only made the wings a more desirable position than any of the better seats in the theatre.

The standards of his theatre were internationally famous, but the form he had created to appeal to French taste was so entirely French that while his style of overture became international—it was Handel's form for the overtures to his English oratorios; Bach adopted it, as did other German composers like Mattheson and Telemann, who knew it at first-hand through their visits to Paris —Lullyan opera never became an international form; it so perfectly performed the function for which it was designed that it remained entirely French.

Just as French opera was an expression of what Louis XIV wanted, or could be persuaded to enjoy, so was the rest of the music of his reign. He did not wish to hear High Mass sung in his chapel but preferred to be present at a Low Mass,

[1] Joseph Addison: *The Spectator*, no. 29, April 3, 1711.

said with the minimum of ceremony. Naturally, however simple his church-going came to be, it had nevertheless to be grand, so that Lully's united court of orchestra was called to join the performance of motets, some of which were so extensive that they tended to make his Low Mass as long as anyone else's High Mass.

The result of Louis XIV's requirements were that while a composer like Charpentier might write masses for the Dauphin's chapel (which he served from 1679 to 1680) and for the chapel of the Princesse de Guise (from 1680 to 1683), his big orchestral motets for Louis's chapel are much more ambitious works, and the *Histoires Sacrées*, the first French oratorios (which give the principles of Carissimi a French accent and musical outlook) remained more or less isolated works. Lalande, who wrote forty-two motets for the royal chapel at Versailles, was a more learned composer than Lully, with, perhaps, a more complex mind; certainly, his music reached almost instinctively towards polyphonic styles. For all that, his motets are as grand, as vigorous and as extensive as those of Lully.

Church-going was, so to speak, the encounter of a divinely appointed king with his divine Overlord; its music was therefore a celebration of Kingship and an act of homage to God. Of course the other people worshipped, and many of them doubtless found it unnecessary to reflect always upon their position *vis-à-vis* their creator either in the way they attended church, in the organisation of the services or in the music which glorified them. But the king's ideas became a standard because noblemen spending most of their time in ceremonial attendance on the king neglected their own musical organisations in which other, perhaps less splendid but more personal, styles of religious expressions might have been cultivated.

Lully had established the style of French opera out of which both the Grand Opera and the lyric drama of nineteenth-century France evolved. With Charpentier and Lalande he had established an objective, stately, grave and earnest style of church music. After 1700, François Couperin established a style of chamber music equally influential for the future of music in France. Couperin was already a well-known organist and composer when, in 1693, Louis personally appointed him to be one of the four organists of the chapel royal; the post was one for a composer rather than a player, as the building of the organ at Versailles did not begin until 1702 and took thirty-four years, and Couperin died in 1733, three years before it was ready. For the chapel he wrote his handful of motets, only two of which required a full orchestra, and the small group of *Élévations*, for one, two or three voices and continuo, sung at the actual climax of the Mass where the liturgy does not ask for music. In 1694 he was appointed teacher to the royal children, and ennobled two years later; after about 1701 he became in fact, if not by official appointment until 1717, *claveciniste* to the king, and the bulk of his keyboard and chamber music dates from the last thirty years of his life.

Couperin's music represents the taste of the Sun King in his prolonged sun-set, while he maintained the formal splendour of his court knowing that the policies to which he had dedicated his life had cost more blood and more money than France could afford. Couperin's music is entirely French in its equivalence between deep feeling and elegance of form and utterance, lucid diatonic melodies with chromatic disturbances in their accompaniments. They are, too, more often than not, genre pieces; they are given picturesque titles which, perhaps, they illustrate although it is often easier to think of the titles as a means of characterising the music or suggesting the state of mind in which it should be heard than to regard them simply as illustrations. To say that anything is sacrificed to elegance or an assumed simplicity is to misunderstand the deliberate compression and concentration which forces these works into complete lucidity.

Ultimately Couperin's work achieves what, in his second set of *Concerts Royaux*, he called a 'reunion of tastes', using the structural dynamics of the Baroque sonata to give further strength and coherence to melodies and rhythms which by nature are French. To do this in instrumental music proved to be quite acceptable to French listeners, and, naturally, it added impressive dimensions to French music by making available to it a range of forms which had previously been regarded as inapplicable to French styles and ideas.

The extent to which all these forms of music, in the theatre, the church and the concert room or the home, depended on the taste of Louis XIV and on his ability to tell good composers from their inferiors is obvious. His place in the history of music is not simply that of a patron who was lucky enough to find first-rate composers and reasonable enough to pay them well, for his influence was more direct. Because he found the first-rate composers who provided the music which appealed to his own educated taste, he laid down the lines along which French music has travelled ever since. There are obvious differences between the genre pieces of Couperin or Rameau and the *Préludes* of Debussy or Ravel's *Gaspard de la Nuit*, but for all that, they are works which share the Couperinesque beliefs in picturesqueness, lucidity and elegance, which contain intensities within forms strong enough to keep them in order, and which always prefer balance to excess and clarity to uncontrolled excitement. We can refer to the France of Louis XIV as the point of departure for all subsequent French music and note that those later French composers whose view of music did not coincide with King Louis's, at whatever period they lived, never had an easy time with their compatriots.

Lully was an abiding influence on French opera, but the strict form he had designed to keep the story in continual movement towards its climax began to relax in the twenty years after his death and to admit Italianate ideas which condoned the expansion of lyrical ideas in far greater freedom, so that they developed in the direction of the aria and, in the works of Rameau (whose contemporaries saw him as an almost vicious revolutionary though to us he is the last great Lullyan) there are passages of florid singing and a distinct break in the progress of the story for reflective, almost self-contained ariettes. Rameau's first opera, *Hippolyte et Aricie*, was staged in 1733, when the composer was fifty years old, and the Lullyans, listening to the rich, detailed orchestration of Rameau's first serious opera—he had written lighter and less impressive works before he had managed to secure a foothold in the *Académie*—were disturbed. Singers became no more than part of the complex texture of Rameau's music, in which the composer looked for musical equivalents to the sounds of the sea, to bird calls, to gentle winds moving in trees, and even to a volcanic eruption. The orchestra of the *Académie* numbered forty-six players in 1713; to Rameau, by the end of his career, with the revival of his *Zoroastre* in 1760, forty-seven were the necessary minimum and some of these were expected to double rarer instruments like the musette. The established woodwind consisted of two flutes, four oboes and five bassoons; Rameau promoted the bassoons from being part of the general bass, indivisible from the cellos, to important melodic roles and important additions to the orchestral colour. He added two clarinets to the normal establishment. The only brass, before his advent, was a single trumpet; many of his scores demand horns, co-opted into the orchestra whenever he needed them. To the Lullyans, Rameau was guilty of pointless elaboration, complications for their own sake and an abandonment of Lully's deliberate purity and simplicity of style, but the Lullyans were eventually won over. It was the intellectual *avant-garde* who refused to come to terms. In 1752, an Italian company had played Pergolesi's *La Serva Padrona*, among other equally light, charming and undemanding works, and had been remarkably successful.

Rameau was writing vast, spectacular operas which took their essential principle from the Baroque age; they required elaborate stage machinery, great choruses and all the paraphernalia of the past to explain the activities of heroes, magicians and supernatural beings. Pergolesi, on the other hand, had composed a delicious trifle with a handful of recognisably human characters, a small orchestra and no need for elaborate settings. In Jean-Jacques Rousseau it found a champion.

Rousseau had come to France from Switzerland and joined forces with the French writers who were known as the *Encyclopédistes*. Grimm, Diderot and d'Alembert, who began with the idea of publishing a translation and adaptation of Ephraim Chambers' *Cyclopaedia* and from that expanded their ideas until they proposed to print an entire account of human knowledge and experience with the most advanced philosophy which could be drawn from it. Their writings were the dawn of a new age, the Enlightenment; the principles of French opera came from an unenlightened past. Rousseau, who was perhaps more notable for eloquence, energy and enthusiasm than for depth and clarity of thought, became responsible for their evaluation of music.

The author of the *Contrat Social*, who deduced an innocence and perfection in the primitive ways of life which had been corrupted by 'advanced' social organisations, approached music with the battle-cry of 'back to nature'. By this, he meant a return to simplicity, to whatever was undemanding and fell easily on the ear; it ought to be possible, he held, to absorb a good composition at a single hearing. Rousseau was something of a composer whose works include an opera written in the pre-Pergolesi French style, *Les Muses Galantes* in 1747. It was privately staged by the Duc de Richelieu, and Rousseau heard it in company with Rameau.

He explained in his *Confessions* that Rameau did not listen patiently to a single
number until an air for counter-tenor. This, Rameau told its composer, was the
work of a master; the rest of the opera was composed by somebody who had
never succeeded in understanding what music is. Rousseau, who was not without
humour and self-knowledge, admitted that the work was 'as dull as it was sublime' because it had been composed according to no system of technique but
only by flashes of genius. As he admitted that he had been helped by François
André Philidor, a good musician and member of a musically gifted family,
it would be interesting to know whose genius intermittently flashed.

The truth about Rousseau as a musician is that he could compose pleasantly
derivative, conventional tunes but was a very inferior technician whose knowledge
of harmony was never more than elementary. The success of *La Serva Padrona*
was a revelation to him; it suggested a charming, delightful simplicity which not
only showed up the grand artificiality of what passed for opera in France but also
demonstrated a style in which his own gifts might realise themselves.

As the supporters of the new Italian *opera buffa* and those of the French tradition formed their ranks and prepared for battle, Rousseau fired a violent salvo
against Rameau, the *Académie* and French music in general. Rameau, the author
of a still-important treatise on harmony, must have been rather dazed when he
read that there is no music except melody, thus harmony is only important in so
far as it is a commentary on melody, that it is not, as melody is, universal but
simply a convention adopted by European musicians. The French, because of the
nature of their language, its angular rhythms and the formation of its vowel
sounds, 'have no music and never will have any'.

What passed as French music was maintained by the *Opéra* itself through a
strict inquisition; as the *Académie* was a monopoly, it was a kind of royal court,
making its own laws, allowing no appeal against them and never concerning
itself with justice or fidelity. It excommunicated (by refusing the operas of) those
who displeased it. From this, Rousseau went on to have a good deal of fun about
stage machinery which had been a source of wonder when it was new, a hundred
years before, but which seemed childish and unconvincing now that everyone was
used to it. The really tragic operas were only those in which ropes broke or the
machinery was mishandled: then the gods and the infernal spirits fell on top of
each other and were killed.

The *Opéra* employed nearly a hundred in its orchestra and chorus, a multitude
of dancers and two or three singers to every role, most of whom drew their salaries
without doing anything to earn them. The principals sang a few performances
of any new work and then left their roles to their understudies. Works were
announced, but the audience, when it had turned up and paid standard prices of
admission, found as often as not that another opera had been substituted for the
one they had paid to hear. The singers yelled or screamed, and they were ugly
of feature and figure, but the audience applauded wildly as soon as it recognised
a rhythm or anything resembling a genuinely melodic phrase. As only melody
mattered, Rameau's rich, inventive orchestration and eloquent harmony were

a complication which, according to Rousseau, did nothing to compensate for the poverty of his melodic inspiration.[1]

Rousseau's case was, of course, an exaggeration of valid defects in the organisation and policy of the *Académie Royale de Musique*, which was an over-conservative body—its earlier violent opposition to Rameau's less than revolutionary developments indicates how hide-bound its attitude was—but it paid its way in spite of its extravagance and maintained an unusually high standard of performance. If it was reluctant to involve itself in anything comparable to *opera buffa* and considered that only exotic or historical subjects were suitable for music, it needed awakening, but Rousseau's diatribe—that of an inferior composer nettled by his failure to make a real impact on the operatic establishment—can be paralleled for unreasonableness by the general attitude of the Enlightenment to the art of the past.

The *Guerre des Bouffons*, the war of the supporters of Rousseau and 'natural' music as manifested by *La Serva Padrona* against the traditionalists, was fought with entertaining vigour but apparently less actual violence than the war of the Lullyans and the Rameauneurs a couple of decades earlier. It resulted in a new situation in which the traditionalists led by Louis XV, and the Italianate innovators led by the queen, each occupied its own side of the theatre and did its best to prevent the music of the rival party from gaining a hearing. The *Académie* continued to stage works in the French tradition, but the struggle created not only a vast library of polemics but also room and an enthusiastic audience for Italian *opera buffa* and, in consequence, a powerful new influence on French style.

Nobody profited more than Rousseau from the limited victory of the innovators. His second opera, *Le Devin du Village*, was staged at Fontainebleau, with the Dauphin among the actors, in 1752 and then, in March 1753, publicly in Paris. As Rousseau thought of music simply as tune with unobtrusive accompaniment, *Le Devin du Village* was an entirely appropriate work for amateurs, but its success in the Paris theatre confirmed its composer's opinion that he had written an opera in a style that all future composers would use as a model. Unfortunately, he was entirely spoiled by success and infuriated that either Louis XV or the Dauphin sang one of his airs in what he described as 'a voice as false as his royalty', forgetting that a mere listener's bad singing of a song he had heard only once proved that he had written the sort of music he believed in, the sort which could be assimilated at a single hearing. *Le Devin du Village* remained in the repertory until 1829, by which time it had been given some four hundred times, but at its last performance some practical critic threw a 1750s style wig on to the stage, apparently to indicate that the opera was equally outmoded. Berlioz, twenty-six years old at the time, was present at this performance and saw a work he heartily detested 'extinguished under a monstrous peruke', but though people accused him of having thrown the wig he disclaimed all responsibility for the action which banished the work.

[1] J.-J. Rousseau: *Lettre sur la Musique Française*, 1753.

Rousseau's third stage work, *Pygmalion*, produced at the *Comédie-Française* in 1775 was a melodrama, in which he gave up the attempt to set to music a language which he believed to be musically impossible, leaving the orchestra to play the melodies that might have been sung if Rousseau had ever mastered French declamation, before the actor speaks them.

The *Guerre des Bouffons* left Paris with a wider style of opera, interested in the goings on of ordinary people as well as in the intense moral problems of heroes and demi-gods; it did not destroy the tradition but expanded it. The destruction of the *Salle du Palais Royal* by fire in 1763 forced the *Académie* to operate in the *Salle des Machines des Tuileries*, in which the conditions of the old theatre were duplicated until in 1770 the new *Salle du Palais Royal*, three times the size of the old, was opened. It held an audience of two thousand five hundred and had a staff of two hundred and seventy-eight, only five of whom were administrators. There were eighteen solo singers and a chorus of forty, nineteen solo dancers and a *Corps de ballet* of seventy-two and an orchestra of sixty-eight as well as choral and ballet masters, accompanists and a stage staff, from designers to stage hands, of thirty-nine.

By royal decree there was no free list, and the prices of admission were designed to suit the pockets of a very varied audience, from 10 livres in the best seats to 2 livres 10 sous in the gallery and pit. As long before as 1697, the *Droits de Pauvres* had added one-sixth to the price of the better seats at the *Académie* in order to reduce cheaper seats by an equivalent amount. On first nights, by the decree of 1770, prices were doubled; they were quadrupled when the king attended.

The 'Rights of the Composer' were revised and fixed by a decree of 1776. In the past, for about a century, he had been entitled to 100 livres royalty on each of the first ten performances of a work and 50 livres for each of the next twenty, or the next thirty if the work were a tragedy. After 1776, he received 200 livres for each of the first twenty performances, 150 for each of the next ten, and 100 for the ten after that, so that his royalty protected him for forty performances. If his work occupied part of an evening, sharing in a double or triple bill, the payments ranged from 80 livres to 60 and then 50. After the fortieth performance, the *Académie* became the sole owner of the work.

The years between Rameau's death in 1764 and the production of Gluck's *Iphigénie en Aulide*, in 1774, were stagnant. Dr. Burney, whose fact-finding tour for his history of music took him to Paris in 1770, could hear nothing of quality in the works he inspected. Though the French were the only people except the Italians who had a national style of opera, 'the serious opera of Paris', he wrote, 'is still in the trammels of Lully and Rameau, through which everyone who goes thither, either yawns or laughs, except when roused, or amused, by the dances and decorations. As a *Spectacle*, this opera is often superior to any in Europe; but, as *Music*, it is below our country psalmody, being without time, tune, or expression, that any but French ears can bear: indeed, the point is so much given up, by the French themselves, that nothing but a kind of national pride, in a few individuals, keeps the dispute [about the relative merit of French and Italian music] alive: the rest confess frankly ashamed of their own music.'[1] Burney was no less a man of the Enlightenment than Rousseau, and although he tried hard to see what in the music of composers like Lully had attracted their contemporaries, he failed to do so. Soon, he concluded, French operatic style must 'give way to the stream of fashion, which runs with too much rapidity and violence to be long stemmed'.

Burney's prediction really meant that there must eventually be a reconciliation between French opera and the prevalent Italian style which, by Burney's day, had become more naturalistic, more immediate in appeal and less ceremonial than it had been when Lully reached the point at which French opera bifurcated from the main tradition. The triumph of Gluck, in France as elsewhere, was to prove short-lived because what Gluck achieved was no more than a period of remission in the fatal illness of the old *opera seria*, not a step forward into the future that was to be dominated by Mozart and Rossini. Even before Gluck had raised the temperature of the Paris theatre to boiling point with his 'reform' operas, the future was foreshadowed by the production of Gossec's *Sabinus* at the *Opéra* in 1774. Five earlier operas by Gossec had been produced at the *Comédie-Italienne*, and he had won a commanding position in French music by work of the utmost importance in the concert hall and in church music before he forced his way through the conservative doors of the *Opéra*, which was to produce seven of his later works.

Gossec, a Belgian born in 1734, had made himself a powerful figure in French music. His qualities as an organiser established the *Concert des Amateurs* in 1770 and revitalised the long-established *Concert Spirituel*—the aristocratic concert society which, since 1725, had given regular performances, first of religious music and then of general programmes, in the Tuileries. His operas, as was natural for those of a composer whose grasp of symphonic structure is remarkably similar to that of Haydn, were not the conservative works dear to the heart of the authorities of the *Académie*; they suggested a line of development which Gluck's exciting incursion into French music only interrupted.

Whatever impact Gossec might have had on the music of the *Opéra* in the 1770s was for a time lost in the battle over the music of Gluck, who had arrived in Paris in 1772, not long after the triumph of *Orfeo ed Euridice* in Vienna. *Orfeo ed Euridice* had brought a successful revolution to Viennese opera after his earlier, conventional works had won great popularity in Italy. He took *Iphigénie en Aulide* as an idea to Paris because of a letter from Vienna published in the *Mercure de France* in October 1772, which explained how Racine's tragedy had been made into a libretto for Gluck. Although the composer spoke French with some difficulty, the letter explained, he had studied the language carefully and had prepared for the composition of a French opera by setting various French texts, and he wanted to know if the directors of the *Académie* would be prepared to produce the opera and, if so, when. He would ask no more for the work than was

[1] Charles Burney: *Present State of Music in France and Italy*. London, 1771.

customarily paid by the *Académie* to other composers whose work had not previously been produced by it.

In the following February, Gluck himself wrote to the *Mercure de France* explaining that the type of libretto provided for him by Ranieri da Calzabigi had enabled him to bring drama back into opera because they were full 'of happy situations, of the moods of terror and pathos which offer a composer the opportunity he needs to compose forceful and moving music'.[1]

To fit his work for the French stage, he intended to discuss it with Rousseau, so that all problems of declamation might be solved, and he hoped to create not only music suitable to the special qualities of the French language but also moving and natural melodies; thus he hoped to break down the distinctions between so-called national musical styles. As the introductory letter explained that Gluck saw nothing intrinsically unmusical in the French language, his obeisance to Rousseau simply meant that he was out to win support from both sides for the question of the proper musical treatment of French, inevitable among a people one of whose abiding concerns is the dignity of their language.

Iphigénie en Aulide, produced on April 19, 1774, was a great success which at once led to the French version of *Orpheus et Euridice*, with the *castrato* part of Orpheus adapted for a tenor. In many ways, of course, Gluck's reform operas are a translation into the styles and idioms of the late eighteenth century of the principles of Lullyan opera. Their directness, their dignified intensity, their tendency to be statuesque and their complete integration of ballet into the drama all look back from a new standpoint at the original principles of opera and a resurrection of Lullyan principles in new forms.

There was no reason for a battle over Gluck's position in Paris. His new style of opera was immediately accepted there. But he had become a protégé of Marie Antoinette, so, to influence the king, Madame du Barry found a composer to rival him, the Italian Nicola Piccinni, whom she brought to Paris. *Armide*, Gluck's third opera, was not a complete success—its third act disappointed his audience—and the traditionalists, deciding that he had made a mistake in setting an old libretto, demanded a revival of Lully's original version. Gluck used his influence with Marie Antoinette, now Queen of France, to prevent this, and then antagonised not only Parisian musicians but the people in general by doing his best to prevent the production of Sacchini's *Olympiade*: what business had a foreigner, whom Paris had gone out of its way to honour, to try to decide what the city should hear? To make matters worse, Gluck told Paris that the now unfashionable Rameau was the greatest composer who ever lived. This, together with the existence of a Piccinni party which had no real reason for existing, as Gluck and Piccinni, perfectly good friends, were both working on Gluckian lines, caused the battle round the composers to rage all the more fiercely and to grow more intense when Piccinni's first French opera, *Roland*, was produced at the beginning of 1778 and became a great success.

[1] C. W. Gluck: *Collected Correspondence and Papers*, ed. Hedwig and E. H. Mueller von Asow. Barrie & Rockliff, London, 1962.

The director of the *Académie*, de Vismes, then had two libretti made on the subject of *Iphigénie en Tauride*, one for Gluck and one for Piccinni. While waiting for the operas to emerge, he ordered a production of Lully's *Thésée* for the pleasure of proving that Lully's work was out of date. It was hissed off the stage. Gluck's fee and royalties for *Iphigénie en Tauride* came to 16,000 livres, so that he asked 20,000 for his next work, *Echo et Narcisse*, was paid 10,000 and left Paris in disgust. Piccinni, whose style was not that of the Gluck reform, was equally successful with *Atys*, an Italian work written before he came to France, and then with his *Iphigénie en Tauride*.

The only results of the war of Gluckists and Piccinnians were, first, the importance to French listeners of the composers' treatment of their language and, secondly, that, as Burney had predicted in 1771, fashion for a time had swept away the traditional operatic style. The battles all began with the literary premises of opera, the words and their organisation, and became musical battles as they moved towards the question of how French words should be treated.

Historically, Gluck was the winner; the grandeur of utterance and dignity of style which are part of his music, together with his musical directness and his determination to harness music to drama had an effect on his followers and are among the many ingredients which went to the making of nineteenth-century French *grand opéra*; despite his objection to the notion of separate national styles, his music helped to create the French style in its next incarnation, as did that of the Italian Cherubini, who at the beginning of the nineteenth century was the next important foreign composer to learn how to compose in a French accent. The available French composers, Gossec, Grétry, Boieldieu and Méhul, were good, inventive musicians whose work demands far more than the oblivion into which it has sunk, but their procedures were never part of a battle. Speaking the French accent by nature, they succeeded in establishing an acceptable compromise. *Opéra comique*, with all attempts at declamatory recitative replaced by spoken dialogue and its music ranging from the fluffiest operetta style to the conciseness, colourfulness and intensity of Bizet's *Carmen*. Whatever nationalists arguments could rage about tradition or innovation in the works presented by the *Académie* and about its corruption or support of the French language, *opéra comique* was not only flexible and versatile; it was also entirely French in its ease and sophisticated simplicity.

After Gluck, the *Académie*'s repertory came to depend on Italian composers—Anfossi, Cherubini, Paisiello, Salieri and Zingarelli, among others, together with Italianised Germans like Johann Christian Bach. A dearth of librettists drove all these composers back to old libretti, so that texts originally set by Lully were reworked in the absence of anything new. This, of course, was entirely unsatisfactory and damaging to the *Académie*; Lully's libretti were carefully and exactly designed for Lully's type of opera, and no amount of adaptation could make them suitable material for Italian composers. French musicians like Gossec and Philidor who were trying to keep French opera alive with considerable injections of Italian music, both needed and worked to libretti of a different type.

The second fire to destroy the *Salle du Palais Royal* theatre, in 1781, drove the *Académie* to a new and smaller home which could not, even filled to capacity, pay the cost of opera productions, and its new theatre was thrown up so quickly that, although its preparation cost 200,000 livres, it had to be expensively strengthened, altered and enlarged. The *Académie* remained in deep water financially until Louis XVI reorganised it in 1784. He wiped out the hereditary privileges which had grown up in a century of existence, and which, among other things, allowed singers to bequeath their roles to their heirs; he instituted prizes for libretti and, in 1787, settled the personnel of the opera at 200 people, revised the regulations and subsidised the *Académie* by levies on all other entertainments from the *Concert Spirituel* to a flea circus. With the coming of the Revolution, the theatre was taken over by the municipality and, like everything else, was used to mount pageants, shows and anything whatever which could serve as Republican propaganda. To do so it began to pile up dignity, grandeur and splendour in a manner which recalled the glories of Louis XIV sometimes incongruously married to the music of the streets.

The development of concert life in Paris, after the foundation of the *Concert Spirituel* in 1725, brought other styles of music—the concerto, the suite and, eventually, the symphony to French audiences. The French suite, growing from collected dance movements out of opera ballets, was a local growth; concertos and symphonies were largely imported from Italy, Germany and Austria. Music outside Paris depended simply on the services of musicians who could not succeed in the capital.

Apart from Gossec's symphonies, works unjustly neglected, little important orchestral music emerged from eighteenth-century France except the symphonies of Franz Beck, who was born in Mannheim in 1723, trained as a violinist at the expense of the Elector Theodore, studied under Johann Stamitz, but had to fly to France after fighting a duel. He settled in Bordeaux, where there was a large German colony, in 1761, and became musical director at the Grand Theatre there, founded a series of concerts, was organist of the city's most important church and, in 1791, he opened the first Bordeaux publishing firm. Beck's symphonies of the 1770s rival the *Sturm und Drang* symphonies which Haydn was writing during the same years; like the symphonies of Gossec, those of Beck deserve rehabilitation. But no other composer of Beck's stature devoted his gifts to any provincial city in France during the eighteenth century.

15　England—Court Music and City Music

The development of English politics and English society had already, in Tudor times, given England its own individual type of musical development. The urge towards the enormous which occupied a lot of attention among composers on the continent had no parallels in English music. The Baroque dramatisation of music was slow to influence the works of English composers. There was little real attempt to find an English dramatic style before 1660 and the restoration of the monarchy. The Baroque instrumental styles—though most of their novelty was assimilated into favourite English forms—were even later in reaching acceptance among English musicians.

For all this, some of the Baroque ideals, the fertilisation of music by poetry (as Wagner was later to call the situation in which music turned to the expression of verbally expressed ideas), the pursuit of expressive intensity, appear in English music no later than in Italian. The composers who for twenty years developed the Ayre, the English solo song with lute accompaniment, were as concerned as any of the Italians of their duty to solemnise a real marriage between music and poetry. Dowland died in 1626, but it is at least possible to see in his non-strophic songs with their continuously developing melodies, their combination of rhetorical declamation with the appeal of tune, an attitude to words close to that of his Italian contemporaries who stripped music down to vocal recitative and figured bass. The differences are that Dowland songs are lyric, not dramatic, and that his accompaniments condense elaborate polyphonic, madrigalesque patterns into music within the capacity of the lute.

In France, the court masque evolved into opera through the ballet. Any train of development parallel to this was brought to a stop in England by the Revolution of 1642 and the outlawing of the theatre by the Commonwealth government from 1649 to 1660. Under James I and Charles I, the court masque in England was as grandiose as it was in France. It utilised singing and the ballet, just as it utilised fine poetry, but its real business was to be visually spectacular. It became an element in plays for the commercial theatre and was acceptable, perhaps, because it was undramatic. It was a new and charming element in entertainment, but it was a decoration adding little or nothing to the real business of the play; the audience did not depend upon it for narrative, action or characterisation—these remained the business of the play in which the theatre masque was an interlude —but they were given dancing, song and music as a bonus added to what they invariably enjoyed. The public theatres could not stage the visual excitements which were the business for which the court masque existed; even if their buildings had been adapted for elaborated stage machinery, they could not have afforded to create them.

The music of court masques alone was expensive beyond the reach of the public theatres. In 1610 the *Masque of the Queens*, a text by Ben Jonson composed by the younger Alfonso Ferrabosco, cost £90 for its musicians alone as there were '13 Hoboys and sackbutts as well as 14 Viollulas' and '12 other lutes, with flutes', '12 musicians that were Preestes, made songs and played', and '15 musicians that played the pages and fooles'; the music was not stinted.

It is in the context of music of this sort and of the ideas of classical drama and music which reached England from Italy, that the declamatory songs of Henry Lawes should be understood. Burney found his music to be 'languid and insipid', and Hawkins decided that his music had neither 'recitative nor air' and 'that a name is wanting for it'. Poets like Milton and Herrick approved of it, for it set out to formulate metre, rhythm and inflection through music; it was not an English style of recitative but an English arioso style, owing something to the English regard for poetry in that it did not use the poet's words simply as matter which could be used to underline a purely musical expression.

There is, too, a certain foreshadowing of the Baroque about the English verse anthem, which came into use in the latter part of Queen Elizabeth I's reign. The dialogues of a solo voice accompanied by viols and a choir with organ accompaniment might have evolved into something comparable to the *concertato* compositions of Italians if the Commonwealth had not, from 1649 to 1660, forced development to follow other tracks.

For at least eleven years church choirs were silent. Organs were taken from many churches, and a considerable number of them were set up in inns and taverns to assist in the entertainment of their clientele. Puritan hostility was directed against church music and against the theatre, and musicians who had earned their living in the playhouses had a bad time; church musicians seem to have been regarded as sufficiently learned to be accepted as teachers, but the author of *The Actor's Remonstrance*, published in 1643, the year after the Civil War started and the theatres were closed, indicated the depth to which he and his like had fallen: 'Our music that was held to be so delectable and precious that they scorned to come into a tavern for less than twenty shillings salary for two hours, now they wander with their instruments under their cloaks—I mean, such as have any—into all houses of good fellowship, saluting every room where there is company with, "Will you have any music, gentlemen?"'

The removal of church organs into taverns, and the knowledge that musicians touted for work in them—nobody attempted to stop them doing so, for the Puritans were not anti-musical and Cromwell, as Lord Protector, kept domestic musicians as the king had done—suggests the beginning of an embryonic concert life about which we know nothing beyond the fact that it existed, just as we know that the unemployed musicians of the Oxford colleges formed their music meeting to play and sing together. Pepys seems to be our best authority for the music of the taverns. The *Diary* mentions the music to be heard at the Dolphin,

the Cock, an unnamed house by the Royal Exchange, the Green Dragon, the
King's Head at Greenwich, the Blue Bells, the Dog and the Black Swan, and
these pleasures all come in the 1660s before the formally organised concerts of
Banister. We do not know what music was played, except that composers did
not alter their ways to suit the new conditions. The Elizabethan madrigal style
continued, for example, in the works of Thomas Tomkins until he died in 1656,
and the consort style was still exploited by John Jenkins until his death in 1678.
Jenkins has been credited with the first English works to be called 'sonatas', but
stylistically it would be hard to distinguish between his fantasias and the works
which have come down to us under the later name. Even Purcell, at the end of
the seventeenth century, found the traditional fantasia to be a completely viable
form but quite unlike the Italian sonata style he set out to exploit in England and
with English materials.

Oddly enough, it was the Puritan's affection for music which almost made it
possible for English people to short-circuit the development of opera through the
masque and the ballet, creating a national operatic style without great indebtedness to any foreign models. Opera was so strange to the English that even an
educated music-lover, like John Evelyn, had to define it when he found it. 'We
went to the opera,' he wrote in his account of his stay in Venice, 'which are
Comedies (and other plays) represented in Recitative Music by the most excellent Musicians vocal and Instrumental, together with a variety of Sceanes
painted and contrived with no less art of Perspective, and Machines, for flying in
the aire, and other wondeful motions. So taken together,' he adds, 'it is doubtless
one of the most magnificent and expensful diversions the Wit of Man can invent.'[1]
Recitative music was known but opera was not, although recitative music was,
to the ideas of the Italians, musically justified because it made opera possible.

Had William D'Avenant been able to carry out his plans, Evelyn might well
have known something of opera before he travelled to Italy. In 1639, Charles I
gave D'Avenant a patent to build a theatre and allowed him 'from time to time
to act plays in such houses to be by him erected, and exercise music, musical
presentments, scenes, dancing or such like'. D'Avenant wanted, it seems, an
all-purpose theatre for plays, opera, ballet and concerts. It was D'Avenant, however, who persuaded the Commonwealth government to allow him to stage
musical entertainments. D'Avenant's aim was not primarily musical; he wanted
to see the theatre in action again, and if he could do so through music he would
happily make use of music.

In 1656 he organised what he called 'The First dayes Entertainment at Rutland
House by declamations and Music: after the manner of the Ancients'. At a cost
of five shillings per head the audience heard a combination of concert, recitation
and reading. Before the curtain rose, 'a concert of music adapted to the sullen
disposition of Diogenes' was played. Then Diogenes and Aristophanes were
discovered, sitting in purple and gold 'rostras'. At great length Diogenes argued
against the value of public entertainment, to be answered after characteristic,

---

[1] John Evelyn: *Diary*. June, 1645.

cheerful music, by Aristophanes. This was Part One, which ended with a chorus accompanied by instruments. In Part Two, a Parisian and a Londoner, each with appropriate introductory music and a final chorus lengthily abused the other's city.

The Siege of Rhodes, which D'Avenant staged soon after, is opera, with music composed by Locke, Henry Lawes, Henry Cooke, Charles Coleman and George Hudson. Its music is lost, and we can judge it only by D'Avenant's libretto as a work which owes nothing to any Italian model. Its subject was, in 1656, modern enough to be almost contemporary; this suggests that its music was equally idiosyncratic. Dent[1] argued convincingly that D'Avenant wrote its libretto originally as a play, in the pentameters standard to English dramatic poetry but, to get the work into performance during the Commonwealth, he adapted his drama to music by breaking the blank verse with occasional shorter lines in Rhyming couplets.

The Cruelty of the Spaniards in Peru was another 'representation', like 'The First dayes Entertainment at Rutland House', but D'Avenant's last pre-Restoration effort, *Sir Francis Drake*, was another opera in the style of *The Siege of Rhodes*. To what extent they owed any popularity they won to the simple fact that they were the only entertainment which had managed to evade the government ban is something we do not know. Two years after the Restoration, in *The Playhouse to Let*, D'Avenant attempted to make a play out of the mere facts that drama was allowed again and that somebody had to provide it. The Playhouse is to be let for a D'Avenant-style opera, and the Tirewoman, who is one of the group of workers in the theatre who make up the *dramatis personae*, is made to say:

> Now we shall be in *stylo recitativo*.
> I'm in a trance when I hear real music,
> And in that trance, inclined to prophesie
> That 'twill bring us inundations of shillings.

But the Tirewoman might as well have been speaking propaganda in prophesying a theatrical success on the basis of experience. Evelyn was taken by his brother to see one of D'Avenant's productions in 1659, amazed that anyone should indulge in such frivolities at a time of political crisis, when the Commonwealth was falling to pieces and renewed Civil War threatened. He found it 'much inferior to the Italian composure and magnificence'.[2]

The Restoration, however, brought in new fashions which prevented the development of D'Avenant's opportunist embryo of a national opera. Charles II had lived in France during the time when *ballet de cour* was evolving into French opera, so that a style of work growing out of free, declamatory arioso passages appealed to him less than the springily rhythmical 'airs' to which he was accustomed, just as he found the polyphonically built English fantasy, or the standard church anthem which followed the styles worked out by the composers of

[1] E. J. Dent: *The Foundations of English Opera*.
[2] Evelyn: *op. cit.* May 5, 1659.

Elizabeth I's Chapel Royal, to be lacking in rhythmic interest. D'Avenant's embryo was unlikely to grow in his court, and D'Avenant, no longer needing to hide his drama behind music, revived *The Siege of Rhodes* as a play.

The London theatre, or the English theatre so far as an English theatre existed outside London, was not dependent upon the king and his court. It stood or fell by public patronage, and the Elizabethan–Jacobean playwrights had commanded a public which cut across social classes. They had used the open, unset, un-localised stage with a sophisticated assurance in matters of technique. Because they had been compelled to write for the loquacious Merchant who takes control of the Induction to Beaumont and Fletcher's *The Knight of the Burning Pestle* as well as for the young men about town who preferred to sit on stools on the stage and flatter themselves that they were connoisseurs of drama, the playwrights had learnt to present action, exciting, funny, violent or formal, as a manifestation of, and influence upon, character. Where, as in France, the drama depended on court patronage, it remained far more classical, conscious of Ancient Greek precedents and determined to observe the rules of probability which Aristotle formulated as the 'unities' of place, time and action. Racine no more than Euripides would have allowed sixteen years to pass in the middle of a play so that a new-born baby could grow into a reconciling heroine, or have allowed an arbitrary bear to devour her escort.

The vicissitudes of English opera, and, indeed, of opera in England, are the result of the English theatrical tradition, with its combination of intellectual depth and easy popular appeal. Its tradition of dramatising character in develop-ment rather than showing developed character in a state of crisis, had created an attitude to drama which Baroque opera did not satisfy. It is possible to imagine a national opera, on D'Avenant's principles, winning the allegiance of English music lovers, but once Italian Baroque opera, and after it early classical opera, became the accepted international standard, the English theatre-goer would not, for the sake of musical pleasure, renounce his earlier delight in the styles and techniques which can loosely be defined as Shakespearean and which have been at the root of all later English drama. Baroque opera, however beautiful its music and elaborate its scenic effects, could not compensate for the loss of human complexity and decisive action.

Thus the eruption of Cambert into English music after his failure in France, and his attempt to form a 'Royal Academy of Musick' on the lines of that which he and Perrin had controlled in Paris, was not enough to make opera seem a natural rival to English drama. His opera *Ariane, ou le Mariage de Bacchus*, was performed in Drury Lane Theatre in 1674 (probably in a new version by Louis Grabu, the inferior French composer who had entered the service of Charles II in 1665) and his *Pomone* was sung in the court theatre in Whitehall in 1674.

Before he had reigned for six months, Charles II granted Guido Gentileschi a licence to build a theatre for a body of Italian musicians who would have the sole right of performing opera in it for six years. Evelyn heard them, but made no comment on this performance. There were six of them, and they cost the king £1700 a year. By 1666 they had discovered the uncertainty of Charles's finances, for they asked him to authorise their payment through a banker so that they would no longer be compelled to 'disturb' him every quarter. When the Popish plot of the late 1670s compelled them to leave England, they had to petition the king for salaries which were four years in arrears.

What they offered, like the Cambert–Grabu *Ariane*, was written and composed without relation to the English dramatic tradition. The Restoration had restored the theatre as a less popular entertainment—in the best sense of the word—than it had been. It was now invariably enclosed, its stage no longer projecting into the auditorium but making a picture behind its proscenium arch. Scenes needed to be built and naturalistically furnished. Audiences were smaller, costs of production higher and admission therefore more expensive, and for this reason its audience and its subject matter became socially restricted; the embarrassments of love and money, the pursuit of sexual pleasure as the aim of life, and heroic tragedy in a sense more classical than the tragedy of Shakespeare and his contemporaries were not subjects likely to appeal so widely as the drama of the great age.

Thus, when Dryden set out in *Albion and Albanius* (an allegorical compliment to Charles II and his brother, the future James II) to write an English libretto, the idea of writing a text for opera combined with the classical fashion of the day invariably resulted in something divorced from English stage tradition even before Grabu's music—clumsily uninventive and markedly insensitive to English poetry—was added to it to ensure its failure.

For all that, Dryden was a major poet and a highly educated one. He could see the special qualities that were required in libretto. Music heightens whatever words are sung to it, so that the Italian habit of singing everything, however trivial or banal, in recitative, seemed pointlessly unnatural, partly because English recitative-arioso was naturally more eloquent than Italian recitative. D'Avenant, in *The Playhouse to Let*, had suggested in 1662 that music could not effectively be harnessed to commonplace expressions:

> Recitative Musick is not compos'd
> Of matter so familiar, as may serve
> For every low occasion of discourse.

By the time Dryden found a great dramatic composer with whom to collaborate in *King Arthur*, he found that the poet had to submit to the composer to achieve the success each wanted. As though to safeguard his reputation, he noted in his Preface: 'But the numbers of poetry and music are sometimes so contrary that in many places I have been obliged to cramp my verses, and make them rugged to the reader, thus they might be harmonious to the hearer.' In a country where the dramatic tradition was literary and poetic, the best playwrights did not come easily to the writing of libretti.

For all Charles II's affection for French and Italian music and the fact that there was, between about 1670 and 1750, a greater number of Italian musicians working in London than anywhere else outside Italy except Vienna, foreign musicians had little direct influence upon English music until the eighteenth century. Those we remember of the semi-operas with spoken dialogue which were the English approach to what was *par excellence* the Baroque form proceeded on quite individual English lines, filling in what seems to be the unbridgeable gap between D'Avenant's opportunist experiments and Purcell's *Dido and Aeneas*.

Between the two are an appreciable number of such semi-operas: D'Avenant's version of *Macbeth*, for example, in 1673, with music once ascribed to Matthew Locke, Shadwell's version of *The Tempest*, with music by Locke, in 1674, his *Psyche*, another collaboration with Locke, produced in 1675, and Blow's *Venus and Adonis*, composed in the early 1680s. To their composers, these were 'operas', a term which had not crept into general use in Italy but which was often applied, usually with a qualifying adjective, to similar works in France. They were written, not for the delectation of the court but for the public theatres whose taste, in the years between the Restoration and the end of the seventeenth century, was governed by the regular patronage of the aristocracy. To them, whatever contained any large amount of music was an 'opera'. 'Opera abroad are plays where every word is sung,' wrote the *Gentleman's Journal* in 1693. 'This is not relished in England.'

Few of these works were given continuous music because the nearest English composers got to recitative was far too expressive to be used for what D'Avenant had called the 'low occasions of discourse'. Music naturally belonged to situations of extreme emotion or to the activities of supernatural powers. Dryden, in the Preface to *Albion and Albanius*, draws a principle from the idea of harnessing an entire text to music: 'An Opera is a Poetical Tale, as Fiction, represented by Vocal and Instrumental Musick, adorned with Scenes, Machines and Dancing. The suppos'd Persons of the Musical *Drama* are generally Supernatural, as Gods, and Goddesses, and Heroes, which are at least descended from them, and are in due time to be adopted into their number.' It was correct for the witches, in the Restoration version of *Macbeth*, to have suitable music, or for the mythological characters of Locke and Blow to sing when mere mortals would only speak. If this meant a harsh limitation on the subject matter of opera, at least it was entirely consonant with the aesthetics of the day and the use of a language which seemed to resist entirely the Italian type of recitative.

Addison, after the failure of his *Rosamond*, which was set to music by Clayton and produced in 1707, became an irreconcilable enemy of Italian opera and invented several of the jokes against it which time has made dear to English Philistines; for all that, in *The Spectator*, he attempted a rational explanation in untechnical language of the reason for the English listeners rejection of recitative:

> ... The tone of (as the French call it) the Accent of every Nation in their ordinary speech is altogether different from that of every other people; as we may see even in the Welsh and Scotch, which border so near upon us. By the Tone or Accent, I do not mean the Pronounciation

of each particular Word, but the sound of the whole Sentence. . . . For this reason, the Recitative Musick, in every language, should be as different as the Tone or Accent of each language; for otherwise, what may properly express a Passion in one language, will not do it in another. Everyone who has been long in Italy knows very well, that the cadences in the Recitativo bear a remote affinity to the Tone of their Voices in ordinary Conversation; or, to speak more properly, are only the Accents of their Language made more musical and Tuneful.

Thus the Notes of Interrogation or Admiration in the Italian Musick (if one may call them) which resemble their Accents in Discourse on such Occasions, are not unlike the ordinary Tones of an English Voice when we are angry; insomuch that I have often seen our Audiences extremely mistaken as to what has been doing upon the Stage, and expecting to see the Hero knock down his Messenger, when he has been asking him a Question; or fancying that he quarrels with his Friend, when he only bids him 'Good Morrow'. . . .

I am therefore humbly of Opinion, that an English composer should not follow the Italian Recitative too seriously, but make use of many gentle deviations from it, in Compliance with his own Native Language. He may copy out of it all the lulling Softness and 'Dying Falls' (as Shakespear calls them) but should still remember that he ought to accommodate himself to an English Audience; and by humouring the Tone of our Voices in ordinary Conversation, have the same Regard to the Accent of his own Language, as those Persons had to theirs whom he professes to imitate.[1]

It was not, originally, the whole idea of opera which English audiences rejected as 'unnatural' but simply that they found the principal of recitative ridiculous, partly because composers were slow in finding an English equivalent. As late as 1728, when Italian opera in its native language had been imported to London for years, Gay could win a laugh when his Beggar, in The Prologue to *The Beggar's Opera*, explains 'I hope I may be forgiven, that I have not made my Opera unnatural, like those in vogue; for I have no Recitative.'

Thus the semi-opera with spoken dialogue, which reached its apotheosis in *King Arthur* and *The Fairy Queen*, seemed to English people—librettists, composers and audiences—to be perfectly valid form. To say that the music remained, or was regarded as, no more than enjoyable decoration would avoid recognition of the fact that in *The Fairy Queen* and *King Arthur*, what is spoken matters only in so far as it speeds us along to the next point at which, according to the English aesthetics of the time, music could make a legitimate re-entry. When French opera abandoned the term 'entrée' for 'scene', and replaced it by 'Tableau' its creators indicated, perhaps without realising that they were doing so, that somehow they had reached a fairly static point in procedure at which what mattered was a richly expressive account of the emotions aroused by the situation; Lully was adamant in demanding libretti which consisted of emotionally effective scenes reached through the necessary minimum of bridging action to be conveyed in his own French equivalent to recitative. His audience

[1] Joseph Addison: *The Spectator*, April 3, 1711.

had little preconceived ideas, for it had no great tradition of tragic drama in which such ideas could germinate, of a stage method like that of the English Elizabethans in which great situations evolved through action. Lully's startling originality was to mould Baroque dramaturgy to French taste, which, in its classicism was as far as can be imagined from that of Shakespeare. Opera in England could not take precisely the same shape because the English dramatic tradition would not let it do so.

Thus it is in *Dido and Aeneas* that opera, rather than semi-opera, reached England in an English composition, arriving in a work written for private performance and not for the public theatre. The libretto was probably printed for the invited audience and it describes the work as 'An opera performed at Mr. Josias Priest's Boarding School at Chelsea by Young Gentlewomen' in the late summer or autumn of 1689. The title page must, of course, have been inaccurate; it seems more than merely probable that 'The Young Gentlewomen' were among the sopranos and altos of the chorus, and among the dancers. They were not the tenors and basses of the chorus; they could not sing the roles of Aeneas and the Drunken Sailor. That any of them could have done justice to the music given to Belinda is hard to believe, and that one of them could cope effectively with Dido's music is nearly incredible. The work was meant for a special occasion; its Prologue and Epilogue (which Purcell did not set) refer to the Glorious Revolution, the settlement of William and Mary on the English throne and, possibly, the agreement of what had been the 'Queen's Party' (whose policy was to make Mary Queen and grant her husband no status beyond that of her Consort) to the idea of a joint monarchy. Precisely why a girls' school chose to perform it when it did so we cannot say; we can suggest, without fearing contradiction, that obviously professional singers were engaged for the leading roles.

Nahum Tate is not among the poets laureate to whom we look back with any frenzy of approbation, but on the basis of *Dido and Aeneas* alone we can remember him as a splendid librettist simply because he condenses the story in such a way that without discarding the aesthetics of his day not a word need be spoken and the music not only can be but needs to be continuous. Narration, so to speak, is firmly embedded in the emotional verse which, in terms of the late seventeenth-century theatre, demands music. The audience invited to its performances may have been one of musical *dilletanti* who could understand the principles involved, but that seems unlikely. Although the work would probably have seemed eccentric if it had been played in a public theatre, in a girls' school which apparently mounted large-scale musical performances from time to time, as other establishments of the same sort seem to have done, its eccentricities were probably regarded as acceptable in the unusual circumstances. There is nothing that the audience can think of as mere recitative because such lines as, for example, Dido's 'Oh Belinda, I am oppressed with torments' or her 'Thy hand Belinda' before her final lament and suicide, entirely justify the extreme intensity with which Purcell sets them. Each of them leads to Purcell's favourite form of an air on a ground bass, and could, perhaps, be marked in any score as recitative;

but anybody can imagine how they would have been set by an Italian or by any composer who regarded Italian recitative as an entirely unavoidable model. The almost wild freedom of Purcell's treatment, and its almost equally wild emotionalism, are a model than a declaration of what English words demand in musical inflection and punctuation as well as a guide to the way in which such demands could be answered.

Dido and Aeneas seems, even to its composer, to have been too special a work and too inextricably involved with special circumstances to become the point of departure for operas of continuous music with a Purcellian approximation to recitative. At any rate, Purcell's two great semi-operas followed it, in 1691, *King Arthur* was produced; in 1692, *The Fairy Queen*. The conditions which made *Dido and Aeneas* possible did not arise again, and English semi-opera continued to be something equivalent to a theatre masque which had somehow taken into itself the necessary spoken dialogue which, in works like *Dioclesian* and *The Indian Queen*, preceded the music to justify it. The music might be grand, eloquent, far more powerful than the spoken portion of the work, but it was a reflection of, rather than the means of achieving, a dramatic situation.

If such works no longer seem viable in the form chosen for them by their composer—and the greatness of *King Arthur* and *The Fairy Queen* stamps every page as the work of a supremely inventive master—we can see them now as theatrical devices by means of which Dryden, and Elkanah Settle adapting Shakespeare beyond recognition, simply created as many opportunities for music as they could within the confines of a single evening. Spectacle, scenic elaboration and the arbitrary juxtaposition of contrasted scenes to evoke contrasted types of music take the place of anything legitimately to be called drama; the only dramatist involved is the composer, who finds unexpected wealth of character, tensions and conflicts in what was designed primarily only to suggest a glorified concert, and it is in the light of what was accepted as operatic by English librettists and English audiences but not by those of Purcell's dramatic genius, that the eighteenth-century struggle to establish Italian opera, and 'opera in the Italian manner' must be seen. Even Handel's very popular *Julius Caesar*, or his semi-comic *Serse*, seemed to many people not a step forward in dramatic music but two steps backwards in dramatic form. Purcellian semi-opera died; Purcellian opera, represented by the lonely miracle of *Dido and Aeneas*, was not pursued. France evolved its national operatic style. England, like the rest of Europe, saw opera as essentially Italian; unlike the rest of Europe, it was able to judge the Italian form as drama because it had a highly developed dramatic tradition in which extreme variety was extremely homogeneous. In this sense, perhaps, it saw the truth about opera—that opera must be musical drama and not simply beautiful and elaborate music sung by gorgeously dressed beings in an incomprehensible language—before any other country in Europe.

In 1702, Nicola Haym, the son of German parents born in Italy and later to be one of Handel's librettists, joined the French composer Charles Dieupart and the English composer Thomas Clayton to produce opera at Drury Lane Theatre.

Their first offering was Clayton's *Arsinoe, Queen of Cyprus*, 'an opera in the Italian manner, all sung'. Although the work came in for a lot of derision from the press, it ran for thirty-seven performances. Clayton, with admirable if simple-minded directness, came to the conclusion that all the trouble with English opera was that it was not 'all sung'; simply to do in English what Italian composers always did in their own language would create true English opera. If, in the words of Locke, 'We have properly no national recitative,' to set English works to the inflective and declamatory patterns of Italian would supply our lack; he did not, in other words, notice that a real problem of English recitative existed and that Purcell had, at least for the purposes of *Dido and Aeneas*, solved it. 'Being recitative,' he explained, 'it may not, at first, meet with that general acceptance, as is to be hoped for, from the audience being better acquainted with it.' At any rate, the commercial success of the work was at least his reward for trying to do something new. Antonio Maria Bononcini's *Camilla*, sung in English, ran for even longer, but *Rosamond*, Clayton's setting of Addison's libretto, was a dismal failure and the reason why Addison, for ever after, seized every possible opportunity for deriding opera.

Opera in other countries had not only the prestige of royal support—the Hanoverian Kings were faithful to London's Italian Opera—but also financial support vastly beyond the £1000 a year which, ever since George I began to subscribe to the Royal Academy of Music, the English opera set up in 1719, had been the king's personal grant towards the performance of opera. £1000 a year was a much greater sum of money than it would be now, but it did not rescue any English opera company from dependence on the money it received as subscriptions or took at the box office.

As opera was the key form in Baroque music, the history of its struggle for birth in England is important, but, while opera fought for existence, other music was accepted and prosperous. The restoration of the monarchy was a restoration of the Church of England and, therefore, of church music. Charles II set about the recreation of the Chapel Royal in 1660. He had no trained choirboys, and many of the gentlemen who had survived the Civil War and the Commonwealth were too old to be of much use, but in Henry Cooke, a singer who had made some reputation as a master of 'the Italian style', he found a 'Master of the Boys' who was not only an efficient and obviously sympathetic teacher but a first-rate talent scout. Cooke, apparently, owed his selection as much to his record in the Civil War, in which he had fought with the rank of Captain, as to his musical abilities, but though he was at the most flattering estimate only a mediocre composer he was also a determined modernist whose ideas were in complete harmony with those of the king. Armed with a warrant to impress boys with good voices, he brought into the choir Pelham Humfrey, John Blow and Purcell, encouraging their progress as singers and instrumentalists but also encouraging and guiding their early efforts as composers. Adult singers, too, were enrolled from the cathedral choirs of Worcester, Salisbury, Lincoln and St. Paul's. By the end of November 1660, Evelyn noted, 'Now was performed the Service with Musique,

Voices &c: as formerly.'[1] Matthew Locke, however, declared that 'For more than a year after the reconstitution of the Chapel, the treble parts had to be supported by cornetts and countertenors, there being not one lad, for all that time, capable of singing his part readily.'[2] Pepys heard the service in the Chapel Royal on one occasion when 'one Dr. Crofts made an indifferent sermon, and after it, an anthem, ill sung, which made the king laugh'. Building a good choir was a lengthy job even for Captain Cooke. It seems that even the music library of the Chapel Royal had been destroyed in some outbreak of Puritan zeal. Nevertheless, when the organisation came to life again it returned to its established repertory of Elizabethan and early Stuart music, at least for so long as it took Cooke to find new music and to persuade the older singers—five remained from before the Civil War—to accept novelties. Thomas Tudway, who seems to have been taken by Cooke into the choir in 1660 when he was ten years old, is remembered for an important collection of service music and anthems which he compiled between 1714 and 1720, as Professor of Music at Cambridge. His Collection is now in the British Museum, and in its notes he describes the changes which rapidly came over music in Charles II's reign: 'His Majesty, who was a brisk and airy Prince, comeing to the Crown in the Flow'r and vigour of his Age, was soon, if I may so say, tyr'd with the Grave and solemn way, and ordered the Composers of this Chappell to add symphonies, ect., with Instruments to their Anthems; and thereupon established a select number of his private music to play the symphonies and Ritornellos which he had appointed.'

This was not the beginning of a policy to remodel church music, for Tudway goes on to explain that 'The King did not intend by this innovation to alter anything in the Established way. He only appointed this to be done when he came himself to the Chappell.' In other words, he could in this way hear the type of music he enjoyed and make the point that his presence at Service made the occasion one of special musical value and rejoicing. 'In about four or five years time,' Tudway mentioned, 'some of the forwardist and brightest Children of the Chappell, as Mr. Humfreys, Mr. Blow, etc., began to be Masters of a faculty in Composing. This His Majesty greatly encouraged, by indulging their youthful fancys, so that every month, at least, and afterwards oftener, they provided something New of this Kind. In a few years more several others, Educated in the Chappell, produc'd their Compositions in this style; for otherwise it was vain to hope to please his Majesty.'

To what extent Charles II's tastes moulded those of such gifted children as Humfrey, Blow and Purcell, and to what extent the king's tastes were simply those of an up-to-date dilettante of the 1660s and therefore in natural sympathy with those of gifted, forward-looking composers is, perhaps, an irrelevance. Evelyn, who was forty-two years old at the time, resented the new style in church music: 'One of His Majesty's Chaplains preached,' he reported, 'after which, instead of the ancient, grave and solemn wind musique accompanying the *Organ*,

[1] John Evelyn: *op. cit.* November 25, 1660.
[2] Matthew Locke: *The Present Practice of Music Vindicated.*

was introduced a Consort of Violins between every pause, after the *French* fantastical light way, better suiting a Tavern or a Playhouse than a Church: This was the first time of change, and now we no more heard the Cornet, which gave life to the Organ, that instrument quite left off in which the English were so skillful.'[1] What Evelyn had actually heard from cornetts, however, was apparently their use to double the treble part because of the weakness of the boys' voices, and what he was missing so pathetically was a hastily contrived procedure which used the instrument simply as a stop gap.

Evelyn, it seems from the *Diary*, was just as interested in music as any educated and civilised man of position ought to be. Pepys, thirteen years his junior, was a real enthusiast who played, sang and composed songs in recitative music. Pepys heard 'violls and other instruments' play 'a symphony between every verse of the anthem' in September 1662, three months before Evelyn's 'first time of change', and although, like Evelyn, he attended the service on December 21, nothing in its music seemed to him to be worthy of mention, though he noted in September that the number of instrumentalists involved was not fixed, but that the music on September 14 'was more full than it was last Sunday'. The King had, by this time, recruited his band of twenty-four violins, in emulation of Louis XIV, but there seems to be no record of the entire band's being brought to accompany the service; as Tudway points out, it was 'a select number' who were employed for church music. Probably, in his distress on December 21, Evelyn did not bother to count but simply, from the sight and sound of the strings, took it for granted that the entire band was present.

With the new elaborations, the anthem tended to grow into something comparable to a short cantata and, oddly enough, its balance of forces tended to change. Purcell, for example, preferred to accompany the solo voice or voices with the organ and to move the strings from the solo music to accompany the choir, perhaps because of the more penetrating voices of strings since the violin had become popular.

The new ideas of the Chapel Royal, however, had little influence on church music in general, or on the music of the cathedrals. Even St. Paul's and Westminster Abbey were a long time before they recovered a full complement of singers although Pepys heard an organ in Westminster Abbey on November 4, 1660, and mentioned in his *Diary* that this was the first time he had ever heard an organ in a cathedral; a month or so later, on December 30, he commented on 'the great confusion of people that come to hear the organ'. Almost a year later, at a time when, according to Hawkins, people of rank used to attend Evensong at St. Paul's so that they could hear the anthem, Pepys went one day to Matins and found 'only a few idle poor people and boys' in the congregation. Gentlemen of the Chapel Royal seemed often to hold a plurality of posts and to serve also as lay vicars at St. Paul's or the Abbey, where as late as 1667 a cornett player was employed to double the trebles.

The provincial cathedrals elsewhere fared worse. At Bristol, in 1663, the

[1] Evelyn: *op. cit.* December 21, 1662.

cathedral staff consisted of three minor canons and six men in the choir. There is no record of the date at which boys returned, and apparently full cathedral music was not restored for some years.[1]

Roger North dealt with the music of 'The Cathedral Churches in the North (except Carlisle which is but a ruin, the east end only and very little if any more than that standing) . . . [They] have the ordinary wind instruments in the Quires, as the cornett, sackbut, double curtaile and others, which supply the want of voices, very notorious there, since we can have none but boys, and those none of the best, as the cornett (being well sounded) doth; one might mistake it for a choice ennuch.'[2]

Parish church music remained simple, rarely offering anything more ambitious than the metrical psalm sung in unison; psalm singing in four-part harmony was rare and even in the eighteenth century the majority of churches were without organs though the instrumental choirs, which are known best perhaps from Hardy's *Under the Greenwood Tree*, began in the eighteenth century to provide a completely satisfactory alternative to the organ, although their technical abilities seem to have been unimpressive and their musical ambitions extremely limited.

The reconstituted Chapel Royal, however, with its school of prodigies—for though Purcell overshadows them, neither Humfrey nor Blow was a negligible composer—was the home of a new style of composition, modern and cosmopolitan, rejecting the English tradition not only in church music but in its entirety. Together with the king's newly organised band of twenty-four violins—by which, like his cousin Louis XIV, he meant strings—the court was the forcing house of a new sort of music. Because the English, at the Restoration, had restored the monarchy and carefully arranged to keep it hamstrung for want of money, the style gained social prestige from the court, but the composers were more occupied with work elsewhere than with music for the king. Court music became little more than the State Birthday and Welcome odes in which fulsomely sycophantic verses were, more often than not, given music of abounding vitality and brilliance. Such works provided not only a technique but a splendidly extrovert style for other odes, like the St. Cecilia's Day odes which became annual public events after 1703, or occasional works like Purcell's *Yorkshire Feast Song*.

Charles II had reappointed Nicholas Lanier to be Master of the King's Musick at the Restoration. Lanier was already an old man—he was born in 1588, the son and grandson of court musicians who had originally come from France. Charles I had made him Master of the King's Musick in 1626. He died in 1666, and was succeeded by Louis Grabu, a musician whose awareness of continental music was not a sufficient compensation for his inferiority as both an executive musician and a composer. In so far as Charles II had a musical policy, it seems to have been twofold: to reproduce the atmosphere of grandeur with which music

[1] J. Graham Hooper: *A Survey of Music in Bristol, with Special Reference to the Eighteenth Century.* Unpublished M.A. Thesis of Bristol University.
[2] Roger North: *Lord Keeper North.* 1676.

surrounded Louis XIV and to bring into English music the new techniques and
new styles of the continent for no better reason than that he enjoyed them. He
was a man who enjoyed music, but only so far as he could beat time to it; the
traditional English fantasy bored him, as he was always ready to point out, and
he preferred light, crisp rhythms and tuneful, harmonised music.

His twenty-four violins and the smaller, select groups of twelve strings which
were a direct but smaller copy of Louis XIV's *Petits Violons* played for the king in
private or in public and travelled with him on official journeys. Five at a time
they played for the services of his Chapel when he was present, and the entire
band was at times used experimentally; in 1668 it was for a time two orchestras
of eighteen men each, each eighteen doing alternate month's duties.

The reaching after continental modes led to the sending of Humfrey to study
in France and Italy, and of John Bannister to France, apparently to investigate
the style and organisation of Louis XIV's string orchestra before taking charge
of Charles II's new group of strings. The early repertory of the English band is
hardly known and the whole ambitious organisation of Charles II's music suffered
considerably from his chronic shortage of money. The salaries of Charles's
musicians were usually and seriously in arrears. In 1667, Grabu had to appeal for
payment in order to avoid arrest for debt; he was owed £450 from the Exchequer,
£145 4s. 6d. by the Treasury and £32 5s. 0d. by the Great Wardrobe. As early
as 1666, Pepys reported a conversation with one of the musicians, John Hingston,
who told him that 'many of the musique are ready to starve, they being five years
behind for their wages; nay, Evans, the famous man upon the harp, having not
his equal in the world, did the other day die for mere want, and was fain to be
buried at the alms of the parish, and carried to his grave in the dark without one
linke, but that Mr. Hingston met it by chance and did give 12d. to buy two or
three linkes. He say all must come to ruin at this rate, and I believe him'.[1]

Charles's intentions were good. He recognised that salaries, at his accession,
were too low to keep his musicians and he raised them to a point at which they
more or less matched prices. The only trouble is that he could not find the money
to pay them, and, in 1666, with unpaid sailors from the Dutch War rioting in
London, the needs of a harpist like Evans could hardly be a pressing concern.

The result, however, was an enrichment of public music in London. The
presence of a number of highly skilled, under-paid and under-employed musicians
meant that they had to go outside their official posts to make money, and this,
in turn, meant the growth of the public concert. While opera was always a
questionable business in English eyes, the public concert, a much cheaper entertainment to mount, rapidly became popular enough to pay its way.

Thus there is no equivalent in England to the Central European *Kapellmeister*
or cantor, busily working for a single patron or institution which demanded all
the work he had time to produce. Purcell wrote for the court, for Westminster
Abbey, where he was organist, for the theatres and for any other patron or group
of individuals who might commission work from him; Matthew Locke, a

[1] Pepys: *op. cit.* December 19, 1666.

generation before, had done the same, and Blow continued to work in the same way after Purcell's death. These external and sporadic patrons enabled the English composer, so long as his work attracted the public, to devote a lot of his time to freelance activity while he held on firmly to a secure though never well-paid post at court, in a cathedral or in the Chapel Royal. Charles II knew, as Elizabeth I had known, that to deny the freedom of his musicians to earn money outside court would have been to make it impossible for any first-rate composer or instrumentalist to accept a position in the king's service.

This, though it explains why there were musicians to provide music for public concerts and to play at such events, does not explain why the public concert began in London before it was considered a possibility anywhere else. Granted that seventeenth-century London was a huge and on the whole wealthy city and that the Puritan banishment of music from the church had denied an appetite which looked for satisfaction elsewhere, on the continent the same appetite was satisfied, as it was in the English provinces, by the private or semi-private meetings of amateurs who wanted to sing and play together. The King's Musick was an efficient and well-drilled body whose members took off their royal livery to augment usually exiguous earnings in the London theatres or concert rooms —the halving of the band so that its members need only play in court during alternate months may equally well have been a concession to their poverty or a recognition of the fact that they could not be dislodged from external commitments. That musicians chose to explore a new way of making money is not hard to explain; the mystery is that the public concert quickly became a musical and social success among listeners many of whom must have been given to making music at home and to have themselves played the works which were the backbone of many concert programmes. 'How and by what means music shot up in such request as to crowd out from the stage even comedy herself, and to sit down in her place and become of such mighty value and price as we now know it to be, is worth enquiring after,' wrote Roger North,[1] about fifty years after Bannister's concerts began, but even he could not answer all the questions.

The early historians, like Burney and Hawkins, describe the concert as a brilliant invention of John Bannister when he fell into disgrace with the king. They do not, in other words, take much notice of the fact that during the Commonwealth music had become part of the business of many inns and taverns. A well-to-do middle class, it seems, could be willing to pay to listen to music in public as well as to play it, and perhaps to pay for it, at home. Nobody can blame Burney and Hawkins for concentrating on the work of Bannister; he advertised his concerts and thus left some record of what he did and where it happened. In their writings, Bannister becomes the hero, dismissed from royal employment because he rudely opposed the king's policy of giving the best positions to foreign musicians. North, rather nearer the actual date and disapproving of what he felt to be the cheapening of music for the sake of mere profit, described his concerts as 'low' and wrote of him without flattery. 'His course of life was such

[1] Roger North: *North on Music*, ed. John Wilson. Novello, 1959.

as kept him poor, and by way of a project to get a little money, he opened a public room in a nasty hole in Whitefriars, where there was raised a compartment with curtains for the music [that is, the performers] and about the room seats by the way of alehouses boxes, but well set off and painted for the company. A shilling a piece, call for what you please, pay the reckoning and "Welcome Gentlemen".[1]

The old historians were quite right about Bannister's resentment of the way in which foreign musicians were preferred at court, but though his opinions seem to have been expressed with considerable force in the king's hearing, he was not dismissed, and both his period of disgrace and his loss of promotion seem to have been due to his doubtful financial character. In 1667, a number of the twenty-four violins petitioned the king to complain that Bannister was keeping for himself money he was supposed to transmit to the players. They accused him of misappropriating about £275 in 1663 alone. Nevertheless, in 1674 he was given grants for liveries due to him in 1665, 1666 and 1667, and a year later he was reimbursed for instrument strings bought over the previous eleven years. Whilst other members of the King's Musick took additional jobs for the sake of pay— John Lily had a private patron, taught privately, acted as a copyist and taught four of the Chapel Royal boys the viol and the oboe—Bannister was simply the most daring and far-sighted of them.

The 'nasty hole in Whitefriars' was Bannister's house beside the George Tavern. The actual music room was made to look as much as possible like the music room of a tavern; the players occupied a curtained alcove at the end of the room, and the audience sat at tables divided by partitions along each wall, as they would have done in a tavern. The musicians were, apparently, 'foreigners' in the old sense of the word, that is, outsiders from the jurisdiction of the London and Westminster musicians guilds, and they played for a fee or a share of the profits. Their programmes were extremely mixed; they played concert music, solos for the violin, the flageolet and the bass viol. The singers sang new songs in the Henry Lawes recitative styles and lute songs. The programme had to be popular, for the whole purpose of the enterprise was to make money. Bannister did well enough to move to Chandos Street at the Westminster end of the Strand after two years, then to Lincoln's Inn Fields and finally to a house near St. Clement Danes, in the Strand.

Bannister regularly advertised his concerts in the *London Gazette,* and his advertisements show that he was ready to use gimmicks to build up an audience. His first concert was announced soberly: 'At Mr. John Bannister's house (now called the Musick School) over by the George Tavern in White Fryers, will be musick performed by the most excellent masters, beginning precisely at four of the clock in the afternoon, and every afternoon for the future, precisely at the same hour.' On January 25, 1674, Bannister advertised that he had moved to 'Shandois Street, Covent Garden'. A week later, a competitor appeared, announcing 'A rare concert of four trumpets marine, never heard before in

[1] *Ibid.*

England. If any person desire to come and hear it, they may repair to the Fleece
Tavern, near St. James's about two of the clock in the afternoon, every day in
the week except Sunday. Every concert will continue one hour, and so begin
again. The best places are one shilling, and the other sixpence.'

Bannister, it seems, had no monopoly of concert-giving because tavern performances seem to have continued, apparently so widely known that it would
have been pointless to advertise them. After his death, in 1679, his son John
continued his apparently profitable work, combining it with his duties as a
violinist in the orchestra of King William and as first violinist for opera performances at Drury Lane. Regular advertisements for another series of concerts
began to appear in the year of his death, when in October, an announcement
explained that the concerts previously given in Bow Street 'would be joined to
those in York Buildings and would be performed in York Buildings'.

York Buildings was a new development, completed in the 1670s, at the Western
end of the Strand, between it and the river. It was named after the Duke of York
who was to become James II while he was still a popular, victorious admiral and
before his real or suspected plans to subvert the Church of England destroyed
his popularity. York Buildings contained the first room in London specifically
intended for music, and it was both fashionable and splendidly decorated in the
style of the times. Its programmes were often both vocal and instrumental; stars
of the opera were engaged to give concerts there, and in 1693 Purcell's *St.
Cecilia's Day Ode*, a couple of months old, was heard. At the same time, music
was regularly to be heard at the Two Golden Bulls, in Bow Street, and at Bedford
Gate, Charles Street, Covent Garden.

North[1] follows the quaint history of one concert society. A group of gentlemen
amateurs met to play together at the Castle Tavern in Fleet Street. Because they
were gentlemen, they played the popular instruments, being mostly violinists,
and hired professionals to play the less gentlemanly parts. They became known
for the quality of their performance; even Roger North approved of them because
they played English consort music in the traditional style, and the landlord
realised that they could be a source of profit. When, however, he began to dis-
courage the gentlemen by filling the room with a paying audience, the gentlemen
gave up, the professionals co-opted colleagues to fill the vacant places and, as the
Castle Concert, before long they too departed to the more fashionable and
commodious hall in York Buildings.

The opposition to public concerts, at any rate as London first came to know
them, was expressed by the old-fashioned Thomas Mace's *Musick's Monument*,
published in 1676. Mace's book actually contained a design for its author's ideal
concert room, a circular auditorium, raked upwards from the curtained central area
where the players sat. As in Bannister's reconstruction of a tavern music room,
the instrumentalists were to be hidden. Mace did not attack concerts on principle; he saw in them a danger of concentration upon what he believed to be the
less worthy qualities of performance, the excitement created by a virtuoso singer

[1] *Op. cit.*

or player, because he rejected the idea of music as sensation and showmanship. Music to him was the voice of thought and of reason; the new music, and the methods taken to propagate it, corrupted it into expressing unbridled emotion and irrational sensation. But Mace looked back longingly to the age when people played soberly beautiful, thoughtful music, and occupied much of his book in explaining how easy it is to learn the rudiments of keyboard or lute technique, or of singing. Real musical appetites, he believed, were being corrupted because those who were conscious of a need for music were seduced by prosperity into the passive world of the concert where they learnt to be satisfied with cheap, catchpenny stuff.

Similar ideas are at the back of North's mind when he considers the concerts he apparently attended at York Buildings:

> Although the best masters in their tones, as well solo, as concerted, showed their gifts, yet I cannot say, whatever the musick, that the entertainment was good; because it consisted of broken, incoherent parts; now a consort, then a lutenist, then a *violino solo*, then a song, and so piece after piece, the time sliding away, while the masters blundered and swore in changing places, and one might perceive that they blundered and swore to spight one another; whereas an entertainment ought to proceed as a drama, fireworks or indeed every publick delight, by judicious steps . . . and concluding in a perfect atone. All of which cannot be done but by an absolute Dictator, who may coerce and punish the republican mob of musick masters.

But, says North in a rare moment of something like humour, the concert givers 'found out the grand secret, that the English would follow musick and drop their pence freely. Of which some advantage hath been made.'[1] Again North pointed out the unwisdom of timing the performances at York House deliberately to clash with the time of theatre performances and thus to set up a struggle for audiences which, he explained, fell away as soon as concerts ceased to be the latest fashion.

Historians dwell lovingly on the concerts promoted and financed by Thomas Britton, the Clerkenwell coal merchant, from 1678 until 1714. Above Britton's coal storage was a long, narrow upper room which he converted into a concert hall. Pepusch played regularly for him, and Handel attended the concerts, and probably played at them, during his first visit to England. Britton, at first, simply invited an audience to make music and to listen to it with him, though eventually he charged a subscription—ten shillings a year—to pay for the coffee which he had previously sold at a penny a cup. The catalogues of his instruments and of his music library survive, and the latter is extremely comprehensive. All the major work, vocal and instrumental, by English composers from the Elizabethans to Purcell were included, with a large number of Italian works spanning the period from Andrea Gabrieli to Corelli and Veracini, and there were omnibus volumes of overtures, trumpet concertos and so on. Britton was operating for pleasure and

[1] *Op. cit.*

not for profit, and it seems reasonable to guess that his often eminent performers were doing the same, so that his taste seems purer than that of rivals who wooed the public in order to make a profit.

Hawkins's description of Britton's concerts (or, in the terminology of the day they should perhaps be called 'academies') allows enthusiasm to obliterate his usual sense of social propriety 'On the ground floor,' he wrote,[1] 'was a repository for small coals; over that was the concert room, which was very long and narrow and had a ceiling so low that a tall man could but just stand upright in it. The stairs to this room were on the outside of the house, and could scarce be ascended without crawling. The house itself was very old and low built, and in every respect so poor as to be a fit habitation only for a very poor man. Notwithstanding all, this mansion, despicable as it may seem, attracted to it as polite an audience as ever the opera did, and a lady of the first rank in the kingdom, the Duchess of Queensbury, may well remember that in the pleasure which she manifested at hearing Mr. Britton's concert, she seemed to have forgotten the difficulties by which she ascended the steps to it.'

By the time that Thomas Hickford, supposed to have been a dancing-master, began to give concerts in what seems at first to have been called 'Mr. Hickford's Great Dancing Room', in 1697, concert manners and planning seem to have reached a point at which North might have begun to approve. Hickford's original room was between James Street and Panton Street, at the back of the Haymarket, and, round about 1700, it was enlarged. The foreign stars of the opera sang there, foreign virtuosi found it the best place because it was in the newly developed, fashionable area between Covent Garden and New Bond Street which grew in the reign of George I—in which to give London concerts and, in 1719, concerts by the Opera orchestra from the Haymarket Theatre began to be given there. The important thing about all its announcements, which duly emphasise them, are the names of the stars of the evening. In 1739 Hickford moved to a new and more fashionable building which had its front door in Brewer Street, Soho, and its back door in Windmill Street. J. C. Bach and Carl Friedrich Abel gave their concerts in Hickford's Brewer Street Rooms from 1766 to 1775 and Mozart played there with his sister on May 13, 1765.

The Bach Abel concerts, which began in Spring Gardens in 1764, were events that neither North nor any fastidious modern music-lover could repudiate. Apart from their own compositions (and Johann Christian Bach was, for England, the leader of a new movement whose compositions do not deserve complete neglect) Bach and Abel introduced the symphony, the new style solo concerto and the pianoforte itself to their audiences. From Spring Gardens they moved to Carlyle House, Soho Square, which had been bought by Mrs. Cornelys, who had been born Theresa Immer, in Venice, had had considerable success as a prima donna, had been Casanova's mistress, had married a dancer who had committed suicide, had married a Dutchman but turned up in England in 1760 without a husband. She had been in England in 1746, as a member of the opera

[1] Hawkins: *op. cit.*

company, but on her return she was about thirty-seven years old and was content to promote balls, masquerades and concerts until, in 1771, she was indicted before the grand jury for keeping a disorderly house; oddly enough, just before the accusation she had begun to challenge the monopoly of the Patent Theatres by giving opera performances in Carlyle House. For the last few years of her life—she died in 1797—she is said to have sold asses' milk from a stall at Hyde Park Corner which she expanded into a breakfast room. Her contribution to music is no more than peripheral but her career adds an enlivening touch of colour, probably of scarlet, to eighteenth-century musical history.

Bach and Abel moved their concerts to the larger hall at Almack's Club, and in 1775 the Hanover Square Rooms was opened. This became the most important of London concert halls, at which Haydn gave his concerts during his two visits to London, and it was the first home of the Royal Philharmonic Society's concerts. Obviously, the concert was a popular London entertainment, but, so far as we are able to follow its history we do so from one point to another in a London expanding rapidly and always ready for new, fashionable developments. In 1772, the Tottenham Street Rooms opened, and provided a new home for the Academy of Ancient Music. The Pantheon, in the newly developed Oxford Street, lying between the modern Great Marlborough Street and Poland Street, opened in 1791 and became a temporary opera house when the King's Theatre was burnt down a few months later. Until then it had been a home for concerts, balls and masquerades.

Obviously, of course, all these were places for the upper classes. They made concert-going a socially elevated occupation. Prices were too high, probably intentionally so, for the lower orders. The socially less favoured, however, were not totally deprived of music, for the popular pleasure gardens—Vauxhall, Ranelagh and so on, like Sadlers' Wells and other places where the classes mingled, offered music often as well rehearsed and sometimes with the same star performers as that to be heard in the concert halls. Music, in any case, was good enough business for rival organisations to set up Pleyel against Haydn in 1792 and for both to do well—Haydn magnificently well—out of a meaningless rivalry.

All this was professional activity supported by takings at the box office. Outside London there was little professional music-making and the few professional musicians were teachers who played with the local music clubs. Only Bath, during the season, of all provincial English cities in the eighteenth century, maintained any professional orchestra other than a group of waits who were in many places still expected to give public performances. Music clubs, like that of Oxford which declined in the 1690s and revived as a primarily instrumental body after Handel's visit in 1733, flourished throughout the provinces. In the seventeenth century, its tastes had been firmly rooted in the past, and its catalogue of music books in 1665 contained only works by John Jenkins, H. Lawes, Coprario, Baltzar, Brewer, Orlando Gibbons and his son Christopher. Brewer may have been alive when the catalogue was drawn up; he was born in 1611. Christopher Gibbons died in 1676 and Jenkins in 1678. Henry Lawes, who died in 1662, was the only one of these composers whose music reflects any mid-seventeenth-century style. This may be why the Oxford Musick Meeting lived for less than thirty years but was resurrected as soon as Handel's visit injected some new blood into it, so that in no more than fifteen years it needed its own hall, the Music Room in Holywell which is noted as the oldest surviving concert hall in Europe.

Those who attended played, if they could, or listened, for the Meeting existed primarily so that amateur musicians could play together. Gentlemen paid a shilling, ladies were admitted free and dogs were not allowed. 'In compliance with the earnest Request of a very considerable number of Subscribers' ran an early announcement, 'it is hoped that Gentlemen will not in future suffer Dogs to follow them into the Room, which are a great Annoyance to the company.'[1]

In Norwich, a lively 'Musick Meeting' began in the early 1720s, and a rival 'Musick Clubb' was formed there in 1736. Norwich was one of the largest and most prosperous cities in England, where, at the beginning of the eighteenth century, a by-law was passed compelling the city waits to play monthly concerts for the citizens. About a dozen music rooms were in successive use in Norwich, and the most likeable and commodious of them is still standing. York, Lincoln and Lichfield had two music clubs each in the eighteenth century, and Hereford probably had three.

Bristol, by 1731, had two music clubs, as well as a Lenten oratorio season given by the professional musicians from the Pump Room at Bath. After 1727, St. Cecilia's Day was celebrated with a concert; at the first celebration, the Utrecht Te Deum and Jubilate were sung, together with one of the Chandos Anthems. Two years later, the St. Cecilia's Day concert was given for the benefit of the cathedral organist, Nathaniel Priest, 'Mr. Priest will not only be assisted by his friends in town,' declared the newspaper announcement of the concert, 'but by several Eminent and Masterly hands from London, Bath, Wells and other Places. The number of performers will be about 30, including voices.' The programme consisted of 'overtures and concertos by Mr. Handel and other judicious Authors', with arias from *Scipio*, *Acis and Galatea* and an oratorio, as well as solos for 'hautboy, German flute and violin', and 'a celebrated piece for two bassoons'. While this music marathon was under way in the St. Augustine's Back Theatre, the rival Music Club was at a concert 'for Mr. Smedley' at the Merchants' Hall.[2]

Something of the musical life of Winchester can be found in the autobiography of the composer, Charles Dibdin. Dibdin was a choirboy at Winchester from 1756, when he was eleven years old, to 1759, and mentioned the regular weekly concerts there in the 1760s. He was visiting the city in 1769 when he attended a subscription concert of the Music Club with a friend. As they were visitors to the city, they were each charged two shillings and sixpence entry fee, but as they were able to play with the orchestra, their half-crowns were returned at the end of the evening.[3]

[1] Jackson's *Oxford Journal*.
[2] Hooper: *op. cit.*
[3] Charles Dibdin: *The Professional Life of Mr. Dibdin.* London, 1803.

Stanley Sadie[1] has traced the growth of music clubs in East Anglia and else-where during the eighteenth century: in 1721, an advertisement in *The Suffolk Mercury or St. Edmunds-Bury Post* proposed that weekly or monthly meetings should be held to perform 'the newest solos, Sonatas, Concertos and Extra-vaganzas extant', though we do not know whether or not as a result of this advertisement subscription concerts started there in 1734. In the 1730s, Great Yarmouth developed both a musical society and a music 'clubb' and Ipswich formed a music society. Even quite small villages, like Debenham, in Suffolk, had some form of musical life. The Debenham musical society met every month 'to perform Handel's oratorios etc.'

Among the available composers only J. C. Bach and Friedrich Abel, his partner, composed specifically for London concerts, the programmes of which are not easy to establish. The music at most of the provincial 'Music Meetings' was largely overtures and concertos of Handel, the concertos of Corelli and Gemini-ani, and whatever similar works they could find. In Newcastle, these were joined by similar compositions by Avison. Mudge, a mysterious figure who may have been a parson in Birmingham or a doctor in Plymouth, was probably in contact with a music club—both the Birmingham clergyman and the Plymouth doctor were members of their local clubs—otherwise he would hardly have published or even written six attractive concertos, the first of which eccentrically requires three singing voices. But until a new style began to reach out from London, the English clubs played an established repertoire. Few composers as talented as Avison and Mudge avoided the lures of metropolitan life and music-making.

From the point of view of modern concert-goers performances, with any visitor who could play joining in the regular ensemble at such meetings, must have been excruciating, but in principle their members played together for fun, in the Chestertonian conviction that anything worth doing is worth doing badly. During the eighteenth century, it seems, amateur enthusiasm declined. A music society was formed in Manchester in 1744, apparently as a way in which the city's Jacobites could meet without rousing suspicion. It consisted mainly of amateurs with two professional violinists and a professional cellist to be the concertino of the concerti grossi they performed, and a professional harpsichordist. It began with a hundred and sixty-five members, each of whom paid a five shilling subscription, rose to a hundred and eighty-one in three months before internal dissensions caused by the 1745 Rebellion halved its membership, suggesting, perhaps, that many Mancunians were Jacobites in principle rather than practice. When the danger passed and concerts again became possible, the membership began to revive, but its last recorded concert was given in August 1745.

Whether or not meetings continued in Manchester but left no trace, in 1777 the Gentlemen's Concerts were inaugurated, the only 'gentlemen' who wished to play were flautists. The Gentlemen's Concerts became professional entertainments which maintained uninterrupted activity until 1920.

---

[1] Stanley Sadie: 'Concert Life in Eighteenth Century England', *Proceedings of the Royal Musical Association*, December 9, 1958.

16 Handel and England

When Handel reached England in 1710, he had recently been appointed *Kapell-meister* in Hanover. For a young man of twenty-five, this was a very impressive appointment, and Handel could very well have settled down to a peaceful and productive life. He had started his career as organist of the Cathedral in Halle, a musically limited post which he left to work at the Opera House in Hamburg. From his Hamburg earnings and his meetings there with Italian noblemen, he had arranged his Italian tour. In Hamburg, and again in Italy, he had met the Englishmen who advised him to visit England.

Apparently the authorities in Hanover felt from the start that it would be difficult to hold him, for Mainwaring, his earliest but in many ways least depend-able biographer, says that the Elector authorised the offer of a salary of 1500 crowns to keep him at court; his actual salary was 600 crowns, or 1000 thaler. Though this made him more prosperous than most court *Kapellmeister*, he accepted the post only on condition that he was allowed to keep promises made before his appointment.

Thus he made his way to England and apparently set out to work according to a preconceived plan. The Earl of Manchester, the English Ambassador in Venice soon to be raised to dukedom, had apparently given the composer intro-ductions to important aristocratic music-lovers in England; so, probably, had John Wych, the English resident in Hamburg. There were a number of German musicians, among them Johann Christoph Pepusch who had been in England for about ten years and Johann Ernst Galliard, both eminent in English music, who became his friends. Probably it was obvious to the Earl of Manchester that no English composer in 1710 had either Handel's inventiveness or the technical competence which equipped him to be a German church composer, an Italian composer of vocal music and a composer of keyboard music in the Italian or German styles. Probably his English admirers told him so. Stretching his leave of absence from Hanover until it lasted for eighteen months, he scored a success in the opera house with *Rinaldo*. This earned him £50 and £811 from Aaron Hill and Johann Jacob Heidegger, the Bavarian-born Swiss impresario, who managed the opera at the King's Theatre in the Haymarket. Out of this he had to pay the orchestra, the members of which earned from eight shillings to £1 for each performance, for the opera's run of thirteen performances, a matter of between £200 and £300. *Rinaldo* was frequently revived, produced in Hamburg, Milan and Dublin and promptly published without recitatives—this was the normal English style—by John Walsh, the most successful and unscrupulous of

English publishers. According to Hawkins,[1] 'Walsh got fifteen hundred pounds by printing it,' but *Rinaldo* was sold at nine shillings and Walsh's print cannot, judging by the scarcity of copies, have been large, so that Hawkins's figure is unlikely to have been accurate.

Handel's next step was to become an officially recognised English composer. He managed to be granted an interview by Queen Anne, 'expressed his sense of the favours accorded to him', says Mainwaring, and, 'Her Majesty was pleased to add to them by large presents, and intimated her desire of seeing him again.'

He had, in other words, set out to become the dominating power in English music. To conquer the Opera House was to win popularity with the educated, travelled aristocracy who constituted the court and who could influence the Crown. We can only guess that this was Handel's plan, for no written evidence of his intentions exists, but his return to Hanover after his interview with the queen and his speedy escape back to England suggest that his Hanoverian salary was only a means of subsidising other activities, and, having proved his quality as an opera composer, he returned to make himself acceptable as a composer of official state works.

It would be interesting to know how Handel managed to escape so quickly from Hanover, but no documentary explanation seems to exist and we are left with speculation. George I, waiting in Hanover, was the legal heir to Queen Anne, whose health was poor and whose admiration for Handel's music was well known. The Elector may have felt that to prevent Handel's return to London could have made difficulties for him, on his accession, for he seems to have made no real efforts to control his absentee *Kapellmeister*.

Handel's return to England in the autumn of 1712 was apparently expected, for the Haymarket Theatre was waiting for an opera from him on November 12, and had to offer a miscellaneous programme, *Il Trionfo d'Amore*, because Handel's *Il Pastor Fido* was not finished in time. *Il Trionfo d'Amore* was repeated on November 15 and Handel's new work reached the stage on November 22. It survived six performances, and had to be replaced by a pastichio, *Dorinda*. 'The musick of this,' its announcement explained, 'is taken out of Severall Italian operas by Nico Haym.' Handel's *Teseo* came into the repertory on January 10, 1713, and was a great success. As the manager to whom Heidegger had entrusted the running of the theatre, Owen Swiney, decamped with the takings after the work had been played twice to capacity audiences, its further success was vital. A note from the Vice-Chamberlain's office, dated February 13, instructs 'the Treasurer or Treasurers' of the theatre to distribute £162 19s. from the theatre takings to the theatre personnel in proportion to the conditions of their contracts. Heidegger, with a success on his hands, persuaded orchestra, singers and theatre staff to carry on and recoup their and the theatre's losses.

It seems that with two successes—*Rinaldo* and *Teseo*—flanking the unsuccessful *Il Pastor Fido*—Handel decided that the operatic situation was satisfactory, and turned to a more difficult part of his plan. By 1713, there was no

[1] Hawkins: *op. cit.*

officially appointed composer to the English Royal Family. The Master of the King's Musick was primarily conductor of the king's orchestra; there were appointments to the orchestra and the Royal Chamber Music, and rather more impressive ones as music teachers to the children of the Royal Family. New music was commissioned as it was needed from the composers who seemed to the king or his officials most likely to supply effective work. It was Handel's aim to show that whatever was needed, he could compose it.

Obviously, as a thoroughly professional composer, he had been studying the English style as it had been a generation before in the works of Purcell and his contemporaries. The first result, written apparently because the War of the Spanish Succession was in sight and would demand celebratory music, was a setting of the *Te Deum*. This was put on one side until it could be useful. An *Ode for the Birthday of Queen Anne*, composed in January 1713, was sung at court on the appropriate date, February 6. There is no document to explain that this was commissioned, so that the composer seems simply to have written it and offered it to the queen. He was ready for the end of the war and the signing of the Treaty of Utrecht. For the peace celebration, after the signing of the Treaty of Utrecht, in St. Paul's Cathedral on June 7, Handel made a setting of the *Jubilate* out of the Psalm *Laudate Pueri*, written in Rome, giving it festive orchestration. Thus, with the still unheard *Te Deum*, he had a setting of the canticles ready for the service.

The setting normally used at such celebrations was that which Purcell had written in 1694, a year before his death, for St. Cecilia's Day. It was generally accepted practice, as Handel must have known, that national celebrations required music by national composers, and nothing but extreme self-confidence could have led him, a foreigner, to put his own works forward for the service at St. Paul's, just as nothing but the queen's command could have put them into a service which she was expected to attend, though it seems natural to suppose that Handel's aristocratic friends had encouraged her decision. Henceforth, the *Utrecht Te Deum* and *Jubilate* alternated with Purcell's setting at St. Cecilia's Day celebrations and were sung at all services which Parliament officially attended. Without being English—he did not seek naturalisation until 1726—Handel had become an English state composer and in return for his 'Utrecht' canticles, the queen granted him a pension of £200 a year.

The accession of George I in 1714 created a situation which Handel's biographers have over-dramatised. According to Mainwaring, Handel had been granted leave from his neglected post in Hanover two years before on condition 'that he returned in reasonable time', and his promise to do so, 'had slipped out of memory'. Handel had been living in the Earl of Burlington's Piccadilly home, among people familiar with court life; the inevitability of his Hanoverian patron's accession to the English throne must have been discussed in front of and probably with him; but for all that, he did nothing to suggest that George I had any grounds for complaint against him. It can hardly have been displeasing to the new king that his *Kapellmeister* had levered himself into a commanding

king was not a retainer for works which he was expected to compose but merely a subsidy. He was to provide the *Water Music*, some movements of which came from earlier works, the *Firework Music*, the canticles for the thanksgiving service after the Battle of Dettingen, coronation anthems, the funeral music for Queen Caroline; but other composers, too, joined him in providing music for these occasions. As music master to the king's daughters, he earned a salary of £200 for specific duties.

On February 20, 1719, Handel wrote to apologise to his recently bereaved brother-in-law for his delay in keeping a promise to visit Halle after the death of his sister. 'I find myself kept here,' he wrote, 'by affairs of the greatest moment on which, I venture to say, all my fortunes depend.' He was referring to his negotiations with the newly formed Royal Academy of Music, which planned to establish opera securely in London and to run it for the profit of the sixty-two wealthy men whose subscriptions of not less than £200 to the joint stock were to organise the company and to finance its first operations.

The Royal Academy of Music was both an artistic and a commercial enterprise. Any company offering shares in the days before the wildly over-subscribed South Sea Company's bubble burst had no difficulty in selling shares to a multitude of enthusiastic would-be investors whose enthusiasm was in direct proportion to their ignorance of the financial principles involved in their activities. Would-be investors believed their high dividends were the natural result of investment. The result of the offer of stock in the Royal Academy of Music, with the king's patronage to the tune of an annual subscription of £1000, was a rush of money. Mainwaring explained that £40,000 was received in promises of subscription; Hawkins and Burney increased the amount to £50,000, and Chrysander, on their authority, gives the higher sum. Deutsch, however, prints a list of the original subscribers and the amount of their subscription,[1] showing that the sum of £10,000 originally intended was over-subscribed by £5600.

The members of the Academy were aristocrats, so that a board of earnest, music-loving amateurs with no professional experience of music and no business experience set themselves to control an extremely complex professional operation. They included Handel's patron the Earl of Burlington, experienced at least in mounting lavish private entertainments, Sir John Vanbrugh, the architect and playwright, and Colonel Blaithwayte, who had been a pupil of Domenico Scarlatti and who, as a child prodigy, had been painted at the keyboard by Kneller. None of them, of course, would have taken part in any sort of business administration, but the arts were a suitable field of activity for aristocrats. They appointed Heidegger to be their business manager and Handel to be the Musical Director of their enterprise at a salary of some £800 a year, in return for which he would recruit a company and direct its orchestra except for the early performances of a new work. Whatever he wrote for the Academy was outside the terms of his contract and would be paid for separately. An official

[1] Otto Erich Deutsch: *Handel: a Documentary Biography*. Adam and Charles Black, 1955.

librettist, Paolo Rolli, was engaged, Giovanni Bononcini was brought to England to play in the orchestra and to compose operas as they were required.

Under a warrant from the Lord Chamberlain, Handel was sent abroad to 'Germany, Italy or other such places as he might think fit' to recruit singers 'either by himself or by such correspondence as he shall think fit'. He was empowered to offer contracts for not more than a year and entrusted to engage the famous castrato Senesino. He had wide powers but was to keep the Court of the Academy informed of his activities, send back copies of any agreements he made and refer back to it any proposals outside the limits of his authority. By the end of 1719 he was back in England without Senesino, negotiations with whom were continued by Heidegger because Senesino's demands had been unreasonable; eventually the celebrated castrato arrived after the Royal Academy had been active for about six months. His unreasonableness must have been extreme, for Handel had, on the authority of the Court of the Royal Academy, engaged the soprano Margherita Durastante for £3000 for a three-month season and an additional £1000 if she would stay for fifteen months.

The Royal Academy of Music began its activities in the King's Theatre in the Haymarket on April 2, 1720, with *Numitore*, a libretto by Rolli set by Giovanni Porta and financed by a subscription of five per cent from the members, called for in the previous December. Its eight years' life achieved a good deal artistically but was a resounding commercial failure which historians used to excuse by pointing out the rivalries which, they held, split the company, between Handel and Bononcini and between the sopranos Faustina (the wife of the composer Hasse, from Dresden) and Cuzzoni. Apart from the fact that the rivalry of Handel and Bononcini existed only in the minds of their rival fans, it is, to say the least, unlikely that the squabbles (reaching on one famous occasion, to fisticuffs and hair-pulling) of two eminent, fiery and equally temperamental *prime donne* ever kept an audience out of a theatre. The Royal Academy of Music failed because its sense of financial reality was never sufficiently developed and because the vast salaries paid to singers and the lavishness of the productions were never tailored to its actual receipts. It was not long before the Court of the Academy was financing its operations by repeated calls for yet another instalment of its members' subscriptions and finding some of the members so reluctant to keep their undertaking that money was extorted from them only under threat of legal action.

The idea of floating an opera company in the hope of financial profit created some enemies for the Academy. The members were not, apart from Vanbrugh, men who had made any great stir in the country by virtue of the service to the state or their participation in public affairs; they were simply aristocratic dilletanti who had begun to show themselves in a new light as men eager for profit. *The Spectator*, still resolutely opposed to opera, found great fun inventing quotations for its stock. 'Yesterday, South Sea Company was 174 Opera Company 83, and a half,' it wrote a few days before the first season opened.[1]

[1] *The Spectator*. March 20, 1720.

Obviously, compared to the South Sea Company, the Royal Academy of Music is regarded as a very paltry investment. A week later it telescoped the names of two tenors, Nicolini and Benedetti, to create an archetypal Italian opera star: 'At the rehearsal yesterday, Signor Nihilini Benedetti rose half a Note above his Pitch when formerly Known. Opera Stock from 83 and a half, when he began; at 90 when he ended.'[1]

Serious attacks were probably less harmful than cheerful ridicule of this sort, but in February, 1721, the periodical *The Theatre* included an article by Sir John Edgar which, after casting the traditional derision upon opera texts, pointed out that as the words of the opera are senseless, the only appeal of the form can be to the desire for profit. Therefore the directors had 'a stock laid in to impose upon the stupidity of their admirers and it is to be expected that there will nightly be a succession of bubbles large enough to those that will part with their cash, as well as their understanding, to support a mechanic and mean profit raised by gentlemen of honour and quality upon ingenuous arts.'[2]

There was another cause for the failure of the Royal Academy of Music; the enthusiastic audience for opera was a socially limited audience of the upper classes. The dramatic principles of Baroque opera were still too far from those of the English theatre to win a large popular audience, and the Royal Academy did not give any very large number of concerts.

Three seasons exhausted nearly half of the original capital through nine demands on the subscribers, some of whom were reluctant to face their obligations. The Court of the Academy warned defaulters categorically that legal proceedings would be instituted against them. Like the earlier threat, however, this produced no action.

For all the difficulties of the directors, the theatre drew good audiences and there was a thriving black market in tickets for the most successful works. Handel's *Otho* was produced on January 12, 1723, and one of George I's gentlemen-in-waiting, Monsieur de Fabrice, wrote to a friend on January 15, the day of the second performance, 'there is such a run on it tickets are already being sold at two or three guineas which are originally half a guinea, so that it is like another Mississippi or South Sea Bubble'.[3] Part of the excitement, of course, was that the famous soprano Cuzzoni made her London debut in *Otho* and connoisseurs were eager to hear her. But inflated prices outside the theatre and splendid profits for the ticket touts did nothing to help the Academy.

On February 16, a month later, the Royal Academy of Music declared a dividend of seven per cent, not bothering to attempt to rebuild its lost capital. The *Daily Courier* expressed the pious opinion that 'If this company goes on with the same success as they have done for some time past, it will become engrafted on some of our Corporations in the City, the Taste of the Publick being so much improved lately.' Cuzzoni chose *Otho* for her benefit on March 26, and

---

[1] *Ibid.* March 27, 1720.
[2] Quoted in Deutsch: *op. cit.*
[3] *Ibid.*

four days later the *London Journal* reported a rumour that 'some of the nobility gave her fifty guineas a ticket'.

Handel's other contribution to the season, *Floridante*, did quite well, and Bononcini added *Crispo* and *Griselda* to the repertoire; Bononcini's were operas in a new, unheroic, charming style unfamiliar to London, and both were great successes. But despite the earlier dividend, on April 8, the Court of the Royal Academy was again warning defaulters of the dire consequences of withholding the subscription so far demanded; in June it was applying for the king's annual subscription of £1000, and for an extra £200 to pay the tax on it; it was given the bare subscription, used it to pay for the redecoration of the theatre and, in November, called for another payment of five per cent by the subscribers.

The season of 1724 brought a masterpiece, *Giulio Cesare*, from Handel, and it packed the house at every performance, but quarrels among the directors and between rival factions—those of composers against those of singers—made the season stormy. Durastante retired after a benefit performance which brought her more than £1000, and this, with her 1200 guineas in salary, suitably ended a great career. Bononcini's contract expired, but the Duchess of Marlborough settled £500 a year on him so long as he would stay in England, so that the Academy's composing staff—Handel, Bononcini and Filippo Amadei, who had been in the orchestra since the first production—remained unchanged. Faustina, joining the company in August 1725, for the following season, demanded and was offered a salary of £2000 a year. The sixteenth and seventeenth demands were made in January and March, 1726; three more demands, and the Academy's money was all gone. The end was drawing ominously near, and an eighteenth demand was made in the following November.

The Court, and its staff, did their best to hold back the inevitable. Bononcini, lately even more popular than Handel, was asked for another work. Handel balanced Faustina against Cuzzoni in *Admetus*, almost tempting them to give attractive displays of *prima donna* temperament which turned into a fight on the evening when Princess Amelia attended. *Ottone*, *Floridante* and *Giulio Cesare*, three of Handel's great successes, were revived. In July, however, George I died and the future of his subscription, vital to the Academy, was in doubt. A nineteenth demand for five per cent was made in October, a demand for two and a half per cent followed in April 1728, and at the end of May the Royal Academy adjourned a meeting until June 5 'to consider of proper measures for recovering Debts due to the Academy, and discharging what is due to Performers, Tradesmen and others; and also to determine how the scenes, Cloaths, etc., are to be disposed of, if the opera cannot be continued'.

On the following January 18, the Court of the Academy decided at last to prosecute defaulters and to 'permit Hydeger and Hendle to carry on operas without disturbance for five years and to lend them for that time our scenes, machines, clothes, instruments, furniture etc.'[1] The Royal Academy of Music was ended.

[1] Diary of Viscount Percival: quoted in Deutsch, *op. cit.*

Handel, only an employee of the Academy, had not suffered from the vicissitudes of his employers. His works had been popular, some sensationally so. His salary had been paid, as had his pension from the Royal Family and his salary as Royal Music Teacher. In 1720, George I had granted him a privilege of copyright to protect him against the activities of pirate publishers. It forbade anyone to 'Reprint or Abridge' his scores, 'or to Import, Buy, Vend, Utter or Distribute any copies thereof reprinted beyond the Seas during the Term of Fourteen Years without the Consent or Approbation of the same George Frederick Handel, his heirs, Executors and Assigns. . . .'

Copyright of this kind had been granted in place of monopolies in the reign of Queen Anne. It was designed to protect any composer or author whose name was a guarantee of profit to the publisher who pirated his work. It was not, however, a fool-proof protection; it was easy for publishers to evade its terms.

Handel had found Walsh eager to publish his work, and had soon discovered that Walsh was unscrupulously avaricious. Whether or not he really suggested that Walsh should write operas and that he should publish them, the story that he did so is a valid comment on their relationship. He brought out *Radamisto* through the relatively new firm of Richard Mears, which produced better prints than Walsh, but did so more expensively. *Radamisto* was hurried out in an edition corrected by the composer apparently to prevent pirated copies of the arias. It was followed by the *Harpsichord Lessons*, brought out by John Cluer; Handel's note explains that he was compelled to publish some of the following lessons 'because surreptitious and incorrect Copies of them had got abroad'.

Handel returned to Walsh for his next three operas, *Floridante*, *Otho* and *Flavio*, receiving £72, £42 and £26 5s. respectively for them. But in 1722 Walsh put out a pirated 'opera of *Radamistus* for a flute' or 'Favourite songs in the Opera . . . of . . . *Acis and Galatea*', published anonymously just after the pirated *Radamisto*. Walsh's agreement with Handel did not prevent him pirating *Radamisto* and issuing *Acis and Galatea*, which Handel had not released. It is not surprising that Handel took his wares elsewhere and thus between 1724 and 1728 his name does not appear in Walsh's accounts. Cluer published *Giulio Cesare*, *Tamerlano*, *Rodelinda* (published by subscription at fifteen shillings), *Scipione* and *Alessandro*. This did not prevent Walsh publishing two sets of 'Favourite songs' from *Tamerlano* almost as soon as Cluer had the vocal score ready. The customary popular flute arrangements—for the flute had succeeded the violin as the proper instrument for a gentleman to play—was prefaced in the authorised edition with a note declaring 'If J. Cluer's name is not on the Title Pages of these Works, they are spurious Editions, and not those Corrected and Figured by Mr. Handel.' Walsh's piracy was so open that the composer realised that his copyright was no protection and allowed Walsh the victory. Publication was obviously something he regarded as a minor concern, so long as the copies of his work in circulation were accurate, for combative as he was he did not fight for long against Walsh's piracy, knowing that whatever he issued would be pirated. His concern was accuracy, not profit, for each of the officially published scores was sold outright.

For the rest of Handel's operatic career, Walsh paid him £26 5s. for each opera, and Handel seems to have made no determined efforts to extort more from his victor. Walsh was prepared to pay considerably more than this for works in English, which indicated that the publisher found a bigger market for works like *Alexander's Feast* and for oratorios. Handel's devotion to opera somehow prevented him from seeing that he was working for a limited audience from a single station of society. He was a man of considerable substance with a considerable amount of stocks in the South Sea Company and a regular income capable of keeping him comfortably alive apart from the fees he received for his occasional works. An anthem for King George I's birthday in 1724 may have brought him only £3 18s. 6d. (Eccles, the Master of the King's Musick, was paid £11 for similar works), but Handel could manage comfortably without fees for such pieces, was generously treated by the Royal Family in other respects and probably wrote his music for royal occasions to keep it clearly in the public mind that he was the dominating power in English music.

It was his personal fortune which he wagered when he and Heidegger decided to carry on providing London with opera after the Royal Academy of Music died. He had, after all, plenty of evidence not only for the popularity of his own works but also for the existence of a loyal opera audience; the flourishing black market in tickets, the public's enthusiasm for the leading singers and the popularity of works revived almost season after season must have encouraged him to carry on; probably, too, he regarded the Court of the Royal Academy as a group of amateurs whose inefficiency had received its just deserts. He had done well out of the Royal Academy; so sanguine and obstinately determined a man, with an inborn love of a good fight, could hardly be expected to change his habits even though careful consideration might have advised him to do so.

It is customary to regard *The Beggar's Opera*, produced at the Theatre in Lincoln's Inn Fields on January 29, 1728, as the last nail hammered into the coffin of the Royal Academy although the Royal Academy had died of financial anaemia before Gay's eccentric masterpiece, fitted with charming popular tunes by Pepusch, had been seen. But *The Beggar's Opera* was not only a very funny play with delectable music in which English political and social life was shown in a distorting mirror, and which still, after nearly two hundred and fifty years, bites deep into the realities of English life. It was witty, it wedded music to action, it abandoned recitative and *da capo* arias, which articulate English theatre-goers regarded as unnatural and undramatic. It was ballad opera which almost any Englishman could enjoy. It attacked the standard form at the point where English audiences regarded it as weakest, the libretto; song after song begins with high-flown, operatically noble words which are mocked by its conclusion:

'If love The Virgin's Heart invade,' sings Mrs. Peacham,
'How like a moth, the simple Maid
Still plays about the Flame!

> If soon she is not made a Wife
> Her Honour's sing'd, and then for life
> She's—what I dare not name.'

The Beggar's Opera did not murder the defenceless Italian form but it was a portent which Handel, who is traditionally supposed to have enjoyed it, failed to heed. He was a gaily self-confident gambler with money enough at his disposal to back his fancy, and in Heidegger he had a partner who had been the only administrative brain in the earlier enterprise.

A visit to the continent enabled him to recruit a company which, if less beglamoured with stars than that of the Royal Academy of Music, was good, well-trained and reliable. Strada, the *prima donna*, was so extremely ugly that audiences nicknamed her 'the pig' and thought nostalgically of the good old days of Cuzzoni and Faustina. Bernacchi, the *castrato*, seemed small beer to the admirers of Senesino, but the new *castrato*, Farinelli, was expected to join the company, and Senesino returned for its second season.

Apparently George II regarded the King's Theatre as the official home of opera in London, so that although Handel and Heidegger were personally responsible for the finance of the opera seasons, he continued to subscribe £1000 a year to them. When their partnership broke up, in 1738, and Heidegger, the actual lessee of the theatre, joined forces with the newly constituted 'Opera of the Nobility', handing the theatre over to the newcomers, the king's subscription went to them. The Heidegger–Handel partnership was never entirely secure; Heidegger was apparently intending to withdraw from it in 1730, after a single year, but, apparently, two quite successful seasons persuaded him to hold on. Whatever his relationship with Handel, who was growing personally unpopular in spite of the appeal of his music, it may have been no more than realism that decided Heidegger to throw in his lot with the new organisation which, like the Royal Academy of Music, had a great deal of money at its disposal.

Opera had become part of a political campaign. The king's patronage and Handel's state works had made him the composer of the Establishment, associated with the materialistic, uninspiring government of Robert Walpole. Opposition to the regime gathered round Frederick, the Prince of Wales, whose quarrel with his father was a public scandal and had driven him from court. The prince himself suggested the formation of a new opera company to oust the Handelian opera of the Establishment.

The battle of the rival operas reached the Press by March 1733, when *The Bee, or Universal Weekly*, printed an epigram in which Walpole and Handel are two 'projectors', who through the Tobacco Excise Bill (which had just been defeated in Parliament) and *Deborah* had set out to milk Englishmen of their money. The leading opposition paper, *The Craftsman*, had the most scurrilous voice. 'The rise and Progress of Mr. H . . . . . L's Power and Fortune are too well known for me now to relate. Let it suffice to say that he was grown so insolent upon the sudden and deserved Increase of both, that he thought nothing

ought to oppose his imperious and extravagant Will. He had, for some Time,
govern'd the Operas, and modell'd the *Orchestra,* without the least Control. No
Voices, no *Instruments* were admitted, but such as flattered his ears, though they
shock'd those of the Audience. *Wretched Scrapers* were put above the best hands
in the *Orchestra.* No Musick but *his own* was to be allowed, though Everybody
was weary of it; and he had the Impudence to assert, that *there was no Composer
in England but himself.*' He had debased the opera until the audience had
deserted him, and had then been forced to pay audiences to attend his Oratorio.
'This accident has thrown him into a *deep Melancholy,*' the article concludes,
'interrupted by raving fits.'

Handel's company, except for Strada, joined the new organisation; Strada
was not invited to do so. Five of the directors of the Royal Academy of Music
became members of the new 'Opera of the Nobility'; the Earl of Burlington was
one of them. For all that, the Opera of the Nobility was primarily designed as a
political move, and the vastly enjoyable scurrility of journalists and pamphleteers
were only incidents in the political campaign of those disgusted with Walpole's
exploitation of power and patronage and, of course, of those in whose direction
the patronage was never extended. Handel was one of the exposed salients of the
Establishment simply because he was German though almost the last thing
George I had done had been to sign Handel's naturalisation papers. Despite the
composer's determination to become as English as possible, English insularity
regarded him as a foreigner and therefore suspect.

The quarrel between Handel and his rivals could be interpreted to suit what-
ever was uppermost in anybody's mind. The *Gentleman's Magazine* of November
1733, advertised a pamphlet magnificently entitled *Do You Know What You
Are About? Or, a Protestant Alarm to Great Britain: Proving our late Theatre
Squabble, a Type of the present Contest for the Crown of Poland; and that the late
Division between* Handel *and* Senesino, *has more in it than we imagine. Also that
the latter is no Eunuch, but a Jesuit in disguise; with other Particulars of the greatest
Importance.* The existence of this remarkable contribution to the operatic duel
was, until recently, known only from its resounding title. William C. Smith
produced an analysis of its arguments in 1964.[1] It advises 'our nobility, Gentry,
and others . . . that before they subscribe, or at least pay any of their money to
H . . . . L, or S . . . n . . . . O, they take especial care to be satisfied, that the
Singers are true Protestants, and well affected to the present Government.'

It is possible, the author explains, to disguise the Mass as an opera and thus
inflict it upon innocent audiences, which have been assaulted by '*A Hymn to the
Virgin,* written by Cardinal Coscia . . . in the opera of Julius Caesar'. The 'hymn'
is the aria *V'adoro Pupille.* The pamphlet goes on to explain that the real business
of Handel and Senesino (who could not possibly be a *castrato* because 'there are
no less than four of the waiting Girls at the opera now pregnant by him') was
not music but religion; Senesino left the composer's company because Handel
made him sing English oratorios, and got him into trouble with the Pope.

[1] *Music Review,* vol. 25, no. 2. May, 1964.

Of course, the text of *V'adoro Pupille* does not mean what the pamphleteer offers as a translation; its librettist was Nicola Haym and not a fictitious Cardinal Coscia. To what extent the author was deliberately fermenting anti-Catholic feeling, and to what extent he believed in his own nonsense is a pleasant matter for speculation. What he demonstrates to a modern reader is the way in which the war of the operas became deeply involved in attitudes and controversies widely removed from music. He suggests an enrolment of the Church party behind Handel because, even if he had, probably unwittingly, attacked English audiences with 'a hymn to the Virgin', he had reformed and gone on to create English, Biblical, Protestant oratorio.

The situation was farcically disastrous for everyone concerned. It involved a nationalist attack on Italian opera, dominated by an Italianised German who was English by naturalisation, by the setting up of a rival Italian opera and bringing the Italianised German Hasse to compose for it. The insular prejudice against Handel was voiced when in 1733, Oxford decided to honour the king's favourite composer and the solid core of Oxford Jacobitism made so much noise in protest that the university authorities had to demonstrate their admiration for his music to prove their loyalty to the Crown. The Jacobite librarian of the Bodleian objected to any invitation to 'Handel, a foreigner . . . and his lousy crew of foreign fiddlers'. In the event, Handel's Oxford concerts consisted entirely of his English works and were greeted with great enthusiasm. Handel was given clues enough, but he was too engrossed in answering a challenge.

Heidegger's association with the Opera of the Nobility left Handel without a theatre. He made an arrangement with John Rich, who had made a fortune at the Lincoln's Inn Theatre out of *The Beggar's Opera* and the series of ballad operas which followed it. Rich had taken over the Theatre Royal, Covent Garden, where he staged plays, ballad operas and ballet; Handel was to rent the theatre for two evenings every week and present Italian opera there. The availability of a *corps de ballet* is apparently responsible for the elaborate ballet music of *Alcina*, which, with *Ariodante*, was produced in his first Covent Garden season.

Slowly Handel was being forced to accept the idea of composing works in English. The spectacular success of *The Beggar's Opera* had a moral which he failed to understand; there was a larger audience for works in English than for works in Italian. English people could accept a style of opera which made some approach to the dramatic tradition which had developed in the theatres they attended. Whenever, as in *Partenope*, in 1730, he attempted to enlarge the boundaries of *opera seria*, his aristocratic audience was unenthusiastic. *Partenope* is an elegant, sophisticated comedy and it was a failure, but apparently the freedom of being his own impresario gave him not only the power to experiment but also the wish to do so.

But also in 1730, Rich's company at the Lincoln's Inn Theatre produced *Acis and Galatea* as an English opera, adding a new character, Corydon (the Lincoln's Inn Theatre did not employ a chorus) to act as a commentator on the action. In 1731, Thomas Arne, the father of the composer, occupied the New

Theatre, across the road from Handel's Theatre in the Haymarket, with an English opera and the new company, too, pirated *Acis and Galatea*, simply it seems because it was the one English work by the acknowledged master of opera which could be produced dramatically. The work was extremely successful, so that, apparently on the musical comedy principle that anything they could do he could do better, Handel revised and enlarged the work and staged it himself before adapting his Cannons Masque, *Haman and Mordecai* into the oratorio *Esther*. A Biblical story could be told in music, but it could not be acted; because it was a religious work, it could be sung in Lent, when plays and operas were forbidden, and thus make a profit out of a theatre which otherwise would be closed. *Esther* was a great success.

A pamphlet purporting to be a letter from Lord Burlington to Aaron Hill, one of Handel's librettists, appeared at the end of 1732 and commented on the introduction of oratorio. 'I left the *Italian* Opera, where the House was so thin, and cross'd over the way to the *English* one, which was so full I was forc'd to crowd upon the stage. . . .

'This alarmed H——L, and out he brings an *Oratorio*, or religious *Farce*, for duce take me if I can make any other Construction of the Word, for he has made a very good *Farce* of it, and put nearly 4,000L in his Pocket of which I am very glad, for I love the Man for his Musick's sake.'[1] The writer goes on to protest against the use in theatres of works which could not be acted, and suggests that if good libretti could be extracted from the Bible, oratorios should be acted and then they would become as popular as operas.

Aaron Hill himself wrote to Handel on December 5, 1732, suggesting that Handel should establish 'Musick upon a Foundation of Good Poetry', thus delivering English music from 'our Italian bondage'. English singers would prove the English language to be as good for music as Italian. What Handel seemed to have realised was only that oratorio could fill the theatre in Lent, when other entertainments were out of action, and thus help him to face the costs of his war with the Opera of the Nobility. In 1732, he produced *Deborah* in Lent; in the following year, *Esther*, *Deborah* and the new *Athaliah* were all performed during Lent, with a new and extremely young Englishman, John Beard (he was born, according to Grove, *circa* 1717), as leading tenor. In 1735, Cecilia Young, who was to marry the composer Arne, joined the company, to be the first soprano in English works while Strada remained the obvious first soprano for Italian works.

The promotion of two English singers pleased those who regarded all foreigners with hostility and preferred English even when the Italians sang better. 'So engrossing are the Italians, and so prejudiced are the *English* against their own Country, that our Singers are excluded from our very Concerts,' wrote *The Prompter* on December 24, 1734;[2] 'Bertorelli singing at the *Castle* and Senesino at the *Swan*, to their shame be it spoken; who, not content with monstrous

[1] Quoted from Deutsch: *op. cit.*
[2] *Ibid.*

salaries at the Opera's stoop so low as to be hired at Clubs! thereby eating some *English* Singer's Bread.'

Even with the additional profits of his Lenten oratorio season to help, Handel ended the 1735 season with a deficit of £9000. The deficit of the Opera of the Nobility was £12,000. Each theatre, if completely full, could earn £240 for each performance. Both companies had thrown everything they had into the struggle and were losing money in the hope that its rival's resources would give out first. The Opera of the Nobility, in addition, was producing opera on the most lavishly spectacular scale; one of its original undertakings—to put opera 'once more upon a good foot'—suggests that Handel and Heidegger had sacrificed spectacle to music.

Handel's accounts with Rich for the first half of 1736 have survived;[1] apparently Handel settled them performance by performance. His season opened with five performances of *Alexander's Feast*, two of *Acis and Galatea* followed, and these were succeeded by two of *Esther*. None of these demands costumes or settings (for, whatever happened to *Acis and Galatea* at other times, it could not be acted during Lent) though the first three performances of *Alexander's Feast* were given before Lent had begun. As they did not clash with dates on which the actors might have performed, the six performances given in Lent cost Handel only the rent of the theatre; his expenses outside Lent, for the first three *Alexander's Feast*, the revival of *Ariodante* after Easter and the season's novelty, *Atalanta*, were £52 5s. 8d. an evening. Chrysander's analysis of these figures shows that the theatre cost Handel £12 an evening, that he paid £7 5s. 8d. for the necessary attendants and £33 to the actors on the evenings when opera supplanted drama. There is no record of the amount he paid to Rich's ballet company for its dancing in *Alcina*, but he did not repeat the experiment of including an obviously expensive suite of dances.

The £370 paid to the actors during the season was an additional handicap Handel had to surmount; the costs of the production, the fees of the singers and the salary of the orchestra were still his responsibility. Although the season of 1735–6 was very popular, the nature of Handel's situation made any considerable profit impossible and he was little by little eating into his investments to meet his inevitable deficits.

Atalanta was written to celebrate the coming marriage of the Prince of Wales, who naturally could not avoid attending; he applauded enthusiastically. Handel wrote the anthem sung at his wedding, and the prince became one of his patrons. This would have been a pleasant end to the ruinous tragi-comedy of the rival opera had it not been impossible for the king and his elder son to be on the same side, so Handel lost the king's support.

Handel's popular English works and his English singers—he had added an English bass to those already prominent in his company—were winning the mastery. Hasse, who disliked England though his works were successful, left London in 1736 and was replaced by Veracini, whose first work for London,

[1] *Ibid.*

Adriano in Siria, was attended by the king. According to Lord Hervey, it was 'The longest and dullest opera that ever the ennobled ignorance of our present musical Governors ever inflicted on the ignorance of an English audience . . . Handel sat in great eminence and great pride in the middle of the pit, and seemed in silent pride to insult the poor dying opera in its agonies.'[1] When the Princess Amelia and her husband attended *Alexander's Feast*, according to the *London Daily Post*, there were 'at least 1300 present'.

Handel, scenting the final victory, set out to annihilate the opposition. Outsiders, seeing most of the game, were less sanguine. The writer, Benjamin Victor, told Matthew Dubourg, the violinist who had become the greatest figure in Dublin music, in a letter dated May 15, 1736, 'The two opera houses are, neither of them, in a very successful way; and it is the confirmed opinion that this winter will compleat your friend Handel's distruction, so far as the loss of his money can ruin him.'[2] Handel, still answering the challenge of the rival opera house, was too busy to realise what the success of his English works really meant. Walsh continued to pay him £26 5s. for each opera as it was produced, but he paid £105 for the score of *Alexander's Feast*. Handel could collect capacity audiences for English works which needed neither costumes, machinery nor stage sets; his operas were not sure-fire successes and cost vastly more to produce.

The instruments for the final destruction of the Opera of the Nobility were *Arminio* and *Giustino*, the works of an exhausted man. *Giustino* suffered, too, from a plot which seemed not far from pantomime. The now-customary Lenten oratorio season was lengthened, by special permission, into Holy Week, and after Easter came *Berenice*. Its first performance was attended by the Royal Family, but by that time, Handel's health had given way. Rheumatism was accompanied by 'a paralytic disorder', some called it a stroke, and for a time it paralysed his right arm.

Both companies were in deep water; the war had not ended in the exhaustion of one side and the consequent victory of the other, for both collapsed almost simultaneously. One of the signs of the end was the departure of Senesino when the Haymarket season ended prematurely on June 11, 1737. Despite his illness Handel stayed in London until September, restoring order to his financial chaos before he went to Aachen to take the cure. Burney[3] describes his situation in the blackest terms: before he left London, he had spent the savings of a lifetime to pay his singers and for a time had been in danger of arrest for debt. It was from these facts that the legend of his bankruptcy arose, but though he was hard hit, he was not bankrupt. His accounts with the Bank of England for the years 1734 to 1739 and 1743 to 1745 have survived. The account begins with a deposit of £2300 in 1732 to which nothing is added but from which heavy withdrawals are made during his years as an impresario—£1300 in 1735, £350 in 1736, and a

[1] Earl of Ilchester (ed.): *Lord Hervey and His Friends*. London, 1950.
[2] Deutsch: *op. cit.*
[3] Burney: *General History of Music*.

final £150 in 1737, leaving a mere £50 to his credit when the storm had subsided. The fate of his fluctuating investment in South Sea Annuities is not recorded.

Handel and the opposition had smashed each other. Senesino and Farinelli both left England in June 1737, but Caffarelli, almost their equal in reputation, had been engaged for the next season; Heidegger, the sole survivor of the opera, had a theatre, a company, no committee of rich, noble patrons, no musical director and no new operas to keep his audience's enthusiasm. Handel, his health restored and ready for action, returned to London in November 1737 and on January 3, 1738, was back at the Haymarket—in some sort of association with Heidegger, who must have been thankful for the death of Queen Caroline in November 1737, because it closed the theatre which was trying to keep open with a single *pasticcio* as its repertory.

In so far as he was the sole survivor, Handel had won the war; there was no one else left to compose new operas. Although he had been seriously ill, and although his rough determination seems to have trampled on too many susceptibilities, Heidegger seems to have had no doubt of Handel's ability to compose popular operas. Obviously the composer had no money to put into a new partnership and was simply Heidegger's employee.

Faramondo, Handel's new opera, ran for only eight performances; it was followed by two more failures. Things went so badly that on March 28, he gave a benefit concert in the theatre; its programme included anthems, and arias and duets from the oratorios. The Earl of Egmont noted in his diary[1] that he counted nearly 1300 in the theatre without including those in the gallery and upper gallery. The audience overflowed, wrote Burney to the extent of 500 people, on the stage; Mainwaring wrote that it brought the composer £1000, but Burney decided that his profit cannot have been less than £800. *Serse*, his next opera, came on April 15, and had only six performances although it is a work of delightful sun and light. The bad season prompted an announcement by Heidegger:

> All persons that have subscribed or are willing to subscribe twenty guineas for an Italian opera to be perform'd next season at the King's Theatre in The Haymarket, under my Direction, are desired to send ten guineas to Mr. Drummond, the Banker who will give them a receipt, to return the Money in case the Opera should not go on, and, whereas I declared that I would undertake the Opera's provided I can agree with the Performers, and 200 subscriptions are procured, and as the greatest part of the Subscribers have already paid 10 Guineas; it is desired that the remaining subscribers will be pleased to send the Money on or before the 5th June next, that I may take my Measures, either to undertake the Opera if the Money is paid, or to give them up if the Money is not paid, it being impossible to make the necessary Preparations, or to Contract with the Singers, after that time.[2]

The money was not paid and, on July 26, Heidegger announced the way in which those who had subscribed could reclaim their money. It was two years

---

[1] Quoted from Deutsch, *op. cit.*
[2] *Ibid.*

before an opera by Handel was heard in London, though when Heidegger announced the abandonment of opera, he was at work on *Imeneo*.

Left on his own, Handel began to compose *Saul*, and no sooner had he finished *Saul* than he embarked on *Israel in Egypt*. On January 16, 1739, *Saul* was played in the Haymarket Theatre, and given five further performances. *Alexander's Feast* was revived in what turned out, as the King's Theatre was otherwise unoccupied, to be an extended oratorio season. The English adaptation of *Il Trionfo del Tempo e della Verita* followed, and *Israel in Egypt* had its first performance on April 4. Each of the oratorios had organ concertos played by the composer between its 'acts'. He had just, according to Charles Jennens, spent £500 on a new organ from which he had a better view of his orchestra and choir. He had not abandoned opera; *Jupiter in Argus*, finished only a week before, was produced for two performances on May 1.

In the October of 1739, Handel's copyright, which the composer had allowed to lapse as though he could not be bothered to attempt any longer to control the publication of his works, was renewed. The renewal of the privilege was due to Walsh's determination to protect his editions of Handel's music. But while the renewed privilege, which was granted for fourteen years, prohibited other publishers from pirating Handel's work, it also gave the composer no option but to sell his works to Walsh.

When Lord Middlesex's opera, with an Italian company, took the Haymarket Theatre from the autumn of 1739, Handel, with a mainly English company, rented the Lincoln's Inn Theatre from Rich and, as he was not at war with the opera at the Haymarket, arranged his times of performance to avoid clashes. His season began on November 27 with a new work, the *Ode on St. Cecilia's Day* and included the new *L'Allegro, il Pensieroso ed il Moderato*, poems by Milton providing the first two parts and an inferior pastiche of Milton by Charles Jennens the third.

His season did well, so he turned almost automatically to opera in his season of 1740-1, giving performances of the new *Imeneo* and *Deidamia*, his last opera, both of which did not appeal to the audience, as well as his secular and Biblical oratorios. By the end of the year, he had composed both *Messiah* and *Samson*. Probably without knowing it, he had finally been pushed from opera to oratorio.

In other words, after more than a quarter of a century spent in supplying a fashionable audience with opera, circumstances had at last forced him to find the subject matter and the style of treatment which the average Englishman could accept with the maximum sympathy.

Whatever persuaded Handel to find the subject matter of the later works in the Old Testament, whether it was only that the Old Testament provided him with strong characters and situations or whether it was some special insight into English character or the suggestion of some unusually acute English friend, we do not know. But no other subject matter could have made so strong an appeal to his adopted fellow-countrymen. The other Protestant countries had neither the knowledge of the Old Testament which first the Anglican Liturgy—the

First Lessons he heard at Matins and Evensong week by week—then the Puritan revolution and the growth of non-conformity, had given to the Englishman. The essential furniture of the English mind was the Bible, to which the educated classes added the literature of the classics.

Englishmen identified themselves with the struggles and triumphs of the ancient Hebrews. Like them, the Englishman was an inhabitant of a tiny country miraculously triumphant over its enemies. Like God's elect, the English had withstood the might of larger continental countries, their trade had grown world-wide and their influence was out of all proportion to their number; they had, they flattered themselves, upheld God's law and had been rewarded for it. Such notions were probably instinctive, and it was, it seems, to this subconscious self-identification with the people of the Bible that Handel's oratorios appealed. The heroes of the oratorios were heroes to his audience.

The works represented no sudden change of policy but only a development of an interest which the composer had been exploiting intermittently at least since he had performed *Esther* in the Lenten closed season for operas in 1732. Handel was a dramatic composer whose treatment of the standard Italian form expanded its conventions; the Old Testament gave him a new range of heroes— Saul, who disobeyed his God and was killed resisting his fate, the broken Samson achieving a final moment of sacrificial courage, Judas Maccabeus destroying his country's enemies as the Duke of Cumberland destroyed the Jacobite invasion. It gave him too, the epic of the Exodus of the Hebrews from slavery in Egypt. As Winton Dean[1] has shown, all but two of the oratorios are conceived as dramas in three acts, with stage directions. No longer bound by the conventions of *opera seria*, Handel adopted new forms for them, abandoned the *da capo* aria except when it was dramatically proper, as in Harapha's aria 'Honour and Arms', in *Samson*. Solo and chorus structures, almost impossible in opera as he knew it, became common and were all moulded to the dramatic situation.

We do not know whether Handel longed for a situation in which his operatic oratorios could be fully staged or not. We do know that he was not satisfied with a single source for his subject matter or a single style of treatment, and that to leave the Old Testament was dangerous for him. There were, too, religious prejudices to face. *Israel in Egypt*, a musical epic telling an episode in the story of a heroic race shocked many who cheerfully accepted *Deborah*, *Athaliah* and *Saul*, in which scriptural texts are tormented into minor eighteenth-century verse; in *Israel in Egypt*, the words of the Bible were profanely sung in a theatre by entirely worldly people who would have readily put on costumes and represented pagan gods, heroes or demons.

Theodora, one of his final works, took its story from the history of the Early Church—possibly some people like the author of *Do You Know What You Are About?* doubted its Protestant sincerity—and Handel, who had won a Jewish audience with *Judas Maccabeus*, explained that the Jews would not care for it because it is Christian and the ladies would dislike it because it is virtuous.

[1] Winton Dean: *Handel's Dramatic Oratorios and Masques*. O.U.P., 1959.

The greatest difficulty he experienced was with *Messiah*, composed in 1741 but not performed till the composer's stay in Dublin a year later, when it was called *A Sacred Oratorio*. *Messiah* is not dramatic but reflective; its hero is Christ himself, for although it contains little narrative, it consists of reflections upon His life. Paul Henry Lang[1] suggests that so unusual a work must have been the result of 'an unusual incentive' and that such an incentive may have been supplied by the invitation of the Lord Lieutenant of Ireland, the Duke of Devonshire, to give three charity concerts in Dublin. The idea of a charity performance may have prompted Handel to consider the feasibility of a work totally unlike any of his other oratorios. Although he seems to have been most highly thought of in Ireland as a church composer—announcing his arrival, the *Dublin Journal* on November 21, 1741, described him as 'a gentleman universally known for his excellent Compositions in all kinds of Musick, and particularly for his *Te Deum*, *Jubilate*, *Anthems*, and other compositions in Church Musick'— what his audience would see as a theatrical treatment in scriptural words of the life of Christ presented a risk he seems to have recognised.

Five months, in which Handel gave two series of very successful concerts of his English secular and Biblical oratorios, passed before Handel performed *Messiah*, and when he did so on April 13, he billed it only as *A Sacred Oratorio*, as though he was nervous about the effect its title would have on audiences. The work was adapted to the resources available in Dublin. The Viceregal Band, directed by the violinist Matthew Dubourg, was his orchestra; it was without the customary woodwind, but the Viceroy's strings had two auxiliary trumpeters and a drummer. His choir included the choristers of St. Patrick's and Christ Church cathedrals, although in January Jonathan Swift, the Dean of St. Patrick's, had previously refused his musicians permission to sing for Handel in a letter of magnificently inventive invective.

Part of the knotty textual problem of *Messiah* is due to the alterations Handel made for performances with London orchestras and different singers. London performances, as they multiplied, induced him to recast some of the solo music —'For he is like a refiner's fire' was either an alto or a bass aria—and the orchestra for the Foundling Hospital performances, which eventually made the work popular through repetition, used an orchestra of strings, two trumpets, four oboes, four bassoons and drums.

Aversion from *Messiah* because the theatre was no place for a meditation in Biblical language on the Life of Christ brought a protest in the *Universal Spectator* on the day of the first London performance, before the work had been heard. It came from a music-lover who claimed never to have deserted Handel. He protested against the mere idea of an oratorio, sung in a theatre and not in a church, given 'the most *Sacred*, the *most merciful Name* of *Messiah*. . . . How will this appear to After-Ages, when it shall be read in History, that in such an Age the People of England were arriv'd to such a Height of *Impiety* and *Prophaneness*, that the most sacred *Things* were suffer'd to be us'd as *publick Diversions*,

[1] Paul Henry Lang: *George Frederick Handel*. Faber, 1967.

and that in a *Place*, and by *Persons*, appropriated to the Performance not only of *light* and *vain*, but too often *prophane* and *dissolute* pieces?' The oratorio was announced not by its name but again as *A Sacred Oratorio*, but the title *Messiah* had been given as its alternative name in Dublin.

Walsh, too, seemed to be doubtful about the work. William C. Smith showed, in *Concerning Handel*, that *Messiah* was engraved by 1749, but the work was not published until 1763, and none of its 'songs' was issued separately. So many associations have grown round the work that a twentieth-century listener, especially a twentieth-century English listener, tends to accept the style of the Handel oratorios, and of *Messiah* in particular, as something intrinsically religious. The eighteenth century recognised the affinity between the great ceremonial chorus—'Lift up Your Heads', 'Hallelujah', 'Worthy is the Lamb'— and a variety of entirely 'worldly' works, just as they recognised the *Messiah*'s Pastoral Symphony as neither more nor less than a Siciliana. Nineteenth-century hagiologists, English and German, decided that such a style is by nature sacred because they knew too little of the Baroque music in which it had its roots and nothing of the music in Handel's operas to which it was related.

Handel's oratorio seasons of 1742 and 1743 were extremely successful. He charged the same prices for seats as he had charged for operas, a policy which seemed to tell against him in the unsuccessful season of 1744–5. 'Handel has set up an Oratorio against the Opera,' wrote Horace Walpole to Horace Mann on February 24, 1743, 'and succeeds. He has hired all the goddesses from Farce and singers of *Roast Beef* from between the acts at both theatres, with a man with one note in his voice, and a girl without ever a one; and so they sing, and make brave hallelujahs; and the good company encore the recitative, if it happens to have any cadence like what they call a tune.' On March 3, he told Mann, 'The Oratorios thrive abundantly. For my part, they give me an idea of heaven, where everybody is to sing whether they have voices or not.'[1]

Walpole seems to have been in a minority, lamenting the dominance of a new, popular, national form over aristocratic, international, Italian opera. The 'goddesses from farces' were Kitty Clive, the comedienne, who sang Dalila (as Handel wrote the name) on February 18. 'The singers of *Roast Beef*' were those who obliged the gallery when it called for the song 'The Roast Beef of Old England' between the acts of the play: Hogarth drew it as it did so. Obviously the links between oratorio and the *hoi polloi* were not pleasing to Walpole's fastidiousness.

For all that, the King and the Royal Family went to hear *Samson*, which had six performances so successful that a subscription was immediately opened for another six. In one thing, Walpole was right; oratorio had at least for the time being vanquished opera. Though Handel's seasons were short, they must have drawn away a considerable part of the opera audience, and in March 1743 the opera found itself to be £16,000 in debt and to have no assets. Its last perform-ance, in April, was a concert of religious music and concertos played in three

---

[1] Horace Walpole: *Correspondence*. London, 1937.

parts like the three acts of a Handel oratorio. The next season was to be managed by the *Dilettanti*, 'a club', wrote Horace Walpole, 'for which the nominal qualification is having been in Italy, and the real one, being drunk'.

It is interesting that in August 1743, for the first time Walsh published a complete Handel work, with all its recitative and choruses, 'The entire Masque of *Acis and Galatea*, as it was originally composed, with the Overture, Recitativos, Songs, Duets and Choruses, for Voices and Instruments.' Subscribers could buy the work for half a guinea; others could buy it in ten weekly parts, nine at a shilling and sixpence and the last at a shilling. The opera and oratorio scores provided the amateur singer with the arias for their own use; possibly the miniature scale of *Acis* may have suggested to Walsh that his customers might wish to collaborate in performances of the complete work.

According to Mainwaring, Handel was ill in the summer of 1743, but he had two new works, *Semele* and *Joseph and His Brethren*, ready for his 1744 season. By this time he had created a special oratorio audience, particularly concerned with heroic virtue, divine law and the sanctities of patriotism. The radiant, serene paganism of *Semele*, obviously an opera in disguise though it is formally as free as the oratorios, worried his admirers. In so far as they felt Handel to be the mouthpiece of what nowadays in America might be called 'White Anglo-Saxon Protestantism', they were disturbed by his delight in what Byron called the 'filthy loves of Gods and of Goddesses'.[1] *Joseph and His Brethren* was moral to the point of sanctimony, and reassured them. He made enough money during the season to buy £1300 of South Sea Annuities—his first recorded investment since the crash of 1738, and he deposited £25 in his account with the Bank of England.

For the 1745 season he had two of his finest works, *Belshazzar* and *Hercules*, ready. *Hercules* was sung on January 5, and Walsh immediately announced its publication. Again Handel's dramatic oratorio style, so firmly associated with religion in his audience's mind, was applied to totally unreligious material. But for the first time since he had forsaken opera, the season went badly. By the middle of January, the composer saw danger looming, and addressed the public on January 17, before the Bible-story *Belshazzar* had a chance to reassure the faithful, with an appeal in the *Daily Courier*:

> Having for a series of Years received the greatest Obligations from the Nobility and Gentry of this Nation, I have always retained a deep Impression of their Goodness. As I perceived, that joining good Sense and significant Words to Musick, was the best Method of recommending this to an English Audience; I have directed my studies this way, and have endeavoured to show, that the English Language, which is so expressive of the Sublimest Sentiments, is the best adapted of any to the full and solemn Kind of Musick. I have the Mortification now to find, that my Labours to please are become ineffective, when my Expenses are considerably greater. To what Cause I must impute the Loss of the publick Favour I am ignorant, but the Loss itself I shall always Lament.

[1] *Don Juan*, Canto I, XLI.

> In the mean Time, I am assur'd that a Nation, whose Characteristick is
> Good Nature, would be affected with the Ruin of any Man, which was
> owing to his Endeavours to entertain them.

He offered to begin the repayment of subscriptions in the following week.

A week later, a second announcement said that, as subscribers had not withdrawn their money, he felt himself bound in gratitude to continue the season
for as long as he could afford to do so, 'Let the Risque which I run be what it
will.'

Belshazzar had its first performance on March 27, and the season came to an
end with its third performance, on April 23. Walsh proceeded with the publication of the new work and Handel's music featured as prominently in London
concerts. It had not become generally unpopular; it was simply his oratorio
season that had crashed.

He was sixty and for more than fifteen years he had been impresario as well as
composer and performer; he had lived well and worked hard, and this second
catastrophe seemed for a time to have finished him. Again his health broke down
and, according to several accounts of his condition in the summer of 1745, his
mind had given way. Biographers again exaggerated the extent of his financial
collapse; he was not made bankrupt, but he offered his two organs at the Haymarket Theatre for sale at considerably less than their real worth; he paid his
singers and his debt to the theatre, clearing his bank account to do so. As in the
earlier catastrophe, there is no record of whether he was compelled to sell all or
some of his investments to do so.

The cause of the collapse of 1745 is still a mystery. On May 25, Horace Walpole wrote to George Montague mentioning that his brother, Edward, 'is perfectly master of all the quarrels that have been fashionably on foot about Handel'[1]
without explaining what they were. Mrs. Elizabeth Carter, a faithful member
of his audience, blamed the collapse on 'fashion'.[2] Whose susceptibilities or
pride Handel had trampled on we do not know. But his oratorio performances
were an expensive pleasure; he charged operatic prices for entertainments
obviously cheaper than opera as they needed neither sets nor costumes. His
expenses—orchestra, chorus, soloists, the cost of rehearsals and the rent of the
theatre—were, however, high enough to justify the cost of admission, and we do
not know if audiences rebelled against prices they may have come to regard as
unjustifiably high. This time there was no campaign of abuse and denigration
against him in the press. He had, however, broken the convention he had created
by the introduction of not merely secular oratorios but of unblushingly pagan
ones into his seasons. We do not know how much these harmed him, but we know
that after his recovery he only once deserted the Bible in his search for a subject
(counting *Judas Maccabaeus*, from the Apocrypha, as a Biblical text) and that
Theodora, in which he did so, was a doubtful financial success.

The resilience which brought him back, after a physical collapse and a nervous
breakdown, to begin again in January 1746, is astounding. With the *Occasional*

[1] Walpole: *op. cit.*   [2] Deutsch: *op. cit.*

Oratorio he recaptured his wayward audience by reflecting the popular view of the Jacobite Rebellion as the Young Pretender gradually abandoned all he had gained in his lightning advance into England six months before. The advent of Gluck, whom Handel seems seriously to have under-rated, as composer at the opera seems not to have affected the popularity of his 1746 season, and though the Duke of Cumberland seems in retrospect to have been far less of a hero than England found him when he annihilated what was left of the Stuart rebellion, *Judas Maccabaeus* spoke for the greater part of the nation.

The *Fireworks Music*, celebrating the Treaty of Aix-la-Chapelle, was publicly rehearsed in Vauxhall Gardens on April 21; 1200 people attended and blocked London Bridge for three hours with what still remains the most disastrous traffic jam on record. The actual performance with fireworks, on April 27, 1749, ended in a serious fire.

In 1749 he began his connection with the Foundling Hospital, and it was for its first performance there, in 1750, that *Messiah* was announced under its proper name; the performance was to inaugurate the organ he had presented to the hospital chapel, where he had been elected a governor. In 1751, his sight failed while he was writing *Jephtha*, and for a time depression drove him into complete inactivity. He recovered sufficiently to finish the work and, when it was performed in 1752, he directed the performance and played the customary concertos between the 'acts'. An operation for cataract, in November 1752, partially restored his sight and he was never totally blind. He was able to mount his oratorio seasons and sometimes could see well enough to work at revisions or alterations of the oratorios he intended to revive. He was at the organ for a performance of *Messiah* on April 6, 1759, eight days before his death.

During the last ten years of his life Handel made a great deal of money. Of his later works, only *Theodora* was a less than complete popular success, and Deutsch[1] notes the deposits and withdrawals in his account with the Bank of England. Not only were his oratorio seasons sufficiently established to be part of the routine of the musical year but he kept them entirely within his own hand, so that nothing in the other theatres could draw his audiences away. Whether by design or art, his subjects were those that his audience could most readily accept in Lent. When he died, his final balance with the Bank of England was £17,000: he left more than £9000 to friends and charities. The Society for the Support of Decayed Musicians, always a favourite charity, was given £1000, and the Foundling Hospital, another cause dear to him, was left the manuscript of *Messiah*.

Only three years passed between the death of Handel and the arrival of Johann Christian Bach, Johann Sebastian's younger son, as composer at the opera. He, too, found that opera in England was an uncertain business, integrated himself into London musical life as he found it and did good work, accepting English taste, without storm and stress. Handel spent much of his life obstinately adhering to policies after his shrewdness—active enough in other

Op. cit.

directions—should have persuaded him to modify them. It was not total dedication which persuaded him to persevere with opera when he knew by experience that English works were more successful, for he abandoned its conventions little by little in his Italian works and, when dramatic principles demanded that he do so, totally in his oratorios. But J. C. Bach was simply a good musician while Handel was gigantic in obstinacy as well as in appetite. J. C. Bach made a good deal of money, and did a great deal of fine work, in the concert hall. Handel's concert music—the two sets of concerti grossi, the opera and oratorio overtures, the *Water Music* and the *Fireworks Music* and the Organ Concertos— were extremely popular repertory works with concert societies in London and all over the country; his total lack of interest in this important and profitable form of music-making simply shows that he never intended to behave like any other composer of his day and to fit into professional life wherever there was space to hold him.

Handel led himself into disaster and then was able to climb out of it only because he combined toughness, aggressiveness and amazing resilience with almost incredible fertility. Whatever was inevitable in his career was made inevitable not by his circumstances but by his character.

17 Music in the Eighteenth-Century Courts

According to Johann Nikolaus Forkel, the first biographer of Johann Sebastian Bach, there were more than three hundred and forty composers working in the German-speaking Europe of 1784; he included them all in his *Verzeichnis Jetzlebender Componisten in Deutschland*, compiled in that year. Other authorities, Marpurg, for example, add to that list. The majority of these musicians were in court employment, craftsmen composers capable of writing acceptably in a socially pleasing idiom but incapable of saying anything outside the elegant platitudes into which eighteenth-century music too easily fell.

They were asked to do no more. They held a recognised, unassailable but unexalted place in the scheme of society, satisfying established tastes. The court appetite for music, from the *concerto grosso* of the beginning of the century to the symphony and solo concerto at its end, dealt in graceful stereotypes, to satisfy which Alessandro Scarlatti wrote more than one thousand works. Telemann had written six hundred overtures and five yearly cycles of church cantatas, apart from all his other works, by the time he was sixty; Carl Heinrich Graun wrote ninety-six symphonies as well as the operas which constituted the bulk of the repertory of the Opera House in Berlin, and Holzbauer, at Mannheim in the second generation of its court's musical eminence, wrote some two hundred and five symphonies and concertos. Hasse, for many years dominating the Dresden opera, simply lost count of the number of his compositions.

All these composers wrote to order, and most of their work was 'occasional music'. When Haydn was asked why he had written no quintets, he simply replied, 'Nobody has ordered any.' If the composer happened to be a *Kapellmeister*, he wrote what was needed—Mass, opera, symphony, a set of dances or whatever it might be—when it was needed. Sometimes, if his conditions of employment allowed him to do so, he sent off a bundle of works to a likely patron hoping to be rewarded with money rather than a gold watch or snuff box. Florian Gassman, who became a leading figure in Viennese music for the ten years before his death in 1774, was paid 100 ducats for each set of six symphonies which he wrote for Count Dietrichstein. Maximilian Joseph, the Elector of Bavaria who came to the throne in 1745, cared very little for the opera carried on in the *Residenztheater* in Munich but a great deal for the private concerts at which he played the viola da gamba. His *Kapellmeister*, Andrea Bernasconi, was left to run the opera without interference, and he made little use of his authority, while the Elector occupied himself with concertos and sonatas written for him by his chamber composers, Wochitzka and Croner, who were paid between 10 and 12 florins for each set of a dozen works.

The court composer, working to order and satisfying set tastes, was simply an upper servant. He might, as Haydn apparently did at Eszterhaza in the 1770s and 1780s, become a favoured upper servant; like Hasse at Dresden or Jomelli at Stuttgart, he might for a time become so important in his patron's scheme of things that his salary was increased and an unusual amount of freedom granted to him; Jomelli, for example, was allowed to adapt and alter the libretti his patron, Duke Carl Eugen of Württemberg, had accepted. But one of Wolfgang Mozart's many reasons for detesting Salzburg was that when he was at the Prince-Archbishop's court he was expected to eat with the valets, his equals in rank, whose conversation bored him.

A *Kapellmeister* himself was a little higher up the social scale, but the conditions of his service had not altered since the Renaissance. He was expected not only to supervise the music of the *Kapelle* but also was responsible for the discipline, behaviour and good manners of its subordinate members and for their appearance always correctly dressed in uniform. He was expected to see that instruments were properly kept and maintained (Haydn, as *Kapellmeister* of three successive Prince Esterhazys, tuned the keyboard instruments himself), and that the library of music, scores and instrumental parts, was kept in proper order. He was to present himself at fixed times to his patron to receive his orders, always in uniform and bewigged. Whatever he wrote was the property of his patron and could not be published or distributed to anyone else without his patron's consent. He could not, therefore, accept commissions from anyone else unless his patron allowed him to do so. Haydn's contract with Prince Paul Esterhazy, in 1761, allowed him to apply for dismissal with, so to speak, six months' notice, but whether or not dismissal were granted was entirely a matter of the patron's decision, and the prince could dismiss him on the spot. Christoph Graupner did not leave the court of the Landgrave of Hesse-Darmstadt in 1721 to become cantor at the *Thomasschule*, Leipzig, simply because, after the post had been offered to him, the Landgrave refused to grant his dismissal. J. S. Bach himself was imprisoned for a month in Weimar because he demanded his release in too peremptory a manner.

Many of these conditions affected the lesser members of the *Kapelle*, restricting their freedom and their ambition. Carl Ditters, for example, who was to be ennobled as Ditters von Dittersdorf, became a member of the orchestra of the Prince von Hildburghausen, at Schlosshof, when he was twelve and became a great favourite. His patron found that in his teens the young musician was capable not only of very good violin playing and of composing lively and charming music but also of thinking-up original entertainments for special occasions. When the emperor visited Schlosshof, the prince ordered a fête in honour of Bacchus, in which twenty-one couples of peasant youths and girls were needed to provide a comic interlude; the young Dittersdorf suggested that the music for this should be played on peasant bagpipes, scoured the countryside for sufficient players whose instruments were in tune with each other, and trained them to play the music of the ballet. He was sent out to gather and train a choir of children in the local schools to take part in the chorus of an opera. But, still in his teens, young Carl took to gambling, found he could not pay his debts, panicked and ran away to Prague where another post had been offered to him. In two days he was arrested and taken back as a prisoner to Schlosshof, where the prince promptly both forgave him and paid his debt.

Naturally, the entire musical climate depended on the character of the patron. A musically ambitious aristocrat of good, educated taste wanted good music. Those whose tastes were undeveloped or frivolous did not want demanding, serious or intense music. The German and Austrian courts kept *opera seria*, for example, alive long after the Italian opera houses, in which *opera seria* grew up, had left the form to die. In 1791, an imperial election led to the commission of *La Clemenza di Tito* from Mozart, the libretto, by Metastasio, having been set by composers of all sorts for nearly fifty years.

At Salzburg, where opera was rarely more than the sort of congratulatory serenata appropriate to a Prince-Archbishop's name day, Leopold Mozart wrote strong vigorous, well-made church music and a large amount of cleverly attractive, amusing light music, like, for example, a concerto for hosepipe and orchestra, a hunting symphony for strings, two horns, dogs and rifle, and, very probably, the 'Toy Symphony' which was traditionally attributed to Haydn.

At precisely the same time, music in Mannheim depended upon a degree of orchestral virtuosity which none of the other court orchestras, and probably no other orchestra in Europe, could rival. During the reign of Frederick the Great, from 1740 to 1786, everything heard in the royal opera house in Berlin or the court at Potsdam belonged in style and spirit to the 1720s and 1730s simply because the king could not enjoy any later music. He was a devoted amateur, probably a good flautist and an enthusiastic if not completely instructed composer. In 1772, when Burney was present at Frederick's court in Potsdam, when the king was sixty years old, the historian heard the monarch play three flute concertos by Quantz. On the following day, the seventy-five-year-old composer explained that the king must just have reached the end of the cycle of three hundred concertos Quantz had provided for him, as one of the evening's three concertos was twenty years old and the other two forty, dating from the years before his accession when, as Crown Prince, he had first collected his musical staff.

In many respects, Frederick was a better patron than many, loyal and more generous to the musicians who served him. He completed and played the flute concerto Quantz had left unfinished at his death in 1773. He paid both Quantz and his *Kapellmeister*, Carl Heinrich Graun, 2000 thaler a year. The least valued but most important of his *Kapelle* was Philipp Emanuel Bach, the court's first keyboard player and official accompanist, who was paid only 300 thaler from 1740 to 1756, when his salary was raised to 500 thaler for the rest of his stay there. C. P. E. Bach's music, in the new expressive sonata style and looking always for greater intensity of expression, meant nothing to Frederick, and C. P. E. Bach was never properly impressed by his royal patron's playing. Frederick allowed himself remarkable latitude in performance, granting himself, for example, freedom to relax the tempo in passages which appealed to him and to hurry through those which he found boring. 'What rhythm!' declared a sycophantic courtier after a royal performance. 'What rhythms!' declared Bach audibly. Frederick must have been irritated by an accompanist whose brand of music criticism was to emphasise in performance any breaches of rule, such as consecutive fifths, in his patron's work. Bach, nevertheless, remained in Frederick's employment until he was offered the succession to Telemann in Hamburg.

Frederick's loyalty to German musicians—after Graun's death in 1759 he appointed a less impressive German to be his *Kapellmeister* rather than a more impressive Italian—has led him to be regarded by some German historians as an early champion of German music. For all that, he staffed the Berlin opera with Italian singers, choosing the best that could be obtained regardless of cost. It was not until 1771, when his opera was run with remarkable economy, that he found a German soprano—Gertrud Elisabeth Schmeling, whom the world came to know as Mara—worthy to be heard in his organisation. But while he believed that German singers were inferior in quality as well as training to Italians, he was convinced that German instrumentalists were superior to any others and that German composers were more 'learned' than Italian. But having chosen his German composers, he rigorously insisted that they composed Italian music in the idiom of the past. Gluck, he informed his sister, 'in my opinion . . . has (1) no invention at all, (2) a poor wretched gift of melody and (3) no accent, no expression—it all sounds alike'.

Like every other German ruler who could afford to do so, Frederick the Great maintained opera. One of his first actions after his accession was to order the building of an opera house; to finance its completion he made a levy of 22,750 thalers on the mail and, after the opera house was opened in 1742, kept the levy in operation as a general theatre tax. The theatre, built for safety from fire over a canal which incidentally made possible stage cascades and fountains, was three hundred feet long by a hundred feet wide, standing alone for ease of access in the centre of a square. Its decorations, paintings and amenities were luxurious in the extreme. Court dress or evening dress was obligatory for the invited audience, but the pit was free to soldiers, citizens of Berlin and anyone else who could pretend to either qualification or find a doorkeeper ready to accept a tip. The orchestra was in court uniform; it greeted the king's arrival with a fanfare of trumpets and waited his signal to begin the overture after he had taken his seat.

Until the Seven Years' War, which started in 1756 and brought a sad deterioration both to Frederick's character and to his finances, the Berlin opera was run with the utmost lavishness in a possibly unconscious rivalry with Dresden, where the Saxon court opera was long established and internationally famous.

The Berlin opera season ran throughout the Carnival, which in Berlin was from Christmas to Shrove Tuesday, and each season saw the production of two new works as well as of revivals from the past. Frederick did his utmost to entice the stars of the Dresden opera to Berlin, but though he failed with the best singers and with Hasse, the Dresden *Kapellmeister*, he won the services of Guiseppe Bibiena, the Dresden stage designer, during every winter from 1751 to 1756.

No account books of the Berlin Opera survive from the days of Frederick the Great, and contemporary anecdotes about its expenses seem to be wildly exaggerated; one source gives the cost of the first two productions to be mounted there as 200,000 thalers, more than any two productions cost in the courts of Dresden and Stuttgart, where finances were not controlled with the dedication to political reality which was even more characteristic of Frederick than was his devotion to music.

In Dresden, where court music had been completely Italianised since the 1660s and where the first opera house had been built in 1666, while Heinrich Schütz was still nominally *Kapellmeister*, political reality was sacrificed to the Elector's appetite for grandeur. In 1719, Frederick Augustus I, popularly and perhaps affectionately known as Augustus the Strong rather for his sexual exploits than his qualities as a ruler, built a new opera house for the marriage of his son, the future Augustus II, to the daughter of the Emperor Joseph I. Augustus I found money enough to collect a company second to none in Europe, and it was to Dresden that Handel made his way when he was sent to recruit singers for the then new Royal Academy of Music in London; because Augustus had temporarily disbanded his opera—quarrels between its German conductor Heinichen and the Italian singers were his excuse though his reason was the emptiness of his treasury—Handel was able to offer London contracts to singers of the stature of Durastante, Senesino and later Faustina, the great soprano who was also an accomplished actress and a beautiful woman.

Augustus II had no intention to live for long without opera, re-established his company in 1726 and in 1731 engaged Hasse as his *Kapellmeister*. He died in 1733, but his son made Dresden music even more splendid, and until the outbreak of the Seven Years' War, Dresden was the centre of court opera at its most splendid. Hasse, a German as completely Italianised as Handel, lacked the force of expression, the range of interests and the varieties of technique and style which made Handel a giant among composers, but his operas precisely suited the tastes of his audience. His operas consist of a succession of beautiful, rather sentimental arias strung together by lengthy passages of recitative; he had little or no interest in ensembles or in writing for the chorus but he gave richly expressive arias to the brilliant singers of the company. By 1756, his *Kapelle* contained nineteen solo singers, several of them internationally famous; he had an orchestra of forty-six, all good players and splendidly drilled; there were seven solo dancers in the ballet company, which was twenty-seven strong. The entire musical establishment of court composers, theatre architects, designers and scene painters, administrative officials and pensioners, added to the instrumentalists and singers, numbered a hundred and forty-six and, in 1756, cost more than 100,000 thalers. Alan Yorke-Long[1] estimated the yearly expenditure on music under Augustus II to be equivalent to £90,000 of English money of the period.

The outbreak of war in 1756 drove Augustus, who was King of Poland as well as Elector of Saxony, to Warsaw; he took with him as many of his opera and ballet companies as possible and let the war take its course; Dresden was first bombarded then occupied by the Prussians. Hasse, given permission by the Elector to publish his works, found that they were destroyed in the fire which destroyed the opera house during the bombardment of the city. The splendid orchestra disintegrated, its members welcome wherever they chose to go. 'It was from the dispersal of the celebrated band,' wrote Burney, '. . . that almost every great city of Europe, and London among the rest, acquired several exquisite and famous performers.'[2]

Augustus II died in 1763 and was succeeded by his son Frederick Christian, who found himself faced with a devastated country and mountainous debts; he pensioned Hasse off with the title of *Ober-Kapellmeister* but forced him to renounce his claim to some 18,000 thalers of back pay still owing to him. Augustus III succeeded to the throne before his father Frederick Christian, a cripple, had reigned for a year. The new Elector was a musician, but he inherited debts of more than 12,000,000 thalers and was in no position to restore the artistic grandeur of his capital. He allowed an Italian *opera buffa* company to reopen the Dresden opera in 1765; the productions mounted there by the Italians cost, of course, only a small fraction of what in the past had been spent on opera in Dresden. For his marriage in 1769 he commissioned an opera from his musician mother's protégé, Johann Gottlieb Naumann—a new setting of Metastasio's familiar libretto *La Clemenza di Tito*—but its cost, about 50,000 thalers, showed him that Saxony could not afford to return to the splendid past although the dowager Electress, Maria Antonia Walpurgis, a Princess of Bavaria and a composer of some accomplishment and unlimited ambition who published her own works under the pen-name Ermelinda Talea Pastorella Arcadia, was eager to preserve the operatic glories of Saxony and to contribute generously to its repertoire.

Dresden had not recovered its glory when Burney visited the city in 1772. 'Everyone is in the utmost indigence,' he wrote.[3] He met Bender, the retired court organist whose small pension was paid at very irregular intervals, and from him discovered that 'most of the nobility and gentry are too much impoverished to be able to learn, or to let their children be able to learn, music. . . . Dresden . . . from being the seat of the Muses and the habitation of pleasure, is now only a dwelling for beggary, theft and wretchedness'. Other countries recovered quite swiftly from the war, but the vast expenses on the arts which put the royal

---

[1] Alan Yorke-Long: *Music at Court.* Weidenfeld and Nicolson, 1954.
[2] Burney: *The Present State of Music in the Netherlands Germany,* etc.
[3] *Ibid.*

family into debt were a heavy burden which Saxony had to carry for a long time, and music had been the most expensive of their pleasures.

The magnificence of Dresden opera inspired Frederick the Great, and Frederick was given charge of the nine-year-old Duke Carl Eugen of Württemberg when the child succeeded to his title. Carl Eugen, handsome, intelligent, unusually gifted and elegant so impressed his formidable mentor that Frederick himself persuaded the Emperor Charles VII to declare the boy of age when he was only sixteen. Württemberg was neither large nor specially prosperous; Stuttgart, its capital, had no impressive cultural traditions and the only eminent musician to have held office there was Johann Sigismund Kusser, who introduced opera to the court in 1698, was appointed *Ober-Kapellmeister* in 1700 but left after a year in office. The *Kapelle* he controlled had thirty musicians. Keiser, the Hamburg opera composer, was there from 1719 to 1722, but left as he did not succeed in gaining an appointment as *Kapellmeister*.

Duke Eberhard Ludwig, who had maintained music with this modest recognition of facts, died in 1733. In four years his successor, Carl Alexander, had more than doubled the number of musicians in court employment, found that he could not afford to keep them and had summarily dismissed the bulk of them. When Carl Eugen came to Stuttgart as a paragon among adolescent princes, he inherited a *Kapelle* of eight singers and thirteen instrumentalists with an obscure Italian, Brescianello, as *Kapellmeister*; he also inherited a constitution guaranteed by Frederick the Great and the emperor, and a regulation limiting the amount of money which could be spent on court music to 5000 gulden a year.

Carl Eugen did not immediately concentrate on music. He corresponded with Voltaire, nourished an instructed love of history with foreign travel to important libraries and archaeological sites, explained to the King of Naples all that was wrong with the long-drawn-out excavation of Pompeii and the chaotic state of the Farnese library, interfered constructively in the organisation of the Württemberg porcelain factories and the organisation of his army, established schools and revised the university curriculum. He seemed to be a true pupil of Frederick the Great.

The first sign of his musical ambition had been his engagement of the once-great soprano, Cuzzoni, in 1745; two years later she ran away, leaving him to pay her debts. When he married in 1748, he was content with the services of a touring company of French actors for the festivities. In 1750, he spent 35,000 gulden on the conversion of Eberhard Ludwig's court opera house into a theatre holding four thousand people, and opened it with an opera by Graun. In the following February, Nicolo Jomelli's *Ezio* was produced, and in the following April came Jomelli's *Didone Abbandonata*. Two years later he engaged Jomelli as *Ober-Kapellmeister* at a salary of 3000 florins which by 1767 had increased to 6100 florins; he had found the composer he needed.

Jomelli, *maestro di capella* at St. Peter's Rome when Carl Eugen engaged him, was thirty-nine and already a successful composer of opera when he went to Stuttgart. He was the last great master of *opera seria*, whose determination to make opera dramatic makes him a forerunner of Gluck although, unlike Gluck, he had no theoretical principles to explain his practices and could work with the old-style libretti which Gluck rejected. His work is dramatically effective, intense and brilliant in the way that Italian audiences understood. At the same time, Ignaz Holzbauer, later to find fame in Mannheim, was engaged as *Kapellmeister* and Carl Eugen, apparently eager to have a concert orchestra as brilliant as his opera, did all he could to entice Johann Stamitz from Mannheim. He would accept nobody less than Gaetano Vestris, the greatest available choreographer, to direct his ballet though Vestris could only spend three months of every year in Stuttgart.

Money was spent in the theatre as though for several years Carl Eugen had lost all touch with reality. When he decided that he would live permanently in his summer palace at Ludwigsburg, an opera house had to be built for him there; the building progressed too slowly to satisfy his plans and he employed his grenadiers as builders' labourers while sending out his cavalry to conscript peasants to join in the work. A theatre was built at his new palace, The Solitude, but simply destroyed when it was complete because its acoustics were unsatisfactory. In 1767, opera and ballet productions cost 22,600 florins and the wages of the *Kapelle*, the ballet and the theatre staff added another 100,000 florins to this; more than a third of the duke's own income and more than a tenth of the entire revenue of the state were spent in the theatre. Six thousand infantry were lent to France for 400,000 florins a year; monopolies of tobacco, salt and the right to mint coins were sold; taxation was increased threefold; cities were compelled to pay tribute to avoid having troops billeted on their citizens; by ceaseless bullying, Carl Eugen forced up his civil list payment from less than 25,000 gulden in 1750 to more than 1,500,000 in 1762.

Unfortunately, for him, however, the constitution which had put an end to his father's extravagance eventually found ways of controlling his. He could imprison the noisiest protesters against new and arbitrary taxes, but he could not prevent his Estates General from appealing for redress to the Aulic Council of the Empire, which sent a commission of investigation which not only saw how justified the complaints were but also discovered that Carl Eugen himself was in debt to the tune of 12,000,000 gulden. For six years he turned a deaf ear to the demands of the Imperial authorities, which Frederick the Great was ready to implement by force if necessary—he was as angry as any teacher could be whose favourite disciple had proved faithless—but little by little the duke returned to common sense. In 1767 he dismissed his French actors and half his ballet company. In 1768, he cut down the size of the opera company and the orchestra. In 1769, Jomelli left Stuttgart, realising that the days of glory there were over; he tried by correspondence to establish his right to the scores of the works he had composed for Carl Eugen, but unsuccessfully. In 1770, the duke accepted the constitution, cut down his *Kapelle* to forty-six singers and players and thereafter depended, for great festivities, on the students of the Military Academy and the Academy of Music and Dancing which he had first established

and then amalgamated into his *Carlschule*. Jomelli's post remained vacant until
an obscure Italian, Boroni, was prepared to accept it at a salary of no more than
2500 gulden. Carl Eugen's projected edition of Jomelli's Stuttgart works was
never published, for no one subscribed to it. In 1776, he was satisfied with a
Kapelle of sixteen musicians augmented by his students, and he lived to 1793,
constructively occupied with educational and social reforms, dutifully attending
the performances of *opera buffa*, French *opéra comique* and *Singspiel* which
appealed to his citizens.

Burney, quick to sense a moral and to make sure that nobody missed it,
deserves the right to pronounce an epitaph on what was in the long run to have
little musical importance, for all that was constructive about court opera in
Berlin, Dresden and Stuttgart, in spite of the fortunes squandered on it, was that
it created a popular audience for the art and a habit of mind which regarded
subsidies from public funds as not only necessary but natural. Burney noted in
1772 that the entire cost of Carl Eugen's music, together with the subsidy to the
Carlschule, was only 66,000 florins. 'It is, perhaps,' he wrote, thinking of the
days in which Carl Eugen sowed his wild oats, 'on occasions such as these, that
music becomes a vice, and hurtful to society; for that nation, of which half the
subjects are stage players, fiddlers and soldiers, and the other half beggars, seems
to be but ill-governed.'[1]

These are the stories of court opera at its most sensational and, perhaps, at its
musically most dubious. Whether the Elector of Saxony and Duke Carl Eugen
of Württemberg were devoted to music or whether they squandered their
wealth on opera because opera flattered them by reflecting their glory it is impossible to say. Their eccentricities employed a large number of musicians but
had no real influence on the development of the art; nothing written by Hasse
or Jomelli depended in any way on the conditions in which they worked and the
facilities available to them.

It was possible, of course, to support opera without either undue extravagance
or any degree of excitement. Munich has an operatic history which goes back
even further than Dresden's; the first opera played there was *La Ninfa Ritrosa*,
by Jacob Porro, produced in 1654, when Porro had been *Kapellmeister* for
twenty-one years. Music in Munich was, too, completely Italianised. Between
Porro's appointment and the end of the eighteenth century, only one German
Kapellmeister was appointed; this was Johann Kaspar Kerll, who held office
from 1656 to 1674 and was probably the most accomplished of the many reliable
mediocrities appointed to the post.

Opera in Munich was never ambitious but it was as expensive as elsewhere;
two operas were commissioned for the marriage of the Elector Carl Albert to
Maria Amalia, the daughter of the Emperor Joseph I, in 1722 cost 200,000
florins. In 1728, the *Kapelle* cost 40,000 florins a quarter. Three of the singers—
the first *castrato*, first tenor and first baritone—were paid 1000 florins each, and
the cost of the costumes for Peli's setting of Metastasio's familiar libretto *La*

[1] Burney: *The Present State of Music in the Netherlands, Germany, etc.*

Clemenza di Tito were 2829 florins, 31 krone. The building of the sumptuous *Residenztheater* by Cuvilliés in 1753 suggests an abounding passion for opera, but the dull Munich fare—provided, apparently, for no other reason than that the Elector was expected to provide it—continued, and it was not until the succession of Carl Theodor, from Mannheim, to the Electorate in 1778 that music in the Munich court recovered the ambition which had marked it in the days of Lassus. We could point to Mozart's *Idomeneo*, produced in 1781, as the first result of Carl Theodor's infusion of new blood.

In many courts, opera was never a central activity. Dittersdorf explains how, while he was in the service of the Prince von Hildburghausen, between 1750 and 1758, opera came to the court at Schlosshof. A certain Piloti, manager of a touring opera company, called on the prince and offered to mount a production then and there for him; Pergolesi's *La Serva Padrona* was chosen to be the work and was hastily prepared, 'with a few violins for the sake of *tempi*', and the performance was given that evening. It was successful enough, though the lack of rehearsal suggests that Schlosshof standards were low, to induce the prince to make a contract with Piloti under which there would be a season of opera productions with daily performances from the beginning of July to the end of October. A large coach house would be used as a temporary theatre.[1]

As *Kapellmeister* to the Bishop of Grosswardein in succession to Michael Haydn, Dittersdorf persuaded his patron to allow him to set up a small theatre in the palace with a surplus of 1400 florins left from the previous year's allowance of 16,000 florins for the expenses of the *Kapelle*. As the bishop enjoyed his theatre, masquerades and balls rather more than was appropriate to his position, in 1769 he was accused of allowing performances in his theatre in Advent and Lent, and was quietly advised by Maria Theresa's private secretary to dismantle his theatre before the Empress felt herself compelled to take action against him.

In Darmstadt, court opera was inaugurated in 1709, while Graupner was *Kapellmeister*; it continued for ten years and then was abandoned until, in 1776, a public opera house was opened and supported by the Landgrave's government.

In Bonn, the Archbishop-Elector Clemens August, after 1723, introduced opera. He was able to exploit an increased revenue (his civil list income amounted to forty per cent more than his predecessor's allowance of a million florins) and foreign subsidies. From France he received 7,300,000 francs, from Holland came 76,000 reichthaler; Austria, too, heavily subsidised his state. He had inherited a *Kapelle* of twenty musicians whose salaries amounted to 8890 florins a year. 'Clemens August,' wrote an early biographer, 'squandered monstrous sums on splendid ornaments, magnificent equipages, furniture and rare works of art . . . operas, dramas, ballets, charlatans, swindlers, female vocalists, actors and dancers. His theatre and opera alone cost 50,000 thalers per annum.'[2]

---

[1] Carl Dittersdorf: *Autobiography*, trans. A. D. Coleridge. London, 1896.
[2] Quoted in Thayer, *Beethoven*.

Maximilian Friedrich, Clemens August's successor, continued his predecessor's lavish musical style. The operas heard at the Bonn court, however, were not the works of his own musicians, but works by popular Italian composers; Galuppi and Piccinni seem to have been specially favoured. Maximilian Friedrich, during these years, had cut down the number of performances and was apparently satisfied with occasional opera performances given by the touring company of Seyler in the Bonn *Komödien Haus*, a two-storey building with the Elector's *Redoutensaal* above an auditorium which many visitors considered too low-built to be worthy of an elegant court.

Whatever financial strains led to this limited operatic fare, the church music and the chamber music presided over by Ludwig van Beethoven, the composer's grandfather, did not suffer. In the year of his death, 1773, the Archbishop-Elector had nine singers, two of them 'accessists' retained without pay and waiting for a salaried post, seven violinists, two violists, two cellists, a double-bass player and four bassoonists; two trumpeters from the Life Guards and two court trumpeters with a court drummer were available.

In 1777, Seyler's opera company left its base in Dresden, where it was in competition with the court opera presided over by the *Kapellmeister* Bondini, and decided to commute between Frankfurt and Mainz, working the towns in between. Seyler had a full-scale company of two hundred and thirty actors, singers and players, and his proximity induced Maximilian Friedrich to commission the formation of a company in Bonn which would play a summer season in Cologne. Into this new company came a large number of Seyler's singers, and opera again became a permanency in Bonn.

A few of the works presented came from among their own ranks. A work by Christian Gottlob Neefe (the best of Beethoven's teachers), who abandoned opera to become court organist in Bonn, was played in 1782. Georg Benda, who had for a time abandoned Berlin and worked with Seyler's company, contributed three works to the repertory. D'Antoine and Schuster, two inhabitants of Bonn, the latter an officer in the Electoral army, each provided a work. For the rest, although the repertory included works by Florian Gassmann, Holzbauer, Hiller, Schweitzer and Michl, and Italian operas by Piccini, Salieri, Paisiello, Cimarosa and Sacchini, the bulk of the works played were French: Grétry, Philidor and Monsigny seemed to be the most popular composers. *Die Entführung aus dem Serail* was produced in the 1782–3 season, providing the twelve-year-old violist-repetiteur Ludwig van Beethoven with what seems to have been his first knowledge of any of Mozart's larger works. It is not, perhaps, fanciful to see in *Fidelio* the influence of the French operas with which the young Beethoven was so deeply concerned in the Bonn orchestra.

The opera, however, died with Maximilian Friedrich in 1784; Maximilian Friedrich, the Elector, left it to die. Like all the small-scale opera companies it had depended on a repertory of familiar works and done nothing for any composers except the two Bonn amateurs. Bonn, apart from its court, was a city of less than ten thousand people, and its operatic history is, in the circumstances, a remarkable story of achievement in a state not specially notable for the concern its rulers displayed for the educational and cultural well-being of their people. But so small an establishment was obviously in no position to commission new works and face the cost of their production.

Oddly enough, it was in the Imperial court in Vienna that opera developed new forms, new techniques and new expressions despite the essential conservatism of Viennese musical taste. The prestige of the world's greatest musical centre attracted every ambitious composer to the city, and the wealth of its nobility created a demand for music which could not be satisfied unless new and startling works were admitted. It was Vienna which nurtured the reform operas of Gluck and the revolutionary operas of Mozart.

Opera reached the Imperial court in the reign of Ferdinand III, who became Emperor in 1637. Ferdinand, a composer of church music whose taste was entirely for Italian music, staffed his *Kapelle* almost exclusively with Italians; Austria, with its territories in Italy, was specially open to an influx of Italian musicians, and until the nineteenth century, Italian music was always strong in Vienna. In 1641, a treatment of the legend of Ariadne and Theseus which mingled *opera buffa* with *opera seria* characters in a most unconventional way foreshadowing Richard Strauss's *Ariadne auf Naxos* seems to have been the first opera seen in Vienna. In 1643, Cavalli's *Egisto* was produced there.

Until after the Thirty Years' War had ended, there was little money to spare for works on a properly Imperial scale, and it was Leopold I, who succeeded to the throne in 1658, who made Viennese opera grand enough for the emperor's court. Leopold, too, was a composer whose oratorio, *Il sacrificio d'Abramo*, began the popularity of oratorio in his capital. He wrote a hundred and fifty-five songs for insertion in the operas and oratorios of other composers.[1] He reigned until 1705, and during his reign four hundred new operas were produced in Vienna by composers like Giovanni Felice Sances and Antonio Draghi; in 1665, Pietro Antonio Cesti was appointed *Vice-Kapellmeister*. Cesti held the post until he left Vienna in 1669. It was Cesti's *Pomo d'Oro* which, at a reputed cost of 300,000 gulden, which was staged to celebrate Leopold's marriage in 1667.

Leopold began the building of a public opera house in 1697, but the theatre was burnt down two years later. His successor, Joseph I, built a second opera house instead of recreating the old one. The *Josephinisches Theater* had two stages, one for spectacular *opera seria* productions during the carnival, the other for smaller-scale works and plays. This was used until the theatre near the Corinthian gate—the *Kärntnertor Theater*, officially the *Städtisches Komödienhaus* and a municipal creation—was built to be used by the opera as well as companies of actors offering folk-type comedies and *Singspiele*. This was burnt down—the common fate of wooden theatres—in 1761. The court *Hofballhaus* was converted into a theatre, becoming the *Burgtheater*, in 1763, and at the same time the court bought the site of the *Kärntnertor Theater*, which became a second home for the opera. The institution had become as much the property of

---

[1] Grove: *Dictionary of Music and Musicians*, fifth edition. Article: Vienna.

the city and its people as of the emperor. Maria Theresa, who became Empress in 1740, had her private passage way from her palace into the *Burgthecter*, but the management of the opera was in the hands of a syndicate of aristocrats who ran it as a commercial enterprise. Metastasio, the great master of the *opera seria* libretto, had gone to Vienna in 1730, had been appointed court poet there and held the position until his death in 1782; his continued existence was in itself a bulwark against change. But innovation crept in as a matter of evolution. While the aristocracy remained devoted to *opera seria*, the rest of the audience, a power increasingly responsible for the finance of the opera, was turning increasingly to the more naturalistic and far less extravagant manners of *opera buffa*. Gluck reached Vienna in 1761, when his ballet *Don Juan* was produced at the *Kärntner-tor Theater*. A year later, *Orfeo* inaugurated the operatic revolution, inspired to originality by the libretto and the teachings of Ranieri Calzabigi. *Orfeo*, *Alceste* and *Paride ed Elena* all had their first performance in Vienna, and though court circles at first found it hard to accept anything which broke with the form established by Metastasio, the works had a great popular success and were profitable enough to induce the syndicate of directors to encourage the revolution to continue.

Joseph II who became emperor in 1781 was prepared to go even further and encourage German opera and *Singspiele*. His enthusiasm for a national style led to the production in 1782 of *Die Entführung aus dem Serail*, with its stylistic leanings both to Italian opera and to *Singspiele*. It led, too, to the development of *Singspiele* in the new suburban theatres, particularly in the *Freihaus Theater*, built in what might be described today as a working-class housing estate. The *Freihaus Theater* provided a home for Emanuel Schikaneder, later to be librettist of *The Magic Flute*. Schikaneder's company played pieces by their manager (who was also a respectable baritone and the company's leading comedian) some of which exploited popular folk-play traditions while others broke entirely from them. But though *Die Entführung* was extremely popular, the court and the aristocracy in general did not share the new emperor's enthusiasm for German opera, and it continued to exist rather precariously in theatres the aristocracy usually failed to attend until the success of *The Magic Flute* made it entirely respectable. Even then almost a generation had to pass and the influence of French opera had to be felt before the repertory of German opera began to rival that of the Italian works which were still the mainstay not only of the Viennese theatre but of theatres throughout Germany. The only other home for German opera was Mannheim where, even before it received the prestige of the emperor's favour, Ignaz Holzbauer had worked towards a German equivalent of *opera seria* between 1753 and his death thirty years later. Opera in Mannheim, however, was a secondary consideration. The great enthusiasm of the Elector Carl Theodor was for orchestral music.

It was the result of Gluck's revolution that Mozart could stage and win acclaim for his three mature Italian operas, *The Marriage of Figaro*, *Don Giovanni* and *Cosi fan Tutte*, bringing *Don Giovanni*, originally produced in Prague, into line with Viennese conditions of casting and production but writing the other two works in response to commissions from the Imperial Opera.

The costs of opera in Vienna were, of course, no lower than those faced by the Kings of Saxony or by Carl Eugen of Württemberg. The emperor, however, was rich enough to stand them without disaster, and throughout the eighteenth century, even before the opera became the business of an aristocratic syndicate, it was administered with a proper regard to financial reality. By 1768 it was, according to Leopold Mozart, managed by a professional impresario '. . . a certain Affligio, who has to pay some 1000 (florins) a year to certain people whom the court would otherwise have to pay. The Emperor and the whole Imperial family pay nothing for their boxes. Consequently, the court cannot say a word to this Affligio, for everything is undertaken at his risk.'[1] Not surprisingly, perhaps, a professional manager seemed to avoid the disasters which haunted all the eighteenth-century well-born amateurs who ventured into operatic finance.

The court musicians responsible for the music of all these operas were also responsible for the multitudinous performances of church music, concertos, symphonies and chamber music which were part of the everyday life of any eighteenth-century court. Outside Vienna, what was new, adventurous and 'progressive' in music came from the courts at which opera was not an all-absorbing pre-occupation, chiefly Mannheim and Eszterhaza. In the 1770s, Prince Nikolaus Esterhazy devoted himself to opera and was thus responsible for the bulk of Haydn's operas; but though we have learnt to value Haydn's operas for their true quality, the type of work expected from him did not demand that he looked far beyond the conventions though his inventiveness as a writer of melody and his mastery of form led him to develop conventional opera a long way along purely musical lines.

Early in the eighteenth century J. S. Bach in Weimar was not only expected but employed to write ambitious church music for a small court at which opera was impossible. At Cöthen, a Calvinist court which had no use for church music, he was expected to provide little beside chamber music. The music at such courts was, and remained, on a very small scale. Baron von Fürnberg, Haydn's first aristocratic employer, was the son of an ennobled physician whose resources ran to a string quartet at his country house during the summer. Haydn's first quartets, Opp. 1 and 2, written for Fürnberg, can, either by accident or design, be played as quartets or, more effectively, by a string orchestra with a double-bass an octave below the cello part and supplying the real bass which is often missing when they are played by a quartet and the cello is allowed to climb into a high register.

Before the middle of the century music had been more important in German-speaking Europe as a servant of religion; its conversion into a social necessity had altered the organisation of the court *Kapelle*. In the seventeenth century it had been based upon the needs of the services of the patron's chapel whether he was Catholic or Protestant. By the end of the eighteenth century, liturgical music

---

[1] Emily Anderson: *Letters of Mozart and his Family*. Letter of July 30, 1768.

was a by-product of the *Kapellmeister*'s activity. Mozart's Masses, Litanies and Vespers appeal to us for their Mozartian qualities rather than for the sense of religion which seems to inhabit only the unfinished C minor Mass and the *Requiem*. Haydn, a composer more religious by nature, found himself under no obligation to compose for his patron's chapel during the years between 1782 and 1796, as the emperor Joseph II had discouraged the use of orchestras in church. But neither Mozart nor Haydn, nor anyone who might have expected church music from them, seems to have been conscious of any sense of deprivation. It seems that what Joseph II did was to interrupt a routine but not to dry up a source of inspiration.

At Weimar, from 1708 to 1717, J. S. Bach was court organist and *Conzertmeister* under the *Kapellmeister* Johann Samuel Drese, and the bulk of his compositions there were for the church. During his brief stay there, the court orchestra expanded while the choir remained small and static. At a small court like Weimar, the number of specialist musicians was limited. The Master of the Pages was one of the two basses; the second bass and cantor was the fifth master in the town gymnasium. One of the two tenors was the Court Secretary. Two of the six trumpeters in the court list of 1716 were court officials, and one of the two violinists named was a secretary. Bach's uncle, Johann Christoph, as a court musician to Count Ludwig Günther of Schwarzburg-Arnstadt, was also one of the Arnstadt *Stadtpfeifer*, played in a *Kapelle* in which the Clerk of the Chambers, the Clerk of the Granary and the Clerk of Works were singers, the Court Actuary and the Clerk of the Kitchen were instrumentalists. Several of the singers were available as instrumentalists when the choir was not in action, and various outsiders, notably three schoolmasters, could be brought in as violinists.

The typical German orchestral work of the first part of the eighteenth century —so far as such work exists—might be one of Bach's Suites or Brandenburg Concertos, which reflected fairly accurately the size of forces available in the average German Court. Apart from great centres—Potsdam, Munich, Dresden and Stuttgart—the multitude of smaller courts were occupied with music on the scale provided by a very small nucleus of professionals with no duties other than musical backed up by court officials whose musical duties occupied only part of their time and whose employment and status depended upon their other official duties.

At about the same time, in 1709, when court opera reached Darmstadt at a time when Christoph Graupner was *Vice-Kapellmeister*, the *Kapelle* numbered thirty; the list includes the three staff employed in the court school, and two boy singers. Among the instrumentalists were the Court Secretary, the Secretary of the Chancellery, the Clerk of the Kitchen, the Cabinet Secretary and the Secretary to the Exchequer. Three members had more menial extra-musical work; one was a 'lackey' and two were servants. This list, however, names only one adult singer and the two boys because the singers of the *Kapelle* were listed in a separate 'Church Book'. Nine of the thirty names on the list are those of court trumpeters, paid from army funds.

In 1718, the list stretches to forty-one names; there are seven trumpeters, one of whom was also a double-bassist. Only one schoolmaster is named, and eight of the orchestra were court officials: they included two chancery clerks, a clerk of the War Ministry, the Court Registrar, the Secretary of the Exchequer and an assistant to the Councillor for War. The additional members included two singers, each listed as a *cantatrice*. The second to be named, Johanna Elisabeth Hessin, was the highest paid member of the Kapelle in terms of money; her salary was 698 florins. Anna Maria Schoberin, the other *cantatrice*, was paid 450. Johann Michael Bohm, whose duties are not listed, earned 600 florins. The Hofkantor received 472. Graupner, *Kapellmeister* since 1711, was paid 675 Reichthaler and allowances of corn, barley, flour, wine and so on to the value of 108 thaler; Gottfried Grünswald, the *Vice-Kapellmeister* earned the same amount in money and allowances. The 1718 list includes two *castrati*; one, Campioli, was paid 400 florins, with 156 Reichthaler for food. The salary of the other, listed as *Der Kleine Castrat*, is not noted.

The changes in the nine years which separate the two lists are the result of the development of opera in Darmstadt, where the custom of entering the names of the regular singers in a separate list from that of instrumentalists accounts for the fact that no tenors or basses are mentioned. By 1767, seven years after Graupner's death, a *Kapelle* list includes three female singers as well as one alto, one tenor and one bass, and divides the orchestra into sections; there are five first and three second violins, one viola player, one cellist and one double-bassist, one flautist, one oboist, one bassoonist and three horn players. Six court trumpeters and two court drummers were available when the *Kapelle* needed them. The city *Musikus* is entered in the list, but his court duties are not described. In the 1718 list, only the bellringer, the double-bassist, a player of trumpet and bassoon and a hornist have their duties described, apart from the court organist, the court trumpeters and the cantor.

The 1767 list specifies a typical eighteenth-century court orchestra. Its representative qualities can be tested by comparison with other orchestras over the same period. In 1709, the Dresden Court Orchestra had four violins, two violas, four cellos, one double-bass, two flutes, four oboes and two bassoons; military trumpeters and drummers could be co-opted whenever they were needed. In 1768, there were fifteen violins, four violas, three cellos and three double-basses, two flutes, five oboes, five bassoons, two horns, two trumpets, two harpsichords and drums. The trumpeters and the drummers had become regular members of the orchestra, not co-opted soldiers.

In 1777, the orchestra in which both Leopold and Wolfgang Mozart were involved in Salzburg could call on between twelve and sixteen violins, four violas, three cellos, three double-basses, two flutes, six oboes, two bassoons and two horns. The orchestra which played for Mozart in Paris on April 11, 1781, consisted of forty violins, ten violas, eight cellos, ten double-basses, four flutes, four oboes, four clarinets, six bassoons, four horns, four trumpets and timpani.

By 1781, Leipzig Gewandhaus Orchestra classified its first and second violinists separately, and had six of each; with these went three violas, four cellos and double-basses, two flutes, two oboes, three bassoons, two horns, two trumpets and timpani. Haydn's orchestra at Eszterhaza in 1783 had eleven violins, two violas, two cellos and two double-basses, two oboes, two bassoons and two horns. When trumpets and drums were needed, they were taken in from Prince Eszterhazy's militia. At the same time, from 1781 to 1783, the court opera orchestra in Vienna had six first and six second violins, four violas, three cellos and three double-basses, two flutes, two oboes, two clarinets, two bassoons, four horns, two trumpets and timpani. By the middle of the century, the idea of the harpsichord as a necessary continuo instrument was dying out. At the Salomon concerts, when Haydn presided over them in 1791, he conducted from the keyboard at which he played a continuo apparently elaborate enough to be interesting, though his orchestra was based on between twelve and sixteen violins, four violas, three cellos and four double-basses. The symphonies call for two flutes, two oboes, two bassoons, two horns, two trumpets and timpani.

The Gewandhaus Orchestra, Mozart's orchestra in Paris and Haydn's in London were not, of course, court orchestras. Salomon's orchestra for the Haydn concerts was not simply an *ad hoc* collection of players assembled concert by concert, for Salomon had been organising his concert series since 1786, introducing symphonies by Haydn and Mozart. The London of 1791 could enjoy opera on Tuesday and Saturday evenings and a concert on every other. Salomon himself led the orchestra for the Academy of Ancient Music, and other players, probably all the orchestra which played for Haydn at Hanover Square Rooms on Friday evenings, appeared on every, or almost every, other evening of the week under some other auspices.

The Gewandhaus Orchestra, Mozart's orchestra in Paris and Haydn's in London inevitably followed the pattern of the court orchestras. The latest and most attractive music, not only for concerts but for ballrooms, was written for court performance. To what extent the orchestra's form was musically inevitable it would be hard to decide. Its quintet of strings—a perfectly balanced homogeneous choir—was inevitable enough, but its trio of woodwind—the clarinet did not become a regular member of the orchestra till towards the end of the century though Rameau's *Zoroastre* had a part for them in 1749 and Arne added them to his orchestra for *Thomas and Sally* in 1760 and *Artaxerxes* two years later—was less than perfectly matched. In the 1770s, Gossec took clarinets for granted in his symphonies, but Haydn despite experiments with the woodwind in his early symphonies—he used cors anglais in Symphony 22, for example, but not flute and oboe—neglected the clarinet until 1792, when he used it in the London Sinfonia Concertante and then, in 1793 and 1794, in the second set of London Symphonies.

The bassoon had belonged to the orchestra since the days before standardisation began simply because it added bite and clarity to the figured bass. It was not until the 1780s that Haydn, in the 'Paris' Symphonies, allowed it independence from the cellos and double-basses. As late as the 1770s, the bassoon part was normally tucked away as part of the general bass line. Flutes and oboes, too, remained tethered to the upper string lines, adding bite and colour or simply sustaining the harmony but allowed little independent activity until the later 1770s. This, of course, was in part due to their imperfect tuning and chancy intonation. Burney's travels through musical Europe led him to make some caustic notes on the quality of continental woodwind tone and intonation.

Horns and trumpets—the latter usually employed only in works of some jubilation—presented only fanfare-type themes or were used to sustain the harmony in powerful *tutti* passages. The art of high clarino playing of which the trumpeters of Bach's Leipzig, for example, had been masters had died with the deterioration of the standards of playing in the *Stadtpfeifer* guilds whose purposes and musical standards were far less relevant to the second half of the eighteenth century than they had been to the first. The absence of trumpets, where they are not mentioned in orchestral lists, means no more than that the patrons involved still regarded trumpeters as soldiers primarily and only as part-time musicians. The city orchestras, like the *ad hoc* orchestra of Mozart's Paris concert, automatically listed their trumpeters.

The semi-professional court orchestra which made use of musically able officials and servants continued as long as music remained a social necessity. When in 1769 the Bishop of Grosswardein found that his opera house had brought him under Maria Theresa's displeasure, he discharged all his *Kapelle* except his organist and two horn players. He asked Dittersdorf to stay, but the composer could see no point in continuing to be a *Kapellmeister* after the *Kapelle* had ceased to exist and asked for his discharge. Within a few months he met the Prince Bishop of Breslau, Count Schafgotsch, who had been driven from his see when Frederick the Great had over-run Silesia and was living on his estates at Johannisberg on an income of '13 or 14,000 gulden per annum'. The bishop asked Dittersdorf to spend the winter with him. 'Musical servants and secretaries, and officials in Johannisberg', composer and patron agreed, could make a string orchestra of about eight players.

Dittersdorf spent the winter of 1769–70 there, and to keep him at Johannisberg, the bishop found him a sinecure as a forester, with the reversion of the post of chief forester, had him created Knight of the Golden Spur and, eventually, ensured his succession to the chief forester's post by obtaining for him a patent of nobility. A rise in the price of timber brought a profit of 1500 florins, and with another 900 florins of the prince's, the orchestra of servants, secretaries and officials was augmented to seventeen, and a tower in the bishop's garden cheaply converted into a small theatre for which Dittersdorf wrote opera, *Singspiel* and oratorios, while his chamber music, concertos and symphonies were played at the bishop's concerts. The existence of a court *Kapelle* and opera did not necessarily mean a megalomaniac disregard of the facts of financial life.

The structure of the court orchestra—flute, oboes, bassoons, horns and strings—seems inevitable because of its purely musical qualities and its potentiality for blends of colour, varieties of tone and dynamic change. It belonged of necessity to the wealthy because, as the experience of J. S. Bach and others in the first half of the eighteenth century had shown, it cost more than the average city could afford to pay. The Gewandhaus Orchestra, for example, did not become an entirely professional body until the mid-nineteenth century, and its finances depended largely on subscriptions or box office receipts. It needed public money, or the wealth of a music-loving ruler, to maintain a fully professional orchestra and to provide it with training and worthwhile music.

In this context, the achievements of the Mannheim Orchestra were as remarkable as they were influential. The Mannheim composers invented comparatively little; the Mannheim school established the four-movement symphony, sandwiching minuet and trio between slow movement and finale. Elector Carl Theodor gave Johann Wenzel Stamitz a place in the Mannheim *Kapelle* in 1743 because Stamitz was a brilliant violinist. Stamitz was made *Konzertmeister* and Director of the Court Chamber Music two years later. His own music combined intensity and fire with the elegance on which his period insisted, and it made demands on its players which few orchestras of the time were able to answer. He built up the Mannheim Orchestra into a virtuoso instrument far more efficient and exciting than any other in Europe, and found that it stimulated him to write yet more demanding music for it.

Perhaps it was natural that he found room in the Mannheim orchestra for a number of gifted compatriots—Franz Xaver Richter, Anton Filz, his son Carl Philipp, amongst others—several of whom were effective composers as well as first-rate players to whom Stamitz gave a discipline and unanimity of style which made possible the mastery of *accelerandi* and *ritardandi* and the sensational dynamic control which created the legend that the Mannheim musicians invented the *crescendo* and *diminuendo*. It was their style of playing rather than the works written for them which dazzled strangers visiting Mannheim. The style, too, travelled; players from Mannheim turned up in the orchestra at Eszterhaza and in important posts in Vienna and Paris as well as in less influential orchestras, whilst composers and conductors who heard them in Mannheim were stimulated to new ideas.

The death of Stamitz, in 1757, left a sensational style to lesser composers who turned its effects into a series of formulae; the music, by an odd but not unique inversion of values, served the orchestral style instead of the style serving the music. When Mozart visited Mannheim in 1778, it was the splendour of the playing rather than the quality of the music played which raised him to enthusiasm; Mozart was, of course, notoriously hard to please.

The other important fact about Mannheim was the height of salaries paid to musicians in the upper echelons of the *Kapelle*. Mozart's mother, his companion on the journey to Paris which took him through Mannheim reported to her husband, 'The leading actor in the theatre, Herr Marshall, gets 3000 Gulden a year, and the most wretched singer, even a beginner gets 600.'[1] 'In the orchestra,

---

[1] Emily Anderson: *Letters of Mozart and his Family.* Letter of December 1777.

too, they get fine salaries. Herr Cannabich, as Director, gets 1800 gulden, Herr Franzl, as *Konzertmeister*, 1400 gulden, *Kapellmeister* Holzbauer, almost 3000 gulden, and in addition they get presents for any new composition.' Not all salaries at Mannheim were so splendid. Fridolin Weber, the court copyist and bass singer, and father of the singer Aloysia, with whom Mozart was at the time in love, was paid 400 gulden a year, about £40. Holzbauer's lordly salary was, of course, about £300 of English money. But Leopold's salary in a post which was Salzburg's equivalent to that of Cannabich, was noticeably less than Cannabich's £180.

The influx of Bohemian composers—apart from the Stamitz team in Mannheim—coincided with the evolution of the symphony into maturity. A generation before, the four brothers Benda had been in the service of Frederick the Great. The elder, Frantisek, internationally famous as a violinist, became *Konzertmeister* in Berlin. His younger brother, Jiri Antonin, became *Kapellmeister* to the Duke of Sachsen-Gotha. Antonin Reicha, born in Prague in 1770, was from 1818 to his death in 1836 Professor of Theory and Composition at the Paris Conservatoire. Vanhal, Kozeluch, Gyrowetz, Vorisek, Gassmann and others worked in Vienna at the height of the classic period.

Bohemia, under Austrian rule and with its national identity firmly repressed since the wars of religion in the early seventeenth century, had no central musical authority apart from the Opera in Prague, a popular institution which the city inherited from the period before the emperor fixed his capital in Vienna. A fashionable nobleman from Bohemia, or any ambitious aristocrat looking for power and influence, spent more time in Vienna than on his own estates, so that there were too few positions open to Bohemian musicians who had been taught thoroughly in schools where music was held to be as important as it was in German schools.

The classical symphony and concerto grew up in the courts where composers were encouraged to work ambitiously in the instrumental forms. If the Elector Carl Theodor and the Eszterhazy princes who employed Haydn had not been attracted to orchestral and chamber music, they would have kept their *Kapellmeisters* and court composers occupied with other work. As befitted men in their position, each supported an opera house. In Mannheim, the townspeople were admitted free to the pit, and Holzbauer experimented with German opera. At Eszterhaza, a world in itself, Haydn wrote twelve operas and was responsible for the performance of many others, for the normal Eszterhaza week had two concerts and two opera performances as well as the prince's own chamber music. In the 1780s six or seven new productions as well as revivals were presented in the Eszterhaza theatre each year. As well as a new work by Haydn in almost every year, works by a large number of other composers—Paisiello, Piccinni, Salieri, Cimarosa, Grétry—were produced. Maria Theresa avowed that when she wanted to hear good opera, she went to Eszterhaza. Opera at Eszterhaza cost a great deal of money; according to the *Diary* of General Miranda, who heard an opera there on October 26, 1785, Prince Nikolaus Eszterhazy spent 30,000 florins a year on his theatre.[1] His singers cost him exactly what good singers would have cost in Vienna, and though the auditorium of his opera house was small, its stage was large and remarkably well equipped.

When Haydn entered Eszterhazy service under Prince Paul Anton, in 1761, his work was at the family's palaces in Vienna and Eisenstadt, where they had already an art gallery and a good theatre. Paul Anton died in March, 1762, and his successor Prince Nikolaus (who was nicknamed 'The Magnificent') had a family hunting lodge at Eszterhaza, in the Hungarian marshes, converted into a palace even more splendid, which he began to occupy in 1765. It was the last word in ivory towers, so remote from any town that the prince, surrounded by his ceremonial army, his court officials, his *Kapelle*, his actors and his army of servants was never bothered by the outside world, except by such representatives of it that he cared to invite. Eszterhaza was so inaccessible that in 1772 Burney did not go there in the midst of his travels although he already knew and admired some of Haydn's work and heard a great deal about him in Vienna. The journey was too expensive and too time-consuming even for a traveller as resourcefully intrepid as Burney.

Once Eszterhaza was habitable, Prince Nikolaus found it attractive to live as monarch of all he surveyed. He lost the habit of dividing his year between Vienna and his own estates. This demanded the permanent attendance at Eszterhaza of his *Kapelle*; few of the orchestra lived in married quarters, for the musicians' house at the new palace could not accommodate musicians' wives, and the plea for leave or for the prince's removal back to civilisation which is supposed to have been made by the *Farewell Symphony* in 1772 was a cry from the musicians' hearts. Haydn turned the geographical disadvantages of his situation to profit. 'At Eszterhaza,' he told Georg August Griesinger, his first biographer, 'not only did I have the encouragement of constant approval, but as conductor of the orchestra I could experiment, find out what made a good effect and what weakened it, so I was free to alter, improve, add or omit and be as bold as I pleased. Cut off from the world, I had no one to bother me and I was forced to become original.'

In other places, chiefly in Mannheim and Vienna, the formal dynamics of the sonata and the symphony were worked out. At Eszterhaza, Haydn established their expressive purposes by creating a clear expressive distinction between the symphony on one hand and the entertainment music of serenades and divertimenti on the other.

But his claim that he had the 'constant approval' of Prince Nikolaus must refer not only to his exploration of formal structures and the freedom he found within them but to the actual materials which he used. Apart from themes adapted from plainchant for symphonies written for performance on particular feast days, folk music style tunes, minuets moving away from court etiquette and themes which seemed to be derived from gypsy music must, at times, have been as surprising

[1] H. C. Robbins Landon: *The Symphonies of Joseph Haydn*. Rockliff, London, 1955.

to an aristocratic audience as the forcefulness and often plebeian vigour of Haydn's work.

Robbins Landon,[1] considering the magnificent *Sturm und Drang* symphonies which Haydn wrote in the early 1770s, with their stormy forcefulness, their strength and harmonic freedom, suggests that the prince's disapproval put an end to this period of adventure. Landon's evidence for this is to be discovered in the nature of the symphonies which followed in the decade after 1774. These are harmonically unadventurous, restricted in the range of tonalities they explore, usually genial and sometimes simply manufactured. The drive and energy of the *Sturm und Drang* symphonies vanished. What remains is masterly but rarely concerned with any intense depth of feeling until the new stimulus of a commission from Paris brought his symphonic ambition to life again. He was, during the years of unambitious symphonies, deeply and exhaustingly occupied with opera.

If such an interruption to Haydn's work happened, it would have been the natural reaction of a patron who did not want to be too much disturbed by a composer suddenly afflicted with a tragic vision. There is nothing in Haydn's known biography to explain the sudden upsurge of tragic feeling in his music in the late 1760s and its departure in about 1774, but, if Landon's suspicions are correct, Prince Nikolaus Eszterhazy endured a great deal of forceful, stormy and disturbing music from his *Kapellmeister* before he demanded that an end be put to this particular vein of expression. There had been a whole series of *Sturm und Drang* symphonies before, as Landon suggests, the prince rebelled.

Nevertheless, the conditions of Haydn's service were such that he would automatically be liable to commands to suit the prince's taste. When he was first appointed *Vice-Kapellmeister*, he was subordinate to the elderly Gregorius Werner, the *Kapellmeister*, in everything which concerned the choir, but he had almost complete control over the orchestra. His status remained that of a superior servant.

In 1765, an order from Prince Nikolaus shows exactly how a *Kapellmeister* could expect to be treated. The Eisenstadt choir, indolent and ill-disciplined, had left the choir loft in disorder. Therefore Haydn was instructed to prepare a catalogue in duplicate of its instruments and music, writing down the names of composers and the number of parts in stock; then to see that the schoolmaster kept the re-catalogued music in proper order and the instruments in good repair. Apparently some of the players had been evading their duty in the church services; Haydn was to see that they attended regularly. During the prince's absence from Eisenstadt, the composer was to be responsible for two concerts a week and to send a fortnightly report of any absentees. He himself was instructed to work hard at composition and, particularly, to compose some new baryton works. A good fair copy of everything he wrote was to be sent to the prince.[2]

[1] *Ibid.*
[2] Joseph Haydn: *Collected Correspondence and London Notebooks* ed. H. C. Robbins Landon, Barrie and Rockliff, 1959.

Apparently the harshness of these instructions (the result of a complaint by Werner, Haydn's immediate superior, about the weakness of Haydn's discipline) was mitigated by the prince's satisfaction with the works he had demanded; they brought Haydn a present of 12 ducats and an order for six more barytone pieces. Haydn's output in his first years in Eszterhazy service was so prolific that it is hard to see any point, let alone any justice, in the prince's rebuke. It is not surprising that he acknowledged mistakes in a score with the explanation that while he wrote it he could barely keep his eyes open. The inaccessibility of Eszterhaza meant that he had fewer opportunities of easing his own burden by putting the works of others into his programmes.

Nevertheless, by 1768 Haydn was beginning to receive privileges which suggest that he must have been entirely in Prince Nikolaus's favour. In 1768, he composed the *Applausus Cantata* for the birthday of an abbot, probably the Abbot at Göttweig, but perhaps at Kremsmünster (as the composer came to believe when, as an old man, he was questioned about the work) or perhaps at Zwetll. By this time, the prince was obviously ready to allow his *Kapellmeister* to undertake external commissions. In the 1770s and 1780s, Haydn was obviously allowed to distribute copies of his works to a number of monasteries in Austria, Bavaria and Bohemia as well as to a number of noblemen. By 1780, no obstacles seem to have been put in the way of his publishing any work which the publishers wanted, and the consequence of this was the spread of his reputation which led to commissions from Cadiz in 1785 (*The Seven Words of the Saviour on the Cross*) and Paris in 1786 (the six 'Paris' Symphonies).

Obviously Eszterhazy prestige was enhanced by Haydn's international celebrity. While it is hard to believe in the close friendship which many biographers have deduced to have been the relationship between Haydn and Prince Nikolaus, the prince was a man of real culture and education capable of realising the greatness of his *Kapellmeister*. Until Nikolaus's death Haydn had his patron's confidence; he began at the beginning again with Prince Anton Eszterhazy, who had no particular interest in music but wanted to hold on to a famous *Kapellmeister* and at last, after his second visit to London, he discovered that his reputation was capable of ensuring that he was treated with courtesy.

Possibly Haydn's achievement was unique because Haydn's situation was unique. He was able to follow his own line of development in spite of the musical seriousness of his aim. That he was able to do so is some indication of the musicality of his first two Eszterhazy princes—and though Anton allowed the Eszterhaza *Kapelle* to run down, Haydn's work had reached out so far that it continued in other places through other hands because Haydn's example had done a great deal to establish a general symphonic style in place of the local styles which had persisted before his work became widely known. His influence exerted itself on patrons as well as on composers; his became the socially acceptable style just as it was the most varied, vigorous and complete.

The work of the Mannheim composers, of Haydn and of Mozart in the last fifteen years of his life, established standards which themselves worked against much that was done by the smaller *Kapelle*. It was not really within the competency of Dittersdorf's scratch orchestra at Johannisberg to play Haydn's *Sturm und Drang* symphonies, or those he wrote for Paris and London, to tackle the *Linz* or the *Prague* symphonies, or Mozart's three final works in the form. Equally, it was beyond the resources of most patrons to spend enough on music to create orchestras that could reach what, through the growing number of public concerts, was winning acceptance as the most effectively composed and interesting work available.

By the end of the eighteenth century the new standard—not of technical accomplishment alone but of musical interest and excitement—transformed the general taste. The light-hearted, comic, semi-divertimento symphonic style of Salzburg and the easy-going relaxation usually offered by early Viennese symphonists like Gassmann, Wagenseil and Monn, lost favour to Haydn and Mozart because they were less exciting and less expressive; the new gaiety was more brilliant and the pathos more intense. It had more to communicate, but to make its effect it demanded more money.

Similarly, the administrative system adopted by the Imperial opera in Vienna reasonably reduced the cost to the emperor's purse in a way that already worked effectively in Italy. In Germany and Austria there was some gap between the popular taste which the providers of *Singspiel* and plays in the folk tradition satisfied and the operatic taste fostered by the Imperial opera. This meant that the emperor was still compelled to pay heavily for his pleasure in the opera house but that a considerable portion of the running expenses was paid in at the box office. By the 1770s even the Holy Roman Emperor was not willing to face the costs of opera unaided.

18 The Rise of the Public Concert

When, in 1712, the *Collegium Musicum* of Frankfurt developed into an organisation which gave public concerts to an audience of subscribers, and was followed after 1721 by that of Hamburg, the two organisations were anticipating an inevitable development by something like fifty years. The growth of the public concert depended chiefly upon two factors: the existence of a public which enjoyed listening to music as distinct from taking part in performances and which could afford to pay for its pleasures, and then on the existence of a municipal authority prepared to support music as a necessary civic amenity. It was the Hamburg city council which provided the citizens' Grand Concert with a hall in which to work.

The creating of Leipzig's Gewandhaus Orchestra follows a similar pattern. Arnold Schering describes the sort of social life out of which it developed:

> There were plenty of connoisseurs with a thorough knowledge of music who played well and could tell good works from bad. Such connoisseurs were found in various strata of the upper bourgeoisie; merchants, doctors, lawyers who had the advantage of higher education. In the homes of such people the better type of *Hauswerk* was played . . . the merits of composers and virtuoso performers were discussed and artists with letters of recommendation were made welcome because the connoisseurs felt that their enjoyment of music laid certain obligations on them.[1]

In 1743 a group of sixteen Leipzig business men formed what, on the precedent of Hamburg, they called a 'Grand Concert' out of the members of the two *Collegia Musica*, that of the city and that of the university. This gave them an orchestra of sixteen strings, three flautist–oboists and three bassoonists; brass and drums depended on the collaboration of the city *Stadtpfeiferei* and the city militia. As director they appointed Johann Friedrich Doles, a pupil of J. S. Bach who was later to succeed his teacher as *Thomascantor*. Some writers have wondered at the way in which Bach, the city's principal musical authority, was by-passed by the concert organisers and have suggested that the composer, embittered by his endless trivial struggles with the Leipzig authorities, preferred to let Leipzig music go its own way. Doles, however, was probably a deliberate choice by the management because he was an up-to-date, Italianate musician and not, like Bach, a mighty survival from earlier musical times.

The Grand Concert was given regularly in the Three Swans Inn, once a week

---

[1] Arnold Schering: *Musikgeschichte Leipzigs; Dritter Band, 1723–1800*, Leipzig, 1941.

in winter and once in every two weeks in summer, until the Seven Years' War in 1756, when the vicissitudes of Leipzig led to its suspension for six years. In 1762, however, Johann Adam Hiller revived the organisation under the more fashionable name *Liebhaberkonzerte*, which usually indicates that a primarily amateur orchestra plays to an audience of subscribers. The regular subscription, rather than the sale of tickets on the night, was necessary because without a known and guaranteed income from subscribers, the concert management was unable to plan a single season's programmes.

Hiller left the orchestra in 1766 to form a choral society with which and the orchestra he gave series of oratorio and choral concerts, too spasmodic, it seems, to demand an audience of subscribers, known as *Concert Spirituel*—the social influence of France counted for a great deal in eighteenth-century Germany—in addition to the established *Liebhaberkonzerte*. He had agitated for a long time for a municipal concert hall, but the war prevented the completion of a plan to build a concert hall with a new theatre in a single complex. In 1781, the Burgomaster caused the unused first floor of the *Gewandhaus*, or Cloth Merchants' Hall, to be lavishly converted into a hall for music; the conversion even included the insulation of the hall itself within corridors built with interior walls designed to add to its resonance. The orchestra was by this time thirty strong—strings, two flutes, two oboes, three bassoons, two horns and two trumpets; the timpanist was either a viola player or a second violinist, whichever of the two was least occupied when the drums were required. Such orchestras continued to depend upon the 'professional stiffening' of the *Stadtpfeiferei* for a considerable time simply because the unfashionable instruments, which could take little part in domestic music-making rarely found accomplished amateur players.

In 1786, however, the professional orchestra of the Leipzig Theatre asked for amalgamation with the Gewandhaus players; suffering from a management which seemed eager to reduce the costs of production by decreasing the size of the orchestra, they felt that they would find safety in numbers and also bring a number of unpaid auxiliary musicians into the theatre pit, thus making possible the expansion of their work into larger-scale operas than had previously been possible, thus insuring their position; they would, too, have some protection from the municipality because they were affiliated to the highly-regarded amateur orchestra. The merger at the same time benefited the Gewandhaus concerts and made possible the creation of the orchestra's pension fund.

There was no single pattern according to which the old, semi-private music clubs were transformed into public concert-giving organisations. In Halle, the university *Collegium Musicum* had been founded in 1694 and continued to function in the traditional way until Daniel Gottlob Türk was appointed music director of the university in 1779. Türk founded a series of concerts played in the basement ballroom of the *Rathaus*. But a Lodge of freemasons had been founded in Halle in 1743; it used music in its ceremonies and apparently included a number of good amateur players among its members, so that it began to promote concerts to which non-members as well as Masons were invited as guests of the members of the Lodge. When the Lodge commissioned a cantata from Türk, the two organisations began to coalesce. Eventually the Masons bought a large house on the Jägerberg, just outside the city, and its ballroom became the concert hall for public concerts in 1810, since which date the *Bergkonzerte* have continued.

Concert societies grew up in quite small and obscure towns as well as in the important commercial or university cities. For example, a *Liebhaber* society was founded in Zittau in 1768; concerts in Güstrow began in 1781, in Haderlein in 1782, in Anklau and in Celle in 1783. This list is not exhaustive; it simply indicates the spread of the habit of concert-giving and concert-going.

The rules of the *Musikalische Gesellschaft* founded in the Germanised Warsaw of 1805 were reprinted with approving comments in the *Allgemeine Musikalische Zeitung* immediately after the Society's foundation, as though at last, after fifty or more years of experiment, an amateur concert society had hit upon the ideal, musically purist scheme of organisation. There would be members—amateur musicians who as singers or instrumentalists would take part in the concerts (refusal to play or sing when requested to do so was to be regarded as tantamount to notice of resignation)—and honorary members who would have no share in the control of the society but who had priority in subscribing to concerts and who could use the amenities of the premises bought with the members' subscriptions; full members paid 1½ thalers a month, honorary members 1 thaler. The society's headquarters had a concert hall, rooms for meetings and relaxation and a library of music books and music periodicals.

The mere payment of a subscription could make anyone an honorary member, but would-be members had to undergo a test to prove their value to the society as either potential performers or as scholars with real musical knowledge before they were elected. The children of members, and any musically gifted children, were admitted to membership because of their potential value to the society in the future. The subscription was low enough to admit members of all social classes; the two musical directors, with a choirmaster and a singing teacher, were professional musicians employed by the society. The administration was in the hands of officials elected not for their place in the social hierarchy: when the society began, a general, a high civil servant, a Polish count and a quarter-master-general in the army all served under the chairmanship of a mere lawyer, while the director of the honorary members was a major in the army.

The list of rules, when it was given in the *Allgemeine Musikalische Zeitung*, had a running commentary of marginal notes by the editor: 'excellent', 'wise', 'severe but sensible', and so on. Apparently the editor regarded the Warsaw organisation as a plan which would combine the best of the old world of musically earnest amateur societies, which existed so that amateur musicians could make music together with serious determination, and the newer organisations which existed to give musical pleasure to mere listeners. In Germany, as the public concert became popular and amateurs addressed their music-making to an audience, many of the larger cities found themselves with *Musikübung* societies of players who met simply for rehearsal and serious musical work with no thought of public performance; they were, so to speak, the old devoted *Collegia Musica* under a new name.

The democratic form of organisation adopted by the Warsaw *Musikalische Gesellschaft* became common among the amateur orchestras and among the choral societies which, in the fifty years after 1775, grew up alongside them and which, necessarily thrown back upon a repertory of choral music from the past, did a great deal to further the exploration of earlier styles than the classical. The Berlin *Singakademie* was formed in 1791, the Leipzig *Singverein* in 1802, the Lübeck *Gesangverein* in 1805; a choral society was formed in Erlangen a year later. The *Cecilienverein* in Frankfurt dates from 1818, and large amateur choirs became active in Halle, Mannheim, Cassel and elsewhere in the 1820s; this list, again, is not exhaustive but simply indicative of progress. During the reactionary years after the end of the war with Napoleon and the Congress of Vienna, the democratic organisation of such societies made them politically suspect; Metternich, the architect of reaction, announced that he would like to find a reason for forbidding their creation, and they operated under police supervision, with all their activities carefully noted. The choirs, however, like the *Liebhaber* orchestras, gave regular performances in public with whatever orchestra was available.

Most of the German political capitals lagged behind in the development of concert music. A concert society was formed in Dresden in 1760 and one in Cassel in 1770, the year in which the Berlin *Liebhaberkonzerte* began with eminent musicians from the court orchestra as its directors. The ubiquitously busy Johann Friedrich Reichardt—composer, conductor, choir-trainer, musicologist and rather unreliable author—founded a *Concert Spirituel* on the original lines of the Parisian organisation whose name it took and whose early principles it applied. Reichardt's concerts, like those of the French organisation at its birth, usually had a religious work or part of an oratorio in its first half and a miscellaneous group of orchestral works in its second; Reichardt, incidentally, pioneered the use of programme books with analytical notes at these concerts.

But the general slowness of public musical organisations to develop in the majority of the German capitals was a result of the overflow of music from the court to the local population; for the musically inclined people of most of such cities, opera—the form which all the courts except that of Mannheim made the centre of their musical activities and supported with most enthusiasm and generosity—was the essential musical fare. The citizens of Berlin, Stuttgart, Munich and so on had little difficulty in finding their way to well staged, professionally performed, up-to-date works which were traditionally accepted as the finest musical and social fruits that expert musicians could produce. Amateur activity would look mean and inefficient beside them, and as late as 1811 Weber wrote sadly about the lack of interest shown by the people of Darmstadt in any efforts to induce them to make music on their own account. As late as 1869, Wagner could write: 'We owe our permanent orchestras to the various theatres, particularly the court theatres, small and great.'[1] He probably remembered, as he wrote this, that his request that the Dresden *Hofkapelle* be allowed to give regular symphony concerts in addition to its duty in the opera house had been turned down in 1848 though he had lucidly shown that for the sake of the orchestra's musical style and the general culture of Saxony, regular professional concerts would have been to everybody's advantage.

Munich, however, found itself provided with regular professional concerts before any other European city except Paris. The leading court musicians who had accompanied the Elector Carl Theodor from Mannheim to Munich had encouraged the formation of a *Liebhaber* concert society in the Bavarian capital 'in order, through the public performance of classical music, to raise public taste above the present liking for bad music'. In the 1790s, the *Cecilienverein*, an amateur choir, had been founded to take part in the performance of oratorios. Public apathy, the war against France, the availability of music at court, to which it was never very difficult for an eager listener to gain admission, and the *Hauskonzerte* of the well-to-do bourgeoisie apparently exhausted the public interest in music. Visiting virtuosi could always find a good audience, and in 1810 performances of *Messiah* and *The Creation* were financed by 'Herr Hatterer, citizen and master-baker, to whom,' said the newspaper *Eos*, 'music-loving citizens and Munich audiences in general owe a great debt.' Though the *Liebhaber* concerts had dwindled in a short time into the private meetings of enthusiastic amateurs, the success of Hatterer's two oratorio performances within a single week, given on Palm Sunday and Good Friday and conducted by Joseph Moralt, the recently-appointed *Konzertmeister* of the court orchestra, prompted a new development without precedent elsewhere in German-speaking Europe.

On October 24, 1810, the then *Kapellmeister*, Peter Winter, the music director, Ferdinand Franzl and Moralt petitioned King Maximilian I for permission to use the court orchestra in public concerts on such evenings as the orchestra had no duties at court or in the opera house—in other words, on some of the greater church feasts when opera was forbidden. Their petition explained that the three principal court musicians believed that 'their plan would benefit the artistic education of the general public'. Maximilian permitted the organisation of the new *Musikalische Akademien* (the use of the almost archaic term 'academy' seems to have been forced on the organisers by the difficulty of finding a name for professional concerts) to be given in the Redoutensaal of the Residenz, five before and five after Lent, with a general subscription of 6 gulden; the king himself subscribed for fifty seats at each concert. The concerts were to be under the administrative control of the court Music Intendant, a fixed reserve of 4,000 florins was to be created from the subscriptions, which were also to pay for the decoration of the hall and the purchase of music; the net profits, once the reserve had been accumulated, were to be distributed among the orchestra, so that the players, whose salaries remained pitifully low, were given a powerful

---

[1] Richard Wagner: *On Conducting (Über das Dirigieren)*, translated by Edward Dannreuther. Reeves, London, 1919.

financial inducement to make the Academy Concerts succeed. The entire court musical establishment of sixty instrumentalists and twenty singers became members of the new organisation, but as the orchestra at that time had six of each woodwind instruments and eight horns it seems very unlikely that any single concert occupied the entire body of players.[1]

The Academy Concerts lapsed during the greater part of 1818 because the king refused to allow the use of the Redoutensaal and the orchestra pleaded pressure of work at court, but in the October of the year they were revived in the theatre, which had a slightly smaller capacity for audiences and therefore added to the cost of subscription to the dearer seats. They were, too, a nuisance to stage directors who naturally regarded opera-free days as a splendid opportunity to get on with their own work. Therefore a cabinet decree in 1825 demanded the building of a Concert Hall, the Odeon, which was opened on October 10, 1828, with a programme of music almost entirely from the works of composers currently in Bavarian court service.

The Odeon was an early example of Munich's classic revival architecture and held an audience of three thousand; the more expensive seats were slightly cheaper than those of the theatre while the cost of the cheaper seats was slightly higher. A hundred and fifteen individual subscriptions were taken out for the first season, together with two hundred and fifty-eight family subscriptions, each for a minimum of four seats.

The Odeon, built primarily as a concert hall for the city, did not only mark the beginning of the emancipation of the orchestra from the opera house; it also marked the growing independence of the city from the court. Its smaller rooms could be used for meetings and any kind of social event while the auditorium did service as a ballroom. It became Munich's first social centre.

The standards achieved by the normal city *Liebhaber* society orchestras must have left a great deal to be desired. At a time when a visitor to Leipzig said that the Gewandhaus Orchestra was like 'the best type of princely orchestra', the *Liebhaberkonzerte* in Breslau were dismissed as 'town gossip with musical accompaniment'. By the time that Weber, Mendelssohn, Berlioz and Wagner arrived and wrote about what they heard, either the standard of performance in the musically more favoured cities had slumped or nineteenth-century ears had grown more demanding than those of eighteenth-century listeners.

But none of these developments, crucial as they eventually proved to be for the future of music, won much attention from contemporary critics, historians or commentators. Charles Burney toured Europe in 1769–70 and in 1771–2 gathering material for his *General History of Music*. In his two accounts of his travels, *The Present State of Music in France and Italy*, published in 1770, and *The Present State of Music in Germany, the Netherlands and the United Provinces*, published two years later, the public concert is hardly mentioned. Burney hurried to the courts, the opera houses and those cathedrals and churches in which

[1] Heinrich Bihrle: *Die Musikalische Akademie München, 1811–1911*. Munich, 1911.

he would hear the new music that would allow him to study the latest developments of styles and techniques; he attended the *Hauskonzerte* to which he was invited apparently as a social duty rather than as a musical pleasure, and he spent some time with the *Accademia* of some of the Italian cities for their historical interest. It was, perhaps, the historical interest of the *Concert Spirituel* in Paris which caused him to attend one of its programmes though by 1770 the original intention of the *Concert Spirituel* had been forgotten. Since excerpts from operas had been admitted into the programmes in 1728, the music heard at its concerts had begun to consist of such excerpts and of symphonies and concertos imported from Germany and Austria. At the *Concert Spirituel*, however, it was possible to hear the pick of the world's virtuoso instrumentalists; appearance there was a necessary qualification for those players who wished to rank high in eighteenth-century eyes.

Burney did not attend the *Concert des Amateurs* while he was in Paris, although the *Concert des Amateurs* was the centre of 'progressive' music in the Paris of his day; it was conducted by Gossec, and the leader of its orchestra was the famous, mysterious Chevalier de Saint-Georges. The organisation moved to premises which were also a Masonic Lodge in 1780, six years before it commissioned the six *Paris* Symphonies from Haydn, and became known as the *Concert de la Loge Olympique*. It was followed, after Burney's visit, by the *Concert de la rue Cléry* and the *Concert Feydeau*, two organisations which attempted to rival the social and musical prestige of the *Concert des Amateurs*. Burney visited Hamburg and Leipzig among other cities which had an active concert life, but if he heard any music in their concert halls he apparently did not consider it worthy of mention.

This neglect is understandable. His English readers would be entirely familiar with the type of music and the style of performance to be found in them. English concert life, since its birth in the last quarter of the seventeenth century, had developed with the times. The Bach–Abel Concerts were in progress at the time of Burney's tours and continued until 1782. The Concerts of Ancient Music, founded in 1776, playing no music less than twenty years old and rooted in the religious works of Handel, had become the socially select 'King's Concert' in 1784, maintaining its original orientation to the music of the past. Various other regular series of subscription concerts existed, and in 1783 a group of European musicians living and working in England—Muzio Clementi, Wilhelm Cramer and Johann Peter Salomon—established the 'Professional Concerts' which operated from 1783 to 1793. Salomon quarrelled with his associates in 1786 and instituted his own concert organisation, to which, in 1791, he brought Haydn. Concerts in the various pleasure gardens—at Marylebone, Ranelagh and Vauxhall—called on the services of the best and most popular singers and instrumentalists, creating an audience not encouraged to show itself at socially exclusive formal concerts. The provincial music clubs, though they tended to keep alive a repertory from the past, bought up-to-date music from the publishers and explored the repertory provided for them by the Bach–Abel Concerts.

Burney had, therefore, no urgent reason to write about concerts in the European cities he visited. The courts, the opera houses and the cathedrals provided new music which, more often than not, he could not expect to hear in England; public concerts anywhere depended upon music generally available to musicians everywhere, not on works specially written for them by their resident composers or the creatively-minded members of their orchestras. Composers took little notice of them because, however popular a composer's work might become at English music clubs, French concerts or German *Liebhaber* societies, he gained nothing from the number of times his works were played; until the later nineteenth century accepted the idea that a composer had a continuing right to a reward for the performance of his works, or until concert societies became rich enough to afford to satisfy their own prestige by commissioning new works, composers might visit a city, play one of their own works at a concert there and receive a fee as a performer; otherwise they had no inducement to work with or for the town orchestras. Burney, and writers in general, could safely neglect them because only a vision of the future could have enabled them to see the future importance of the concert hall.

It was Mozart, and even more decisively Beethoven, both living as freelance musicians in Vienna, dependent on their earnings from as wide a variety of sources as they could create for themselves, who made the public concert into a vehicle for important new music, and they did so rather in spite of than because of the complex musical situation of Vienna. The nobility of the Empire spent a considerable part of each year—the social season embraced autumn and winter—in the capital, each bringing with him his *Kapelle* or whatever domestic musicians he employed. At the same time, though no firm evidence about them can be found, Vienna seems to have had a considerable pool of freelance professional players, apart from the members of the various theatre orchestras, always looking for work and living, probably, as Haydn had lived when he was expelled from St. Stephen's Cathedral choir; he had given lessons, sung tenor in the Cathedral High Mass, played the violin in church and monastery orchestras and had spent each evening playing wherever he could—at noblemen's *Hausmusik* for a fee, or in street serenading parties for whatever he could collect from busking.

During the season, the opera and *Hausmusik* occupied almost every evening of the week. During March, 1784, when Mozart was a great popular favourite, according to the list of his engagements he sent his father, he had hardly an evening free; he gave two of his subscription concerts and he had planned the first of two concerts in the *Burgtheater*; the second was to take place on April 1 and the first, fixed for a Sunday evening, had to be postponed because Prince Liechtenstein was giving an opera performance in his palace and had 'bribed or seduced the best players of the orchestra'.[1]

It was not unusual for noblemen to co-opt members of the professional orchestras to take part in their *Hausmusik*; when Beethoven was living in his house, Prince Lichnowsky gave regular chamber music concerts on Friday

[1] Emily Anderson: *The Letters of Mozart and his Family*. Macmillan, London, 1938. Letter of March 20, 1784.

mornings; Schuppanzigh, who played the violin in the *Burgtheater* orchestra and
was to conduct the concerts in the Augarten Pavilion at the end of the century,
regularly led the ensemble of professional musicians who played for Lichnowsky,
so that the Friday morning concerts were not a nobleman's eccentricity but were
given at a time when he could secure reliable professional musicians who spent
their evenings in the theatre. Aristocratic *Hausmusik* in Vienna, to the surprise of
Beethoven's doctor friend, Franz Gerhard Wegeler, and of the musician and
writer Johann Friedrich Reichardt, was remarkably free and easy. The intellectual,
social and musical elite of Vienna attended Lichnowsky's Friday morning
concerts and mixed on terms of complete equality with the professional
musicians when the music had ended and the company had lunch together;
Wegeler thought this social free-and-easiness well worth mentioning when he
came to write his *Biographische Notizen über Ludwig van Beethoven* in 1838.

With so much music available, the Viennese middle-class amateurs did not
hasten to form musical organisations of their own. It was not until 1782 that
regular amateur concerts—the first regular concerts that Vienna was given—
were organised by Philipp Martin in the Pavilion of the Augarten, a royal park
given over to the public by the Emperor Joseph II. Mozart's brief association
with these concerts was his first public activity in Vienna after his dismissal by
the Archbishop of Salzburg from his post in the Salzburg court music, at a time
when, it seems, he still realised that to make his way as an unattached composer
and virtuoso pianist he needed to explore every possible professional opening he
could find. He described the plans for Martin's first season in a letter to his
father:

> This Martin has got permission from the Emperor under Charter (with
> a promise of his gracious Patronage) to give twelve concerts in the Augarten
> and four serenades in the finest open space in the city. The subscription
> for the whole series is 2 ducats. So you can imagine that we shall have
> plenty of subscribers, the more so as I am taking an interest in it and am
> associated with it. Assuming that we get only a hundred subscribers,
> then each of us will have a profit of 200 gulden (even if the costs amount
> to 200 gulden, which is not very likely). Baron van Swieten and Countess
> Thun are very much interested in the plan. The orchestra consists
> entirely of amateurs with the exception of the bassoon player, the trum-
> peters and the drummer.[1]

Mozart's later letters give us no idea of the progress of the concerts or the end of
his association with them; we do not know if his probably over-sanguine financial
expectations were realised. A letter after the first of them, at which a symphony
(according to Deutsch,[2] No. 34, K. 338) and the Concerto in E flat for Two
Pianos, K. 365, were played, dismisses the event very casually, mentioning only
the members of the nobility who were present and saying nothing about the
music except that it went 'fairly well'.

[1] *The Letters of Mozart and his Family.* Letter of May 8, 1782.
[2] Otto Erich Deutsch: *Mozart, a Documentary Biography.* A. and C. Black,
London, 1965.

Precise records of Viennese concerts at the turn of the eighteenth century would be very interesting because of the number and variety of occasional events which the public could attend apart from those which were primarily meant for the nobility and remained socially exclusive. Artists themselves could hire one of the theatres, as Mozart hired the *Burgtheater*, to give concerts for their own benefit, inviting whatever solo players were free to take part and using the theatre orchestra. Franz Bernard Ritter von Kees, until his death in 1795, and then Baron Gottfried van Swieten, friend and patron of Haydn, Mozart and Beethoven, ran an aristocratic concert society which failed to survive van Swieten's death in 1803. The Society of Noble Amateurs, though it sounds like a socially exclusive *Liebhaber* concert society, financed concerts at which the bulk of the musicians were professionals, and admission to its concerts was not narrowly exclusive; its greatest glory was the first performance of Haydn's *The Creation* in 1798. At such concerts, however, and at *Hauskonzerte* with a mainly professional orchestra, noblemen who wanted to play or sing did so, apparently on terms of equality with the professional players. Prince Lobkowitz played and sang at his own *Hauskonzerte*, van Swieten occasionally conducted. So did Raphael Georg Kiesewetter, the highly born civil servant in the Austrian war ministry who was one of the prime movers in the creation of the *Gesellschaft der Musikfreunde* and the Vienna Conservatoire; Kiesewetter seems to have been an indispensable bass singer and a violinist of professional standard; he was from time to time a conductor even at public concerts as well as at his *Hauskonzerte*, which for twenty years after 1817 explored the music of the Renaissance and the Baroque periods.

The musicians themselves constituted the *Tonkünstersocietät*, which gave two or three charity concerts each year. Membership was a notable distinction offered to composers and players who, in the opinion of the society, could further its aims. Its concerts were often on a very large scale, and to be invited to perform at one, as Mozart and Beethoven both did before they were elected to membership, was to be awarded the accolade by the musicians of Vienna. The Society did not form its own orchestra until late in the nineteenth century but it recruited its players *ad hoc* from the theatre orchestra, the emperor's court orchestra, the *Kapelle* of whatever noblemen were in Vienna at the time and, apparently, from the freelance pool.

When Mozart, in 1784, launched his own series of subscription concerts in the hall of the Tratternhof, he collected a hundred and seventy-six subscribers in spite of the large number of rival attractions available to Viennese music lovers. It would be interesting to know a great deal more about these concerts than has been left on record; with some descents to mere conjecture, we know with some degree of certainty which piano concerto was composed for which concert; we know that he paid a rent of three ducats for the three concerts of his 1784 season, and that the subscription was six gulden; the gross receipts amounted to more than a thousand gulden. We know from the subscription list that Mozart's audiences were drawn from the nobility and the official class; the ordinary bourgeoisie, who flocked to hear *Die Entführung aus dem Serail*, is not represented among the names Mozart collected.

But we know nothing of the expenses involved after the rent had been paid. Almost certainly Mozart collected an amateur orchestra and whatever professional assistance his players needed; we do not know what the conditions of rehearsal were, or how much they cost him; we have no notion of the profit he achieved. However, it is sensible to assume that the series made a profit, because in the following year Mozart doubled the number of concerts and took the hall of the Mehlgrube (the Flour Mill) for six subscription concerts in the Lent of 1785. This time he raised a list of only a hundred and two subscribers, but these were enough to console his father, who was in Vienna for the first concert, for Wolfgang's lack of a regular post. He described the first concert in a letter to his daughter:

> A great many members of the aristocracy were present. Each person pays a souverain d'or [about $13\frac{1}{2}$ gulden, more than double the previous year's subscription] or three ducats, for these concerts. Your brother is giving them in the Mehlgrube and pays only half a souverain d'or each time for the hall. The concert was magnificent and the orchestra played splendidly.[1]

Leopold said that the first concert brought a profit of 559 gulden, and Leopold was a cautious man where money was concerned, never given to his son's flights of blind optimism. He worried about his son's professionally irregular way of life but was almost reconciled to it by his experiences in Vienna in 1785.

Other works, notably his preoccupation with opera, kept Mozart from attempting another series of subscription concerts until 1789, when his subscription list carried only one name, that of van Swieten; the rest of his aristocratic admirers were simply not interested. By this time he was playing less frequently at other musicians' concerts, but his operas were the most popular works in the repertory of the German theatres and were beginning to make an impact outside German-speaking Europe. There is no explanation of his fall from the resounding triumph of *Don Giovanni* in Vienna in 1788 to the subscription concerts aborted by lack of support only a few months later.

The opera appealed to a wider audience than the restricted class of Viennese concert-goers. It may be that the aristocracy, whose support as patrons, concert-givers and sponsors of performances was vital to him, abandoned Mozart because his political opinions (on the evidence of *Le Nozze de Figaro*) were suspect, his moral attitudes (on the evidence of *Don Giovanni* and *Cosi fan tutte*) were dubious and his religious beliefs (on the evidence of his fervent adherence to Freemasonry) were wickedly unorthodox: the case is argued by Robbins Landon,[2] persuasively but with no supporting evidence, as an interpretation of established fact—Mozart's swift and disastrous fall. But it is more probable that

---

[1] Emily Anderson: *op. cit.* Letter of March 14, 1785.
[2] H. C. Robbins Landon: 'The Decline and Fall of Wolfgang Amadeus Mozart', in *The Viennese Classical Style*. Barrie and Rockliff, the Cresset Press, London, 1970.

Mozart, the pianist-composer whom fashionable Vienna had found indispensable between 1782 and 1785 had suffered from over-exposure in a situation and society not designed to support the work of a freelance. His concert music was too intense, too violent and too 'learned' for the average Viennese aristocratic music lover; even Joseph II had accused him of writing 'too many notes' in *Die Entführung aus dem Serail*, by no means the most complex of his works, and he himself was unwilling to undertake such tasks as bored him, like teaching, or to attempt to live within his income. In addition, subscription concerts of the sort he gave were new to Vienna; they set up a new, demanding but unsensational type of entertainment in rivalry to the more relaxing, spectacular type of concert at which the Viennese connoisseurs could listen to their favourite works and to their favourite virtuosi doing exciting things; Mozart's concerts failed, perhaps, because they asked too much of their aristocratic patrons.

Though business-like shrewdness is not one of the qualities we normally associate with Beethoven, Beethoven managed his business affairs far more shrewdly than Mozart and continued to make an artistic and financial success of a hazardous freelance existence. Like Mozart he rapidly became the favourite Viennese pianist, lionised in the houses of the great; it seems even that his tendency to aggressive discourtesy endeared him to a nobility used to complete subservience, as though Beethoven gave them a rare opportunity to congratulate themselves on their ability to penetrate his roughness and rudeness to the integrity and genius lying beneath these socially deplorable failings. Beethoven, with his tendency to fall in love with attractive but noble female pupils, taught for as long as he could hear and was ready for any musical work even though it brought duties which Mozart, a few years before, had found intolerable, and by 1796 he was as much in demand in the houses of the great and the public concerts of other musicians as Mozart had been a dozen years before. In 1795 he made his public debut at a concert of the *Tonkünstlersocietät* and impressed the general public no less than he had previously delighted the nobility. He was sufficiently occupied both as a composer and as a pianist to have had no reason to risk financing a public concert until 1800, and by that time his reputation in Vienna was made: he was accepted as a great musician and talked about as a striking personality. His first concert, in the *Burgtheater*, included music by Haydn and Mozart as well as his own First Symphony, the C major Piano Concerto known (from its publication before his earlier B flat major Concerto) as 'No. 1', and the Septet, op. 20.

Writers after the event have found in Beethoven's failure to compose a symphony until he was thirty years old (apart from a juvenile beginning dated 1785) a probably unBeethovenian significance. If Beethoven took so long to write a symphony, they suggest, it can only have been because he found qualities of intensity and profundity in the form which earlier composers had never realised and which he had previously felt himself incompletely equipped to handle. They feel that, like Brahms, he had come to the conclusion that 'a symphony is not a joke'.

It is never a joke, of course, for a composer to commit himself to a work for orchestra in a four-movement form without some immediate prospect of performance and payment, for such a work robs him, for whatever length of time it occupies his mind, of the prospect of incidental earnings. The symphony was the central point of the vast number of court concerts for which Haydn was responsible at Eszterhaza; it was as a composer of symphonies that he became best known to the world at large and it was symphonies which both the *Concert de la Loge Olympique* in Paris and Salomon in London wanted from him; therefore Haydn wrote a very large number of symphonies. Twenty-seven of Mozart's symphonies were written for court performances at Salzburg in the ten years before his dismissal, and we can find specific occasions for all the other symphonies of his maturity except the final three. He wrote twenty-seven indisputable, mature piano concertos because the central feature of his concerts was a piano concerto; the demand created the supply.

Until Beethoven gave a concert of his own, there was no demand for his first symphony, and it would be hard to see it as a more decisive work than many of the earlier piano sonatas, or the op. 18 string quartets and the C minor Piano Concerto, which were written at about the same time. He was a practical composer who had almost worn out the B flat concerto with repeated performances before he wrote the C major concerto to replace it in his programmes. Later in life he planned his concerts to match his output: at first he wrote what was actually needed for the commitments he had on hand, and he would probably have continued to do so had he made his way into the *Kapellmeistership* he expected to be his fate. Left to survive as a freelance, his later concerts became something like retrospective exhibitions of the major works of a number of years. He never, like Mozart, committed himself to series of subscription concerts which might turn, in his audiences' view, into the presentation of 'the mixture as before'.

Thus, at the *Theater an der Wien*, in 1803, his programme consisted of the First and Second Symphonies, the Third Piano Concerto and the oratorio *Christus am Oelberg*. We have no account of the finances of the event, but Beethoven's net profit from it was 1800 gulden. In 1808, in the same theatre, a deaf composer attempted to play the Fourth Concerto and the piano solo in the Choral Fantasia and make his way through them by sheer technique and experience alone; this was his last appearance as a solo pianist, and it was a comic sort of tragedy with the pianist-composer forgetting that he was not conducting from the keyboard. Apart from the probability of accidents at any Beethoven concert, there was no routine; even apart from the presentation of at least two major works at each his concerts grew bigger in scope, to be regarded as red letter days in the Viennese musical calendar.

To what extent Beethoven deliberately composed for the general public it is impossible to say. The length of the *Eroica* makes it an impossible work to perform after dinner for the sake of social relaxation in a princely *salon*. When he wrote to Count Oppersdorff to describe the Fifth Symphony, after expanding

the orchestra to include piccolo and trombones in the work's finale, he said:
'this combination of instruments will make more noise, and a more pleasing
noise, than six kettledrums'.[1] A more pleasing noise is a nicely subjective
description, for what is more pleasing depends upon the way in which it fills its
purpose; what is more pleasing in a large public theatre or concert hall is not
necesarily more pleasing in the music room of a nobleman's residence. The letter
suggests that unless Beethoven's growing deafness had undermined his sense of
aural reality, he must have been thinking of music played in far larger auditoria
by larger and larger orchestras necessary to convey the strength and violence of
his major orchestral works. Obviously Beethoven expected a proportional increase
in the number of strings, for in the 1820s he pointed out to the Archduke Rudolph
that the Seventh Symphony could not make its proper effect with a domestic
orchestra of about four violins. There were, of course, purely musical reasons
for the admission to the orchestras of trombones, the only brass instruments
capable of playing any melody or supporting the harmony through complex
modulations.

The standard orchestra of early nineteenth-century Vienna could not, it seems,
supply all Beethoven's demands. Spohr, in Vienna as director of the orchestra at
the *Theater an der Wien* in 1813, was invited to play in the concert which gave
the Seventh Symphony its performance in the Redoutensaal, and left his description of Beethoven's peculiar and ineffective conducting style. 'All who could
fiddle, blow or sing,' he wrote,[2] 'were invited to assist, and not one of the most
celebrated artists of Vienna failed to appear. I and my orchestra, of course,
joined.' The programme also included *Wellingtons Sieg*, or *Die Schlacht bei
Vittoria*, which English people like to call the 'Battle Symphony', the most
elaborate, lengthy and musically dubious of Beethoven's pot-boilers; it had a
splendidly triumphant if brief career, became the excuse for a number of
Beethoven concerts and earned its composer a good deal of money. It turned
up again at the concerts on January 2 and 4, 1814, when the programme
was repeated, and again at the charity concert for war victims in February
1814, when the Eighth Symphony was played. Actually, Spohr's account of the
December performance fails to mention *Wellingtons Sieg*, perhaps a too eccentrically vulgar work for so seriously high-minded a musician, but he dwells on the
success of the Seventh Symphony, the allegretto of which was encored at all
these performances. The charity concert had raised 4006 gulden net profit, and the
later performances were equally crowded and enthusiastic though it is in the
nature of charity concerts to have unusually high admission costs and Beethoven's
later profits were unlikely to be so remarkable.

The finances of these events are not completely recorded, but a certain amount
of piecemeal information remains. They were essentially a gamble when he, or
some of his wealthy friends, decided to finance them and bring out new works;

[1] Emily Anderson: *The Letters of Beethoven*. Macmillan, London, 1961. Letter
166, of March 1808.
[2] Ludwig Spohr: *Autobiography*. English translation, Reeves and Turner, London, 1878.

the first performance of the Seventh Symphony was sponsored by a group of Beethoven's rich friends and patrons. The culmination of such concerts came in the *Kärntnerthor Theater* on May 7, 1824, when the Ninth Symphony was heard for the first time in a monster concert which included the Overture *Die Weihe des Hauses* and the *Kyrie, Credo* and *Agnus Dei* of the Mass in D, played as 'Three Latin Hymns' to defeat the prohibition against the performance of liturgical music in the theatre.

By 1824 Beethoven had reached a state in which he seems to have found it all but impossible to make up his mind about any practical problem. The Ninth Symphony's premiere was first offered to Berlin; an eloquent petition from loyal Viennese friends and patrons persuaded him to allow Vienna to hear it first, but he was almost defeated by the question of where to mount the performance and, when all arrangements were made, quarrelled with his friends and assistants and ordered them to cancel the concert when it was too late for them to do so. Eventually it took place in the *Kärntnerthor Theater*, which cost him 300 gulden for rent and services; the choir and orchestra, both augmented by amateurs— the orchestra eventually contained twenty violins, ten violas, twelve cellos, twelve double-basses and double woodwind, overflowing from the orchestra pit on to the stage—cost 400 gulden more. The concert was a triumph and its gross receipts were 2200 gulden, but when all expenses were paid Beethoven was left with only 420 gulden. A second performance on May 23, a Sunday, set the Symphony in a somewhat lighter programme (it included, for example, the aria *Di tanti palpiti* from Rossini's *Tancredi*); the second performance was organised by the theatre management, who offered Beethoven a fee of 1200 gulden and a half share in all profits over that figure. Exceptionally pleasant spring weather seems to have left the public unwilling to spend the afternoon in the theatre, and though Beethoven was compensated for his low earnings from the first concert, the management lost 800 gulden.

While Beethoven was giving the concert new status by making it the vehicle for his largest and most ambitious works, other amateur societies in Vienna, grew, flourished as gorgeously as they were able and withered again during the quarter-century of his public career. Most of them played his music as well as they could and he regarded their efforts with neither enthusiasm nor gratitude, not only because they did not pay him for the right to play his works but also because some of them played atrociously. The most important of these societies, the *Gesellschaft der Musikfreunde*, proved to have the power to adapt itself as conditions changed and to be a continuing benefit to music ever since its foundation.

It grew out of the *ad hoc* committees of noblemen, noblewomen and musicians set up to mount charity concerts in war-stricken Vienna. As the war made it increasingly difficult for the nobility to support their own individual orchestras, opera companies and choirs as they had done in peacetime, those involved in planning great concerts to aid war victims came together with a group of notable musicians and Josef Ferdinand Sonnleithner, the librettist of *Fidelio* and

Secretary of the court theatres, to organise a musical society in place of the domestic music they had lost. The *Gesellschaft* became active in 1813 with the aim, according to its statutes, of 'the advancement of music in all its aspects'. A conservatory was planned and opened in 1817 under the direction of Raphael Kiesewetter, the bassist-violinist-conductor-musicologist whose career in the civil service had ended with the war and whose administrative experience as well as his founder-membership of the *Gesellschaft* made him the obvious man to bring the new organisation to life. Public taste was to be elevated, young musicians encouraged and, when necessary, given financial support; the *Gesellschaft* established a public music lending library and its own periodical. For a long time it did not bother to buy premises of its own but met in Sonnleithner's house for business and in the Redoutensaal for its concerts though it regarded public performance, in a city where music was always available, as less important than the other aims it had announced.

The *Gesellschaft* concerts did not form their own orchestra but collected the usual semi-amateur orchestra to play almost always under the direction of a professional and highly regarded conductor. Kiesewetter was one of the few amateurs to direct one of its concerts; his programme, in 1816, was the first to include a work by Beethoven, but it began a period of nineteen years in which almost every concert included a major Beethoven work.

In 1817, the year in which the *Gesellschaft* founded the Vienna Conservatory, a group of its influential members also instituted regular series of chamber concerts, which they called *Abendunterhaltungen*, to which members of the society and their invited guests only were admitted, turning chamber music for the first time into another form of public music. The *Abendunterhaltungen* performed songs and a few instrumental works by Schubert during the last twelve years of his life, and was the first organisation to allow his voice to be heard beyond the large circle of bourgeois and aristocratic friends who gathered to listen to his music in private.

Purely professional concerts were not heard in Vienna until 1842, when the composer Otto Nicolai, at that time *Kapellmeister* of the Imperial Opera, gave a concert with the opera orchestra in the Redoutensaal on behalf of the widows and orphans of past members, instituting an annual pension fund concert still known as the 'Nicolai Concert'. It was not until 1860 that the orchestra followed the example set in 1811 by the Munich court orchestra and obtained permission to give regular concerts at times when the members were free from their duties in the opera house and thus transform themselves into the Vienna Philharmonic Society.

In spite of Beethoven's glorification of the public concert, in those cities where opera was linked to a court and to displays of social grandeur, orchestral music continued to take second place to dramatic music. There is no reason whatever to regard opera as an 'aristocratic' form and the symphony as in some way essentially 'middle-class', but it was in the towns where opera was not a special entertainment fervently supported by royalty and the socially great that the concert achieved parity of esteem with the socially grander form. Wagner's failure to establish regular professional concerts in Dresden in the 1840s shows that the officialdevoti on to opera persisted long after Beethoven's death.

19   Composer and Publisher

Only the development of concert societies in the second half of the eighteenth century can account for the boom—the term is hardly extravagant—in music publishing which accompanied it. In England, where the public concert had been established in 1672, music publishing had been a profitable business by the time of Handel: on the continent, its growth was slower simply because the market for public music was slower to develop.

In 1745, Johann Gottlob Immanuel Breitkopf had inherited the publishing house which his father had established in Leipzig in 1719, and had turned from its originally forbidding output of theology, philosophy and history to publish music. Schott, of Mainz, began business in 1770; André, of Offenbach, who was later to buy the bulk of Mozart's unpublished works from his widow, started to publish music in 1774. Simrock, in Bonn (the firm eventually moved to Berlin) was publishing music by Beethoven from 1794 onwards. Schlesinger, of Berlin, opened in 1810; his son spread the business to Paris in 1823. C. F. Peters bought the Leipzig business of Hoffmeister and Kühnel (a branch of a Viennese firm) in 1814.

Hummel, a firm founded in Amsterdam in 1760, opened branches in Vienna and Berlin in 1774. Sieber, of Paris, who specialised in imported German and Austrian music, began operations in 1771. The Viennese publishers whose output included so much that is of supreme musical value all came into existence in this period, Torricella in 1775, Artaria in 1776 after nine years of dealing in imported music and art reproductions. In 1783, Hoffmeister began business, and the houses of Mollo and Mecchetti were both in action by the end of the century. The great Italian publisher, Ricordi, established his business in 1808. The boom affected England: Bland, who in 1787 went to Vienna to buy works from Haydn, and who traded a good razor for a Haydn string quartet, established his business in 1762. Longman and Broderip, whose relations with Haydn became for a time less friendly, had begun to publish music by 1767. Forster, a member of a family of violin makers, turned to publishing in 1781. In 1783, Robert Birchall added music publishing to his activities as owner of a music circulating library. Clementi, the Italian composer-pianist who had settled in London and bought an interest in Longman and Broderip's, opened his own publishing house and piano factory in 1798. In 1811, the house of Novello and Company opened, specialising at first in cheap editions of music for Roman Catholic and Anglican church choirs and from necessity creating an invaluable collection of almost forgotten works by Renaissance and seventeenth-century composers, European and English.

The mainstay of any music publisher's business was inevitably the amateur market for instrumental solos, chamber music, songs and vocal pieces for small ensembles, everything that could be used as *Hausmusik*. There is no evidence that in the late eighteenth century the amateur market expanded so rapidly that it made room for so many newly-established businesses; accounts of domestic music-making in the cities of the early seventeenth century, like Schering's account of the musical activities of the Leipzig bourgeoisie,[1] suggest that it remained more or less unchanged. It seems that the new supply of works came into being to satisfy the demands of the new *Liebhaber* concert societies, the *Musikübende* associations and all the new bodies of musicians which needed a steady flow of new works to appeal to their audiences.

Until the end of the eighteenth century, the publishers did what they could to cut the cost of their products. Breitkopf, whose interest in printing techniques may have been one of his reasons for becoming a printer and publisher of music, developed a new fount of improved movable types for printing music; they were difficult to set because of their large number and complexity, but they were far cheaper than the standard method of engraving on copper plates. Breitkopf's new types could produce large numbers of orchestral parts very quickly and very cheaply, and they were used in 1754 to print the full score of a *pastorella*, *Il Trionfo della Fedelta*, by the Electress Maria Antonia Walburgis of Bavaria, who wrote as 'Ermelinda Talia Pastorella Arcadia'. Naturally, its results, though less ugly than those of earlier music printed by a similar method but with more primitive types, were less beautiful than good engraved music or even than the copies engraved on pewter by English publishers like John Walsh, who had avoided the use of copper at the beginning of the century in order to cut costs. Other publishers adopted and adapted Breitkopf's improved types for cheap music like orchestral parts.

Music printing by lithography for a time seemed to be a more effective way of producing attractive music at a lower price. It was developed by Aloys Senefelder, who worked in Ingolstadt and Munich, and was taken up by the Munich firm of Falder; Falder wrote to the Augsburg publisher Gombert that what he called 'chemical printing' could produce music at only a quarter of the cost of engraving on copper plate. André, Breitkopf and Härtel (in 1796, Christoph Breitkopf, Immanuel's son, had taken Gottfried Christoph Härtel into partnership with him) and Ricordi all for a time used Senefelder's method, which was patented in England in 1801; Senefelder established his own *Chemische Druckerei* in Vienna in 1803.

Lithography was easier than engraving or type-setting; perhaps that is why publishers eventually abandoned it. Composers could use it to produce scores for themselves. Weber, as a small boy, learnt the technique from Senefelder, and when he was sixteen he wrote to Artaria, in Vienna, 'I can engrave music on stone in a manner equal to the best English engraving on copper plate.' As late as 1845, Wagner used lithography to print the four hundred and fifty pages of *Tannhäuser*,

[1] See above, p. 314.

noting on its title-page *Als Manuscript von der Hand des Componisten auf Stein gedrückt.*

Neither movable types nor lithography eventually replaced engraving. The cost of an individual printed page is almost infinitesimal once the cost of printing notes or words upon it has been met. To make five thousand copies, sharing the originally high cost of engraving or printing between them all, adds little to the cost of making five hundred; movable types and lithography forced down the price of printed music while the demand was growing, but the eventual size of the demand made possible return to engraving which added little to the cost of the individual copy of a work printed by later methods.

At the same time, the sale of music in manuscript copies continued. During Mozart's lifetime, more of his music circulated in manuscript copies sold in Vienna by Traeg or Lausch, to say nothing of Sukowaty, a professional copyist who made a profitable side-line out of making and selling extra copies of popular works, than appeared in print; most of those which appeared in print emerged in copies published without Mozart's authority. The historically fascinating *Thematic Catalogue* issued by Immanuel Breitkopf between 1762 and 1787 in six parts and sixteen supplements lists works for sale which, its title-page notes, '*che trovanno in manuscritto*'. The catalogue identifies works by their incipits (which in spite of Breitkopf's title are by no means always their themes) so that readers would be able 'to differentiate works from one another as one differentiates books by their titles.'

It was difficult, Breitkopf pointed out, to build up a truly comprehensive stock of works and hard to 'wrest them from certain musicians'. He makes it clear that some of the works he was selling came from sources other than their composers, apologising to 'connoisseurs and amateurs of music, and even to composers themselves' for unavoidable errors in the ascription of certain works. He promises, should a later edition of his catalogue be necessary, to correct as many errors as he can. Therefore he appeals to the users of the catalogue for help, and to composers for guidance:

> If famous composers would not themselves mind compiling a catalogue of their practical works, and would be kind enough to send it to me, I would not only acknowledge it with many thanks but would also continue my endeavours, all the more encouraged in proportion to the possibility of relying on the accuracy of such communications. It would not matter that I might not yet possess the items that appear in such a catalogue, because I would at once take steps to acquire these, should there be any demand for them among music lovers.[1]

Obviously, Breitkopf did not regard publisher and composer as partners. Many of the composers from whom it was difficult to 'wrest' works held court positions in which permission to publish anything they had written had to be obtained from reluctant patrons. When Duke Carl Eugen found that he could no longer

---

[1] Immanuel Breitkopf: *Thematisches Verzeichnis*, Postscript to Part 1. Leipzig, 1762. Translated and edited by Barry S. Brook, Dover Books, 1966.

maintain his vast musical establishment at Stuttgart, he refused to allow Jomelli to take any copies of the works he had written for the Württemberg court on leave to Italy with him, afraid that his *Kapellmeister* might be planning to desert. Jomelli pointed out that Hasse, in Dresden, was recognised to have an undisputed right to his own scores and had been allowed to plan a collected edition at his patron's expense, but this did not alter Carl Eugen's determination. Haydn, when he first entered the service of the Eszterhazy family, was under contract not to publish his music without the Prince's permission. Mozart, in the 1780s, was convinced that his works were simply his stock-in-trade as a performer, and was so conscious of the danger of a work falling into other hands that he took only orchestral parts and a rough note of the solo with him to concerto performances, so that the work would be meaningless to any outsider into whose hands the manuscript fell. When financial stringency forced him to approach Prince Fürstenberg through the Prince's valet, Sebastian Winter (who had been Leopold Mozart's servant) and the Prince bought the symphonies K. 319, K. 338 and K. 425 (the *Linz*), with the Piano Concertos K. 451, 459 and 488, Mozart sent the works with a covering note:

> The compositions I keep to myself and a small circle of music lovers and connoisseurs (who promise not to let them out of their hands) cannot possibly be known elsewhere as they are not even known in Vienna. And this is the case with the three concertos I have the honour of sending His Highness. . . . I must ask His Highness not to let them out of his hands.[1]

Beethoven's earliest piano concertos, the B flat ('No. 2') of 1795 and the C major ('No. 1') of 1797 were not published until 1801; both were very popular works and Beethoven had, apparently, played them in public until he feared they were growing stale. But he did not publish them until he had the C minor Concerto, No. 3, ready for performance.

The composer's interest did not coincide with that of the publisher, whose profit depended upon his ability to satisfy the demand for the latest music. The publisher would happily buy whatever a known composer was ready to sell and assume that he had bought all the rights in a work which, to the eighteenth-century mind, had twice been paid for by the time it reached his hand. A patron had demanded it or commissioned it, so that the publisher's payment was a bonus to the fortunate composer. What the publisher could not get from a composer he would obtain in any way he could, possibly from an already existing edition published in another city probably without the composer's authority or the payment of any fee to him. In that case, all the second publisher had to do was to buy a printed copy of the work he wanted. If the work did not exist in print, a copyist with access to it was rarely unwilling to make extra money by selling an authorised copy to anyone who asked for it.

Both Haydn and Mozart were aware of the depredations of copyists. Mozart, with his deep-seated objection to letting his music go beyond his control—at one point he dreamed up a scheme whereby he would rent a theatre and mount his

---

[1] Emily Anderson: *The Letters of Mozart and his Family.* Letter of September 30, 1786.

own operas, thus collecting for himself the profits from his work which, in Prague and Vienna, went to the theatre managements—wrote to his father:

> The Salzburg copyists are as little to be trusted as the Viennese. I know for a positive fact that Hofstetter made two copies of Haydn's music. For example, I *really* possess the last three symphonies he wrote. And as no one but myself really possesses these new concertos in B flat [K. 450] and D [K. 451], and no one but myself and Fräulein von Ployer, for whom I composed them, those in E flat [K. 449] and G [K. 453], the only way in which they could fall into other hands is by this kind of cheating.[1]

In 1787, when Artaria was preparing to publish Haydn's six String Quartets, op. 50, he accused the composer not only of having sold subscription copies of the set (a procedure upon which he and Artaria had agreed) but also of having sold a manuscript copy to Leopold Lausch, the Viennese dealer in manuscript music. The composer replied indignantly:

> I do assure you, on my honour, that they the quartets were not copied by my copyist, who is a most honest fellow, whereas your copyist is a rascal, for he offered mine 6 gold ducats this winter if he would give him the *Seven Words*. . . . Although you have everything copied on your premises, you may be swindled all the same, for the rascals put a piece of paper *a parte* under the music, and thus by degrees they secretly copy the parts they have in front of them.[2]

Artaria's indignation was justified, for to the eighteenth-century mind the pirates were taking over what he regarded as his market; he believed that he had bought the sole right to sell in it when he took over the composer's rights in a work at the time of its purchase. The composer, to his way of thinking, had been paid twice—once by the patron for whom a work was written or by the fees he earned by playing it at concerts—and again by any publisher who decided to handle his work and bought it; therefore the composer had no cause for complaint if the work appeared from any other source while the publisher lost money. In this case when Artaria received a set of string quartets from Dittersdorf in 1788, he received the following letter:

> No one here has the quartets (not like the ones by Haydn which you printed) which not only the Prince here in Breslau but various other people had bought before, in manuscript copies, for 6 ducats.[3]

Haydn, of course, fought back. He had apparently suffered in the same way before. He suggested that Artaria forced Lausch to appear before the Mayor of Vienna (an old friend who had helped Haydn in similar circumstances) and forced to name his supplier, who could then be arrested. It may be said, to excuse the copyists, that those in court employment were normally the most badly paid of the whole badly paid musical establishment. Independent copyists were no better off. The bill for copying the parts of Beethoven's Eighth

---

[1] Anderson: *op. cit.* Letter of May 15, 1784.
[2] H. C. Robbins Landon: *The Collected Correspondence and London Notebooks of Joseph Haydn.* Barrie and Rockliff, London, 1959. Letter of October 7, 1787.
[3] *Ibid.* Editor's note to the letter above.

Symphony and the vocal trio *Tremate, empi, tremate*, op. 116, for his concert in February, 1814, came to 90 gulden, 24 kreuzers for four hundred and fifty-two sheets of music; a kreuzer was worth about a halfpenny, so that the copyist received something like sixpence-halfpenny per sheet of music.

As the composer had already profited as much from his composition as he would have done in the days before the growth of publishing, the Breitkopfs, Artarias and Schotts of the late eighteenth century did not feel that there was anything morally dubious about profiting themselves from his work without offering him any reward in proportion to what they hoped to receive when they issued the music of a celebrity. Therefore a work might be republished several times in different places, and then played at concerts all over Europe, without further reference to its creator. There was not only no legislation controlling performing rights; there was no conception of the idea that they could, or should, be recognised. There was, too, no effective system of copyright; even the type of royal Privilege which had failed to protect Handel from exploitation by publishers had become extinct because of its ineffectiveness.

It was inevitable that the contrariety of their aims for a long time bedevilled the relationship between composer and publisher; it was equally inevitable that the two should attempt some dubious practices to improve their position. In addition to the difficulty of tracing the true composers of all the works that reached them, it seems as though publishers soon realised that certain names on a title-page sold works more quickly than others. Breitkopf's *Catalogue* suggests that somebody had soon realised that the popularity of Haydn's work made his name an effective selling point, for by the time Breitkopf's final supplement appeared the catalogue listed ninety-six symphonies composed by him though the best authorities have demonstrated that by 1787 he had composed no more than eighty-odd. In 1789, the composer Adalbert Gyrowetz attended a concert in Paris in which a symphony by Haydn was to be played; when it began, he was surprised and hardly pleased to recognise it as a work of his own. Eighteenth-century publishing methods were responsible not only for a good deal of chicanery repaid in kind by the composers but also for a multitude of problems of text, ascription, date and bibliography which occupy musicologists today. Dedications and even *opus* numbers were usually affixed by publishers and not by composers, so that even as late as 1828 and the music of Schubert, *opus* numbers can be more misleading than helpful.

Thus the source of the bulk of the works which Breitkopf (the obvious example for discussion because of the thoroughness of his *Thematisches Verzeichnis*) sold either in manuscript or, after 1768 (when he began to list imported printed music, mainly from Amsterdam, London and Paris in his supplements) and other publishers can rarely be traced, it is clear that the composer gained little from publication; at best it worked only indirectly to his advantage—a printed copy of an attractive work might easily fall into the hands of a potential patron ready to commission new works from him. But English publishers, for example, were prepared to pay well for the prestige of bringing out editions of unfamiliar music by international celebrities like Haydn. So were publishers everywhere, and while what was published in Vienna was as unlikely to reach Leipzig, Berlin or Bonn as music from any of these cities to reach Vienna, publishers found that a system based on the uncontrovertible principle that dog does not eat dog worked more profitably than a free for all in which everybody pirated everybody else's publications. By the 1780s, publishers had begun to think in terms of spheres of interest; private arrangements between them to deal in each other's editions were operated by the firms which had bought exclusive rights from the composers involved: Artaria, for example, issued music in London through the firm of Longman and Broderip, and the important houses had their systems of alliances with publishers in other cities and other countries.

Sir George Smart, the English composer who was a publisher's son, toured Germany and Austria in 1825 for the sake of his musical education; while listening to music and meeting musicians, he was also doing business as the agent of Robert Birchall, looking for works which would suit English taste so that Birchall could issue them in London. His diary records visits for this purpose to Artaria and Mecchetti in Vienna, to Breitkopf and Peters in Leipzig, to Schlesinger in Berlin and to Simrock in Bonn. It obviously did not occur to him that his fellow composers might well resent the buying and selling of their works to bring profit to their publishers but with no reference to their own wishes or profit.

The composer brought up in the eighteenth-century system of patronage tended to share the publisher's view and to think of publication as a pleasant irrelevancy; he earned his living by writing new works whenever they were needed. Gluck in his Paris period could afford to be traditionally casual about the fate of his works in print because he was in no way dependent on the money they brought to him. He had a salary of 2000 gulden a year from the Emperor as court composer and, as a traditionalist turned revolutionary, he could demand high fees for anything he wrote; the success of his works in Paris—for bitter controversy has never emptied a theatre—added a good deal to his already comfortable income. There is no reason to disbelieve the Dedicatory Letter he wrote to Duke Giovanni di Braganza, which prefaces the score of *Paride ed Elena*, in 1770:

> The sole reason that induced me to publish my music for *Alceste* in 1769 was the hope of finding imitators who would follow the new trail and summon the courage to eliminate the abuses which have crept into Italian opera and bring it as near to perfection as possible.[1]

But Gluck, caring little about publication—*Alceste* was three years old in its French version and two in its Italian before he bothered to publish it—found that his casualness created an embarrassing situation for him when, in 1774, having disposed of all the rights in *Iphigénie en Aulide* to the *Académie Royale*

[1] Hedwig and E. H. Müller von Asow: *The Collected Correspondence and Papers of Christoph Willibald Gluck*. Translated by Stewart Thomson. Barrie and Rockliff, London, 1962.

de Musique, the publisher Le Marchand brought out a volume of its airs and claimed that he had bought the right to do so from the composer.

Nevertheless, traditional casualness was not an effective approach to a cut-throat, buccaneering type of business enterprise, but Dittersdorf, writing a charming, lively *Autobiography* at about the time of Mozart's death, manages to neglect the subject almost completely. Mozart himself paid no attention to his father's pleas that he should write pot-boilers for the Paris publishers to make some money out of what proved to be an uneconomical visit:

> As for composition, why, you could make money and gain a great reputation by publishing works for clavier, string quartet, and so forth, symphonies and possibly a collection of French airs with clavier accompaniment, like the one you sent me, and finally operas.[1]

This having no effect, and Paris proving to be anything but a source of wealth, Leopold returned to the subject a few months later:

> If you have not got any pupils, well then, compose something more. Even if you have to let your work go for a smaller sum, why, this will help to make your name known in Paris. But let it be something short, easy and popular. Discuss the matter with some engraver and find out what he would like to have.[2]

Wolfgang, who found teaching a bore when it meant spending time with aristocratic ladies and their children and could be bothered only with gifted pupils, was equally disinclined to flatter French taste by writing to suit it. The sort of professionalism which would have made a Handel or a Bach regard such composition as an interesting stylistic challenge meant nothing to him, and together with his dislike of letting his repertory evaporate through publication seemed to go a disinclination to make money by arranging and adapting works which he had written and left behind. He arranged with Torricella, for instance, to arrange a piano score of *Die Entführung aus dem Serail* when the opera was a great success in 1782, but Torricella's edition was too late to rival another brought out by Lausch, as though the composer could not regard the piano score as a matter of urgency. Even Artaria's authorised publication of the six *Haydn* Quartets, for which he paid Mozart 100 ducats, was challenged by Torricella's unauthorised edition of six early quartets. He published some clavier works through Hoffmeister, but paid no attention to the publisher's warning that he must write something simple if he wanted Hoffmeister to handle it. It was, apparently, only Torricella's unauthorised advertisement of sets of parts of his concertos K.413, 414 and 415 and Traeg's issue of others in 1783, which led him to try to find a publisher for these works, and he wrote to Sieber, in Paris, apparently feeling that works published in Paris would not endanger his activities in Vienna; Sieber refused and the works went to Artaria, but did not appear until 1785, after Torricella and Traeg had taken the cream off the market.

[1] Anderson: *op. cit.* Letter of February 16, 1778.
[2] *Ibid.* Letter of August 13, 1778.

A failure to understand the importance of publishing or to come to terms with the circumstances of life as a freelance was one of the elements of Mozart's tragedy.

Spohr's early adventures with publishers provide a tale of exploitation which he accepted as inevitable. He wrote his first Violin Concerto as a boy of fourteen in the orchestra of the Duke of Brunswick and played it on tour with such success that he wanted to publish it, and sent it to Breitkopf and Härtel:

> For the consolation of the young composer who can find no publisher for his first work, the conditions upon which the above-named firm consented to undertake its publication may be mentioned. I had myself given up all claims to payment, and only stipulated for some free copies. The firm required, however, that I should buy one hundred copies at half the selling price. At first my youthful artist-pride rebelled against such dishonourable conditions, as I deemed them. But the wish to see the publication of the Concerto so expedited that, upon our return to Brunswick I might be able to present my Duke with a copy, joined to the hope that he would make me a present, assisted me to conquer my sensitiveness.[1]

In a sense, a number of free copies to present to potential patrons could seem more important than a fee to composers who believed that their livelihood depended upon their tenure of a reasonably well-paid post in which they would be given as much artistic freedom as the age could accept. The composer's war against the publisher broke out when Haydn, among whose main qualities was an invincible peasant shrewdness, found that he was losing money to publishers all over Europe. His music began to appear in print in the 1760s, when French publishers began to issue scores and parts of his early symphonies. How these works travelled to Paris is a mystery, and there is no evidence that Haydn knew of them. Many of them appeared before the *Applausus* Cantata, written for an Austrian monastery in 1768 and according to all surviving evidence the first work which Prince Nikolaus Eszterhazy allowed him to write for an external patron.

The Haydn works which came out in Paris encouraged first Hummel, of Amsterdam, and then the English firms of Bremmer, Longman and Broderip and Forster, as well as other French houses, the new firm of Sieber among them, to exploit Haydn's popularity by publishing any of his works they could find. Naturally, they made no more effort than the original Paris publishers to recompense the composer. By the 1780s, when Austrian and German publishers were equally ready to exploit Haydn's work, the Austrian monasteries to which he had regularly sent manuscript copies of his works had begun to buy printed editions. These were cheaper than a copyist's manuscript but brought nothing to the composer; Haydn at once realised that he must take a business-like interest in the fate of his works.

The first music Haydn himself published in Vienna—they were possibly the first works he took any steps of his own to publish—were six Piano Sonatas

---

[1] Ludwig Spohr: *Autobiography*. Cassel, 1861; English translation, Reeves and Turner, London, 1878.

issued by the firm of Kurzbock in 1774. He seems to have thought first of the profitable domestic market. In 1779 he arranged that Artaria should publish his works as they were written, with a regular right of first refusal should anything Haydn offered not fit in with his plans. For a time he insisted that Artaria should always delay publication until the clients who expected his music in manuscript would be satisfied, but many of the various external patrons apparently decided that a copyist's manuscript of a work due to appear in print would not give them any sense of personal, privileged possession, and transferred their orders to Artaria, so that what Haydn gained on the roundabout of publication he lost on the swings of distribution.

The arrangement with Artaria was eventually profitable to both parties, but it was not without its storms. Artaria treated Haydn fairly, in a way which seems to set him on a higher moral plane than most of his fellow-publishers—he refused to accept unauthorised copies of Haydn's works and bought only from the composer, telling Haydn when and from whom he had received offers of his star composer's work—but it was a long time before Haydn succeeded in convincing him that immediate financial advantage was not the only criterion to be observed when he was dealing with a very popular composer. In December, 1781, Haydn planned a subscription edition of the String Quartets op. 33 to precede Artaria's publication of the set. A month later, before all the subscribers had received their copies, Artaria announced his published edition. Haydn had himself refused a subscription from Hummel to protect Artaria's edition from piracy, knowing that once the music reached the rival publisher he would at once prepare his own pirated edition, but Artaria, instead of protecting the composer, had made it seem that the subscription was no more than a catch-penny trick to make money out of works he had already sold. He angrily told Artaria that this greed had cost him more than 50 ducats, suggesting that eight or nine subscribers had withdrawn their subscription to wait for the printed edition. After this storm, in 1784, the subscription for the op. 50 String Quartets was managed smoothly; Haydn told Artaria that he had made 100 ducats from the subscription and had refused a publisher's offer of the same amount to accept Artaria's offer of 300 gulden; but Artaria was asked to wait three months for the manuscript of the works and actually waited three years for the scores of the last two quartets.

Haydn kept Artaria waiting, but grew indignant if his publisher were not sufficiently brisk. When Artaria was slow in producing a collection of six Overtures eventually issued as *Sei Sinfonie a gran Orchestra opera XXXXV*, Haydn told him that he could have had 40 ducats for the collection if he had not entrusted it to his Viennese publisher. Whether it was to keep Artaria up to scratch or not, or whether Artaria had refused the works, Haydn sold Symphonies 76, 77 and 78 to Torricella in 1784. Shortly before the appearance of the three Torricella symphonies, Boyer had written to Haydn from Paris asking for new works. Possibly this suggested to the composer a way of exploiting the foreign rights in his works and making use on his own behalf of the publishers' limited spheres of influence. He explained to Boyer that his patron objected to the sending of autograph scores out of Austria but pointed out that a copyist's manuscript was easier to work from than an autograph score, and ended with a laudatory description of the three symphonies due to be published by Torricella. These were bought not only by Boyer but by Forster in London, so that Haydn had three fees, Torricella's, Boyer's and Forster's, for the one set of works. But Torricella went bankrupt in 1785, and Artaria took over his property, including the three Haydn Symphonies.

Artaria had his own agents in London, Longman and Broderip, whose handling of the three symphonies suffered from Forster's acquisition of them. A year later, Haydn's association brought serious trouble to him and to Artaria. For £70, Haydn sold Forster *The Seven Words of the Saviour on the Cross* and the *Paris* Symphonies; Artaria bought them, too, and in the course of time they reached Longman and Broderip from the Viennese publisher. Forster had, apparently, wished to guard against a situation of this sort, for he had insisted upon Haydn's signature to a contract which included the words:

> I hereby certify and declare that the said Guilaume Forster is the sole proprietor of the said works, and that I sold them to him as such, and that I cede and transfer to him all my rights and covenants therein.[1]

In 1787, Artaria complained to Haydn that these dealings behind his back were wrong because, when he bought a work, it was understood that he bought exclusive rights in it and that any profit which it made through any of the channels of distribution he created for it was his alone. At the same time, Forster demanded that the composer made clear his possession of the English rights in any works he had bought from Haydn. It was clear that Forster and Haydn both regarded the declaration Haydn had signed as applicable only to England, and that Artaria had every other right that he could exploit. Artaria had only himself to blame, Haydn wrote, for it was the publisher's greed which had forced the composer to seek outlets beyond him. If he were adequately paid for what he sold to Artaria, he would not have seized the opportunity to negotiate separate English rights. He continued:

> No one can blame me for trying to secure some profit for myself after the pieces have been engraved; for I am not properly recompensed for my work, and have a greater right to get this profit than the other dealers. Therefore you will see that the contracts are more carefully drawn up, and that I am sufficiently remunerated. If you lose GENERALLY because of this, however, I shall find a way to recompense you in another way.[2]

In other words, Artaria was to pay more for his works, and then Haydn would do something in return, possibly hand to the publisher more easily sold music for the amateur market.

Forster's situation remained unpleasant, and Longman and Broderip brought an action against him which was still in progress in 1791, when Haydn was in

---

[1] H. C. Robbins Landon: *op. cit.* Letter of ?, 1786.
[2] *Ibid.* Letter of November 27, 1787.

England and was called to give evidence. His letter to the English publisher when the storm broke is one it would be kind to call disingenuous:

> It is not my fault but the usurious practices of Herr Artaria. This much I can promise you, that as long as I live neither Artaria nor Longman shall get anything from me, directly or indirectly. . . . But you must realise that whoever wants exclusive rights in six new pieces of mine must pay more than 20 guineas. In fact, I have a contract with someone who pays me 100 guineas or more.[1]

Haydn had demonstrated that he could see the unfairness of his situation; he had unscrupulously gone round its provisions to do himself justice, but if he had not established a way of protecting his foreign rights he had at least found a way of screwing high fees from a publisher who wanted his work. The break with Artaria which he mentioned to Forster lasted for no more than six months, and then he offered his Viennese publisher three string quartets or three piano trios for 25 ducats. There is no further mention of the extremely generous English publisher whose terms seemed to have been mentioned only to inspire Forster to similar generosity. From then onward, Haydn demanded higher fees, and when Artaria protested at the fee of 24 ducats for the piano Fantasia in C, suggesting that a work in only one movement could not be worth so high a fee, the composer simply said that the Fantasia was priced according to the effort it had cost him, and that he would not reduce the price by a single halfpenny. Haydn's music sold well enough, we may assume, for Artaria and other publishers to meet the composer's demands.

Whatever his early difficulties with publishers—though in the twenty years which succeeded Haydn's quarrel over foreign rights Haydn dealt quite peacefully with Traeg, Breitkopf and Härtel and others as well as Artaria and did so on his own terms—only the number of unauthorised copies of his work before he himself decided to take the situation in hand, can explain the spread of Haydn's European fame during the 1770s and early 1780s. He spent the better part of a quarter of a century, with only brief visits to Vienna, in a remote palace in an inaccessible corner of the Hungarian marshes, but in 1785 the canons of Cadiz Cathedral commissioned *The Seven Words of the Saviour on the Cross* from him. A year later, he was asked for six symphonies by the *Concert de la Loge Olympique*, in Paris; also in 1786 the King of Naples commissioned the concertos for lyra organizzata. In 1787 the publisher Bland made his way from London to Vienna to buy Haydn's works, and in 1790 John Peter Salomon planned Haydn's visit to London. In all these places his name was known and his music admired, and his way of life was by force of circumstances so remote that only publication can have made his work so well known.

We can deduce something similar about the music of Beethoven: as soon as his orchestral works were available in print, they were played in Leipzig. When the Frankfurt Museum Concert Society was formed in 1808, it introduced works by Beethoven in its first season and, like the Gewandhaus Orchestra, kept up with

[1] *Ibid.* Letter of February 28, 1788.

his output as soon as new works became available. The London Philharmonic Society included three of his symphonies in its first season in 1813. The *Musikverein* founded in Innsbruck in 1818, and the Graz *Musikverein* were determined players of Beethoven's music, and when the Graz organisation evolved into a *Musikverein* for the whole of Carinthia in 1828, its first concert included the *Egmont* Overture and the Second Symphony. In 1828, the newly formed *Société des Concerts du Conservatoire* in Paris played the *Eroica* Symphony at its first concert and the Fifth and Seventh Symphonies during its first season. Beethoven's exploitation of an effective publishing industry was the only means by which his music could so quickly attain international popularity.

The circumstances of Beethoven's life after deafness had ended his career as a virtuoso pianist forced him to depend far more on publishing for his livelihood than it had been necessary for any of his predecessors to do. His last public performance was the tragic fiasco of 1805, the premiere of the Fourth Piano Concerto. He had already given up playing at private concerts because they were more revealing of his condition than concerts in public. He had a number of patrons prepared not only to commission works from him but also to see that he lived comfortably, but he had no regular income and therefore he needed to make what money, and what reputation outside the nobility, he could by regular publication.

Before he had been two years in Vienna, he began to publish regularly. He issued a number of easy-going, well-written works which could appeal to amateur pianists; he seems to have carried with him a considerable stock of such works written in Bonn and to have a complete confidence always to be able to produce as many of them as he needed. From the first he acted as though the publisher had no justification for his existence except his ability to serve a composer and to do as he was told. In 1793 he wrote a letter protesting against mistakes in Artaria's engraving of his Variations on *Si vuol ballare*, Figaro's aria in act one of Mozart's opera (WoO 40). A year later he wrote to Simrock, in Bonn, an old friend, complaining that Simrock should not have engraved his *Variations on a Theme by Count Waldstein* (WoO 67) without the composer's agreement. 'What would you think of me,' he asked, 'if I were to act in the same way and sell these variations to Artaria although I know that you are engraving them?'[1] Apparently Simrock had sent him a proof, as he points out a serious mistake in the engraving, but the letter treats the copy he received as a finished copy and complains that he should have two dozen complimentary copies, on the grounds that Artaria had not only sent him twelve copies of the earlier set of variations but had paid a handsome fee for them as well. But he offered to find Simrock a publisher in Vienna to act as his agent, and in a few months put the Bonn firm in touch with Traeg.

Beethoven's quickly-achieved position as a social favourite helped him when the Piano Trios, op. 1 were published by subscription in 1795. The subscription

---

[1] Emily Anderson: *The Letters of Ludwig van Beethoven*. Macmillan, London, 1961. Letter 10 of June 18, 1794.

list carried a hundred and twenty-three names, many of them impressively aristocratic, representing the social, intellectual and musical *élite* of Viennese high society. Almost all the great names associated with Beethoven throughout his career—Kinsky, Lichnowsky, Lobkowitz, Rasoumovsky, Waldstein and so on—appear on it. The subscription price was one ducat, of which Artaria was paid one gulden for printing the work, leaving the composer a profit of about seven shillings on each volume. The op. 1 Trios were the most ambitious works Beethoven had so far published, which may explain why they appeared by subscription and not as a direct publication. But by 1797 the publishers were taking his more serious works apparently without misgivings while he continued to put into practice Leopold Mozart's advice to the young Wolfgang to publish 'short, easy pieces' for the sake of money and prestige. They helped to build up Beethoven's reputation with the middle-class audience which did not hear his playing or many of the works which he wrote for his originally aristocratic clientele.

Though Artaria published the first works Beethoven issued, he soon began to sell music to any publisher who would pay for it, not only to those who asked for it but, at times, soliciting the attention of others who did not to his latest works. Simrock, Traeg, Mollo and Hoffmeister as well as Artaria issued his music in the 1790s, Breitkopf and Härtel joined in the competition in 1802, and were rapidly joined by the Viennese firm of Cappi and the newly formed *Kunst und Industrie Comptoir*. In this position, with his music widely known through its distribution to publishers in so many cities and through them to their associates and agents, he was in a position to play publishers off against each other and so push up his fees. Beethoven was always ready to hector publishers from the height of an unchallengeable moral superiority while behaving as badly as any of them, but while he had no compunction against playing the games according to the rules they had invented, he was still suffering from firms which published his work and delayed payment for it beyond any reasonable time, as Clementi in London did, and from undisguised piracy: Artaria had no compunction about bringing out his own edition of the String Quintet op. 29 which Breitkopf and Härtel published in 1802.

Nevertheless, Beethoven's situation by the end of the eighteenth century justifies the claim he made to his doctor-friend Franz Gerhard Wegeler, a native of Bonn whom Beethoven had met again in Vienna and with whom, after his return to Bonn, he carefully kept in touch for a time. The letter is well known as that in which he first describes his growing deafness:

> My compositions bring in a good deal; and I may say that I am offered more commissions than it is possible for me to carry out. Moreover, for every composition I can count on six or seven publishers, or even more if I want them; people no longer come to an arrangement with me. I state my price and they pay.[1]

The technique of exploiting the exploiters is revealed in Beethoven's letters. For the two sets of Piano Variations, op. 34 and op. 35, he asked 50 ducats from

---

[1] *Ibid.* Letter 51 of June 29, 1801.

Breitkopf and Härtel in 1802. A year later he offered George Thomson, the Edinburgh publisher, six sonatas for 500 ducats. In 1804, he sent a list of works to Thomson with a symphony and a quartet priced at 20 ducats each. All the works in his list had already been published in Austria or in Germany; the high price of the six sonatas was the result of his awareness of how high English prices were. In 1805 he asked 700 gulden for the *Eroica* Symphony, The *Waldstein* and F major Sonatas, op. 54 and op. 55, all of which were published by the *Kunst und Industrie Comptoir*.

In 1808 he demanded 900 gulden from Breitkopf and Härtel for the Mass in C, the Fifth and Sixth Symphonies and the Sonata for Cello and Piano, op. 69. The prospect of his appointment as *Kapellmeister* to Jérôme Bonaparte, king of the newly created state of Westphalia moulded out of a group of North German principalities by the French, prompted him to ask Breitkopf to hold up the publication of the Mass, which had not been issued, until his journey through Leipzig on the way to his new post, and the concert he would give on his way, had helped to publicise the work. In 1809, having changed his mind about the *Kapellmeister* post, he lifted the embargo on the Mass so that it could appear at the same time as *Christus am Oelberg* (which Breitkopf had been holding for a considerable time) but at the same time he added 250 gulden to the price of the works they held and had bought on the grounds that Simrock had offered him 100 gulden for the Mass alone and that the new firm of G. A. Steiner in Vienna, for the sake of getting Beethoven's name into his list, would certainly pay more, and so would other Viennese firms. He thus pushed his original agreement with Breitkopf and Härtel out of the way. Incidentally, the collapse of Viennese money at this time was making him very careful about entrusting anything to the Viennese publisher, who would pay him in a grossly inflated currency; until the situation began to stabilise itself in 1813, in spite of his letter to Breitkopf and Härtel about the potentially high fees available for him in Vienna, he published little of importance through any of the Viennese houses, and in dealing with firms outside Vienna, he tended to quote prices always in internationally acceptable ducats.

Publication, he had obviously come to believe, was a business in which the devil was sure to take the hindmost, and if he needed an excuse for sharp practice, he could justifiably point out that Clementi had bought the English rights in the Violin Concerto, its adaptation for Piano, and the *Coriolan* Overture in 1807 but that two years of laborious correspondence were necessary before he succeeded in extorting his fee from the London publisher.

New firms, eager to get hold of any unpublished work he had ready, were drawn into the ring as soon as they appeared, and their eagerness helped him to play his game victoriously. Not only Steiner but Schlesinger, Mecchetti, Starke and Schott all issued works by Beethoven which, whenever possible, he published in London or through Thomson in Edinburgh. He set his fees according to the scale and complexity of each work he wished to sell, but the number of publishers angling for his work enabled him to force higher and higher fees from all the business men whom he had drawn into his ring or who had joined it of their own free will.

Beethoven's offer of works to George Thomson in 1802 seems to have been his first attempt to take control of the foreign rights in his music, and his method was simply that which Haydn had tried. It was hardly more likely to succeed for Beethoven in the long run than it had for his great predecessor; it would, he knew, be better to fix a system which was agreed by both parties. That, perhaps, may have been what was in Beethoven's mind when, in 1806, Breitkopf and Härtel tried to persuade him to make an agreement by which they would become the sole publishers of his music. This would have put an end to the irregular auction he had established by distributing his works to every publisher who was willing to deal with them, but Beethoven, apparently aware that it might be possible to come to an arrangement which allowed him control of his royalties outside Germany and Austria, answered that he was prepared to sign a contract by which he sold to them and to no other German publisher providing that they accepted his right to accept satisfactory offers from publishers elsewhere; he would then sell to Breitkopf and Härtel at a lower fee any works which he had handed over to other publishers. If they would accept this idea, they could start their association with him on this new basis at once; the *Rasoumovsky Quartets*, op. 59, the Fourth Symphony, the Fourth Piano Concerto, *Christus am Oelberg* and *Leonore*, the original version of *Fidelio*, were all ready for publication.[1] *Christus am Oelberg*, which Breitkopf and Härtel wanted, apparently, whatever final arrangement were reached, stayed in their hands, as we have seen, for five years.

Breitkopf and Härtel looked, it seems, carefully at this revolutionary proposal and decided that it needed clarification. If the composer's explanation was satisfactory, they would be prepared to make a contract with the composer to buy all he had to publish for three years: unfortunately, Beethoven's clarification seems more obscure than the original offer:

> As for a three-year contract, I should be willing to make it with you at once, if you would agree to my selling several works to England or Scotland or France. It would be clearly understood that the works *you* received *from me* or which I sold to you would belong to you alone, that is to say, would be exclusively and wholly your property, and would be quite different from those for France or England or Scotland. But I should have to be allowed to retain the freedom to dispose of other works as well to the countries I have just mentioned. In Germany, however, you would be the owner of my works and there would be no other publisher Whatsoever.[2]

Whether the letter was meant to leave Beethoven a large area for manœuvre and was deliberately disingenuous, or whether its obscurities are simply the result of Beethoven's clumsiness with words, it left a number of conundrums for Breitkopf and Härtel to solve. If the works which Beethoven wrote for publishers

---

[1] *The Letters of Ludwig von Beethoven*. Letter 134 of September 3, 1806.
[2] *Ibid*. Letter 137 of November 18, 1806. Beethoven's italics.

in England, Scotland or France were to be 'quite different' from those he would agree to sell to Breitkopf and Härtel, what were 'the other works' he demanded freedom to dispose of abroad? Was he expecting more commissions like Thomson's request for arrangements of English, Scottish and Welsh airs, or was he suggesting that he must be allowed to sell in other countries works which Breitkopf and Härtel had bought? The rights which were to be 'exclusively and wholly' the publishers' property seem, in a mere couple of sentences, to dwindle into no more than the German rights. Eventually Breitkopf and Härtel bought *Christus am Oelberg*, but did not publish it until 1811. They did not help Beethoven to create a precedent which allowed the composer to restrict the rights which any publisher bought when he chose to publish a work.

The idea lay on one side for a year, apparently developing in Beethoven's mind, for when the composer suggested it to Simrock in 1807, it had become a good deal more thorough:

> I intend to sell the following works to a firm of publishers in France, to one in England and to one in Vienna simultaneously, but on condition that they shall not appear until a day to be fixed. Thus I shall obtain the advantage to be derived from the speedy publication of my works with benefit to myself and to the various publishing firms concerned in the matter of price.[1]

The works involved in this offer included some that Breitkopf and Härtel had not taken a year before—the Fourth Symphony, the Fourth Piano Concerto and the *Rasoumovsky* Quartets—and also the Violin Concerto, its adaptation for piano and the *Coriolan* Overture. They were published in Vienna by the *Kunst und Industrie Comptoir* in 1808 and 1809. After his letter to Simrock, Beethoven offered them on the new conditions to Pleyel in Paris and Clementi in London but won no support for his idea of simultaneous publication in three countries; his efforts to find a fair and rational way of dealing with his valuable foreign rights was unacceptable to publishers, although he was prepared to accept three rather lower fees from each of the publishers concerned in order to make more money from the three together. The result was that he continued to sell works wherever he could for as much as he could and leave the publishers to sort out the difficulties, if any arose, for themselves, as Haydn had left Artaria and Longman and Broderip to deal with the problem of Forster's editions. His works were too valuable a property for publishers to boycott them when he wilfully plunged them into complications, for the idea of their limited spheres of interest still persisted and they handled their foreign markets through the agency of publishers in the other countries concerned as they had been doing since the middle of the eighteenth century; they could, therefore, adjust the complications of duplicated editions for themselves or simply grin and bear it, as they grinned and bore the issue of pirated editions. To their way of thinking, Beethoven was simply another pirate who had to be tolerated because they could make a decent profit out of anything he put into their way, and his jugglings with his works did

[1] *Ibid.* Letter 141 of April 26, 1807.

not, apparently, cost them enough money to make a decisive quarrel with him worth while.

The almost pointless complexity of Beethoven's dealings with publishers in the last ten years of his life are, perhaps, a different matter from the earlier determination not to suffer at their hands or to let his works go for less than he knew that they were worth. High-minded biographers, convinced that an artist's character should be quite as noble as anything he creates, were shocked by the deceits, chicaneries and falsities through which he tried to sell the Mass in D for as much as he could possibly get. In 1819, the work enters his correspondence as a potential asset; he asked his friend Ferdinand Ries, who had settled in London, about the possibility of publishing the work there; it was, he said, nearly finished. He was, too, obviously aware that this was a great work and was determined to sell it for something like a sum commensurate with the labour it cost him. Actually, though the bulk of the work was written by 1820, it was not until 1823 that he was reasonably satisfied with what he had done and prepared to put an end to the process of adjusting and revising details in the score; the bulk of the correspondence and the negotiations he initiated took place before the work was ready for a publisher.

In February 1820, he offered the Mass to Simrock for a fee of 125 louis d'or—more than 200 ducats—and demanded an early reply so that, if Simrock did not want it, he could immediately offer it to someone else. Nevertheless, he repeated his offer to Simrock in March and July, and in August said that he was ready to send the work to the copyist as soon as he had Simrock's first remittance; while waiting for Simrock's decision, he said, he had refused a fee of 200 gold ducats for Simrock's sake. There is nowhere any surviving evidence of this rival and generous offer. In September, 1822, Simrock was told that the work was not for him because four separate Viennese publishers had each offered him 1000 gulden—a negligible increase in price—for the work; again there is no evidence to support his claim. In the meantime, however, he had offered it to Schlesinger, in Berlin (in November 1821) and to Peters (in June 1822) on precisely the terms that he had proposed to Simrock. Peters were prepared to pay what he asked when they received the manuscript; this, of course, was impossible, for the composer was not yet sufficiently satisfied with the work to let it go. He began to mention first a second Mass, and then a third, the sale of which he could negotiate at the same time while building up interest in the Mass in D. These Masses may have been works which he intended someday to write, but they had no actual existence when, in 1823, he told Peters that he had not yet decided which of the three they were to have. While all this was in progress, he drew Diabelli into the team of publishers who were expected to compete for the work, offering it still at the original price of 125 louis d'or. As he began to collect subscriptions for the publication, he involved Schott in the plan and eventually sold the Mass to him at the fee all his competitors were ready to pay.

The object of these almost pointless negotiations, which show Beethoven in anything but an admirable light, had been to induce one of the publishers to offer more than the composer asked for the sake of obtaining a work which was the object of such keen competition; it was not achieved. In terms of its period, the Ninth Symphony was an almost impossible, hardly comprehensible work, but the Mass in D was quite impossible and entirely incomprehensible; no publisher handling it could have believed that it was a road to high sales and quick profits. Beethoven's fee was high to begin with, and it seems that the competition existed only in his mind; the calmness with which the publishers waited for him to make a decisive move suggests that they simply did not trust him and were not ready to commit themselves until they had the work in their hands.

Neither Haydn nor Beethoven created a system which was generally accepted by publishers or followed by composers. They were able to exploit publication as a new medium, in the way that they did, simply through the force of their characters and the popularity of their work. Spohr, arriving in Vienna in 1813, had published a good deal of music without any serious attempt to make publishers' fees into a salient feature of his earnings. He came to an agreement with Johann von Tost, who had been a violinist in Haydn's orchestra at Eszterhaza until he married a wealthy woman and had set up as a manufacturer and business man. Tost had taken Haydn manuscripts to Paris to publish them there on the composer's behalf but also to use them to establish himself in musical society; he now proceeded to do the same with Spohr, buying in advance everything Spohr was to write for three years. Tost undertook not to publish the works but to have them performed at musical parties. Spohr charged him 30 ducats for a quartet, 35 for a quintet, and so on, and Tost apparently made the works very popular both in Vienna and elsewhere. When the expiry of their agreement came and the manuscripts were returned to him, Spohr was able to write, 'I now sold the whole of the returned manuscripts to two Viennese publishers, and from their having acquired a great celebrity by their frequent performance, I received a considerable sum for them.'[1] Spohr sold his works on the basis of their popularity, not, like Beethoven, on the strength of his reputation; when he had done so, he did not regard the fee he received as a matter of any great moment.

Until a binding and internationally accepted system of copyright was worked out and took the force of law (a development of the late nineteenth century), the composer continued to be at a disadvantage in any dealings with publishers, though by his middle-age Brahms, among other composers, was able to make a decent income from publications alone. Beethoven, living in an age when the social framework within which music functioned was changing, and unwittingly helping to bring about the changes by his composition of works on a scale which demanded public performance before a mass audience, and by his eagerness to circulate his music in print as early as he could and thus creating a modern, challenging repertoire for the concert platform, set a pattern which his successors gradually found themselves compelled to follow.

[1] Spohr: *op. cit.*

20 The Liberated Composer

Neither Mozart nor Beethoven saw himself as a new kind of composer, a specialist working outside the normal system of court or ecclesiastical patronage. Mozart, although his attitude to an official appointment seems to have been ambivalent, spent his life waiting for the official appointment worthy of his gifts and at the time of his death was court composer to the Emperor—a post which entailed minimal duties but brought him an annual salary of 800 gulden—and had been appointed Assistant *Kapellmeister* of St. Stephen's Cathedral, at his own request, with the expectation of the post of *Kapellmeister* when it should fall vacant. As late as 1808, when deafness had made any part in active music-making impossible for him, although he still attempted to conduct his works, Beethoven was apparently ready to accept the post of *Kapellmeister* offered to him by Jérôme Bonaparte; the offer shows a singular lapse in both men's sense of reality, but Beethoven only rejected the post when he had secured a legally binding contract from the Archduke Rudolph, Prince Kinsky and Prince Lobkowitz to pay him the annuity they had suggested. It was no one's fault that the war and its results prevented the subsidy from keeping him as comfortably as a professional musician could hope to be kept.

Neither Beethoven nor Mozart was really a failure as a freelance. At the end of his life, crushed by debts and penury, Mozart was earning more than twice as much as his careful father had ever earned and was regarded as a great, if over-intellectual, composer. Fecklessness, a love of luxury and a total incapacity for dealing with the problems of everyday life destroyed him. Beethoven was unable to master practical circumstances; it is as though his skill in subjugating publishers and his dominating power over the people who knew him were something apart from everyday existence and not applicable to it. If impracticality left him living in squalor with one pair of boots occasionally 'under house arrest' as he put it, squalor was never the result of grinding poverty but rather of a neurotic dread of poverty which came, perhaps, from his deafness, and the sense of isolation deafness creates; a dread of poverty, and his determination to leave as much money as possible to his nephew Carl, made him complain of an illusory lack of money. The cheque for £100 which he begged from the Philharmonic Society in London to help him in his last illness went uncashed, and his estate, apart from personal effects—some of considerable worth—was valued at 9885 gulden; 7441 of these were safe in bank shares.

The nineteenth century invented the legend of the great, unappreciated genius, struggling not only with his daemon but also with the incomprehension,

350

neglect and contempt of his contemporaries. The world came to believe itself to be too stupidly and insensitively blind to appreciate living greatness though there is no indication that a master like Haydn was other than justifiably proud of having made his way in the world after starting from utter poverty. It is interesting to try to trace the reasons why the world accepted the idea that genius be too great for it.

Court patronage did not end in the lifetime of Beethoven, as a result of the Napoleonic Wars or for any other reason. From Weber, through Spohr and Wagner to Brahms, Richard Strauss and, as late as 1913, Reger, important composers were in court service. The customary simplification, that the courts were no longer able to support music, is really untenable. The lesser aristocracy lost their power of patronage; the greater did not.

What actually happened is far more complex. Before the Congress of Vienna set out in 1814 to undo the revolution, the ecclesiastical states were secularised, their territories handed over to more powerful nearby states. After 1802, Bonn, with its court opera and orchestra, Salzburg, with a *Kapelle* of more than sixty musicians, and Würzburg all lost their professional musicians. So did Eichstätt, a diminutive prince-bishopric on the road between Munich and Nuremberg, where the sixteen players of the court orchestra had been responsible for forming a concert society among the citizens. So did Grosswardein, Breslau and other cities which had, in the past, employed musicians sometimes of great eminence.

The Congress of Vienna carried the rationalisation of the map of Central Europe still further. The Imperial Free Cities lost their pre-war status and privileges, though this, after a century in which the nobility dominated the arts, had little effect on music. A hundred and twenty-one of the once-independent German states lost their independence and became merged with their greater neighbours. The Princes—the Kinskys, Lichnowskys, Lobkowitzes and Eszterhazys—were no longer rich enough to support music by maintaining great musical establishments of their own, and they never really recovered their pre-war wealth, for the riches of the future depended upon industrial power and not on the mere possession of land. Many of those who had before maintained impressive musical establishments had to express their enthusiasm for music in other ways, as many of the nobility of the Empire did through membership of the *Gesellschaft der Musikfreunde*. King Ludwig II of Bavaria could support Wagner royally, to the destruction of his private fortune if he chose; his Bavarian people were by no means eager to join in his acts of patronage by allowing Wagner (whose demands were entirely insatiable) to spend public money. Thus there was far less patronage to go round; the Congress of Vienna could restore the political system of the past, but it could not restore the vast aristocratic wealth on which the past had depended. Just as the Imperial and Royal Opera of Vienna had already, before the Revolution, become a group of theatres managed by a commercial management on behalf of the court, maintaining its artistic and social standards by admitting a paying audience to take some of the burden of its support off the Emperor's shoulders, court establishments began to grow into national institutions.

In Dresden, for example, the alliance of Saxony with Napoleon's empire nearly brought an end to the opera when France's power crumbled away and the Russians occupied the city in 1814. Prince Repnin, the Russian governor-general, prevented the destruction of the court opera and musical establishment by putting them under public control; the return of the Saxon monarch King Friedrich August, in 1817, meant that the theatre was again called the Court Theatre, but it remained a public organisation dependent on money taken at its box office as well as on government funds supplied by the new king. August Friedrich's support of German opera and his appointment of Weber as *Kapellmeister* responsible for raising the standard of German opera in Dresden until it was as high as that of the Italian opera can be seen as a two-edged stroke of policy; it both proved his patriotism and won the support of a new audience. The court theatre in Munich was destroyed by fire in 1818; when it was rebuilt and reopened in 1828, it was no longer simply the *Hoftheater* but the *Hof und National Theater*; it was a public theatre and no longer one to which the public were admitted simply by the grace of the King.

But the *Kapellmeister*—for the traditional title continued to be bestowed—found that his functions had changed. The publication of music had created a repertory which he was expected to play. He was no longer a musician whose authority rested upon his power to compose as much pleasant, fashionable music as was wanted whenever it was wanted; to all intents and purposes he had become a court conductor whose primary task was to see that the growing repertory—its standardisation was a very slow process—was adequately rehearsed and performed. The nineteenth-century *Kapellmeister* whom we remember as a composer did not write primarily for the organisation he controlled. Even *Euryanthe*, one of Weber's German operas, had its first performance in Vienna; Spohr's oratorios and symphonies were written for German or English musical festivals, or for institutions like the Philharmonic Society in London, for which he wrote his Second, Sixth and Eighth Symphonies over a period of some twenty years; his last six operas were first performed at Cassel, where he was *Kapellmeister*, but they represent only a fraction of the operatic repertory he conducted there. Weber, Spohr and Wagner owed their *Kapellmeister* posts to their efficiency as conductors and organisers; their prestige as composers helped them to secure their posts only because prestige as a composer was more clearly understood in the early nineteenth century than mastery of the new technique of conducting a large orchestra. Conducting seems still to have been a mystery to most people when Berlioz wrote his essay *Le Chef d'Orchestre, Théorie et son Art* in 1848, and the essay *Über das Dirigieren* which Wagner published in 1869 was his attempt to show people exactly what are the interpretative qualities needed in a conductor.

The idea of a specialist composer who had no other musical function began with Beethoven not because Beethoven wished to restrict his activities to composition but because deafness compelled him to do so. Schubert had no intention of remaining a freelance composer with a considerable following among the Viennese artistic bourgeoisie and lesser nobility; his operas and church music were all aimed at proving his qualifications for a regular, salaried post. But the breakdown of the old system, restricting the number of posts available and, by demanding a new expertise from the *Kapellmeister*, put the available posts beyond the reach of many. It seems unlikely that the born bohemian Schubert, with a defective sense of punctuality and little interest in performing the works of other composers, would have been an effective *Kapellmeister* of either the old or the new style.

The breakdown of the old system took the composer effectively out of practical music-making unless he were also a virtuoso instrumentalist or conductor. It robbed him not only of his opportunity to work in close collaboration with other musicians but also of his chance to forge a close, potentially creative association with his audience. That is to say, it took away his direct social function (which all composers had enjoyed since the business of composition had been recognised as something different from skilled performance). After Beethoven, the composer as composer—but not as *Kapellmeister*, conductor or virtuoso— found himself standing outside society and consoling himself in whatever way he could for his alienation. He became seer, prophet, 'unacknowledged legislator of the world' (like Shelley's poet) simply because he no longer worked of necessity in any direct relationship to the world in which he lived, a world represented by an audience which knew and understood his aims, which would sympathise with his experiments and which he could lead. If he was not, like Schubert, constitutionally a bohemian, unwilling to conform to social convention, he was drawn into bohemianism partly because the world wanted him to reject normality and partly because it never paid him in a way which made normal, conventional life natural to him. He was either a spoiled social idol or a man living as best he could from exiguous earnings. He became the entirely free man, that is to say, a man in no way indissolubly tied to the normal courses of society.

The romantic symbol for the entirely free man was the brigand or the corsair; Byron found it and Berlioz accepted it with delight. The Brigand disdained the normal uses of society and rejected its laws because they were irrelevant to his needs and their fulfilment. The artist's brigandage, his alienation from the normal courses of the world, was approved by the world because it was intellectual and emotional, never actual. The course of history had set the composer apart from the normal system of work and wages, of money-making, with their concomitants of social responsibility and social necessity. Therefore only by seeing him as a born outsider could society forgive itself for its lack of genius, its lack of creativity; the uncreative, everyday personality, building industries or working in them, making laws or considering the way in which they were observed, excused its lack of creative power by accepting, as an article of faith, the remote unpracticality of the creative mind; who, it wanted to know, would run our world if we were all artists, and how on earth would we manage if there were no industrialists, sewage men or factory hands, shop-keepers and clerks? The question is, of course, a valid one. Society, which had no direct use for the artist, put him in a position where he could not conform to common social usages and then forgave his inability to do so because it had no immediate need of him. Thus the angry, rebellious Haydn of the *Sturm und Drang* period was forgotten and the profound, high-spirited master who, in the *London* Symphonies, seemed to order the entire gamut of human experience, was seen as a good-natured, amusing 'Papa' capable of little more than slight orchestral jokes. Mozart's arrogance, fecklessness and impracticality were forgotten, and the society of his day (which treated him better than it treated many musicians) was blamed for the tragedy which was rooted in his personality. Society could not blame itself for Beethoven's deafness, but the nineteenth century made deafness a symbol of the neglect and contempt it believed that any great composer ought to suffer.

The Beethoven legend was already in circulation when Berlioz visited Vienna in 1846 and conducted, standing where Beethoven had stood, in the *Redoutensaal*. He remembered the story of a performance in 1820 of the Seventh Symphony, played to an audience of fifty. He did not ask who played, where the concert was given or whether it was one of the frequent Viennese concerts at which an amateur orchestra simply read through a work at sight. Nor did he bother to ascertain that the Seventh Symphony, by 1820, was already a very familiar repertory work by virtue of its great popularity. He did not stop to consider that at its first performance, the *allegretto* had been encored and that its impact was such that the work was repeated three times in four months. He needed to believe the legend of the neglected, suffering genius.

The creative mind is a comparatively rare phenomenon, and when it is recognised it is admired to the point of idolatry; it becomes necessary to the uncreative majority to believe that the genius is poor, misunderstood or uncomprehended, neglected, mentally strong enough to survive contempt and derision but physically as well as socially stricken, probably, for some reason that never reveals itself, by tuberculosis. By convincing the world that the creative artist is not as other men, it convinces him that he is better, with different and more exigent needs; it helps to make him into an egocentric monster like Wagner.

Before the Revolution and its aftermath, the composer worked within a small society—a court, a cathedral, a provincial city like Leipzig. He wrote for people whom he knew, offering something of immediate value to them. The age after Beethoven's was that of Liszt and Paganini, and it is to say the least arguable that the virtuoso's 'general public' proved as restrictive as the patronage of any prince. Paganini kept his devotion to Beethoven's Concerto and chamber music out of sight, for such music would not have given him any occasion for the pyrotechnics which his audience expected. The writings of men like Berlioz and Charles Hallé suggest that the enthusiasm of an audience could make Liszt capable of performances of Beethoven's music which twisted and falsified the composer's ideas to make the pianist's skill the centre of the audience's devotion.

Music had passed from the stage at which it was a social necessity to become a remote, esoteric delight thundered out by vast orchestras or dispensed by virtuoso players and singers. It became increasingly the pleasure of a cultured *élite* rather than an immediate communication between men and women. It was not long before the ambitious composer discovered that the provision of dance music and easy-going entertainment was beneath his dignity, and a divided society was left to make do with a divided art; social necessity was served, not by Brahms and Wagner, Verdi and Bruckner but by the Strauss family and its waltzes and polkas; and the Strauss family were, after all, great masters of their style. Before very long, anything with the right rhythm would do to fill up the social time for music.

A Note on Currencies
referred to in this volume

The values given here are all approximate. They make no attempt to indicate any of the fluctuations of the exchange rate or of the various European currencies in relationship to each other. They take no account of the fact that the gold and silver standards upon which European currencies were based were themselves hardly more than approximate in different countries.

Despite the varying gold standard of seventeenth- and eighteenth-century Europe, gold coins had a reasonably firm international value, so that the following table, which refers primarily to the second half of the eighteenth century, can base itself upon the internationally accepted standard of the ducat, which at the time was worth about nine shillings of English money.

1 ducat, in Germany and Austria, $= 3\frac{1}{2}$ thaler
$= 3\frac{1}{2}$ florins
$= 4\frac{1}{2}$ gulden
$= 72$ groschen
$= 270$ kreutzer
in Italy, $= 6\frac{1}{4}$ lire
$= 1\frac{1}{4}$ scudi (according to Venetian rates of exchange)
in France, $= 11$ livre
in Spain, $= 375$ maravedi
$= 11$ real 1 maravedi

1 sequin, current throughout Italy, was slightly more valuable than a ducat (approximately 9s. 6d. of English money).

Other gold coins which were internationally valid were:

1 pistole (originally Spanish) $= 7\frac{1}{2}$ gulden, approximately 15s.

1 Friedrich d'or (originally Prussian) $= 8$ gulden, approximately 16s.

1 carolin (originally Bavarian)
1 Louis d'or (originally French) $\Big\} = 9$ gulden, approximately 18s.

1 souverain d'or (originally Austrian) $= 13\frac{1}{2}$ gulden, approximately 27s.

To attempt to suggest the value of these currencies in purchasing power would be entirely futile. The best the reader can do is to remember that, while Goldsmith's village parson was 'passing rich on forty pounds a year', an investment of £1000 in The Royal Academy of Music—the operatic venture which in 1719 appointed Handel to be its director of music—was the necessary condition of membership and ensured that the members would belong to the social *élite*.

Apart from any other considerations governing the purchasing power of money, the cost of gold itself has risen by some 400 per cent in the last two hundred and fifty years, so that both English and European salaries of 1750 tend to seem, in modern terms, no more than derisory.

Some indications of purchasing power may be gained from a variety of unrelated facts. In Bach's lifetime in Leipzig, a florin would buy: 1 lb beef, 2 lb bread and a pair of soles for a man's shoes.

A document in the Public Record Office gives the English value of the ducat in 1670 as 3 shillings, 10 pence. Burney regarded the ducat as the equivalent of 9 shillings.

In the 1780s, Dittersdorf, discussing concert finances, described 860 German thaler as the equivalent of 1290 florins in Vienna.

In assessing Beethoven's estate in 1827, nearly seventeen years after Austria's financial collapse in the Napoleonic war, the Austrian officials regarded the present of £100, sent to the composer by the Philharmonic Society in London, as 1000 florins.

Bibliography

Hermann Abert: *W. A. Mozart*. Leipzig, 1919–21. Edited and revised by Anna Ameli Abert, 1956.
Emily Anderson: *The Letters of Mozart and Family*. Macmillan, London, 1938.
The Letters of Ludwig van Beethoven. Macmillan, London, 1961.
Richard Batka: *Die Musik in Böhmen*. Bard, Marquardt & Co., Berlin, 1906.
Anthony Baines: *Musical Instruments through the Ages*. Pelican Books, Harmondsworth, 1961.
R. H. Bainton: *Here I Stand*. Hodder & Stoughton, London, 1951.
C. H. Collins Baker and Muriel I. Baker: *The Life and Circumstances of James Brydges, First Duke of Chandos*. Oxford University Press, 1949.
Ilse Barea: *Vienna, Legend and Reality*. Secker and Warburg, London, 1966.
Dénes Bartha and László Somfai: *Haydn als Opern Kapellmeister*. Verlag der Ungarischen Akademie der Wissenschaft, Budapest, 1960.
Richard Baum and Wolfgang Rehm (ed.) *Musik und Verlag*. Bärenreiter, Kassel, 1968.
C. Cannon Beekman: *Johann Mattheson, Spectator in Music*. Yale University Press, 1947.
Hector Berlioz: *Memoirs*, translated and edited by David Cairns, Gollancz, London, 1969.
The Conductor. Supplement to *Traité de l' Instrumentation*, 1848. English translation by John Broadhouse. Reeves, London, 1917.
Heinrich Bihrle: *Die Musikalische Akademie München, 1811–1911*. Munich, 1911.
Wolfgang Boetticher: *Orlando di Lassos und seine Zeit*. Bärenreiter, 1958.
Aus Orlando di Lassos Wirkungskreis. Bärenreiter, 1963.
Werner Bollert: *Sing-Akademie zu Berlin*. Rembrandt Verlag, Berlin, 1966.
Noel Boston: *The Musical History of Norwich Cathedral*. Friends of Norwich Cathedral 1963.
Morrison Comegys Boyd: *Elizabethan Music and Music Criticism*. University of Pennsylvania Press, 1946.
Nanie Bridgman: *La Vie Musicale au Quattrocento*. Gallimard, Paris, 1964.
Manfred Bukofzer: *Studies in Medieval and Renaissance Music*. Norton, New York, 1950.
Music in the Baroque Era. J. M. Dent, London, 1948.
Charles Burney: *The Present State of Music in France and Italy*. London, 1771. Edited by Percy A. Scholes, Oxford University Press, London, 1959.
The Present State of Music in Germany, the Netherlands and the United Provinces, London, 1775. Edited by Percy A. Scholes, Oxford University Press, 1959.
A General History of Music (four volumes, London, 1776, 1782, 1789). Dover, New York, 1957.
Norman Carroll: *Bach the Borrower*. Allen and Unwin, London, 1967.
Adam Carse: *The Orchestra in the Eighteenth Century*. Heffer, Cambridge, 1950.
George Chandler: *Liverpool*. Batsford, London, 1957.
Liverpool under James I. Brown, Picton and Hornby Libraries, Liverpool, 1960.
A.-E. Cherbuliez: *Die Schweiz in der Deutschen Musikgeschichte*. Verlag von Huber, Fraunfeld und Leipzig, 1932.
Pierre Citron: *Couperin*. Editions du Seuil, 1956.
H. A. F. Crewdson: *The Worshipful Company of Musicians*. Constable, London, 1950.
A. Dandelot: *La Société des Concerts du Conservatoire, 1828–1923*. Paris, 1923.
Christopher Dearnley: *English Church Music 1650–1750*. Barrie and Jenkins, London 1970.
Norman Demuth: *French Opera*. Artemis Press, Sussex, 1963.
An Anthology of Musical Criticism. Eyre and Spottiswoode, London, 1947.
E. J. Dent: *Opera*. Pelican Books, Harmondsworth, 1940.
The Foundations of English Opera. Cambridge University Press, 1928. Second edition, Da Capo Press, New York, 1965.
Mozarts' Operas, A critical study. Oxford University Press, London, 1913.
Otto Erich Deutsch: *Handel: A Documentary Biography*. A. and G. Black, London, 1955.
Mozart: A Documentary Biography. English translation by Eric Blom, Peter Branscombe and Jeremy Noble. Adam and Charles Black, London, 1965.

Karl Ditters von Dittersdorf: *Autobiography*. Translated by A. D. Coleridge. Bentley, London, 1896.
Frederick Dorian: *The History of Music in Performance*. Norton, New York, 1942.
Alfred Einstein: *Mozart: His Character, His Work*. Translated by Arthur Mendel and Nathan Broder. Cassell, London, 1956.
Robert Elkin: *The Old Concert Rooms of London*. Edward Arnold, London, 1955.
F. G. Emmison: *Tudor Food and Pastimes*. Benn, London, 1964.
Christiane Engelbrecht: *Die Kasseler Hofkapelle im 17. Jahrhundert*. Bärenreiter, Kassel, 1958.
David Ewen (ed.): *Romain Rolland on Music*. Dover, New York, 1959.
Günther Fleischauer and Günther Lange: *Georg Philipp Telemann; Leben und Werke*. Beiträge der gleichnamigen Ausstellung im Kunsthistorischen Museum, Magdeburg, 1967.
Foakes and Rickert: *Philip Henslowe's Diary*. Cambridge University Press, 1961.
Hans Gal: *The Composer's World*. Thames and Hudson, London, 1965.
William Gamble: *Music Engraving and Printing*. Pitman, London, 1923.
Karl Geiringer: *The Bach Family*. George Allen and Unwin, London, 1954.
Haydn; a Creative Life in Music. George Allen and Unwin, 1947.
Josef Gmelch: *Musikgeschichte Eichstätts*. Eichstätt, 1914.
Max Graf: *Composer and Critic*. Chapman, London, 1947.
Donald J. Grout: *A Short History of Opera*. Oxford University Press, 1947.
A History of Western Music. J. M. Dent, London, 1962.
Grove: *Dictionary of Music and Musicians*. Fifth edition, edited by Eric Blom, Macmillan, London, 1954.
Heinrich Habel: *Das Odeon in München, und die Frühzeit des öffentlichen Konzertsaalbaus*. Walter de Gruyter, Berlin, 1967.
John Harley: *Music in Purcell's London*. Dennis Dobson, London, 1968.
Alec Harman, Antony Milner and Wilfred Mellers: *Man and his Music* (4 volumes). Rockliff, London, 1958. One-volume edition, Barrie and Rockliff, London, 1962.
Frank Lloyd Harrison: *Music in Medieval Britain*. Routledge, London, 1968.
Phyllis Hartnoll (ed.): *Shakespeare in Music*. Macmillan, London, 1964.
John Hawkins: *A General History of Music*. London, 1776: Dover, New York, 1963.
Friedrich Heer: *The Medieval World*. Translated by Janet Sonderheim. Weidenfeld and Nicolson, London, 1962.
Ernest Eugene Helm: *Music at the Court of Frederick the Great*. Oklahoma University Press, 1960.
Fritz Henneberg: *The Leipzig Gewandhaus Orchestra*. Dennis Dobson, London, 1966.
J. Hennings: *Musikgeschichte Lübecks; Weltliche Musik*. Bärenreiter, Kassel, 1951.
Angus Heriot: *The Castrati in Opera*. Secker and Warburg, London, 1956.
Hajo Holborn: *A History of Modern Germany, 1648 to 1840*. Eyre and Spottiswoode, London, 1965.
A. K. Holland: *Henry Purcell*. Penguin Books, Harmondsworth, 1948.
Mátyás Horányi: *The Magnificence of Eszterháza*. Barrie and Rockliff, London, 1962.
Arthur Hutchings: *The Baroque Concerto*. Faber and Faber, London, 1961.
Georg Kärstadt: *Die Extraordinarien Abendmusiken Dietrich Buxtehudes*. Verlag Max Schmidt-Römhild, Lübeck, 1962.
Sylvia W. Kenney: *Walter Frye and the Contenance Anglois*. Yale University Press, 1964.
Joseph Kerman: *Opera as Drama*. Oxford University Press, London, 1956.
A. Hyatt King: *400 Years of Music Printing*. British Museum, 1964.
Karl Kobald: *Altwiener Musikstätten*. Amalthea Verlag, Vienna, 1911.
Bernhard Krick: *St. Thomas zu Leipzig; Schule und Chor*. Breitkopf and Härtel, Wiesbaden, 1963.
Henry Cart de Lafontaine: *The King's Music*. Novello, London, 1909.
H. C. Robbins Landon: *The Symphonies of Joseph Haydn*. Rockliff and Universal Edition, London, 1955.
Essays on the Viennese Classical Style. Barrie and Rockliff The Cresset Press, London, 1970.
Beethoven. Thames and Hudson, London, 1970
H. C. Robbins Landon and Donald Mitchell (eds.): *The Mozart Companion*. Rockliff, London, 1956
Paul Henry Lang: *Music in Western Civilisation*. J. M. Dent, London, 1942.
George Frederick Handel. Faber and Faber, London, 1967.
Jan la Rue (ed.): *Aspects of Medieval and Renaissance Music*; a Birthday offering to Gustave Reese. Norton, New York, 1966.
Peter le Huray: *Music and the Reformation in England, 1549–1660*. Herbert Jenkins, London, 1967.
Hugo Leichtentritt: *Music, History and Ideas*. Harvard University Press, 1938.

360   Bibliography

Rene Bernard Lennerts: *The Art of the Netherlanders*. Arno Volk Verlag, Cologne, 1964.
Alfred Loewenberg: *Annals of Opera, 1597–1940*. Heffer, Cambridge, 1943.
Eric Mackerness: *A Social History of English Music*. Routledge and Kegan Paul, London, 1964.
Manchester: *Court Leet Records of the City of Manchester*.
J. S. Manifold: *The Music in English Drama*. Rockliff, London, 1956.
James E. Matthew: *A Manual of Musical History*: Grevel, London, 1892.
Wilfrid Mellers: *Music and Society*. Dobson, Second edition 1950.
Dominikus Mettenleitner: *Musikgeschichte der Oberpfalz*. Amberg, 1867.
    Musikgeschichte der Stadt Regensburg. Regensburg, 1866.
Ernest H. Meyer: *English Chamber Music*. Lawrence and Wishart, London, 1946.
Gotbert Moro and Ambros Wilhelmer: *Zur Musikgeschichte Kärntens*. Klagenfurt, 1956.
H. J. Moser: *Geschichte der Deutschen Musik*. Breitkopf and Härtel, Wiesbaden, Sixth Edition, 1964.
    Die Evangelische Kirchenmusik in Deutschland. Verlag Carl Meresburger, Berlin, 1954.
H. J. Moser and Carl Pfatteicher: *Heinrich Schütz*. Concordia Press, St. Louis, 1959.
Hedwig and E. H. Mueller von Asow: *Collected Correspondence and Papers of Christoph Willibald Gluck*. Translated by Stewart Thomson. Barrie and Rockliff, London, 1962.
Paul Nettl: *Luther and Music*. Muhlenberg Press, Philadelphia, 1948.
Elisabeth Noack: *Musikgeschichte Darmstadts vom Mittelalter bis zur Goethezeit*. Schott, Mainz, 1967.
Grace O'Brien: *The Golden Age of Italian Music*. Jarrolds, 1948.
Alfons Ott: *Tausend Jahre Musikleben*. Prestel Verlag, Munich, 1963.
Reinhard G. Pauly: *Music in the Classic Period*: Prentice-Hall, New York, 1965.
Eberhard Preussner: *Die Bürgerliche Musikkultur*. Bärenreiter, Kassel, 1950.
    Die Musikalischen Reisen des Herrn von Uffenbach. Bärenreiter, Kassel, 1949.
Richard Petzoldt: *The Leipzig Thomaner Chor*: Dennis Dobson, London, 1966.
Gustave Reese: *Music in the Middle Ages*. J. M. Dent, London, 1940.
    Music in the Renaissance. J. M. Dent, London, 1964.
H. F. Redlich: *Claudio Monteverdi, His Life and Works*. Translated by Kathleen Dale, Oxford University Press, 1952.
Alec Robertson and Denis Stevens: *The Pelican History of Music*. Pelican Books, Harmondsworth. Volume 1, 1960; Volume 2, 1963.
Michael F. Robinson: *Opera Before Mozart*. Hutchinson University Library, London, 1966.
Roland-Manuel: *Histoire de la Musique*. Encyclopédie de la Pleiade, Paris. Volume 1, 1960; Volume 2, 1963.
Fr. M. Rudhart: *Geschichte der Oper am Hofe zu München*. Daltwer, Freising, 1865.
Stanley Sadie: *Concert Life in Eighteenth-Century England*. Proceedings of the Royal Musical Association, 1958/59.
Arnold Schering: *Geschichte des Instrumental Konzert*. Breitkopf and Härtel, Leipzig, 1905.
    Studien zur Musikgeschichte der frühen Renaissance. Breitkopf and Härtel, Leipzig, 1914.
    Musikgeschichte Leipzigs. Leipzig, 1941.
Ernst Fritz Schmidt: *Musik am Hofe der Fürsten von Löwenstein-Wertheim-Rosenberg*. Freunde Mainfrankischer Kunst und Geschichte, E.V., Würzburg, 1953.
Friedrich Schmidt: *Das Musikleben der Bürgerlichen Gesellschaft Leipzigs*. Musikalisches Magazin, Langensala, 1912.
Percy A. Scholes: *The Puritans and Music in England and New England*. Russell and Russell, New York, 1962. Oxford University Press, 1934.
Willi Schuh (ed.): *Schweizer Musikbuch*. Atlantis Verlag, Zurich, 1939.
Ulrich Schwetzke: *Hundert Jahre Bergkonzerte*. Halle, 1910.
Karl Senn: *Der Innsbrucker Musikverein*. Innsbruck, 1918.
Heinrich Sievers: *Die Musik in Hannover*. Sponholtz Druckerei und Verlaganstalt, Hannover, 1961.
Joan Simon: *Education and Society in Tudor England*. Cambridge University Press, 1966.
William C. Smith: *Concerning Handel*. Cassell, London, 1948.
Philipp Spitta: *Johann Sebastian Bach*. Translated by Clara Bell and J. A. Fuller-Maitland. Dover, New York, 1951.
Ludwig Spohr: *Autobiography*. Kassel, 1860; English translation, Reeves and Turner, London, 1878.
W. Stahl: *Musikgeschichte Lübecks: Geistliche Musik*. Bärenreiter, Kassel, 1952.
Vladimir Stepanek, Bohumil Karasek and Ladislav Sip: *Geschichte der Tschechischen und Slowakischen Musik*. Orbis. Prague, 1964.
Denis Stevens: *Tudor Church Music*. Faber and Faber, London, 1961.

Robert Stevenson: *Spanish Music in the Age of Columbus*. Martinus Nijhoff, The Hague, 1960.
Spanish Music in the Golden Age. University of California Press, 1961.
Oliver Strungk: *Source Readings in Musical History*. Norton, New York, 1950.
C. S. Terry: *Johann Sebastian Bach*: Oxford University Press, 1958.
Bach's Orchestra: Oxford University Press, 1958.
Johann Christian Bach (second edition edited by H. C. Robbins Landon), Oxford University Press, 1967.
Alexander Wheelock Thayer: *The Life of Ludwig van Beethoven*. Edited by H. E. Krehbiel, New York, 1921–25. New edition, Introduction by Alan Pryce Jones, Centaur Press, New York, 1960.
Ernst Tittel: *Oesterreichische Kirchenmusik*. Verlag Herder, Vienna, 1961.
Ernst Valentin: *Georg Philipp Telemann*. Bärenreiter, Kassel, 1952.
Richard Wagner: *On Conducting*. Munich, 1969. English translation by Edward. Dannreuther. Reeves, London, 1969.
Horst Walther: *Musikgeschichte der Stadt Lüneburg*. Hans Schneider, Tutzing, 1967.
Ernest Walker: *A History of Music in England*: Oxford University Press, 1907. Third edition, edited by J. A. Westrup, 1952.
George F. Warner: *Manuscripts and Muniments of Dulwich College*. Longman Green, London, 1881.
John Warrack; *Weber*. Hamish Hamilton, London, 1968.
Carl Maria von Weber: *Sämtliche Schriften*. edited by Theodor Hell. Berlin, 1908.
Hildegard Weber (ed.): *Das Museum: Einhundert fünfzig Jahre Frankfurter Konzertleben*, Kramer, Franfurt am Main, 1958.
Max Weber: *Rational and Social Foundations of Music*. South Illinois University Press, 1958.
C. V. Wedgwood: *The Thirty Years' War*. Cape, London, 1947.
Ludwig Wegele: *Musik in der Reichsstadt Augsburg*. Die Brigg, Augsburg, 1965.
Elwyn A. Weinandt: *The Choral Music of the Church*. Free Press, New York, 1965.
J. A. Westrup: *An Introduction to Musical History*. Hutchinson's University Library, London, 1955.
Thomas Whythorne: *Autobiography*. Edited by James M. Osborn. Oxford University Press, 1961.
John Wilson (ed.): *Roger North on Music*. Novello, London, 1959.
C. von Winterfeld: *Johannes Gabrieli und sein Zeitalter*. Berlin, 1834.
Walter L. Woodfill: *Musicians in English Society*. Princeton University Press, 1953.
Simon Townley-Worsthorne: *Venetian Opera in the Seventeenth Century*. Oxford University Press, 1954.
Alan Yorke-Long: *Music at Court*. Weidenfeld and Nicolson, London, 1954.
Percy M. Young: *Handel*. The Master Musicians, J. M. Dent, London, 1947.
The Concert Tradition. Routledge and Kegan Paul, London, 1965.
Franklin B. Zimmerman: *Henry Purcell, 1659–1695; His Life and Times*. Macmillan, London, 1967.

Index

MUSIC AND SOCIETY
SINCE 1815

Music and Society
Since 1815

HENRY RAYNOR

This edition first published in 1978 by
TAPLINGER PUBLISHING CO., INC.
New York, New York

Published by arrangement with Schocken Books, Inc.,
200 Madison Avenue, New York, N.Y. 10016

Library of Congress Catalog Number: 78-58318
ISBN 0-8008-7238-X

Contents

Introduction and Acknowledgements

Revolution at the end of the eighteenth century and reaction after 1815, with the consequent upheavals in European society and politics, left the musician and especially the composer without a recognised place in society or an understood social function; it seemed only too easy for the world to continue without him. Left without an audience, he had to challenge the 'great masters' for the attention of the public, and in doing so he had to write 'great' music, on a bigger scale than the masters themselves. The public was to be met, and if possible subjugated, in huge opera houses and large concert halls if the composer was to earn his living, so that orchestras and choruses had to grow if they were to be sufficiently imposing in auditoria built to hold thousands.

At the same time, both musical developments and social conditions created a specialised 'light music', taking away the 'serious' composer's traditional function as an entertainer and widening the gulf between him and his audience, compelling him to concentrate on huge sensations and often painful extremes of emotion. As European religion declined and composers dwelt almost exclusively on the tremendous and the intense, the 'serious' composer, like Berlioz and Wagner, began to find in art, and especially in music, the only safe repository of spiritual values.

The composer, dispossessed by social and political conditions of his natural audience, became conscious of the imperfections of the society by which he was surrounded and to which he wished entirely to belong; his cure for social imperfections could only be through music. The salvation of the nation, the brotherhood of man, the power of nature, the sanctity of art: these became the themes for the nineteenth-century composer. Therefore he was, in a sense that his predecessors had never been, concerned with politics; he became aware of, and sought to exploit and develop, national musical characteristics. He found, often enough, a definite political role to play.

These are the trains of thought which this book attempts to follow into the twentieth century as it considers the social and political pressures under which the composer functioned until the patterns of European society and culture were broken into fragments by two world wars, revolution, the continuous dehumanisation of life in an age of industrial mass production, advertising and mass communications.

The development of music in these conditions poses questions which tempt the historian to moralise; not even Gibbon could totally resist the temptation, while Macaulay, like Spengler and many others, accepted it gratefully. In so far as a wish to preserve inherited standards of excellence in music, in historical enquiry, in society and in its politics (matters in all of which inherited standards are anything but static or reactionary) tend to promote moralising, the author apologises in advance if he has unthinkingly yielded to a natural temptation and drawn too many morals.

I am deeply grateful to a multitude of friends who, in discussion or general conversation, or in correspondence, often without knowing that they were doing so, have guided my hand and suggested answers to problems while stimulating my attempt to probe the relationship between music and the world it inhabits, reflects, expresses and interprets.

I am specially grateful to Stainton de B. Taylor for putting at my disposal his researches into the musical history of nineteenth-century Liverpool.

To Martin Roth, Esq., for finding me a way through the quagmires and thickets of nineteenth-century European currencies:

To A. C. Stock, Esq., who has taken care that my translations from French shall be plausible:

To David Cairns, Esq., to Messrs Victor Gollancz, Ltd, for permission to quote from Mr Cairns's translation of the *Memoirs of Berlioz*:

To Messrs John Calder for permission to quote from *The American Symphony Orchestra*, by John H. Mueller:

To John G. Pattisson, Esq., of Messrs Barrie and Jenkins, for unfailing patience and encouragement:

And, as always, to Ellie, who has reduced German translations to accuracy, reprimanded verbosities and demanded the rationalisation of occasional stray pronouns.

HENRY RAYNOR

Reigate, Surrey: June, 1975

I

The Decline of Court Patronage

The Europe of the Old Regime, of the sometimes benevolent despotism and of the classic ideal, began its protracted dissolution with the outbreak of the French Revolution in 1789. As the old world dissolved, the system of musical patronage which had persisted since the renaissance dissolved with it, for though the Congress of Vienna set out in 1814 to revitalise the corpse of pre-revolutionary Europe, it could not restore the aristocratic wealth on which not only the social and political life of the eighteenth century had depended but which had also made possible its artistic achievements. In 1803 Beethoven's patron and friend Prince Lobkowitz had supported the orchestra which gave the first performance of Beethoven's *Eroica* Symphony; after 1812 Prince Lobkowitz was apparently satisfied to be an active member of the newly formed Vienna *Gesellschaft für Musikfreunde*.

As the huge aristocratic fortunes evaporated, a savage inflation and post-war depression after 1815 made the support of a paying audience essential to the satisfactory performance of opera and of large-scale orchestral music. Beethoven had developed the habit of addressing his symphonies and concertos to the general public; his successors followed him in this because his example set the fashion for larger and larger orchestras essential to satisfactory performances in auditoria large enough to permit the general public to hear a composer's message. The general public had to be invited because the special public to whom the court musician had addressed his communications assembled less and less frequently in princely salons and music rooms. Music and musicians turned to the general public for support because the traditional patrons were no longer able to play their traditional role in music with anything like their old lavishness. Patrons who before the revolution had created musical organisations to serve their individual taste found that they needed to make room for paying audiences to augment the subsidies they were able to grant to their orchestras and opera houses. Such subsidies, which in the past had come from the personal income of a royal or noble patron, began to come to music directly from taxation or indirectly from civil list payments to a ruler; orchestras and opera companies began to become, in fact if not in name, state or national musical organisations.

At the same time, the number of such musical organisations decreased during the Revolutionary and Napoleonic Wars and though the work of the

Congress of Vienna itself, which accepted its inability to put every clock everywhere back to 1788; it accepted, for example, the secularisation of ecclesiastical states and prince-bishoprics, the destruction of the Imperial Free Cities and the absorption of a number of smaller states by their larger neighbours; a hundred and twenty-one of the minor German states lost their old independence, and with it their traditional musical establishments.

Eichstätt, a tiny Prince-Bishopric between Nuremberg and Munich, can serve as an example. The city's musical history dates unsensationally back at least to 1293. The Eichstätt *Kapellmeisters* seemed to have maintained an unbroken tradition of complete mediocrity and the *Kapelle* they directed was never large or important; by the 1750s it had seventy-three singers, including those of the cathedral choir, and sixteen instrumentalists. These musicians were responsible for the cathedral services as well as for the Prince-Bishop's court concerts, *Singspiele* and what Joseph Gmelch, the Jesuit historian of music in Eichstätt, calls 'little Italian operas'. In 1799 the members of the *Kapelle* were chiefly responsible for the organisation of a concert society which met every week in the Black Bear Inn; the society had the collaboration of the city's *Stadtpfeifer* band and of local amateur musicians. Travelling virtuosi passing through Eichstätt and presumably hoping for an invitation to play before the Prince-Bishop, took part in its concerts. The city's geographical position suggests that such visitors may well have been both numerous and eminent, but Gmelch's history mentions none of them by name.[1]

With secularisation, in 1802, the city lost virtually all of its professional musicians except its *Stadtpfeiferei* and those directly attached to the cathedral; though some may have stayed in Eichstätt to earn their living as music teachers, some fifty lost their court employment. The local amateurs and the *Stadtpfeifer* kept the concert society going under the direction of the cathedral *Kapellmeister*. Events at Salzburg, where Leopold Mozart and Michael Haydn, as well as the rebellious younger Mozart, had been employed; at Bonn, where the Archbishop Elector had a claim on the services of Beethoven until he was driven from his capital by the French; at Groswardein, where Dittersdorf had been *Kapellmeister*; at Breslau where both Dittersdorf and Michael Haydn had served, and at Würzburg, a city with a musical history as unexciting as Eichstätt's, paralleled the musical history chronicled by Gmelch.

None of these cities had any influence upon the music of their age, for Mozart and Beethoven were the only composers of decisive influence to have worked in an ecclesiastical state, and of all the ecclesiastical states only Bonn could afford to finance music as lavishly as the royal courts, with a busy opera house and opera company. The disappearance of the ecclesiastic states and of numerous minor dukedoms, principalities and kingdoms

[1] Joseph Gmelch: *Musikgeschichte Eichstätts*. Eichstätt, 1912.

reduced the number of court establishments requiring professional musicians, but quite possibly made available the number of performers needed to organise music in the larger towns on the post-revolutionary, post-Beethoven scale. The extra demands made by Beethoven and his successors may well have absorbed many of the players whose occupation in the minor states had gone. It is impossible to estimate the hardships imposed on professional musicians by the political events of the post-revolutionary settlement. At the same time, however, the demands of amateurs, especially those of the rapidly rising bourgeoisie, for musical instruction offered considerable opportunities for employment to those who could earn their living as teachers. What has been called the 'democratisation' of music thus provided some alternative outlets for the abilities of musicians thrown out of employment by political readjustment.

The major states, which naturally retained their musical establishments, were forced to accept change. The concert remained a minor consideration in those cities, notably the political capitals, where opera was the traditional centre of musical life, as it was in every Italian city which could support a company even of the lowest standard. But even such institutions as the Imperial and Royal Opera, in Vienna, found themselves forced to depend upon supplies of money from which their box offices to augment the subsidies poured into them by the ruler or by the state. The Court Theatre in Munich, for example, was burned down in 1818 and reopened two years later under the new and significant title *Hof und National Theater*: it too had passed from the sole control of a monarch and become a theatre which, in spite of a heavy subsidy, needed to earn a considerable income from the sale of seats; whilst an Intendant appointed by the King from among his courtiers was its supreme authority. His control of the theatre did not cover its repertoire or any of its musical activities, and he interfered in its management only when it ran into difficulties.

The Dresden Court Opera became a public institution in 1814; Saxony's alliance with Napoleon I brought the Saxon Royal House, and the Opera House which had been its pride, close to dissolution as French power crumbled. But Prince Repnin, the Russian Governor of Saxony appointed by the victors, prevented the disbandment of the orchestra and opera company by placing them under public control. When the monarchy returned, under the Peace Treaty of 1817 and the coronation of Carl Friedrich I, the theatre again became the Court Opera, but its traditional title did not prevent its dependence upon paying audiences; the appointment of Weber two years later as *Kapellmeister* of a newly established German Opera to run in conjunction with the traditional Italian Opera under its *Kapellmeister*, Francesco Morlacchi, was a political and financial move designed to add to the popularity of a royal house suspected of lack of patriotism; at the same time, it sought to develop and exploit a new audience whose patronage would contribute to the heavy expenses of the theatre. German opera owed a great deal to Carl Friedrich's use of its popular appeal as a means of winning public support; the German audience's enjoyment of opera in its own language, too, eventually came to mean a growth of support for opera in general, sung as a matter of course in German translation.

The post-war settlement, therefore, opened a new era for composers; they no longer looked for a *Kapellmeister*'s post which would bring them in touch with an audience. It became their duty to serve but demanded that they found an audience from among the general, concert- and opera-going public. But at the same time it demanded a return to pre-revolutionary styles of government. Throughout central Europe and the Austrian dominions in Italy, and in the southern Italian Kingdom of the Two Sicilies, the aim of the authorities was to preserve and consolidate their restored power, ruling on eighteenth-century lines through nineteenth-century instruments of coercion. Anything that questioned official established policy was to be suppressed as prejudicial to religion, morality or good order. The composer's appeal to the public was not allowed to step outside narrowly drawn limits of what was politically and socially acceptable to an old regime conscious of the fundamental dangers of its position.

Austria, which in the eighteenth century had been the centre of progressive music largely because of the Imperial family's musical enthusiasm and the frequent presence at court of a nobility which accepted opera, concert and chamber music as social necessities no less important than dance music, became the centre from which reaction spread. Joseph II, who died in 1790, had been among the most liberal of benevolent despots. The revolution in France and its aftermath had withdrawn the liberalism which he had encouraged, and Francis I, who became Emperor in 1792, had been persuaded both by events and by his political advisers to suppress whatever in the circumstances of the day could be regarded as politically dangerous. In 1810 his Chief of Police, Baron von Hagen, had taught him that too rigid a suppression was itself politically dangerous because it closed safety valves, so that the Emperor had instructed his censors not to forbid works by scholars, even when they contained new discoveries, unless those discoveries were likely to have an adverse effect on religion or morals, or to encourage subversion. But the relatively liberal von Hagen was succeeded in 1815 by Count Sedlnitzky (the bogeyman of the revolutionaries in 1848), whose harsher repression grew from an utter fear of anything new as likely to lead to political or religious dissent or even to encourage criticism.

Repression, therefore, was already powerful in Austria when, in 1819, the conservative dramatist Kozebue was assassinated by a liberal student. As the universities were the centres of political unrest, Kozebue's murder led to concerted action among the German states led by the Austrian Chancellor, Count Metternich, whose policy dominated Europe between

Napoleon's overthrow and the revolutions of 1848. With King Frederick William of Prussia, Metternich evolved a policy of added repression for the entire German-speaking world and Austria's Italian possessions. Their Carlsbad Decrees, of 1820, extended the censorship to pamphlets, magazines and newspapers, previously exempt, and proposed a Pan-German Commission to enquire into conditions in the universities in order to prevent revolutionary teaching and activity within them. Metternich wished the commission to be empowered to withdraw suspected revolutionaries from their own states for trial, but Frederick William sensibly believed that a supra-national authority would create more problems than it could solve among German rulers jealous for their independence, while at the same time it would foment the disorders it was intended to stifle. Metternich, of course, disavowed any wish to interfere in the content of university education but only to preserve the discipline of students and their teachers; but in place of the Pan-Germanic Commission he proposed, each state appointed a special official to control political activity in its universities. Naturally, purely arbitrary lines were drawn between the legitimate teaching of philosophy, politics and history and what was officially regarded as their corruption into seditious criticism of existing practice. Similar lines were drawn between valid artistic expression and the apparent encouragement of disorder.

The result was that until after 1848 the intellectual life of Central Europe became almost dormant. Political and social circumstances encouraged the exploitation of national myth and legend in works like *Der Freischütz* and the German romantic opera represented by such works as E. T. A. Hoffmann's *Undine*. As it became impossible to compose the successors to such socially orientated operas as *Le Nozze di Figaro* and *Fidelio*, which reflected too precisely and with too cutting an implied criticism of existing political conditions, music, as a serious study, tended to concentrate on the past. Mendelssohn and the choral society movement began the rediscovery of the choral works of J. S. Bach, and the result of political repression was not merely the extension of the repertoire into the forgotten world of baroque composition but also the writing of a number of crucial, monumental works of what came to be known as 'musicology'. Such critical biographies as Carl von Winterfeld's *Johannes Gabrieli und sein Zeitalter* (1834), Otto Jahn's *Wolfgang Amadeus Mozart* (published between 1856 and 1859) and Chrysander's *G. F. Handel* (the three volumes of which appeared between 1858 and 1867) combated the idea, tacitly encouraged by the repression, that the arts are simply ornamental appendages to 'real life' by carefully linking the artistic achievements of their subjects to the conditions and society of their day.

The repression set out also to create an unbridgeable chasm between the 'safe' educated classes and the rest. In 1821 an Austrian newspaper reported an address by Francis I to teachers at the Lyceum in Laibach:

> I do not need savants but good honest citizens. Your task is to teach
> young men to be this. He who serves me must teach what I order him.
> If anyone cannot do this, or comes with new ideas, he can go, or I will
> remove him.[2]

Consequently, both education and the censorship grew narrower and increasingly obscurantist, and until after 1848 the view of what could be treated as specialised learned writing, or as purely creative artistic work, became too restricted to permit the publication of, for example, a medical book which, purely in passing, referred unflatteringly to the state of the roads in Carinthia. A poem by Franz Grillparzer nearly brought his dismissal from the civil service and his play *König Ottakars Gluck und Ende*, in 1825, described the resistance of King Ottakar of Bohemia against Rudolph of Habsburg in a way which seemed to suggest that the Habsburg was simply an earlier Bonaparte; it reached the stage in Vienna only after its author had almost despaired of its success and his own future. Schiller's *Piccolimini*, which deals with events in the Thirty Years War, was forbidden, and his *William Tell* was produced in Vienna only after it had been ruthlessly cut in an apparent attempt to disguise the fact that its hero was a Swiss rebel against Austrian rule. 'Musicians are lucky,' wrote Grillparzer in one of Beethoven's Conversation Books, 'they don't have to bother about the censors. But if only the censors knew what the musicians are thinking as they compose.'

Mètternich's system not only utilised the Empire's large and efficient force of secret police; he himself set up a private force responsible to and reporting to him personally. In 1815 Beethoven was a disillusioned Francophile who had become a patriotic Austrian republican. He had risked arrest during the French occupation by his refusal to play to an audience of officers of the army of occupation; under the Metternichian regime he chose Schindler, a student revolutionary who had spent a year in prison for taking part in a political riot, as his secretary-confidant and his friends tried in vain to quieten the loud political complaints and criticisms he made in public places. Apparently Beethoven escaped arrest because he was a celebrated eccentric rather than a political opponent to be taken seriously. His Conversation Books made clear his eager interest in what officially passed as sedition: his enthusiasm for libertarian political theory and the enthusiasm for England which he based on a possibly exaggerated belief in the liberty of English political life. He talked proudly of the banned books which he owned and had read.

Between 1814 and 1819, when the repression at its height was joined by a disastrous post-war depression, Beethoven fell into a relative silence; he

[2] C. A. MacCartney: *The Habsburg Empire, 1790–1918*. London, 1968. p. 212.

ceased to compose any of the large public works on which his reputation was based and which had won him his great popularity. This silence is usually blamed upon ill-health, private unhappiness and the troubles brought upon him by his unfortunate nephew Carl. But it may well be that the dead weight of a detested political system had a great deal to do with his failure to complete large public works like the Mass in D, which he began in 1818 and could not finish for five years, and the Ninth Symphony, begun in 1817 but not completed until 1823. During these years of repression and poverty Beethoven's output consisted chiefly of a handful of songs and three piano sonatas—*Opp.* 90, 101 and 106; even the mighty *Hammerklavier* in B flat (the use of the German equivalent to 'pianoforte' in the titles of *Opp.* 101 and 106 seems significant in the intellectual and social climate of the immediate post-war years) is a private work, not addressed to the general audience which had greeted the meretricious *Wellingtons Sieg* with frenzy and had made the Seventh Symphony, composed in the hopeful days when Napoleon's power began to totter, into its favourite among his large-scale works.

After 1822, when the slow increase of prosperity slightly reduced the burden on the Austrian people, the large public works began again with the Mass and the Ninth Symphony. But even the text which Beethoven chose for the choral finale of the Ninth was dangerous in the age of Metternich and the political circumstances of Beethoven's day. Beethoven's vision of joy in a world where all men are brothers uses a poem which Schiller had originally intended to be an 'ode to Freedom' (*Freiheit*) but which the poet had tactfully changed to 'Joy' (*Freude*).

To attempt to analyse the effect of political repression on the music of composers who suffered it—Beethoven and Schubert were the most immediately affected—would be foolishly subjective. Beethoven was, in these difficult years, trying to solve the problems set by his guardianship of his nephew; he was, too, reaching a state of mind in which any decision outside those demanded by composition was becoming increasingly difficult to him. But his hatred of the political situation seems to have been a factor not only in his failure to continue the composition of public works but also in the sense of alienation from everyday concerns which bothered and baffled the friends who worked to arrange the performance of the Ninth Symphony.

Schubert was active in the Vienna of the same period, and most of Schubert's work was not addressed to the general public. Without a patron, unable to find a church post or to keep the only position in the Imperial Opera which was ever offered to him, Schubert seems to us to be an entirely unpolitical personality, but his death in 1828 removed the last major composer Austria had produced before the repression or was to produce until the rise of Bruckner. The city's musical prestige and its long tradition continued to ensure that Vienna would act as a magnet to composers from outside

Austria, but until after the revolution of 1848 Austrian composers, in the
words of Stendhal, turned away from serious considerations and devoted
themselves to the 'sweet sensuality' of light music, the operas of Rossini, the
development of the waltz and the exploitation of nostalgia. 'In Vienna,' wrote
Stendhal, 'sensual pleasures, less likely to trouble the Government, took possession of the people.'[3]

The post-war period was one in which amateur orchestras flourished and
amateur choral societies were founded, all, according to the authorities,
fraught with political dangers. The choral societies in particular seemed
to be not far from active sedition because choirs were run on democratic
lines, the members themselves electing directors and committees of management, working with an enthusiasm and success, which, the Austrian and
German authorities believed, could easily be applied to political ends; for
any efficient democracy, even in music, implied a criticism of autocracy.
Metternich himself said that he would have liked to prohibit choral
societies, but he left them in existence not as a useful safety-valve for the
public spirit of their members but because action against them would draw
attention to the dangers they represented. Nevertheless, throughout Austria
and Germany such organisations had to submit to careful police control.

Because repression was inescapable, even so unpolitical a musician as
Schubert was influenced by the situation. The strict control upon the lives
of students and the intelligentsia which followed the assassination of
Kozebue involved Schubert directly. His close friend and sometime school-
fellow Johann Senn (two of whose poems, *Selige Welt* and *Schwannenge-
sang*, Schubert made into *Lieder*) came under police suspicion because of
his regular meetings with a group of fellow intellectuals in a Vienna inn. In
1820 the police searched his lodgings, confiscated many of his papers and
arrested him, together with the friends, Schubert amongst them, who were
in his lodgings at the time. Senn was imprisoned for fourteen months but
the composer escaped with no injury but a black eye after a night in gaol.[4]
Schubert, a friend arrested and the censorship interfering in the libretti of
his operas *Die Verschworenen* and *Der Graf von Gleichstein*, did not live
outside the world's troubles. In 1824 he enclosed a poem of his own,
Complaint to the People, in a letter to his friend Franz von Schober; the
poem bemoans the inactive, insignificant life of 'the youth of the present
time'. 'Me too,' he writes, 'these times are fast to ruin bringing' while the
people creep about 'sick and decrepit', dismissing the ideals and actions of
youth as 'mere dreaming'.[5]

[3] Stendhal: *Letters on the celebrated composer Joseph Haydn*, by
'A. C. Bombet'. English translation, London, 1817. Letter 1.
[4] O. E. Deutsch: *Schubert, a Documentary Biography*. London, 1946.
pp. 128–9.
[5] *Ibid.* p. 375.

Metternich's intelligence system operated effectively outside German-speaking Europe, and as national feeling grew in Italy, the Austrian authorities gripped their subject provinces as relentlessly as they could. Berlioz, a student at the French Academy in Rome after his success in the Prix de Rome in 1831, wrote from Rome to Charles Duveyrier, professional librettist and editor of *Le Globe*. Duveyrier was a social reformer, a follower of Saint-Simon; that probably is why Berlioz's letter fell into the hands of Metternich's police: 'among schemes for the political reorganisation of society, I am convinced that the plan of Saint-Simon is the most effective and most thorough,' he wrote. '. . . I believe that there is nothing to prevent my uniting my voice and my efforts with those of others for the amelioration of the conditions of the largest and poorest class of people.'[6] The official response to this letter, probably found by a Metternichian agent as it made its way across the Austrian territories to an addressee known for his journalistic support of liberal policies, was a letter from Metternich to Count von Lutzow, the Imperial Minister in Rome, in which a copy of Berlioz's letter was enclosed:

> I take the liberty of sending you the enclosed letter, which came to me through a secret channel and must therefore be for your personal information only. My reason for sending this copy to you is that I should like to point out to Your Excellency the dangerous tendency towards fanaticism indulged in by its writer, a disciple of Saint-Simon and, apparently, a student at the French Academy in Rome. I am sure, my dear Count, that you will think it suitable to inform the Papal authorities of this young man's views and to warn students who are subjects of his [Austrian] Imperial Majesty resident in Rome of his dangerous influence, warning them against contact of any kind with this young man. Should M. Hector Berlioz, on his departure from Rome, visit the Imperial Embassy to ask for a visa into the Austrian states, Your Excellency will, of course, be obliged to refuse his request.
>
> Metternich.[7]

The July Revolution in France in 1831 had, naturally, stimulated the discontent of Italians against their Austrian overlords so that any French student would be an object of interest and suspicion to the Austrian authorities in Italy, but the modern reader cannot but admire a spy network which found its way so far down the political scale that it examined the correspondence of obscure music students.

Even in France itself it was possible to plunge accidentally into political hot water. In 1844 Berlioz and Isaac Strauss (whom Berlioz called 'the

[6] H. Berlioz: *Correspondance Générale*. Flammarion, Paris. Letter of 28 July 1831. p. 476.

[7] André Espials de la Maistre: *Hector Berlioz and Metternich*, in *Oesterreichische Musikzeitschrift*, 1953, *Heft* 12. Quoted in Georg Knepler: *Musikgeschichte 19 Jahrhunderts, Band* 1. p. 303.

Maestro of the fashionable balls') planned a three-day festival to salute the
end of the Exhibition of Industrial Products. The musical events would
take place in the Exhibition's vast Hall of Machines. The Minister of Trade
accepted Berlioz's proposal, but the Commissioner of Police refused his permission until the composer persuaded the Minister of the Interior to order
the police to sanction the festival. Berlioz recruited a huge choir and
orchestra and drilled his battalions to perfection in a series of rehearsals.
The final concert included music by Beethoven and a hotch-potch of
'modern' works, and a vast, frenziedly enthusiastic audience left Berlioz
with a net profit of 800 francs and an urgent summons to attend the office
of the Commissioner of Police. He had, he was told, 'secretly added to the
programme a piece of music calculated to arouse certain passions which the
government is endeavouring to suppress'.

The offending item was a chorus from Halévy's *Charles V*; it had
a crudely nationalistic text apparently condemning the policy of friendship
with England which Louis Philippe was sedulously fostering at the time,
and it won the loudest applause of the afternoon. Berlioz explained that
Halévy, nettled at being the one important French composer left out of the
programme, had persuaded his publishers to approach Berlioz and have the
omission remedied; Berlioz had chosen the offending chorus because it was
both effective for the huge number of performers and easy to prepare; although it had not been included in the preliminary announcement of the
concert which had been submitted to the police, it had not been 'secretly
added' to the programme because it had been advertised for a week on the
festival posters. 'Nevertheless,' wrote Berlioz, 'from that time a censorship
of programmes was established, and today you cannot sing a romance by
Berac or Mlle. Peyer in a public place without a licence from the Ministry
of the Interior countersigned by a Superintendent of Police.'[8]

The censorship did not directly affect the composer of instrumental
music except in so far as it imposed an atmosphere of intellectual sterility
on European life, and this naturally affected composers. It was, however,
the composer of operas who had to tread carefully; it is noticeable that
Weber and his German successors were little concerned with the political
and social realities which had been the basis of *The Marriage of Figaro*
and *Fidelio*. Weber's *Der Freischütz*, in 1821, is not far from being
the operatic equivalent to the 'Gothic' novel which had become popular in
Britain at the end of the eighteenth century set in a German society of folk
tales and folk superstitions; the same spirit animated, and the same substance gives a foundation to, such works as Marschner's *Der Vampyr*, of
1828, as well as the operas of E. T. A. Hoffmann. The other strand
of popular nineteenth-century opera with which the composer could deal in

[8] Hector Berlioz: *Memoirs*; translated and edited by David Cairns;
London, 1969. p. 365.

safety was the historical romance; Weber's *Euryanthe*, produced in Vienna
in 1823, was an early example of the vast number of operas set in a remote
and largely unreal past as well as in a strange country; these works choose
history as a starting point but have less interest in the interpretation of
historical reality than in the use of history as a source of sensational stories.

Historical romance was a manifestation of a new spirit in the arts which
stretched a considerable distance beyond music. It was in part a result of
Scott's novels and their remarkable vogue throughout Europe, but it grew
as well from the historical, or pseudo-historical, plays of Schiller, in which
history is subservient to dramatic effect and Schiller's enthusiasm for what
he felt ought to have happened. Rossini composed his *Elisabetta, Regina
d'Inghilterra*, in 1814, the year before Scott began his literary career with
Waverley and sixteen years before he handled the same situation as Rossini's
opera in *Kenilworth*. History allowed the censored composer to deal with
serious subjects in settings which would not disturb his political overlords.
In Italy, opera was the essentially popular form of theatre, and a scrupulous
attention to historical truth was no more essential to the composer of
romantic opera than it is to the creator of a cinematic historical epic.
Often enough, 'historical romance' in opera lies outside the boundaries of
'real' history, as it does in Bellini's *Norma*, a work which, although it deals
with the struggles of a subject people to gain their freedom, seems to have
annoyed none of the authorities who were adept in finding a contemporary
significance in any dramatisation of the careers of historical personages in a
genuinely historical setting. Actually, it is perhaps *I Puritani* which gives
the most truthful reflection of the romantic composer's attitude to history;
the events it describes did not happen, but history might have been more
enjoyable if they had done so, as though a strange romance about a cavalier's
engagement to a puritan girl, and the danger to their happiness of his
attempt to rescue a persecuted queen from her rebellious subjects, has more
dramatic vitality than the actual struggle of the English Civil War.

Donizetti and his librettists plundered European history for plots which,
romanticised out of reality, directed attention to things which, if they had
ever happened, would have happened a long time ago and preferably a long
way away. *Pietro il Grande, Anna Bolena, Lucrezia Borgia, Rosamunda
d'Inghilterra, Maria Stuarda, Belisario, Roberto Devereux* and about half a
dozen other Donizetti operas take plots not from a nation's history but from
the myths which spring up around the actual history of every nation; it is
clear that the composer who set *Emilia di Liverpool* in its heroine's hospice
for travellers in the mountains near Liverpool was not prepared to have his
romantic aspirations and emotions crushed by a too slavish observation of
mere physical reality; it was emotional reality which he looked for.

The attractions of England and English settings to the Italian composers
of romantic operas who had never visited the British Isles is a fascinating

aspect of the romantic outlook which it is hard to explain. The Tudor period in particular, with its melodrama, its richness of character and setting, its brutalities and splendours, was especially dear to them; it offered them not only the baffling figure of Elizabeth—a heretic but a glorious heretic, adored, feminine and unmarried—but her rivalry with her beautiful, catholic, persecuted cousin. It had, perhaps, a special relevance to an Italy aching for independence because it emphasised the national spirit and independence of England. It is hard not to think, too, of Italian composers and librettists fascinated by the huge and successful heresies of Henry VIII and his younger daughter while they were heartbroken at the tragedy of Mary Queen of Scots as they saw it through the distorting filter of Schiller's play. Schiller, after all, gave the world the essential unhistorical scene which the theatre demanded—the confrontation of Mary with Elizabeth.

Even more than in Italy, opera in Austria was a source of political danger. Revolutionary passions might too easily be inflamed by music linked to a dangerous story. Count Sedlnitzky's police kept dossiers on all the artists, writers and composers active in the Empire, noting their political allegiances and any record they had of activities which might imperil the Empire. The activities of the censors ran to almost hilarious extremes. Meyerbeer's *Les Huguenots*, historically one of the most important of operas, could not be seen and heard by the Austrian public because the strife between catholics and protestants in sixteenth-century France might direct their sympathies in the wrong direction, so that *Les Huguenots* could not be produced in Vienna until it had been fitted out with a new libretto and had become *The Ghibellines of Pisa*, in which thirteenth-century rebels were identified by their singing of Luther's hymn *Ein feste Burg ist unser Gott*. There was a period, after the battle of Solferino, when the word 'Rome' was forbidden on the Austrian stage, so that a production of *Tannhäuser* in 1859 sent its hero for absolution to the Pope simply '*dort*' (there), and the forbidden name was avoided.

Verdi, whose historical melodramas cannot be mistaken for historical fantasy and whose plots were often uncomfortably close to the realities of nineteenth-century, unliberated Italy, found that the Austrian censorship had strong teeth and a natural readiness to bite. Almost by accident, with the chorus of exiled Hebews in *Nabucco*, Verdi became the mouthpiece of Italian nationalism; the sufferings of his own country made possible the lament in the opera which won not only tears but the lasting devotion of Italian audiences. Verdi's choice of libretti, too, was not simply the need to find sensational plots in old, unhappy, far-off things and battles long ago. *La Battaglia di Legnano*, in 1848, sailed dangerously close to the wind by dealing with the defeat of the Emperor Barbarossa by the Lombard League in the twelfth century—a dangerous subject in the days of Italy's struggle for independence, and Verdi knew that the opera might be unacceptable to the authorities in its original form. He wrote to his librettist, Salvatore Cammarano: 'If the censor should not pass it, do you think that, with the title and locale *etc.* changed, all or most of the text could be retained?'[9] Even in Verdi's years of galley slavery—the period of ten years from 1842 in which he wrote at least an opera a year—a complete opera was too considerable an enterprise to be put at risk by a cavalier attitude to the prejudices of the censorship. *La Battaglia di Legnano* was produced in Rome in 1849, but then it disappeared from the stage to reappear as *L'Assedio di Haarlem*, an opera about the Dutch resistance to the Spanish occupation of Holland in the sixteenth century. Both composer and librettist were careful, in *Luisa Miller*, to avoid the dangers of a straight adaptation of Schiller's *Kabale und Liebe*; the danger of Schiller's critical attitude to life in a minor German court of the eighteenth century evaporated, however, when the courtiers and officials turned into the gentry and peasants of a Tyrolean village.

The censorship was moral and religious as well as political, so that *Stiffelio*, in 1850, had to be changed from the story of a priest whose moral character had some doubtful aspects to a story about a politician whose private life impeded his usefulness. It was *Rigoletto*, however, and *Un Ballo in Maschera* which caused most perturbation both to the composer and to the censors who had to deal with his work, simply because both operas reflected harshly upon monarchy and envisaged circumstances in which the assassination of king might be a laudable, heroic action. *Rigoletto* is a version of Victor Hugo's *Le Roi s'amuse*, and the censors condemned it for 'revolving immorality and obscene triviality'. These flaws in its character disappeared, however, when Victor Hugo's king was turned, on the advice of the censorship, into a mythical Duke of Mantua. *Un Ballo in Maschera* is an adaptation of Eugene Scribe's play *Gustavus III* and deals unequivocally, if with less than total historical accuracy, with the character of the Swedish king and the assassination plot against him. Not only did the libretto suggest that a king could be morally reprehensible; at the same time it sympathised with his murderers. Verdi refused to accept the censors' advice that the plot be transplanted to the middle ages or the early renaissance; such a period, he declared, would not suit his music, and a plan to transfer the action to sixteenth-century Pomerania still left the plot hinging upon the assassination plan; the presence in the *dramatis personae* of a fortune-teller treated not as a charlatan or as a figure of fun but as a character with real dramatic power and validity was, compared to this, a minor if dangerous feature of the work. Eventually, to save the opera's life, eighteenth-century Sweden became Massachusetts shortly before the War of American Independence and the morally unstable king was transformed into a mere Governor-

[9] Giuseppe Verdi: *Letters*; selected, edited and translated by Charles Osborne. London, 1971. p. 55.

General of the colony, a mythical Riccardo, Earl of Warwick.

If these Verdian problems suggest nothing to us more than the absurdity of a short-sighted, repressive political censorship, they at least show the frustrations to which a great dramatic composer was subject. But their effect went deeper: the only way in which a composer in the first half of the nineteenth century could establish himself financially and win a reputation was through opera. The censorship meant that he was either to risk a series of headlong collisions with the authorities or to accept that his work could never be more than a pleasant decoration of the surfaces of life and to work in a vacuum where political and social realities no longer applied and the relationships of his characters were falsified by their removal from social reality. The deliberate stultification of opera closed one of the doors to success to the composer, and its effect can be seen in the failure of the German opera houses between the death of Beethoven and the rise of Wagner to produce a single work not necessarily on their level but even on the lower level of Bellini and Donizetti.

Virtuosity was the only other direct road to success, a term which in this connection is synonymous with acceptance. A Liszt, a Paganini and a Mendelssohn (the latter a universally gifted young man with a considerable family fortune and no essential need to earn a living) could win acceptance through their superlative quality as instrumentalists. There was, of course, another and more indirect route to acceptance—that through criticism. The 'democratisation' of music, the opening up of both opera house and concert hall to the general public and popular taste, enhanced the importance of the critic who, like Berlioz, could write with wit and elegance as well as musical knowledge. Berlioz disliked writing criticism in spite of his superlative gifts as a writer. Schumann, probably the most gifted and lucid of writers on music in the Germany of his period, was probably the most powerful advocate the mid-European romantic composers ever found. The direct routes to success and acceptance, open in the eighteenth century to every fertile, hard-working composer, was effectively closed to all but the most obstinately gifted of his successors in the early nineteenth century.

2

The Romantic Composer

The political readjustments of the early nineteenth century and the declining fortunes of the aristocracy left the composer in search of a social function. This meant that he was left without an actual audience with whom to communicate. Published music increasingly provided the surviving court orchestras with works by composers who had already established their reputations so that orchestras had little need for a *Kapellmeister*, an all-round composer who could provide music whenever it was needed for church, opera house, Milord and Milady's private music-making and whatever concerts were to be given; they needed a conductor whose abilities as an executant and administrator were of more immediate consequence than his possession of interesting creative gifts. That being so, how was the composer whose secondary gifts as executant or conductor were less developed than his creative ability to find the audience which, by its approval of his work, gave him both his social function and the power to earn his living?

Spohr, born in 1784, and Weber, two years younger, adapted themselves to the new situation. Spohr undertook his first concert tour as a violinist when he was only fourteen, became leader of the Duke of Gotha's orchestra in 1803 (he had already been a member of the Duke of Brunswick's orchestra, suffering from an unmusical Duchess), and continued his career as a soloist during his periods of leave, incidentally gaining an impressive reputation as a conductor. From 1812 to 1815 he conducted the orchestra of the Theater an der Wien, and in 1817 took over the direction of the Frankfurt Opera. In 1822 he became Court *Kapellmeister* at Cassel, where he spent the rest of his life. The bulk of his compositions were in no way connected with his official duties: his violin concertos were the stock-in-trade of his concert tours; his symphonies were written for the German musical festivals or for organisations he conducted outside Cassel, three of them for the Philharmonic Society in London; his oratorios were commissioned by the German Festivals or for English organisations—*Calvary* for London and *Der Fall Babylon* for the Norwich Festival; the last six of his eleven operas were first produced in Cassel, but their composition was not demanded by his contract there. He was, officially, a conductor, who composed as and when it pleased him to do so.

Weber was a successful concert pianist in his teens; at the age of eighteen he became director of the orchestra at Breslau, an institution like the

Gewandhaus Orchestra in Leipzig, run by the wealthier citizens of the town;
but an eighteen-year-old conductor has little power to exert authority over
older and more experienced musicians. In 1807 he became secretary to the
brother of the King of Württemberg, a position which made it possible for
him to draw attention to his compositions and seemed likely to secure the
production of his opera *Silvana* (the third opera he had written but the first
to have any opportunity of being brought to the stage). Unfortunately Weber
fell foul of the autocratic, unmusical King Friedrich. His experience of a
luxurious court bleeding a poor country with limited resources and little
intellectual life caused, first, his arrest for insolence (he directed an old
woman looking for the Court washerwoman to the King's private room)
and then his exile after a financial muddle for which his father, not he, was
to blame. For a time he lived in Mannheim and then in Darmstadt as a freelance pianist and composer before undertaking another concert tour in 1811.
Two years later he settled down in Prague as director of the theatre
orchestra.

Weber was an efficient administrator and, born into a theatrical family,
one of those musicians gifted with a clear sense of what is effective on the
stage, not only in singing and acting but in design, décor and the minutiae
of production. In 1817 he accepted the post of *Kapellmeister* of the new
German Opera at Dresden, where his duties were to create a company and
direct its performances. Any additions he might make to its originally very
limited repertory were only incidental to his primary duties as a conductor-
administrator.

The speediest way to success was unusual ability as a soloist. Chopin, an
unusual personality of great charm, with an original style of composition
which demanded an unusual and magical style of performance, founded his
career on the success he won in Paris, where the revolution of 1830 took the
aristocracy out of the centre of musical patronage as it took them from the
centre of government; the bourgeoisie which replaced the old ruling class
was touchingly eager to believe what the intellectuals told it so long as it was
told nothing disturbing. Chopin, with the support of powerful critics and,
in Germany, of Schumann, the critical voice of rebellious youth, was able
to live comfortably, not as a frequent giver of concerts and recitals but on
the profits of his publications and on the proceeds of his lessons to the very
well-to-do. Liszt, handsome, phenomenally gifted, with a personality like
a firework display, dazzling everybody with whom he came into contact,
discovered, as Paganini had discovered before him, that the musical world
was his for the taking. Brahms was a redoubtable pianist who, by putting
his own works into his concert programmes, could convince publishers that
his music could become profitable and supplied them not only with piano
pieces but with songs, exploiting the growing amateur market.

The position of the composer who had no marked abilities as instrumentalist, conductor or administrator was far less profitable. Schubert's life was contemporary with the second half of Beethoven's, and it shows very clearly what the new situation meant to a composer of supreme genius who could not impose himself on the world as soloist or conductor. The situation was unprecedented: from any worldly point of view, no career was ever so unsuccessful as Schubert's, but to write of him as a neglected genius is hardly accurate. His songs and piano music were known to a rather influential circle of friends in the minor aristocracy and the upper bourgeoisie of Vienna. The well-known picture by his friend Moritz von Schwind includes not only the composer but a number of identifiable people who have gathered to listen to his music. They include not only Vogl, the leading bass of the Imperial Opera who introduced many of Schubert's songs to the Viennese public, but other well-known singers. A group of writers includes Grill-parzer and Mayrhofer; there are members of the official class and, present at least in spirit is Schubert's pupil Karoline von Esterhazy, whose portrait hangs on the wall. Von Schwind's picture, painted some years after Schubert's death, assembles the people who at one time or another attended his musical evenings and none of them seems to be a nonentity. It is, of course, significant that despite the eminence of some of those who attended such musical evenings that the events were '*Schubertiaden*', named after the composer and not after some eminent friend.

The essential fact was that the musical situation of the early nineteenth century provided no way in which Schubert could earn a living. He was indisputably the greatest Central European composer of the generation which followed Beethoven. His education, at the Cathedral Choir School and the Imperial Seminary, was superior to that which Haydn had received at the Choir School some three-quarters of a century before. He had become, it seems, a respectable pianist and violinist and a promising conductor, but he was never the type of virtuoso who could accumulate a fortune by tramping round the international celebrity circuit. As a boy he had composed songs and piano music, chamber works for his family and friends, and orchestral music for the school and other amateur orchestras; he had composed other orchestral works before he reached his First Symphony, in 1813, when he was sixteen, and seven operas before he was twenty. In 1816, the year of his Fourth and Fifth Symphonies and about a hundred songs (*Gretchen am Spinnrade, Der Erlkönig* and *Heidenröslein* had been composed a year earlier, in the excitement of his first discovery of Goethe's poetry), he left school and became a schoolmaster, though he soon fled from that uncongenial occupation. His salvation from that time onwards depended upon his either securing a church appointment or a success as a composer of operas, and from this date his church works and later operas were composed to stake his claim to any suitable vacancy. In 1818 the Kärntnerthor Theater management commissioned *Die Zwillingsbrüder*, which was kept unproduced for eighteen months by Joseph Weigl, whose *Schweizerfamilie* was so popular that his influence in the theatre, where he was *Kapellmeister*, was unassailable; Weigl had no intention of encouraging young men who might undermine his popularity. *Die Zwillingsbrüder* ran for six reasonably successful performances and earned its composer 500 florins, about £20 in the English money of the day.

Die Zwillingsbrüder seems to have convinced the opera management that Schubert could be useful. It commissioned an aria and a duet from him to be added to Hérold's *La Clochette* when it was produced in Vienna as *Das Zauberglöckchen* and then set him to work on the incidental music for *Rosamunde*, the play by Helmina von Chezy. A year later, in 1822, his opera *Alfonso und Estrella* was commissioned when its composition was almost complete, but in spite of the commission it was not produced. *Die Verschworenen* and *Fierrebras* were both composed in 1823. *Die Verschworenen*, a one-act work, ran into trouble with the censors because its title, 'The Conspirators' (apparently as much of the work as the censors read), suggested that it might have a dangerous political theme; actually, it is based on Aristophanes' *Lysistrata*. Rechristened *Das Häusliche Krieg* the censorship sanctioned its production, but it had not been commissioned and it remained unproduced. The librettist of *Fierrebras*, Josef Kupelweiser, was secretary to the Directors of the Kärntnerthor Theater and the work was announced in the press as a forthcoming attraction, but Kupelweiser left the theatre staff before the production was due, and the opera's hopes departed with him. In the last year of his life Schubert worked on the sketches of yet another opera, *Der Graf von Gleichen*, which he apparently abandoned because the censorship objected to its libretto.

Schubert's failure in the Opera House had nothing to do with the quality of his music. His *Lieder*, for example, are essentially and effectively dramatic in the sense that they paint a situation or create a character within a dramatic situation; the operas, apart from their wealth of music, are as stageworthy, to say the least, as anything by the successful composers whose works were seen in Schubert's Vienna; but within the Kärntnerthor Theater the power struggle, which became inevitable when opera ceased to depend upon the will of an all-powerful patron, was waged with the odds heavily against any newcomer who threatened to become a dangerous rival to established composers. Schubert had one champion within the company, Vogl, who was instrumental in securing for him the commission for *Die Zwillingsbrüder*; the delay in its production Schubert himself blamed on the machinations of the resident powers. 'In spite of Vogl,' he wrote, 'it is impossible to outwit such *canaille* as Weigl, Treitschke *etc.*'[1] Obviously the

[1] Letter of 19 May 1820 to Anselm Huttenbrenner. In Deutsch: *op. cit.* p. 117.

belated production established the composer's claim to consideration and led to his work on *Das Zauberglöckchen* and *Rosamunde*.

This measure of success, not unpromising for a young man in his early twenties, seems to have prompted his application in 1821 for a post as composer or conductor at the Opera. He was supported by impressive testimonials from a Court Secretary, Ignaz von Mosel, from the Court Music Intendant Count Moritz Dietrichstein, from the Court *Kapellmeister* Salieri and from Weigl, *Kapellmeister* of the Opera. Perhaps because Schubert, at twenty-four, had no professional experience of work in the theatre, his application brought him only the offer of work as a coach; this at least provided him with a foothold in the theatre on which an ambitious, practical, determined young man could have based a career, but the accounts of the Kärntnerthor Theater record only one payment to Schubert for undertaking duties as a coach; in April 1821 he was paid 50 florins (about £2) for coaching a young singer in the part of Dorabella in Mozart's *Cosi fan Tutte*. According to Leopold Sonnleitner, nephew of Joseph Sonnleitner, director of the Theater an der Wien, librettist of the original version of Beethoven's *Fidelio* and one of the founders of the *Gesellschaft der Musikfreunde*, Schubert was unable to observe rehearsal times, 'punctuality and the mechanical nature of the work were vexatious to him'. 'Schubert,' he wrote, 'was extremely fertile and industrious in composing. For anything else that goes by the name of work he had no inclination.'[2] It seems that Schubert's casual attitude to what he must have regarded as boring hack-work closed the door on any hopes of more valuable or creative work as a member of the theatre staff. According to Anton Schindler, Beethoven's friend, confidant and dogsbody, Schubert applied again, five years later, when he was twenty-six, for a conductorship at the Kärntnerthor Theater, and was asked to write a lengthy *scena*, with orchestral accompaniment, for the soprano Nanette Streicher and chorus. The music proved to be too difficult for the soloist, but in spite of entreaties Schubert refused to make any alterations and stormed from the theatre taking the score with him.

If twentieth-century readers regard such an action as a demonstration of unshakable artistic integrity, in 1826 it would have seemed to be no more than a rudely unprofessional tantrum and another reason for keeping Schubert out of any responsible post in the theatre. Schindler's account of the incident, however, was not published until 1857, and though many people who would have been involved in the actual event were still alive to read what Schindler wrote and not one challenged his veracity, no Schubert work of sufficient bulk to be the *scena* has survived, and Schindler is known to have been an unreliable biographer.

Though Schubert's dealings with the Opera were a series of disappoint-

2 Quoted in Maurice J. E. Brown: *Essays on Schubert*. London, 1966. pp. 130, 132.

ments, they were the most profitable of his ventures, though that says very little. He earned occasional fees as a pianist and accompanist at private and public concerts; between 1818 and 1824 about 1000 florins came to him from lessons, and the rest of his income was earned by his publications; Deutsch reckons his total earnings during his professional career of more than twelve years as 7638 florins, and to this should be added some 350 florins paid to him by the Kärntnerthor Theater the details of which were not available when Deutsch compiled his list.³ During Schubert's lifetime his publications included one of his string quartets, the E flat Piano Trio, three of his piano sonatas, one of the duets for violin and piano, a group of works for piano duet, a large number of smaller piano pieces, some part songs, one Mass, three slighter, motet-type church works and a hundred and eighty-seven songs.

Derisory as are these earnings—some £350 for his entire life's work—some of Schubert's music became well known. Some of his church works were heard outside Vienna as well as in some of the city churches, so that in 1825, during a holiday in Upper Austria, he could write to his parents: 'I find my compositions everywhere, especially at the monasteries of St. Florian and Kremsmunster.'⁴ Some of his songs were heard at concerts in Vienna, especially at the chamber concerts, or *Abendunterhaltungen,* of the *Gesellschaft der Musikfreunde,* where the A minor String Quartet, the Octet and several of his part songs were performed. Schubert was apparently held in high regard as a composer by the *Gesellschaft,* which in 1826 elected him to membership and awarded him 100 florins for his services to the Society. These, apparently, were simply his readiness to hand over works for performance; apart from this reward, such performances would earn a composer nothing.

Schubert's only public concert of his music, on 21 March 1828, brought him a net profit of 192 florins, not quite £8. Its programme consisted of the first movement of the String Quartet in G major, five songs sung by Vogl, the Serenade for soprano and female voices, one of the Piano Trios, the duet *Auf dem Strome* and the *Schlachtgesang,* for double male-voice choir. Several musical periodicals from outside Vienna—for example the *Allgemeine Musikalsiche Zeitung* of Leipzig, the *Abendzeitung* of Dresden and the *Allgemeine Musikalische Zeitung* of Berlin (all of which, with other periodicals, from time to time reviewed Schubert's publications enthusiastically)—noticed the concert with enthusiasm; the Berlin paper noted the 'numerous audience' and the 'resounding applause' with which the music was received and mentioned that several items were encored.⁵

³ Deutsch: *op. cit.* pp. 932–3. Brown: *op. cit. Schubert and the Kärntnerthor Theatre.* pp. 127–38.
⁴ Deutsch: *op. cit.* Letter of 25 July 1825. p. 757.
⁵ Deutsch: *op. cit.* pp. 756–7.

Of Schubert's orchestral music, only the two Italian Overtures were heard during his lifetime at professional concerts, and these, with the *Rosamunde* Overture, were published in piano duet form, but towards the end of his life he was beginning to negotiate for the publication of other orchestral works. But if his music was known in Upper Austria, his fame must have been spread by his published music; the monasteries may have added his Mass in C and a group of Offertory motets to the repertoire after these works, the first of Schubert's church music to reach print, had achieved publication, but that was not until two months after he had written to tell his parents that his music was known in St. Florian and Kremsmunster. It is, of course, possible that the C major Mass, one of his other early Masses or some of his miscellaneous pieces had reached the monasteries in manuscript copies. His symphonies, to all intents and purposes, were unknown; the Sixth was played by an amateur orchestra in 1817, when it was new, but the incomplete Symphony in E (No. 7), the 'Unfinished' B minor (No. 8) and the 'Great C Major' (No. 9) remained unknown until long after Schubert's death.

Thus, without any system of copyright and no acceptance of any performing right, it was possible for Schubert to have a more than local reputation and a considerable local following but remain unable to earn a living. Schubert could dispose of piano music and songs to the publishers, but what he received from publication could hardly be described as a living. His published works were addressed to the amateur market, and his supply of songs seems to have outstripped the publishers' capacity for issuing them. Schubert's publication did not benefit him as effectively as Beethoven's publication of works of all kinds, including deliberate pot-boilers for amateurs, benefited their composer; but Schubert never had the aristocratic patronage which eased Beethoven's way in his early years in Vienna and enabled him to gain international recognition while still a young man.

The German song, when Schubert began to compose, had little to show for itself except the seventy or so songs of Beethoven which are the true precursors of the German *Lied*. Though *Lieder* were Schubert's most effective material for publication, his songs were outside the conventions of his age and tradition. Any age of great song-writing, like the Elizabethan period in England, depends upon the existence of an extensive body of lyrical poetry to serve as its raw material, and before Schubert's day German lyric poetry barely existed. Goethe was born in 1749 and Schiller ten years later; Schubert discovered the poetry of Schiller when he was fourteen, in 1811, and the works of Goethe four years later; in the year of his death he discovered the poetry of Heine, his exact contemporary. Schubert's appetite for song texts devoured lyrics by a number of minor poets whose work varies from the effective to the merest composer-fodder.

Carl Loewe, born a year before Schubert and outliving him by more than forty years, was a reasonably successful composer of operas, and he also left a collection of three hundred and sixty-eight songs, mostly in ballad style and many of them extremely attractive. To compare Loewe's songs with Schubert's is to discover the novelty of the Schubertian *Lieder* style, not only in its command of an unprecedently rich harmonic vocabulary but also in its economical creation of situation and character and, chiefly, in the chamber-music-like perfection of the balance of its two equal partners.

Mendelssohn and Schubert were prolific *Lieder* writers, as was Brahms; Hugo Wolf is accepted as a master on the basis of his songs alone. The *Lied*, that is to say, was established by Schubert, and it offered challenges to vocal style, literary insight and musicianship which are hardly the simplest way of catering for the taste of the amateur public. Schubert's dedication to *Lieder* was a matter of emotional compulsion rather than the not-unpraiseworthy desire to turn an honest penny or two whenever he needed it. The impulse which created German lyrical poetry led to the flowering of *Lieder*, which shows a new sensitivity to words among the composers of the early nineteenth century.

A little later Wagner was to write of the necessary fertilisation of music by poetry. By the time that Schubert died, not only had this new sensitivity created the *Lied* but Berlioz had embarked on the early concert overtures in which his musical impulses were drawn into focus by works of literature—*Waverley*, *King Lear* and *Rob Roy*. The *Fantastic Symphony* was performed less than eighteen months after Schubert's death. The new alliance between literature and music was to develop in the 1840s into the symphonic poems in which Liszt adapted the techniques of symphonic development to as close a parallel as can be achieved to narrative style in order to communicate his sense of the emotional significance of stories and poetry.

To declare any essential connection between the composer's new awareness of literature as a musical stimulus and the search for new audiences forced upon him by social and political conditions, would be to state more than we can ever have sufficient information to know. But it may well be that subconsciously—for no composer of programme music has suggested that his approach to literature was a deliberate attempt to create a community of feeling with an audience which might otherwise find it difficult to come to terms with what he had to communicate—the romantic composer realised that the shared experience of literature was a means of approach to listeners otherwise hard to reach.

Berlioz, whose programme music does not deal in narrative but in the expression of his emotional response to literature, lacked an audience sympathetic to his aims and familiar with his idioms, the type of audience which Mozart and Beethoven could expect for their concerts; and while there is no objective evidence that programme music was his means of finding a starting point from which he and his audience could begin a co-operative exploration of new musical territory, the history of the *Fantastic Symphony* suggests that its sensational programme was devised to put the audience into a frame of mind in which each listener could understand an exceedingly original musical conception. The symphony's main theme, its '*idée fixe*', is the final version and expansion of the melody of a song written in his teens; the grotesque, lurching *Marche au Supplice* was composed, two or three years before he thought of the symphony, for the unfinished opera *Les Francs Juges*; it is cyclically related to the symphony by the simplest scissors-and-paste method; the March is interrupted and the melody of the '*idée fixe*' inserted immediately before the movement's closing bars. Obviously this music had not previously been associated in Berlioz's mind with a sensational story about unrequited love, drugs and opium nightmares. The work was finished as neither more nor less than a strange musical experience when Berlioz, aware of the new romantic interest in drugs and their effect on the human mind (de Quincey's *Confessions of an English Opium Eater,* for example, was published in 1821), added a story 'about' the symphony to guide the listener through its unusually hectic emotional world. The story is not the point at which the experience starts but that at which the symphony ends.

'The fertilisation of music by poetry', then, can be seen as a happy coincidence in which the composer's new literary interests could appear as the ally of his own art, capable of establishing a means of communication between composer and audience. In Berlioz's mind, programme music was the use of familiar, appropriate literary ideas to define the type of purely musical communication he had to make. It was Liszt, Liszt's disciples and Richard Strauss who went further to re-create literature in music.

Berlioz was a considerable prose writer and as such responsible for a great deal of the essential mythology of the romantic age. The great composer, it seemed to him, is inevitably misunderstood and neglected, inevitably condemned to defend himself against the attacks of philistines and ignorant obscurantists; he is inevitably lonely because the world cannot understand originality. When Berlioz conducted in the Redoutensaal in Vienna, standing where Beethoven had stood, his mind was full of the sufferings of his heroic predecessor but not particularly attentive to the facts of Beethoven's career.

It was in this large and handsome hall [he writes] that Beethoven first performed his masterpieces, now worshipped throughout Europe but at that time received by the Viennese with contempt. Count Michael Wielhorski told me that he was one of an audience of fifty which in 1820 heard the Symphony in A performed! The Viennese were busy going to Salieri's operas. Puny creatures! A giant had risen among them but they were happier with dwarfs.[6]

[6] Berlioz: *op. cit.* p. 375.

To ask why Berlioz did not mention the performers of the Seventh Symphony at this notably inauspicious concert, whether the orchestra and conductor were professionals or whether this was one of the Viennese concerts at which an amateur orchestra gave an optimistic sight-reading to the work, or to have expected him to remember that the Seventh Symphony had been enormously popular at its first performance in 1812 and repeated several times at Beethoven's own concerts would have been as pointless as reminding him that in 1820 the Viennese might well have been listening to Rossini's operas but that Salieri had composed nothing for the theatre for about twenty years. The point of his outburst is that by the time Berlioz reached Vienna, in 1845, it had become necessary for him to see the great composer as a sacrificial victim offered up to the self-seeking meanness of an academic establishment and the mean-minded narrowness of an inartistic general public.

Berlioz's sufferings were real enough. Henry Chorley read Berlioz's articles and occasionally quoted them in his own music criticism; he referred several times in his *Music and Manners in France and Germany* (1841) to Berlioz as an obviously important but apparently difficult composer, but admitted that during his visits to Paris he had tried unsuccessfully to hear some of Berlioz's work. He noticed that in spite of its reputation for obscurity, Berlioz's music had a great influence in Paris and described him as 'the idol of the younger critics'.[7]

All Berlioz's major works were greeted with excitement: the single performance planned for *Romeo and Juliet* and the *Symphonie Funèbre et Triomphale* turned by public demand into three performances. *Benvenuto Cellini* and *The Damnation of Faust* were his only real failures.

'The Overture was extravagantly applauded,' wrote Berlioz of the first performance of *Benvenuto* on 10 September 1838, 'the rest was hissed with exemplary precision and energy'.[8] Berlioz knew, of course, that he had not insured the opera by buying the support of the singularly efficient claque of the Paris Opéra. *Benvenuto Cellini* is an unorthodox work, making few concessions to the conservative, restricted taste of the Paris public. *The Damnation of Faust* was played on two successive Sundays in the November of 1846. The whole venture—fees, rehearsal costs, publicity, ushers and attendants, box office staff—was undertaken at his own risk. He had to pay excessive rent for the Opéra Comique, the only suitable auditorium available. None of his singers was a star, only members of the theatre's regular company. Paris was in the grip of a financial depression and there had been rioting in the streets; further to deter the audience, the weather was execrable. 'For all the number of people who came,' wrote the defeated

---

[7] Henry F. Chorley: *Music and Manners in France and Germany.* 3 volumes. London, 1841. Vol. 2. p. 301.

[8] Berlioz: *op. cit.* p. 245.

composer, 'it might have been the most footling opera in the company's repertoire.'[9] The 'progressive', Berliozian critics applauded; the opposition, realising the extent of the catastrophe—the number of unfilled seats— decided that they had heard the last of an unruly perverter of public taste. Berlioz rescued himself from the debts he had incurred by a concert tour in Russia and made a vow, which he was unable to keep for very long, never again to mount a concert in Paris.

If two disastrous failures seems comparatively little foundation for the ironical despair of the Berlioz of later years, the mere practicalities of his success provide a reason for it. His first concert, in 1829, which included the *Waverley* and *Francs Juges* Overtures, the *Dance of Sylphs* from the *Eight Scenes of Faust* and the *Resurrexit* of his early Mass as well as Beethoven's E flat Piano Concerto, made him a net profit of about 150 francs (about £3). He hired a hall, paid copyists, orchestra, choir and conductor, under-took the management of publicity and the box office, and what was left over was for his own use. Critical acclaim and widespread heated discussion are not capable of supporting life. Almost all Berlioz's successes were won at concerts which he himself financed; the choruses he used were the professional choruses of the theatres; he undertook months of work for a negligible financial reward. For *Romeo and Juliet* the hall was sold out so that he issued corridor tickets for the overflow. Part of the débâcle of *Faust* was that the rent of the Opéra Comique was 1600 francs and the copyists' fees were enormous, so that he came to believe that the venture would justify itself only through a success as crowded as that of *Romeo*. It was the finances of the performance, not its reception by the audience, which were ruinous.

This is the context in which Berlioz's sense of failure can be understood; it explains his bitter, ironic desperation at his unwanted though successful career as a critic; it explains the perhaps apochryphal story of the dream symphony he dared not write. He woke one morning, shortly before his wife's death, clearly remembering a Symphony in A which he had been composing in a dream; he could remember its entire first movement, an *allegro* in two-four time, and was going immediately to write it down.

> I suddenly thought: 'If I do, I shall be led on to compose the rest. My ideas tend to expand nowadays, so this symphony could well be on an enormous scale. I shall spend three or four months on the work [I took seven to write *Romeo and Juliet*], during which I shall do no articles, or very few, and my income will diminish accordingly. When the Symphony is written I shall be weak enough to be persuaded by my copyist to have it copied, which will immediately put me a thousand or twelve hundred francs in debt. Once the parts exist, I shall be plagued by the temptation to have the work performed. I shall give a concert, the receipts of which will hardly cover the costs—that is inevitable these days. I shall lose what I haven't got, and be short of money to provide for the poor invalid, and no longer able to meet my personal

9 *Ibid.* p. 416.

expenses or pay my son's allowance on the ship he will shortly be
joining.' These thoughts made me shudder and I threw down my pen,
thinking: 'What of it? I shall have forgotten it by tomorrow.'[10]

He dreamed the symphony again on the following night, suffered and over-
came the same temptations, and then the music left him for ever.

There was little prospect of Berlioz earning regular sums of money
through the publication of his works; only a handful of songs and vocal
ensemble pieces with piano accompaniment was likely to appeal to the
amateur public, and the huge scope of his most popular works precluded
their having any extensive sale in print. But to set against this there was
the great prestige of his huge ceremonial works, the *Messe des Mortes,* the
Symphonie Funèbre et Triomphale and the *Te Deum.* The first two of
these were official commissions. The Minister of the Interior, de Gasparin,
commissioned the *Requiem* in 1836 as part of a plan to restore the prestige
of French religious music by commissioning new works and sponsoring
their performance. Unfortunately the Director of Fine Arts—'he was unable to concede real merit to any music except Rossini's,' complained
Berlioz—was not musically adventurous so that for a time he doubted the
possibility of the commission ever becoming more than a verbal promise
which might easily be dishonoured. Nevertheless, the confirmation of the
commission arrived and its performance was planned for the ceremony
commemorating the dead of the Revolution of 1830. Then de Gasparin
fell from power, and Berlioz, writing in the tradition of French ceremonial
music at its most grandiloquent, planning music to saturate a lofty,
resonant building, had already had parts copied and rehearsals in progress
when the musical part of the commemoration was cancelled.

The problem of how to extract his own fee of 4000 francs, about £80—
he considered it 'niggardly for the occasion but was not prepared to
haggle'[11]—but also the copyists' fees and the cost of the rehearsals took
second place for a time to the necessity of arranging a performance of the
work. The death of General Damrémont in Algeria gave the Ministry of
the Interior an opportunity to push the *Requiem* on to the Ministry for
War; the Ministry for War was ready to accept financial responsibility for
a performance but not for the composer's fee. Cherubini, whose own
Requiem was customarily sung at such ceremonies, then had to be bribed
by the rank of Commander of the Legion of Honour to surrender his right.
The performance was a great musical success, so that Berlioz at last had
time to address himself to the question of his unpaid fee, but it was not
until six weeks after the performance and eighteen months after the

[10] *Ibid.* p. 470.
[11] Hector Berlioz: *A Selection from his Letters.* Selected, edited and
translated by Humphrey Searle. Letter of 17 April 1837 to Adèle
Berlioz, p. 64.

granting of the commission that, by threatening to publish the details of his negotiations with the two ministries, he extorted the money for which he had worked.

The commission for *Symphonie Funèbre et Triomphale* in 1840 to commemorate the tenth anniversary of the July Revolution came to a composer already made suspicious by the shoddy treatment he had received over the *Requiem,* so that the rumour that the musical part of the celebration was to be cancelled after he had written the first movement of the *Symphonie* left him prepared for the worst. The rumour was false, however, and the composition and rehearsals went ahead as planned. Berlioz had been offered 10,000 francs for the composition and the expenses of its performance; these included the copying of parts and the selection and rehearsal of orchestra and choir. The ceremonial went against the music; the first movement made little effect as it was played on the march to the *al fresco* ceremonies in the Place de la Bastille, and the dismissal of the National Guard from the Square during the second movement effectively destroyed the work's impact. Fortunately, the management of the Salle Vivienne, where the rehearsals had taken place, booked two further performances after the spoiled première, and from these Berlioz collected a respectable fee, so that his profit from the work was 2800 francs; it obviously paid Berlioz not to act as his own impresario.

The *Te Deum* was written without a commission, and after its completion in 1849 Berlioz had considerable difficulty in arranging its performance in conjunction with an event of sufficient magnitude; even an appeal to Napoleon III for support did Berlioz no good. In 1855 it was played at the closing ceremonies of the Paris Exhibition, with orchestral and choral forces matching Berlioz's demands and 200 drums in the final apotheosis.

Nothing that Berlioz did enabled him to secure a way of life in which he could devote himself to composition. His salary as Assistant Librarian and then as Librarian of the Conservatoire was, like most musical salaries, minimal, and his concert tours, successful as they were, did not bring him enough money to make him secure. A concert in Gotha, in 1855 for example, brought him 300 thalers (about £45), but though it was obviously cheaper to mount a concert in Germany with an established orchestra than to follow his Paris custom of assembling and drilling an *ad hoc* body of performers for each of his concerts, his tours in Germany, Austria and Russia were financed by himself and taken at his own risk; it was only in England that he conducted as the result of definite invitations with his fees guaranteed. Thus, despite his detestation of journalism (a detestation which must as often as not have been modified by his pleasure in a job superbly done) he could never escape the uncongenial demands of a secondary career followed with an honesty that closed against him the doors of many whom he treated with uncompromising disdain. Even his foreign tours had to be material for articles—racy, sardonic and witty—invaluable as accounts of musical conditions in the mid-nineteenth century.

Schubert and Berlioz, outside the system, demonstrate the near-impossibility of a free-lance career. Mendelssohn, whose music exactly met the taste of nineteenth-century Europe, was a member of a wealthy family even before he could live comfortably from his achievements as composer and conductor. Liszt, when his days of virtuoso touring ended, became *Kapellmeister* at Weimar with a conventional *Kapellmeister*'s salary of 400 thalers a year. This was about £100 in the English money of the period. The leader of the Opera orchestra at Leipzig, in the 1820s, also earned 400 thalers; the various section-leaders earned 200 thalers and the rank-and-file players a mere 150. For rehearsals they were paid eight groschen, with 16 groschen for dress rehearsals. The entire orchestra cost the Leipzig Opera about £900 (6000 thalers) a year, even when extra rehearsals were called, but it played for a hundred and ten operas and a similar number of plays.

Salaries in the court orchestras were not appreciably higher; a court orchestra consisted of *Kammermusiker,* seniors whose positions were permanent, and *Accessisten,* probationers, who waited until death or promotion among the higher ranks emptied a space which they could fill; their salary until they joined the ranks of the *Kammermusiker* was round about 150 thalers a year. Therefore orchestral players everywhere, however onerous their orchestral duties, were willy-nilly teachers in order to earn enough to survive. Both Berlioz and Charles Hallé described their hardships when the 1848 revolution in France scattered their wealthy pupils and closed the theatres. Hallé wrote:

> In Paris by far the greatest part of a Musician's income was invariably derived from teaching; and so it was with Chopin, Heller, many others and myself; but from the day after the Revolution, the pupils disappeared, and at the end of the week I could only boast of one. . . . The audience at our third concert did not number fifty people, although every place was subscribed for.[12]

Hallé, like Berlioz, found himself in England and settled there, to England's great musical advantage. Berlioz returned to Paris, though not by design, on the day that the National Assembly voted a grant to enable the theatres to reopen.

> Inadequate relief, [he wrote] above all to the musicians! A first violin at the Opéra was lucky if he earned 900 francs a year; he lived by giving lessons. It is hardly to be supposed that he could have saved on a very brilliant scale. Now their pupils have gone, what is to happen to such people?[13]

[12] C. E. and M. Hallé: *The Life and Letters of Sir Charles Hallé.* London, 1896. p. 92.
[13] Berlioz: *op. cit.* p. 45.

Naturally, a *Kapellmeister's* salary was not commensurate with the skills he was expected to employ or the amount of work he had to face. Spohr, at Cassel, was paid 2000 thalers (not quite £300) with six to eight weeks' leave in a year in which he could follow his international career as violinist and conductor. His duties included the direction of the Court Opera and occasional court concerts as well as the administration of the entire musical establishment. In addition, he formed and directed an amateur choir and established regular orchestral concerts for the townspeople.[14] His publications and the fees he received from external engagements augmented his salary.

Weber's yearly salary at Dresden was 1500 thalers (about £220), equal to that of Morlacchi, *Kapellmeister* of the parallel Italian Opera in Dresden. But when Weber drew up the outline of the German opera company he was engaged to establish he noted that the first soprano would have to be paid 5000 thalers, the second soprano, the first and second lyric tenors and the dramatic tenor would each command a salary of 2000 thalers, while two additional woman singers could not be expected to accept engagements at less than 1500. Singers were more expensive than *Kapellmeisters*, though the proceeds of Weber's operas added to his exiguous earnings and in 1820, when he was offered the post in Cassel which Spohr eventually accepted, the Dresden authorities offered an extra 300 thalers a year to keep him in the city. To prevent jealousy between the two Dresden companies, Morlacchi's salary rose by the same amount.

The great success of *Der Freischütz* made it possible for Weber to demand more money from theatres eager to produce his operas. The original production of *Der Freischütz* brought the composer 80 Friedrichs d'or from the Berlin Opera in 1821, to which another 40 Friedrichs d'or were added before the first performance; a Friedrich d'or was worth about sixteen shillings in the English money of the time. When *Der Freischütz* reached its hundredth performance in Berlin, a hundredth performance signifying an epoch-making success, the management offered Weber an honorarium of 100 thalers; this he regarded as an insult, pointing out that the theatre had already made about 30,000 thalers from his work. But Vienna paid him 300 Friedrichs d'or for *Euryanthe,* but out of this sum he had to pay the cost of travel to and life in Vienna during the rehearsals of his opera. Covent Garden offered him £500 for *Oberon*; in addition he was offered £225 to conduct four orchestral concerts and there was a suggestion of an additional concert for his benefit. Until Weber realised that the cost of living in London was far higher than in Dresden or Vienna, he felt that fees so munificent would make him a rich man. But though he stayed in London as the guest of Sir George Smart, he had occasionally to spend money, and dinner with a friend—soup, fish, mutton cutlets with beans,

[14] Spohr: *op. cit.* Vol. 2. p. 141.

and beer—cost him all of six shillings (21 groschen, 4 pfennigs), he
pointed out in a horrified letter to a friend.

Lortzing, born in 1801, composed operas which were an immediate
success in the German theatres, but he kept their scores in his own hands
to avoid the sale of his rights to theatres which could then cut and mangle
his works before hiring scores to other theatres, hoping to mount performances from which the composer would receive no fee at all. He refused
an offer made by Leipzig Opera in 1840 for his opera *Hans Sachs*:

> I cannot allow my opera for the fees your manager declares he paid
> Marschner—though I doubt it, because Ringelhardt used to pay 100
> thalers for every opera by Marschner—for I should be ashamed to tell
> people about it when I get 30 thalers from the smallest company. I had
> to pay more than 16 reichthalers in copyist's fees for *Zar und Zimmer-
> mann*. So simply for your sake I shall drop three Friedrichs d'or and be
> content if your manager finds that price satisfactory. The fee I mention
> is paid by any municipal theatre of importance.[15]

Zar und Zimmermann is one of the permanent successes of the German
theatre, and Lortzing's scale of fees for it ranged from 10 to 20 Louis d'or,
according to the size and prestige of the theatre wishing to produce it; a
Louis d'or of the 1840s was worth approximately £1. But for *Der
Wildschütz*, a great success in 1842, he could extract no more than 6 Friedrichs d'or from the theatre in Coburg. Lortzing's operas were played
repeatedly all over Germany while their composer wore himself out with
overwork in small theatres with inferior companies.

The publication of a successful opera—unsuccessful operas remained unpublished unless their composer was rich and foolish enough to publish
them at his own expense—made little difference to the composer's financial
well-being. Marschner's *Der Vampyr*, a great success in Leipzig in 1828,
was one of the most successful operas inspired by popular 'gothic' horror
stories; Marschner sold it outright for 220 thalers. Lortzing, departing
from his usual custom, offered his *Caramo*, produced in 1839, to Breitkopf and Härtel for 100 Friedrichs d'or, a price which the publisher
thought excessive, although Lortzing was by that time a very popular
composer.

Unlike Beethoven, who had made a not inconsiderable income from publishing his works, other composers had not yet learned how to exploit publication to their own advantage. They were unwilling, or unable, to write
pleasant pot-boilers for amateur players and thus ensure the publisher of
the profit on their minor works which would pay for the symphonies and
concerts which would enhance their prestige. Spohr reached print when he
was in his early teens and ready to hand over his music for a number of
complimentary copies to impress actual and potential patrons.

[15] Hans Gal: *The Composer's World.*

Those composers who could publish their music in England could expect higher fees than they could obtain on the continent, but those fees were the result of the higher cost of living in England, where food prices had made Weber wince. Ewer and Ewer had offered Mendelssohn £250 for the English rights in *Elijah*, and after the composer's death had added £100 to their offer for the sake of the composer's widow. But the fantastically popular *Elijah* had the weight of the large English choral societies to guarantee a profit for the publisher.

> One of the greatest difficulties in the early days of music publishing [wrote William Boosey] was to know how adequately and fairly to pay a composer and mitigate one's losses in case of failure. Many instances occurred of the purchase of valuable copyrights, at the price of a mere song, in works which often resulted in a very big profit for the publisher. The English firm of Chappell gave £100 for all the publishing rights in Gounod's *Faust*, which was a great and lasting success, so they paid £1,000 for his next opera, *Mireille*, which was a total failure.[16]

Until later in the century, when a workable system of international copyright was worked out, and the paying of performing rights accepted as a matter of justice to the composer, publication could be a way of augmenting a composer's income but was a way of earning a living for only a very few who had seized the public imagination. Brahms made a respectable income from publication by virtue of the small pieces on which his relationship with publishers was based; so long as he supplied them with music that was immediately profitable, they would deal with large-scale, less profitable works for the prestige they gained from the handling of major symphonies and concertos although elaborate full scores were extremely expensive to produce and the market for them was necessarily limited. Publication could, for a composer whose style was original, be a positive danger. Berlioz, whose major works would have been a doubtful source of profit, decided that the *Francs Juges* Overture in print did him only harm; it was played by conductors who had no real understanding of his demands and performed travesties of his intention, so that he wrote to Schumann:

> I am afraid I should lose the esteem of musical people for ever if, by premature publication, I exposed my symphonies, while they are still too young to travel without me, to the risk of being mutilated even more than my overture.[17]

It is less than fair to the publisher to regard him always as an un-

[16] William Boosey: *Fifty Years of Music Publishing*. London, 1931. pp. 23–4.
[17] Hector Berlioz: *Letters*, translated by H. Dunstan. London, 1882. pp. 131ff.

scrupulous money-grubber. In 1831, at the request of Wagner's teacher, Breitkopf and Härtel published a piano sonata by the young Richard Wagner; they paid the eighteen-year-old composer a mere 20 thalers, but at least they took the trouble to encourage an unknown beginner whose efforts were unlikely to bring them much return. Simrock paid Dvorak 300 marks for the first set of *Slavonic Dances* in 1878, when Dvorak was completely unknown in Germany. The dances became extremely popular and Simrock did very well out of his generosity; eight years later Dvorak refused the same sum for the D minor Symphony (No. 7), but Simrock doubled his offer while urging the composer to write some more Slavonic Dances.

Judged simply as a source of profit, Simrock found, Dvorak was a doubtful blessing; when he received the score of the G major Symphony (No. 8), in January 1890, the publisher wrote to the composer explaining the economic facts of life:

> If only I did sufficient business with your symphonies to be repaid for my enormous expense! But this is far from being the case as I am thousands down on them. . . . If the performances are successful, the composer always thinks that his work will sell well. You were successful here over Bülow's performance of your D minor Symphony, but subsequently not a single copy, not even a piano version, was sold.[18]

Neither performance nor publication replaced the loss the composer had suffered when the old system of patronage broke down, musical employment no longer was offered to him and he was left to find his own audience. He could become a popular hero adored by audiences wherever he appeared but still, like Berlioz, be involved in a hopeless struggle with intractable economic realities.

While the composer was left to depend upon his ability to find the audience for whom his music was intended, social and political circumstances made it difficult for him to do so. The educational policies fostered in the period of repression—from 1814 to 1848 and for some considerable time, in some states, afterwards—deliberately cut as many of the means of communication as possible between the intelligentsia and the common people. The man of culture had no direct access to communication with a working class brought up, according to the dictates of Francis I, to be simply good, honest citizens who knew their place and were contented with it. The composer found himself confronted by a social system which demanded that he found his audience but denied him the facilities for doing so. For the first time, the composer was edged into a position not simply dissatisfied with society but actively hostile to it. The social situation drew composers to the 'progressive', liberal side in politics.

[18] John Clapham: *Antonin Dvorak*. London, 1966. pp. 16, 19ff.

> I think that there is a big difference between revolution and reform.
> Reform is what I look forward to in all things—life, art, politics, road-
> making. Reform is intended to get rid of ill-usage and tries only to
> remove everything which hinders progress.[19]

The words are those of Mendelssohn, not, on the surface, the fieriest or
most discontented of nineteenth-century composers. Since Beethoven had
poetically embraced the millions in the exaltation of the Ninth Symphony,
it was to the millions that the composer spoke, and to cry like Mendelssohn
for reform was to look for a political and social system which ceased to
divide him from his audience. He did not need to rationalise his aspirations
in this way; to be aware of the educational system of Germany and
Austria—or for that matter of Britain—in the 1830s and to speak for
reform was to make unavoidable implications about the musical situation.

In 1848 Schumann, who was influenced by the writers who became
known as 'Young Germany' and who married the emotionalism and un-
worldliness of the Romantic Movement to the liberal ideal of freedom,
ceased to write in a strain similar to Mendelssohn's because in 1848 he
could not avoid the sight of the eggs being broken as they went into the
omelette, and he drew back from the prospect of violent change with his
social principles in ruins; if the alternative to repression was destruction,
death and the end of the cultural traditions which had created him, the
result could only be despair and withdrawal for social concern. Heine, the
poet with whose lyrics Schumann most identified himself, spoke for him:
to remake the world on juster lines would remove the poets and musicians;
utilitarian potatoes would replace laurels and roses. His *Buch der Lieder*,
Heine suggested, would come in handy in a greengrocer's shop for any
tradesman who wanted to wrap up his cabbages. Lortzing, composing his
'revolutionary' opera *Regina* in 1848 (the work was not seen on the stage
for fifty-one years), introduced striking workmen into his cast of characters,
but even he wrote of them from a respectable, middle-class angle; they
were the agents of destruction and anarchy acting in the names of freedom
and justice. While the social situation drove the artist into the progressive,
liberal camp, the revolutionaries drove him out again into a no-man's-land
where all political action became pointless if it was not wicked. The artist
may love freedom in theory, but he cannot exist without tradition.

The case of Wagner, in Dresden, is the extreme example of the artist
driven into political action. Wagner believed art to be the only possible
unifying force in an age which had lost the inspiration of religion and in
which politics were only unprincipled expediency; the arts would bring
back the true spiritual values with which conventional religion had lost
contact. United by music into the *Gesamtkunstwerk*, which would bring

[19] Felix Mendelssohn: *Briefe aus dem Jahren 1833–1847*, edited by
V. J. Rietz. Leipzig, 1864. pp. 72–3. Letter to Rebekah Dirickler.

together poetry, the dance, drama, painting and design in the service of music, the arts would regenerate the shoddy, cheap-jack nineteenth century, returning it to the path of truth and salvation. In his powerful but illogical mind—for Wagner was a clear thinker only about music and musical problems for all the power and fertility of his imagination—Wagner could see no other hope for the world and felt it to be his destiny to provide the means of salvation.

Dresden, where he was *Kapellmeister* and where, despite his known financial unreliability, he had a good deal of official support and encouragement, was to be the point from which regeneration spread. He drew up plans to reorganise and reform music in Dresden; his schemes were clear, sensible, economical and fundamentally unpolitical. They would not only have made Dresden a city in which music of all kinds could be heard at its best; they would have improved the desperate lot of singers and instrumentalists in court employment. They were dismissed without discussion. Wagner found new ideas irresistible: he was aware of the teachings of socialists, communists and anarchists, and new ideas were attractive to him to the extent that they seemed to have clear musical consequences, so that if his mission of salvation was hindered by corrupt or old-fashioned courtiers who stood in the way of his duty, the revolution would aid him and was therefore to be supported. Into the sketches for *Siegfrieds Tod,* the single opera which eventually developed into the monumental *Der Ring des Nibelungen,* went Wagner's revolutionary fervour roused by the obscurantism of the Saxon establishment: Siegfried, the redeeming hero, owes something (as Bernard Shaw pointed out in *The Perfect Wagnerite*) to the powerful figure of Bakhunin, the anarchist leader.[20]

To think of Wagner, the revolutionary activist of the Dresden barricades of 1849 as an anarchist, socialist or communist would be to give him command of a system of ideas which he seems never to have envisaged. The revolutionary Wagner who was driven into exile with a price on his head was simply a revolutionary composer looking for the society which would make it possible for him to realise his mission, not a dedicated rebel who happened incidentally to be Court *Kapellmeister* and composer of three unusual operas which were refining and developing Meyerbeer's style of grand opera. Wagner always had a typically German devotion to the idea of leadership; actually, through his belief in music and its regenerative power, he felt himself to be the leader in whom he most devoutly believed. In 1863, faced with a failure so total that he seems for the first time to have realised it as disaster, he was saved by Ludwig II of Bavaria, and his subsequent royalism was never really inconsistent with his revolutionary past. The artist–philosopher–king Ludwig, a strange, handsome boy in his teens, would lead the work of regeneration, himself led by the composer–

[20] G. Bernard Shaw: *The Perfect Wagnerite.* London, 1898. p. 48.

philosopher Wagner who could forge the redeeming *Gesamtkunstwerk*. Who nominally led was an irrelevancy so long as Wagner himself led the leader, the composer–philosopher–poet–vegetarian–anti-ecclesiastical–anti-semite designing the world of the future. It says everything for the power of Wagner's personality that his extra-musical doctrines were taken seriously by serious thinkers for nearly half a century.

The mere composer, with no elaborate if tangled philosophy to expound, had few other roads to explore except those which enabled him to create sufficient excitement to be taken notice of. The nineteenth century became the age of continual expansion. Wagner's attempt at a simple, economical repertoire opera became the five-hour gorgeous agony of *Tristan and Isolde*. Everyone's orchestra, except that of Brahms, became larger, everyone's palette more gorgeously coloured, everyone's symphonies longer and more demanding until, at the close of the century, we reach Strauss's *Ein Heldenleben*, Mahler's Eighth Symphony and Schoenberg's *Gurrelieder*. Sensation and extreme emotional intensity became necessities, and the startling thing about how much of the most sensational nineteenth-century music is the extent to which composers turned sensationalism to valid musical ends.

The composer in the nineteenth century, a man with no recognised, essential social function, could accept that he was an outcast, wandering through life in bohemian ineffectuality, or he could think of himself as the prophet of a new age in which his value would be recognised; he could see himself as, in Shelley's phrase, an 'unacknowledged legislator of the world'. But he could find no clear line of action outside music to which he could dedicate himself. Reform, opposed by repressive authority, led to revolution: it was the nature of authority to oppose reform. Revolution, if successful, would overthrow the traditional world of music which provided the centres from which the composer could preach his necessary, disregarded doctrines. The only escape from alienation, therefore, in a corrupt, philistine world is the fellowship of art itself, which must therefore direct its attention to the visionary and ideal rather than the practical. These are the ideas which pervade the serious music of the nineteenth century until they reach their conclusion in Schoenberg's statement that audiences are necessary to make music sound well; in an empty hall, music does not make the proper effect; in other respects, audiences are simply a nuisance.[21] The composer can only find his own, sympathetic, ideal audience, cultivate his own garden and withdraw himself from a world in which his aims and ideals are irrelevant.

[21] Arnold Schoenberg: *Letters*, Faber, London. Letter of 23 February 1918 to Alexander von Zemlinsky.

3

Musical Standards
in the Early Nineteenth Century

Our mental pictures of early nineteenth-century music-making are perhaps more glorious than the reality ever was. We think of Haydn at Esterhaza, with all the materials and trained personnel necessary to a composer ready to his hand and the approval of a musically-minded prince to stimulate his work. In Vienna Joseph II was at least a knowledgeable connoisseur of music, and in Munich the Elector Theodore was interested enough to attend the dress rehearsal, as well as the première, of Mozart's *Idomeneo*. On Friday mornings in the 1790s Prince Lichnowsky listened to chamber music played by the best instrumentalists he could find in Vienna, giving his protégé Beethoven the opportunity to write and hear works composed for these morning concerts. Prince Lobkowsky, an enthusiastic bass ready to take part in public performances, had his own orchestra, and in 1803 it gave the first performance of the *Eroica* Symphony, probably unaware that it was opening a new age. There were many patrons, of course, like Dittersdorf's first employer, Prince von Hildburgshausen, active and benevolent but, reading between the lines of Ditterdorf's *Autobiography*, with less than superfine musical tastes. There was a considerable number of lesser nobility involved in the life and work of Mozart and Beethoven.

Nevertheless, it is unlikely that any of the concerted music which such devoted patrons heard would have seemed to us to be played in a satisfactory way. Outside the opera house, where the co-ordination of so many diverse functions made rehearsal obligatory, performances seem to have taken place with the minimum of preparation. Mozart's concerts in one or other of the Viennese theatres seem to have been rehearsed, as was the first of the concerts in 1781 in which Mozart collaborated with Phillipp Martin in the Augarten Pavilion in Vienna, but not even Leopold Mozart's letters from Vienna during his visit in 1785 mention any rehearsal for the subscription concerts which his son was giving during the visit. Even Mozart seems to have taken for granted a system which put concert programmes on to the platform with at best the minimum of rehearsal. In 1781 he wrote to his father that on the previous day he had played a solo and accompanied the arias at a concert given by the Archduke Maximilian, Archbishop Elector of Cologne, who had instructed him to arrive after the guests were assembled, and caustic as Mozart could be about the musical tastes and demands with which he was confronted, he

36

mentions this unprepared performance as a matter of course.[1] He seems
not to have been worried when his own music was played unrehearsed, for
he mentions that the violinist Franz Mendel played his music a sight
better than any other violinist in Vienna.

When Spohr, as director of the orchestra at the Theater an der Wien,
took part in the concert in 1814 when Beethoven conducted *Wellingtons
Sieg* and the Seventh Symphony, he gave a shocked account of Beethoven's
eccentricities as a conductor, his disappearance behind the desk at a
pianissimo, during which, apparently, his arms were held motionless across
his chest, his leaps into the air at a *sforzando* and so on. If Beethoven had
conducted a rehearsal, such antics would have been equally noteworthy
then, so the implication is that either there was no rehearsal or that
Beethoven had been satisfied to take over a performance prepared by someone else, or that Spohr was altogether too eminent an instrumentalist to be
asked to rehearse.[2] None of these dubious ways of preparing a performance
would have seemed particularly negligent to the composer, who in 1818
wrote a hurried note to Carl Czerny asking him to play the last two movements of the Concerto in E flat (the *Emperor* Concerto) at a concert 'the
day after tomorrow' without mentioning a rehearsal; Czerny, of course,
knew the work—he had given its first performance—but Beethoven's letter
simply explains that two of the 'hymns' (by which he apparently means
movements from the Mass in C) could not be adequately rehearsed in time
and the Concerto movements were intended to take their place. It seems that
choirs needed rehearsal but that distinguished instrumentalists did not.[3]

In 1819 Franz Xaver Gebauer, the organist of the Augustinerkirche,
added a 'Concert Spirituel' to the end of his weekly choir practice; at this,
he conducted choir and orchestra through choral and orchestral works
played at sight, without any preparation at all. As Gebauer's programmes
included Beethoven's symphonies in spite of their unusual difficulty, the
results must have been unusually unsatisfactory. Beethoven, nevertheless,
attended some of them, for in 1821 he wrote to the publisher Sigmund
Anton Steiner asking for two tickets for what (in Emily Anderson's translation) he describes as 'lavatory concerts'.[4]

Spohr's *Autobiography* offers interesting testimony as to the court concerts in which, as a youth, he played either as soloist or as orchestral
musician to the German nobility. When he was fourteen he was invited to

[1] Emily Anderson: *The Letters of Mozart and his Family.* London,
1936. Letter of 17 November, 1781.

[2] Spohr: *op. cit.* Vol. 1. p. 186.

[3] Emily Anderson: *The Letters of Beethoven.* London, 1961. Vol. 2.
p. 775.

[4] *Ibid.* Vol. 2. p. 935.

play before the Duke and Duchess of Brunswick. The Duke himself was a violinist, but the Duchess played cards, so that the orchestra, stationed on a thick carpet to deaden the sound, was never allowed to reach *forte* and trumpets and drums were omitted from any score they tackled. 'One heard therefore the words "I play", "I stand" and so forth, much louder than the music.'[5] Appointed to the court orchestra, there was an evening when young Spohr grew over-excited by the music and forgot the embargo on *fortes*; his arm was 'seized by a lackey who whispered, "Her Highness sends me to tell you that you are not to scrape so vigorously." '

In 1807 Spohr played at Stuttgart to the King of Württemberg, who throughout the performance played cards at a table from which a semi-circular segment had been removed to accommodate his corpulency; the episode is one of the few in the *Autobiography* which indicated that the earnest, high-minded Spohr actually had a sense of humour.

E. T. A. Hoffmann, the novelist–composer, animated the generation of Schumann, the generation following his own, by his writings. Hoffmann, the archetypal German romantic, invented an ardent, imaginative and daring musician, *Kapellmeister* Kreisler, to represent the new and explora-tory world of music confronted, baffled and stultified by meaningless traditions and conventions, his imagination, learning and seriousness dis-qualifying him from success. Kreisler, who came to fictitious life between 1820 and 1822, experienced among the German provincial bourgeoisie private concerts as bizarre as those Spohr experienced at Brunswick and Stuttgart. As a local *Kapellmeister*, Kreisler could never escape these often hilariously painful events designed with snobbish inanity to allow the vain to show off their more or less imaginary talents.

When all the eating and drinking have finished at the Röderleins' dinner, Kreisler discovered, the seniors settle down to cards while the younger guests rush to the two young Misses Röderlein, who try in vain and with no real determination to escape the invitation to sing, pleading colds and lack of practice. It is possible, for Kreisler, who is their teacher, to guess what the songs and arias they attempt are meant to be. Their performance gives the card players, from the far end of the room, opportunity to join in. ' *"How much I loved, how happy I was!"* . . . "Pass!" *"When I never knew the pains of love"* . . . "Follow suit!" '

After the amateurs have exhausted their repertories somebody remem-bers that the *Kapellmeister* had left some music in the cloakroom, with his hat. He is therefore compelled to send for it and to begin to play Bach's *Goldberg Variations*, but his audience begins to drift away at Variation 3; after Variation 5, even his two pupils, the Misses Röderlein, find their

[5] Spohr: *op. cit*. Vol. 1. p. 10.

loyalty exhausted, and he has one listener left. After Variation 30, Kreisler is left alone to play Bach to himself.[6]

Kreisler's sorrows are all, in a sense, social comedy, but the Röderlein *Hausmusik* introduces a new note into writing about music; this is the bourgeoisie aping the manners of a decaying aristocracy, rejecting great music but insisting on popular works to show off their culture. Middle-class amateurs whose standards of taste are complacently third-rate, like a nobility which accepts great music played by its domestic musicians so long as their efforts are painlessly unobtrusive, are the signs of musical deterioration. It is obvious that the Misses Röderlein would not have missed the opera and the meetings of the local concert society, applauding and condemning enthusiastically for the wrong reasons.

Hoffmann's fictitious account of middle-class standards is borne out factually by Weber, who was concerned with the problems of the travelling virtuoso and decided that musicians needed a guide book to the conditions they were likely to find in the various towns through which they passed. He began the compilation of a *Musikalische Topographie* in the completion of which, he hoped, other musicians would join. Because he intended only to provide necessary information for touring instrumentalists, whose work would be largely with the amateur orchestral societies, he did not deal with the theatres in any of the cities whose musical facilities he described. His aims were purely practical, not critical; he notes the authorities who should be approached for permission to give a concert, the capacity and cost of the available hall or halls, the facilities for advertisement, the unavoidable expenses, such as the fees to be paid to any professional players needed in the orchestra (naturally, he expected the concert orchestras to be predominantly amateur), the advisability of arranging a subscription before his arrival, the season, day of the week and time of day when a concert would be most profitable, the days of the week when the hall would be unavailable, the price that could be asked for tickets and the profits that could be expected. The quality of performance, he writes in his notes on Basel, compiled in 1811, is something that he does not care to judge on the basis of his limited experience of music in the city. 'But as dedication and real love of music are generally lacking, little is done about standards.'[7]

Two years earlier he had dismissed Stuttgart fairly cursorily. 'As there are neither amateur theatres nor concerts in existence, it does not pay artists to come here.' The King's *Kapellmeister*, Franz Danzi (the son of the celebrated composer who had migrated with the Elector Theodor from Mannheim to Munich), had written excellent German opera. Its *Konzertmeister*, Abeille, composed charming music, and its second *Konzertmeister*, Sutor,

---

[6] E. T. A. Hoffman: *Johannes Kreislers, des Kapellmeisters, Musikalische Leider. Sämtliche Werke, Band 1.* pp. 24–6.

[7] C. M. von Weber: *Ausgewählte Schriften,* edited by G. Altmann. p. 119.

had composed an opera of which the critics had approved. For the rest, two amateurs were the only musicians in the city worthy of note.[8] It was equally impossible, Weber decided, to write enthusiastically about Darmstadt. The Archduke Ludwig I, he wrote in 1811, had done much to improve the playing of his own orchestra; he attended its rehearsals, following the music from the score, correcting errors or slipshod performance. But the townspeople depressed Weber. The Archduke allowed local amateur musicians to meet in the palace for rehearsal three times a week, but they looked on this privilege as an unwelcome court duty and never touched their instruments on any other day. Only a tiny handful of townfolk attended these rehearsals as listeners, and neither they nor the players had any interest in the private music-making which 'must always be the foundation of genuine musical achievement and real musical appetites'.[9]

Unfortunately, Weber's *Musikalische Topographie*, potentially a source book of the greatest possible historical value, remains incomplete, but it shows how, while concert music remained in most places the concern of amateur musicians, with professional players only for the less popular and less domesticated instruments, standards could hardly be high enough to achieve successful performances, or even a clear impression, of works as difficult as the Beethoven symphonies; Beethoven's music, nevertheless, was played all over Europe. It is worth while to remember that the Ninth Symphony was far too much for the Philharmonic Orchestra of London, the completely professional, international and highly regarded organisation for which it was written. Many Beethoven performances must have been little short of appalling. Weber himself conducted the concerts of the Prague Conservatoire Orchestra, a body of students, in 1814 when he was Director of the Conservatory; with it, he introduced Beethoven's Seventh Symphony to Prague; the experienced professional orchestra of the Opera had too full a schedule to undertake concert work.

The public concert had been the invention of middle-class amateur musicians in towns where there was no opera or where, as in Leipzig, opera had never developed the social pre-eminence it gained from its status as an entertainment designed primarily for the nobility. As the nineteenth century made opera increasingly dependent, even in Vienna, Dresden, Berlin and Munich, and the other great courts, on the support of a paying audience, brilliancies of singing, stagecraft and orchestral sound became more important to the success of a work than they had been in earlier days. From this point of view, the great opera houses maintained standards apparently far higher than those of almost every regular concert orchestra.

The determination to popularise opera, however, led managements into remarkable acts of disloyalty to any composer whose work might outstrip the conventions with which the audience was familiar. In London, where all

[8] *Ibid.* p. 124.   [9] *Ibid.* p. 137.

public music-making depended on success at the box office or on the support of wealthy subscribers, Sir Henry Bishop became director of music and house composer to Covent Garden in 1810; his success led to the offer of the directorship of music at the King's Theatre in the Haymarket in 1816, and for two seasons he held both posts. In 1825 he moved to Drury Lane Theatre. Bishop wrote a large number of operas and semi-operas designed to suit the taste of London audiences, but in addition he made other men's music as immediately palatable as he could to early nineteenth-century prejudices. In 1812 he added music to Arne's *Comus*; in later years, Boeildieu's *Jean de Paris*, *Fidelio*, *Don Giovanni* (renamed '*The Libertine*'), *The Marriage of Figaro*, *The Barber of Seville*, *Der Freischütz* and *William Tell* (first known as *Ninette* at its première in 1830 but transformed into *Hofer*, *The Tell of the Tyrol*, for a revival in 1838) were all presented to English audiences after they had been filtered through Bishop's style and usually interfering hand. Juggling with opera texts was a familiar occupation in censor-ridden Europe, but although the interpolation of new arias in any work—to suit the voices of the available singers for example—was a commonplace—Haydn, Mozart and many others were responsible for such interpolations—in the opera houses in London and Paris, the 'adaptation' of successful works to suit new conditions was almost a major industry. Bishop's version of *William Tell*, for example, turned the *ranz de vaches* which follows the storm in the Overture into a contralto aria in the body of the work. So much was altered, added and changed in Bishop's versions that it would be easy to believe that the adapter regarded other men's music as little more than a suitable context for his own.

Bishop was more objectionable than his French counterpart—François Henri Joseph Castil-Blaze—simply because Castil-Blaze's activities were far more restricted. As a translator of German libretti into French, Castil-Blaze was unusually gifted, but Auber, Boeildieu and Hérold all wrote operas which he to some extent travestied. His greatest distinction, however, was to draw the fire of Berlioz—Bishop was lucky in that he seems to have had no critic with either Berlioz's passion for authenticity or his knowledge of the originals which Bishop spoiled—over the first French production of *Der Freischütz*, which was produced at the Odeon Theatre as *Robin des Bois*, which, to Berlioz, was 'a great travesty, hacked and mutilated in the most wanton fashion'.[10] Berlioz, who had previously savaged Castil-Blaze for his treatment of Gluck's *Alceste*, was outraged to find that 'the plunderer of the masterpiece was richer to 100,000 francs'. Nevertheless, *Robin des Bois* was published before *Der Freischütz*. Castil-Blaze reorganised the order of the numbers, rescored whatever did not please him, rewrote the vocal line in various places, cut passages from Weber's score and inserted a duet from *Euryanthe* with his own accompaniment to Weber's vocal parts. 'And a

[10] Berlioz: *op. cit.* p. 86.

wretched sailor,' wrote Berlioz, 'gets fifty lashes for a minor act of insub-ordination!'

Castil-Blaze answered Berlioz with the classic apology of the arranger. He explained in the *Journal des Débats* that it was 'common knowledge that foreign operas cannot succeed on the French stage unless they conform to our dramatic standards. . . . The object of my endeavours has been to make this splendid masterpiece known in France.'[11] Berlioz, of course, was not appeased and likened *Robin des Bois* to a travesty of Mozart's *Die Zauberflöte*, which had been played in Paris as *Les Mystères d'Isis*, arranged by a German, Lachnith, who more or less rewrote Mozart's work and added to it snippets from other operas, turned the music of a chorus into an aria, converted arias into ensembles and generally spoiled a masterpiece. It was the reworking, adaptation and reinstrumentation of works he revered which led Berlioz to appoint himself leader of an unofficial *claque* applauding and booing on behalf of the composers of desecrated masterpieces.

Whilst the major opera houses provided performances effective in their own terms when they distorted or totally falsified a composer's style and purposes, the smaller theatres simply did their best. Wagner, in charge of the chorus at the tiny opera in Würzburg in his first musical post as a young man of twenty, had fifteen singers with whom to manage the vast choral effects of Meyerbeer's *Robert le Diable*. Eighteen years later, in 1841, Henry F. Chorley heard a performance of *Les Huguenots* with a chorus almost as weak and an orchestra with too few strings to balance Meyerbeer's scoring.[12] The triumph of French grand opera in the 1830s, which converted it into the fashionable international style, added to the repertoires of the small German and Austrian theatres a number of works which they could not fail to produce, although *Les Huguenots*, for instance, demands five solo singers of the highest quality, a huge orchestra and a choir which can effectively represent huge, opposed groups of catholics and protestants; whatever its demands, it was seen for fashion's sake wherever an opera management was determined to maintain the loyalty of its patrons. Naturally, managements with little money regarded the chorus as the most easily expendable element in a production, and as late as 1882 Mahler conducted a performance of Gounod's *Faust* at Laibach in which the 'Soldiers' Chorus' was replaced by a single bass who marched across the back of the stage singing Luther's Chorale *Ein feste Burg ist unser Gott*.[13]

The habit of reorchestration continued into the mid-century. In many theatres it was simply a matter of adjusting the score to replace instruments which the orchestra of smaller theatres did not contain, but Berlioz, in Lon-don for the Great Exhibition of 1851 as one of the international jury of the

[11] *Ibid.* p. 89. Editor's footnote.
[12] Chorley: *op. cit.* Vol. 2. p. 94.
[13] Henry-Louis de la Grange: *Mahler*. London, 1974. p. 84.

Musical Instruments section, wrote about London music for the *Journal des Débats*:

> That composers are great masters, armed with great authority, that they are called Mozart, Beethoven, Weber or Rossini, matters little. Mr. Costa has for a long time thought fit to give them lessons in instrumentation, and, I say it with regret, Balfe has followed his example. The two orchestras [of Covent Garden and Drury Lane theatres] include three trombones, an ophicleide, a piccolo, a big drum and cymbals; in their opinion, such things are there for use. In Mozart's masterpiece, while Don Juan's private band is playing the naive music of the *Cosa Rara*, an incredible solo on the ophicleide has been introduced.[14]

Berlioz noted the use of trombones and ophicleide in the accompaniment to Marcellina's aria in *The Barber of Seville*, their appearance at large in *The Marriage of Figaro* and their general indispensability. When he saw *Die Zauberflöte* at Covent Garden he noted with sarcastic amazement that Costa had been satisfied with Mozart's orchestration; all he had done was to add four bars to the Priests' Chorus in Act Two.

The concept of opera as 'Drama in music' meant little to the nineteenth century until the example of Wagner's Bayreuth Festival performances began to be felt in the 1870s and 1880s. House lights blazed throughout the performance on stages that remained open through the intervals and the scene changes. Mahler, in 1897, demanded the dimming of the house lights in the Vienna Opera during the action, and had the curtain closed at the end of each act; Toscanini, appointed to La Scala, Milan, in the following year, introduced the same custom there.

To consider the state of opera throughout the first sixty years of the nineteenth century is to understand the fanatical zeal which Wagner, Mahler and Toscanini brought to the task of reforming it. In most opera houses the orchestra sat behind the conductor as he faced the stage from immediately in front of the proscenium with no direct control of the orchestra. Even Hans Richter, accepted in Bayreuth as the most loyal of Wagner's disciples, accepted this situation in Vienna; it was Mahler who moved the conductor's desk back to the front of the orchestra to give the conductor complete control of every element of the performance, especially necessary in such works as *Fidelio* and the operas of Mozart, where the orchestra's contribution to the work is no less important than that of the singers.

The concert, until later in the century, had little of the prestige which the opera claimed, but the concert had one major virtue which opera lacked. The concert behaved with almost exemplary loyalty towards the composers whose works were played. The concert orchestras did not deal in adaptations of standard works meant to add to their popularity with audiences unfamiliar with their style or purposes.

[14] A. W. Ganz: *Berlioz in London*. London, 1950. p. 108.

The most celebrated concerts in Germany were those of the Gewandhaus Orchestra in Leipzig, organised by the city's wealthy music-lovers. In the late eighteenth century the largely amateur concert orchestra had been amalgamated with the orchestra of Leipzig Opera, which meant that it had become predominantly professional, though when Mendelssohn became its conductor in 1834 it still had amateur members; Mendelssohn's timpanist, for example, was a theology student at the university. In 1827, when the fourteen-year-old Richard Wagner returned from Dresden to his birthplace, he had already fallen in love with *Der Freischütz* and heard, among other music, the overture to *Fidelio*. In Leipzig, Mozart's *Requiem* converted him to a composer he had previously rejected because he rejected everything, like Mozart's operas, which had an Italian text. A performance of Beethoven's *Egmont Overture*, in Leipzig, sent him to Beethoven's piano sonatas, and in January 1828 he heard his first Beethoven symphony, the Seventh.

The Gewandhaus Orchestra at that time was still directed by its leader; a conductor only appeared when the orchestra was joined by a choir, and the conductor was, by appointment, director of the choir, not of the orchestra. On Good Friday, 1830, Wagner was present for the first time at a performance of the Ninth Symphony (a work which had been played in Leipzig several times before). The leader made his way as best he could for the first three movements; *tempi* were extremely slow because the orchestra could not play the work at the speeds Beethoven had marked; a good deal of the playing was extremely ugly and incoherent. The arrival of a conductor for the last movement did little to improve matters. Christian August Pohlenz, the conductor in question, was well known in Leipzig, a teacher of singing, organist of the Thomaskirche and conductor of the *Singakademie* and various other choral societies. His intervention in the Ninth Symphony when young Wagner heard it did not improve matters. The youth knew the work well from the score, but for one of the few times in his life he almost began to doubt himself; the music which on the page had appeared to him to be beautiful, miraculously logical and monumentally powerful emerged to his ears as a chaos of uncoordinated sound. Wagner's self-doubts did not last for long—it was beyond Wagner's nature to doubt himself for long—but the performance was possibly the most valuable music lesson he ever received.

For all that, in the context of its time, the Gewandhaus Orchestra deserved its high reputation. It represented, wrote Henry Chorley about ten years later, 'the most perfect expression of the musical spirit of Germany'.[15] It had always been adventurous: Beethoven's name had first appeared in its programmes in 1799, when the aria *Ah! Perfido* was sung at one of its concerts, and his works had come to Leipzig almost as quickly as they had become available. Mendelssohn, its first great conductor, ardent and

[15] Chorley: *op. cit.* Vol. 2. p. 99.

high-minded, was the ideal musician for serious-minded Saxon music lovers, and though both Berlioz and Wagner had reservations about his quality as a conductor, the orchestra which Chorley heard was considerably better than that which Wagner remembered with dismay.

'The concerts,' Chorley continued, 'are but indifferently provided. The Gewandhaus, a moderately sized room, is infinitely too small for the audience who crowd it and pay their sixteen groschen for entrance (think of such a concert for two shillings!)' But not even Mendelssohn, it seems, could achieve all that should have been possible. Berlioz went to Germany in 1841 believing that German *tempi* were invariably slower than those set by French conductors, but he found that Mendelssohn used faster *tempi*— Wagner regarded them as excessively fast—than those heard in France. Mendelssohn admitted that he erred on the side of speed to prevent the instrumentalists getting bogged down in music too difficult for them.

Berlioz's account of musical conditions in Germany during his concert tour of 1841–2 follows some quarter of a century after Weber's *Musikalische Topographie*, and Berlioz set out not to study the musical life of the amateur concert societies but to describe his work as a virtuoso conductor, a passionate leader of modern music, with the best available opera and court orchestras. His quality as a conductor—the clarity of his beat, his painstaking patience and the decisiveness of his intentions, together with the charm, wit and dignity of his personality—won the devotion of the orchestras he met as he made his way from musical centre to musical centre where, with the exception of Leipzig, the orchestras were primarily concerned with opera and where professional concerts were rarities. But the orchestras could rarely satisfy all Berlioz's demands: 'We tried in vain,' he wrote of his concert in Leipzig, 'to procure three additional instruments, cor anglais, ophicleide and harp.'[16] Six months earlier, he discovered, Mendelssohn had been compelled to send to Berlin for the harps he needed in his incidental music to *Antigone*. But Berlioz found the Gewandhaus itself 'admirable' and the orchestra to consist of 'capital musicians', and so well disciplined that a programme which included the *King Lear* and *Francs Juges* overtures, the Rondo and Caprice for Violin and Orchestra and the *Fantastic Symphony*—all works new to Leipzig—could be prepared in two rehearsals; at the concert the orchestra played 'faultlessly'.

'Almost everywhere I went in Germany,' he wrote, 'I found discipline and alertness combined with real respect for the *maestro*.'[17] The administrators whom he met and the orchestras which he conducted were dedicated and enthusiastic, determined to give him every ounce of their skill and co-operation. His only general dissatisfaction was with chorus masters, too many of whom were bad pianists and too few of whom were thorough enough to arrange sectional rehearsals even when the music proved difficult.

[16] Berlioz: *Memoirs.* p. 295.   [17] *Ibid.* p. 264.

In Frankfurt, where the orchestra served both the Opera and the regular concerts of the *Museum Gesellschaft* (in which, until 1861, it was joined by amateur players, Berlioz found that the orchestra consisted of eight first and eight second violins, four violas, five cellos, four double basses, two each of the woodwind, four horns, two trumpets, three trombones and timpani. 'The identical force of forty-seven players is, with minor variations, found in every German town of the second rank,' he wrote.[18] When he heard it in the Opera House—for his Frankfurt concerts, planned to open its German tour, had to be postponed till its end—he judged it to be first-rate. 'Not a nuance escapes it, the various timbres blend into a harmonious body of sound free from all trace of harshness, it never falters, its ensemble is precise; it plays like one instrument.' He found a similar orchestra at Stuttgart, 'full of energy and fire, and fearless sight-readers'.[19] It too managed a concert which included the *Fantastic Symphony* after only two rehearsals. But on the road to Stuttgart he had called at Hechingen, where he found only eight violins, three violas, two cellos and two double-basses in the strings. The Weimar Orchestra, in preparation for Berlioz's visit, had assembled all the extra string players that could be found to provide him with twenty-two violins and seven of each of the lower strings.

At Dresden he found 'the richest combination of musical resources that I had encountered since coming to Germany'. He had the services of the orchestra and chorus of the Opera, a military band, a famous tenor (Tichatscek, a great Rienzi and Tannhäuser), Wächter (the first Dutchman in Wagner's *The Flying Dutchman*) and Wilhelmine Schröder-Devrient, whose combination of a fine voice and great dramatic sense made her a great Leonore in *Fidelio*. Unfortunately he found, too, in the orchestra an oboist whose tone was remarkably good but whose sense of style was antiquated and who had a passion for adding ornaments to everything he played. Berlioz protested against this at the second of the four rehearsals, but the oboist returned to his customary tricks at the concert. The leader of the double-basses moved him not to anger but to pity, for he was so old that he could hardly 'support the weight of his instrument' and was no longer able to reach some of his notes.[20]

In Berlin, Berlioz found an orchestra of fourteen first and fourteen second violins, eight violas, ten cellos, eight double-basses, four each of the woodwind instruments, four each of the brass, timpani, bass drum, cymbals and two harps. Everything in Berlin's musical life appealed to him. In Hanover, on the other hand, there were only thirteen violins and three double-basses, with the rest of the orchestra built in proportion. The players were competent but lacking in warmth and feeling; while the Dresden players had been eager to rehearse Berlioz's programme until they knew the music

[18] *Ibid.* p. 270.   [19] *Ibid.* p. 275.
[20] *Ibid.* p. 305.

(after four rehearsals they were ready for a fifth if the composer considered it necessary), some of the Hanover players resented his demand for two rehearsals.[21]

Berlioz's concert tour of 1841–2 took in Mannheim, Hamburg, Brunswick and Munich, important cities with celebrated orchestras and proud musical traditions; players seem to have regarded the visit of so dangerous a musical revolutionary as a challenge to their ability even before Berlioz's personality and ability began to impress them. It may be that the temporary escape from Paris, where his music had impassioned supporters but was opposed by the critics and the academic establishment as well as by the Opéra management, may have influenced the composer's judgement of musical standards, because in Germany his music was accepted and he was offered the wholehearted co-operation and sincere admiration of those musicians with whom he came into contact.

In Brunswick and Dresden, for example, there was no professional concert organisation and no satisfactory concert hall, so that Berlioz gave his concerts in the theatre. An amateur *Konzert Gesellschaft* existed in Dresden, and soon after its creation, in 1821, it had invited Weber to become its director. Weber accepted the invitation but soon found that his official duties and his unsatisfactory health left him no time to train the orchestra of the *Konzert Gesellschaft*; he told the members that he had flattered his powers when he had accepted their invitation.[22]

Concerts in cities like Dresden, where court institutions had been or were in the process of being transformed into public organisations, were rare and special events in the lives of the professional musicians whose real preoccupation was the opera. In the 1840s, when Wagner was *Kapellmeister* at Dresden, the orchestra gave a concert every Palm Sunday for its Pension Fund. Occasional concerts had been given since Weber's successor, Karl Gottlieb Reissiger, had introduced concert music as a spare-time activity for the already overloaded orchestra, but the traditional Palm Sunday concert was a major event of the official musical year, and the standard of symphonic playing in Dresden can be judged from the fact that Wagner's performance of Beethoven's Ninth Symphony, on Palm Sunday 1846 (not the first performance of the work in Dresden or by the *Staatskapelle*), was the first to establish the work in the minds of the Dresden audience as a necessary masterpiece rather than as a piece of remarkable eccentricity by a composer whose sufferings had driven him out of touch with reality. More than that, Wagner's performance impressed visitors like Mendelssohn's assistant in Leipzig, the Danish composer-conductor Niels Gade, although the Ninth Symphony had been played in the Gewandhaus programmes since

[21] *Ibid.* pp. 346–7.
[22] Karl Laux: *The Dresden Staatskapelle*, translated by Lena Jaeck. London, 1964. p. 39.

the 1820s. It was Berlioz and Wagner in Germany and England, as it was Habeneck in France, who removed the impression that Beethoven's last symphony was simply a work of wild incoherence occasionally played out of devotion to its great composer.

In Vienna, in 1845, Berlioz heard one of the charity concerts of the *Gesellschaft der Musikfreunde*, with more than a thousand performers. He was more concerned about the Viennese habit, common both to musicians and to audiences, of closing the ears to all music later than Beethoven's than by anything he heard at the concert, but he was full of enthusiasm for the huge orchestra, which played with fire and accuracy, each of its amateur members arriving note-perfect for the first rehearsal. The orchestra at the Theater an der Wien, where newcomers like to make their Viennese débuts, was not, he noted, as good as that at the Kärntnerthor Theater, where the Court Opera functioned with Otto Nicolai as *Kapellmeister*. The Opera Orchestra began to give public concerts under Nicolai, in 1842, beginning its transformation into its dual personality as orchestra of the State Opera and Philharmonic Orchestra, eventually expanding to the size at which it is virtually a double orchestra capable of serving both the opera and the concert hall. It was this orchestra that Berlioz conducted in his concert in the Redoutensaal, not in the hall of the Conservatoire, where the Opera Orchestra's concerts were normally played.

In 1847, recouping his fortunes after the disaster of *The Damnation of Faust*, he found a 'large and well-rehearsed orchestra and chorus, and a military band to boot' in St. Petersburg. With these he gave two hugely successful concerts of his own music before setting off to Moscow. His first concert had brought him 18,000 francs and the second was equally successful. In Moscow he found 'third-rate musicians, incredible choristers and some bizarre obstacles' but an enthusiastic audience; he made a profit of 8000 francs.[23] In both cities all the musicians he needed were put at his disposal for as many rehearsals as he thought necessary.

With Berlioz's declaration that he could secure fine performances with existing European orchestras so long as he was given adequate rehearsal time, it seems that it was the organisation of European music rather than the accomplishment of musicians which was responsible for the deficiencies about which he, like Wagner, Schumann and many others, inveighed. Some of these deficiencies were due to the slowness of orchestras and their organisers in realising how the novel, enlarged scale of music since Beethoven had created the need for new methods of performance and the presence at any concert of a capable conductor. Conducting, in the modern style, remained more or less a mystery even to most of the people who practised the art until in 1856 Berlioz wrote his essay *Le Chef*

[23] *Op. cit.* pp. 422–4.

d'Orchestre, Théorie et son art and Wagner his essay *Über die Dirigieren* in 1869.

Since the nineteenth century addressed music to the general public gathered in large concert halls, the conductor had become necessary. He needed to be a skilled performer with a specific technique and skills which he did not necessarily share with other musicians. The small orchestras which had been responsible for court concerts and court opera in the eighteenth century could be adequately controlled by a player at the keyboard or by their leader or *Konzertmeister* from his desk at the head of the violins. In 1821 Paganini conducted the first performance of Rossini's *Matilde di Shabran* from the leader's desk when the conductor fell ill after a series of troublesome rehearsals. Mendelssohn was expected to conduct his music for the Philharmonic Society when he first visited London in 1829 from the keyboard of a piano which had already become redundant when Haydn directed his symphonies in the Hanover Square Rooms in the 1790s. Spohr claimed to have been the first musician to conduct the Philharmonic Society concerts with a baton in London during his first visit to England in 1820. In the theatre, with a greater number of players to direct over a greater area, conducting was accepted as necessary; Weber conducted *Oberon* at Covent Garden with a rolled-up paper instead of a baton.

Musically, too, a *Konzertmeister* at the first violinist's desk or a *Kapellmeister* at a keyboard could do justice to a well-rehearsed performance of a pre-Beethoven symphony; his activities could do no harm and possibly a great deal of good even though he had no special qualifications as a conductor. The idea of a time-beater was not new, but the special techniques required by the conductor of a large orchestra were not understood by, for example, Beethoven, who conducted until 1812, although by this time he could not clearly hear most of what was done by the orchestra; apparently he had no clear ideas about the indication of *tempi* and was almost, according to Spohr's account, exclusively interested in expression. Berlioz suggested that orchestras adopted the benevolently dishonest practice of paying no attention to his excessive gesticulations.

Both Wagner and Berlioz wrote with great respect of François Antoine Habeneck and the orchestra of the Société des Concerts du Conservatoire, which Habeneck founded, and conducted for the first twenty years of its life. The Ninth Symphony in Leipzig had, according to Wagner, been a chaotic disappointment in 1830. In Paris, about ten years later, he heard Habeneck conduct a performance which seemed to him to be superb in spite of his inborn conviction that French musicians were temperamentally incapable of understanding the introspection and *Innigkeit* of German music.

The orchestra of the Society was founded in 1828; it had fifteen first and sixteen second violins, eight violas, twelve cellos, eight double-basses, four flutes, three oboes, four clarinets, four bassons, two trumpets, four horns, four trombones, a timpanist and a harpist. To it was attached a professional choir of seventy-nine voices. It gave, according to its constitution, seven concerts in a season that began every January, giving an opportunity to prize-winning students of the Conservatoire to appear in its concerts as soloists or as composers. As well as the seven concerts of its official season, it played a programme every year for the players' concert fund.[24] The hall of the Conservatoire originally, at the foundation of the orchestra, accommodated a thousand and seventy-eight listeners.

Habeneck's pre-eminence as a conductor of the symphonic repertoire was based on thorough and painstaking rehearsal. The Ninth Symphony, when Wagner heard it in Paris, was a performance which had been rehearsed for several months until every member of the orchestra knew and understood his part. 'The orchestra,' said Wagner, 'has learnt to look for Beethoven's *melody* in every bar.' Habeneck was a stern disciplinarian and a fine orchestral trainer, and though Berlioz lists him among the 'barbarians' who, like the musicologist Fétis, presumed to 'correct' Beethoven's music, he made no complaint against the concert in 1832 when Habeneck conducted his *Fantastic Symphony* and its sequel *Lélio*. Habeneck silenced the double-basses at the beginning of the scherzo of Beethoven's Fifth Symphony and was condemned by Berlioz for this, saying that the cellos sounded better alone—a decision which probably owed more to the poor quality of the Paris double-basses than to Habeneck's philistinism.

Habeneck lived before the days when conducting became a skill which combined technique with mystique in more or less equal proportions; once a tempo had been firmly established, he would stop and treat himself to a pinch of snuff while the orchestra carried on. Berlioz, at the first performance of his *Requiem*, noted that he ceased to conduct and took snuff just at the point in the *Dies Irae* where the tempo broadens out for the entry of the four far-flung brass groups of the *Tuba mirum*, leapt to his feet and gave the beat himself; writing many years later, he saw the incident as an indication that Habeneck had joined in the determined persecution of everything that he did.

Habeneck's masterly conducting of the Beethoven symphonies was achieved by conducting with a violin bow from a first violin part in which essential cues had been noted; he conducted at the Opéra not from a full score but from a double-stave version which contained only the vocal line and the most essential strand of accompaniment. In modern terms, Habeneck was barely a conductor at all, for the proper technique, its invention and codification, was largely the work of Berlioz and Wagner. Berlioz's essay

[24] A. Dandelot: *La Société des Concerts du Conservatoire, 1828–1897.* Paris, 1923. pp. 29–30.

of 1856, which was added to the 1844 *Traité d'Instrumentation* as an epilogue, remains a fine textbook. It starts from the fact that a bad singer or solo instrumentalist ruins his own part, but a bad conductor ruins an entire work. He wrote:

> A conductor should *see* and *understand*; he should be *agile* and *vigorous*; he should know the composition he conducts and the nature of the instruments; he should be able to read a score.[25]

If it seems remarkable that Berlioz should need to point out facts so blindingly obvious, he does so because he wrote when conducting was a new technique not properly studied but left to what Wagner called 'professional routine'. Berlioz admits that as well as 'a special talent' the conductor needs other abilities which are

> almost indefinable and without which an impalpable barrier rises between him and those who he directs, the faculty of transmitting his feelings is denied him, and therefore power and authority, the directive action, completely escape him.

But he still has to point out that

> the making of any noise whatsoever, either by the conductor's baton on the desk or by his foot on the platform, is to be universally condemned. It is worse than a bad habit—it is a barbarism.

Obviously in 1856 the basic facts needed to be stated firmly.

Berlioz's essay deals precisely with matters of fundamental technique, with methods of beating time clearly yet in a way which prevents monotony of rhythm. He considers the control of scattered forces in the opera house or concert hall, the use of the metronome, the control of sub-conductors. He does not attempt to teach the indefinables of musical sensitivity but restricts himself firmly to knowledge of the kind that can be imparted.

Wagner's essay is as different from Berlioz's as Berlioz was from Wagner. What can be imparted by a textbook seems to have little interest for Wagner, because anybody could teach it. He set out to show how musical understanding and sensitivity can be transmitted by the conductor through an analysis of what he regarded as the common faults of German conductors; he considers not only the almost sacred German classical symphonies and the problems they pose but also the failings of German performances of the operas of Rossini and Bellini. The faults he discovers he attributes to two main causes—the incapacity and insensitivity of conductors who cannot sense the true *tempo* of a work; everything depends on this. The Paris performances of Beethoven's symphonies under Habeneck had been great because the orchestra, knowing and understanding the music, could

[25] Berlioz: *On Conducting*, translated by John Broadhouse, London, 1917. p. 3.

project its melodic line from bar to bar throughout whatever complexities of harmony and orchestration a long movement offers. German conductors who could neither sing nor understand real singing were incapable of bringing out a complex, varying melodic line; they did not understand such things as melodic phrasing and left a work like the Ninth Symphony to exist without any clear melodic continuity, regarding the music as sacred because they did not understand it. The tradition of Mendelssohn, the elegance and polish of which had got rid of 'a good deal of rawness and loutishness' preserved an academic rather than a living tradition of performance, though Mendelssohn's penchant for over-fast *tempi* suggested a dangerous lack of sensitivity. The essential Wagnerian teaching is conveyed through his analysis of standard performances of music by Haydn, Mozart and Beethoven; the essay is about musical sensitivity, not about the technique of conducting.

Berlioz's beat was clear and immediately legible, Wagner's more elaborate, designed to convey unusual subtleties of rhythm and *rubato*. London orchestras, trained for years by the bandmaster methods of Costa, who dominated both opera and concert hall in London for almost forty years, never understood Wagner's requirements, and his season as conductor of the Philharmonic Society was disastrous. Those who managed to grasp his style, however, were enthusiatic about it:

> The old flautist, Furstenau, of Dresden, told me that often, when Wagner conducted, the players had no sense of being led. Each believed himself to be following freely his own feeling, yet they all worked together wonderfully. It was Wagner's mighty will that powerfully but unperceived had overborne their single wills, so that each thought himself free while each followed the leader, whose artistic force lived and worked in him.[26]

The Wagnerian doctrines spread through Europe as his career achieved the apotheosis of Bayreuth and his disciples took more or less complete control of European music. But mere familiarity with the nineteenth-century orchestra created a real understanding of the problems of balance, control and interpretation involved in the conductor's work.

But in all fields of music-making the same faults were observable in the earlier years of the symphony. The permanently based string quartet hardly existed before the violinist Joseph Joachim founded his string quartet in 1869 and established real standards of chamber-music performance. Spohr played a vast amount of chamber music wherever he went, but he found the later string quartets of Beethoven to be completely baffling. To his mind, a quartet was a work in which he, as first violinist, was accompanied by the most satisfactory musicians who could be found to fill up the other desks. Even Berlioz was worried when, as a young man,

[26] Felix Weingartner: *On Conducting*, translated by Ernest Newman. Leipzig, 1925. p. 11.

he discovered that he could not make sense of the posthumous Beethoven quartets simply by studying their first-violin parts. The habits of the eighteenth century prevailed for fifty years into the nineteenth century, although music had long outgrown them.

4

The Virtuoso

Possibly the difficulties of eighteenth-century travel were all that restricted the activities of the great eighteenth-century virtuoso players. Eighteenth-century singers travelled widely, but tended to contract themselves for a season to whatever theatre offered them the most profitable terms. Instrumentalists moved on more quickly from their concerts but tended not to devote too much of their time to touring. Mozart's colleagues from Salzburg, Ignaz Leutgeb, the horn player and Anton Stadler, the clarinettist, for example, discovered that they could live well enough in Vienna without committing themselves to the rigours of long, extensive tours; Leutgeb helped to finance his freelance career in Vienna by running a cheesemonger's shop. Johann Simon Hermstedt, who played Spohr's clarinet music, toured with his composer, as did Weber's clarinettist, Heinrich Bärmann. But their tours were less frequent and less extensive than those of Spohr, and Weber travelled further in his early years as a concert pianist. Maria Theresia von Paradis, the blind pianist whose father, an Imperial Counsellor, was a nobleman, played in Paris in 1784, travelled on to London, staying there for five months and meeting all the best people before she returned to Vienna through Brussels and the major German courts. A single tour could establish a reputation, after that, further travelling seemed pointless.

The traveller made his way over appalling roads—the only record of a concert from which Paganini's audience went away disappointed refers to his appearance at Stuttgart on 3 December 1828; he had arrived in the city in the early hours of the morning after his coach had overturned. The touring musician was rarely able to plan a concert more than a week ahead, and his first advance publicity came from the gossip of travellers making their way over his route a day or two before him. He would send his business manager ahead, if, like Paganini, he could afford to employ one, to book a hall or rent a theatre, come to terms with the local orchestra and arrange as much publicity as time allowed.

Major cities stood outside this haphazard progress as fixed points by which his intermediate activities could be governed. In them, dates of arrival would be fixed in advance, other performers booked and possibly even a rehearsal arranged. But the traveller making his way, say, from a long-fixed performance at Nuremberg to another at Munich would pass through Eichstätt, giving himself time there to play to the Prince-Bishop's court if his offer to do so were accepted, and possibly to arrange a concert with the amateur orchestra of the city. His chances of planning any of this ahead were very limited; he was not, however, completely governed by the repertoire familiar to local musicians in small towns, for nobody would worry if the local orchestra sat down to play at sight the accompaniment to a concerto they had never seen before. He could, of course, maintain some sort of contact with the musicians of cities where he had already given a successful concert and, through them, plan ahead in spite of the difficulties of travel in the pre-railway age, which in Germany continued into the 1840s. The need for such a book as Weber's planned *Musical Topography* becomes obvious as we realise that the musician was hoping to play in places where had had no musical contacts whatever and where the facilities for concert performance were not known to him.

But just as Beethoven appeared to the early nineteenth century as a type of composer without precedent, above and outside all precedents by virtue of his genius, subject to no law but that of his own inspiration, so the super-virtuoso appeared a being as remote from normal considerations as was Beethoven. Paganini reached Vienna in 1828, the year after Beethoven's death. He was a physical wreck; in addition to acute and sometimes crippling digestive troubles and a nervously over-intense temperament, he suffered from tuberculosis. He did not even look like other men; he was emaciated to the point at which that it seemed as though he wore clothes to keep his skeleton from falling apart; black eyes glittered from a yellow-skinned, cadaverous face on each side of which hung long, lank black hair. His platform manner added to his strangeness; he bowed stiffly, like a marionette whose strings had suddenly been released, and he walked in a peculiarly stiff, wide-legged way. Of course, he played the violin as it had never been played before; his G string had an effective range of three octaves, and he produced harmonics the like of which were unheard of. His varieties of bowing and his left-hand pizzicato were equally new.

Legends accumulated round him. Imprisoned for murdering his wife or his mistress—nobody was quite sure which—men said that he had spent his years of imprisonment perfecting his playing because he could neither read nor write, so that less strenuous ways of killing time were not open to him. His peculiar walk was due to the years in which he had paced his tiny cell with a criminal's iron crossbar chained between his legs. The G string on which he performed incredible solos, including an entire sonata he had dedicated to Napoleon I, was made from the intestines of his wife or mistress, whichever of the two had been his murder victim. The more observant, or the more imaginative, saw the devil standing beside him on the platform, guiding his bowing arm or his left hand or both. He had won his mastery at the price of a Faustian bargain with the Evil One.

The terrifying, Mephistophelian Paganini—who seems to have been a man of great charm and considerable culture as well as lively intelligence—was forty-six before he began to travel outside Italy. The publicity stories, wherever they came from (and he himself protested that he disliked them), did nothing to decrease the size of his audiences; they turned him from a mere musician into a sensation appealing to crowds who would never have dreamed of attending a concert by a mere celebrity, like Spohr. When he started to move outside Italy he began to declare that the legends were an affront to his dignity as an artist, but they seem to have worried him not at all while he was establishing his reputation as a wonder man, and, ridiculous as they are, they stamp him with the seal of the romantic age; one can imagine the young Berlioz, if he had thought of the story first, composing another symphony of 'Episodes in the life of an artist' (the subtitle of the *Fantastic Symphony*) in which the artist sells his soul to the devil for the sake of superhuman skill, murders his beloved and makes a miraculous G string from her intestines. Even the streak of morbidity in the early romantic movement and its typical works is paralleled by the morbidity which is one of the elements of Paganini's life.

From the age of thirteen, when he played at a concert in Genoa to finance his further training, he had been almost continuously active, though for some three years (the years of mystery which prompted the story of his imprisonment for murder) he had apparently retired into the house of an aristocratic mistress, and from the age of nineteen until he was twenty-two had given the world nothing but compositions. He had been *Maestro-di-capella* in the court at Lucca while Napoleon's elder sister, Marianne Elise Bacchiochi, and her husband were Prince and Princess there. In 1809 he gave up court service, playing wherever he could earn money, never completely healthy, driven sometimes into retirement to recoup his health, gambling and wenching inexhaustibly. An action for abduction against him—though the girl he supposedly abducted seems to have been a prostitute who recognised that an abduction charge would be an easy way to make money from him—caused him some trouble and cost him a great deal of money but has nothing to do with the legend of his imprisonment. In 1814 he bought an annuity for his parents at a cost of 20,000 lire, and for the rest of his life his brothers and sisters depended upon him for frequent financial help.

He had not made so much money by exercising the highest musical taste. He had a genuine love for the music of Beethoven, whose chamber works he loved to play in private, but his public concerts contained no music of this sort, but only the almost impossible works he composed for himself, one or two popular virtuoso concertos by his contemporaries and, at times, farmyard imitations; he imitated the braying of an ass so effectively in Ferrara that his audience suspected that he was making a comment on them, and drove him from the city; they had refused to take the singing of his current mistress seriously. In Leghorn he arranged a concert without asking the co-operation of the Orchestral Society, so that the concert started belatedly, with only four of the orchestra present. In such a situation Paganini was at his best; he could spend the evening proving that he needed no orchestra. He was always happy to dazzle his public by carrying through a programme almost unaccompanied.

He made use of the most astounding gimmicks; in Lucca, as leader of the orchestra, he directed an entire opera with only the two lower strings in place on his violin; he fascinated audiences by his willingness to carry on a work after a string had broken on his instrument rather than interrupt the music and fit a new string, and though both his compositions and his playing were genuinely creative, he seems to have enjoyed the breaking of strings for the opportunities they gave him to stupefy an audience by his ability to play without them. His G string solos may have begun as gimmicks, but they became a vehicle for the melancholy poetry which haunts his slow movements.

Spohr, the conservative purist, wrote:

> Connoisseurs say that it cannot be denied that he certainly possesses a great dexterity with the left hand, in double chords and in passages of every kind, but the very thing by which he fascinates the crowd debases him to a mere charlatan. . . . That by which he captivates the Italian public consists, on a nearer enquiry, in a succession of feats . . . viz: in flageolet tones; in variations upon one string, in which, for the purpose of imposing more upon the audience, he takes off the other three strings of the violin; in a peculiar kind of *pizzicato*, produced with the left hand without the help of the right hand or the bow; and many tones unnatural to the violin, such as the bassoon tone, the voice of an old woman, etc., etc.[1]

This was the result of hearsay, Spohr defending traditional values against an opponent whom he had never heard. When, later, Paganini played in Cassel, Spohr was present at the concert and gave the famous traveller a dinner without becoming a wholehearted admirer. 'His compositions,' wrote Spohr, 'and his execution I found a strange mixture of the highly genial and childishly tasteless.'[2] The Victorian translation of Spohr's *Autobiography* is not without its eccentricities; it seems that both Paganini's compositions and his playing seemed to the German virtuoso to be brilliant and to have genius, but at the same time to be disfigured with circus tricks of the sort that could only appeal to a child. To Spohr, revolutions in violin technique were irrelevant to real musical considerations because the violin as it had reached his generation could already do everything which it

[1] Spohr: *op. cit.* Vol. 1. p. 280.
[2] *Ibid.* Vol. 2. p. 168.

needed to do, its limitations having been laid down in the works of the classical masters.

To understand Paganini's influence on the course of music, it is not only necessary to note the expansion of technique which, notwithstanding the doubts of old-fashioned musicians, provided the entire string orchestra, as well as the violin, with a vast expansion of their vocabulary; it is also essential to consider the personality which gave rise to the highly coloured legends and made him a figure of wonder and terror; the sense of the dangerous, the uncanny and the superhuman which he imposed on his audiences was not only a valid part of the romantic atmosphere of the period; it was also a potent influence on new audiences and on a vast number of his successors. Meyerbeer and Rossini both admired and liked Paganini; Schubert wrote to his friend Anselm Huttenbrenner about a concert of Paganini's in Vienna: 'In the *adagio* I heard an angel sing.' The adagio was that of Paganini's D minor Concerto.[3]

This was Paganini away from home, where he disciplined himself to express his personality through music and not through the sort of frivolous cleverness which had often appealed to Italian audiences and where his influence was greatest. In central Europe. France and Britain he seems to have been no longer content simply to amaze huge audiences by his ability to do what had never been done before even when it was hardly worth doing. Wherever there was an audience he played to it, so that even in England he travelled to concerts in provincial towns where Spohr and Mendelssohn had never troubled to make themselves heard. All over Europe he doubled admission fees to his concerts and still packed the hall for every appearance; only the English resisted his demands after pointing out that admission prices in London were already nearly twice as high as those in theatres and concert halls even in the continental capitals. He made 20,000 florins out of his concerts in Vienna and averaged £1000 a night for his appearances in London; even in provincial cities like Norwich he packed halls in spite of prices as high as fifteen shillings a seat. His demands brought him a reputation for extreme avarice; in London in 1831 he refused to play at the benefit concert for the famous bass Lablache unless he were given one-third of the gross takings. He never became, or wished to become, a popular or beloved figure; he preferred his audiences to regard him with some dread. Occasionally, unaccountably but in a way which did no harm to his strange reputation, he would give concerts for charity so long as he was not importuned to do so; he could, apparently on impulse, attend a performance of Berlioz's *Harold in Italy* and at its close kneel at Berlioz's feet and two days later send him a cheque for 20,000 francs. The story has been denied, first by Paganini's adored son and then by others who wished him to be consistent in his miserliness, but it has not been disproved.

[3] Deutsch: *op. cit.* p. 737.

Between the man Niccolo Paganini and the diabolical public enchanter
was a great, and apparently calculated, gulf. Canon John Edmund Cox of
Norwich was his host and apparently his English secretary while he stayed
in the city, and Cox noted the difference between the private musician and
the public showman:

> In private—*for he had the violin constantly in his hand*—he would sit
> down and dash off by the hour snatches from the compositions of the
> best masters and give readings of such originality to passages that had
> been heard again and again, such as they have never been supposed to
> possess by any other player. As an instance of this, he, one morning
> while I was writing several notes for him, commenced the first motivo
> of Beethoven's Violin Concerto. To write then was impossible, and he,
> seeing how entranced I was, asked me whether I knew what it was. On
> my replying in the negative, he promised, if it could be managed, I should
> hear the whole movement. . . . On the last night . . . one gentleman . . .
> at a signal from the 'Master' sat down at the pianoforte and drawing a
> crumpled piece of paper from the inner pocket of his long black dress
> coat, began to play. Instantly I was on the alert, for I remembered the
> notes and his promise rushed back upon me.[4]

Paganini's activities in Britain alone were more exhaustive than those of
any other international celebrity. He played in Great Yarmouth, went from
there to Dublin, stayed in Ireland to visit Carlow, Clonmel, Kilkenny,
Waterford, Cork, Limerick and Belfast. From there he crossed to Scotland
and appeared in Edinburgh, Glasgow, Ayr, Kilmarnock, Perth and
Dundee. In England he gave concerts in Brighton, Clifton, Cheltenham,
Bristol, Bath, Liverpool, Manchester, Leeds, Sheffield, Chester, York,
Birmingham, Winchester and Southampton before returning to France and,
for a time, commuting between Paris and London to satisfy his admirers
in both capitals. His aim, he said, was to leave his natural son, Achillino
(who was later legitimatised), 2,000,000 lire, and after he returned to Italy
in 1835 he was almost burnt out, incapable of any extended effort. He died
in 1840, leaving Achillino all the money a son could require and the world
a legend.

The influence of Paganini extended itself through his personality as well
as his genius as a violinist; in future there was to be an inescapable equation
between powerful, eccentric personality and supreme virtuosity. 'The
grand manner' on the concert platform is part of Paganini's legend. But
the influence of Paganini's compositions, though they seem to need his own
personality to give them their full effect, went equally deep; they underlie
much of the string writing of Berlioz and Wagner. He is one of the
Personalities re-created by Schumann in *Carnival,* and Schumann used six
of the solo violin *Caprices* of Paganini as bases for his Concert Studies
op. 10. Liszt's *Études d'exécution transcendante,* the *Grandes Études de*

[4] J. E. Cox: *Musical Reminiscences.* London, 1872. pp. 196ff.

Paganini and his *Grande Fantaisie sur la Clochette* are works in which
the master pianist set out to do for his instrument what Paganini had done
for the violin. Brahms's *Paganini Variations* and Rachmaninov's *Rhapsody
on a Theme by Paganini* are only two of the memorable acts of homage
paid to his genius by later composers.

Not even Liszt travelled so extensively. After Paganini, the old virtuoso
route round the courts of Central Europe, with visits to Paris and London,
was no longer the most profitable route an instrumentalist could follow. Of
course, any musician with a great reputation could collect audiences in
Winchester, Bath or Norwich: the question was whether he needed to drive
himself so hard as Paganini had done. Until Paris, London, Vienna and
Berlin were tired of him, why should he endure the miseries of travel to
smaller towns and less profitable concerts? Paganini's labours went beyond
what was necessary; a couple of extra concerts in London—and there was
never a time when he could not command a capacity audience paying more
than the usual cost of admission to listen to him with bated breath in any
capital in Europe—would have made him as much money as his exhausting
journeys through the provinces, and this was a fact which he was quite
shrewd enough to realise; his determination to leave every beaten track
seems to have arisen from an inner compulsion to conquer every audience
he could reach, no matter at what cost in exhaustion and what danger to
his health came from reaching it. His determination to make his son rich—
the rationalisation with which he explained his endless labours—could as
easily have been served in the relative comfort of half a dozen great cities.
Paganini was apparently under some compulsion to conquer wherever roads
could lead him; not for him the establishment of a reputation among connoisseurs in a few historic, politically important cities.

It was Liszt who followed most closely in Paganini's footsteps. A
beautiful and fantastically gifted child, he had played in Vienna in 1822,
when he was eleven years old, and had, perhaps, been kissed by Beethoven
(more probably in private than, as the legend insists, at a public concert).
At twelve he reached Paris, at thirteen he appeared for the first time in
London and at fourteen his opera *Don Sanche* was produced in Paris. He
continued to tour until his father died, in 1827, and then he seemed to lose
any sense of the direction in which he might develop. The arrival of
Paganini in Paris in 1833 gave his art and personality the target they
needed, the possibility of leading a revolution in keyboard technique as
startling as Paganini's revolution in violin playing.

The pianistic revolution could not have taken place had it not been for
developments in pianoforte design and building notably by the Parisian
manufacturer Sebastian Érard. Iron-framed pianos gave the player a new
range of dynamics and a wider range of colours; Érard's double-escape-
ment action made possible the effects of speed and glitter through which

Liszt and his contemporaries transferred to the piano the effects and figurations inspired by Paganini in genuinely pianistic equivalents. The arrival in Paris of Chopin, in 1832, and the emergence of Berlioz's music, joined with the style Liszt had already developed, combined together to create the superman-virtuoso of the piano.

But while it is Liszt who is remembered as the supreme pianist, he was one of a remarkable generation of piano virtuosi. Mendelssohn, a splendid pianist, was born two years before Liszt; Chopin was a year Liszt's senior. The aristocratic Sigismund Thalberg, illegitimate son of Count Moritz von Dietricstein and Baroness von Wetzlar, was a year Liszt's junior. Adolf Henselt, in the eyes of some Liszt's superior but the victim of a shyness which would not let him play in public, was born a year later, in 1813, and Ferdinand Heller in 1814. It is almost as though the now perfected piano—for only Steinway's increase in the instrument's sustaining power and volume, an innovation of the 1850s, remained to be developed when the Liszt generation took command—created the possibility of the masters it needed. Their popularity, and the awe in which they were held, was increased by the rapidity with which the piano became the universal, all-purpose domestic instrument. It was the piano which young ladies automatically learned as a social duty, and it was the piano which enabled the serious amateur to come to terms with the orchestral repertory through transcriptions. The general fascination with the piano and its masters encouraged the pianist to take the risk of giving solo performances.

It is difficult accurately to chart the rise of the piano as the essential amateur all-purpose instrument. Shudi, the London instrument-maker, was producing about nineteen harpsichords and twenty pianos a year in the 1770s. Stein, of Augsburg, whose pianos pleased Mozart, produced a similar number. Broadwood, the London maker who learned his trade from Shudi, created about seven thousand square pianos and one thousand grands between 1782 and 1815. By the end of the nineteenth century there were about thirty piano-makers in London, and Broadwood, the most successful of them, had begun to use steam power and methods of mass production at a time when there were, according to a Scottish author, John Russell, in his *A Tour in Germany and some of the Southern Provinces of the Austrian Empire* (published in 1828), about sixty-five piano-makers in Vienna, none, however, using Broadwood's mass production techniques.

By the middle of the nineteenth century, Broadwood was making about two thousand three hundred instruments a year and Collard, the firm originally established by Muzio Clementi, about one thousand five hundred. France produced about a third of the entire English total, but the largest and most successful of Vienna's one hundred and eight piano-makers were producing some two hundred pianos a year. The piano was so firmly entrenched in amateur musical life that chamber music had drifted out of the home and was becoming the preserve of ensembles of professional players like the Joachim Quartet. As early as the 1830s, Mendelssohn had written to Zelter that there were 10,000 pianos in Vienna. A few days before he had been irritated in Munich by 'young ladies quite able to perform some adequate pieces very nicely' but who 'tried to break their fingers with juggler's tricks and rope dancer's feats of Herz'. Herz's music was flashy, empty showman's work, and Mendelssohn, the handsome, elegant darling of the salons, tried to convert the Munich girls to Beethoven's sonatas.[5]

Ignaz Moscheles, born in 1794, claimed to be the first pianist to have played in public without an orchestra, but when he did so, in 1837, he shared the programme with singers to avoid the danger of the monotony which his friends thought likely to afflict a solo performance. In 1839 Liszt began a series of solo performances, which he called 'Musical Soliloquies', in Rome. In a letter to Princess Belgiojoso he discussed his innovation: 'My impudence is so limitless that I am quite capable of importing my Musical Soliloquies (I cannot think of another name for these inventions of mine) to Paris.' He sent the Princess a note of his programme—his own transcription of the *William Tell* Overture, his Fantasy on *I Puritani*, some of his pieces which were billed as 'Studies and Fragments' and an improvisation on a given theme. All the music was by Liszt or arranged by him, probably for the reason that other men's music might not give him sufficient opportunities for display. When Liszt gave his first solo performance in London, the concert, in the Hanover Square Rooms, was announced as a 'Recital', apparently the first use of the term in publicity, though Dunneley's *Dictionary of Music,* published in 1825, had used the name 'recital' for a solo vocal performance.

Liszt's recitals were as much social events as they were concerts. It was possible to eat, drink and smoke between the items and the seats were arranged so that the audience could move at ease about the auditorium. Liszt would go to the piano and play for a time; then he would descend into the auditorium and talk to friends or to those lucky enough to be presented to him. Then he would play a little more, interspersing the entire programme with socialising descents into the auditorium. The programme invariably ended, of course, in London as in Paris or Vienna, with an outburst of the sort of hysteria associated in the eighteenth century with the singing of *castrato* opera stars and in the twentieth by the performances of 'pop' idols. It was a half-smoked cigar by Liszt that was retrieved by an aristocratic lady in his audience and carried round in her corsage until the day she died. Much of his appeal, apparently, was sexual, and nobody who wrote of his performances found it possible to isolate his musicianship from his personality; at the piano the paradoxes, inconsistencies, severities, in-

[5] Mendelssohn: *Letters,* edited by G. Selden-Goth. Elek, London, 1947.

dulgences and the charlatanism which went cheek by jowl with his devoted musicianship were all displayed.

The display was unusually lucrative. Wagner, when he was the merest acquaintance of the man who was to be his first and most devoted champion, was in Paris earning his living by the dreariest musical hack-work when he heard a Liszt recital and discussed it in an article for the *Abendzeitung* of Dresden:

> Liszt recently gave a concert here. He appeared alone; nobody else played or sang. The tickets cost twenty francs each, and he earned a total of ten thousand francs, with no expenses. He is soon to give another concert. What assurance! What infallibility! I am speaking of the speculative aspect; his playing is so assured and infallible that it is not worth wasting a single word on that.[6]

Liszt's programme of show pieces and transcriptions was not of the sort that could appeal to Wagner at his sunniest, and the penniless composer with a sense of his destiny and the sanctity of great art could not, perhaps, avoid the note of rancour when he found Liszt making great sums of money by cheapening and making a sensation out of the art he served.

Though Liszt's contemporaries had fervent supporters—some of them were popular enough to appear as his rivals—it was the hysterical sensationalism that accompanied Liszt, rather than his importance as a composer whose considerable creative power overflowed into performance, which made Liszt a legend while his rivals, apart from Chopin and Mendelssohn, are simply names in the history books. Chopin's originality—a quality which the twentieth century often finds it hard to appreciate—and the long, self-propagating melodic lines he developed from Italian *bel canto* opera were as startling as the unorthodox beauty and expressiveness of his harmony. Mendelssohn's letters, for example, dwell with delight not only on the beauty and appeal of Chopin's music but also on the remarkable keyboard style which Chopin had developed—he could not have learned it from any of his teachers—in order to embody his own music. Chopin used the sustaining pedal, for example, to secure *pianissimo legato* passages. Chopin himself gave few public concerts but lived on his earnings as a teacher with an extensive practice among the wealthy, by his performances at the private concerts of the rich and by the money made by his publications. When he played to an audience he avoided the startling, eye-catching mannerisms of Liszt.

Thalberg, too, whose speciality was so to surround a melody in the middle of the keyboard with fantastically elaborate arpeggios that listeners could not understand how two hands could achieve his effects, deliberately

adopted a very restrained manner. Liszt's playing tended to be a dramatic
struggle in which he was pitted against mighty forces which only a super-
man could defeat; Thalberg made virtuosity sound easy, but Liszt, perhaps
more shrewdly for the effect he had upon audiences, acted out both the
technical problems he surmounted and the emotional responses the music
demanded from him. Neither Liszt nor Thalberg played much apart from
their own bravura works in public; Thalberg seems hardly ever to have
gone beyond them, though those who heard him play Beethoven sonatas in
private ranked him above Liszt because he never added his own embellishments to the music.

The works through which Liszt conquered the musical world in the
1830s were his own, and they extended piano technique in every direction
beyond anything that had been thought possible before his appearance.
Other men could do one or other of the things he did superlatively well,
but he alone could manage them all. The works which he wrote to demonstrate his abilities are more than a meretricious exploitation of a phenomenal
technique, and even at their most spectacular they express something deep
in Liszt's personality—the virtuoso's delight in his mastery. Even the
operatic fantasies—a type of composition extremely popular in the days
when he was the lion of the keyboard with the longest mane and most
musically intimidating roar—become re-creations by Liszt of other men's
thoughts. The later Liszt blazed strange harmonic trails, was an orchestral
innovator and pioneered techniques of symphonic narrative, but the early
Liszt was essentially an interpretative artist; where he was not interpreting
the music of other composers, he was interpreting the nature of the piano
itself, and other people's music, when it became the basis of a Liszt work,
reappeared as his own view of the notes with which he had been provided.
When he played music by Beethoven he used the notes set down on paper
for him with a freedom which many of his contemporaries condemned and
which would be unforgivable to twentieth-century ears. It was from Liszt
more than from anyone else that the idea grew of the interpretative artist's
right to freedom of expression through other men's music.

Until 1840, when Liszt played music by other composers he was more
likely to play his own transcription of one of their orchestral works than to
embark on a piano piece. His piano versions of the Beethoven symphonies
appeared far more frequently than any of Beethoven's pianoforte works in
his programmes. There is no record of Liszt's attempting any of Beethoven's
concertos except the G major and the E flat (the *Emperor*), and the sonatas
he chose to play, apart from the *Hammerklavier op.* 106, were the
extremely popular works with titles, like the so-called 'Moonlight'; he
seems to have played only five Beethoven sonatas in public. He acknowledged a debt to Chopin, but played little of Chopin's music. When, at a
Beethoven concert, the audience demanded his transcription of the Skating

Scene in Meyerbeer's *The Prophet,* he obeyed the public; he was, he said, its servant.

The *Hammerklavier Sonata,* regarded as an impossible and incoherent work, was the work with which he chose to declare his superiority over Thalberg, when Thalberg challenged his mastery of the Paris audience. According to Berlioz, who followed the performance from the score, the performance made a previously unintelligible work appear for the first time as great music. A sight-reader of almost incredible swiftness, he was capable of fine performances at sight from manuscript orchestral scores; he achieved such performances at sight of the Mendelssohn Concerto in G minor and Grieg's Piano Concerto as well as with Grieg's Violin and Piano Sonata, in each case to the amazed delight of the composer. Joachim, the great violinist of the nineteenth century, enjoyed first performances with Liszt but said that at every later performance the piano part would become subject to more and more elaborate embellishments until in the end it was as much a Liszt paraphrase as a performance of another man's music.

The legend which Liszt alone, of the great generation of virtuoso pianists, left behind him has done as much as his enormous body of compositions to keep our interest alive; there is no doubt that, like Paganini, Liszt was conscious of the need to dominate his audience by dazzling it and playing upon its emotions, but the audiences which feared Paganini loved Liszt. We do not know the extent to which the excitement of contact with an almost hysterical audience affected him so much that he stretched interpretative liberty into licence; Berlioz wrote that an intense responsiveness of temperament was responsible for inducing Liszt to play magnificently whilst distorting Beethoven, whom he as well as Berlioz worshipped. In private, Berlioz noticed, Liszt played Beethoven's music as powerfully as he would play it to an audience, but with the discipline that Berlioz found natural in approaching the works of a great master.

Charles Hallé was already a fine pianist when, in 1836, at the age of seventeen, he settled in Paris and became a friend of Liszt, Berlioz and Chopin. In the late 1880s Bernard Shaw wrote of him with the admiration he refused to mere showmen pianists:

> Sir Charles is not a sensational player, but nobody who heard him play the *largo* of this sonata [Beethoven's op. 10 no. 3] has ever accepted the notion that his playing is 'icy and mechanical'. Is there any audience in the world that would come to hear [Anton] Rubenstein play a Beethoven sonata for the twentieth time? Yet Hallé is always sure of his audience. . . . The reason is that he gives you as little as possible of Hallé and as much as possible of Beethoven.[7]

[7] G. Bernard Shaw: *London Music in 1888–89 as heard by Corno di Bassetto.* London, 1937. p. 41.

For a time, Hallé had been swept off his feet by Liszt's example. He first heard the great magician at the concert in which Berlioz first conducted the *Marche au Supplice* from the *Fantastic Symphony* in its orchestral dress and then Liszt played his transcription of the same movement. The example could not be resisted, and Hallé found himself in hot water with the Paris critics in 1844 when he played Beethoven's E flat Concerto at a Conservatoire concert and copied Liszt, by playing in octaves passages written in single notes; but Hallé was never really a showman and learnt to judge Liszt accurately. He wrote:

> If before his marvellous execution one had only to bow in adoration, there were some peculiarities of style, or rather of musicianship, which could not be approved. I was very young and most impressionable, but still his tacking on the finale of the C sharp minor Sonata [the '*Moonlight*'] to the variations of the one in A flat *op.* 26 gave me a shock in spite of the perfection with which both movements were played. Another example: he was fond of playing in public his arrangement for piano of the scherzo, 'The Storm', and the finale from Beethoven's *Pastoral Symphony*. 'The Storm' was simply magnificent, and no orchestra could produce a more thrilling tempest. The peculiarity, the oddity, of the performance consisted of his playing the first eight bars of the scherzo, rather more quickly than they are usually taken, then the following eight bars, the B major phrase, in a slow *andante* time.[8]

This was written by Hallé later in life, when he was a devoted classical pianist almost crowded out of concert life by his work as a conductor. On the unveiling of Beethoven's statue, in Bonn, a year after his infection by Lisztian excess, Hallé heard Liszt play the E flat Concerto again. 'I think he must have felt equal scruples,' wrote Hallé, 'for . . . he adhered most scrupulously to the text, and a finer and grander reading of the work cannot be imagined.'[9]

The virtuoso introduced a new element into instrumental performance. He won a new audience through his mastery of showmanship, transferring to the concert hall from the opera house the element of danger and physical excitement. By doing so he not only captivated new audiences but enlarged the orchestral vocabulary and extended the composer's range of colour. They led the way not only to more and more startling individual feats but to the virtuoso orchestra and the dazzling effects of such movements as the 'Queen Mab' scherzo in Berlioz's *Romeo and Juliet* Symphony. In an age of public music, they were their own, and music's, most effective publicity agents.

[8] C. E. & M. Hallé: *op. cit.* p. 38.   [9] *Ibid.* p. 85.

5

The Commercialisation of Opera

Once, when opera was an entertainment designed for monarchs and their courtiers, public taste mattered little to the providers of opera except in the Italian theatres where the public's support was financially necessary. In most German and Austrian court theatres the general public was originally admitted free of charge so long as it conformed to accepted standards of dress and behaviour. It was only when the public's contributions were demanded that they were in a position to call the tune and influence the repertoire.

As early as 1768, the Royal and Imperial Opera in Vienna had been put under the care of a commercial manager who, in 1768, turned down an opera by the twelve-year-old Mozart. Leopold Mozart, in Vienna with his children for the first time since the beginning of the concert tour which had taken them across Germany and France to London, wrote to the Chancellor of his Archbishop in Salzburg about the new situation at the Vienna Opera: [1]

> The theatre is farmed out, or rather entrusted to a certain Affligio, who has to pay some 1,000 [florins] a year to certain people whom the court would otherwise have to pay. The Emperor and the Imperial family pay nothing for their boxes. Consequently the court cannot say a word to this Affligio, for everything is undertaken at his risk.

Mozart, with his son's work turned down, seems to have found the new system objectionable, but it took much of the cost out of the hands of the court and left businessmen to undertake the administration.

The rising cost of opera after the Napoleonic Wars produced a new type of opera management in Italy and Germany, the type which was already familiar in the Italian theatres. In 1821 the Imperial Court in Vienna leased the management of the Kärntnerthor Theater, the home at that time of the Opera, and the Theater an der Wien, to an Italian, Domenico Barbaja, who had started life as a waiter, had managed a circus and had taken charge of the gambling rooms attached to the Scala Theatre in Milan. With the profits he made from the gaming rooms, he bought control first of the San Carlo Opera in Naples and then of La Scala itself, and he ran

[1] Anderson: *The Letters of Mozart and his Family*. Letter of 27 July 1768. Vol. I. p. 190.

both these Italian theatres in conjunction with his two Italian companies. In Vienna he had almost complete freedom of action under the supervision of the Court Chamberlain; artists and repertory were solely his concerns unless and until for any reason he became subject to some official complaint; such a complaint, in the terms of his management, could only be a fall in the public's esteem for the opera.

Barbaja was commonly regarded by the Viennese to be an illiterate barbarian concerned not with music but with money, but his record in Vienna is not discreditable. He exploited German operatic successes and took *Die Zauberflöte* on to the stage of the Kärntnerthor for the first time, invited Weber to conduct *Der Freischütz* there and commissioned *Euryanthe* from him. Josef Weigl, *Kapellmeister* of the Opera, who had won a great success in 1809 with *Die Schweizerfamilie*, was commissioned to write *Die eiserne Pforte* in quite a different vein to a libretto adapted from a tale by E. T. A. Hoffmann. Barbaja commissioned the ill-fated *Alfonso und Estrella* from Schubert.

But five years before Barbaja had accepted office in Vienna, Rossini's music had already created a sensation there, and Rossini had worked under contract to Barbaja, as manager of the San Carlo Opera, expected to compose two operas a year and assist in the management of the theatre; Barbaja had been rewarded in 1816 by the incredibly popular *Otello*. It was therefore natural that Barbaja, whose primary duty was to fill the theatre, should take Rossini to Vienna in 1822, and the visit was a triumph; it entirely vindicated Barbaja's policy of holding on to the support of popular German composers while encouraging the taste for Italian works. At the same time, he kept the company under firm discipline and dismissed its less efficient members. In spite of his reputed lack of education and culture, Barbaja was a gifted judge both of singing and of theatrical effectiveness; and he understood the taste of the public. Apart from his functions as a new broom in a dusty opera house, he introduced the Italian system of regular subscription throughout the season and brought to Vienna the best available Italian singers. He did not only ensure that the theatres under his control did not run at a loss; he permanently influenced Viennese taste. Although his rule lasted for only nine years, he established a system and a policy for his successors to follow.

In Paris the situation of the Académie Royale de Musique, by this time familiarly known as the Opéra, demanded more radical changes. The traditional battle of French opera against Italian styles had led to the opening of a theatre for Italian opera, established in 1829 in the Théâtre Italien after functioning in several other Paris theatres, while the Opéra Comique, already a venerable institution founded in 1715, occupied a variety of theatres in succession; its speciality was not comic opera but opera with spoken dialogue in place of recitative. Serious opera, with sung dialogue, elaborate ballet and a high degree of scenic grandeur, belonged to the Opéra itself. It had survived the revolution and the Empire, first as the Théâtre des Arts and then as the Académie Impériale de Musique. Napoleon had reimposed the tax on all other entertainments which had provided a major part of its subsidy, drawn up regulations to control its personnel and compelled its staff to make good any deficit on their yearly accounts. Productions at the three state theatres—the Opéra, the Opéra Comique and the Comédie Française—were controlled by the Ministry of the Interior. Since 1807, the Opéra management was in the hands of a Director, a Treasurer, and Inspector and a Secretary-General, all members of the Opéra staff, but a government Inspector of Theatres had supreme power over all the theatres of Paris. The restoration of Louis XVIII had changed but the name of the institution, which again became 'Royale' instead of 'Impériale', and it remained under the nominal control of a puppet director under the authority of an all-powerful Superintendent.

The Opéra, its management after the Restoration hamstrung by a Superintendent, the Vicomte de la Rochefoucauld, whose chief preoccupation was the respectability of the *corps de ballet* (he ordered that the skirts of the ballerinas be lengthened), ran more and more heavily into debt in spite of a lavish subsidy. The tax on other entertainments brought in some. 300,000 francs a year to add to the annual state subsidy of 750,000 francs, but in 1827 it had to apply to the King for another 996,000 francs (almost as much as its official income) to make good its debts. The July Revolution of 1830, with the enthronement of the Orléanist dynasty and its 'Citizen King by a triumphant bourgeoisie, put the reins of power into the hands of the financially experienced business men of the middle class. The new regime had no wish to diminish the prestige of the Opéra—indeed, the new government wished the Opéra to shine as the great showplace of French culture—but it saw no point in a management which was incapable of organising a year's work within an extremely generous budget. In 1831 the government announced that: 'The administration of the Académie Royale de la Musique, known as the Opéra, shall be entrusted to a manager–entrepreneur, who shall manage it for six years at his own risk and fortune.' The subsidy would continue, decreasing during the Director's reign from 810,000 francs in his first year to 760,000 for the next two years and finally to 710,000 for the rest of his period in office.[2] What the government wanted was primarily a business man as director to manage the theatre within the limits of the subsidy; if the new Director happened also to be a musician, so much the better. If he ran the theatre at a profit, so much the better for him; if he ran it at a loss, the loss was his own. At the same time, the conditions of the appointment insisted that: 'The entrepreneur shall be able to

[2] William L. Crosten: *French Grand Opera; an art and a Business.* New York, 1948. p. 18.

maintain the house in that state of splendour suitable to this national theatre.'[3]

The appointment of a commercial manager to provide the necessary financial expertise and business experience was in itself an indication of the way in which the audiences in all European theatres were changing as the middle classes began to share power with the aristocracy if not entirely to supersede the traditional arbiters of taste. Benjamin Lumley, the London solicitor who became manager of the King's Theatre in the Haymarket, the traditional London opera house since the days of Handel, noted the change in his *Reminiscences of the Opera*:

> The Opera House—once the resort and the 'rendezvous' of the *élite* of rank and fashion, where applause received its direction from a body of cultivated, discriminating 'cognoscienti', and the treasury of which was furnished beforehand by ample subscriptions in reliance upon the provisions made by the manager—now mainly depends for support upon miscellaneous and fluctuating audiences. . . . Boxes, which of yore were lent to friends if not occupied by the possessor, are now, it is well known, sold for the evening to any stranger who wishes to attend the performance.[4]

Lumley's unsubsidised theatre was, of course, more completely at the mercy of its audience than any continental theatre which backed its manager's presentation of opera with reasonable financial support, but the symptoms of social change which made Lumley's work in London especially hazardous were present in all the major European opera houses. It was in Paris that a new operatic style was evolved to exploit them.

The first director appointed in Paris under the system worked out in 1831 was Dr Louis Véron, born in 1798, the son of a stationer who had qualified in medicine, written a book about children's diseases and made a fortune out of a chest ointment bequeathed to him by an apothecary friend. Abandoning medicine for journalism, Véron had founded the *Revue de Paris*. Totally ignorant of music, a small, fat, scrofulous dandy, Véron put himself forward for the Directorship of the Opéra by explaining 'how a brilliant and skillful direction of the Opéra might be politically valuable at the beginning of a new reign'. The Opéra could attract foreigners by its musical quality and, by 'displaying crowded audiences in a sumptuous theatre, could demonstrate the order and tranquillity brought to France by the new order.'[5]

With the support of a corruptible press which he recognised as well worth

---

[3] *Ibid.*

[4] Benjamin Lumley: *Reminiscences of the Opera*. London, 1864. Introduction, p. viii.

[5] Auguste Véron: *Memoires d'un Bourgeois de Paris*. Quoted in Crosten: *op. cit.* p. 19.

the money it cost, with a cool sense of efficiency which economised by reducing the size of orchestra, chorus and *corps de ballet* while paying astronomical salaries to star singers, and with the aid of a *claque* as efficiently organised as everything else in his theatre—its leader was granted tickets to key points in the theatre for distribution to his subordinates and allowed to attend rehearsals to judge those points at which applause could be most effective—Véron set out to make the Opéra pay its way and earn him a fortune. In his attempt, he was instrumental in the development of a form of opera calculated to exploit the taste of the well-to-do bourgeoisie, who had nothing of the strict conservatism of the old aristocratic audience with their long exposure to the French operatic tradition. The new audience consisted of self-made business men and members of the professions who found themselves at last with time for amusement and the money to pay for it. Many of them lacked any extensive education; they wanted their eyes pleased and their ears tickled. Véron, in his *Mémoirés*, declared:

> The Revolution of July is the triumph of the Bourgeoisie. This victorious middle class will be anxious to reign and to amuse itself. The Opéra will become its Versailles, and it [the middle class] will rush there to take the place of the great lords of the exiled court. The plan to make the Opéra at once brilliant and popular appeared to me to have a fine chance of success.[6]

The fact that the first Director of the new dispensation was a man who could easily have stood as a symbol of the conquering middle class and its standards naturally meant a change of orientation not only in the works produced at the Opéra but in the standards of manners and conduct prevailing there. French opera since its foundations had been formal and dignified; it had made little effort to exploit or express deep emotions; its triumph was the expression of society, not the investigation of personal joy or tragedy. The place for intimate emotional expression was the Opéra Comique or the Théâtre Italien. What was performed at the Opéra under Véron extended the French tradition in accordance with the ideas of the July Revolution. The German poet, Heine, writing from Paris as a journalist, noticed the new attitude when he set out the reasons for Meyerbeer's domination of the Opéra after the triumphs of *Robert le Diable* and *Les Huguenots*. He wrote:

> Meyerbeer's music is more social than individual; the grateful present, that sees its own inner and outer discoveries, its own dissensions of the spirit, its own needs, its own hopes, reflected in his work, celebrates its own passions and enthusiasms when it applauds the master.[7]

[6] *Ibid.* quoted in Crosten: *op. cit.* p. 20.
[7] Heinrich Heine: *Uber die französische Bühne. Sämtliche Werke, Band.* xi. Quoted in Ernest Newman: *The Life of Richard Wagner.* London, 1933. Vol. i. p. 259.

Traditionally, whatever was performed in the Opéra was transformed
to suit French taste, and the groundwork for Véron's revolution had been
laid in the 1820s. In 1825 Rossini had composed *Il Viaggio a Reims* for
the Théâtre Italien; it had not been successful. A year later he turned his
Maometto II, written for the San Carlo Opera in 1820, into *Le Siège de
Corinthe* for the Paris Opéra itself, emphasising these elements of the
libretto which could make the work appear to be a story of national, public
action. The tale of the Greek girl who refuses to marry the Sultan of Turkey
because he ill-treats her people was reorganised to achieve a French emphasis on a national, political struggle instead of on the love story which
is its Italian *raison d'être*; emotions were simplified and large-scale scenes
were introduced to exploit the French love of spectacle and dramatic
choruses. *Le Siège de Corinthe* was so complete a transformation of its
Italian original that, retranslated into Italian, audiences in Italy accepted
it as a new work. In 1827 *Moise in Egitto*, also written for Naples, was transformed into *Moïse et Pharaon*, taking over the ballet from *Armide*
(Rossini's only Italian work with a ballet) to bring it into line with French
demands. *Le Comte Ory*, with a libretto by Eugène Scribe, the father of
the nineteenth-century French libretto who found the correct literary forms
for the operatic prejudices of his fellow countrymen, gave Rossini his first
French text in 1828, exploiting his genius for frivolously effervescent gaiety.
In 1829 *Guillaume Tell*, an unwontedly clumsy adaptation of Schiller's
drama by Etienne de Jouy, improved by Hippolyte Bis and polished up
by Armand Marrast, never really won the heart of the French audience,
though its six hours' length contains a wealth of splendid music. Rossini
adapted himself to French taste but never ceased to be Rossini the inexhaustibly fertile and unmistakably personal.

The critic and musicologist Joseph d'Ortigue, a friend of Berlioz, whom
he succeeded as music critic of the *Journal des Débats*, wrote a study of the
controversy which arose in France over Rossini's music, *La Guerre des
Dilettanti*; it provided an explanation for Rossini's failure completely to
subjugate the Paris Opéra after annexing every other opera house in
Europe:

> Rossini's music is far from being universal in its appeal. One must already
> be something of a dilettante and have reached some degree of musical
> civilisation to appreciate it. The people, as well as the genuine music-
> lovers, can remember an air by Mozart, by Mehul or by Gretry. Rossini,
> like Voltaire, writes for semi-scholars, for the people who can remember
> a cavatina. . . . His music is too refined, too far removed from simplicity;
> it is too artificial. It can perhaps become popular among a certain type of
> clever people, but I doubt if it can ever appeal universally.[8]

Ortigue, writing of Rossini as a disturbing newcomer to French music,

[8] Joseph d'Ortigue: *Le Balcon de l'Opéra*. Paris, 1833. p. 23.

offers an unusual angle of approach to a composer whom the twentieth century is rarely prepared to consider intellectually, but it seems to have been the naturally Italianate exuberance of Rossini's melody, its use of florid decoration at points where a French composer would write an eloquently simple vocal line, which disturbed the French critic in spite of the inventiveness and brilliant panache of the music. Such a style, at the Théâtre Italien, could be adorable, but the Opéra, the home of the French tradition, saw it as a brilliant disturbance.

The real pointer to the future of French opera was Auber's *La Muette de Portici*, known to English and Italian audiences as *Masaniello*, taking its name from the heroic peasant, who, avenging his dumb sister for the cruelty and betrayal of a lecherous aristocrat, saves his people from the tyranny of an alien monarchy. *La Muette de Portici* was produced a year before *Guillaume Tell*; Auber, normally a composer of graceful, stylish, light operas, manages in it to cope with big choral masses confronting each other in conflict in the way that French audiences demanded and at the same time to capture the emotions of all those European audiences who were permitted to see so inflammatory a work. It was *La Muette de Portici* which in 1830 precipitated the riot which turned into Belgium's struggle for independence. Auber's music is not a matter of powerful, large-scale structures. The grandeur and the passion were basically scenic rather than musical, and its plot takes a story of personal suffering and makes a national, political work from it; if Auber had been capable of deeply passionate, introspective music, such music would have been out of place, so that the excitement of the work came from its big, fundamentally simple, choral confrontations and the opportunities it gave to designers to create impressive stage pictures. It was closer to the French tradition than *Guillaume Tell*, which determinedly personalises great political issues, making Tell a hero and Gessler flamboyantly a villain while throwing in a pair of lovers whose personal story is caught up in great political events.

This style, rather than any individual work, was the foundation on which Véron built, knowing that the audience he had to win was not musically sophisticated. The English critic Henry F. Chorley visited Paris for the first time in the Véron period and immediately became an ardent francophile. He described the Opéra orchestra in glowing terms; after discussing each section individually—the tone of the wind instruments, he notes, 'partakes somewhat of that thin shrill which seems generic to all wind tones (the human voice included) in France'—but concludes,

> there is a uniform and well-proportioned care in finish, and consent of execution—an understanding with the chorus—an understanding with the singers—a sensitiveness as to every nice gradation of tone, slackened or hastened, never displayed by our most sensitive orchestras.

The Opéra orchestra is 'a machine in perfect order', because of the quality of Habeneck's conducting.[9]

In other words, Véron's economising on numbers did not detract from high standards because he maintained the best men he could find in the essential posts. Habeneck was worth his hire whatever Habeneck cost. The best available singers were kept under contracts which satisfied them (and incidentally seem to have been responsible for a considerable inflation of the fees paid to leading singers all over Europe); the leading dancers were Maria Taglioni and Fanny Elssler. The old prohibition on admission back stage was relaxed so that members of the fashionable audience—optimistic young men and their seniors who ought to have known better—could delight themselves with glimpses, if no more, of the young ladies of the ballet at close quarters. The Opéra balls, previously occasions of great formality, became functions marked by a delicious freedom in manners. The theatre itself was gorgeously redecorated.

Véron did not pander to the tastes of a rich, philistine public; he shared them. Véron's audience did not want formalised or simplified stage settings but looked for a high degree of accurate representation. The stage was darkened and the curtain was lowered (important innovations) while scenes were changed. Gas lighting, introduced in 1822, already allowed the designer a new range of effects including dawns, sunsets and twilights. Under Véron, flat backcloths were replaced by concave representations of the world behind the stage, with scenes continued on them in careful perspective. Edmond Duponchel, an architect and archaeologist who eventually succeeded Véron as Director, and Pierre Ciceri revolutionised the art of stage setting; for the first act of *La Muette de Portici* they created a Mediterranean beach leading by a flight of huge stone steps to the palace of the Spanish viceroy and with a view of Vesuvius in the distance; in the last act, at the summit of Vesuvius, the dumb girl Fenella casts herself into the crater of the erupting volcano. *Guillaume Tell* presented splendid Swiss landscapes and the lake across which Tell rowed to safety, but nothing so breathtaking as the eruption of Vesuvius.

The opera libretto, with its insistence on political, social or religious themes, naturally dealt with its materials from the point of view of the new middle class and its monarchy: kings and aristocrats are corrupt and cruel —it was to escape from a detested aristocratic seducer that Fenella chose to die so spectacularly. Eugène Scribe was the most prolific writer in the French theatre of the time. Auber (in *La Muette de Portici*), Suppé, Rossini (in *Le Comte Ory* and *Guillaume Tell*), Halévy (in *La Juive*), Meyerbeer (in *Robert le Diable, Les Huguenots, Le Prophète* and *L'Étoile du Nord*), Donizetti (in *Les Martyrs, La Favorite* and *Don Sebastien*) and Verdi (in *Les Vêpres Siciliennes*) all wrote successful operas to his texts,

[9] L. Chorley: *op. cit.* pp. 17ff.

as did many others, including the Polish Moniusko, and he found time to write plays and vaudevilles. He had an infallible sense of what was theatrically effective in terms that Véron's audience could accept. Not only did his texts demonstrate the wickedness of the aristocracy and the stalwart, virtuous independence of their opponents; Scribe's libretti also integrated ballet into the dramatic action and built each to a climax which involved a scene of pageantry, huge dramatic choruses and the participation of several principal singers with fine voices. The weakness of Scribe's libretti is that their excitements tended to work to a formula, that his great scenes of procession and pageant were often peripheral to the action and could, with little sense of strain but with some adaptation of costume, be transferred from one work to another. Even the social orientations of his plots created similarities both of character and incident.

For all that, Scribe was the architect of 'Grand Opera', for it was the text of *La Muette de Portici, Robert le Diable, Les Huguenots* and Halévy's *La Juive* which created the form and demanded the style of treatment which dominated Europe until Wagner's early operas began to replace it. If the dignity, formality and pageantry of Scribe's libretti is as old as French opera itself, his delight in visual effects won the half-educated, as Ortigue called them, to delight in the opera.

Véron ruled the Opéra until 1835, less than the period originally offered to him but long enough to enable him to retire with a fortune of 900,000 francs. When he took over the theatre the average receipts for each performance had been between 1100 and 2000 francs. *Robert le Diable,* in 1832, raised the average evening's takings to between 9000 and 10,000 francs. He maintained this standard of financial success without winning much gratitude from the musically educated. 'The name of Véron will live for ever in musical history,' wrote Heine. 'He has beautified the temple of the Goddess, but he has turned her out of it.'[10] His successors could not rival his financial success; they shared Véron's ignorance of music but not his genius for publicity or his immediate identification with the tastes of the 'common man'. Duponchel, the architect–archaelogist–stage designer who followed him, achieved only one success on the scale of Véron's—that of Meyerbeer's *Les Huguenots* in 1836, and in his days the decline began. He was succeeded by Léon Pillet, whose mistress, the *prima donna* Rosina Stoltz, was, according to Berlioz, the directrice of the Director, and Pillet failed to revive the suffering theatre. Louis-Victor-Nestor Roqueplan shared the directorship with Duponchel from 1847 to 1849, after which Roqueplan reigned alone for five years. Berlioz, whose relationship with successive directors is described in his *Memoirs* in a special tone of amused scorn, dismissed them all with contempt:

[10] Heine: *op. cit.*

> Musically speaking, they are all heathen Chinese who happen to believe
> themselves gifted with unusual taste and discernment, thus embodying
> the fatal combination of unshakable confidence in themselves with
> profound ignorance and barbarism.[11]

Only an angel of forgiveness could have written of the successive directors
without bitterness after the treatment Berlioz received from them, but in a
theatre which had been designed to depend upon smash hits the departure of
Véron began a period in which the smashes became far more notable than
the hits and Berlioz, intermittently, became the chronicler of the decline.

> The Opéra, that large theatre with its large orchestra, with its large
> choruses, its large government subsidy, its numerous staff, its huge sets,
> imitates the sorry bird of the fable on more than one score. Sometimes it
> is to be seen motionless, sleeping on one leg; at others it goes on some
> vague, flustered trek, looking for food in the merest trickles. . . . However
> urgently it strides, it will never reach its journey's end, the more so as
> it does not know itself in which direction it should go.[12]

The Ninth 'Evening' of Berlioz's *Evenings in the Orchestra* is devoted
to a comparison between opera in Paris and opera in London, where
Berlioz had recently endured some startling experiences as conductor of
the company created by the conductor Jullien at Drury Lane Theatre.
Opera in London, dominated by an eccentric with a streak of charlatanism
and a genius for publicity, is simply a joke which, try as he will, Berlioz
cannot take seriously, but the Opéra in Paris is a national disgrace, to be
scarified and scourged with all the scornful rhetoric Berlioz could command.
Cardinal Mazarin, at the birth of French opera, had declared, 'The Opéra
sings, it does not pay', but Berlioz inverted the cardinal's dictum: 'The
Opéra pays, but it does not sing.' It is in love with mediocrity, passionate
in its adoration of the trite, bludgeoning its broken-spirited audience into
submission. He declared:

> The heavy guns were brought out to shake its [the audience's] drowsi-
> ness, it was given chest Cs of every sort, bass drums, organs, military
> bands, antique trumpets, tubas the size of engine funnels, bells, cannon,
> horses, canopied cardinals, gold-spangled emperors, diademed queens,
> funerals, weddings, banquets and everywhere the famous canopy, the
> magnificent canopy, the plumed and feathered canopy, borne like Marl-
> borough by four officers, then jugglers, skaters, choir-boys, censers,
> monstrances, crosses, banners, processions, orgies of priests and naked
> women, the bull Apis, an army of calves, screech owls, bats, Hell's five
> hundred devils, all there for the asking, the final earthquake, the end of
> the world . . . the whole interspersed with a few colourless cavatinas and
> a lot of claquers.[13]

[11] Berlioz: *op. cit.* p. 446.
[12] Berlioz: *Evenings in the Orchestra*, translated by C. R. Fortescue.
London, 1963. p. 118.
[13] *Ibid.* p. 120.

Music had become a pointless decoration for an uncoordinated stage spectacle, and stage spectacle, with no dramatic motivation, had lost its power to excite because it had worn out every spectacular trick of which it was capable. So long as the money flowed in, the directors did not care, but Véron's successors, unable to find more exciting tricks than those already worn threadbare, had nothing on which to pin their faith but expensive star singers. The Meyerbeer style had exhausted itself.

Meyerbeer had arrived in Paris with the score of *Robert le Diable* in 1830. He was forty years old and had for a time been one of Weber's comrades at Darmstadt in the attempt to rejuvenate German music and establish German romantic opera. He had written three German operas in his twenties, then the Rossini craze had swept him off his feet and he had gone to Italy to study the Italian style, which meant to write operas as Rossinian as he could make them, but, alas, without Rossini's stylish and elegant excitement. His six Rossinian operas had some success and the last of them, *Il Crociato in Egitto*, had been played in Paris in 1826. He met Scribe, who gave him the libretto of *Robert le Diable*; in 1830 he returned with the score complete. In spite of some doubts, the Opéra accepted it.

The July Revolution and Meyerbeer's demands for more and more rehearsals—it took five months of preparation to get the opera on to the stage —held up the production until November 1831. In *Robert le Diable*, Scribe had managed to find a place for every ingredient which Véron's audience —'business men, professional men and politicians, all looking for distraction and eager to prove that money could replace nobility of birth' was Véron's own description of them—could enjoy; the synthesis of thrills and sensations provided by the libretto had never been attempted before. The first act offers a gambling scene; then the heroine is tormented, sadistically enough to titillate but not to distress; then comes a ballet of the ghosts of debauched nuns; there follows a scene in which the entire court is put into an enchanted sleep, and the opera ends with a magnificent cathedral wedding and a brilliantly designed transformation scene.

Meyerbeer's music dresses all this brilliantly. According to Ortigue, it is 'a marriage of unusual happiness between Weber and Rossini, Italy and Germany'.[14] Although the only really original feature of *Robert* is its splendid orchestration, his successfully eclectic style enabled him to match everything in a libretto with the appropriate musical expression. His German training helped him to build up big scenes into convincing musical forms, so that in respect of sheer theatricality *Robert le Diable* eclipsed *Guillaume Tell* and *Le Muette de Portici*. Even the orchestration (which so impressed Berlioz that his *Traité de l'instrumentation et d'orchestration modernes*, published in 1843, before Meyerbeer's final operas had been produced, can cite no scores but Meyerbeer's for a large number of

[14] Ortigue: *op. cit.* p. 183.

orchestral effects which later became common practice) is simply an inventive response to the demands of the dramatic moment which such effects accompany. If the music's cleverly calculated effectiveness is close to being meretricious it delighted the public, proving that, like Véron, Meyerbeer was immediately capable of feeling exactly as his audience felt. The total effect of *Robert le Diable* was to give the public what *La Muette de Portici* and *Guillaume Tell* (really a far greater though sometimes flawed work) had been struggling to find for it.

Having found the necessary formula, Meyerbeer's later operas followed a similar plan. *Les Huguenots* begins with an orgy of catholic noblemen; Act Two includes a ballet of bathing beauties; Act Three sets a protestant chorus in direct opposition to a catholic chorus, has a gipsy ballet, a duel and a wedding procession. Act Four provides the solemn blessing of the daggers to be used in the St. Bartholomew's Day massacre and a spectacular love duet. By Act Five, the real drama has ended, but we are still allowed to watch the massacre itself. *Le Prophète* has a skaters' ballet, a coronation scene, an exorcism and a final explosion to settle the fate of most of the characters: in a sense, Meyerbeerian opera is never very far in spirit from the Hollywood screen epic of the great days, but it includes a good deal of spectacular incident written into the libretto because each act must achieve a great climax involving crowds of people and a huge orchestra.

Meyerbeer set out to please his public, and to do so used every trick available for the intensification of atmosphere and every style which could be judged appropriate. He was not, hovever without artistic conscience; he worked slowly, preparing each of his Paris operas with painstaking historical research to establish the right atmosphere, but the limits of his imagination made it possible for him to accept Scribe's formulae, just as his sincere though limited artistry made it possible for him to apply those formulae with complete sincerity. In his own day, his music was deemed irresistible both in power of expression and grandeur of design. Chorley, a devout traditionalist who loved Beethoven's symphonies and the operas of Rossini, Bellini and Donizetti, was overwhelmed by Meyerbeerian opera as soon he encountered it, but he did not pretend to overlook its weaknesses. He wrote:

> I can content myself with studying, for their own intrinsic dramatic force or melodic sweetness, the *Fidelio*, or the *Euryanthe* of Weber, even when cut down to the meagre shadow of a pianoforte arrangement; but I must see Meyerbeer's operas as well as hear them, and at the Académie Royale. . . . There are only about three separate items—Isabelle's two cavatinas in *Robert* and the couplets of the Page in *Les Huguenots*, which are effective in a concert room.[15]

[15] Chorley: *op. cit.* Vol. i. p. 45.

Manner, he explains, is 'all predominant'; musical substance takes second place.

The Italian composers who accepted commissions from the Opéra—all those who had won a great reputation at home and whose works had begun to travel—were expected to compose a grand opera on Meyerbeerian lines and scale. Donizetti was at work on *Polliuto*, for the San Carlo Opera, when Duponchel asked him for two new operas. Donizetti asked for a libretto by Scribe but rejected the first that he was offered in terms which sound like a total rejection of the principles of grand opera. 'I want a characteristic drama with two or three interesting and moving situations that will be outside the ordinary [things] done a thousand times in Italy',[16] but not suggesting any interest in the scenes of spectacular pageantry and disaster which were essential in Duponchel's theatre. *Polliuto*, for which Corneille's drama *Polyeucte* had been Italianised by the librettist Salvatore Cammarano, telling the story of a Christian martyr, might offend the authorities in Naples and could, perhaps, in that case be adapted to the needs of Paris. As he feared, it did not suit Neapolitan restrictions and was therefore transformed into *Les Martyrs* and given the full Parisian treatment; its choreography was designed by Corati, and six designers worked on the sets, the second of which was based on a painting by Delacroix of a great square in Mytilene. *Les Martyrs*, produced in 1840, was followed in the same year by *La Favorite*, a conversion into grand opera of an unproduced work *L'Ange de Nisida*; to reach the stage of the Opéra, it jettisoned a character and divided its first act into two so that it could reach the four acts which were the smallest acceptable size for grand opera. Its ballet employed both Carlotta Grisi and Petipa in a *pas de deux*.

Donizetti seems to have coped with professional aplomb in the task of adapting his works and style for the Opéra. Verdi, in 1854, found it difficult to assume a French accent and objected to Scribe's libretto for *Les Vêpres Siciliennes* as a travesty of history, its inaccuracies dishonouring to Italy.[17] At the end of a year's struggle with an unsympathetic libretto, the style of grand opera which he felt to be undramatic, and the musical standards of the Opéra, which disappointed him, he tried unsuccessfully to have his contract cancelled. For all that, *Les Vêpres Siciliennes* was a great success, achieving, according to one critic, French operatic form without losing Italian ardour. Each act has its grand spectacular scene and the work ends with the Italian massacre of their French overlords signalled by the ringing of the bell for Vespers. The complete work lasts six hours, but they are six hours of middle-period Verdi, authoritative in their energy, melodic power and superb vitality. Translated into Italian and reshaped to Verdi's requirements, the work scored a success in Italy.

[16] Quoted in H. Weinstock, *Donizetti*. London, 1964. p. 136.
[17] Geoffrey Toye: *Giuseppe Verdi*. London, 1931. p. 93.

In the twelve years between *Les Vêpres Siciliennes* and *Don Carlos*, the death of Scribe had made room for librettists who, if less infallible than Scribe in their presentation of theatrical high points, were disposed to use their materials more freely and with less regard for a basic formula. The Italian revision of *Don Carlos*, however, is tauter and swifter than the original French form of the opera; in both versions, Verdi's instinctive command of dramatic reality was at war with the preconceptions of grand opera as dramatic pageant, and in each Verdi won his victory though at some cost to the incidentals of his work. By the time that Verdi was called to Paris, the Meyerbeerian form was international; before 1840 Chorley had found that the audience in the Leipzig Theatre—and Leipzig is, in one sense, the centre of the German musical tradition—was 'as devoted to French opera as the other towns I visited', though Chorley remained convinced that only the Paris Opéra could cope with the vast scenic, choral and orchestral demands of Meyerbeer's French works. Chorley's account of the small-scale production of *Les Huguenots* in Leipzig[18] must have compared very favourably with the performance of *Robert le Diable* in Würzburg in 1833, when the young Richard Wagner, in his first post as chorus repetiteur of the Würzburg Theatre, drilled a chorus of fifteen singers through Meyerbeer's gigantic score.

In one form or another, often shorn of the visual excitements which French audiences found indispensable to a production, grand opera became the only effective alternative to the *bel canto* opera of Bellini, Donizetti and early Verdi. The German opera of the 1830s and 1840s was so essentially German in outlook, attitude and atmosphere that, after Weber, there was nothing to win international popularity until, in the 1850s, the early works of Wagner began to win acceptance. As Heine had clearly seen, grand opera in general, its Meyerbeerian form in particular, was essentially 'contemporary', its social preoccupations and its subject matter reflecting, though often in strange disguises, the preoccupations of the nineteenth century, together with a certain vulgarity of style endemic in the period itself but expressed at its most highly developed in Paris after the 1830 Revolution. To put the point in its simplest terms, nothing by Rossini, and not even the ardour, vehemence, vitality and beauty of Weber's operas, instigated a revolution; it was the musically light-weight *Le Muette de Portici* which helped Belgium to win independence from Holland, and it did so because it dressed up the preconceptions and the social ideals of the nineteenth century in attractive historical clothes.

At the same time, there are few masterpieces of nineteenth-century opera across which the shadow of Meyerbeer does not fall. Berlioz's Troy is destroyed to music infinitely more subtle and indisputably more original than anything by Meyerbeer, but the idea, like that of the ballet of the Car-

18 Above, p. 42.

thaginians celebrating the glorious reign of Dido, is a Meyerbeerian conception, and there is a sense in which *Aïda,* and not *Les Huguenots,* is the greatest Meyerbeerian opera. Meyerbeer did not consciously aim at a *Gesamtkunstwerk,* a Wagnerian union of all the arts through music, but his operas are the unconscious move of a clever, clear-minded composer towards a future that he could not foresee through mere intelligence.

Wagner, whom Meyerbeer tried ineffectually to help, in 1855 wrote *Opera and Drama* to work out his own finished, personal stylistic aims. He attacked Meyerbeer as an opportunist composer who had no aims beyond exploiting his audience, but he could not dismiss his apparently unprincipled predecessor. 'Only the most perfect works of art,' he wrote, 'are worthy to be set beside the love duet in *Les Huguenots*', and at the end of his life, when Meyerbeer's failure to help him had grown in Wagner's mind to a deliberate attempt to hold him back, and Meyerbeer's Jewish birth had put him beyond the Wagnerian pale, Wagner still shamefacedly admitted the power of the fourth act of *Les Huguenots*; most of Wagner's set pieces, from the conception of the grand operatic *Rienzi* to the Grail scenes of *Parsifal,* owe a great debt to Meyerbeer. The style which was developed in Paris as a means painlessly to hold the attention of the relatively unmusical was the last important stage on the road to Wagnerian music drama.

Commercial managements, however, faced the future only by accident. They existed to keep theatres solvent and therefore crowded. As they did so, they accidentally replaced royal control with a complex system of internal politics based on the dynamic stresses, attractions and repulsions of a number of powerful, possibly indispensable, subordinates. A musical director, a stage designer, a choreographer, *prime ballerine* and, above all, star singers with great popularity and natural gifts, were the powers whom every director had to placate: the singers often exercised an authority out of all proportion to their musical understanding and were able to exert direct control over everything a company did. A composer's success in those opera houses where great reputations were made depended on the skill with which he could manoeuvre these various, antagonistic powers into working in his favour; the mere quality of a score was rarely enough to decide its future; the support of a powerful coalition of the theatrical powers counted more than quality in the composer's search for success. It was natural that the nineteenth-century opera house should become known as a centre of intrigue, conspiracy and double-dealing.

The story of the failure of Berlioz's *Benvenuto Cellini* and its apparently deliberate sabotage by the Paris Opéra after the work had been accepted is perhaps the best known of the many stories of skulduggery which surround the opera, and Berlioz's subsequent dealings with the Opéra's successive directorates reinforces its effect. Duponchel accepted Berlioz's opera simply because Berlioz was the critic of an influential newspaper, the *Journal des*

Débats, and a close friend of its proprietors, Armand and Édouard Bertin. Apart from Berlioz's own uncompromising criticism, no director could afford to have an influential newspaper among his enemies, so *Benvenuto* was to be produced and to fail, so that the Bertins and Berlioz would be convinced of Duponchel's right-mindedness. When rehearsals started, Habeneck, fine conductor though he was, could not catch the lightness and élan of the 'Roman Carnival' scene, but, according to Berlioz, the music itself won over the orchestra when he had taken the players through it. By this time, however, it was clear that Duponchel wanted the work to fail and professed to find the orchestra's change of front simply comical. When the chorus discovered that the Carnival scene gave ample opportunity for horse-play with the dancers, Duponchel was never in the theatre to enforce discipline, and Berlioz, merely the composer with no authority over the production, had no right to do so himself; he was forbidden, like every other composer, to take an active part in the rehearsal of his work. Berlioz knew, of course, that the rehearsal time allotted to *Benvenuto* was insufficient for a really polished performance.

None of the impediments, however, would have long stood in Berlioz's way had he taken the trouble to ingratiate himself with a director painfully aware of the rough side of Berlioz's tongue and the point of his pen. At the first performance some of the audience professed to find the line 'In the early morning, roosters crowed' too unpoetic and banal to be heard without laughter, and that was the end. *Benvenuto* was murdered after three performances; after a riotous first night there was no reason why the director should keep it on the stage until it made friends among the audience, although most of the critics wrote favourably of it. Berlioz, realising this, withdrew his opera.

The débâcle of *La Nonne Sanglante*, a Scribe libretto handed over to Berlioz in 1847 by the new directorate of Duponchel and Roqueplan, shows how powerless a great composer could be made by a management determined to control him. Berlioz had used his influence, and that of the Bertin brothers, to establish the new directorship, which in gratitude offered not only Scribe's libretto but also the assistant conductorship. But the statutes of the Opéra forbade the performace of works by members of its staff, so that the libretto was withdrawn from Berlioz and handed over to Gounod; then they manoeuvred Berlioz into refusing the assistant conductorship; they circulated the story that he had demanded the musical directorship of the theatre and attempted to oust its exciting musical director, actually a close friend on whose behalf Berlioz had refused any post more exalted than that of assistant conductor when, at the beginning of their negotiations, Duponchel and Roqueplan had offered it to him. Their final discovery was that the only post available for them to offer to Berlioz was that of chief coach, a post so junior that they knew he could do nothing but reject it. Thus a dangerously inflammatory conductor and composer was kept out of a theatre which sorely needed him.

A commercial manager whose position owes itself to his abilities as a business man cannot be expected to encourage works which lose money. If Duponchel had persisted in keeping *Benvenuto Cellini* in the repertoire, and given audiences a chance to come to terms with its originality, the whole course of Berlioz's future life might have followed a different pattern. But commercial managements exist to see that all possible seats are filled on all possible occasions, and they themselves were subject to a harsher dictatorship than their own. Opera in the nineteenth century existed first for its audience and then for the singers who drew the public. Just as the ballet of the period existed to show the grace, lightness and essential pathos of a *prima ballerina*, the purpose of opera was to give the greatly gifted tenor and soprano a chance to shine and to thrill the audience by doing so; from *Norma* to *Le Prophète*, through all the operas of Donizetti, it was the soprano and tenor—the former with an almost obligatory mad scene—who filled the house, and they had to be pleased. It had been possible for Handel, rehearsing Cuzzoni, to threaten to throw her out of a first-floor window, but Cuzzoni was a great soprano who was paid £2000 for her singing. The aggressive Handel was merely a paid musical director, not responsible for any financial loss if she hurt herself on the pavement or simply, following the age-old, infallible method of the great singer, felt too ill too sing; fortuitous ill-health is the singer's most powerful weapon when circumstances seem adverse. However dearly a director loved an opera, he was forced to love his audience still more dearly, and the audience came to hear a great voice doing something brilliant more often than it came to hear an opera. So long as the singer was preferred to the work, the singer had his way.

The singer's temperament, like that of the virtuoso instrumentalist, was always a fact to be reckoned with because of the nervous intensity of a singer's work and the potentially disastrous effect of nervous strain on a fine voice. A singer was not expected to be calm and untempestuous, for a placid singer suggests that he or she lacks the histrionic attitude to life which wins an audience's devotion.

Benjamin Lumley, the solicitor-manager of Her Majesty's Theatre, arrived in the Haymarket as legal adviser to his predecessor, Laporte, who, learning that his conduct of the opera was likely to be subject to interference by Queen Victoria, suggested the drafting of a courteous letter to justify his management. 'I have been at war all my life with the Semiramides, Anna Bolenas and such queens,' he said, 'but I did not expect to have the honour to oppose a real queen.'[19] 'War' was not a serious exaggeration of the relationship between managers and singers who could always feel ill or plead

[19] Lumley: *op. cit.* p. 8.

a cold to evade obligations which displeased them. Laporte managed the London opera at a time when all real decisions were made by his leading singers, whom Lumley called a 'cabal', because they found themselves able through their popularity to dictate the repertoire and the casting of operas. Lumley's own struggle against their arbitrary rule and usurped authority finally led to the foundation of a second Italian Opera at Covent Garden in 1846; the new company was one in which the real power lay with the singers, who worked through a management appointed to express their intentions.

The power of the singers can be seen in the case of Sir Michael Costa, an Italian who had settled in England and imposed discipline if no high degree of interpretive skill on the opera orchestra. In 1842 he composed an opera, *Alma*, for Her Majesty's, and it won some success; another opera, *Don Carlos*, had failed two years later. In 1846 the Philharmonic Society, belatedly recognising its orchestra's need for a skilled permanent conductor, offered the post to Costa, who accepted it in spite of his heavy commitments at Her Majesty's; Lumley promptly offered him an increase in salary commensurate with the fees he would earn from the Philharmonic Society, but refused Costa's demand that his new contract should include his right to compose an opera and a ballet in alternative years for Her Majesty's. The opera owed Costa a great deal, probably not less than it owed to any of the stars of a golden age of singing, but Lumley accepted his resignation without a qualm when Costa found that his terms were refused; his secession was not in any way comparable to the catastrophe which followed the resignation of any leading singer whose tyranny led Lumley to desperate measures. Almost inevitably, Lumley's sixteen years in control of the opera at Her Majesty's, where he had brought all Europe's leading singers and established Verdi as a popular composer while maintaining all the old favourites of the repertoire, ended with the manager heavily in debt.

The composer accepted and endured the power of the star singer. Rossini was musical director of the Théâtre Italien in Paris when, in 1832, the manager, Severini, decided to stand up to the demands of the legendary Malibran. The *diva*, convinced that her departure would empty the theatre, offered to cancel her contract, convinced that her offer would not be accepted. To her surprise, she was replaced by the young Julia Grisi, new to France and not yet adored. 'Monsieur,' said Rossini to Severini, 'you have just thrown away 100,000 francs a year.' He knew that he was the most admired and successful composer of the day, but he also knew that any popular singer had powers that he would be a fool to attempt to resist.

Berlioz follows the absurdity of singer worship to its logical conclusion. The tenor Duprez, at the height of his fame, was paid 100,000 francs a year. Berlioz elucidates:

this means that he sings perhaps seven times a month, which means that he appears in eighty-four performances a year, and earns something like 1,100 an evening. Now, supposing his role is made up of eleven hundred notes or syllables, this represents one franc a syllable. Thus, in *William Tell*.

'My' (one franc) 'presence' (two francs) 'perhaps will seem to you an outrage' (nine francs).

'Matilda,' (three francs) 'my indiscreet steps' (five francs) 'have boldly dared to make my way into your presence!' (thirteen francs).

Total, thirty-four francs. Your words are golden, my Lord!

Given a wretched *prima donna* whose miserable pittance is only 40,000 francs, Mathilda's reply naturally comes cheaper (in commercial parlance), each one of her syllables only reaching the eight sous price bracket.[20]

In the *Journal de Débats*, where this financial analysis originally appeared, Berlioz contrasted the rewards of the singer with those of the composer who has given the singer a reasonably attractive role:

At the time of Louis XIV, who created the Académie Royale, the principal artists had a revenue of 4,000 francs, the author's share, for a grand composition, was 100 francs. At present, this same share, for the first forty representations, has amounted to 250 francs; and if it had kept pace with the monstrous increase of which we have had a specimen in the salary of 100,000 francs recently received by Duprez (for instance), it should have reached 2,500 francs.[21]

Commercial opera was, in the last resort, singers' opera; the composer remained, in the eyes of both management and public, the necessary functionary who provided singers with the means of delighting their audience. That he could do so most effectively by observing routines and conventions while providing the stars with opportunities for their most effective vocal tricks went entirely against the attitude of the nineteenth-century composer, who had learned that in all other musical fields the primary necessity was to work with the utmost originality and emotional intensity. Opera needed the heroic determination of Wagner to break the moulds which delighted semi-musical audiences attending performances for the sake of fashion, and the effect of Wagner's work was not only to establish new forms for musical drama but to revivify opera in general.

[20] Berlioz: *Evening in the Orchestra.* pp. 81–92.
[21] Berlioz: in the *Journal des Débats.* Translated by Henry Chorley: *op. cit.* Vol. 1. p. 163.

6
Choral Music in Germany and England

As the nineteenth century transformed the orchestra into a predominantly professional body and as composers gave it duties which amateur instrumentalists found increasingly difficult, building the orchestra as they did so up to a size that except in large cities precluded amateur performance, the hitherto professional choir was transformed into an amateur body. Amateur choirs were linked to professional music-making through their performances of oratorios and liturgical works which needed the participation of an orchestra. While oratorio belonged to the concert hall, the choirs gradually took liturgical music out of church, breaking its links with public worship.

It is possible to link the rise of the German choral societies with the political situation on the Metternichian reaction as well as in the greater social freedom which followed the French Revolution. The Handel revival which spread across Europe in the closing years of the eighteenth century and the Bach revival of the 1830s both influenced the growth of the choral movement, as did 'colossal' works for massed voices and orchestra encouraged by the early music festivals. The researches of such historically minded scholar-connoisseurs as Baron van Swieten, patron of Haydn and Mozart, and of Raphael Kiesewetter, civil servant and amateur musician in Vienna, who after 1817 helped to found the Vienna Conservatoire and whose private concerts explored a wide range of choral music from Lassus and Palestrina to Bach's *Magnificat*.

The earliest of the great German choral societies was the Berlin *Singakademie*, which grew from the singing class held in Berlin by Carl Friedrich Fasch from 1787 onwards; the class, originally of wealthy bourgeois ladies, was one of Fasch's ways of augmenting the exiguous salary he received as a Berlin court musician when he found that, after the Seven Years War, it had lost a great deal of its value. In 1791 Fasch's class began to meet in the garden of an official in the Prussian War Ministry and to accept men into its membership; four months later, in October 1791, it was heard in public for the first time, singing in the Marienkirche. In 1796, when Beethoven visited Fasch in Berlin, its original membership of twenty-seven had expanded to ninety; when Fasch died in 1800 it had grown to a hundred and forty-seven singers.

Carl Friedrich Zelter, friend of Goethe and of the Mendelssohn family, succeeded Fasch. Like his predecessor, Zelter had a more than scholarly interest in the music of the past; Fasch had composed a great deal of music in the style of the early baroque composers, while it was Zelter who fired Felix Mendelssohn's enthusiasm for the choral works of Bach and was instrumental in initiating the 1829 revival of the *St. Matthew Passion*, which Mendelssohn conducted. He broadened the base of his work in Berlin by forming the *Liedertafel*, a men's singing club which met once a month for supper and the singing of its members' compositions. As the repertoire of the *Singakademie* expanded beyond unaccompanied choral works to embrace oratorios, Zelter organised an orchestra to take part in its performances. When he died, in 1832, the *Singakademie* had three hundred and fifty-nine members.

A similar organisation was created in Erlangen in 1806, and in 1807 J. F. Reichardt formed a choir in Weimar—he based it on the family of friends with whom he stayed in the city—to sing Handel's *Messiah*, and the choir remained in being after this inaugural performance. A *Singanstalt* came into being in Dresden. A Leipzig *Singakademie* was formed in 1802, and another in 1805; in 1817 the two began to work together, creating a choir of about a hundred and fifty voices. In Cassel the *Baldweinische Singinstitut* began operations as a choral society for 'young people of good family'; it took its name from its founder, a Cassel cantor active in the concert life as well as the church music of the city. A choral society was formed in Mannheim for the *Singende höhere Töchter* and the *Musikalische Bürgersöhne* of the citizens. A *Singakademie* founded among the students of Halle University numbered three hundred and seventy-one members by 1829. A Lübeck choral society formed to take part in oratorio performances was founded in 1816, and in Frankfurt the *Cecilienverein* was founded in 1818 and soon began to co-operate in oratorio performances with the already established orchestra of the Museum Concert Society. In 1823, when he had been *Kapellmeister* in Cassel for only a year, Spohr founded a *Cecilienverein* 'after the example of the majority of the larger towns in Germany, to strive towards the same noble aim, to awaken and cultivate a pure and correct taste for music of an exalted and earnest character'.[1] Similar amateur choral societies came a little later in Austria; the *Singschule* of the *Musikverein* in Carinthia began operations in 1849, and the *Singverein* of the *Gesellschaft für Musikfreunde* in Vienna was founded in 1858. The Vienna *Singakademie* was founded in 1863; until these organisations began their work, choral music in the Austrian cities was the duty of the theatre choruses.

The work of Hans Georg Nägeli in Switzerland was contemporaneous with that of Fasch and Zelter in Berlin. Nägeli, born in 1773, was a colleague and disciple of the educationalist and social reformer Pestalozzi, and his work ran parallel to that of Fasch and Zelter in a different social con-

[1] Spohr: *op. cit.* Vol. 2. p. 147.

text and with precise social aims as important to him as its musical purposes. Nägeli's organisation of singing classes began in the schools of Switzerland because singing together, he believed, should produce a sense of social unity and purpose while awakening the taste for good music and a sense of spiritual values. Among adults, it seemed to Nägeli, a problem of leisure was beginning to make itself felt; what was the adult to do with leisure hours his limited education could not immediately employ? How could that leisure be used both to enrich a working man's life, add to his enjoyment and be socially advantageous?

In a country where there was no organised musical life outside a handful of large towns—Zürich, Basel and Berne in particular—and where the musical traditions of the people consisted of folk songs and the psalm tunes permitted in Calvinist worship, and where there were three native languages and a variety of local traditions, Nägeli wished to use choral music as a means of social enjoyment sugaring the pill of spiritual uplift and social improvement. In 1805 he formed the Zürich *Singinstitut*, which included a mixed choir and a children's choir, and its public performances were designed to show what could be done by the sort of organisation he had created as a musical and social amenity for the general public.

Since 1792 Nägeli had been publishing music as a necessary educational service (it was he who roused Beethoven's fury by adding four bars to the first movement of Beethoven's Piano Sonata *op.* 31 No. 1) and composing keyboard pieces and songs for use in schools. His primary interest in his *Singinstitut* was pedagogical, and what he learned from the *Singinstitut* became the foundation of his *Gesangbildunglehrer,* the textbook of the choral societies formed all over Switzerland and affiliated to the *Singinstitut* in Zürich; from the individual choral societies came the *Allgemeine Schweizersiche Musikgesellschaft* with its headquarters in Lucerne. From Nägeli's work developed a number of music festivals which were held by large choirs founded to copy his original *Singinstitut,* assembling singers from all over their locality. Oratorio performances on a choral scale almost as massive as that of the Handel Festivals in London (though Haydn's *The Creation* was the favourite work of the Swiss choirs) were heard in Zürich, Winterthur, Aaraus, Schaffhausen and St. Gallen. Between 1808 and 1867 the *Musikgesellschaft* was responsible for festivals not only in the large cities, Zürich, Basel, Berne and Lucerne, but in any centre where a large number of members and member choirs could gather.

Nägeli's work, like the whole of the Pestalozzi movement, coincided with and expressed the spirit of the new political organisation of Switzerland which gave the state its modern structure. These changes were hotly debated and the creation of a democratic state, paradoxically, divided a country which had before seemed reasonably united in spite of differences of language, religion and culture. Nägeli's belief in the unifying influence of music was prompted by political conditions of the sort which require social rather than political cure, and the growth of the Swiss festival movement had precisely the social influence for which he had designed it.

Music festivals in Germany, too, encouraged the growth of choralism, though they had no clearly stated aims outside the desire to make music. In 1810 Spohr was invited to direct the first festival at Frankenhausen; the twenty-six-year-old conductor–violinist–composer was, apparently, asked to take charge because of his position as leader of the court orchestra at Gotha nearby. Spohr's efficiency and style had impressed the Frankenhausen cantor, Bischoff, who in 1804 had raised a choir of eighty to sing *The Creation* with the court orchestra from Gotha; the festival was simply designed to involve a still larger number of participants in two great musical events. The festival choir which Bischoff collected came from Weimar, Rudolstadt, Gotha and Erfurt as well as from Frankenhausen and several other nearby towns. The orchestra, with twenty players from Spohr's orchestra in Gotha as its foundation, numbered one hundred and six. A hundred singers were present at the rehearsal of *The Creation*; ninety-nine of them took part in the actual performance on the second day of the festival. An orchestral concert included an overture by Spohr and his Clarinet Concerto in E flat, played by his friend Hermstedt, with Beethoven's Fifth Symphony as its climax.[2]

In 1814 the French military governor of Erfurt ordered a festival to celebrate the birthday of Napoleon and commissioned Spohr's oratorio *The Last Judgement* as its main feature; Spohr, as the festival's musical director, made his own orchestra the nucleus of a large festival orchestra and co-opted Bischoff to create a properly numerous choir. The fact that an oratorio on a very large scale was to be the main feature of the festival itself presupposed the availability of large amateur choirs.

Spohr was in Vienna during the second Frankenhausen festival; the third, in 1815, celebrated the defeat of Napoleon with his cantata *Das befreite Deutschland* and Gottfried Weber's *Te Deum*. In 1818 Spohr was involved in the first Lower Rhine Festival; most of his soloists were musicians who had taken part in his two Frankenhausen festivals, with a large orchestra and a huge choir recruited throughout the festival area. In 1820 he directed a festival at Quedlinburg, where the big choral work was *The Last Judgement* by J. C. Friedrich Schneider, himself in later years director of Festivals at Magdeburg, Nuremberg, Strasbourg, Halle, Wittenberg, Halberstadt, Dessau, Köthen, Koblenz, Hamburg, Zerbst, Meissen and Lübeck. Such festivals were organised for the people of the area in the centre of which they took place and depended upon the performance of one or more big choral works; many festivals were isolated events, not repeated year after year, but they were all rooted in the activities of choral societies

[2] Spohr: *op. cit.* pp. 140ff.

which could band together for spectacular events. In 1826 the indispensable
Spohr was in Düsseldorf for the year's Lower Rhine Festival, and though
none of his later oratorios was written as a German festival commission, he
continued to be involved in the festival movement until 1848, when he was
in his middle sixties; festivals of Nordhausen, Hesse, Brunswick, Dader-
born, Cassel itself and Lucerne all claimed his attention at one time or another.

Mendelssohn, a greater composer, as efficient, dedicated and charming as
Spohr, became no less indispensable to the major German festivals and an
enthusiastic supporter of all their activities. In Frankfurt, in 1832, he wrote
to Zelter in Berlin about the excellence of the St. Cecilia Society, which,
he said:

> would alone make it worth while to be in Frankfurt. The singers work
> with such enthusiasm and precision that it is a sheer delight to listen to
> them. It meets once a week and has two hundred members. Besides that
> Schelble [the choirmaster] has a small group of about thirty voices who
> meet at his place every Friday and he works with them at the piano;
> little by little they prepare his favourite compositions which he dare not
> give directly to his big chorus. I have heard a great deal of lovely music
> there, several of Bach's 'Sunday Services', his *Magnificat* and the great
> Mass. Just as in your own Academy, the female singers are always the
> more eager; the males sometimes leave something to be desired; their
> heads are full of their business affairs. . . . In the big society, I heard,
> among other music, the motet [sic] *Gottes Zeit ist die allerbeste Zeit,*
> which we used to sing at your Friday nights.[3]

Both the choirs and the proliferating festivals were self-propagating. A
combination of local patriotism, local pride and the determination to keep
up with whatever musical Joneses had recently distinguished themselves,
ensured that they spread. Apart from their bringing new audiences into
contact with orchestral as well as with choral music, they were directly
educational, creating in their members and would-be members not only the
ambition to join effectively in exciting performances of great music but also
the incentive to undergo the training their ambition demanded.

Possibly too the appeal of choral music in German-speaking, Metternichian Europe was that it allowed each individual member, man or woman,
to become involved in the thoroughly democratic processes that were denied
to him in political life. In the choral societies all decisions, democratically
arrived at, were the results of general votes of all the members; in a sense this
gave the choral societies political implications unwelcome to the authorities.
The fact that large and efficient organisations could function successfully by
democratic methods suggested a criticism of the authoritarianism by which
Central European states were controlled. At the same time, the regular meet-

[3] Mendelssohn: *Letters*, edited by G. Selden-Goth. Elek, London,
1947. Letter of 15 February 1832. p. 189.

ings of large bodies of men and women could very easily, in the eyes of governments and police, cloak other and less innocuous purposes, so that the German and Austrian choral societies were hemmed in by police regulations.

In 1816, at a time when individual decisions were completely circumscribed by political control, Zelter published the principles and rules of the Berlin *Singakademie* in a pamphlet, *Grundriss der Verfassung der Sing-Akademie zu Berlin*. Whoever wished to join the Society had to apply to its Director and give an audition. Then he would be subject to election by the existing members of the Society. The business administration was in the hands of three members, one of whom should be Treasurer, and all three were elected by their colleagues, so that the Society offered an opportunity to members to exercise possibly unused talents in carrying out not the wishes of a Director (though he himself was elected by the members from whatever professionally qualified choral conductors were available) but the decisions of their fellow members.[4]

The Lübeck *Gesangverein* formally organised itself in 1819. It began its public career in November 1820 with a performance of the vocal sections of Johann A. P. Schulz's incidental music to Racine's *Athaliah* and a Mass by Haydn. The latter work was repeated a month later, sharing the programme with Mozart's *Requiem*. The *Gesangverein*'s original statutes apparently dealt only with the timing of rehearsals and concerts, but later statutes, drawn up in 1832 under the influence of a new Director, Gottfried Meyer, decided that eight members—four women and four men—were to be elected as a committee of management; they examined the new statutes and offered them for the approval of all the members. Matters of finance were to be decided by a general vote.[5]

The Carinthian *Musikverein*, with its headquarters in Klagenfurt, was a much larger organisation, responsible for orchestral and chamber concerts as well as the organisation and staffing of a conservatoire. Its choir was an outlet for many of the would-be members who were not instrumentalists. Its statutes, drawn up in 1827, show the attractively democratic principles on which such societies worked. The entire *Musikverein* was to be controlled by an elected president and a committee of five, all of whom were to hold office for three years and could then, if they wished, offer themselves for re-election. The various officials, too, held their posts as the results of election, and new members were elected to the Society. The process of voting was carried out with exaggerated punctiliousness; voting papers, correctly filled in and endorsed by the member's signature, were kept under

---

[4] Werner Bollert (editor): *Singakademie zu Berlin*. Berlin, 1966. pp. 61ff.

[5] Johann Hennings and Wilhelm Stahl: *Musikgesichte Lübecks*. Cassel, 1951. *Band 1 (Weltliche Musik)*. pp. 211ff.

lock and key (in a case with two locks and two key-holders) until the time
had come for the count. Incorrectly used voting papers were not counted,
and votes received after the closing date were not scrutinised but added to
the majority.[6] In so far as the Carinthian *Musikverein* and the other societies
prospered during the Metternichian repression, they provided a valuable
lesson in practical democracy.

Possibly the democratic methods adopted by amateur choirs and musical
organisations in general seemed all the more deplorable to the rulers because they drew their membership largely from the educated middle classes
who were, perhaps subconsciously, troubled by the problem of leisure which
Nägeli had set out to solve for his poorer fellow countrymen. The register of
Fasch's original singing class in Berlin survives, and, writes Friedrich
Herzefeld:

> The names are less interesting than the titles that accompany them. We
> find a Mrs. Medical Councillor, a Mrs. Legation Councillor, a widowed
> Mrs. Court Councillor, a Mrs. City Councillor, a Mrs. Ministry of
> Justice Councillor, a Mrs. Privy Councillor, a Mrs. Court of Appeal
> Councillor, a Mrs. Education Councillor, a Mrs. Privy Council Secre-
> tary, a Mrs. Doctor and a Mrs. Rector's Widow as well as a member who
> is simply described as 'Madam'.[7]

The German Karl Halle, in the throes of his transformation into the
English Charles Hallé, settled in Manchester in 1848, and in 1850, eight years
before the foundation of the orchestra for which he is remembered with
veneration, he had found

> So many amateurs with fair voices and an ear for music that I was able
> to found the 'St. Cecilia Society', in imitation of the German *Gesang-
> verein*, which dwelt in my memories since the days of my childhood. It
> consisted of ladies and gentlemen of the best society, at first about fifty
> in number.[8]

Hallé's St. Cecilia Society grew, he writes, from year to year and after 1858
was an adjunct to the performances of his orchestra.

The Hallé Orchestra, however, rooted itself in a city where music was
traditionally lively. Hallé had established himself in Manchester as a
teacher and recitalist and had then taken over the conductorship of the semi-
professional orchestra of the Gentlemen's Concerts there; the Gentlemen's
Concerts was an organisation which could trace its history, perhaps a little
deviously, to the earlier Music Club of the eighteenth century.

[6] Gotbert Moro and Ambros Wilhelmer: *Zur Musikgesichte Kärntens.*
Klagenfurt, 1956. pp. 52ff.
[7] Friedrich Herzefeld: *Sing-Akademischer Alltag*, in Bollert: *op. cit.*
p. 11.
[8] C. E. and Marie Hallé: *The Life and Letters of Sir Charles Hallé.*
London, 1896. p. 116.

Music in Liverpool, on the other hand, grew almost entirely out of the impetus provided by amateur choral societies. Liverpool was both large enough and prosperous enough to be visited by famous singers and the great touring instrumentalists; intermittently it enjoyed performances of opera. Its home-grown music, however, was choral, and orchestral work existed to support choirs in their performances of oratorio. Music festivals held in 1784 and 1790 were concerned with choral music, and from them grew the Apollo Glee Club, which continued to meet for close on a century. The later Festivals of 1830 and 1833 rested primarily on the work of two societies, the Liverpool Musical Society, a semi-professional orchestra, and the Cecilian Society, a choir, both active from the early 1800s and both directed by local organists, meeting in Liverpool churches. For the 1836 Festival, at which Mendelssohn's *St. Paul* was heard for the first time in England, the Festival Choral Society was founded. In 1831, when it was heard in public for the first time, singing Handel's *Jephtha*, it numbered twenty-six sopranos, fifteen (male) altos, twenty-three tenors and thirty-five basses. The necessity for an orchestra to join in its activities meant the expansion of the Music Society's orchestra with whatever musicians were available, many of them normally active in orchestrally-minded Manchester. The orchestra existed to provide the necessary accompaniment to choral music.

While choral music in London depended on the professional choirs of the theatres and the opera (so that the finale of Beethoven's Ninth Symphony had to be translated into Italian for the work's first performance in England in 1825) and it was not until 1881, in a performance of Berlioz's *Romeo and Juliet*, that an amateur choir was heard in a concert of the Royal Philharmonic Society, the music of massed voices had been an English passion at least since the later eighteenth century and the early Handel Festivals. Haydn in the 1790s and Berlioz in the 1840s had been overwhelmed by the effect of several thousand children's voices singing in unison in St. Paul's Cathedral simply because the musical effect was one with which they were entirely unfamiliar. Outside London, Manchester and Liverpool, the development of the amateur choirs in England was a matter of carefully designed 'social engineering'. Hallé's middle-class singers and the Church of England choralists of Liverpool were not typical of the large choral societies of the industrial towns which provided probably the vast majority of the English people with their only real contact with music.

To say that English choral music in the nineteenth century was largely the result of a union between music and nonconformity as they acted together on a depressed and degraded working class is hardly an exaggeration. John Wesley, the founder of Methodism, was a member of an extremely musical family which in the next two generations was to produce two of the finest English composers of their day, his nephew Samuel and Samuel's son,

Samuel Sebastian. But whatever interest John Wesley felt in music was controlled by his vocation; he wanted hymns which the simplest and most illiterate people could remember and sing to simple, emotional or rousing tunes 'with the spirit and understanding'. Wherever Methodist congregations met, they sang lively or moving tunes while the Church of England, outside the cathedrals, provided little music except settings of the metrical psalms.

Methodists taught the children of their congregations to sing, and Wesley demanded that care be taken in their training, but anthems and any elaborate music were forbidden; the whole congregation was to sing and not to sit silently while others sang to it. Methodism, and nonconformity in general, were urban, industrial movements wherever there was a working class alienated by its conditions and its lack of either education or any place in the traditional society of the past from the Anglican religious tradition. Methodism conquered the new industrial working class in new towns, or in the old towns which industry swelled to bursting point. It was a relief from squalor and deprivation, and it is at least arguable that music attracted people to Methodism as much as Methodism attracted people to music. Music unites; singing together, Wesley knew, individual men and women become a community, a congregation. There was no Methodist activity, from vast open-air services to the small, intimate 'Class Meetings' for instruction and discussion, which did not demand hymn singing. In the minds of a vast number of English people, Methodism created a feeling that music, to be worth while, was inextricably tied to worship.

It was from Methodism, too, that the appetite for education developed. In the early nineteenth century the new working class came to be convinced that the way out of its misery was through education. By learning, the workers could win promotion, and from promotion better positions, better wages, better housing and a hope for the future. Those who were not totally dehumanised by their lot developed an enthusiasm for education which led to the foundation of a variety of institutions to provide the opportunities for 'Self Help' that they needed. In 1823 the London Mechanics' Institution opened to offer specialised practical knowledge to workers whose aim was to make themselves more useful to their employers and thus reach a position where they could earn higher wages. The example of London was rapidly followed in other towns and cities throughout industrial England. But the specialised, practical training which had been the first aim of the Mechanics' Institutes proved to be less than their members needed; classes in Latin and the classics, and in both music and mathematics, were rapidly formed, and music became a popular subject. Naturally, more often than not the music studied was vocal music.

The autobiography of Thomas Cooper, a Leicester cobbler, provides an example of the musical enthusiasm awakened by the Mechanics' Institutes.

Cooper was a Methodist and a Chartist, self-educated to the point at which he became a newspaper reporter. In 1834, while he was still in his twenties, he went to Lincoln to teach Latin in the Mechanics' Institure there; he had a gift for languages and rapidly found himself teaching French as well. He had not long been involved in his educational work when what he called 'a new attraction' demanded his attention:

> A few young men wished to form a choral society and asked me to allow them the use of my schoolroom for rehearsals. I consented readily, and became a member of the new society, taking my stand, weekly, as a tenor singer in the choruses. My heart and brains were soon on fire with the worship of Handel's grandeur, and with the love of his sweetness and tenderness. They made me their secretary; and my head went to work to make the music of the choral society worth hearing in old cathedralled Lincoln.[9]

Cooper became the moving spirit and the recruiting officer of the Society. He made the best sight-reader in the city, who was also the 'most experienced in the music of Handel', its conductor; found an alto and a bass capable of leading their sections of the choir and of singing solos; enlisted the cathedral organist as a viola player, and found the best cellist in Lincoln to lead the cellos. In the first year of the Society he raised £200 for its support and obtained permission for its performances in a church in the centre of the city. The Society sang *Messiah, Judas Maccabeus, Israel in Egypt, Solomon*, The Dettingen *Te Deum*, Haydn's *The Creation* and music by Mozart and Beethoven. Later, the Society bought drums, a slide trumpet and the nucleus of a library—Arnold's complete edition of the work's of Handel, Mozart's *Requiem, The Creation* and Beethoven's *The Mount of Olives*. There was a committee of performers, but it was content to leave the business of the Society in the hands of the enthusiastic, and better educated Cooper.

Other institutes were equally active. Music classes were available at Institutes in York and Newcastle, amongst many others. The Miles Platting Institute, in one of the most squalid parts of Manchester, founded in 1836, offered a class for instrumental music. The music teacher at the Manchester Mechanics' Institute formed a group of those who attended his class into a glee and psalm singing group. In Bradford a special committee of the music class, meeting with the general committee of the Mechanics' Institute, began to organise the weekly concerts for the working classes in 1845.

It would, no doubt, be cheap irony to suggest that working-class enthusiasm for music was fostered by employers because music was an inexpensive alternative to drunkenness, supported for this reason by nonconformist employers because sober, music-loving employees are more

[9] Thomas Cooper: *The Life of Thomas Cooper*, written by himself. London, 1872. p. 107.

efficient than the drunken and dissolute. Nevertheless, while music became an instrument in the hands of those who saw it as a way of enriching deprived lives, it was also a tool in the hands of 'do-gooders' whose interest was in its social effects and not in the art itself. The result was that some employers began to encourage musical activities among their employees. An American visitor to Robert Owen's community at New Lanark, where children under ten were sent to school instead of to work, noted that children were taught to sing there. Samuel Gregg, at Bollington, in Cheshire, opened a mill in 1832 and began to provide amenities for his workers, among them a singing class which rapidly became popular. From the singing class grew a weekly glee class and a much larger choir which met twice a week to sing sacred music. Before long, Gregg's workpeople had founded a brass band and, with their employer's support, taken up other instruments.[10]

The general educational level of the working-class singers was responsible for the various simplified methods of notation which evolved into the system of Tonic Sol-fa eventually worked out by John Curwen, a nonconformist minister and educationalist, in his book *Singing for Schools and Congregations*, published in 1843 to assist those who were intimidated by conventional musical notation. Parallel with the work of the choral societies, Joseph Mainzer, a German musician who had instituted large-scale singing classes for the poor in Paris, moved to England and continued his work in this country. His example was followed by John Hullah, who originally set out to train singing teachers for the schools but found himself with large, enthusiastic classes of members of the general public. With a choir formed from his London classes, Hullah gave a series of ambitious concerts, four of which, in 1847, were designed as a history of English choral music.

The alliance with nonconformity continued. When the Huddersfield Choral Society was formed in 1836 it refused membership to anyone who attended the secular, politically orientated Owenite 'Halls of Science'. The first of the great London choral societies, the Sacred Harmonic Society, began in 1832. The violinist-critic John Ella noted its origin in his *Musical Sketches*: 'The Sacred Harmonic Society first held its meetings for choral practice and prayer in a dissenting chapel.'[11] The chapel was that in Gate Street, Lincoln's Inn, but after two years the officers of the society secured the use of the smaller of the two halls in the Exeter Hall complex, in the Strand. Exeter Hall was the citadel of Methodism, and its statutes permitted it to be used only for religious purposes or the meetings of charitable societies. Apparently the activities of the Sacred Harmonic Society were religious enough to satisfy the authorities, who soon permitted it to use the

[10] E. D. Mackerness: *A Social History of English Music*. London, 1964. pp. 129–32.
[11] John Ella: *op. cit*. London, 1869. p. 428.

larger hall, which seated 3000 in its auditorium, for a charity performance of *Messiah*. It continued to use Exeter Hall until 1880, its performances of oratorios and of Haydn's *The Seasons* apparently being acceptable to the hall's management. By 1837, the Society's choir and orchestra numbered five hundred, and when Sir Michael Costa became its conductor ten years later it increased its membership to seven hundred. By this time, apparently, the members had began to feel that their first conductor, Joseph Surman, could not realise their musical ambitions.

The Sacred Harmonic Society was an extension to London of the main feature of northern industrial music, the huge amateur choir. Ella, writing in the 1860s, spoke of the change which such bodies had brought to the performance of the great choral works:

> During the early part of my professional employment in the orchestra of the King's Concert of Ancient Music [Ella played the violin in the Ancient Concerts from 1832 to 1848] the principal female choristers were brought from Lancashire. These ladies, who were supposed to have finer voices and a more intimate acquaintance with the *chefs d'œuvre* of the sacred composers than the theatrical choristers in London, were adequately remunerated to remain the whole season in town and sing exclusively in twelve concerts. . . . Choral societies are now increased to such an extent that if it were required to bring together in London a thousand good treble voices and choristers, I do not apprehend there would be the slightest difficulty.[12]

Wagner, during his unhappy tenure of office as conductor of the Philharmonic Society Concerts in 1855, heard several of the Sacred Harmonic Society's concerts and, despite his dislike of London and everything that happened there, could not bring himself totally to condemn the Society's activities; their atmosphere was, to him, strange and not altogether congenial:

> The oratorios given there [in Exeter Hall] nearly every week have, it must be admitted, the advantage of the great confidence to be gained from frequent repetition. Neither should I refuse to recognise the great precision of the chorus of seven hundred voices, which reached quite a respectable standard on a few occasions, particularly in Handel's *Messiah*. It was here that I came to recognise the true spirit of English musical culture, which is bound up with the spirit of English protestantism. This accounts for the fact that an oratorio attracts the public far more than an opera. A further advantage is secured by the feeling among the audience that an evening spent listening to an oratorio may be regarded as a sort of service and is almost as good as going to church.[13]

Among the few critics to show any sympathy to Wagner as a composer

[12] *Ibid.* p. 141.
[13] Richard Wagner: *My Life.* 'Authorised translation', London, 1963. pp. 634–5.

was George Hogarth, music critic of the *Daily News*, of which his son-in-law, Charles Dickens, was editor. Hogarth was Secretary of the Philharmonic Society at the time of Wagner's visit, and it is interesting to see that Wagner's diagnosis of the 'true spirit of English music' is stated very forthrightly, and with entire approval, at the end of Hogarth's *Musical History, Biography and Criticism*. Though he was deeply involved in English music-making, Hogarth's delight in the art seems to be for its ethical values, as he interprets them. He refers less to the musical standards of the opera or of London's concert life than to the process of moral reform through choral singing:

> The cultivation of a taste for music furnishes to the rich a refined and intellectual pursuit, which excludes the indulgence of frivolous and vicious amusements, and to the poor, a *laborem dulce lenimen*, a relaxation from toil, more attractive than the haunts of intemperance. . . . In the densely populated districts of Yorkshire, Lancashire and Derbyshire, music is cultivated among the working classes to an extent unparalleled in any other part of the kingdom. Every town has its choral society, supported by the amateurs of the place and its neighbourhood, where the works of Handel, and the more modern masters, are performed with precision and effect, by a vocal and instrumental orchestra consisting of mechanics and workpeople. . . . Their employers promote and encourage so salutary a recreation by countenancing, and contributing to defray the expenses, of their musical associations; and some provide regular musical instruction for such of their workpeople as show a disposition for it. . . . Wherever the working classes are taught to prefer the pleasures of the intellect, and even of taste, to the gratification of sense, a great and favourable change takes place in their character and manners. . . . Sentiments are awakened in them which makes them love their families and homes; their wages are not squandered in intemperance, and they become happier as well as better.[14]

Hogarth wrote in 1835, before the choral movement had grown to its greatest extent, and if it is difficult to estimate how many of the industrial working class were saved by singing from pauperdom, drink and degradation, the moral fervour behind English music in the nineteenth century is clear from the words of Hogarth, the activities of so many employers and the determination of the English people to associate good music with religion rather than with musical quality. The choral movement, with its insatiable appetite for works to religious words, together with the activities of a number of publishers, most effective of whom was Vincent Novello, who in 1811 made himself publisher in chief to the choral societies by producing the necessary supply of cheap vocal scores that the choirs needed, prove the movement's importance. It gave the English composer, out of touch with most continental developments, a reason for existing. The nineteenth cen-

[14] George Hogarth: *Musical History, Biography and Criticism*. London, 1835. pp 430–1.

tury is littered with the remains of well-meant if dull choral works, of the highest possible ethical and religious intentions, composed at an age when choral music flourished but England looked elsewhere for its operas and concert music.

7

Concerts and Orchestras

The orchestral music of Haydn and Mozart, and the power exerted by Beethoven's symphonies wherever they were heard (as well as the curiosity about Beethoven's music created by critics and commentators in places where concert music was not regularly available) gave the concert a new prestige equivalent to that of the opera. Cities where concerts had been established in the eighteenth century found themselves regarded for the first time as among the centres of musical life. Until Beethoven's contribution to musical expression was understood, listeners in the 1830s and 1840s found nothing in the other works available to them equal in importance to the symphonic world of the dead master for all its apparent obscurity of utterance and technical difficulty. The spread of European concert life was largely the result of the determination of early nineteenth-century musicians and their audiences to understand Beethoven. The musical necessity of performances of the concert works of Beethoven, Haydn and Mozart virtually created the 'standard repertoire'.

Possibly, too, it would not be merely fanciful to regard the orchestra, expanded by Beethoven and both enlarged and refined by Berlioz, Liszt and Wagner, eventually transformed by Mahler and Richard Strauss into a small army of musicians as an essential expression of the personality of the nineteenth century. While artists in general looked away from the age of industrialisation, the orchestra reflected the character of the age not so much in what it did as in what was and still is. The age of great orchestral forces designed to exploit new, compulsive powers of tone had begun in the age of the Napoleonic armies, winning an empire not only by their commander's unprecedented military genius but also by a new conception of warfare which depended on the precise co-ordination of many disparate specialist functions. The ensuing age was, increasingly and ever more ubiquitously, the age of industrial expansion which, in a sense, applied to peacetime occupations the same employment of masses individually skilled but all necessary to the complete achievement of more and more production of more and more necessary materials. The co-ordination of diverse specialist functions in the orchestra could be regarded, in its manner of work but not in the purposes for which the work was done, as the perfection of industrial method; the orchestra was a combination of sixty, eighty, ninety or even more highly skilled workers offering contributions to a task even more complex and difficult to co-ordinate than the diverse tasks of workers in any industrial process. There was a sense in which the symphony orchestra reflected the character of European industrial civilisation.

The creation of the Philharmonic Society in London in 1813 was, perhaps, natural in a city where the public concert dated back to the late seventeenth century. Regular London concerts with trained professional musicians suffered a prolonged interval after Salomon's third season of concerts had come to an end in 1796, after the glories of the seasons to which he had brought Haydn and killed off the rival organisation, the Professional Concerts which were the true forerunners of the Philharmonic Society. The Professional Concerts had been the creation of a group of professional musicians, most of them—like Clementi, Wilhelm Cramer and Salomon himself—who began to give public concerts after the Bach–Abel concerts had come to an end. The struggle of Salomon against the 'Professionals' during Haydn's first visit to London, each attempting to capture a numerically restricted audience, ended in the collapse of the 'Professionals', and after Salomon's 1796 season no organisation remained to provide regular concerts in London.

In 1813 thirty musicians, including J. B. Cramer, Clementi, J. A. Moralt, Ferdinand Cramer and Salomon, with a number of native musicians, among whom were the composers Attwood, Bishop, Dance, Horsely, Knyvett, Smart, Shield and the younger Samuel Webbe, set out to provide a new concert society. Among them were Charles Neate, who had met Beethoven and for a time became the new Society's intermediary with him, and Vincent Novello, whose determination to publish cheap editions of music for catholic choirs recovered large quantities of otherwise unobtainable music from the renaissance and Tudor periods.

The Philharmonic Society gave its first concert in March 1813, determined from the start to provide London audiences with the best modern music; this meant, before all else, the symphonies and overtures of Beethoven. Symphonies by Haydn and Mozart appeared frequently in the programmes, each of which at first included choral items and chamber music; solo vocal and instrumental pieces were not permitted until 1830, when Beethoven's concertos were allowed to take their place in the repertory. The Philharmonic Society was largely responsible for the introduction of Mendelssohn's music to England and commissioned his C minor Symphony as it had previously commissioned Beethoven's Ninth. Later composers who wrote for the Society included Spohr, who conducted his own works during his visits to London, and Dvořák. From time to time it did what it could to encourage native composers, but without finding much British work to set in its programmes.

The concerts, however, depended for their existence on subscriptions and on box-office receipts. The early concerts were given in the Argyle Rooms, which held audiences of eight hundred; these were burnt down in 1830, and after two years in the concert room of the King's Theatre the Philharmonic Society settled in the Hanover Square Rooms, which again accommodated audiences of only about eight hundred; this meant that subscriptions and admission charges had to be high and that the audiences were as a result socially exclusive. Though the concerts never had the social prestige of the opera or of the long-established Concert of Antient Musick, which had been in existence since 1776, continued until 1848, admitted no music which was less than twenty years old and numbered members of the royal family in its membership, attendance at the Philharmonic Society's concerts implied a degree of wealth and a social position. When, in 1869, the Society moved its concerts to the new St James's Hall, which could accommodate audiences of two thousand one hundred and twenty-seven, the Society could offer unreserved seats for five shillings or half a crown. The critic H. F. Chorley greeted this influx of new listeners with no enthusiasm; he wrote in the *Athenaeum* that, in losing their exclusiveness, 'the Philharmonic Concerts have lost their distinctive charm and the Society its only *raison d'être*'.

The Philharmonic Society created no orchestra for its own exclusive use but depended, so far as possible, on the orchestra of the opera, engaging its members not for a season but for individual concerts. From the start it was at the mercy of the deputy system, accepting the fact that members previously engaged would accept any more lucrative engagements that offered themselves, either for rehearsals or for the concert itself, sending a deputy to fill their places. At first the concerts were directed by members of the Society, sharing control of the performance from the leader's desk and from the keyboard of a piano on the desk of which lay the score; the piano, of course, was a redundant survival of the old days of the *basso continuo*. Spohr, visiting London for the first time in 1820, claimed to be the first musician to conduct the Philharmonic Society's orchestra with a baton, though Mendelssohn, in 1829, was 'conducted like a young lady to the piano' (so he wrote to his sister Fanny) to conduct his C minor Symphony. Although conducting in the modern style became customary in the 1830s, no specialist permanent conductor was appointed, and in 1843 the critic J. W. Davison suggested in *The Musical Examiner* that the decline in the Society's fortunes which had prevented the commissioning of new works and the open rehearsals of works submitted to it was in part at least due to the need of a permanent conductor who should be able to take full control of performances. In 1845 Sir Henry Bishop, not a specially auspicious choice, became conductor for a year; ill-health made it impossible for him to complete a single season, and in 1846 he was replaced by Michael Costa who, by virtue of technical competence and strict orchestral discipline, seemed to dominate English music through the mid-century.

The possibility of an audience less socially restricted than that served by the Philharmonic Society is proved by the success of Promenade Concerts, immediately acceptable to London audiences because they brought to England an idea already successful in Paris and made no exorbitant demands on the attention of a largely untutored body of listeners. In December 1839 a series of 'Promenade Concerts à la Musard' (Musard being the conductor of such concerts in Paris) began at the Drury Lane Theatre with an orchestra of sixty musicians. The capacity of the theatre— well over two thousand—permitted the attendance of a whole class of people who could not afford to attend the Philharmonic Society's concerts. The conductor of the series, Negri, offered programmes guaranteed not to alarm the most timorous: each concert normally consisted of four overtures, four waltzes, four quadrilles and a piece for a solo wind instrument.

The natural consequence of their success in a musical world dominated by the need to make a profit at the box office was that a rival series of concerts began, a month after Negri's, at the Crown and Anchor Tavern; the conductor was the violinist Eliason, who was almost indiscreetly ambitious— most of his programmes contained a complete symphony. The Crown and Anchor, however, could not accommodate audiences large enough to ensure success, and it may be that Eliason's audiences were not prepared for so much concentrated listening as was demanded of them, so that the series failed.

In the autumn of 1840, Eliason embarked upon another series, this time at the Lyceum Theatre, with the French Louis Antoine Jullien as his assistant conductor, while a smaller and less successful series occupied the Prince's Theatre, and in the winter Philippe Musard himself took over Drury Lane with a series of *Concerts d'hiver*. The informal, not too demanding concert was, it seems, sufficiently established at a time when the Philharmonic Society existed in permanent financial anxiety. In 1841 Jullien himself took over Drury Lane Theatre for his own Promenade Concerts and achieved almost unparalleled success; during his ascendancy, other conductors tried to rival him with concerts based on a similar pattern of music-making, among them Balfe, with his National Concerts, but nothing disturbed Jullien's command of his huge, devoted audience; that command was won by a fine orchestra and choir, skilled programme building and, above all, by his combination of brilliant showmanship, blatant sensationalism and genuine musicianship; whoever else appeared on his platform, he was always a star of sufficient luminosity to outdazzle any of his guests. Elegantly eccentric, with splendid moustaches and luxuriant black hair, he had a gilt armchair behind him on the podium, and into this he would sink exhausted after acknowledging the applause. At the climax of any work he would seize a violin, or perhaps a piccolo, and play with the orchestra.

Each concert included a quadrille, usually linked by its title to some great topical event, and in this a military band, or two, or three, or on special occasions even six, would join. There was a good deal of the charlatan about Jullien and his determination to become the focal point of the audience's attention by showing how great a man—a combination of Napoleon and Svengali—a real conductor must be. But he conducted music by Beethoven to audiences who would never have dared to set foot in the Hanover Square Rooms, proving that the music of Beethoven was special and precious by putting on a pair of white gloves, brought to him on a silver salver, and using a jewelled baton; the performances, however, were scrupulously rehearsed and accurate. Whilst Eliason had failed to win a popular audience for symphonic music, Jullien's unblushing showmanship succeeded to such effect that he plunged into the recklessly disastrous venture of the ill-prepared opera season at Drury Lane, to which he brought Berlioz as conductor for the first time in England, and later into even more grandiose catastrophically ill-founded schemes. But he created audiences for others to sustain, and in this way was responsible for developments in more normal musical fields.

The history of such organisations as the Philharmonic Society, not only in England, is normally one of enthusiasts determinedly creating a body of musicians dedicated to an up-to-date musical style; the style of its founders, however, becomes a norm and without anyone's realising it, the taste of the founders becomes an orthodoxy beyond which no particular expansion is acceptable. The Orchestra of the *Société des Concerts du Conservatoire* began operations in 1828 and gave authoritative performances of the Beethoven symphonies which delighted the hearts of both Berlioz and Wagner. Its association with the state-supported conservatoire and its use of a hall which seated more than a thousand listeners made its financial situation less precarious than that of the Philharmonic Society in London, but both these once almost revolutionary organisations had, within thirty years of their creation, begun to face criticism for their reactionary attitudes and their neglect of new music.

In London the New Philharmonic Society was founded in 1852; its prime mover was Henry Wylde, organist, Professor of Harmony at the Royal Academy of Music, and, in 1863, Gresham Professor of Music. The New Philharmonic Society, according to its prospectus, intended to provide 'more perfect performances of the works of the great masters than have hitherto been attained'. The prospectus continued:

> The growing taste for the arts, more especially for music, in this country, demands a new institution where the greatest works by the greatest masters of all the ages may be heard by the public at large. . . . Exclusiveness, the baneful hindrance of all progress in art, will not be tolerated in this society. . . .

The New Philharmonic does not entertain the opinion, acted on by an older institution, that no schools but those which can be called classical are to be considered capable of affording pleasure, and that such schools can only be enjoyed by a select few amateurs and artistes.

The New Philharmonic Socety was controlled by Wylde and a committee not of professional musicians but of socially eminent and wealthy concert-goers. It was, at first, able to use Exeter Hall, with an auditorium capable of holding more than three thousand, for its concerts. Thus, although its orchestra was built to the scale of twenty first violins and although it engaged a professional choir, its subscription for the six concerts of its inaugural season was only two guineas—one guinea for professional musicians—and single tickets for the cheaper parts of the auditorium were within the reach of working people.

Originally, the New Philharmonic Society was an outstanding success. The concerts of the first season were conducted by Berlioz, popular in England since Jullien had first brought him to London. The first concert included movements from his *Romeo and Juliet,* and the season contained two revelatory performances of Beethoven's Ninth Symphony which were the first in England to do justice to the work; the clarity, incisiveness and insight of Berlioz's conducting, added to the more humdrum fact that the work was, in Berlioz's manner, scrupulously rehearsed, secured a triumph. The cost of the sectional and choir rehearsals, and the seven full rehearsals, was not, however, something the New Philharmonic Society was inclined to repeat as a matter of course for difficult works.

In the second season the orchestra was matched to the scale of twenty-four first violins; Berlioz was replaced by Peter Joseph Lindpainter, who shared the conductorship with Wylde until his death in 1856. In 1858 Wylde became sole conductor. Already by 1854 the concerts moved from their insecure base in Exeter Hall, where the authorities of the Methodist Church had never been completely easy in their consciences at housing mere orchestral concerts—the hall was designed 'for religious meetings and the activities of charitable associations'—and in 1857 they were driven to the Hanover Square Rooms, where concerts on their original scale were out of proportion both to the orchestral accommodation it offered and to the hall's acoustic qualities; the move naturally impeded the idea of social inclusiveness. Eventually, with the opening of the St. James's Hall in 1858, Wylde moved his organisation there, and continued as conductor and manager until his retirement in 1879. The German-born William Ganz, who had come to England as an orchestral violinist, opera rehearsal pianist, accompanist and conductor before the New Philharmonic Society was born, took over the New Philharmonic Society's activities, converting it into 'Mr. Ganz's Orchestral Concerts' and continuing the New Philharmonic Society's traditional devotion to the works of Berlioz; it was, too, at Ganz's concerts that the *Dante* Symphony of Liszt had its first performance. By the 1880s, however, the New Philharmonic Society's pioneering functions had been taken over by the Crystal Palace Concerts, conducted by August Manns.

The Crystal Palace Concerts took place in an auditorium—originally a transept of the huge exhibition building—large enough to accommodate those who could not afford to pay even the lower prices charged at West End concerts, and the hall was even able to find room for the army of singers and instrumentalists assembled for the monster Handel Festivals of the late nineteenth century with as many as two thousand performers in choir and orchestra. Apart from the apparently considerable merits of Manns as a conductor—he was, it seems, clear and decisive and a sensitive interpreter of a wide range of music. His programmes included not only works by Schubert, Schumann, Raff, Liszt, Brahms and Smetana previously unknown in England in his programmes but also found room for works by Sullivan, Mackenzie, Parry and Stanford, the forerunners of 'the English musical renaissance' before such composers could hope for a hearing at any of the longer-established London concerts. To insist upon the importance to nineteenth-century concerts of the size of the auditoria they frequented is not, of course, to note a mere triviality; concerts which had to survive more or less entirely through takings at the box perforce depended either on high prices or on the availability of a hall large enough to allow the sale of tickets at prices within the financial reach of the more or less poor.

By the end of the nineteenth century, England was a land in which music was heard by audiences with a considerable social range; there was space for the *hoi polloi* at the various Promenade Concerts and the Crystal Palace; the New Philharmonic Society played to audiences socially inferior to those of the 'old' Philharmonic Society as well as to patrons of the older Society, and the opera catered for the wealthy. But at the same time England was '*das Land ohne Musik*'. In Wagner's season as conductor of the Philharmonic Concerts he conducted a single English work—a symphony by Cipriani Potter which he did not find as detestable as he found most new music. Berlioz conducted a symphony by Charles Lucas for the New Philharmonic Society, but perhaps tactfully wrote nothing about it. The rest of the music, some of it, in the Philharmonic Society's palmy days, commissioned from the famous, came from foreign composers. Conductors and soloists were mostly foreign.

England's dependence on foreign musicians was not restricted to the concert hall and the opera house. John Ella, founder of the Musical Union which gave chamber-music concerts from 1845 to 1880, was music critic of the *Morning Post* and from time to time wrote for other periodicals. He quotes the remark of a Venetian soprano in a story by Balzac that England and France robbed Italy of the best singers: *'Paris les juge et Londres les paye'*.[1] The English public, he declared, 'is often the victim of *charlatanerie*, and its patronage most shamefully abused by the importunities of the most inferior talents with letters of introduction'.[2] 'Most of the pianists, getting their guinea per lesson in London, would receive in Vienna not more than six shillings,' Ella declares. '. . . I have known a *maestro di canto* from Naples obtain a number of pupils on his arrival in London, at one guinea per lesson, who, to my knowledge, in his native city was glad to give seven lessons for the same amount.'[3]

Nevertheless, Ella, organising his own concerts in London, depended on foreign musicians, not necessarily for their superior accomplishments. He tells the story of an English lady who called on him one morning without an appointment: she had dreamed that she was playing the piano at a Musical Union concert and was determined to make her dream come true. She insisted upon playing a Hummel sonata to Ella, who was surprised by her performance but felt compelled to reject her offer. 'My expenses,' he said, 'are considerable, the subscription very low, and without attracting visitors by the engagement of new and eminent professors from the continent, I could not afford to pay my artists.'[4]

After thirty-two years of Musical Union concerts, Ella in 1877 provided some statistics: at his concerts seventy-four pianists, a hundred and two string players and twenty-seven wind players had appeared at his concerts:

> Analysis: Englishmen, forty-eight; French, thirty-one; Germans and Austrians, sixty-four; Italians, fifteen; Belgians, fourteen; Hungarians, eight; Poles, three; Russians, five; Dutch, eight; Swedes, one; Spanish and Portuguese, four.[5]

Ella's assemblage of foreign artists, however, included Mendelssohn, Dragonetti, Moscheles, Thalberg, Hallé, Ernst, Sivori, Piatti, Sainton, Joachim, Leopold Auer and Anton Rubinstein; in the nineteenth century it would have been hard to find any more illustrious collection of instrumentalists.

While foreign musicians increasingly dominated London music throughout the nineteenth century, provincial music-making followed the eighteenth-century pattern of semi-amateur performance in most towns and cities, with such events as the Three Choirs Festival of such cities as Norwich, Liverpool and Birmingham to diversify the fare and bring together local amateur choirs with professional orchestral musicians from London and solo singers of international reputation. The establishment of

---

[1] Ella: *op. cit. Italian Opera.* p. 350.
[2] *Ibid.* p. 105. *Composers and teachers of music at home and abroad.*
[3] *Ibid.* p. 104. *Foreign musicians in London.*
[4] *Ibid.* p. 332. *A Lady's Midsummer Night's Dream.*
[5] *Ibid.* p. 434. *The Musical Union (1877).*

'modern' concert societies in English towns and cities when and where it came, yielded English music into the hands of Central European musicians and the musical attitudes they brought with them.

Liverpool had a Festival Choral Society with a choir a hundred strong and its own semi-professional orchestra when, for reasons which have never been made really clear, the Liverpool Philharmonic Society was founded in 1840. The founders were Liverpool business men who controlled the organisation of their foundation in everything except its musical policy. In three years the Society had outgrown its first home, 'Mr Lassall's Saloon', a dancing academy, and moved to the hall of the Liverpool Collegiate Institute. Its first concert included overtures by Kalliwoda and Auber, the *Macbeth* music attributed to Matthew Locke and a sextet for flute, clarinet, horn, cello, double-bass and piano by Onslow; the rest of a long programme consisted of madrigals by Morley and Wilbye and choruses by Rossini and Bishop, but with no star singers to dazzle the audience with spectacular arias. The early conductors were local church organists.

With the move to the new hall in 1843, Jacob Zeugheer Hermann was appointed conductor. Born in Zürich in 1805, Hermann had studied in Munich, where he had founded a string quartet with which he had toured from 1824 to 1830, and had first reached Liverpool to give six concerts there on his way to Scotland and Ireland. In 1830 he had tired of a nomadic life and settled in the north of England, becoming conductor of the Gentlemen's Concerts in Manchester from 1831 to 1838. Hermann based his programmes on the familiar continental music of the day; from 1844 onwards, symphonies were regularly played in Liverpool programmes, but audiences continued to enjoy 'selections' from the popular operas—*Fidelio, Der Freischütz,* Balfe's *The Bohemian Girl,* Wallace's *Maritana,* Rossini's *Semiramide* and Spohr's *Jessonda.* Mendelssohn's choral works were as popular in Liverpool as they were everywhere else. Amateur players gradually disappeared from the orchestra, their places taken by professional players imported from London. A single year at the Collegiate Institute was enough to convince the Society that its concerts needed a larger hall with better acoustics, and in 1844 the foundation stone of the Original Philharmonic Hall was laid. In 1849 the Hall was opened; it accommodated audiences of 2100 and an orchestra and choir of 250.

The rules of the Society were, perhaps belatedly, published in 1845. A committee of not more than thirty-six members, including the Secretary and the Treasurer, would control the Society's business. There were to be four 'full-dress' and six 'undress' concerts a year; 'full-dress' concerts would be distinguished by performances of 'metropolitan talent' (usually singers of international reputation). The Society's insistence on dress was, apparently, part of a yearning for the social exclusiveness which at that time was beginning to worry London musicians, but it was the decision of

Liverpool business men who wanted their society to reflect their own social attitudes and ambitions. In their pursuit of social grandeur the Society's rules, and some later regulations, go to great and sometimes barely intelligible trouble. They declare:

> No gentleman within seven miles of Liverpool, not being a member, or a member in the family of a member, shall be admitted to any concert.

When the Philharmonic Hall was opened, those not wearing evening dress were banished to two side galleries; evening dress was obligatory in stalls and boxes: great care was taken to be sure that the right people were in the right places and that the wrong people did not obtrude on them. Until the original hall was burned down in 1933, a list of 'Gentlemen having the *entrée*' was displayed in its corridors, and, until 1909, when it was 'temporarily suspended', an intimidating notice was repeated from time to time in the programmes:

> The attention of proprietors and those who rent boxes and stalls is drawn to the following regulation, which will be strictly enforced:
>
> No gentleman above twenty-one years of age residing or carrying on business in Liverpool or within ten miles thereof, and not being an Officer of the Army or Navy, or Minister of Religion, is admissable to the Boxes or Stalls unless he be a Proprietor, or member of the family residing in the House of a Proprietor, or have his name upon the List of Gentlemen having the *Entrée* exhibited in the corridors.
>
> Resident Gentlemen who are not Proprietors can acquire the Right of Purchasing Tickets or of making use of Proprietor's Tickets during the season on the Payment of an Entrance Fee of 10s. 6d.
>
> N.B. Gentlemen above twenty-one, although members of the family residing in the house of those who *simply rent* Boxes and Stalls, are only admissable after payment of the Entrance Fee.[6]

Apparently, though earlier accounts do not mention the fact, it was possible for those who wished to do so to buy their own boxes or stalls rather than simply to subscribe to them; this was the system later to be used for the Royal Albert Hall in London. The members of the Liverpool Philharmonic Society seem to have been agitated by the possibility that 'proprietors' might pass on their rights to the socially unacceptable, and one suspects that a small audience of the acceptable would please the committee more than a hall thronged with the *hoi polloi*. It is possible to assume that the suspension of these regulations in 1909 may have been the result of diminishing audiences as the rights of original proprietors were inherited by children or grandchildren who did not wish to make use of them. Mere subscribers, who '*simply rented*' their seats, could not, however, claim any particular rights; their subscriptions could not be transferred to

---

[6] W. A. Argent: *The Philharmonic Jubilee: Half a Century of Music in Liverpool.* Liverpool, 1889.

members of their families without the payment of a new entrance fee by the recipient of the subscription.

When the twenty-nine-year-old Karl Halle (born at Hagen in Westphalia but a member of the Parisian *avant-garde* which included Berlioz, Liszt and Chopin) was driven from France by the revolution of 1848, he planned to settle in London and quickly established himself there as a concert pianist and teacher. Before long he left the Metropolis, invited to 'take Manchester in hand'. A year later, he was given the conductorship of the Gentlemen's Concerts in his new home. He had already established his chamber-music concerts, which, because of the large German colony in Manchester, rapidly drew a satisfactory audience; in 1849, their first season, Hallé (as he had become) won sixty-seven subscribers; after four years they filled a hall which held an audience of 450 and had a waiting list of over a hundred would-be subscribers. His first chamber-music concert in Liverpool, incidentally, was played to an audience of eleven, but by 1852 his Liverpool concerts were prospering.

The Manchester 'Gentlemen's Concerts' were, like the Liverpool Philharmonic Society's, administered by a committee of members; the conductor was a salaried official responsible for no more than musical policy and performance, limited in respect of both by the finances made available to him by the committee. It says much for Hallé's impact that in 1849 the committee accepted the almost ruthless conditions he advanced before accepting the conductorship; he was empowered to discharge inefficient members of the orchestra, recruit new ones, rehearse works until he was satisfied with the quality of performance before including them in a concert programme. When he had first attended a Manchester concert in 1848 to hear his friend Chopin play with the orchestra, he almost fled the city; he was fresh from the Conservatoire Orchestra's concerts in Paris and the conducting of Berlioz. In the September of 1848 he himself played with the orchestra; his performance in Beethoven's E flat Concerto was only part of a programme which included songs by the soprano Grisi (whom Hallé accompanied in Beethoven's *Adelaide*), Mario, the tenor, and Tagliaficio, the bass. Zeugheer Hermann returned from Liverpool to conduct, but the standard of orchestral playing was no better than when Hallé had first attended a Manchester concert. Hallé was, it seems, an unusually gentle man of great simplicity and kindness, but he would not accept the conductorship until his conditions were met.

In 1857 Manchester held an 'Art Treasures Exhibition', for which the authorities determined to create a first-class orchestra and empowered Hallé to engage the players capable of forming such an orchestra from London and from the continent to play with the best of his local musicians. Rather than disband an orchestra which had proved itself to be effective after the closing of the exhibition, Hallé planned a series of weekly concerts to keep the new ensemble together. He gave his first concert in January 1858, realising that he would have to create an entirely new public. He could, perhaps, depend upon the support and patronage of the members of the Gentlemen's Concert Society, but his success as concert promoter would depend upon the appeal of his new organisation to a much wider public. Those who had been fascinated by the quality of music heard at the exhibition had not attended specifically to listen to the orchestra, and the higher prices he would have to charge when his orchestra was no longer a subsidised feature of the exhibition would, perhaps, be a strong deterrent: thirty concerts, he decided, would be enough to decide on the success or failure of his scheme. He announced his programmes in advance, hoping for the patronage of many to whom orchestral music was unknown, depending in part on arousing the interest of a public which, he knew, had no notion what the words 'symphony' and 'concerto' implied, and pressed on with his plan in a manner which seemed foolhardy even to his well-wishers. His autobiography, with its naively direct account of the early struggles, is superior to any retelling of the tale:

> Beethoven's Symphony in C major headed the first programme and was vehemently applauded by the meagre audience. The loss upon the concert was a heavy one, and was followed by similar losses week after week, until my friends were debating whether for the sake of my family I ought not to be locked up, and I myself began to feel rather uneasy. It was not before nearly half the series of thirty concerts had been given that things took another aspect; the audience gradually became more numerous and more appreciative; at last full houses succeeded each other, and the day after the thirtieth concert my managers and dear friends, Messrs. Forsyth Brothers, brought me with the statement of my receipts and expenses ten brand-new threepenny bits, the profits of the whole series— a penny per concert! Perfectly satisfied with this result, which I considered most encouraging, I at once made arrangements for a second series to be given during the winter season of 1858–9.[7]

The Hallé Concerts were the personal responsibility of their founder–conductor. Until he reached his seventies Hallé had no committee of management sharing the financial burdens of the concerts and taking a share in their control. Hallé was not bound by the social preconceptions of well-to-do Mancunians as to the types of people who could enjoy orchestral music and those whose social status made them virtually untouchable. The advertisement of the first concert read:

> Reserved seats 2s. 6d., Gallery and body of the hall (unreserved) 1s., Subscription for a series of eight concerts 20s.[8]

[7] C. E. and Marie Hallé: *op. cit.* pp. 131–2.

[8] Michael Kennedy: *The Hallé Tradition.* Manchester University Press, 1966. p. 30.

It was Hallé's policy always to have some seats available for the lowest-paid members of the Manchester community, and these seats were never empty. The social exclusiveness of concert societies in London, copied by the Liverpool Philharmonic Committee, seem to have been imposed by their own members, not by limitations of public taste. Hagen, Hallé's birth-place in Westphalia, where his father was organist and director of the town's amateur orchestra and choral society, was not an industrial town and Hallé did not, therefore, grow up inside a rigid class system, so that the various boundaries which separated Englishmen seem to have meant nothing to him, and the idea of appealing to a concert audience on the basis of social class apparently never occurred to him. According to his son and daughter, who completed his *Autobiography* and edited the correspondence which is added to it; he specially treasured the appreciative letters he received from the occupants of the cheaper seats: one such letter was 'written on a narrow sheet of paper such as is found in most workshops'. It is signed 'An Operative' and was accompanied by a gift of 'two yards of fine white flannel', the gift of a workman who in November 1873 had attended his first concert and offered the conductor his tribute.[9]

Hallé's son and daughter meditated upon their father's achievement:

> How many a factory hand or office clerk in the busy towns of Manchester and the North of England may have owed his only knowledge of what was beautiful to the music he had an opportunity of hearing at my father's weekly concerts during the dreary winter months.
> It is impossible to believe that some element of refinement has not developed in the large audience of working men who, standing packed together in great discomfort, have yet listened for hours, and evidently with much appreciation, to much intricate and delicate music; or that the taste thus formed in one direction should not have its effect in others, and possibly have coloured their whole lives?[10]

The Hallé, as a permanent orchestra engaged by the season, set new musical standards which by the 1880s startled London audiences whom the orchestra regularly visited. London concerts were bedevilled by the 'deputy system' which elsewhere continued as something unavoidable until, in 1911, Henry Wood took a firm stand against it and created an orchestra which was bound by contract to play at all the concerts for which he booked it.

At the same time, Hallé was destroying the social pattern which in the past had restricted the availability of music in Manchester to gentlemen and ladies, just as the social pattern restricted the availability of concert music outside the traditional Promenade Concerts to those who could pay highly for a seat and dress well enough to occupy it without causing con-

[9] Hallé: *op. cit.* p. 144.   [10] *Ibid.* p. 143.

sternation to those sitting nearby. Hallé did not, as Henry Wood was to
do after 1895, when he took charge of the Promenade Concerts, educate
the musically illiterate in his audience by leading it through shoals of light
music to easy classics and from them to the profundities of Bach, Haydn,
Mozart and Beethoven. The Hallé policy was simply to play great music
as well as his orchestra could play it, and his audience—'operatives',
'factory hands', Lancashire business men and exiled German textile merchants nostalgic for the life they had enjoyed in Germany—accepted his
offerings enthusiastically.

The Hallé and the Liverpool Philharmonic Society naturally handed
over provincial music-making to German domination, just as London
opera had been ceded to the Italians and London concerts to Germans. The
only alternative to foreign domination would have been a stultifying pro-
vincialism more harmful than indoctrination into the music of Beethoven,
Mendelssohn, Brahms and Wagner. German domination of the concert hall
brought up English musicians on the most adventurous and stimulating
music available; all that was needed was a group of composers strong
enough to resist domination while up-to-date enough to profit from its example. When at the end of the nineteenth century Elgar arrived to lead
English music back into the world of musical adventure, English musicians
and their audiences were able to take their place in the mainstream and
not simply to fight their way out of a remote musical backwater.

In Paris the formation of the *Société des Concerts du Conservatoire*, in
1828, created the orchestra which was responsible for what seems to have
been the best, most conscientiously prepared performances of Beethoven's
symphonies to be heard at that time in Europe. Berlioz, however, after his
first visit to London, spent 1850 and 1851 attempting to create a Philharmonic Society similar in organisation to that of London in order to bring
Paris musicians and music lovers up to date with works which the Conservatoire concerts neglected. Though anything which Berlioz attempted
was almost sure to be attacked by the heads of the French musical establishment, his plan to promote new music within the context of the great
masterpieces of the past succeeded sufficiently for him rapidly to build up a
first-rate orchestra and choir, to be paid from the profits of the concerts in
which they took part. The first concert was an unprecedented success, making a profit of 2700 francs. This, however, was to be divided into equal
shares for ninety orchestral players and a hundred and ten choralists; the
chorus master took three shares and Berlioz four. In return for this, Berlioz
had undertaken the administration and publicity, rehearsed the music, composed works to be played and arranged others; while the players and singers
each received thirteen francs, his reward was fifty.

Even the most exemplary loyalty could not ensure the regular, industrious attendance of singers and players at rehearsals and performances for

so low a fee, and the fact that, although his music invariably drew large, and mostly enthusiastic, audiences, his colleagues, notably Pierre Dietsch, the chorus master, had compositions of their own to include in the programmes, less appealing to the public than those of their flamboyant leader. Berlioz, unusually generous in such matters, was prepared to conduct such works, planned to give performances of any new works composed by Prix de Rome winners on their return to France and, in order to increase the profits, allowed room in one programme for a new and not specially gifted Italian *prima donna*; he even accepted payment for the inclusion of a new work by a wealthy amateur composer. But the public wanted to hear music by Berlioz and the great familiar classics, so that the Society survived only for about eighteen months. It had, however, proved the possibility of an alternative organisation to the Conservatoire Concerts if finance could be assembled to keep it alive; in this it led the way to the concert organisations of Pasdeloup, Colonne and Lamoureux.

The *Société des Jeunes Artistes*, the first concert of which was conducted by Jules Pasdeloup, the Society's founder, in 1851, was fortunate in having a conductor who could treat his musical duties as a hobby. Pasdeloup, who had collected notable prizes from the Conservatoire and was a completely equipped musician, had entered the Civil Service; in 1848 he became Governor of the Château of Saint-Cloud, a post which took him among the rich and influential while paying him generously both in money and in leisure. Like Berlioz, he had discovered the need for a new orchestral organisation to give a hearing to the works of new composers, himself included. In 1858 Berlioz described the concert situation in Paris in a letter to Henry Litolff which justified his and Pasdeloup's attitude:

> The *Société des Concerts du Conservatoire* was instituted under the best possible conditions. It has the right to an excellent concert hall; its instrumentalists are in general the most skillful musicians to be found in Paris. . . . But the Conservatoire Society has limited its aims to conserving a certain number of masterpieces by the famous dead; for the Society, the living do not exist. Its aims are splendid nevertheless; it does its duty with dignity, and the works which are heard in its concert hall, and the composers who make their way through the hall of Society of the Conservatoire concerts are treated with respect as they cross its threshold, just as French officials look at the Great Pyramid in which the Egyptians, through the ages have conserved the mummies of their Pharaohs.[11]

Pasdeloup, Berlioz continued, conducted the concerts of the *Société des Jeunes Artistes* 'with zeal and devotion', but the Society was handicapped by the limited number of rehearsals that was possible in preparation and by the fact that musicians of its orchestra had to earn their livings else-

[11] Berlioz: *Correspondance Générale*: edited by Pierre Citron. Flammarion, Paris, 1972. Vol. 1. p. 209.

where. He painted a touching picture of Pasdeloup's players crawling exhausted to a morning rehearsal after playing in a ballroom until the small hours.

The experience of conducting the concerts of the *Société des Jeunes Artistes* convinced Pasdeloup that his real vocation was not composition but conducting; he introduced Paris to the symphonies of French composers, gave the first performance of Mozart's *Die Entführung aus dem Serail* in a concert version, and brought Schumann's orchestral works into his programmes. The '*Jeunes Artistes*' of his orchestra were ex-students of the Conservatoire who had not yet found their way into regular orchestral employment and from 1861, rechristening his concerts '*Concerts Populaires*', he challenged the Conservatoire Concerts by mounting his own programmes at the same time, on Sunday afternoons. After the Franco-Prussian War of 1870, his organisation was given a government subsidy of 25,000 francs per annum, and continued in Paris until 1884. The advent of stage performances at Sunday matinées in the Paris theatres had by that time seriously weakened his grip on his audience.

Édouard Colonne, his successor, was at first a violinist in the Opéra Orchestra and then a member of the Lamoureux Quartet; he had his first experience of conducting at Pasdeloup's concerts. In 1873, with Hartmann, a publisher, he founded the *Concert National*; in the two seasons for which these concerts continued, Gounod's *Redemption* and Massenet's *Marie Magdaleine* had their first performances, and in 1874 Colonne set out to create an organisation of musicians which would appeal to the public by its performances of works by younger composers. What began as the *Concerts du Châtelet* eventually became the *Concerts Colonne*, and although they were at first overshadowed by Pasdeloup's *Concerts Populaires*, their attention to the music of Franck, Massenet and Lalo, amongst the composers of a younger generation at a time when Pasdeloup was inevitably growing out of touch with the style and tastes of the young ensured him a following which remained dangerously limited until, in the 1880s, he revived the works of Berlioz, which had been suffering almost total neglect.

Charles Lamoureux, the violinist founder of the Quartet in which Colonne played second violin, opened his career as a conductor in 1873, with performances of oratorios previously unknown, or virtually unknown, in Paris—*Messiah* in the first year as well as *Judas Maccabeus*; Bach's *St. Matthew Passion* followed in 1874 and Massenet's *Eve* in 1875. The *Société de l'Harmonie Sacrée* which he founded for these performances was based on the model of the London Sacred Harmonic Society and performances which he heard at German festivals. From 1872 he was second conductor of the Conservatoire Concerts and from 1877 to 1879 conductor at the Opéra. Disputes about details of performances in large organisations made him determined to work independently, and in 1881 he founded the

Nouveaux Concerts, which became known as the *Concerts Lamoureux.*
Like Pasdeloup, he was a fervent Wagnerian, but he advanced the repertoire
beyond that of Colonne to the music of D'Indy, Royer, Chabrier and
Debussy.

The establishment of a regular concert life in those German cities
traditionally devoted to opera was, on the whole, a slow development.
Occasional concerts, or even more frequent events arranged for the benefit
of favourite performers, and concerts arranged to enable a touring virtuoso
to make his presence felt were not a substitute for the sort of concert familiar
in Leipzig, the hall of the Paris Conservatoire or the homes of the Philharmonic and New Philharmonic Societies in London. For one thing, the
orchestras of the old German capital cities were heavily engaged in the
opera houses, and the underpaid musicians had little, if any, time, after the
teaching which made their livelihood possible, to undertake new musical
activities. Nevertheless, to the musicians of the German and Austrian opera
houses in the first half of the nineteenth century it was obvious that the most
exciting and valuable new music—which in most places continued to be the
works of Beethoven—belonged to the concert hall. Enthusiasts like the
leaders of the Munich Court Orchestra, who added regular concert performances to their duties in 1810, and, like Spohr in Cassel, won audiences
for their concerts. Wagner's career in Germany before his exile in 1849 is
full of determined though fruitless efforts to enrich the music of the cities in
which he served with regular series of concerts in a way which would benefit any underpaid orchestral musicians of the theatre orchestras which he
conducted; but he was met either by lack of interest from players on whom
he depended or by the obscurantism of political or municipal authorities.
As conductor of the Opera in Riga in 1838, when he was twenty-five, he
addressed a letter to the members of the orchestra proposing that they undertook regular annual concert series.

With the apparently unenthusiastic support of the theatre manager, Karl
von Holtei, who was ready to release the orchestra on Tuesday evenings,
when the stage was normally given over to spoken drama, Wagner proposed
six subscription concerts in a first season. The subscription would be four
silver roubles and admission an extra rouble. He himself would conduct the
concerts but would take no remuneration; the entire profit would be divided
among the players; leaders, who might appear as soloists, would receive a
larger share than the rank and file. The Riga players, twenty-four men, were
warned that an inaugural season might not be specially rewarding, but later
seasons would probably work to the financial as well as the musical advantage of the players.

> The project should be in itself an advantage to an artist through its very
> concept of a perfectly organised body, as we may now call our orchestra,
> which may display its ability for independent development. For what

true musician would not be distressed to see such a fine ensemble used for nothing but routine and never of its own accord venture on what gives deep enjoyment and inspiration?[12]

Wagner's signature is followed by twenty-four others, apparently those of the entire orchestra, prepared unanimously to follow their conductor's lead. The plan, however, came to nothing, perhaps because of the lack of enthusiasm of Holtei, who dismissed Wagner six months later.

In a much stronger position as *Kapellmeister* in Dresden Wagner set out to add an active concert life to the traditional operatic life of the city. Maria Schmole, daughter of Ferdinand Heine, costume director of the Dresden Court Theatre during Wagner's *Kapellmeistership*, wrote in 1895 of Wagner's occasional concerts with the Opera orchestra as though they were events quite fresh in her memory and not recollections called up after half a century:

> By the consummate performance of musical works which he put on the programme of the so-called Palm Sunday Concerts, he probably laid the foundations of the subscription concerts of the Dresden Court Theatre Orchestra which in our time are enjoying a fame and attendance not surpassed by any town in Germany.[13]

Wagner's attempts to create a concert organisation in Dresden were frustrated by the power of opera in a city where it absorbed all the attention of a royal patron and of an audience familiar not only with the ever-growing Italian repertory but also with the German repertory which the Kings of Saxony had cultivated since the end of the Napoleonic Wars. The great virtuosi visited Dresden and played to the court and the public. Amateur orchestras of varying quality existed for their own pleasure rather than for the benefit of the public, but any orchestra attempting to pay its way without a regular scheme of subscriptions was hampered by the fact that in Dresden no concert hall existed capable of accommodating an audience large enough to make concerts financially viable. The theatre, rarely available for concerts, was the only auditorium large enough to support an orchestra except at excessively high prices.

In addition, the Court Orchestra was unwilling to encourage any rival ensemble; its single annual concert, played on Palm Sunday each year for the benefit of the widows and orphans of past players, was, to the orchestra's mind, sacrosanct. The musicians believed that any multiplication of public concerts would steal the audience of the all-important pension concert. Audiences, too, preferred the familiar music of Italian opera to the still unexplored music of the symphonic tradition.

[12] Wagner: *Letters—The Burrell Collection*, edited by John N. Burke. Gollancz, London, 1951. The letter to the Riga Orchestra is given on pp. 341–3.
[13] *Ibid.* p. 128.

Wagner reached Dresden in 1842, but before his abortive plans for regular concerts with the Court Orchestra had been worked out, Ferdinand Hiller, a thirty-three-year-old composer whose achievements at that time outshone Wagner's, came to Dresden in 1844 intending to make a position for himself in the city's music-making. He had won a great reputation as a pianist in Paris and as a conductor in Leipzig and Frankfurt. He arrived in Dresden after his lifelong friendship with Mendelssohn had broken down and brought his work in Leipzig to an end. With no official standing in Dresden despite his popularity, he began to establish himself by collecting as good an orchestra as he could from unattached musicians there. Although there was no suitable hall, he found an appetite for orchestral concerts which, despite high prices, were profitable enough to continue until Hiller had made his rough and ready ensemble into a satisfactory orchestra. In 1847 Hiller's organisation failed, partly because of the limitations of his audience and partly because of the hostility of the Court Orchestra and its *Kapellmeister*. Wagner had little faith in Hiller's interpretative powers and he was determined to bring concert music into the Court Orchestra's normal sphere of activities.

On Palm Sunday, 1846, Wagner conducted Beethoven's Ninth Symphony for the Pension Fund Concert after enormously painstaking rehearsal (the double-basses alone had twelve individual rehearsals). The work, which the Dresden authorities had expected to empty the theatre, was so successful that it took more money than had ever been gained from a Palm Sunday Concert in the past and its performance became almost a tradition for the Pension Fund Concert. Wagner's attitude had not changed since he had tried to find room for symphony concerts in the Riga orchestra's schedule: the symphonies of Beethoven, he believed, were a necessity for orchestras and for their audiences; to neglect them was to neglect the possibility of mastering modern orchestral style; to play them correctly it was necessary to understand them and to convey that understanding to every member of the orchestra; to understand them was to be musically enlightened and spiritually enriched. There were other works from the past of almost equal value. Modern opera, on the other hand, was usually meretricious, showy and still awaiting its Wagnerian redemption.

The hundred-page report, *Die Königliche Kapelle betreffend*, which Wagner sent to the authorities at the beginning of March 1846, is like all his musical thinking—exhaustive, precisely worked out and entirely practical. It lists the deficiencies of the orchestra and the additional instruments needed if it were to do justice to 'modern' works; it points out the shamefully low salaries of the players and the excessive overwork to which, partly as the result of bad planning, they were subjected, and provides a reasonable cure for this. He describes the inadequacy of the orchestra pit in the Opera House —neither the tone nor the ensemble could be satisfactory while the orchestra's depth was only a quarter of its length; and the music desks were an old-fashioned nuisance.

But these immediate practicalities are followed by Wagner's insistence that the orchestra, for the sake of its style and the cultural life of the city, should give regular concerts. At least six concerts should be given in the winter months so that the masterpieces of instrumental music which are the glory of the German school could be played to the Dresden public. Wagner believed that regular concerts would not decrease the takings of the Palm Sunday Concerts but that greater familiarity with the symphonic repertoire would make the Pension Fund Concert, which could be given a specially ambitious programme, more popular than it already was. The overworked orchestral players, after a rationalisation and reorganisation of their duties in the Opera House and the Royal Chapel, would support the proposed venture, which would cost the court authorities nothing, if the profits of the concerts were divided among them. As Wagner admitted, the King could not increase the orchestra salaries, the concerts would bring the players a much-needed increase in pay.[14]

Wagner's plea for reform was rejected, but at the beginning of 1848 he was able to conduct three concerts with the Opera Orchestra. Unlike Hiller, Wagner depended on the music of the past; choral works by Palestrina and Bach belonged, in 1848, to the special sphere of the 'Historical Concert', and the only modern composer represented in Wagner's 1848 programmes was Mendelssohn, who had died two months before the first of Wagner's programmes. After 1848, orchestral concerts in Dresden again depended on the initiative of two freelance musicians, Kunze and Hartung, who inherited the organisation which Hiller had abandoned, with the result that they were able to play the symphonies of Beethoven and other difficult 'modern' works without being forced into a financially ruinous multiplication of rehearsals. Their auditoria were public gardens and on Saturday afternoons the Brulschen Terrace; such auditoria were to their obvious financial advantage; they could count on a much larger subscription audience and fewer expenses. The profitability of symphony concerts was amply proven before the Court Orchestra undertook to provide them regularly.

It was natural that Wagner, exiled to Zürich after 1849 and with no other way of earning his living, should involve himself in the music of the Zürich opera and of the *Allgemeine Musik Gesellschaft* there. It was equally natural that he should attempt to put the affairs of both organisations on a more satisfactory musical footing while providing for improved pay and conditions for the players. Though he refused the vacant conductorship of the Zürich Opera in 1851, he secured the appointment of Karl Ritter, a devoted disciple who turned out to be hopelessly incompetent. Wagner, whose

[14] Ernest Newman: *The Life of Richard Wagner*. Vol. 1. Cassell, London, 1937. See pp. 464–9 for a summary of the entire memorandum.

sense of musical responsibility was as highly developed as his sense of responsibility to people was lacking, found himself morally bound to take over Ritter's duties until he was relieved by the arrival of Hans von Bülow, a born conductor still in his twenties. Wagner worked behind Bülow until the young man resigned and Wagner decided that he had discharged his responsibilities to the management.

From 1850 onwards he appeared at concerts of the *Allgemeine Musik Gesellschaft*; his first appearance was to conduct Beethoven's Seventh Symphony in a vastly distended programme of vocal and instrumental trivia. The orchestra consisted of thirty free-lance musicians, teachers, *Stadtpfeifer* and outsiders, with a handful of local amateur players. Wagner, accepted as a great figure in the musical world, with *Tannhäuser* going the rounds of the German opera houses, was in great demand as a conductor in Zürich, conducting the more ambitious works in the *Gesellschaft*'s programmes. His audience noted the difference between the results he obtained from the orchestra and those obtained by others, and he was induced to conduct three concerts of his own music there in May 1853, but despite a great success, Wagner had decided that music in Zürich needed a total reorganisation. The city was too small, he realised—it had some 33,000 inhabitants in 1850—to support separate orchestras for the opera and for the *Musik Gesellschaft*, so in 1855, as the most distinguished musician in the city, he drew up a plan as thorough, practical and generally advantageous as that for Dresden to rationalise Zürich's musical resources. The two orchestras should be united and the resulting ensemble used both for opera and concerts. This would provide players enough for the larger modern operas and an orchestra capable of doing justice to the concert works of Beethoven and his successors; he remembered that he had been compelled to collect players from far and wide for his concerts in 1853. These plans cut across vested interests in both organisations; their ambition was noted, but not their practicability, and they were never implemented. It was Winterthur, a smaller town than Zürich, which became the centre of Swiss concert life in the later 1850s, simply because there was no conflict there between the interests of an opera and those of a concert society; thus a group of mainly young enthusiasts were able to build a concert society which, after 1863, followed an entirely un-Wagnerian line, following the tradition of Mendelssohn, Schumann and Brahms.

German cities where opera did not traditionally dominate musical life developed concert organisations with greater ease than Dresden or Berlin. The wealth of Lübeck had enabled the city to equip itself with eight town musicians to undertake the traditional *Stadtpfeifer* duties. A secondary guild of twenty-one musicians, the *Rollbrüder* and *Kostendbrüder* existed to take part in church music and municipal ceremonial. In addition to these, there were the regimental musicians of Lübeck's own militia. The City

Fathers, realising that the musicians could not earn their livings simply by fulfilling their traditional duties, encouraged them to join with the theatre musicians to set up a *Liebhaber Konzert* Society, thus creating something which both in its organisation and its composition was more or less equivalent to a concert orchestra; it provided ten concerts each winter at a subscription of 20 marks a season. The exigencies of war in 1808 and 1809, and between 1811 and 1815, temporarily put an end to their activities, but the orchestra survived, and the Lübeck Senators themselves paid the fees of musicians qualified as *Stadtpfeifer*; there were ten in 1825, fifteen in 1829.[15]

Although the Senate insisted that the status of the *Stadtpfeifer* should be preserved, Lübeck had really created what to all intents and purposes was a City Orchestra which, because of the great simplification of church music and the meaninglessness of traditional *Stadtpfeifer* duties in the nineteenth century, functioned almost entirely as a concert orchestra before its civic organisation was officially brought into line with the facts of its existence in 1873.

Public concerts in Augsburg, comparable to those of Lübeck, followed a similar pattern. With twenty-seven musicians to carry out the duties of the *Stadtpfeiferei*, it was natural that the town musicians should involve themselves in any profitable or potentially profitable concert scheme, but it was not until the Free Cities lost their independence and Augsburg was incorporated into Bavaria in 1810 that the Augsburg musicians formed themselves into an orchestra with the principal purpose of giving subscription concerts under the aegis of the city Senate.[16]

The historically 'great' orchestras developed later to vindicate Wagner's conviction that any orchestra, for the sake of its quality and musical standards, should be involved in both opera and concert music. Vienna remained without regular, professional concerts until the success of the annual Pension Fund Concert—the 'Nicolai Concert' inaugurated by Otto Nicolai, conductor of the Court Opera from 1842 to 1847—led in 1860 to the organisation by the orchestra itself of the Vienna Philharmonic Orchestra, through which the members of the Opera Orchestra became a concert-giving organisation, self-governing and appointing its own conductor, at times when it was not engaged in the theatre. The consequent expansion of the orchestra's numbers was beneficial to both aspects of its work. The Philharmonic Orchestra remains the central and most respected Viennese orchestra, but its double life inevitably restricts its scope and led to the formation of ensembles free from operatic duties—the *Konzertverein*

---

[15] Eberhard Preussner: *Die Bürgerliche Musikkultur*, Bärenreiter, Cassell, 1950. p. 152.

[16] Ludwig Wegele: *Musik in der Reichstadt Augsburg*. Die Brigge, Augsburg, 1965. pp. 163-4.

Orchestra in 1900 and the *Tonkünstler* Orchestra in 1907. The two amalgamated in 1922 to form the Vienna Symphony Orchestra.

In Munich, too, the Musical Academy concerts, twelve a year, given by the Court Orchestra since 1810, proved insufficient to satisfy the public appetite for orchestral music, and lesser organisations added to the official concert season. In 1893 the piano-maker Franz Kaim formed an orchestra of seventy-five musicians who gave twelve concerts a year and evolved first into the Munich *Konzertverein* and eventually into the Munich Philharmonic Orchestra.

Berlin, too, owed its regular professional concerts in the nineteenth century to the initiative of its court musicians. Anton Bachmann, one of the players in the Prussian Court Orchestra, founded the first orchestra—a semi-professional organisation, to give public concerts in Berlin in the late eighteenth century, and amateur orchestras multiplied throughout the following century while the Court Opera Orchestra, as the *Königliche Hoforchester*, gave fairly regular symphony concerts. The Berlin Philharmonic Orchestra, free from operatic entanglements, was founded in 1882 and the Berlin Symphony Orchestra, the deliberately modernising force in a city where music had become conservative, in 1908.

The social composition of audiences had not bothered German concert-giving organisations. Just as music had traditionally been the solvent of social differences in Vienna, where Beethoven behaved with a sense of superiority to the nobles with whom he associated and who met musicians on terms of relative equality, so it was taken for granted in Germany and Austria that the artisan class would be no less comfortable at concerts than was the bourgeoisie; the availability of orchestral concerts at prices within the reach of the relatively poor prevented the development of a class to whom music was unfamiliar and intimidating. When Sterndale Bennett, the most notable English composer of the early and mid-nineteenth century, first played in Leipzig, 'he was prepared,' wrote his son, 'to find music more widely cultivated than in England', and he noted the greater respect paid by intellectual Germans to music. The affectionate filial biography continues:

> He also observed that in Germany a love for [music's] more advanced forms was to be found in all classes. On the evening when he made his début at Leipzig he espied the man who blacked the boots at his lodgings sitting in the gallery of the Gewandhaus.[17]

The boots later explained that attendance at the Gewandhaus Concert was a pleasure for which he saved his spare money and to which he eagerly looked forward.

Concert life in the nineteenth century, however, depended increasingly

[17] J. R. Sterndale Bennett: *The Life of William Sterndale Bennett*. Cambridge University Press, 1907. p. 101.

on the exploitation of a repertoire often restricted by limitations of taste either in the audience or on the part of the conductor. Neville Cardus remembered how the petition of younger members of the Hallé audience to Hans Richter, that the orchestra should pay some attention to the works of Debussy and 'modern French composers', was dismissed by the great conductor's sweeping assertion, 'There is no modern French music.'[18] Usually, however, the limitations were those of the audience; a very brief research into the concert statistics of almost any major orchestra, as well as the accounts of musical controversies, demonstrates the general resistance against new music which delays the acceptance of many composers into the repertoire.

For this reason, the development of orchestral concerts throughout Europe was of comparatively little direct help to the composer, who had to be popular before his music was played but who was denied the opportunity of popularity until his music was heard. Any symphony after the death of Beethoven was necessarily a major undertaking simply in the amount of time it exhausted; to produce the full score of a work lasting for more than forty-five minutes is a singularly time-absorbing task, and the composer who undertook it in the nineteenth century was compelled to do so, as often as not, with no certainty of earning any money from his labour; probably he had neglected more immediately profitable work in order to bring to birth a probable white elephant. The mere economics of the task, even more than the mystique of the symphony as in some sense the greatest, most profound and demanding of forms, probably inhibited the would-be symphonist. John Shedlock, the pianist and music critic who died in 1919, wrote of Brahms a month after the composer's death in 1897:

> There was, however, a higher step to take, and that was to write a symphony. Mozart, Schubert, and Mendelssohn, while yet boys, rapidly wrote off symphony after symphony, but when they grew to manhood they took longer over such works, and were far less prolific. Beethoven was more than thirty years old when he published his first Symphony in C, and before the C minor of Brahms appeared the latter had passed his mature age of forty.[19]

One of the usual facts about the creative mind in youth is its almost inordinate ambition: Wagner's first acknowledged work, when he was in his early teens, was a poetic tragedy with a huge *dramatis personae*, many of them dead and resurrected in the last act. Britten, we are told, wrote a huge oratorio, *The End of the World*, as a small boy at his prep school. What Brahms wrote as a child it is not ours to know. To speak of a form as the

[18] Neville Cardus: *Second Innings*. Collins, London, 1950. p. 127.
[19] J. S. Shedlock: *Brahms. Monthly Musical Record*, May, 1897. Quoted in Norman Demuth: *An Anthology of Musical Criticism*, Eyre and Spottiswoode, London, 1947. pp. 282–3.

most serious, intense and profound is to offer a challenge immediately accepted by the young. The symphony had no special quality when Beethoven worked for more than fifteen years before he composed one he was prepared to acknowledge; but he was a professional musician living upon his earnings; until he had a practical reason to compose a symphony, he did not bother to do so but composed what the world needed from him.

Brahms was well enough aware of the symphony as a challenge; his first attempts at Beethovenian intensity. But when he declared that 'a symphony is not a joke', he may not have been thinking of the spiritual and emotional depths of the task; it may have been the economic and practical aspects of the task, its long, time-consuming demands, that disturbed him: it can never be a joke to withdraw for a considerable length of time from the activities which enable a man to earn his living even if the result is as friendly, charming and companionable as the Second Symphony which Brahms composed within a year of the passionately intense First. This does not suggest that Brahms was inhibited from writing a symphony until he felt himself emotionally and spiritually capable of answering the Beethovenian challenge. The First Piano Concerto which he wrote in his twenties was a practical work; he earned a great deal from his appearances as a concert pianist, and it measures itself against a properly Beethovenian seriousness; he wrote a symphony as soon as his career was sufficiently advanced to allow him time to do so and to regard the work as a probable source of income. One of the difficulties of the nineteenth century was that it neglected to attend to, and still tends to prevent us from considering, the practicalities of musical life. Writers still prefer to give their attention to the imponderables of inspiration about which they cannot know, although mundane practicalities provide us with valid reasons for many of a composer's activities.

The composer had, one way or another, to secure a career in order to win a hearing for the work on which his career was to rest. The nineteenth century distrusted music composed on commission on the grounds that inspiration cannot be booked in advance. There was, too, so far as concert organisations were concerned, the danger of providing time in a programme for music which might antagonise patrons; the prospect of commissioning new music was even more dangerous than that simply of rehearsing and performing it. Thus, it may have been a sentimental wish of concert promoters to encourage young composers, but it was no essential part of their duty to do so. The purpose of an orchestral concert, even outside Britain and the United States, where concert finance was an insoluble problem and depended entirely upon what could be taken at the box office, was to play the music which most pleased the audience.

8

National Music

Until the nineteenth century, music was generally regarded as an international language. Its technical vocabulary was Italian, and from the time of the early baroque European music in general had evolved its styles and technical devices from the developments initiated by Italian composers. Court opera was opera in Italian both in Weber's Dresden and in Victorian London, no matter who composed it and where it was staged. In 1855 Queen Victoria suggested to Wagner that *Tannhäuser* should be translated into Italian so that it could secure a production in London.

French music had in one sense always been French; it had served the social and political purposes both of the Bourbon monarchy and of the revolutionary governments, and its styles had been determined by its subjugation to the French language and French prosody, so that its melodic idioms could barely survive the translation of libretti and lyrics into any other language. These facts did not prevent French music exerting a powerful attraction on German composers, among others, in the early years of the eighteenth century. English music, too, had its national idiosyncrasies. In England as in France Italian-type recitative sounded unnatural and either incongruous or simply ridiculous when applied to English words for any dramatic purpose. In England the tradition of consort music for a long time withstood the development among English composers of the Italianate sonata. Jenkins, in England, had published 'sonatas' before Purcell published his trio sonatas in 1683 with the declaration that by doing so he 'endeavour'd a just imitation of the most fam'd Italian masters'. Both Jenkins and Purcell were unable or unwilling to eradicate specifically English traits from their Italianate works; early English sonatas often move like fantasies, in free polyphony, use biting false relations in their harmony, as English composers for a couple of centuries had done, admitted modal flavouring to their harmony and interchanged expected iambs with trochees, or trochees with iambs, as, for example, the Agincourt Song had done in the early fifteenth century and as Purcell did innumerable times in his vocal music. But music, in spite of such local eccentricities, aspired, as Purcell's words show, to the state of an international language which might be legitimately spoken with a variety of local accents by members of different races. In the late eighteenth century the international idea had conquered; music was a European application of Italian techniques and styles.

The international idea began to collapse in the early nineteenth century. Embattled nations, or nations subjugated by a foreign invader, began to think of music as an expression of their own national personality, a way of voicing their own national aspirations. In the *Adieux* Sonata (*op.* 81a), Beethoven's *au revoir* to the Archduke Rudolf when in 1809 that most exalted of his pupils left Vienna to escape from the advancing French, Beethoven set out the first movement with the instruction *Adagio*, leading to *Allegro*; the second movement is *Andante*, with additional German instructions, *In gehender Bewegung, doch mit Ausdruck*; the third movement is *Vivacissamente, in lebhaftigen Zeitmasse*. The next sonata, *op.* 90, written in 1814, retains such Italian terms as *ritard., in tempo, crescendo, sempre diminuendo* and so on; its main instructions are in German: *Mit lebhaftigkeit und durchaus mit Empfindung und Ausdruck; Nicht zu geschwind und sehr singbar vorzutragen*. The 1816 and 1819 sonatas are the two for *Hammerklavier*, the generally accepted Germanism for pianoforte.

Beethoven's Italian was not always as fluent as it might have been, and as his primary instructions to a pianist become more detailed and complex, it might have seemed natural to him to set them out in his own language, although he had previously been happy enough with such conventional Italianisms as *con espressione* and *cantabile*; his German directions usually have an acceptable Italian equivalent which Beethoven had been happy enough to use in the past. The Napoleonic invasions which turned Beethoven from a simple revolutionary into a patriotic Austrian revolutionary seem to have made him feel that his own language was a perfectly satisfactory way of telling pianists how he wanted his music played.

The urge towards nationalism in German and Austrian music before 1815 appears in other *dicta* than Beethoven's. Weber, writing with little if any evidence beyond Bach's keyboard works, twenty years or so before the so-called 'Bach Revival', wrote:

> Sebastian Bach's characteristic attitude, in spite of its rigidity, was clearly romantic and fundamentally German.[1]

In the context of 1811, the date of Weber's remark, the later composer can hardly have been thinking of the melodic and rhythmic idioms suggested to an eighteenth-century German master by the language of the text which occupied him. 'Clearly romantic' and 'fundamentally German' are given as characteristics of the music itself, part of its special personality.

It was, perhaps, natural that, because Central European nationalism was prevented from finding any expression in political life, it expressed itself vehemently through the arts. For some years a considerable part of Germany had been given unity by Napoleon; there was, beyond and including that, a huge and potentially powerful area in the heart of Europe which used a

---

[1] Weber: *Ausgewählte Schriften.*

common language and shared most of the same aspirations; the complex
which was to become the German Empire presented a more or less homogeneous state, united by language and culture but forced by political
organisation into political disunity against the will of its people; even the
idea of an Austro-German Empire uniting all German speakers seemed
anything but unreasonable until the power and ambition of Bismarckian
Prussia put such a union beyond the bounds of practicality.

The idea of German unity, however, had awakened before Napoleon's revolutionary rationalisation of the map of Central Europe. It preceded
Beethoven's use of a German musical vocabulary and Weber's statement
about the essentially German nature of Bach's music. The writers and
thinkers of the Enlightenment in Germany, notably Johann Gottfried
Herder (1784–1803) and Johann Gottlieb Fichte (1726–1814), had taught
that nationalism manifested a unity of culture rather than any political
situation. If, declared Herder, the German-speaking word achieved a
unity of education and culture, these would inevitably generate political
unity. It was the personality of the German *Volk* and their consciousness of
a common culture which would create the less essential unity of political
organisation. Then Fichte, treading in the footprints of Immanuel Kant,
believed that a nation was not simply the aggregation of people living in a
defined geographical area but a spiritual unity achieved by the creation of
a shared culture and shared aspirations forged by the various pressures—
religious, social, economic and political—to which they were subjected.

The collision of this cultural and idealistic nationalism with war and the
political ambitions of Napoleon's France forced the German people if not to
find political expression for their spiritual unity at least to justify the political
endeavours of their rulers. As ex-members of Napoleon's empire, the German states came each to renounce not the political absolutism which was
their political tradition but the supra-national ideas—of the Holy Roman
Empire and even of the recent Napoleonic Confederation of the Rhine—
which had lingered on as a sentiment even though eighteenth-century
absolutism had largely destroyed their reality. Although during the years of
French dominance the old German patchwork was largely reorganised and
rationalised, and although many parallels to Napoleonic social and
economic law were applied to the German states, an entirely unpolitical
concept of nationalism made Germany return willingly to the pre-
revolutionary *status quo*.

The refusal of the Congress of Vienna to allow Austria any foothold in
Western Europe destroyed the last vestiges of the Austrian Emperor's
traditional authority as Holy Roman Emperor and left the tangle of German states without a centre, creating a gap which remained until 1870 and
the creation of the German Empire under Prussian leadership. The German cultural unity, existing despite differences of religion between the

various German states, the unity of a national language, national folklore and national traditions, all of which Herder and Fichte exalted as the reality of unity, became realities looking for political expression.

From their foundations, the German choral societies found it natural to sing folk songs and songs in folk styles. *Des Knaben Wunderhorn*, the anthology of German folk poetry which provided texts for Mendelssohn, Schumann, Brahms, Mahler and Schoenberg, as well as numerous lesser composers, was collected by Ludwig Achim von Arnim and Clemens Maria Brentano and published between 1805 and 1808. Earlier collections of folk music, like that published by Herder in 1778 and 1779, had brought together popular songs from various nations; *Des Knaben Wunderhorn* is totally and exclusively German. Such anthologies, like Beethoven's choice of a German rather than an Italian musical vocabulary, indicate the national feeling that was eventually to force itself into political expression and find itself continually frustrated in the age of the reaction. To Hegel (1770–1831), the state, its policies and the order it enforces, were the only real embodiment of the national culture which to Herder and Fichte had been realities transcending any political expression. Hegel laid it down as the duty of the state to ensure the independence of art, philosophy and religion, but it must be the state itself, and not its incidental culture, which embodies the national personality. Thus, in the writings of the most decisive German philosopher of the early nineteenth century, political nationalism became a matter of urgency.

The outcome of this sense of national unity thwarted by a threadbare, repressive political system underlay the longing for national unity which persisted until the creation of the German Empire. The patchwork of German states, lacking a capital or any cultural, political or educational centre, seemed to express its individuality most effectively through music rather than through literature and the nebulous political structures which tacitly denied the unity its people felt; it created a potentially dangerous sense of national inferiority.

The much-travelled young Mendelssohn, on his first visit to Britain, found himself staying in Llangollen and so persecuted by Welsh harpists that he wrote a letter home violently rejecting the whole notion of 'national' music, a term by which he seemed to mean little beyond Welsh harps and folk songs, Scottish bagpipes, alphorns and Swiss yodelling. Conscious nationalism in music, he wrote to Zelter from Paris in 1832, was simply the intrusion of politics, which bored him, into art. The Germans talked interminably of politics because the disunity of Germany made them feel inferior to other nations, but it was their ceaseless grumbling which caused the sense of disunity of which they were so conscious.[2]

[2] Mendelssohn: *Letters*. Edited by G. Selden-Goth. Elek, London, 1947.

In this, Mendelssohn was for once out of tune with his times. Wagner, Mendelssohn's junior by four years, grew up with a childish prejudice against Mozart's music because most of Mozart's opera libretti are Italian: Weber's music he loved because it, and the libretti of Weber's operas, are German in language, style and atmosphere. It was a performance of Mozart's *Requiem* in Leipzig in 1828 which opened his eyes to Mozart's greatness. In 1834 Bellini's *I Montecchi ed i Capuletti*, in Leipzig, left him with ideas which he explained fully in the *Autobiographical Sketch* nine years later:

> Though I could see no great merit in Bellini, yet the stuff out of which his music was made seemed to me to be better suited to spreading the warm glow of life than the calculated pedantry with which we Germans, as a rule, achieved only a laboured make-belief.[3]

By this time, Wagner was convinced that he had been born to save German opera and had reached the conclusion that the way to do so might be learned from the Italians. In the June 1834 issue of a Leipzig magazine, the *Zeitung für die Elegante Welt*, Wagner turned to the plight of German opera, thinking in entirely nationalistic terms:

> We are too intellectual, too learned, to create warm, human figures. Mozart could do so, but he animated his characters with the beauty of Italian song. Since we have come to despise this, we have wandered further and further from the path that Mozart beat out for the salvation of our dramatic music. Weber never knew how to handle song, nor does Spohr understand it much better. But song is the organ through which a human being can communicate himself musically; and so long as this is not fully developed, he lacks genuine speech. This is where the Italians have an enormous advantage over us; with them, beauty of song is second nature.[4]

The fault of German opera composers, Wagner declared, was that none of them 'has known how to win for himself the voice of the people'.

The essence of Wagner's thought is national. German, French and Italian music each have their individual characters, and the character of German music had lost, not the learning for which it had always been celebrated, but the reality of its connection with German popular melody. But while it is fairly easy for a modern listener to isolate French, Italian or English music by their national characteristics, so much of the *lingua franca* of music in practice is German that its national character often escapes us. The use of an English, French, Spanish or Italian folk tune immediately advertises the tune's place of origin, we miss the profound nationalism advertised by Papa-

[3] Quoted in Ernest Newman: *The Life of Richard Wagner*. Cassell, London, 1931. Vol. 1. p. 110.
[4] *Ibid*. p. 111.

geno's arias in *Die Zauberflöte* or the closeness to folk song of very many of Schubert's *Lieder*; *Die Zauberflöte* and even *Fidelio* seem to owe their nationality to their libretti rather than to their music, and Germanism becomes a matter of various imponderables like attitude and atmosphere, not of any specifically German tradition.

The nationalistic aspect of Wagner's *Rienzi*, like its political aspect, therefore tend to escape us. It is, however, the musical statement of Wagner's political attitude. Rienzi, 'the last of the tribunes', rises from the people to defend them against the tyranny of a corrupt aristocracy. The libretto was written before Wagner abandoned his post in Riga and was at least partly translated into French ready for exploitation in Paris when Wagner slipped away from his creditors there. Neither Wagner's praise of the popular liberator–leader nor various lines altered by the Saxon censor for the work's first performance in Dresden would have ruffled a single feather in Paris, but before the Dresden production the censors found it necessary to insist on a variety of alterations. 'Not only Rome shall be free,' cries Rienzi in the original version of the libretto, published in Wagner's *Collected Writings*: 'All Italy shall be free. Hail to united Italy!' The censor was not enamoured of either the idea of freedom or that of unification, which could easily be applied to Germany; to prevent audiences from making that dangerous identification, not concern for Italy (which the censor, like Metternich, may have regarded as no more than 'a geographical expression'), Rienzi's declaration was changed. 'Not only Rome is great!' he cried in the Dresden production. 'All Italy shall be great. Hail to the ancient greatness of Italy!'

Wagner's openly nationalistic occasional works, the *Huldigungs Marsch* for his patron Ludwig II of Bavaria and the *Kaisermarsch*, celebrating the Prussian victory over France in 1870 and the long-delayed unification of Germany, are not impressive works; they celebrate the political nationalism which has nothing much to do with the composer of *The Ring*, in which the mythology of the German people becomes a means of universalising a nationalism far deeper than its overtly political expression. *The Mastersingers*, in which the *Volk* themselves, richly and lovingly depicted, makes the people the guardians of artistic tradition and artistic progress. Wagner at his greatest became a mouthpiece of the doctrines expounded long before by Herder and Fichte. Political considerations, which Wagner confused with the progress of his own cause, and mixed up with memories that made him loathe France and celebrate Prussia's victory in 1870 with mean-spirited glee, always show Wagner at his least likable.

If the German national style is not, like other national styles, immediately identifiable through its musical expression, it nevertheless had popular manifestations which now seem strange to us. In 1863 the *Gesellschaft der Musikfreunde* in Vienna awarded a first prize to Joachim Raff's

First Symphony, *An das Vaterland*. The composer provided the work with
a fairly detailed programme:

> First movement: *Allegro*. Image of the German character; ability to
> soar to great heights; tendency towards introspection; mildness and
> courage as contrasts that touch and interpenetrate in many ways; over-
> whelming desire to be pensive.
> Second movement: *Allegro molto vivace*. The outdoors; through Ger-
> man forests with horns calling; through glades resounding with folk
> music.
> Third movement: *Larghetto*. Return to the domestic hearth, tranfigured
> by love and the muses.
> Fourth movement: *Allegro drammatico*. Frustrated desires to work for
> the unity of the Fatherland.
> Fifth movement: *Larghetto—Allegro trionfale*. Plaint; renewed soaring.

It is the naivety of this programme which makes the work sound at least
faintly ridiculous, and there is no reason why Raff's symphony *An das Vaterland* should be any less musically valuable than a symphonic poem by
Richard Strauss. Though it has meant nothing to the world for a century or
so, its importance to our argument is that a composer born in Zürich but
educated in Germany and spending his career in the latter country should
choose a nationalistic subject for one of his first major works and should win
a prize for doing so. In Raff's mind, it seems, 'The Fatherland' was
a theme as important and stimulating as the struggle with fate, life and
death, love or any of the other favourite subjects of nineteenth-century composition.

Nationalism in German music was never a conscious effort to find
a national voice, for the national voice already existed. German music
simply set out to express a national reality which its creators believed to
exist in all aspects of their lives except the political. Brahms, born in Hamburg, where memories of the city's old independence as a member of the
Hanseatic League seemed to have more influence than the struggle for
unification and leadership in a united Germany, preferred to live in Vienna
in spite of Vienna's complete dissimilarity from the earnestness and
emotional sobriety of northern Germany. But the Austro-Prussian War of
1866 left him equally annoyed with both of the combatants because the
question of whether Prussia or Austria should lead the inevitable united
Germany seemed to him to be meaningless. Yet Prussia's victory in the
Franco-Prussian War of 1870 stirred him to his foundations; he told Georg
Henschel, the singer-conductor who was later to settle in England, that his
first impulse on the outbreak of war had been to join the army. Count Bis-
marck, the architect of the German Empire, became his hero, and he greeted
the victory over France with his *Triumphlied*, a choral and orchestral work
with biblical words which identified the cause of German nationalism with
Old Testament Hebrew patriotism.

The German conviction that the music produced by German composers has a certain national quality on which each individual composer of worth stamped his own individuality created new problems in the minds of some German musicians. The belief that German music is of its nature more intellectual than other music was old enough—Burney drew attention to it in the 1780s—before anyone began to think systematically about music as the natural expression of national character. By the 1830s, it seemed natural to ask if the musicians of other nations could ever truly understand German music. Wagner, during his first stay in Paris, was properly impressed by the performances of Beethoven's symphonies which he heard from Habeneck and the Conservatoire Concerts Society Orchestra, but there were questions to be asked, he felt, on a deeper level than that of the accuracy and injustice to the text of these performances; surprised by the quality of these French communications of Beethoven's essentially German spirit, he wrote:

> They love to admire and applaud things beautiful and unknown from abroad. As witness the reception that has been so quickly accorded to German instrumental music. Though, apart from this, whether one could say that the French completely *understand* German music is another question, the answer to which must be doubtful. Certainly it would be wrong to maintain that the enthusiasm evoked by the Conservatoire orchestra's performance of a Beethoven Symphony is affected. Yet when one listens to this or that enthusiast airing the various opinions, ideas and conceits which such a symphony has suggested to him, one realises at once that the German genius is very far from being completely grasped.[5]

It would, probably, have been anything but difficult to hear equally startling examples of incomprehension from German listeners to a German concert. Wagner himself wrote uncomprehendingly of Haydn's symphonies, and Schumann, like many of his contemporaries and successors, did not see a great deal in Mozart's instrumental music beyond its elegance and shapeliness, while Spohr, and many of his generation, could not come to terms with the later music of Beethoven.

Because German music was apparently more intellectual than the music of other nations, it was not difficult for German musicians to feel that they had grasped the totality of French or Italian music, for the difficulty faced by French audiences and musicians when confronted by Beethoven's symphonies was not simply the foreignness of different musical languages but the German habit of thinking in music more deeply than musicians outside Germany found it necessary to think. This is a point which has some validity, but it became a point to exaggerate at the time when music was the central unifying force of a politically disunited people. Music was the out-

[5] Robert L. Jacobs and Geoffrey Skelton: *Wagner writes from Paris.* George Allen and Unwin, London, 1973. p. 36.

ward and audible sign of the essential cultural unity of the German people; it was never in any sense a weapon in the political struggle for German unification.

In Italy the long story of the *Risorgimento* is given a musical commentary by the operas of Verdi. To what extent Rossini intended his Moses, leading his people from bondage to the Promised Land, or his William Tell, heroically confronting a foreign tyrant, to express the political realities of Italian life in the early nineteenth century, nobody can say. It was Honoré de Balzac who claimed that during Moses's prayer in the last act of the opera he was watching the liberation of Italy.[6]

The Italy of Verdi's youth makes Metternich's remark that Italy was not a nation but simply 'a geographical expression' not a mere gibe but a statement of fact. The Italian states spoke no central language but a number of related dialects; Italy had neither a central language nor a literary tradition of its own. In Naples and Piedmont the official language was French; in the Papal States it was Latin. The Austrian provinces—Lombardy, Venice, Parma, Tuscany and Modena—were governed in German. The Milanesi spoke in a dialect not immediately or completely comprehensible to the users of the Ligurian dialect in their north-west or to the Parmigiani, who provided Verdi with his mother tongue in Roncole and Bussetto, where he worked as a young man. Travelling from Roncole or Busseto to Milan as a student, Verdi needed not only a passport but also a language in which to make himself understood. Verdi was fourteen when in 1827 Alessandro Manzoni published his novel *I Promessi Sposi*, and sixteen when he read that masterpiece. *I Promessi Sposi* is to a large extent the beginning of modern Italian, moulded from the Tuscan of Dante and fitted out with acceptable new and compound words. Music, as Verdi inherited it from tradition, had a special position in Italian life because it was not a dialect but a national language which cut across the various local differences of dialect and custom. Italian music insisted, as did German music, upon a fundamental unity of style and spirit inevitably clamouring to become political unity.

Therefore Verdi, who by virtue of creative genius dominated Italian music for the last sixty years of the nineteenth century, could not stand apart from the political struggles of his age. Unlike Wagner, he made no effort to involve himself in political action and his membership of the Italian parliament, accepted to please Cavour, whom he idolised, seemed to him to be only a sardonic joke. His beliefs and aspirations were totally expressed in music, so that many of his works seem to be either a reflection in terms of romantic opera of the struggle for unification or of the political problems that were inescapably part of the struggle. Whilst Wagner could see in the

[6] Quoted in Francis Toye: *Rossini; a Study in Tragi-Comedy*. Norton, New York, 1963. p. 131.

elaborate vocal style of Bellini the essentially melodic Italian musical
tradition, Verdi's melodies begin at a point closer to the music which might
be sung in streets and taverns; even the superb choruses which mark climatic
moments even in his early operas are in this sense the voice of the Italian
people united in musical style though in nothing else. The problems which
had to be solved by the *Risorgimento*—the impossibility of independence
without unification, the futility of either under any absolutist rule—are reflected in the music of Verdi the liberal patriot. In a country with no
literary tradition, Verdi and his music, in its patriotism, its sense of Italy as
a musical nation, its enormous vitality and inexhaustible energy spoke for all
Italians.

To Verdi, the divided group of states, many of them under alien control,
which comprised a narrow Mediterranean peninsula were never a geographical expression; in his mind Italy was a nation. Its divisions existed
without reason or justification as an attempt to deny its nationhood. To what
extent he set out deliberately to write the music of the *Risorgimento* nobody
knows; it seems that it was simply the music of the great chorus *Va,
pensiero*, in *Nabucco*, which led his audiences to feel that the music of the
ancient Hebrews in exile spoke really of a divided and suffering Italy; we
do not know that Verdi, as he wrote the music, identified himself with the
sorrows of his characters in their Babylonian captivity. His choice of subject
matter often invited the audience to break into the patriotic ecstasies which
greeted *I Lombardi* and *Attila* when they were new. If he did not intend to
be the mouthpiece of the *Risorgimento*, he nevertheless chose subjects apparently motivated by his consciousness of Italy's sufferings, and neither he
nor his librettists can have been unaware of the effect of such correspond-
ences on his audiences. He was exploiting the political situation to win an
audience if he was not inflaming it to advance and possibly secure his own
political aims.

Nabucco was produced at La Scala, Milan, in March 1842. It was accepted as a revolutionary work—revolutionary less in its technique than in
its early-Verdian quality of almost brutal directness and emotional intensity.
In a country where political discussion and argument were stifled, the
chorus of exiled Hebrews seemed to early audiences to be their own cry of
pain. With Austrian help, a rising in Naples had been crushed in 1820; in
the following year, rebellion had been suppressed in Piedmont. In 1831 the
Pope had appealed for Austrian assistance to smash a rising in the Papal
States. An abortive rebellion in Piedmont had failed in 1833. The music of
the Hebrew chorus was the music of Italian liberalism conscious of the
parallel between Sion and Italy; the parallel was no secret.

The situation seemed perhaps rather less dark in 1843, when *I Lombardi*
was staged at La Scala. The battle cry of the crusaders—'Today the Holy
Land will be ours?—was interrupted after early performances with shouts

of approval from the audience. The police were unable to prevent the giving of a number of encores, although encores were forbidden; everyone knew that the Lombardian crusaders were the Italians of 1843 and the stage Saracens were the Austrian troops on whom the disunity of Italy depended.

Before *Attila* reached the stage of La Fenice Theatre in Venice, in 1846, a combined rising in Naples, the Papal States and Tuscany in 1843 had failed and a revolt at Rimini been defeated. In *Attila* a Roman general cried, 'You can have the Universe, but leave Italy for me.' Again the performance was interrupted with cries of enthusiasm. The struggles of 1848, with the almost irrelevant conflict (in terms of Italian unification) of monarchists and republicans and the defeat of a rising in Lombardy, seem to be reflected in *La Battaglia di Legnano* in 1849. This was an immediate and dangerous comment on the current situation, with the troops of the Emperor Barbarossa defeated by an Italian army and its hero, imprisoned in a tower, leaping to freedom to join his compatriots with a cry of *'Viva Italia!'* which roused the audience to repeated cheers; at every performance the fourth act, the battle and victory, had to be repeated.

It is not only the nationalism of the *Risorgimento* but also the doctrine of liberalism in politics—Verdi's anti-clericalism does not appear much in his work, except in *Stiffelio*, until *Don Carlos*, in 1867—which motivated much of his writing. *Les Vêpres Siciliennes*, written for Paris in 1855 and revised for Milan a year later, is about national liberation. *Un Ballo in Maschera* justifies the assassination of a king although censors insisted on reducing his rank. In 1849 Charles Albert of Piedmont had abdicated in favour of his son Victor Emmanuel, so it was after *Un Ballo*, ten years later, that the name 'Verdi' appropriately became an acronym for *'Vittoria Emmanuele Re d'Italia'*, and the shout *'Viva Verdi!'* saluted more than a patriotic composer. By the time that *Don Carlos* was composed for the Paris Opéra in 1867, the struggle was all but won and only Rome stood outside the Italy which Mazzini, Cavour, Garibaldi and Victor Emmanuel had created. But Don Carlos harps still on the theme of liberation; the Netherlands, say its Spanish heroes, must be free, as Italians, we gather, must be free. Because Verdi was a great dramatist, the tortured King Philip is created with sympathy and compassion, but he is wrong, just as the Church, in the awesome figure of the Grand Inquisitor, is wrong. More consistently than Wagner's, Verdi's politics have moved along in parallel to his work, adding to its vitality.

Beyond its effect as an expression of thwarted national will, music to Verdi is national by virtue of the tradition to which it belongs:

> Our composers are not good patriots [he wrote in 1889]. If the Germans, stemming from Bach, arrive at Wagner, they are doing as good Germans should, and that is fine. But for us, descendants of Palestrina, to imitate

> Wagner is to commit a musical crime, and we are doing something useless, even harmful.[7]

Verdi looks back to Palestrina, whose work was probably the earliest Italian music of which he was aware, as the beginning of the tradition which he himself served, the necessary foundation for the vocal style which is intrinsically Italian and which all Italian composers should serve:

> Palestrina cannot compete with the very daring harmonic discoveries of modern music, but, if he were better known and studied, we might write in a more Italian manner, and might be better patriots (in music, I mean.)[8]

Music in Germany and Italy reflected the struggle for unity of states divided by the will of the great European powers; in other states, notably Poland, Hungary and Bohemia, national music was the music of an unlettered, unpolitical class of peasants and artisans. National rhythms, harmonic and melodic idioms and tastes in instrumental colour were not features of the music of the educated Poles or Bohemians, let alone of the great generality of trained musicians. For the first time since Haydn, the idea of national resurgence after the collapse of Napoleon's empire again made it natural for the composer to look at and refer to idiosyncrasies of national style.

Such idiosyncrasies became increasingly important in the countries dominated by the Habsburg Empire, where educated culture was German in outlook and language, imposed on educated classes who saw in these essentially foreign attributes the only way to realise their ambitions; in Hungary and Bohemia the nobility, usually more at home in Vienna than in the territories from which they drew their titles, positions and wealth, German culture and German music, inevitably disregarded the plebeian music of the indigenous populations. Thus, inevitably, individual folk styles became symbolic of the national identities the subject provinces were determined to assert and the master races to forget. Poland, to Russia, Austria and Prussia, was simply a nuisance so long as Poles regarded it as a nation: the culture of Hungary and Bohemia, to the Austrians, was simply a crude irrelevance.

Thus, a composer like Chopin, who adopted and glorified national rhythms in polonaises and mazurkas, became a heroic patriot who, according to legend, travelled always with a precious cup full of Polish earth among his luggage, although he seems in reality to have preferred Paris to all other cities as a home. Politics impinged on his life, as they impinged on the lives of all nineteenth-century musicians. The Warsaw friends of his

[7] Verdi: *Letters*. Selected and edited by Charles Osborne. Letter to Franco Faccio, 14 July 1889. p. 206.
[8] *Ibid*. Letter to Giuseppe Gallignani, 15 November 1891. p. 249.

youth lived in a ferment of liberal revolutionary politics and, apparently, felt him to be indissolubly of their number. His departure to Paris was delayed by the nationalist rising in Warsaw in 1830, but Chopin's letters of that time seem to concentrate more on his need to explore wider musical worlds than to suffer for the agony of a native land which, since 1772, had been partitioned between Austria, Russia and Prussia, a division exploited after 1815 for the sake of Metternichian *Real-politik*. The fact that Chopin's nationalism was active only in his affection for the dances and musical idioms of his people, and that he took no active part in their struggle, cannot lessen the extent to which his work supported their political aims and won sympathy for Poland though his exploitation of what was naturally Polish in music. Moniusko, Chopin's contemporary, was a lesser composer and occupies a lower place in our musical awareness, but he was, in a sense, more consciously a mouthpiece of Polish nationalism than Chopin in the sense such a work as Vaughan Williams's *Hugh the Drover* and Kodály's *Hary Janos* are consciously English and Hungarian respectively. Moniusko's *Halka*, produced in Wilno in 1848, finds its inspiration in Polish life, legend and folk customs as it finds its musical inspiration in the idioms and rhythms of Polish folk music; in spite of amateurish dramatic construction, it opened the road to a distinctively national operatic style which neither Moniusko in his later works nor any of his successors have successfully trodden.

The real battle for musical nationalism was fought out in the Austrian subject provinces. 'The conflict between a supernational dynastic state and the national principle had to be fought to a finish,' writes A. J. P. Taylor, 'and so had the conflict between the master and the subject nations.'[9] Poland had been divided among greater powers—Austria, Russia and Prussia—in 1772 to insulate Austria against any Russian advance in Central Europe, only the core of the Polish kingdom remaining. Kosciusko's rising against Russia was crushed by the three great Powers although, according to Thomas Campbell,

> Hope for a season bade the world farewell
> And freedom shrieked when Kosciusko fell!

The rest of Poland fell with its would-be liberator, and naturally the Congress of Vienna ratified the destruction of Poland. Chopin's generation was close enough to the memory of a free and independent Poland to struggle bitterly against its subjugation, but it was harder in the Central European subject provinces of the Austrian Empire to find any sense of national individuality or national culture like that to which the discontented Poles could look back for inspiration. Any sense in which Liszt, a willing expatriate

[9] A. J. P. Taylor: *The Habsburg Monarchy, 1809–1918*. Hamish Hamilton. London, 1948. p. 7.

who towards the end of his life spent part of each year in Budapest, was a Hungarian nationalist can only have been very limited, but he wrote what he believed to be Hungarian works because the enjoyment of exotic national idioms was a new taste to be savoured for the sake of the expressive intensities which could be drawn from it.

Liszt in the *Vormärz*, the period before the revolutions of 1848, believed the gipsy music of Hungarian cafés and street bands to be the traditional music of the Magyar people; Brahms, about a decade later, made the same mistake. It was natural for them both to fall into error because any high culture in the Habsburg dominions was essentially Austro-German. Paul Ignotus describes what he calls the 'estrangement' of the Hungarian aristocracy from their national traditions:

> Their withdrawal from the intellectual life of the country, however, seemed total; at one time the chief patrons of Hungarian arts and letters, by the end of the nineteenth century they had lost absolutely all interest in them. . . . Some were well-versed in the philosophical trends of German-speaking Central Europe but hardly noticed those in their own country.[10]

The real centre of aristocratic life—Hungarian, Bohemian or in any of the subject provinces—was Vienna, as it had been in the days when Haydn, as *Kapellmeister* at Ezterhaza, had written music that would have come just as naturally to him—even when, for the sake of high spirits, he was writing *alla Ongarese*—in Vienna or London. Music and drama were what could be found in the capital, and the gipsy fiddlers of Hungary, bending over the supper table to play 'in the ear' of a fashionably dressed lady while his accompaniment second violin, viola, cello and dulcimer or cimbalon, kept time with him from a suitable distance, lacked metropolitan dignity, but the fierce, often fiercely melancholy music, the *czardas*, with its alternations of wild high spirits and wild melancholy, developed from earlier folk dances, was often far from genuine. It resembled the many Irish songs composed in New York for American singers and became, in spite of its dubious ancestry, a powerful nationalist propaganda. The stranger music of a Hungarian peasantry was left for Bartók and Kodály to discover in the twentieth century; Liszt, like his fellow countrymen and Brahms, accepted the gipsy music as the traditional idiom of his people.

If, as may well be the case, he exploited it for the sake of its piquancies and exoticisms rather than as the true voice of his native land, Liszt's fellow countrymen regarded his music as national, expressing their hatred of Austrian authority. After the creation of the Dual Monarchy (by which the Austrian Emperor took the title King of Hungary and gave Hungary some outward show of independence) it manifested their dislike for the pretence that simply masked the continuation of Habsburg dominance. In

[10] Paul Ignotus: *Hungary*. Ernest Benn, Ltd. London, 1972. p. 80.

Liszt's later years he was almost totally disregarded by the official 'establishment'. His *King's Song*, an attempt at a Hungarian national anthem, was not played at the opening of the Royal Opera House in Budapest in 1874 because, according to the Superintendent, Frigyes Podmowiczky, 'its motives are borrowed from a well-known revolutionary song'. To the people of Budapest, Liszt was Hungary's greatest composer and a national hero, and this slight against him led to a demonstration in his favour outside the theatre.[11] Liszt thought himself a nationalist composer in spite of his cosmopolitan way of life and his apparent inability to find a home either among or away from his fellow countrymen. Arguing backward from the discoveries of Bartók to the late piano works of Liszt, with its strange harmonic conundrums, it is possible to see in his work another nationalism quite different from his flamboyant delight in the pseudo-nationalism of Hungarian rhapsodies.

The position in Bohemia, and indeed throughout the provinces which were later to become Czechoslovakia, was more complex. The Bohemians, and the rest of the Czechs for that matter, had always been an extremely musical people; from the Middle Ages onwards, Bohemian musicians had supplied Germany and Austria with fine musicians. The Benda family had been prominent in Frederick the Great's Berlin; the Mannheim School, which had influenced Mozart, was largely the creation of a group of Bohemian musicians, and such composers as Dussek, Reicha (who after 1818 spent the last eighteen years of his life at the Paris Conservatoire and was possibly the most influential teacher of his day as well as an extremely prolific composer) to say nothing of Vanhal, Kozeluth, Gyrowetz and Tomascek, composers far from negligible but overshadowed, as every other composer working between 1770 and 1820, by the work of Haydn, Mozart and Beethoven.

None of these composers, however, owed his reputation to his work in his own country. The nobility of the Central European Slavonic lands was a largely artificial creation, owing its way of life, and often its origin, to the Empress Maria Theresa. Like Beethoven's patron Prince Lobkowitz, their homes were in Vienna and their culture the international culture of the eighteenth century. An absentee aristocracy, they concentrated their musical life on Vienna and were almost infinitely remote from the way of life and the folk culture of their homeland. Even the gifted musicians of Bohemia and the other Austrian provinces could not earn their living at home among their own people.

It was the success in Bohemia of *The Marriage of Figaro* and of *Don Giovanni* that began the renaissance of Bohemian music and encouraged musicians to exploit recent political reforms. Joseph II, the most enlighten-

[11] Bence Szabolski: *The Twilight of Ferenc Liszt*. Translated by Andras Deak. Hungarian Academy of Science, Budapest, 1959.

ed, it seems, of 'Enlightened Despots', had abolished serfdom, granted religious toleration, permitted the publication of a Czech newspaper and allowed the Czech language to become a subject for study at the Charles University in Prague, although Czech was never taught at any lower levels in the schools. More influential still was the growth of industry in the Czech provinces and the consequent rise of a bourgeoisie which took its culture from the way of life of the German cities. Napoleon's empire had created areas in the Austrian dominions where the native population found itself thrust by war and French conquest into contact with Germans and Frenchmen rather than with Austrians; naturally, the doctrines of liberal nationalism spread like an epidemic through Austria's subject provinces.

It was Germany and not France, however, which provided the model for emergent Czech nationalism. In 1807 a German Opera House opened in Prague, and in the following year the Prague Conservatoire was founded. It is significant that from 1813 to 1816 the *Kapellmeister* of the Opera was Weber, and that Weber also conducted the orchestra of the Conservatoire. For some reason, composition was not taught at the Conservatoire, which did nothing to stimulate interest in a national musical style, although it turned out a considerable number of virtuoso instrumentalists, perhaps as a consequence of the neglect of theoretical teaching and the study of ideas.

When Weber went to Prague in 1813 his determined effort to modernise the Opera's repertoire brought in not only his own works but operas by Rossini and the French composers, so that in the long run it was amateur opera companies and amateur concert organisations that started the exploration of Czech idioms and Czech life as a subject for libretti. The 'successful' works by Czech composers of Weber's day were operas like Weigl's *Die Schweizerfamilie*, which was so successful in Vienna that its composer became *Kapellmeister* of the Imperial Opera. But in spite of the traditional draining away of Czech talent towards Vienna or the northern European courts, the first steps towards an individual Czech style (itself an amalgam of various styles present in the folk and popular music of what became Czechoslovakia) came in the 1820s, and the failure of that style to develop any further for a quarter of a century was not the result of any lack of enthusiasm or even the lack of any central Czech musical tradition; it was the irruption into Bohemian musical life of an influence as powerful as that of Mozart.

> Before any real native voice could be heard, [writes Brian Large] Prague was invaded by a number of visiting artists, notably Berlioz, at the request of a dissatisfied clique forced to look abroad for inspiration. After Berlioz came Liszt, then Wagner. Music was reborn, but not by Bohemians—by French, German and Hungarian visitors whose influence began to stifle everything Czech.[12]

[12] Brian Large: *Smetana*. Duckworth, London, 1970. p. 25.

The inspiration brought by such visitors was influential enough, and eventually beneficial—the national schools which developed in the second half of the nineteenth century came into the world with a sense of the orchestra which they had learnt from Berlioz. It was the political ambitions of Bohemian musicians—they wanted and were prepared to work for independence outside the Austrian Empire, and saw the unifying effects of their national music as a weapon in their hands—which released them from their inhibitions by turning them to explore the possibilities of folk song and folk dance. Smetana, who was twenty-four when the revolutions of 1848 shook the European establishments and the Austrian Empire with them, saw Austria struggle to hold on to her Italian provinces and was stimulated by the sight to demonstrate his own sense of Bohemian nationality. Smetana's operas take their plots from Czech history, Czech national myth and Czech folk customs; *Libuse*, the essential national myth, became an opera he wished to see preserved for national occasions. But for twenty years or more, before his operas reached the stage, his choral orchestral and piano music exploits, as often as not, Czech idioms and rhythms. Occasionally they are written to openly nationalistic texts.

Smetana, perhaps, was more politically conscious than any other composer. His letters refer to such political phenomena as the growth of Czech influence on the *Reichrat* (the consultative assembly originally designed by Metternich and set up in 1851 to support the Emperor's absolute rule with a show of popular consent). The elections of 1859, Smetana declared, gave enough strength to national opinion for the Czechs (never, in Smetana's correspondence, Bohemians and Moravians but always members of a single nation) to insist that the demand for national independence be continually reiterated until official Vienna, which he saw as entirely destructive of the Czech way of life, was compelled to take notice.[13] Both to Smetana and to Dvořák, the fact of their Czech birth was a reality which gave a special national character to their music. The difference between the two is, perhaps, that Smetana wanted Czech music to be established for its own sake, while Dvořák fed national ideas into the European mainstream.

Musical nationalism in Russia had other than political sources. Russia, in what may have been a somewhat ramshackle way, was united, independent politically and ranked among the great powers; its musical revival was a matter of national pride rather than of any political demand. The Russian musical tradition, both in folk song and dance and in liturgical music, had lost whatever influence it might once have had because of the westernising policy adopted by the Czars since the seventeenth century. Czar Alexis Mikhailovitch, the father of Peter the Great, began the *rapprochement* with the West which was ruthlessly accelerated; Peter left Russia in 1697 for

[13] Frantisek Bartos: *Bedrich Smetana; Letters and Reminiscences*. Translated by Dorothy Rustridge. Artis, Prague, 1956. p. 113.

a year and a half's tour of the West and then set out to complete the creation of a Westernised Russia from first-hand experience of Western society, industry and customs. Western music, especially Italian opera and *Singspiele*, became the models for Russian composers. The Empress Elizabeth Peter's successor, appointed the Italian Francesco Araja to direct music in her court, and Araja held office continually until the murder of Peter III and the usurpation of his wife, Catherine the Great, in 1762. Araja, seven years before this, had composed the first opera to a Russian text, a work representative of Westernising demands through its subject matter, *Cephalus and Procris*.

The policy of westernising Russian music so far succeeded that, by the time of Catherine the Great, every aristocrat had his own musical establishment performing Italian or German music.[14] Catherine was as resolute a westerniser as any of her predecessors. She brought Galuppi, at the height of his fame and influence, to St. Petersburg in 1766. Galuppi controlled the music of the Imperial Court Chapel as well as of the court's secular events, and among his pupils was Dmitry Stepanovich Bortniansky, who returned to Italy with Galuppi in 1768, to continue his studies at Catherine's expense. In Italy he had three operas successfully produced before he returned to Russia in 1779, where the court composers were successively Paisiello and Traetta; Martin y Soler and Cimaroso followed in their footsteps, and it was not until after the death of Catherine and the reign of Paul I that Bortniansky, in 1796, found an official position in Russia. Paul I made him director of the Imperial Court Chapel, a post in which he wrote Italian style music for the Russian liturgy. Erstignei Ipalovich Fomin, Mikhail Martinsky and Vassily Paskewitch, Bortnianski's contemporaries, wrote opera equally Italianate in style, their training having been no less Italian than Bortniansky's. Their models were the inferior Italian works of a period which is, to modern listeners, that of the operas of Mozart. Vladimir Stassov, writing more than half a century later, saw in these works some appetite for Russian national music crushed to the conventions and tyranny of the court:

> The fact that we were so long in producing an art music of our own was due solely to the unfavourable conditions of Russian life in the eighteenth and nineteenth centuries, when everything national was trampled in the mud. Nevertheless the need for national music was so widespread that even during the time of Catherine the Great . . . one of our poor composers after the other tried to incorporate folk melodies into his poor operas.[15]

Nevertheless, not only the audience for such works, but the composers

[14] R. A. Leonard: *A History of Russian Music*. Jarrold, London, 1956.
[15] Vladimir Stassov: *Selected Essays on Music*. Translated by Florence Jonas. Cresset Press, London, 1968. p. 71.

themselves, were wedded to an Italian style and Italian taste, accepting models considerably behind those acceptable in the Europe of Mozart, Beethoven and Rossini. In Russia, Gluck's reform operas apparently won little approval though his earlier, conventional works, were popular. The next model, after the assassination of Alexander I in 1801, was Boieldieu, who went to the Imperial Opera as conductor in 1803 and was succeeded by Daniel Steibelt, a German who had worked successfully as a conductor in Paris, in 1808; two years later Steibelt was promoted to become *Maître de Chapelle* of the Imperial Court. Among Steibelt's Russian pupils was Alexis Nikolaievich Verstovsky, the most successful composer yet to be produced by Russia.

Verstovsky, born in 1799, had a conventionally cosmopolitan training. The Irish John Field, the Italian Tarquini and the German Böhm were his teachers for piano, singing and the violin respectively. His own compositions began to attract attention in 1818; in 1824 he was made Inspector of the Imperial Opera in Moscow, and between 1828 and his death in 1862 he composed six operas, the third of which, *Askold's Tomb*, produced in 1835, became so popular that for some years it eclipsed even Glinka's *Ivan Susannin (A Life for the Czar)* produced a year later.

The composers who followed Verstovsky, Glinka among them, belonged to a class which had not previously been much occupied in the arts. The recent history of Russia, its encounter with the might of Napoleon in particular, had created a new sense of national pride and national purpose, especially among the growing middle class which provided the country's legions of bureaucrats and civil servants, its middle-class shopkeepers and business men who had previously been too few and too unregarded to have much influence on any aspect of Russian life. The shock of war had become the seed from which conscious patriotism grew among a class which was not involved with the court, and therefore with the deliberate Italianism which court music expected. The use of popular-style melodies in *Askold's Tomb*, the work of an official musician, suggested that at last a truly national music had been born, but Stassov, summing up the achievements of the National School in an essay written in 1883, almost sourly put Verstovsky's into perspective:

> Half a century ago the Russians firmly believed that they had achieved their own national, truly Russian, music. The reason for this was that they had a 'national anthem', which had been written on commission by Lvov and was being ardently disseminated, and also Verstovsky's opera *Askold's Tomb*, whose quasi-gypsy, quasi-popular melodies excited many listeners. But the belief that these constituted a national music was only an illusion. Neither the anthem nor the opera had any national character, and despite the expectations of the authorities and the public, they did not give rise to any national music or school of composition whatever.[16]

[16] *Ibid.* p. 66

The real Russian nationalist school, with and following Glinka and Dargomiszky, were all, as Verstovksy had been, amateurs born outside court circles and therefore not indoctrinated with the Western tastes which they came to despise. Glinka, born in 1806, was a country gentleman who spent four years in the Ministry of Transport and Communications before retiring at the age of twenty-three. He had studied the piano and the violin, brought up on German music until, in 1830, he went to Italy, where he came to the conclusion that his future was to write opera, not in the Italian style but for his own people. His only formal study of composition was undertaken during a year's stay in Berlin, where he broke his return journey from Italy in 1834. *Ivan Sussanin* was produced in 1836; aristocrats in the audience, brought up on German and Italian music, dismissed Glinka's work, with its contrasting Russian and Polish melodies, as 'coachman's music', in other words, unfit for aristocratic ears. But the use of an episode from Russian history and the combination of Russian-style melodies with a conventional operatic technique, all written with vividly colourful orchestration, persuaded the unaristocratic audience that at last a composer had found the real music of Russia. Glinka's second opera, *Russlan and Ludmilla*, its libretto pieced together by the composer himself from a poem by Pushkin, never won the same popularity.

Dargomizhsky, nine years younger than Glinka, was another country gentleman trained as an amateur pianist. His only consistent training in composition came from the notebooks in which Glinka had worked out the exercises set for him during his year of study in Berlin. After a series of minor successes in the theatre with works based on Russian subjects, he was close to fifty years old when, in the early 1860s, he came into the orbit of Balakirev and reformed his style according to the tenets of the deliberate, conscious nationalist school which owed its dogma to Balakirev. The result was Dargomizhky's last opera, *The Stone Guest*, based on Pushkin's treatment of the Don Juan legend and produced in 1872, three years after its composer's death. *The Stone Guest* became extremely influential because of the precision and accuracy with which it did justice to Russian rhythms and prosody.

Of the brilliant group who came together as 'The Kuchka', 'The Mighty Handful' or 'The Five' in the generation after Glinka, none was academically trained, all tended to despise academic training, none was originally a professional musician and all were provincials. This meant that though all of them were well-trained instrumentalists, their impressions of music as a living art came not from the operas and symphonies heard at court or in aristocratic circles generally but from the songs and dances of the serfs and peasantry on the estates where they grew up. The music they studied formed a second, more superficial, level of experience, less immediate and less personal to them than the music of their own countryside. The similarity of their backgrounds and upbringing made it natural for them to cluster together round Balakirev, the most prolific in ideas and the most unusual in personality; it was equally natural for them to look scornfully at the Russian Musical Society founded in 1854, and bringing more up-to-date Western music to St. Petersburg. Out of the Russian Musical Society the St. Petersburg Conservatoire grew in 1862; its staff and its pupils did not accept or for a moment take seriously Balakirev's conviction that tradition and saturation in the music of the past was the only training a composer needed. Nevertheless, the Russian Musical Society began to bring into its programmes the works of the Balakirev group, all of whom studied with their leader, who taught them only what he himself would have done with the materials of their compositions. Rimsky-Korsakov, as a pupil-disciple of Balakirev, lived to find that his hero's teachings were not sufficiently comprehensive to be fully useful to him. Balakirev, he wrote:

> should have given me a few lessons in harmony and counterpoint, should have made me write a few fugues and explained the grammar of musical forms to me. He could not do so, as he had never studied systematically himself and considered it unnecessary. As a product of the Conservatoire, Tchaikovsky was viewed rather negligently if not haughtily by our circle.[17]

Tchaikovsky, at various times, expressed similar uncertainties about the procedure of the Balakirev 'Mighty Handful' and its leader; their lack of training, he felt, and the absence of real mental discipline in their music, led often to the squandering of brilliant ideas and the crippling of remarkable talents.

The essential amateurishness of the 'Handful', from which only Rimsky-Korsakov escaped, did not prevent the creation of several indisputable masterpieces, although most of the members remained amateurs composing in the intervals of their extra-musical careers. For a time, the group dominated St. Petersburg music, as the Russian Musical Society fell into the hands of Balakirev, who, though he did not remove Western works from its programmes, never found it necessary to arrange for the performance of any works earlier than Beethoven's but regarded it as a point of principle to see that a Russian work was included in every programme. The only work by Bach to appear in the Musical Society's programmes during the years of nationalist control was, perhaps inevitably, conducted by the more academically-minded and disciplined Rimsky-Korsakov. Amateurishness was both a strength and a debilitating weakness of his colleagues and explains why so much of his time was spent in clearing up and making practical the works of his fellow nationalists.

Tchaikovsky, with his Europeanism and his unfashionable devotion to

[17] Rimsky-Korsakov: *My Musical Life*. Translated by Jonah A. Jaffe. Knopf, New York, 1942. p. 34.

Mozart, was never an official, exclusive nationalist, but it may be that, acting, so to speak, the Dvořák to their Smetana, he advanced the cause of Russian music by building the necessary bridges between it and the central tradition. He chose Russian subjects for some of his operas and found folk melodies and national rhythms valuable. But he never considered the wholesale rejection of European influences or sympathised with the excesses of the 'Mighty Handful'. It was with him, and with other composers who achieved the synthesis of the unmistakably Russian with the generally European, that the future of Russian music really lay, so that the symphonies of Glazounov, Prokofiev and Shostakovitch follow not from the exclusiveness of the Balakirev group but from the Tchaikovskyan synthesis. The greatest work of the 'Handful' is, it seems, that of Mussorgsky, greatest in songs and operas, reaching a style of melody which is the outcome of Russian speech, 'a reincarnation of recitative in melody'. But the outcome of that was that Mussorgsky's operas were known until the mid-twentieth century in the tidied, smoother versions prepared by Rimsky-Korsakov when he assembled their disorganised fragments.

Nationalism, however, was a nineteenth-century necessity, affecting music in Spain, in Britain, where the collection of English folk songs showed the way to Holst, Vaughan Williams and other refugees from an outworn European style, and eventually in America, after Charles Ives had used the music of his youth, revivalist hymns and popular melodies, to create the musical reality of the United States.

9

The Great Schism

Until the nineteenth century, the idea that 'light' music is something essentially different in nature from 'serious' music would have been meaningless. The professional composer of the eighteenth century had to be as willing, and ideally as capable, of providing music for amusement or for social relaxation as he was of writing a mass or a church cantata, and the specific gravity of his music ideally depended on the music that was expected from him for any particular occasion. Leopold Mozart, who never found life at Salzburg intolerable, wrote rather academic church music and a considerable number of light, humorous and occasionally freakish works because such music was expected of him. Dittersdorf, in spite of serious operas and oratorios, could be seen as a 'lighter' composer than Wolfgang Mozart because his various patrons required light-hearted music from him rather more often than they asked for serious works. Sets of dances by Mozart or Haydn seem to have occasioned neither composer any pangs of conscience, just as Schubert's dance music for piano seemed to him to be quite natural music to compose and to publish. Beethoven's sets of minuets, German dances and *Ländler* have all the essential character of light music. It was Chopin, Schumann and Brahms who refined dance music into abstraction, just as it was Lanner and the two Johann Strausses who decided never to venture beyond what is enjoyably light, though the younger Strauss sometimes gave almost symphonic emotional depth to the introductions and codas of his waltzes. But Chopin, Schumann and Brahms are accepted as invariably and incurably 'serious' musicians while Lanner and the Strausses were accepted as specialists in 'light' music who could not be expected to write 'light' sonatas, string quartets and symphonies, although earlier musicians had done so; they could not be expected even, in the way of Mozart, to write a Mass with its *Kyrie* in waltz-time.

This precise and now tidy distinction between music for amusement and what for the want of a better name passes now as 'serious' music (Malcolm Arnold's Second Symphony, because it is a symphony, is 'serious' in spite of its hilarities and the rhythmic jokes that it plays on the listener) asks questions which permit no simple explanation. The Marxist critic, noting the general decline in Viennese music, and to a lesser extent of Central European music generally, from the end of the Napoleonic Wars until the triumph of Wagner and the rise of Brahms, is inclined to see the decline of power as a result of the post-revolutionary reaction in politics. Serious thought about life and, consequently, about society was likely to give offence to governments. Therefore musicians turned to the great music of the past, rediscovering Handel, Bach and works of power and beauty which could no longer shock tender political sensibilities; or they spent their time with the romantic extravagances or glorious flippancies of Rossini, Bellini and Donizetti. Or there was the spectacular grand opera of Meyerbeer, emasculated, as was often necessary, into political conformity.

The move towards charming, easy-going dance music, as satisfying to listeners as to dancers, came first from Vienna. Weber and Schubert had composed waltzes before the first master of the dance, Michael Pamer, and his disciples Lanner and the elder Johann Strauss first set Vienna, and then the rest of Europe, dancing to the slightly distorted three-four time of the Viennese waltz. It was in 1814 that a disillusioned diplomat in Vienna, asked about the progress of the Congress of Vienna, said that Congress did not progress, it only danced. Lanner joined Pamer's orchestra in 1813, when he was twelve years old, and Strauss, three years Lanner's junior, played with it until, in 1819, he joined the trio—two violins and a guitar— which Lanner had formed two years before. The quartet thus formed had become an orchestra playing in the Prater before the two quarrelled in 1825 and Strauss broke away to form his own orchestra, eclipsing both his master and his friend.

The Viennese waltz was an offshoot of the Viennese musical tradition; though both Lanner and the elder Strauss were virtually self-taught both as violinists and as composers, they united the tradition of Austrian folk dance with the legacy of the Viennese classics. Elegance and taste, with sentimentality never denied its place but always kept under control, were as important as high spirits. Both Lanner and Strauss introduced their waltzes with a musical prologue, Strauss briefly with a flourish, Lanner often with a quasi-symphonic, poetically emotional introduction. The younger Strauss, who usurped his father's title, 'Waltz King', before the elder Strauss was prepared to abdicate, was a trained musician whose juvenilia include church music. The second Strauss took his orchestra, and his waltzes, to France, England, Russia and the United States. His father's music had intoxicated Wagner during Wagner's first stay in Paris, and Strauss the Second was greeted with critical approval by the critic Hanslick, Wagner's most irreconcilable enemy, but lost the critic's advocacy when he introduced Wagner's music into his Viennese programmes, which, naturally, demanded some occasional relief from dance rhythms. The younger Strauss showed in the introductions to some of his waltzes—*The Blue Danube* and the *Kaiserwaltz* for example—that he knew and loved Wagner's music, and understood Wagnerian orchestration, which he applied to his own smaller orchestra. More ambitious than his father, he composed operettas which, at their best, are great (if the concept of 'greatness' in music has any real meaning) in their unique expression of things which more serious masters have never really wished to express; no other music creates the alcoholic goodwill of a successful party so perfectly as the finale of act two of *Die Fledermaus* with a waltz which celebrates, if not the essential brotherhood of man, at any rate the temporary brotherhood of the good-naturedly tipsy.

If the cult of light music, started in Vienna, had been restricted to the German-speaking nations when they were condemned to silence by the Metternichian reaction, the Marxist explanation might stand as a complete account of its origins. But light music, often of genius, came from Offenbach (and from others) in Paris. From 1839 onwards, Offenbach was supplying the Paris stage with complete operettas, one-act plays with music, and cabaret sketches more than thirty years before the younger Strauss invaded the theatre. Among Offenbach's vast collection of stage works are several unique masterpieces like *Orphée aux Enfers, La Belle Hélène, La Vie Parisienne* and *La Périchole*, and, like the younger Johann Strauss, he was followed by an army of imitators. Strauss's disciples lack the refinement and inventiveness of his music, and its exact balance between sentiment and undue sentimentality, while Offenbach's imitators rarely possessed in any marked degree the technical finesse and elegance of his music, while no other composer has achieved the heartless, glittering frivolity of his finest scores; emotion he reserved for *Les Contes d'Hoffmann*, the final and technically unfinished work which he rightly described as an opera.

The need for light music in the nineteenth century, not only in Austria, Germany and France, in countries of great political agitation and up-heaval, but also in countries where music was as free as the circumstances of commercial music-making would allow it to be, seems to need other than political and social explanations. The effect of Beethoven's work was to make unprecedented demands not only on instrumentalists but on their audiences. The *Eroica*, writen in 1803, lasts almost as long as any two symphonies by Haydn and Mozart; the Ninth Symphony lasts half as long again. The intricacy of such music, its demands on the resources of the average violinist or oboe player, its demand for more and more rehearsal time, tended to put this music in as much a class of its own as Mahler's Eighth Symphony or Schoenberg's *Gurrelieder* are in the late twentieth century; such works, before the days of the long-playing gramophone record, could not become familiar, and familiarity is a necessary ingredient of devotion to any music. But Beethoven also demanded an unprecedented concentration and development of the musical memory if the problems set in the early pages of his major works are to be heard to have a convincing solution at their end.

Chamber music, especially the companionable string quartet, played by amateurs in their homes, probably without rehearsal and intended simply for their pleasure, became the vehicle for Beethoven's most exalted thought and complex structures, not uningratiating to the ear but baffling to the traditional understanding of musical grammar, syntax and logic. Schubert, too old in the 1820s to be diverted from his own paths by the works of Beethoven's third period, was the last composer outside Italy not to feel the Ninth Symphony as an inescapable challenge and the late quartets as invitations to a world which he must enter; he was, with Mendelssohn, the last composer to invite the attention of amateur chamber musicians. However close to normal experience the chamber music of Brahms may be, however heartful and melodious that of Dvořák, the music of such composers demands a technical expertise beyond that of the amateur quartet. The popularity of the piano as everybody's all-purpose instrument meant a decline in the number of amateur string and wind players—the world ceased to be crowded with enthusiastic amateur flautists—and the number of amateur ensembles of all kinds decreased; the technical demands of the nineteenth-century composer kept at bay all but the most accomplished players.

In this situation, as a direct descendant of Beethoven, Wagner appeared as the composer who not only demanded unusually large orchestras exactly balanced, but also listeners who could hear the end of *Götterdämmerung*, late on Friday evening, as a fulfilling recapitulation of music heard early on the previous Tuesday evening. Beyond that, he imposed upon Europe an aesthetic which exalted music from the status of a delightful and moving art to a religion, to be treated with an invariable devotion and seriousness, with no room for pleasantry and relaxation. The music lover who could listen with pleasure, or even with a sense of revelation, to the symphonies of Haydn and Mozart could come to terms with Wagner only when he was able to recognise the final cadence of *Tristan und Isolde* as the necessary resolution of a harmonically baffling harmonic statement made in the work's opening bars. Listening, like playing, had become much harder, and whilst Wagner won the complete devotion of those who were capable of learning his ways, there were music lovers who could not do so. Light music, within the tradition which Europe had developed, was an alternative course to the ever more demanding works of the serious composers. It was, in addition, socially necessary; somebody had to write the music of relaxation and social enjoyment. If Beethoven, by the time that Strauss and Lanner had begun to delight audiences in Vienna, no longer felt disposed to enliven all and sundry with dance music, and Wagner bypassed that area of music altogether, less exalted composers had to fill the breach. As music became the romantic composer's substitute for religion and its most earnest composers became less and less willing to do anything which derogated from the divine dignity of their art, they ceased to regard it as belonging to a world which urgently needs music, however ephemeral, for social life and activity.

The worlds of light music and serious music are not, for all that, mutually exclusive. Brahms, for example, though for a long time he was regarded as a composer of almost unfathomable profundity and super-human intellect, was an admirer of the younger Strauss; Bruckner's scherzos usually stand in a clear relationship to Austrian folk music and Mahler could never, even in his most ecstatic moods, break contact with the music of the Vienna streets and inns, the Schrammel groups of fiddlers, guitarists and accordion players, the buglers and trumpeters of the barrack square. It has always been popular, even in a work as sophisticated as *Wozzeck*, to connect the opera house to the music of streets and dance halls, but the nineteenth century made the journey between diverse musical worlds far more difficult. It is not only that there will always be people who are musically underdeveloped, just as there will always be people to whom mathematics, beyond its simplest operations, is a matter of insuperable diffi-culty and those who seem by nature incapable of using any language but their own. The development of light music towards ever-increasing simpli-fication and of serious music into increasing abstraction and specialisation has created a schism so that it often easy to see the two as acrimonious armies engaged in hostilities across the divide.

The example of English music in the nineteenth century provides a clear demonstration of the development because, perhaps, by the 1820s English music had been more or less buried by the popularity, among the wealthy, leisured patrons of the opera and the London concert hall, of foreign musicians and European styles. Such English forms as the glee, music essentially for small amateur groups of singers, held their own and until the middle of the century provided music admirably fitted to its social and artistic purposes, while the English symphonies and oratorios of the period are no more than dutiful reflections of the style and ideas more pointedly used by Beethoven and Mendelssohn; Sterndale Bennett, a composer of considerable originality and technical expertise, who married the English tradition to the techniques of Mendelssohn and Schumann, was driven into teaching and administration while his music was forgotten. In Britain, how-ever, the development of an industrial working class, bred in towns created simply to satisfy the demands of industry or into poor areas of existing cities decayed into centres for industry, produced a whole population which for generations grew up divorced from any traditional standards of culture, general or musical. When Dickens, as a young journalist, reported the amusements of the working classes in the essays eventually published as *Sketches by Boz* in 1836, he found the London working classes preserving the manners of the well-to-do and aping their social superiors in the song and supper rooms with glees interspersed by solo songs, like the comfortable Bohemians of Thackeray's *Pendennis* and *The Newcomes*, novels of the 1850s. The early music halls, beginning in the middle of the century, provided at first opportunities for concerted singing of the same sort, with solo songs and occasional excursions into 'serious' music. The first London performance of Gounod's *Faust*, as a piece in concert form, was early in the 1860s at the New Canterbury Music Hall in Lambeth. But whatever the quality and zest of the concerted singing and the degree of public interest to be aroused by performances of opera, there was always Little Swills, the archetypal comic singer of Dickens's *Bleak House*, ready to attend the inquest on the mysterious suicide, held in the Sol's Arms; such material would enable Little Swills to entertain the habitués of the same pub later that evening with a topical comic song with a nonsense refrain. The song and supper rooms had their singers of often extemporary, topical comic songs, and while the music halls and their audiences were never averse to easy and directly melodious songs from opera, or to the more spectacularly acrobatic feats of *coloratura*, their strength eventually came to be the artists they created, for whom songs were written reflecting colourful, eccentric personalities, with easy sentiment or socially pointed derision, growing from, or creating, a folk tradition much further from the concert hall or the opera house than the waltzes of Strauss, which are never more than a stone's throw from the hall of the *Gesellschaft für Musikfreunde* in sentimental, music-obsessed Vienna. The music hall invented a style of popular song developed from the tastes, habits and manners of the industrial working class who grew up with no contact with the world of high culture except, perhaps, the language of the authorised version of the Bible.

The music halls eventually created their community, an entirely classless one, not through its music but through the startling, flamboyant and extraordinarily gifted people who became its stars. Their gifts were not, perhaps, primarily musical, although one of their central abilities was to be able to project songs, comic, satirical, pathetic or simply sentimental, with the maximum point. There was no essential way from the music hall to works which conveyed other, and perhaps even more important, aspects of life than the everyday experience of a working-class audience which understood why Marie Lloyd's old man, engaged in a moonlight flit, told her to follow the van without any undue waste of time. It is not that the wealthier patrons of the 'halls' necessarily became aware either emotionally or intellectually of the world in which a tandem bicycle became a more suitable wedding conveyance than a coach, or of the pathos of entering a workhouse where, after forty years of happy married life, they would be parted from their old Dutch. It was the 'star quality' of a handful of great entertainers whose gifts were often for satire—they lived in Trafalgar Square, with four lions to guard them, or watched the activities of Burlington Bertie, who rose at ten-thirty and walked down the Strand—which were the life-blood of the music hall. If offered membership of a classless community and created a social unity almost without attention to the music or poetry which it used.

The publication of *Hymns Ancient and Modern* in 1860 seems to have added the final ingredient to English popular music. The compilers of that anthology included in their collection a considerable number of hymns from the Latin liturgy, with their original plainsong melodies somewhat unsympathetically harmonised, but these seem to have made comparatively little impression on the congregations which used the book; it was the more stirring or more sentimental tunes which were most often heard and many of these were held in common with the nonconformists. Probably any enquirer looking, in the 1880s and 1890s, for music which was universally known to the English would have turned to the Victorian hymn tunes, which, close on a century later and in a period of religious decline, are still in the mind of almost every Briton. To strike chords in the average English heart, the composer need only turn, deliberately or unconsciously, to the idioms and harmonic procedures of Victorian hymn composers. The popularity of these melodies did not, perhaps, entirely depend on their being given week by week to a captive audience in church or chapel but because many of them seem to express, in sturdy if limited rhythms or in sweetly lachrymose melodies, certain essential English attitudes. *Hymns Ancient and Modern* became virtually a national possession perhaps twenty years before the greatest days of the music hall, and the music of the anthology (as the old habit of prefacing Football Association Cup Finals with the singing of the hymn 'Abide with Me' indicates) created a musical taste perhaps even more universal than the music hall. From the meditations of Mrs Waters, the heroine of Ethel Smyth's opera *The Boatswain's Mate*, to pop songs, the cadences of Victorian hymnology haunt English popular music.

In so far as music creates a social unity among its hearers, so that such composers as the two Johann Strausses and Offenbach preserved a corner of the central musical tradition, the development of English music into two largely antipathetic styles lessened the possibility of such unity. The Victorian hymn melody, sung with whatever sincerity or fervour, was not really a means of entry to any wider musical tradition, though the chorales of Lutheran Germany had opened doors to more extensive musical horizons. Hymns were the only contact which the huge and largely illiterate population of Britain outside the choral societies had with any type of musical experience.

Because of this, the English composer who can justly be classed with the Strausses and Offenbach achieved enormous, deserved popularity. Arthur Sullivan was in no way inferior to the continental masters of light music. It could be argued that in inventiveness and range of emotional expression he was possibly Offenbach's superior. While the 'Savoy Operas', in which he deals with the libretti of W. S. Gilbert, are not his only worthwhile music, the 'operas' maintain a remarkably high musical level; their elegance of melody, harmony and orchestration is rarely less than delightful, Sullivan's gift as a parodist is made all the more effective by its restraint, while his lyrical gift seems almost inexhaustible. But the Savoy Operas are the work of 'Gilbert and Sullivan', relegating the composer to a junior partnership in the enterprise; Gilbert was invincibly and almost arrogantly of the middle class, almost its laureate. The situation of the English theatre in the late nineteenth century insisted that the Savoy Operas were written for and enjoyed by middle-class audiences, by tradition the most eager theatre-goers; they became available to a wider public, of course, but the wider public of the theatre gallery and the amateur performance aimed at and implicitly accepted nineteenth-century middle-class values. This Gilbert and Sullivan opera reinforces the old-fashioned conviction that the upper-classes are amusingly effete, that foreigners are quaint and the working class unamiably funny; the coster, as a matter of course, jumps on his mother; middle-class spinsters past their first youth are, equally 'of course', a subject of unparalleled hilarity. The Savoy Operas perform the important incidental feat of creating a community out of a mere audience, but their influence is largely a narrowing one, offering membership to a small, closed world.

The brass-band movement in England and Wales was to reach a similar musical restrictedness. The bands rose in the areas, and among the class of people, who created the choral societies, so that band music was part of the early nineteenth-century appetite for self-help, for moral and material improvement. Like many of the choral societies, many of the brass bands grew out of nonconformity. The band formed at Stalybridge, in Cheshire, began its recorded history when it played as a reed band at the laying of the foundation stone of a local Sunday School on 24 June 1815. The members of the band had created it for their own pleasure and practised in the house of one of the members, but their understood allegiance to the chapel was marked by the membership of the son of the local minister who had himself blessed the organisation at its foundation.

The poverty of most of the members of the early bands restricted them to reed instruments, notably cheaper than brass, but employers were as quick to see the benefits of bands as they had been to encourage choral singing. In 1816 an employer, John Foster, became a member of the group which was later to evolve into the Black Dyke Mills Band while it was still restricted to reeds. Foster's took the band over, and in 1854 converted it into a brass band. The Besses o' th' Barn Band, equally celebrated in brass-band circles, began life as a string band in 1818; in 1854 it changed to brass. Because of their alliance with nonconformity, many brass bands added the adjective 'temperance' to their name; the Bramley Old Band, which began with reeds in 1828, took up brass instruments in 1836 and became the first such organisation proudly to describe itself as a 'temperance' band. At Brown's iron works, at Blaina in Monmouthshire, a brass band was created in 1832, the employers apparently buying the instruments, which were all imported.

William Gardiner, a Leicestershire hosiery manufacturer who died in 1853 (he made a pair of stockings for Haydn and wove the notes of the Emperor's Hymn into them), was an amateur editor of music, composer of religious music and translator of biographies of Haydn and Mozart. In his reminiscences he provides a splendid picture of a factory band in Derbyshire:

> The Messrs. William, George and Joseph Strutt of Derby, men of great wealth and acquirements, employ nearly the whole population of Belper. . . . To give a higher taste to the work people at Belper, Mr. John Strutt (the son of George) has formed a musical society by selecting forty persons, or more, from his mills and workshops, making a band of instrumental performers and a choir of singers. These persons are regularly trained by masters and taught to play and sing in the best manner. Whatever time is consumed in their studies is reckoned into their working hours. On the night of a general muster, you may see five or six of the forgemen, in their leather aprons, blasting their terrific notes upon ophicleides and trombones.[1]

Apparently as early as the middle 1830s a band had become a source of pride, prestige and, possibly, advertisement, to the workplace which sponsored or even created it. There are numerous other records of similar bands created, financed and encouraged by employers. The Strutts found that their better musicians were likely to be enticed away from the mills as soon as they were fully trained, either to jobs in mills with rival bands or to become teachers of their instruments. The poaching of good players to build up rival bands became common practice, as did the advertising of industrial jobs restricted to players of instruments in short supply at whatever mill offered the vacancy. The Strutts found it necessary to arrange that 'members of the orchestra are bound to remain at the works seven years'.

The organisation of brass bands rather than of any sort of concert orchestra was a matter of simple practicality. To train foundry men and other manual workers into reasonable string players would have been too time-absorbing a scheme to have been of any great value; string players are unlikely to emerge from among men who undertake heavy work with their hands, and it takes less time, even with the most promising material, to create effective brass players who can enjoy themselves by playing than to make violinists and cellists.

The nineteenth-century centres of adult education in England, the Mechanics' Institutes and Lyceums, planned originally to increase the

[1] William Gardiner: *Music and Friends*. London, 1838. Vol. 2. pp. 511–13.

efficiency of workers, and their chance of escape from the most degrading work by increasing their basic knowledge, found themselves rapidly answering demands for a variety of what would now be called 'cultural' subjects. Musical teaching, in singing classes and the teaching of brass instruments, became extremely popular additions to the austerely practical aims of the educators. At first, the bands played arrangements of glees and of music from operas and oratorios. As the century progressed, they became increasingly satisfied to live in a world of their own in which the popular selections from popular operas, and the popular overtures, joined works written for bands competing in the various local or national competitions which tended to become the real purpose of the bandsmen's efforts. Since 1853, when the first National Brass Festival was held in the Belle Vue pleasure gardens in Manchester, the bands have followed a path some distance from either the developing tradition of popular music or the world of orchestral concerts, paying comparatively little attention to works composed for them by such musicians as Elgar, Vaughan Williams, Holst and Bliss (among many others) active in wider musical worlds. For all that, a considerable number of brass bands can be regarded as virtuoso ensembles, and any effective band makes music with a splendid, extravert panache.

The nature of light music is to offer simplifications and dilutions of styles and methods which are presented with due and natural weight in the opera house and the concert hall, but while Sullivan, for example, was rarely contented with clichés or banalities in his early orchestral works or his operettas, in his writing for a popular audience, which inevitably included the church audience of hymn singers, he could descend to the level of 'Onward Christian Soldiers' or 'The Lost Chord'. The divorce of the popular audience from any music which could stir its imagination, since the music hall abandoned the glee and their forays into opera, together with the absence of music from upper-class education in Britain, and the inanity of what was presented as musical education for the state schools established in the days of compulsory education, made a decline in standards as inevitable as the eventual rooting of English popular music in hymnology.

The rise and enormous popularity of the drawing-room ballad presented to British audiences, round about the first ten years or so of the twentieth century, prove the existence of composers who could plug like telephone operators without difficulty into customary channels of popular sentiment and whimsy, producing some works to which we can listen with an indulgent smile and others which we find intolerable. Every age produces its music, of all degrees of weight in considerable bulk and, if it is lucky, manages to achieve a handful of masterpieces. The production of ephemera is natural and necessary; what ultimately became depressing about so much English light music was the way in which it unerringly found its way to the lowest common denominator of taste and sentiment. The result is that music-hall songs, the best of which were created to exploit the voice, style and personality of a particular star who was often concerned to make a social rather than a purely musical point, often had not only a far greater vitality of style and rhythm but also, in their own way, a far more convincing musicality.

Thus English popular music came to inhabit a backwater from which it was difficult to reach any mainstream. The story of American popular music echoes that of English light music until it reaches the late nineteenth century, when the music of American negroes became not simply quaint but intellectually and socially acceptable. Ragtime became an international style; it reached England before the first World War, and jazz, its development, with an intellectual structure of its own, followed without any interval. Part of its appeal was the fact that it grew out of a clear social situation and expressed social realities; the high spirits, humour and ebullience of the jazz style matched the natural optimism of an America which, until the 1920s, could think of little reason for pessimism; after the first World War, when the United States for the first time learnt what were to be the realities of twentieth-century life, the pathos of American negro music found its place in the jazz-oriented style which became the world's popular music for not only the social amusements of the Western world at large but also for such works as the operas in which Kurt Weill found music for Berthold Brecht's vision of the final paroxysms of capitalism. This music, which occupied the dance bands of the United States and Europe, was in itself another simplification; it diluted the Afro-American music which demands a receptiveness which the listener to popular music is usually disinclined to reach; it was the music of black America simplified for white Americans.

Light music is invariably a simplification of things current, or recently current, in other musical spheres, and the jazz-orientated music which became an international style for the twentieth century was a reaction against the negative politeness and lack of vitality which had befallen the descendants of the Strausses, of Offenbach and of Sullivan. It succeeded a music of unexciting mildness and effete good manners—the good manners which are entirely negative and not a refinement of passion and energy. In the United States the new style was always a natural way of musical speech, and it can be listened to with pleasure in songs that are its classics; it was more exclusive than the domestic Wagner of the younger Strauss and opened no doors into more extensive musical worlds, so that it trapped lesser composers into routines of composition which diluted its basic African style with nothing stronger than water, so that whilst a composer like Kurt Weill could use the American popular style with point and wit, the bulk of mid-twentieth-century light music offered nothing to reflect any social reality, to engage the mind or even to startle the listener. Jazz itself demands attentive listening; it has its forms and its musical order as well as its open spaces for often outrageous instrumental virtuosity. What came to replace it in the 1960s was a popular style far more undernourished than any of the earlier dilutions of more demanding styles. 'Rock' and 'pop', the 1950s reaction and its 1960s offspring, are styles in which every other element of expression is sacrificed to the often spurious vitality of mechanical rhythms.

This music became the music of adolescence, a fact which gives it unusual social significance. The American cult of youth is probably a natural result of the development of a society built by immigration from all the European countries of adults who cling to their own languages and national traditions in the land which they adopted only to find that their children, born or at least educated in the United States, speaking the language of the new home-land and mastering its culture, become the guides and leaders of their parents. If a 'generation gap' (to use today's cant phrase) is an inevitable, naturally unobjectionable though sometimes irritating part of the business of 'growing up', it became in the United States an unnatural situation in which adult experience tended to yield to youth's mastery of new linguistic and social ways, a mastery too easily exploited by advertisers, politicians or any-one who found advantages in the exploitation of inexperience. It created an attitude—as twentieth-century attitudes tend to spread from the United States—which became international.

Thus pop, in its various manifestations, came to balance the attitude of those serious composers who found their natural speech in music too far re-moved from that of their hearers to win a reliable audience and who there-fore ceased to regard musical life as a tripartite agreement between com-poser, performer and audience; as much of what might appeal to the young because of its novelty, its daring and its brilliance in the concert hall became too complex for assimilation, the music of the young became increasingly elementary, undernourished in style and limited in vocabulary.

Therefore pop tends to have a restrictive influence on its natural audi-ence. It began as a reaction against the tepid, jazz-orientated style of the 1930s and 1940s, which, by the 1950s, had very little vitality left with which to appeal to the young. The successful composers in the style (they deserve, perhaps the epithet-begging term, 'great'), Gershwin, Jerome Kern, Cole Porter and a few others, were either dead or reaching the end of their careers, and though many of their songs have survived them, light music lives on novelty succeeding novelty. The weariness of their style opened the door for the mechanically rhythmic style of 'Rock 'n' Roll' in 1954 and 1955, and for the musically more interested period of 'skiffle', in which the young made music for themselves with whatever instruments—home-made if necessary—were available. The piano, for the first time since jazz had become respectable, ceased to count, for even a poor piano is not only a relatively costly instrument but also one not easily transportable to concerts or easily mastered by a musician whose contribution to any event depends on enthusuasm rather than training.

Skiffle was, by the nature of its performers, a return to a more lyrical style than rock, and it asked for a very small instrumental group: guitars, one for melody, one to provide the bass and one to join a percussionist in marking the rhythm, together with whatever instruments could be available in the style of primitive jazz, like a tea chest bass and a corrugated washboard in the 'rhythm section' became the source of a music meant for its own performers rather than for an audience; it was a style through which enthusiastic young amateur performers could explore and expand their own musicality. Any material simple enough appealed to the performers and turned the attention of many groups of young and almost self-trained musicians towards folk music, creating a passion that grew, bifurcated and survived its division. There were, among folk musicians of the new generation, those with whom music went hand in hand with social and political dissatisfactions; they saw in many folk songs an attitude to life and to society which could be applied to the present and suggest a style in which the ills of twentieth-century life could be expressed; both in Britain and in the United States, for many folk-song enthusiasts, the term became one which combined a genuine love for old music with an adherence to pacifist, left-wing, generally 'progressive' political and social beliefs often naive but admirable in their sincerity and dedication. Whilst most of the music of the young celebrated nothing beside the experiences of youth, and these in often pathetic simplification, the enthusiasm for folk song created a large number of young musicians whose music was closely related, even if naively related, to social realities. Other folk-song enthusiasts turned to extreme puritanism, rejecting any modernisation of their chosen musical way by accompaniment or adaptation. Whilst skiffle was trodden underfoot in the 1960s by the triumph of pop, the new folk-song revival, both in Britain and in the United States, continued to hold its broad front—from the singers whose concern is social protest to those who maintain a strictly purist attitude—throughout the pop period.

Rock 'n' Roll was unremittingly noisy music, utilising the brass of the standard 'dance band' as well as percussion. Skiffle and pop slimmed down the band to a group with the guitar as its standard instrument; the skiffle group was content with 'acoustic' guitars, but pop demands the electronic instrument which compensates in the eyes of young players and their audiences for its limited range of colour and effect by its capacity for filling any auditorium with overwhelming sound. It is loud, simple, appealing in its concentration upon elementary music and elementary words. In the hands of the Beatles, who for a time were not only the most celebrated musicians to rise to power through this style but also its most resourceful musicians (a fact which has led many authorities to exaggerate their attainments to the point of silliness), these elementary musical facts created a harmonic style which enriched what was essentially old-fashioned and never very far from the harmonic processes of Victorian hymnology with passing notes, or passing chords, which provided the sophisticated listener with a pleasant surprise.

The style, however, is international. The fact that the Beatles spoke and sang in a regional English accent no more impeded their success in the United States than an American accent reduced the appeal of popular translantic stars, and Europe seems to breed groups whose natural language for performance is English or Americanised English. Part of the appeal of the Beatles was that they appeared on any stage simply as four unexceptional young men who did nothing beyond the capacity of anybody who put his mind to such achievements; there was nothing obvious in their performance (their talent being kept carefully undercover) to indicate that these were hardly four ordinary young men with whom the audience could not completely identify.

The Beatles' original rejection of performance gimmicks died, perhaps through shrewd management, perhaps as a result of the adoration of their 'fans', until, since their departure, tricks of performance are probably more important than the quality of a song within the idiom in deciding any group's success. Pop is the first music to depend on gramophone and tape recording rather than on live performance for its success; thus it is forced to become a part of a complex business and financial world and to run the risk or face the consequences of commercial exploitation. One historian of the 'pop scene' (it is worthy of note that pop needs its own verbal as well as musical language) noted that pop is largely determined by changing fashions.[2] Pop not only created fashions in dress, hair-style and externals; it creates and discards musical fashions in a determination always to have something different that can be applauded by an audience inexperienced enough to believe that 'latest' is necessarily synonymous with 'best'. Nevertheless, while maintaining the illusion that this is any young person's music, shorn of the difficulty and the mystique of traditional musicians, the Beatles' later, more ambitious and often attractive records co-opted the services of orchestral musicians playing instruments usually outlawed by the basic principles of pop. A number of admirable instrumentalists took part in such recorded performances without acknowledgement, adopting an anonymity which seems at times to be a deliberate attempt to cheat the young.

The creative and performing world of pop music is dominated by the 'charts' which, week by week, estimate the most popular songs available by a calculation of their commercial success through sales. The charts in themselves suggest that what is most popular is often most widely advertised and

[2] Richard Mabey: *The Pop Process.* Hutchinson Educational. London, 1969. p. 38.

most frequently heard by radio from the stations which exist to provide the young with a ceaseless flow of their music. There was a period in the late 1960s when, for more than a month, the charts in Britain were headed by an innocuous and undistinguished waltz tune, sang unusually 'straight', celebrating the 'good old days'. 'Those were the Days', the song in question, delivered a message dogmatically unsympathetic to most pop songs and their audiences in a style which adolescents normally deride; but it was extremely popular for a considerable length of time. More recently, a Welsh hymn tune has held pride of place, played not by a conventional 'group' but by a military band; if such phenomena suggest that conditioning by advertising has not been totally successful among the pop audience, it also suggests the reverse proposition—that the pop audience accepts whatever advertisers insist that it enjoys. At the same time, the advertising of pop music suggests to an inexperienced young devotee that whatever happened before or happens outside the closed and inevitably commercial world of pop is irrelevant to the lives of those who accept exploitation.

Thus the attractive idea of pop as an international style which has its audience among the young and will develop with them is made doubtful by the methods used to promulgate the music. Pop has not been a static form, and it has created players and composers whose ambitions are not satisfied by its strict conventions. Its development, however, has led to the emergence of a 'progressive' pop which depends on relatively untrained composers with little experience of music outside their own speciality; the liveliest and most imaginative pop music comes from the world of the groups working directly for audiences within a convention which, like all conventions, can be strictly observed or cleverly expanded. Nevertheless, those whose primary concern is the quality of music and its communication cannot but be anxious about the commercial pressures on pop music. 'Is it, or was it,' writes Richard Mabey, 'a spontaneous creation at all? Or has it been skilfully manufactured by an adult world that wants as much as possible of its offspring's £1,000,000,000-a-year spending money?'[3]

As long ago as 1934, in *Music Ho!*, Constant Lambert predicted the death of the listener who, in the terminology of the time, he described as 'middle-brow' as distinct from the devotee of jazz and jazz-orientated dance music on the one hand and the concert and opera-goer on the other. He was prophetically envisaging a world in which music and musicians were driven into one or other of two camps—the totally undemanding and usually uncreative on the one hand and the increasingly remote and 'serious' on the other, with no means of communication between the two. Recent developments have left no space in life for salon music, for the palm court orchestra or the cinema organist; there is no twentieth-century, post-

[3] *Ibid.* p. 35.

World War Two equivalent to the Victorian ballad in any country of Western Europe. In so far as this disappearance is the consequence of the commercialism which seems likely to prevent the liberation of pop from its commercially profitable conventions, the present situation is sinister; our light music is tied to commercial interests while the *avant-garde* musician eagerly accepts the notion of a divorce between the composer and the audience with whom it is his duty, as it should be his pleasure, to communicate.

10

Music in the United States

Because the bulk of the earliest settlers in what became the United States were British, the pattern of music-making among Americans at first followed the pattern created by musicians in English cities. By 1750, some sort of concert system was growing in a number of American cities; perhaps Charleston, in South Carolina, was musically the most advanced of them simply because it was closest to England in manners and social customs; life in South Carolina offered more leisure than life in the New England colonies, and none of the southern states developed the intolerance to any form of public entertainment which had to be combated in Massachusetts and which spread throughout the northern colonies. Concerts in Charleston, and subsequently in the other major cities, were semi-amateur events in which music teachers and the orchestra of the theatre collaborated with enthusiastic amateurs. Charleston, though small, with some eight thousand people in 1750, was the wealthy 'gateway' to the richly agricultural south. Before it developed any orchestral organisation its citizens founded a St. Cecilia Society for the performance of choral works, and the town's musical pre-eminence, perhaps, explains why Theodore Pachelbel, son of the great Nuremberg organist, who emigrated to America in 1733 to become organist at Newport, Rhode Island, and was responsible in 1736 for organising the first concert in New York of which any record remains, moved to Charleston a year later, when he was given a benefit concert there, and remained for the rest of his life.

New York's music was, apparently, waiting for someone like Pachelbel to bring it to life. The size of its population, the extensiveness of its business interests and its growing wealth made it a good city for immigrant musicians who realised that, whatever other possibilities might open up for them, the essential foundation of their American careers would be a teaching practice as extensive as they could make it.

Puritan Boston, too, had at least occasional concerts from 1731, and even Quaker Philadelphia, where music was at first distrusted as merely a worldly amusement, began to regard music as permissible in 1757. Twelve years later, an opera house had been opened there and the gentlemen of an amateur orchestra began to play with the theatre's professional orchestra on opera nights.[1]

[1] Gilbert Chase: *America's Music*. McGraw Hill, New York, 1955. p. 84.

Semi-professional music-making continued in a growing number of American cities, as it does in the United States to this day in many community orchestras which flourish in cities which cannot support a completely professional orchestra: European visitors to the concerts of the Fort Worth Symphony Orchestra as recently as 1969 would probably have been startled to find three nuns, properly habited, among the orchestra's violinists; further investigation of the orchestra would have revealed that while many of the players earned their living as teachers of their instruments —no other regular musical work is available to them—many of the players are completely amateur. The structure of such orchestras, except for the presence of a salaried music director-conductor, has hardly changed since the early days of music in the United States. It was in a relatively few cities of the industrialised, commerically active and affluent states of the north-east that completely professional orchestras arose in the second half of the nineteenth century and brought with them a new and often fruitful form of patronage.

Boston, for example, has a musical history which reaches back to the early eighteenth century. The first regular, professional orchestra to be heard there grew up round the German Gottlieb Graupner in 1810; it followed in the footsteps of a predominantly amateur Euterpe Society. In 1815 the Handel and Haydn Society, an amateur choral society with its own orchestra, began a long and fruitful history, devoted to 'cultivating and improving correct taste in the performance of sacred music'. University music at nearby Harvard, first effectively organised in 1808, grew into the concert-giving Harvard Musical Association. The Handel and Haydn Society, in 1823, commissioned an oratorio from Beethoven, who took the offer seriously enough to note it, although he never began the composition.

In 1842, however, the professional musicians of New York, most of whom played in the orchestras of the city's theatre, decided to establish their own orchestra and concert society on the model of the Philharmonic Society in London. Less than fifty years before this date, New York, for all its financial and commercial importance, had counted for less in commercial prestige than Boston and for less as a business centre than Philadelphia. But since the Erie Canal had been opened to traffic in 1825, New York had grown enormously and had some four hundred thousand inhabitants by the 1840s. Its growth had attracted immigrant musicians eager to establish themselves in regular employment, so that a large number of theatre musicians, most of whom were also teachers, were looking for ways of satisfying musical ambitions and of augmenting their salaries by organising regular orchestral concerts. The death in 1838 of Daniel Schlesinger, a musician popular in New York, had been the occasion of a memorial concert given by an orchestra of sixty instrumentalists gathered mostly from the New York theatres. Despite what seems to have been the barest minimum of rehearsal, the concert was successful enough to demonstrate an appetite for such events. By 1842, the Philharmonic Orchestra, a co-operative body, had been built, and it gave its first concert in the December of that year.

The original members of the orchestra created a self-governing organisation, employing a salaried conductor whom they elected, and paying a librarian; the members divided the profits of the concerts among themselves at the end of each session, all members taking equal shares. Thus the concerts were necessarily a spare-time occupation of the players, who continued to depend for their livelihood on their work in the theatres. The orchestra met only at rehearsals or concerts, and necessary business discussions consumed the exiguous rehearsal time, so that players not attracted by business discussions often did not bother to attend. Naturally, when members found themselves facing a clash of engagements, it was the Philharmonic Concert, the less profitable of any two engagements, which took second place. The orchestra originally gave membership to any musicians who wanted it—twenty-two violinists and four cellists, for example, at one stage of its early history. Its audience, most of the members subscribers whose advance payments made the whole operation possible, was both fashionable and generous, but it did not provide sufficient money to entice good players from Europe. Nor were the musical ambitions of the audience as high as those of the orchestra, so that the quality of the programmes had to be diluted to win audiences sufficient to support the concerts. In addition, distances in the United States militated against any comparison of one orchestra with another, and, therefore, of any comparison of standards. Though there was considerable musical activity in both Boston and Philadelphia, there was no competition between orchestras and no improvement evolving from comparison of standards and methods; the United States did not, therefore, at that time create patrons exigently demanding the highest standards of performance.

In 1848 a group of central European musicians, exiles from the revolutions of 1848, reached the United States and banded themselves together as the Germania Orchestra. As unsuccessful revolutionaries or sympathisers with unsuccessful revolutions, their music did not stop at Beethoven and Mendelssohn but went on to Wagner and Liszt; they had been members of efficient European orchestras and, beginning from Boston, they toured the United States, reaching as far from the east coast as St. Louis, suggesting orchestral standards at that time out of reach of any American orchestras. Eventually the members of the Germania Orchestra went their individual ways, joining existing American orchestras to the orchestras' advantage. Carl Bergmann, one of the Germania's cellists, became conductor of the New York Philharmonic and, in the words of Theodore Thomas, the first American conductor to impose high standards on his players; Bergmann, said Thomas in an address when he left New York to take charge of the new

Chicago Symphony Orchestra in 1891, was 'the first conductor to give us an insight into our great composers'.[2]

Louis Antoine Jullien, if he did nothing quite so high-minded as Bergmann, showed American audiences what a really well-drilled, thoroughly rehearsed ensemble of good players was capable of. Looking for fresh worlds to conquer and another wealthy audience to enthrall, in 1853 Jullien took the key members of his London orchestra to play to American audiences recruiting American instrumentalists as he arrived to tour the United States from Boston to New York with divers concerts on route, travelling as far as New Orleans. During a two-month stay in New York he conducted nightly concerts with programmes perhaps rather less ambitious than those his London audiences had come to enjoy; he had visited the United States to create the sort of audiences he had found and educated in England, and succeeded in doing what he wanted. Those who attended his concerts were struck by such everyday matters as the fact that his violinists bowed together—some indication, perhaps, of the standards of orchestral playing which his visit disturbed.

It was Theodore Thomas, the son of German parents who arrived in the United States in 1845, when he was ten years old and who played in Jullien's orchestra when he was eighteen, who did more than anyone else to raise American musical standards. In 1863 he formed an orchestra with which he gave regular concerts in New York and *al fresco* light music concerts in Central Park. The orchestra was his own, founded, organised, paid and trained by Thomas himself with the support of wealthy sympathisers. Because his orchestra was paid a regular salary and not simply working for a share of the box-office takings, its players rehearsed and played together with a regularity the New York Philharmonic could not achieve. Thomas and his orchestra, moreover, toured indefatigably, creating an audience for regular concerts in Cincinnati and Chicago as well as playing in musically conscious centres like Boston and Philadelphia.

Thomas had joined the New York Philharmonic Society in 1852, and in 1877 was elected its conductor; the following year he became Director of the Cincinnati College of Music, an institution inspired by the annual festival concerts he gave there. In 1879 he returned to New York to conduct the Philharmonic and to revive his own orchestra. In 1891 he became conductor of the Chicago Orchestra, which changed its name to the Theodore Thomas Orchestra, and then, in 1902, it became the Chicago Symphony Orchestra; Thomas kept the conductorship until his death in 1905.

Thomas's own orchestra had created a specifically American form of musical finance. His concerts could not be supported to his own satisfac-

[2] John H. Mueller: *The American Symphony Orchestra*. John Calder, London, 1958. p. 33.

tion simply by the proceeds of the box office, although he played to large audiences, and as a professional musician, popular and well paid though he was, he could not afford to finance it himself; the money he needed came from wealthy patrons of music who were prepared to back their faith in music, or in the abilities of Theodore Thomas; or in both.

When Thomas was offered the conductorship of the New York Philharmonic in 1877 the offer was an attempt to rescue an ailing institution which had come to depend for support on its prestige rather than on the quality of its performances. Members who had for the sake of their livelihood to regard the Philharmonic as a mere second string, and a weak one at that, could not attain the standards imposed by Thomas on his fiercely drilled players; absenteeism alone was enough to ensure that. Nor was the Philharmonic Orchestra's repertoire, designed not to startle old-fashioned audiences whose attitudes were as much social as musical, sufficient to maintain the level of excitement and interest which other concerts had reached. The result was the creation of the New York Symphony Orchestra in 1878. Not only did it seem that a city of well over a million inhabitants could happily support two orchestras; the Symphony Orchestra's motive power was its founder, Leopold Damrosch, German by birth, who had found his way to New York as conductor of the Arion Männersanverein after some conducting experience in Breslau. Damrosch was a friend of the 'progressive' school in German music and believed that he could find not only finance for a rival orchestra to the Philharmonic but also audiences for more adventurous concerts than the Philharmonic presented. The acceptance of the Philharmonic conductorship by Thomas meant that the admirably trained instrumentalists of the Thomas Orchestra were mostly unemployed—Thomas had taken the best of them with him to the Philharmonic—so that Damrosch had the foundations of an orchestra from the players whom Thomas could no longer occupy. With the financial guarantee of men who were great powers in American finance, and the adherence of New York 'Society' won by his natural geniality and friendliness, Damrosch set out to enliven New York's music in spite of the enmity of Thomas, who explained to Damrosch that it was his habit to 'crush' anyone who ventured to oppose him.

The infirm Philharmonic suffered another severe blow in 1883 with the establishment of the Metropolitan Opera House; the greater glamour of opera and a determination that it would bring the greatest European stars to New York, so that opera in America should have the same prestige as opera in Milan, Vienna or Dresden, created excitements beyond those of the concert hall, and New Yorkers who had felt that their social position had been kept up by attendance at the Philharmonic—after all, it had the prestige of being one of the world's oldest concert societies—was overshadowed by the social glamour of the opera, which drew audiences, publicity and funds from the wealthy within a considerable area round New York.

The splendour of the Metropolitan overshadowed all earlier attempts to provide New York with opera, and crushed all later operatic ventures for a long time to come. The repertoire of the 'Met' was always popular; new or controversial works were resolutely avoided, while those which had won the adoration of audiences everywhere were produced with the greatest possible lavishness not only in the quality of singers but in costumes, décor and all the ancillary services of opera. Efforts to provide opera at prices which the average New Yorker could afford failed, in spite of determined efforts, until 1944, when the New York City Opera presented its first short season and succeeded to so marked an extent that it has grown to create its own stars and to follow a policy far more adventurous than the Metropolitan dared to implement until the lesser house had shown that tastes were less circumscribed than the Metropolitan's tradition had imagined.

Damrosch's early days with the New York Symphony Society were not easy, and membership of the Symphony Orchestra, like membership of the Philharmonic, necessarily occupied only part of a player's time, so that the new orchestra had many of the problems of absenteeism which weakened the old. The final departure of Theodore Thomas from the Philharmonic Society in 1891, when the veteran conductor moved to Chicago to establish the Chicago Symphony Orchestra, enabled Damrosch to secure the financial backing of several of the legendary rich of the United States who had previously supported Thomas during the days of his independence. With Carnegie, Vanderbilt, Rockefeller and Morgan ready to finance a more ambitious policy, Damrosch brought Adolf Brodsky from England to lead the orchestra, established daily rehearsals and announced his new ensemble as 'the only permanent orchestra in New York'. Unfortunately, despite the fabulous wealth of his patrons, by 1898 the guarantee fund they had established was exhausted, and for four years the Symphony Orchestra's concerts were abandoned.

By this time, however, the Boston Symphony Orchestra was established on a firmer basis than either of the New York ensembles. In 1881 Henry Lee Higginson, the son of a wealthy Boston financier, decided to organise a permanent orchestra of sixty musicians to whom he would pay a regular yearly salary while subsidising the concerts they would give. He anticipated a deficit of $50,000, to meet which he was ready to provide a capital of $1,000,000. There was a considerable audience for music in Boston, a city which regarded itself as the cultural capital of the United States, and in the surrounding centres like Harvard; concerts in Boston and in Harvard were anything but infrequent, and the Handel and Haydn Society operated on a guarantee fund created by wealthy Bostonians. Higginson, originally a would-be concert pianist who had studied in Vienna, created a new system of patronage; like an Esterhazy prince he would completely support the orchestra, employing its personnel on a permanent basis to give weekly concerts of 'the highest type' of music; admission prices were to be low and the conductor himself was to be solely responsible for the ensemble's artistic policy. Unlike an Esterhazy, Higginson stuck scrupulously to the rule he had established and never sought to usurp the conductor's artistic primacy. He took care of the financial and extra-musical administration even when, in the orchestra's early days, Wilhelm Gericke (whom Higginson brought from Vienna to be its second conductor) followed a policy of dedicated, Mahlerlian ruthlessness in his determination to achieve the highest musical standards, dismissing unsatisfactory players and replacing them with instrumentalists brought from Germany and Austria.

Gericke's predecessor, the baritone–conductor–composer Georg Henschel, had been thirty-one when he conducted the Boston Symphony Orchestra's first concert, and though he lacked the experience needed to achieve standards comparable to those which Gericke pursued, his enthusiasm, panache, dedication and likable personality made the concerts popular. It was Gericke who made a real, disciplined ensemble out of players who often played for other organisations under a variety of conductors and were unaccustomed to severe orchestral discipline; Higginson supported him by refusing permission to his orchestra to play for any other concerts except those of the Handel and Haydn Society. Having worked himself into a breakdown by 1889, Gericke was replaced by Nikisch for four years, and then by Emil Pauer. In 1898 Gericke returned, and in 1900 a new concert hall, Symphony Hall, was built by public subscription. Until Higginson's death in 1919, not only did he remain totally responsible for the increasingly huge expense of the orchestra but ensured that the conductors, whom he personally selected, were musicians of the highest calibre. Influenced by the anti-German feeling aroused by the first World War and a political scandal which rose around Karl Muck, conductor from 1906 to 1908 and again from 1912 to 1918 (Muck found himself in a controversy over the demand that he should play the American National Anthem before concerts), Higginson, whose personal tastes were almost exclusively for the German classics, appointed Henri Rabaud in 1918 and Pierre Monteux in 1919, supporting their widening of the orchestra's repertoire in a city where music, to most listeners, meant German music and where Monteux's delight in works by Debussy and Stravinsky was anything but immediately popular and where his undemonstrative, bandmasterly style disappointed audiences who wished to see a conductor expressing and visibly shaping the music by gesture.

Higginson was able to leave no endowment for his orchestra; its maintenance had left him with little money to leave as he had been forced, during the last few years of his life, to face annual deficits of about

$100,000. Since his retirement from business, he had recruited three hundred guarantors to ensure the orchestra's continuance and the maintenance of its high standards, but their guarantee was not sufficient to face the huge annual deficit, and it was left to the very wealthy to fill Higginson's place.

In 1895 the Cincinnati Symphony Orchestra came into being. It was the indirect offspring of Theodore Thomas's earlier tours in a city which had a considerable German population with the usual vocal groups—*Liedertafel*, *Liederkranz* and *Männerchor*—which were the result of German-American nostalgia for a lost fatherland. Since 1873, Cincinnati had been the scene of regular biennial festivals given by Thomas and a stalwart patron, Mrs Maria Nicholas Longworthy. In 1878 a College of Music was opened, financed by a group of extremely rich citizens, and for its first two years Thomas was appointed its director at a salary of $10,000. Among Thomas's great qualities seems to have been a stubborn intractability which had made him a magnificent musical pioneer incapable of compromise; he was also apparently incapable of working under direction, and after two years he was replaced by a virtual nonentity.

Naturally, Cincinnati had had regular concerts before 1895, mounted by orchestras which rose and failed to survive. The most notable had been a Philharmonic Orchestra, inaugurated in 1857, on the same co-operative lines as the New York Philharmonic and sharing with its model the difficulties which naturally afflict any orchestra whose members are compelled to earn the bulk of their livings by other activities and therefore to sacrifice it whenever they are faced by a clash of interests. A private patron organised an orchestra and choral society in 1865, building it a small concert hall; other patrons, led by a Mr. Springer (who himself paid $200,000 towards the cost), built a larger hall for concerts and festivals in 1875. The permanent orchestra eventually founded in 1895 was planned by a group of women who organised its finance by private benefactions. In 1909 pledges of support to the extent of $50,000 a year for each of the next five years were secured, the players were offered contracts holding them for a complete season and the young Leopold Stokowski, who had arrived in the United States from England in 1904 and was quite literally at the beginning of his exciting conducting career, was appointed conductor.

The next of the major orchestras to appear was that at Philadelphia, another city which had a musical history antedating the American War of Independence. Philadelphia had never been without an orchestra, though it had never employed musicians who rivalled the prestige of those of New York and Boston; the formation of a Musical Fund Society in 1820 had led to regular concerts and performances of opera, mounted to 'care for decayed musicians and their families'. In 1856 the Germania Orchestra, another self-governing ensemble organised on the lines of the New York

Philharmonic, was as active as the Musical Fund Society; neither body, however, had any financial organisation or the ability to reach the standards set by Damrosch with the New York Symphony Orchestra and Gericke with the Boston Symphony Orchestra, both of which visited Philadelphia regularly. Local patriotism, a considerable force in American life in the nineteenth century, was outraged and in 1900 the President of the Musical Fund Society called a meeting to raise funds to establish a permanent orchestra, and guarantors contributed $15,000 to support an inaugural season of six concerts to be conducted by Hans Scheel, who had been assistant to Hans von Bülow in Germany and had already made an American reputation in Chicago and San Francisco. Like Gericke, Scheel created a new orchestra, dismissing players and replacing them with experienced instrumentalists from Europe. Money continued to be supplied by the guarantors, satisfied by the response to the first season, and a Women's Committee, formed in 1904, undertook the task of raising funds and persuading the public to regard the orchestra as a social necessity. Scheel died in 1907, and after an unimpressive interregnum of five years, Stokowski was appointed conductor. Stokowski, by a combination of musical brilliance, ruthlessness, charm, good looks, expert knowledge dressed up as eccentric charlatanry, and remarkable organising ability was able to make the orchestra the most famous in the United States if not in the entire world and to mould it into a superb virtuoso instrument. He secured endowments substantial enough to allow ample rehearsal for novelties and for familiar works and to recruit the finest players he could find. For the first performance in America of Mahler's Eighth Symphony, in 1916, Stokowski found additional funds to the extent of $15,000 and, by skilful publicity, was able to make a profit on nine repeated performances in Philadelphia itself and in both Boston and New York. Stokowski's twenty-four years with the Philadelphia Orchestra were full of excitements whipped up to keep the orchestra in the public eye, to make it newsworthy, to attract attention; Stokowski made the orchestra a regular broadcasting attraction in the early days of radio, took it into the television studios for the first television symphony concert in the history of American broadcasting, gave ambitious seasons of opera—the one area where his enterprise and flair failed—and became a film actor in order to take his orchestra into the world of cinema in the sentimental little film *A Hundred Men and a Girl*. In Walt Disney's *Fantasia* he lent the orchestra to cartoon treatments of Bach, Beethoven and Stravinsky, amongst other music, only to find when the film was completed that the visual interpretations which were a counterpoint to his performances were not entirely sympathetic to his view of the works involved.

Stokowski proved that an American orchestra, given a Stokowski to conduct it, could survive financial storms and flourish. But for all the sensationalism of his work in Philadelphia, the apparent charlatan was a superbly sensitive expert in sound quality and tone colour, an undaunted champion of new music who refused to surrender his right to experiment both in repertoire and in the organisation of the orchestra.

But by the time that Stokowski was demonstrating to Philadelphia that the musical life was a matter of irrepressible excitement, the self-governing orchestral financing itself from box-office receipts could no longer hope to survive in the climate which had brought Nikisch to Boston and Arthur Seidl and Gustav Mahler from Leipzig and Vienna respectively to New York; Stokowski's career in Philadelphia was an object lesson to all American concert organisations in the art of establishing a symphony orchestra, building its repertory and integrating it into the community it served. It proved, too, the importance of finding conductors who would create an atmosphere of almost dangerous excitement and vitality.

The want of a sufficiently compelling conductor forced the New York Symphony Orchestra into silence between 1898 to 1903, and in 1907 falling attendances and the visits of the secure Boston Symphony Orchestra almost destroyed the New York Philharmonic. In 1901 Andrew Carnegie had become President of the Philharmonic Society, and Walter Damrosch, Leopold's son, had accepted its conductorship in 1902; together the new President and the new conductor worked to reorganise the now historic orchestra; Carnegie established a fund which would guarantee the Society $25,000 a year for four years on condition that the orchestra would reorganise its establishment and enlarge its governing body of fifteen players to include seven representatives of the new financial powers who would assist them, make changes in personnel and give more and more thoroughly rehearsed concerts; the established board of governors, determined to remain masters of their own orchestra, refused, Damrosch withdrew his acceptance of the conductorship and revived the New York Symphony Orchestra. The Philharmonic carried on with the support of John D. Rockefeller and relays of guest conductors, and with the adventitious excitements such changes of personality and style inevitably bring. Most of the concerts of 1906 and 1907 were conducted by Vassily Ilyitch Safonov, whose brilliant handling of Russian music at first created a deserved sensation but eventually showed Safonov's limitations in the works of the German and Austrian repertoire to which the Philharmonic subscribers were wedded. The 1907 concerts were badly attended and the orchestra at last realised that its co-operative, democratic methods could not survive in the new, high-powered world of American twentieth-century music.

In 1908 Mrs. George R. Sheldon, the wife of a banker and republican politician, assembled representatives of 'the best families in the city' to save the Philharmonic and raised a fund of $90,000 for three years; among the contributors were Carnegie, Pierpont Morgan and Joseph Pulitzer. The conditions of this subsidy were harsher than those originally offered by

Carnegie five years before. The self-governing status of the orchestra, its right to frame its own policy and to elect conductors were all to go; old players were to be replaced by new; a board of control would be established by the financial powers on which the orchestra would be represented and more concerts, all more thoroughly rehearsed, would be given. Safonov was to be replaced by Mahler, who had conducted the German repertoire at the Metropolitan Opera for the previous two seasons and whose mastery in the opera house had dazzled New York. When Mahler died, in 1911, after storms and disillusionment, Pulitzer also died, leaving almost a million dollars to the Philharmonic on condition that it established itself as a permanent orchestra, created a list of a thousand contributing members, reduced its prices of admission and kept its programmes 'not too severely classical'. A new, still rather obscure but thoroughly efficient conductor, Joseph Stransky, was appointed. Stransky, with programmes weighted towards Liszt, Wagner and Dvořák (composers of whom Pulitzer thoroughly approved), played to standing room only.

As the basic conditions of twentieth-century music put an end to the orchestral democracy of the New York Philharmonic, the retirement and death of Higginson ended the era of individual patronage. Higginson had spent a vast fortune to support the Boston Symphony Orchestra for more than thirty years, maintaining an ensemble of the highest class while following a policy of musical non-interference. Unlike the great patrons—the Frederick the Greats and the Prince Nicholas Esterhazas of eighteenth-century Europe—and unlike Joseph Pulitzer too, he had never demanded the inclusion in programmes of music he liked and the exclusion of music which did not appeal to him. By the time of his death, not even his dedication and determination could preserve financial autocracy; the supply of instrumentalists from Europe had dried up as a result of the first World War and the American Musicians' Union, strengthened by the new demands for American players, fought a long-drawn-out and ultimately successful war against the concert organisations for rates of pay which themselves defied the individual generosity of the greatest of patrons. Though patrons whose wealth, like that of Carnegie, Rockefeller, Morgan and others, is belittled by the use of the adjective 'wealthy', provided vast sums for the support of American orchestras, the task of financing music in the United States was a job for committees of millionaires, not for single men of great wealth working alone.

With the development of group sponsorship came the growth of Ladies' Committees formed by the wives of wealthy patrons who tended to represent culture and 'Society' as their husbands represented finance; such committees tended to become thorns in the flesh of conductors and musical directors. Alma Mahler described with some eloquence the way in which her husband's originally indulgent amusement at the activities of the

Ladies' Committee of the New York Philharmonic Society turned to rage when he found that the Committee tried to limit his authority as musical director, attempting to control his programme planning and backing its wishes by appeals to the governing body of the orchestra.[3] A Ladies' Committee which, in times of crisis, would be both persistent and effective in raising funds and which kept the orchestra in the minds of the most affluent and influential members of 'Society' was not an organisation to be treated with Mahlerian disrespect. Mahler, whose refusal to compromise in Vienna had led him to disregard the wishes even of members of the imperial royal family, found that he lacked the qualities necessary for dealing effectively with a Ladies' Committee; the young Stokowski had them, and moulded a Ladies' Committee in Philadelphia into a powerful source of financial and other support for his orchestra.

But the intensely competitive organisation of American music, especially of its orchestras, insisted always on the finest performers directed by the most spectacular conductors, even when the spectacular element in the conductor's work was the almost complete, calm immobility of a Fritz Reiner. Mahler, Toscanini and Mengelberg conducted in New York, with the young John Barbirolli and Rodzinski. In Boston Karl Muck was succeeded by Monteux, Koussevitzky and Charles Munch; Rodzinski and Kubelik conducted the Chicago Symphony Orchestra and when, after twenty-four legendary years, Stokowski left Philadelphia, he was succeeded by the almost equally glamorous Eugene Ormandy. The Cleveland Orchestra, founded in 1918 as a reliable second-rank, provincial ensemble, in 1946 found the formidable Georg Szell to raise it to a place among the great orchestras of the world. In America a conductor had to be flamboyant, romantic, eloquent, extravagant in one way or another; he had to dominate not only an orchestra but also its audience. The triumph of the Nazis in Germany and Austria sent not only Schoenberg and Hindemith to teach in the United States and to exercise a momentous influence on American taste; Klemperer, Reiner, Szell and Bruno Walter were America's profit from the Nazi revolution. The situation in twentieth-century America was like that of nineteenth-century England until the second World War persuaded the United States audience that native talents were not to be neglected or derided, but the United States provided the cream of the musical profession with possibilities of the richest rewards and the greatest adulation. As early as 1892, the critic Eduard Hanslick had sourly written in his journal: 'America may not be the promised land of music, but it is the promised land of musicians.'[4]

The consequences for the American composer were rather similar to

[3] Alma Mahler: *Gustav Mahler: Memories and Letters*. John Murray, London, 1946. p. 115.
[4] Hanslick: *Aus dem Tagebuch eines Musikers*. Berlin, 1892. p. 58.

those which had arrested the development of English music a century before. The New York Philharmonic Society, at its inception in 1842, included among its rules an attempt to encourage the work of native composers:

> If any grand orchestral compositions, such as overtures or symphonies, shall be presented to the Society, they being composed in this country, the Society shall perform one every season provided a committee of five appointed by the Government [of the Society] shall have approved and recommended the composition.[5]

The rule, of course, makes no mention of the nationality of the composer, but only of the place of origin of the work, so that the encouragement to American music was no more than minimal. Anyhow, the first conductor of the New York Philharmonic Orchestra who seems to have paid any real attention to the possibilities of American Music was Mahler, who in 1910 conducted concerts of English and American compositions.

Protests against the German hegemony exercised over New York concerts had come long before. In the 1850s William Henry Fry and George Bristow, the first American-born composers to handle nineteenth-century orchestral forms convincingly, protested intemperately about the exclusion of American works from the Philharmonic Society's programmes, forgetting the occasional minor work which had won a hearing at Philharmonic concerts. Bristow resigned from the Society and its orchestra, in which he played as a violinist, to show his condemnation of what he called 'the systematised effort to extinguish American music'. In the first forty years of its life, the Philharmonic had made itself responsible for single performances of three of Bristow's symphonies and two of his overtures, but for all that Bristow and Fry (a critic as well as a composer who joined in Bristow's protest) were more successful than most of their contemporaries in winning something of a hearing; other organisations did less even than the New York Philharmonic Society to foster American music, and apart from the five works heard at Philharmonic Concerts, Bristow's opera *Rip van Winkle* ran for four weeks in New York, and as conductor of the amateur choral society, the Harmonic Society, he was able to conduct his cantata *Eleutheria*.

Fry was born in Philadelphia in 1915, studied composition with a French musician and, though he began composing in his early teens, became a journalist and critic. In 1846 he began a six-year stint as a European correspondent to various papers in the United States, returning eventually as music editor of the *New York Tribune*. His opera *Leonore*, based on Bulwer-Lytton's *The Lady of Lyons*—a large-scale work in what at the time was the latest and most flamboyant Italian style—was played at Philadelphia in 1845; a production in Italian by an Italian company was heard

[5] John H. Mueller: *op. cit.* p. 266.

in New York in 1858. His four symphonies, each written to a programme of considerable naivety, were taken up by Jullien, apparently to attract American audiences.

After Bristow and Fry, the most successful American composers were Bostonians, or musicians educated at Harvard and indoctrinated by the German classicism which dominated Boston music. They studied in Europe and several of them, like Daniel Gregory Mason, George W. Chadwick and Horatio William Parker, wrote works which were heard here and there in Europe and were not totally neglected in the United States. Edward MacDowell not only studied at the Paris Conservatoire, at Stuttgart and at Wiesbaden, but lived in Germany for four years after his studies ended; he taught the piano at Darmstadt. His compositions won some attention in Europe, and he returned to America with a higher prestige among his fellow countrymen than any earlier American had achieved among his own people. His works, too, were given occasional performances but they did not become part of the repertory.

If, in the first forty years of its life, the New York Philharmonic played only half a dozen works by American composers and found no place for any of them in its repertoire, the Boston Symphony Orchestra, between its foundation and 1914, when its history was written, played thirty-two works by native composers though none of them, not even those by Mac-dowell, found a regular home in its programmes, though the composers favoured by Boston were followers of the German classical tradition, far more Central European than American in their outlook. Between its creation in 1892 and its thirty-third birthday in 1925—precisely as long a period as that which measures activities in Boston—the Philadelphia Orchestra had given first performances to only four American works, although Stokowski, after his appointment in 1912, had tormented conservative Philadelphian ears with a large number of new European works and works by European expatriates to America, although much of the music he fought for seemed to his audiences almost offensively obscure.

The appetite for American music which first developed in the 1850s was part of the general agitation that established Americans began to feel at the mass immigrations which began with thousands of victims of the Irish potato famine who arrived in the United States in 1846; it continued with the flood of refugees from the abortive revolutions of 1848. The White, Anglo-Saxon Protestant settlers, faced with a flood of Roman Catholic Irishmen, and followed by an influx of Central Europeans many of whom were also Roman Catholic, noticed that immigrants tended to settle together and to maintain the culture and habits of their homelands rather than to assimilate and become native-born Americans by some act of will; in the face of so much immigration, what had become American national tradition seemed to be at risk and unlikely to survive, so that music which might be called American because of the nationality of its composer, whatever his stylistic preoccupations, seemed to be one of the possible lines of defence against European encroachments. But music composed in America could not sufficiently grip the affections of American listeners to replace the un-American works on which Americans, however proud of their Anglo-Saxon traditions, had grown up. The American music which won American hearts is better represented by the songs of Stephen Foster (the archetypal 'light' composer of mid-nineteenth-century America) than by the serious efforts of more intellectual American composers. Foster listened to the music of black Americans and refined it into a style compounded of Victorian balladry and negro folk music. Somehow, and not with any abundant sense of logic, this itself seemed to be a weapon in the service of the apparently endangered national heritage. Foster died in 1864, before either Bristow or Fry; his work predates the American Civil War, but it has retained its hold in affections in the United States and beyond.

Daniel Gregory Mason was the most determinedly classical of the classical school which developed in mid-nineteenth-century Boston, partly as the result of the traditional intellectual climate of Boston and partly the result of Higginson's choice of conductors for his orchestra. Mason, born in 1873, suggests in his opinions a representative of his parents' generation. On Thanksgiving Day, 1895, he wrote in his Journal:

> Thank God Wagner is dead and Brahms is alive. And here's to the great classical revival of the twentieth century in America.[6]

In *Music in my Time* he expressed his antipathy to 'excess, unbalance and romantic exaggeration' in the works of composers like Wagner, Tchaikovsky, Liszt and Strauss whose greatness he could not deny.[7] Mason, nevertheless, wrote that what he called 'the Anglo-Saxon element' in American life had become a 'minority element' in American national character.[8] But that belief did not alter his love of the minority element or prevent his realisation that American culture must inevitably adopt some degree of eclecticism. It is such an eclecticism in its earliest stages which is the strength of Foster's relatively unambitious music: the basic style comes from an undemanding European manner, but to it is married a semi-negro style. It is, in Foster's work, alive and native while its European background is simply acquired after a time-lag. At the same time, the New York Philharmonic in its early days had been as busy in its exploration of Beethoven's music as the London Philharmonic Society had been in its early days, and the audiences it

---

[6] Quoted in Gilbert Chase: *op. cit.* p. 101.
[7] Daniel Gregory Mason: *Music in my Time*. Macmillan, New York. p. 101.
[8] Daniel Gregory Mason: *Tune in America*. Knopf, New York, 1931. p. 160.

had won put up a resistance to new music—that of Brahms as well as that of Wagner—even more conservative than that of any European audience. In nineteenth-century America music belonged to the past, and only music from the past was regarded as serious and important.

While the importance of Foster is that he created a synthesis of Afro-American music with a tradition of European light music, both elements in his style were considerably diluted, but all the same he hit upon a style intrinsically American, though his highest motive for doing so seems to have been only to give refinement and respectability to what most of his contemporaries would have considered to be the music of rough, uncultivated entertainment. As negro music became a matter of more sympathetic interest and greater understanding, it added itself to the extensive stock of American raw materials at the composer's disposal, though, until the end of the century, he was disinclined to use them and unable to see their value for any purpose beyond that of easy-going entertainment: Puritan hymnology, both European and the work of early American composers who made the European hymn tradition into strangely primitive harmonic structure, transplanted folk song, especially English folk song, transatlantic song of every sort, including the indigenous styles of the United States, even American Indian song and dance, and Afro-American styles learned especially from negro religious music, with its idiosyncratic attitude to rhythm: it was the task of the American composer to find a style embracing as many of these remarkably disparate elements as possible, and the most influential of the available styles rapidly became jazz, which, because it was the most immediate, vital and inescapable, became part of the American musical atmosphere from the beginning of the twentieth century. Jazz in Europe, in the hands of composers like Kurt Weill, was an exotic importation, appearing always like a sort of quotation introduced when special points had to be made, but in the United States it was almost the only indigenous music which could be heard everywhere and belonged to the States and not to one of its various ethnic groups.

Thus, Charles Ives's creation of a personal style from the popular music of his youth, the music of white New Englanders—patriotic songs, revivalist hymns and so on—all treated with a total disregard for academic tradition and fortuitously discovering principles and ideas that European composers like Schoenberg were to reach through a painstaking reappraisal of first principles, wrote works which for more than fifty years was dismissed as the eccentricity of a musician who no one needed to take seriously. Even the Third Symphony, composed in 1911, with its beautifully treated if basically unsymphonic evocation of traditional American puritanism through its moving use of revivalist hymns, made little impact. It was the development of music which synthesised jazz and the European tradition which persuaded Americans to take their own music seriously.

Gershwin's *Rhapsody in Blue*, given its first performance in 1924 by Paul Whiteman's jazz orchestra and not by a team of musicians dedicated to 'serious' music, made 'symphonic jazz' respectable. Gershwin's Piano Concerto and Aaron Copland's *Dance Symphony*, heard in halls dedicated to the symphonic tradition, won interest rather than respect and acceptance when they were both heard for the first time in 1925. At the I.S.C.M. Festival of 1931 in London, Gershwin's *An American in Paris* won only disapproval, though it was greeted with enormous acclaim when it met its natural, American audience; thirty years later a dead Gershwin could expect the approval of international audiences who no longer dismissed jazz as a strange and musically illiterate dialect; the work was helped, of course, in the United States because it had the prestige which came from a performance by the Boston Symphony Orchestra and the conducting of Serge Koussevitzky.

Americans themselves were slow to accept American music:

> In the twenty-five-year period 1925–50 the names of 280 American composers appeared on regular subscription programmes of the ten oldest major symphony orchestras. Of these, 136, or fifty per cent, have been played by only one orchestra each, while only eighteen composers, or six per cent, have been heard in nine or ten orchestras. It is therefore apparent that most of the quota of American composers is consumed in purely token performances of local and regional interest.[9]

These were the circumstances which led Aaron Copland to complain as recently as 1941:

> I have no quarrel with the masterpieces. I think I revere them and enjoy them as well as the next fellow. But when they are used, unwittingly perhaps, to stifle contemporary effort in our own country, then I am almost tempted to take the extreme view and say that we should be better off without them.[10]

One of the effects of America's participation in two world wars was an increased self-confidence which affected attitudes to the arts as well as to politics; the music composed in the United States by American composers for American audiences seemed at last to be as worthy of attention as any other music. In the years before the second World War the most frequently played American composer was Charles Martin Loeffler, Alsatian by birth, trained in Paris, naturalised American in 1887 when he was twenty-six and totally French in his attitudes. Loeffler died in 1935. Second to Loeffler, John Alden Carpenter, born in 1876, was a pupil of Amy Fay, herself a pupil of Liszt; for a time he studied with Elgar. He was a graduate of Harvard and properly influenced by Bostonian classical ideals. He died

[9] Mueller. p. 176.
[10] Aaron Copland: *Our new Music*. Whitlesey House, New York, 1941. p. 134.

in 1951. The third favourite among American composers was Ernest Schelling, born in New Jersey in the same year as Carpenter; Schelling made a sensational reputation as a *Wunderkind* pianist in Philadelphia, studied under Bruckner and Leschitizky, among others, and wrote decently traditional music which owes nothing to its American origin.

After the second World War, however, the most popular—in the sense of widely performed—American composers were Copland, Barber and Gershwin. In common with many British composers of their generation, Copland and Barber did not study in Germany but in Paris, with Nadia Boulanger, opening themselves to a range of influences more susceptible to novelty and experiment than their predecessors. Copland and Gershwin both wrote overtly American music, although Copland's 'national' style represents only the more 'popular' side of his work and is matched by more difficult and learned works. Barber, whose reputation began in Europe before it was established in American concert halls, is not in any direct sense a musical nationalist. Statistics like those of Mueller quoted above do not, of course, explain whether it was Copland's American music which won audiences or whether his more austerely abstract music gained an equal response.

The activities of Schoenberg, Hindemith and other established European refugees to the United States naturally met the rising confidence of American composers and created an appetite among them—and to a lesser extent amongst audiences—for 'advanced' styles. Schoenberg and Hindemith were both inspiring and inspired teachers whose influence made 'advanced' music intellectually respectable, while Weill, working in the American theatre, influenced both opera and the elaborate, sentimental American 'musical', the United States' equivalent to Strauss operetta, to Offenbach and to Gilbert and Sullivan. If there is something a little dubious about the libretto of the greatest of all post second-World-War successes, *Oklahoma!*, with its mystique of the Land and the Folk, the athleticism and spareness of its music might not have been possible if Weill had not found a refuge in the United States. Only Bartók, driven from Hungary to America, seems to have been able to exert no direct influence upon the course of musical history in his new homeland.

If American composition became respectable in the 1950s, the American orchestras have been unmistakably American since the end of the first World War, with a brilliance that is strictly national and a virtuoso quality that European orchestras have rarely tried to achieve. This style is in part the gift of conductors, for until after the second World War any major American orchestra looked for a conductor who, having won a great European, preferably German, reputation, was given a degree of authority uncurbed, as conductorial tyranny is normally curbed in Europe, by a variety of imponderables of custom and orchestral tradition; nowhere else had a conductor had so free a hand to make what he wished of an orchestra, so long as he was supported by the committee which manages the orchestra's business affairs, and the adherence of orchestras, as he is in the United States.

In one point at least American concert organisations have shown a fore-sight not often in evidence elsewhere. The Children's Concert, unknown in Britain until the 1920s, when Sir Robert Mayer brought the idea home with him from the United States and the Children's Concerts of the New York Symphony Orchestra, is as old-established in the United States as the orchestras which perform such concerts. Children's Concerts have an influence exerted in many directions. With relatively few orchestras, and therefore little live music for most American children, a conductor capable of holding the attention of children while amusing them and winning their respectful admiration, could, in the person of Leonard Bernstein, become a television star presenting not only children but adults as well with an in-sight into the delights and excitements, as well as the intellectual founda-tions, of music. In Europe, where habits of concert-going and respect for music are traditional, such concerts may be of little importance. In Britain and America no work has been more valuable.

The finances of American concerts and opera, for all their dependence on the generosity of very rich Americans, are no more free from strain than comparable English organisations, and are equally concerned about success at the box office. Music in the United States benefits from the support of powerful trusts and foundations, like the Ford Foundation's huge grants to opera in New York, Chicago and San Francisco to support productions of American operas,[11] and the patronage of individuals, but little public money is used in support of the arts in America though municipalities often help by providing auditoria and with them the necessary rehearsal facilities. The Federal government helps through fiscal regulations which, while exempting donations to charity from income tax, regards money given to any cultural purpose as a donation to charity.

This does not prevent American orchestras from the necessity of work-ing to an exhausting schedule; the programmes of the New York Phil-harmonic Orchestra, for example, are each repeated on four successive eve-nings. Erich Leinsdorf, interviewed in London on his appointment as con-ductor of the Boston Symphony Orchestra, quoted the Bostonian witticism that the orchestra's schedule of work is 'all right for three orchestras and six conductors'. In Boston the audience likes to see its principal conductor in action at most concerts, and Leinsdorf's tenure of office bound him to conduct twenty-one concerts in the first six weeks of his first season. The Boston season, at the time of his arrival in 1962, included twenty-four sub-scription concerts played on Saturdays and repeated on Sundays, Tuesday

[11] Wallace Brockway and Herbert Weinstock: *The World of Opera.* Methuen, London, 1963. p. 388.

subscription concerts played in Cambridge, Massachusetts, and Sunday and Monday series of concerts.[12]

A multiplication of orchestras to lighten the burden on the musicians who carry it is made impossible not only by the money that is available for music but also by a shortage of players. There is no extensive pool of American musicians available in any of the major cities on which an orchestra could be based, so that except for the great established orchestras, music is necessarily served by community orchestras of amateurs with professional stiffening because no totally professional orchestra can be created without financial guarantees which are still impossible to maintain. When Toscanini, the idol of audiences in the United States, retired from the direction of the National Broadcasting Company Orchestra, created for him in 1936 when he left the New York Philharmonic, his players were naturally reluctant to disband an orchestra with a great international reputation and attempted to form themselves into a self-governing organisation on the lines of the London Symphony Orchestra. They were totally defeated by the facts of American financial life which left them with no funds except those which could be received from subscribers and the box office.

[12] Erich Leinsdorf: interviewed in *The Times*, London, 14 March 1962.

Music in a Fragmented Culture

The nineteenth century created the musical environment in which twentieth-century musicians and listeners have grown up. The opera and concert organisations, the system of chamber-music performances and recitals, and the alternative attractions of musical comedy, variety, popular music on all its various levels and the 'pop' music which is unlike all other forms of music in that it is addressed to a particular age-group although it claims listeners outside its special, selected audience: all these are developments of musical phenomena which first manifested themselves in the nineteenth century.

The twentieth century has modified the system without changing or substantially adding to its essential nature. The late nineteenth-century orchestra of Straussian or Mahlerian dimensions has lost much of its attraction for composers, who have found their way to smaller ensembles depending more often on contrasts of tone colour than on the blended colours of the late nineteenth century, but this development had already begun in the works of Mahler. As early as 1906, while Richard Strauss was still writing operas on a more than Wagnerian orchestral scale, Schoenberg had composed his first Chamber Symphony in E major 'for fifteen solo instruments', and Stravinsky followed during the first World War with *The Soldier's Tale*, first produced in 1918. In his autobiography Stravinsky explains his choice of instruments—violin, double bass, clarinet, bassoon, trumpet, trombone and percussion—as forced on him by the exigencies of wartime, which had dried up his resources and made it impossible for him to recoup them through the composition of the sort of large-scale work on which his reputation was based. Nevertheless, it is possible to see *The Soldier's Tale*, after more than half a century, as a liberation from the large orchestra, which became increasingly less important to many composers. Mahler's orchestras—and Mahler died in 1911—may have been numerically huge, but Mahler was an honorary member of the future in that his scoring is selective and often enough two or three contrasted instruments playing in counterpoint to each other convey everything he wishes to say.

Stravinsky's explanation of the small, selective chamber group of *The Soldier's Tale* became incomplete because even Stravinsky himself wrote increasingly for smaller orchestras, often unusually constituted, and the interest in smaller ensembles grew after the first World War had ended.

From the composer's point of view, smaller ensembles offered the possibility of more performances, and therefore greater financial rewards than the nineteenth-century orchestra, as well as the musical profits of new and attractive styles. The full weight and saturated tone of the post-Wagnerian orchestra became a matter often for special occasions and seemed to leave little new for the composer to do; the great masters of the orchestra in the twentieth century have been disciples of Mahler, who used the orchestra selectively for the sake of contrasted colours and not simply for the sake of its overwhelming power.

Thus the large orchestra ceased to be the natural, all-purpose ensemble it had been for nineteenth-century composers. The French composers of the 1920s, and English composers of the same period, like Bliss, spent as much time writing for oddly assorted *ad hoc* groups—like the soprano, flute, clarinet, bassoon, viola, harp and double bass of Bliss's *Madame Noy*—as with the full orchestra. In one sense, such music, like that of the original version with reciter of Walton's *Façade*, is a virtuoso composer's music for virtuoso players. In Germany Hindemith was composing *Gebrauchtmusik* ('utility music') for whatever group of players might find themselves together and need something to play, including not only sonatas for all the wind instruments, except tuba and piano, a concerto for piano and twelve solo instruments and one for cello and ten solo instruments.

When Britten, after the triumph of *Peter Grimes* in 1945, turned immediately to chamber opera with *The Rape of Lucretia*, he advanced practical and economic reasons for his decision to use an orchestra of twelve—five solo strings, five wind, percussion and harp, with no chorus. Opera on this scale would not be tied to large theatres in which complete orchestras can be accommodated, with stages large enough to permit the deployment and movement of a large chorus; chamber orchestras of Britten's dimensions could fit into almost any theatre in comparatively small towns and thus reduce the expense of producing opera while adding to the social relevance of the art by seeking, and possibly winning, new audiences. Chamber opera was not a totally new conception; Holst's *Savitri* and *The Wandering Scholar* were twentieth-century precursors of *The Rape of Lucretia*, and a considerable number of forgotten works from the late eighteenth century could fall within any reasonable definition of the form, but Britten and other contemporary composers have provided a growing repertoire of modern works within the not entirely rigid limits which Britten has observed. But however practical the original aims of *The Rape of Lucretia* and succeeding chamber operas were, the imaginative scoring and the originality and beauty of the effects that Britten has gained from his small ensembles suggest that whatever his primary motives may have been in reducing the scale of opera, his achievements in the form leave the listener to suppose that, perhaps unconsciously, the real motive may have been an artistic one. In any case, the extent to which Britten's chamber operas have widened the appeal and the subject matter of opera, and the distance over which they have carried it to new audiences, are not easy to calculate.

The interest in smaller orchestras of possibly mixed constituents was shared by many concert-goers. The success of the Boyd Neel Orchestra after its foundation in England in 1932, and of similar continental groups— I Musici in Italy, the Moscow Chamber Orchestra and the Stuttgart Chamber Orchestra, as well as a considerable number of similar orchestras all over Europe—meant the exploration of a new repertoire; by the end of the 1940s, almost forgotten composers like Vivaldi had won a place in modern concert programmes and, equally significantly, in gramophone record catalogues; the precise orderliness of the baroque concerto took its place in general musical experience. The unity of musical outlook, which had been shared by musicians and their audiences throughout the nineteenth century, was further broken by the revival of the baroque to add to the confusion caused by the Great Schism which had taken away from the musical centre those whose taste was for the purely entertaining.

At the same time, the situation of the composer had to some extent become easier than it had been. Though the social vacuum into which he had been compelled to live throughout the nineteenth century still existed, and though he was still virtually compelled to silence until he found a willing audience, society became increasingly ready to pay him for whatever work he did which gave pleasure.

Attempts to reward the composer, and other artists, through copyright laws have been made since the seventeenth century. The music of Heinrich Schütz, for example, was protected through copyright throughout Saxony, and George I granted Handel a copyright in 1720. But Handel's music could legally be issued in pirated editions though he had the King's 'licence for the sole printing' of his work for fourteen years, after which each passed in its turn into the public domain. Schütz's music had found its way into the hands of unauthorised printers as soon as published copies were available to be bought. Any special licence of this kind was so indefinite and poorly drafted, from any modern point of view, with no clear notion of how a work could be given real protection, that neither Schütz nor Handel, for all the century which passed between the grants in their favour, had any real safeguard against the pirating of their published work. George I's special grant to his favoured composer afforded Handel no more protection than he would have had from the general copyright act which was introduced in Queen Anne's reign.

As country after country introduced increasingly effective copyright arrangements, the problem came to be that of protecting works from exploitation in foreign countries. The English composer and publisher George

Smart, for instance, made business trips to Europe after the Napoleonic Wars, visiting publishers to buy from them, not from their composers, music which he believed would have a good sale in England. It was this situation that led Beethoven to sell limited rights to his publishers, reserving to himself the right to dispose of music already sold to German or Austrian publishers, exploiting his work in other countries to his own, if limited, advantage.

Foreign copyrights were a composer's headache. In 1855 Verdi, whose works were invariably published by Ricordi, in Milan, discovered that England had granted foreign composers the right to profit from the publication of their works in England, so that Verdi had been able to sell scores to English publishers. Then a case in the House of Lords had decided that this right was accorded only to those foreign composers whose countries had copyright agreements with Britain; Milan was not one of them, and the decision made it possible for British publishers to issue Verdi's scores without even consulting, let alone paying, him.

> During my two visits to London [he wrote in September 1855] it was suggested that I should apply for citizenship of either England or France, or even Piedmont (because France and Piedmont have international agreements with England), but I prefer to remain what I am, that is to say, a peasant from Roncole, and I prefer to ask my government to make an agreement with England. The government of Parma has nothing to lose in an agreement of this kind, which is purely artistic and literary[1]

The situation was not brought under control until the decisions of the Berne Convention of 1886, which decided that all the signatory countries should grant internal copyright protection to their nationals, and that foreign works should be protected within every country which subscribed to the Convention. Neither Russia nor the United States of America, however, did so, and Russian publishers of serious music proceeded to protect their composers—in the case of authors, whose work needed a translator, protection was a more difficult business—by setting up branch houses in France and Germany. The United States was satisfied by making bilateral arrangements with countries which had accepted the Berne Convention.

The protection given by a genuinely international system of copyright depended on the sale of works published. Composers of songs and piano music which caught public attention and could be sold as sheet music profited immensely; in England publishers promoted 'ballad concerts' at which popular songs composed to safe formulae with words that appealed to the popular sentiments of late Victorian England were sung by admired, and often justly admired, vocalists who were paid a royalty on each performance for their assistance in promoting sales. Ivor Newton wrote of the legendary Dame Clara Butt:

[1] Verdi: *op. cit.* p. 100.

Her mastery of ballads was doubly profitable for her. Her audiences loved them as she did, and she contracted with publishers to sing them, receiving a royalty on the sales of those she made popular; I believe that every copy sold of 'Abide with me' brought her threepence. When I asked her why she had dropped one highly popular song from her programmes, she explained that she had made a contract with its publishers for a royalty on sales which continued for seven years; the contract had now expired, and she was not prepared to go on advertising the song.[2]

Exploitation of this kind could produce sales of vast quantities of songs which won popular acclaim and were consequently a welcome source of income for the composer, who himself received a royalty of from ten to fifteen per cent on every copy sold. The publisher regarded it as his duty no less than his profit to sell as many sheet music copies of a composer's songs or small piano pieces as possible.

But though the composer of operas, symphonies, concertos and so on was at last protected so far as publication of his work was concerned, obviously he was in a far less favourable position. Even if an opera or a symphony rapidly became popular (and 'popularity' is a relative term; it rarely means for a symphony what it means for an undemanding song which any amateur can sing for fun), it could be expected to sell only a limited number of copies. An aria which could be published separately, as sheet music, with a piano accompaniment, would sell far more copies than a complete vocal score, just as a vocal score, or a piano transcription of an orchestral work, could rightly expect to sell more copies than its orchestral score. As the bulk of performances of any extensive new work, or relatively new work, are given not from published parts bought by a concert organisation but from parts hired from its publisher, the necessity for the composer's prosperity was payment not so much by the number of copies sold as by the number of performances given for so long as the work is protected by copyright.

The French had realised this as early as the late eighteenth century. In 1776 Beaumarchais was largely responsible for the creation of a *Société des Auteurs et Compositeurs dramatiques*, the members of which permitted performance of their plays and operas only by managements who paid them a royalty on each performance; this became a standard arrangement for composers in France. Berlin adopted a similar system early in the nineteenth century, and the Austrian and other German theatres followed suit. A similar recognition of performing rights in all music arose in France after 1850, brought about by a composer of light music who, hearing music of his played in a restaurant where he was dining, refused to pay for his dinner on the grounds that he had not been paid for the use of his music; the case came to court and the composer won it. The right of the composer, after this, to control the performance of his music, and to expect to profit

[2] Ivor Newton: *At the Piano*. Hamish Hamilton, London, 1966. p. 83.

from that performance, led to the setting up, in May 1850, of the *Agence Centrale pour la Perception des Droits des Auteurs et Compositeurs de la Musique*. Richard Strauss, more than anyone else, was responsible for the creation of a similar society in Germany in 1903, and international copyright acts were revised to recognise the right of composers to authorise the performance of their works in exchange for a fee.

English publishers operated the system of royalties on sold copies of music more extensively than other European companies so that they were at first unhappy about the principle of a performing right. Such a system, they felt, would be likely to reduce the number of performances of any new or relatively new work by throwing performers back, for the sake of economy, on works in the public domain and thus indirectly injuring the sale of copies from which the successful composer of popular works could expect to earn a valuable sum and the publisher a no less valuable profit. It was the development of recorded music which persuaded William Boosey, himself a music publisher, that the composer's situation had radically changed by virtue of technical and scientific progress. He wrote:

> I was beginning to be aware that probably, eventually a composer's performing rights might be even more valuable than his publishing rights.[3]

In 1911 a new Copyright Act added to the composer's rights that of controlling reproductions of his work by any mechanical means, and his right to authorise performances. Towards the end of 1913 composers and publishers (whose own rights might be threatened by unauthorised performance) began to discuss the creation of a society which would protect copyrights by controlling performances and preventing those that were unauthorised, with the result that the Performing Rights Society was registered in March 1914, the publishers involved in the Society having vested in it the performing rights of a large number of works of all kinds. Naturally, much of its time and energy was spent in ensuring that copyrights in the most popular kinds of music were not infringed, but 'serious' composers too benefited from its operation. Copyright in mechanical reproduction had been reorganised in 1908 and 1909 in all the countries which accepted the Berne Convention; these agreed to safeguard performers' rights in mechanical reproduction, so thus the actual player was in a stronger financial position than he had ever been before.

Recording, however, had other than financial effects on the composer; Edison's phonograph, which made its first recognisable sounds in 1877, had originally been nothing but an ingenious toy. The invention in 1888 of a shellac disc in place of Edison's cylinder as the recipient of the recording, revolving on a turntable to transmit the sounds imprinted on it, led to a

[3] William Boosey: *op. cit.* p. 175.

great multiplication of recordings. Before the first World War Adelina Patti recorded 'Home Sweet Home'; Calvé made records, as did Melba from 1904 onwards. Tamagno and Maurel, the first Otello and Iago of Verdi's opera, can still be heard. In 1905 Jean de Reszke recorded two discs, but permitted the release of neither, although even in those early days voices could be recorded with tolerable fidelity while instrumental tone was not satisfactorily captured until the development of electrical recording in the 1920s, by which time a considerable library of Melba and Caruso records already existed. Both Melba and Caruso made considerably more money from the recording of passages from Puccini's operas than did the composer himself.

The early gramophone record was an expensive pleasure: to listen to a sixty-year-old Patti sing 'Home Sweet Home' cost £1. But mass production and skilful advertising succeeded in lowering prices by increasing demand until in the 1930s Woolworth's sold seven-inch records for sixpence each, while to listen to Chaliapin, Paderewski, Kreisler and Casals and the great singers and instrumentalists, or to Toscanini and Stokowski, Weingartner and any of their peers on ten- or twelve-inch records cost only a few shillings for up to ten minutes' music. Electrical recording and reproduction conveyed instrumental and orchestral tone accurately enough to satisfy ears that were more concerned with the music played or sung than with concepts of 'high fidelity'. The gramophone became not only a source of easy-going entertainment but an invaluable tool in the hands of the musical historian and a means to knowledge for the student. Elgar conducted his own works; so did Rachmaninov and all composers who had won recognition in the concert hall since the technique of recording had developed sufficiently to allow a trustworthy account of their performance. Of equal historical value are many recordings of music of all kinds which preserve performances by the great interpretative artists of the past and those which present the evolution of popular styles from ragtime through jazz to the dance music of the 1920s and 1930s and on to the pop of the 1960s and 1970s.

The gramophone record, however, introduced a new style of advertising into our musical life. Any artist, soloist, or conductor, who catches the public imagination can be exploited by publicity machines simply to sell records. As the public interest almost inevitably precedes the records of any 'serious' musician, it is in the realm of 'popular' music that performer's reputations are likely to be established through the skilful advertising of records before they have made any genuine appeal to the public; the recording of any pop group may not precede the group's first, exploratory appearances in public, but recording and a position in the 'charts' of each week's most popular discs is the way to, and not as it is for 'serious' musicians the consequence of, celebrity.

The growth of recording, which by the 1930s was producing complete versions of the more popular and manageable operas, the still admirable recordings of the Mozart Opera Society, recorded versions of the standard symphonies and concertos, the offerings of the Sibelius Symphony Society and the Beethoven Sonata Society, as well as quantities of choral, chamber and solo instrumental music, naturally aroused the pessimism of many musicians. Why, it seemed natural to ask, travel to hear a work played by X, Y or Z in some discomfort and the price of a seat when for no more than the cost of a ticket you could obtain a more or less permanent recording of the work in an interpretation by Schnabel or Kreisler, Toscanini, Furtwängler or Walter, or sung by the finest singers of the day? The pessimists, of course, undervalued the atmosphere of the concert hall, the appeal of participation which is the concert hall's special quality and the sense that live performance is an important communication to listeners delivered from the composer through the performers.

Actually, the effect of recording and later of broadcasting was to extend rather than diminish the attractiveness of 'live' musical events. Nevertheless, after the doubtful advantages of recording, the advent of broadcasting in the 1920s was greeted with dismay, especially in England, where the concept of broadcasting as a public service dedicated to providing everybody with the best of everything flooded the air with music of all sorts available all the time. While conductors like Sir Thomas Beecham and Sir Hamilton Harty prognosticated the end of the public concert, Constant Lambert was moved to write in 1934 about the stultifying effects of what he called 'the appalling popularity of music':

> In the neighbourhood where I live, for example, there is a loudspeaker every hundred yards or so, and it is only rarely that they are tuned in to different stations. If they are playing the foxtrot I most detest at one corner of the street, I need not think that I can avoid it by walking to the other end. At times there is a certain piquancy in following a tune in two dimensions at once, so to speak—to buy one's cigarettes to the first subject of a symphony, to get some scraps of development as one goes to the newsagent, and to return home to the recapitulation—but the idea of the town as one vast analytical programme, with every paving stone a bar line, soon palls.[4]

The misuse and cheapening effects of music, which Lambert noticed, turned out to be side effects of the musical policy of broadcasters. Actually, if there were (and still are) those who conduct the trivia of their lives while radio or record player offer them the Ninth Symphony or *Tristan und Isolde*, the late Beethoven quartets or the *Art of Fugue*, if a balance sheet of the good and ill effects of broadcasting could be drawn up, it might

---

[4] Constant Lambert: *Music Ho!* London, 1934. Pelican Books, Harmondsworth, 1948. p. 169.

easily show that both the record and the loudspeaker have served music faithfully and well, although both have made it possible to use great music as a negligible accompaniment to other activities. It is perfectly reasonable to think of works like (in the words of W. H. Auden):

> Those divertimenti which
> He wrote to play while bottles were uncorked
> Milord chewed noisily, Milady talked.[5]

as background to a meal or the completion of a crossword puzzle, but it is too easy now for the vacant corners of minds to be made receptacles for the late Beethoven quartets, or *Cosi fan Tutte, Don Giovanni* or *Die Meistersinger*. If every cloud has a silver lining, it has been justly pointed out, every silver lining had a cloud.

Furthermore, the permanent availability of a vast 'serious' repertoire through the radio, the long-playing gramophone record and, more recently, the tape recorder has robbed too much music of the sense of occasion which is part of the experience of great works. The question of how often we should hear the Ninth Symphony or the *Missa Solemnis, Götterdämmerung* or *Tristan und Isolde*, Mahler's Eighth Symphony, the Mass in B minor or the *St. Matthew Passion* is subjective; but it is a real and difficult question; huge works, some of the greatness of which is imparted by their sheer size, should perhaps always be events rare enough never to lose their power from over-familiarity. There is, too, an equally real question to be asked about the continuing validity of a record player's unvarying reproduction of the same performance; in the realm of 'live' music performances cannot be unvarying and identical, just as no 'live' performance can be expected to reach the state of unnatural perfection achieved by recordings constructed piecemeal from the splicing together of innumerable short lengths of tape; it is significant that many of the most communicative recorded performances are faulty and less than perfectly balanced preservations of particular performances played in the presence of a less than perfectly silent but usually excited audience. A performance can never do more, and perhaps should never do more, than represent its player's response to music at a particular time, in a particular hall, with particular colleagues on a particular occasion.

The coming of the long-playing record, which appeared in the United States in 1948 and in Britain a year later, containing up to or even more than half an hour's music on each side, was probably responsible for the greatest expansion of the repertoire ever achieved. It is natural enough that there should be a multiplicity of recording of important and popular works, all of which are capable of a variety of valid interpretations which may vary in tempo, dynamic scale, accentuation and phrasing. But together with the

[5] W. H. Auden: *Metalogue to the Magic Flute.*

natural multiplication of great music has come the exploration of works
rarely if ever heard in the concert hall and the opera house. The *Tristia* of
Berlioz, for example, are, like many other works known by name rather
than by actual performance, recorded when a conductor with an established
reputation (and therefore the ability to attract buyers) shows a special sympathy with their composer's style. The popularity of Mahler's music in
England since the early 1950s probably owes a great deal to the discovery
that a fine and much-admired singer, Kathleen Ferrier, had a special sympathy for *Das Lied von der Erde* and the *Kindertotenlieder*. But it is
equally arguable that recording companies, looking for new works to catch
the record buyer's ear, found that Mahler's orchestral style exploited the
record's technical qualities effectively. At the same time, the record has
fanned a minority interest in medieval music into something already large
with unexpected repercussions on popular music. A good deal of the most
extremely radical music of the 1960s and 1970s is, too, given a wider
audience by recording.

Recording under modern conditions and with modern techniques, however, fosters an appetite for a type of perfection which is not only capable
of creating a liking for performances which win total exactitude of performance at a cost in communicative vitality, thus becoming inimical to music
itself. The record collector is too often asked to concentrate on qualities of
reproduction which in the context of a moving performance in hall or opera
house would not capture our attention but would be subsumed in our response to the music as communication. There are record-makers and record-
buyers for whom music exists only as an adjunct to the exercise of the techniques of the recording studio.

To draw any final balance sheet of drawbacks, to consider 'the appalling
popularity of music' (which means, as Lambert pointed out, that music is
heard without being listened to) and the pressures of advertising applied to
what might be great and with equal vigour to what might be merely trivial,
and to set these things against the enrichments brought by recording and
radio, is impossible. Broadcasting, perhaps more effectively in Britain than
in most countries, has led to the commissioning of works from both established and young struggling composers looking for their audience. Some
of the music thus created has been important and interesting; some has
been artistically successful; some of it has been deservedly forgotten. But
any composer develops by composing, so that every commission is important, whatever the result it produces might be. If an unascertainable number
of radio listeners and record-buyers misuse the music that is available 'on
tap' (and there is, perhaps, a degree of unjustifiable superiority in claiming
that any use of music is a misuse), an equally unascertainable number has
found the same music to be a valuable enrichment of their lives. The
'appalling popularity of music' of all kinds, from the most exalted to the

most trivial, has made it possible for large numbers of musicians of all
sorts to live by their art and to contribute whatever they have to contribute
to general pleasure and enrichment. Music as a profession is a more rewarding way of life for musicians than it was in the past.

The development of broadcasting led the BBC, in 1930, to create its own
Symphony Orchestra on terms which would have seemed normal to the
members of major continental orchestras but which were, in the Britain of
the early 1930s, not only new but almost ideally benevolent. Musicians in
the various BBC orchestras—for regional symphony orchestras were
formed after the establishment of the major London orchestra—were
granted not seasonal but annual employment on contracts which made music
as safe a profession as any other, with the possibility of more than adequate
rehearsal time and regular studio work interspersed with regular public
concerts. The BBC could afford to organise an orchestra on these, for
England, lavish lines while the Hallé, the Liverpool Philharmonic, the
Bournemouth and Birmingham Orchestras and the Scottish National
Orchestra could afford to give their players contracts only for the season
and the London orchestras had never completely thrown off the deputy
system. The London Symphony Orchestra, founded by dissidents from Sir
Henry Wood's policy of no deputies allowed, prided itself, as a players'
co-operative formulating its own policy and electing its own conductor, on
the freedom its players maintained to avoid the compulsions of a policy
which gave the players security at the price of freedom. It led a hand-to-
mouth existence, never far from financial disaster, as did the London
Philharmonic Orchestra established by Sir Thomas Beecham in 1932,
collecting many of the finest players in Britain and establishing standards
of virtuosity rarely achieved in the days before the second World War by
any British orchestra. Box-office finance and the support of wealthy patrons
left every British orchestra except those of the BBC to struggle for survival.

By the end of the second World War, the appetite for music and for all the
arts in Britain, which up to that time had been as effectively self-supporting as they could, more than justified the creation of the Arts Council,
created to organise and disburse government subsidies to artistic enterprises.
Together with this, local governments were empowered to raise and spend
money to support the arts. The result was that the provincial orchestras
could be organised on the same effective lines as those of the BBC or, for
that matter, the continental orchestras. Though the provincial orchestras are
not left to serve audiences simply in their own city but play in wide areas
around them, and though subsidies both from local government and the Arts
Council are parsimonious when compared to those offered in support of
opera companies and orchestras in Europe, they have helped to make music
far more available, and far more widely attended, than it was when broadcasting first offered the listener his choice of music.

The same experience is, to some extent, that of the United States, though radio in America has not felt itself very conscious of any duty to win audiences for the arts; its commercial basis meant that from the start concert and opera broadcasts were a matter of prestige rather than of artistic or social duty, but the introduction of music to audiences otherwise deprived of it had the same effect as it has had on the eastern side of the Atlantic.

At the end of the 1920s the cinema too found a voice and by doing so plunged the entire musical world into consternation. Wherever the film became popular—and that is almost everywhere in the 'civilised' world—it had employed musicians. If, in any local cinema, an indefatigable pianist accompanied each film with a musical commentary made up of works and pieces which seemed appropriate to his or her mind, larger and more expensive cinemas employed orchestras which not only accompanied the film on show but proved to be popular enough to occupy the stage and make music on its own account. Naturally, like restaurant orchestras, cinema orchestras varied both in quality of performance, quality of repertoire and in composition. But the conductor Eugene Goossens gives an account, in his autobiography, *Overture and Beginners*, of conducting sixty-five members of the London Symphony Orchestra throughout a performance of *The Three Musketeers*, the work of the fantastically popular Douglas Fairbanks Senior, when it was screened at Covent Garden in 1922. Seven years later the music critic Edwin Evans explained:

> It is estimated, on the basis of union statistics, that picture theatres, great and small, are now providing between three-quarters and four-fifths of the paid musical employment in the country. . . . For about fifty-nine hours weekly, music is being performed in upward of three thousand cinemas, and for shorter periods in perhaps a thousand isolated halls. Setting aside all aesthetic considerations in favour of a purely objective view, one may say that the cinema is at present the most important musical institution in the country.[6]

Cinema orchestras, the more or less resident musicians of many cinemas, created their musical commentary on the films (working out two programmes a week in most suburban and provincial cinemas) which consisted of either their leader's or their conductor's compilation and adaptation of familiar melodies from light music, popular symphonies and overtures or whatever seemed to convey the substance of the episode with which they were linked; occasionally a score was composed specially for the film to be seen, but such specially composed scores were rarely more stimulating than the usual arrangements by local musicians. Only in Russia, and for such special prestige films as Eisenstein's *Battleship Potemkin*, were the scores of particular musical value.

[6] Edwin Evans: 'Music and the Cinema'. In *Music and Letters*. Vol. X. January 1929. p. 69.

The destruction of 'live' cinema music by the talkies was a disaster for all cinema musicians, especially dire in England and the United States. But the musical influence of such orchestras had rarely been powerful; it seemed to mean little to audiences. The film score itself was gradually to have a considerable influence on 'serious' composers through the money it brought them. Originally love scenes often decided that their point of departures, musically speaking, was some special intensity from *Tristan und Isolde*; moments of extreme dramatic tension looked back to Tchaikovsky, horror and terror moved the film composer, if not towards the structures of Schoenberg and his followers, at least to their vocabulary of extreme dissonance.

By the 1930s, composers from the concert hall and the opera house were beginning to be called in to provide suitable music for films. In England Walton wrote his first film score, for *Escape Me Never*, in 1934. Bliss composed the score for the film of H. G. Wells's *Things to Come* a year later. Walton went on to deal with another ten films in scores that rightly yielded music for concert suites. Vaughan Williams found a rewarding discipline in working to a rigid time-table of the film shot. Shostakovitch had written film scores since 1928, Prokofiev found himself working for the cinema in 1924 and went on to a splendid partnership with Eisenstein in *Alexander Nevsky* and the *Ivan the Terrible* trilogy. In the United States Copland and Vergil Thomson have provided memorable music for films; French composers—Milhaud, Auric, Sauguet, Honneger, Ibert among them—composed for the cinema in the great days of the French film.

For the successful film composer the cinema provides a very profitable field of action, and the composer who is regularly demanded by the cinema finds himself pleasantly removed from the anxieties and uncertainties which are an inevitable part of the freelance composer's normal lot without, necessarily, cheapening his style or making unwilling concessions to audiences which cannot listen to his music in the concert hall.

But the protection of a composer's now multiplied rights, though it is elementary justice, depends upon the extent to which he can win a hearing. A composer of any nationality can live by composition provided that he becomes successful enough to receive commissions from films and from other sources, especially if he can feel confident that a work can look forward to a second and third performance. An enquiry into the situation of the British composer[7] in 1974 suggested that out of five hundred composers of all ages and all kinds in Britain, ten could afford to live by the proceeds of their work. The rest were compelled to earn money outside music or, more appropriately, as orchestral musicians or teachers of music; some worked as editors of music, wrote criticisms or undertook any musical hackwork they could find. A questionnaire submitted to five hundred and seventy-five com-

[7] *Observer Magazine*, 6 January 1974.

posers in 1971 revealed that their average earnings from composition for the previous year had been £357; the 'serious' composers among them earned an average £185.[8] A similar enquiry into the composer's ways and means in the United States revealed that a similar situation existed across the Atlantic. Though there is no available study of the economics of composition in Europe, a study of programmes in continental countries suggests that the 'serious' composer in Europe is in a position similar to that of his British or American contemporary. The conductor, the successful player and the teacher are all more than likely to earn more money from teaching than all but the few composers whose work proves popular enough to win frequent hearings and recordings. This, however, can hardly be regarded as a serious flaw in our musical system; the composer is properly occupied with the practicalities of music and gains from his struggles with them.

The distance between modern 'light' and entertainment music on the one hand and the work of such composers as Stockhausen, Cage, Boulez and Maxwell Davies on the other, together with the large spectrum—from Henze, Britten, Shostakovitch, Malcolm Arnold and Walton (remembering that while critics are inclined to regard Walton as a Grand Old Reactionary there are still devoted listeners and concert-goers who find his music too radical and 'modern' for their taste) almost defies the composer to win an audience along any wide front. The old attitude to music, acceptance of a tradition perpetually expanding under the pressure of every major composer's personality and aims, no longer has any wide authority. The criteria which we can apply to more or less all the music that has survived from, say, the age of Dunstable in the early fifteenth century and persisted until the music of composers whose activities began in the 1930s no longer applies to much of the new work we hear; to apply those standards to much of the music of Messiaen and most of that of Boulez and Stockhausen would be to invite invalid judgements, leaving aside the deliberate limitations of style and vocabulary adopted by composers like Gershwin. The traditional criteria apply more effectively to Rock 'n Roll and to pop, for example, than they do to much of the *avant garde* work of the '60s or '70s; the criteria by which we judge, or should judge, electronic music are not those we should apply to music by Britten, Orff, Penderecki or Shostakovitch, diverse as their music is. There are few composers who have Britten's gift for writing melodies which can be immediately accepted and enjoyed together with the self-discipline which leads him to simplify and refine whatever he composes until it comes as close as it can to its audience for all its originality of sound and style. The enormous amount of music permanently at the disposal of the modern audience, whatever individual tastes exist within that audience, makes it unnecessary for the listener to come to terms

[8] Alan Peacock and Ronald Weir: *The Composer in the Market Place*. Faber, London, 1975.

with any type of composition with which he is unfamiliar, so that musical conditions themselves assist in the separation of musical society into a multitude of coteries variously overlapping.

Music, however, creates societies. Any audience which undergoes a similar experience through a performance is welded, however temporarily, into a community, so that the attraction of such events as the carnival 'last night' of a London Promenade Concert season is only partly musical, though it is music which makes the carnival possible despite the fact that much of the music heard appeals to traditions only partly musical in themselves; these traditions are often worn, but music raises them to a power which restores their validity. This social power of music is exemplified over and over again in works of all periods: Bach's use of Lutheran chorales in his church music and the popular gaiety of the last movement of Berlioz's *Symphonie Funèbre et Triomphale* are examples from far extremes of musical style and aspiration. A similar unifying power is felt in the hysterical adulation which is poured out over some outstanding performers, from Maria Callas to Leopold Stokowski, from Frank Sinatra to the Beatles. But that is a power which 'serious' Western music has all but lost in the second half of the twentieth century.

Any attempt to organise music on behalf of society and set it to serve social ends make little appeal to musicians and to music lovers. In our state of shattered culture what concept of 'society' should music be organised to serve? By forbidding this or that manifestation of music as 'decadent' (a Hitlerian notion) or 'formalistic' or 'socially divisive' (two terms close together in political thought) is not, in the aftermath of the liberal age, a pleasant or a tenable idea. A work like Britten's *War Requiem*, for example, manifesting an inherited tradition and a common hatred of war, creates unities which may possibly be temporary but which are nevertheless consciously held; but performances of Mahler's Eighth Symphony or Schoenberg's *Gurrelieder* or, almost certainly, Havergal Brian's *Gothic* Symphony, indeed of any massive work which ends in a blaze of triumph, creates the terms under which we listen to them and thus imposes unity on us. The atheist and the agnostic, the unitarian, the quaker, the protestant and the catholic all respond to, say, the Mass in B minor or the end of *The Dream of Gerontius* more or less as Bach and Elgar compel them. Such responses operate infallibly so long as the audience shares some musical awareness with the composer and recognises the tradition of thought in which he has written so that it, so to speak, grasps the basic terms of the composer's vocabulary: music is self-sufficient with this one proviso, that it can be a foreign language and therefore exclude those who have no fundamental grasp of its grammar and vocabulary. Possibly music cannot create but only serve the society which it needs and which needs it. The young listener whose musical awareness is restricted to pop is not sure to respond to Bach any more than would be the listener, if such a being exists, who had heard no music except electronic compositions.

It is natural that absolutist government should wish to win the voice of the arts. Jewish music virtually ceased to exist in Hitler's Germany, in so far as music by Jewish composers within the European tradition can be validly classed as 'Jewish', just as all the musical styles and organisation of the Bourbon court in France was harnessed to serve the purposes of Napoleon's empire. In the same way, music in Soviet Russia is, so far as it can be, harnessed to clear social purposes evolved from a clear political philosophy. Russian music should be 'realist', objective not subjective, expressing the voice, ideals and nature of the people, not an unrestrained, solitary individualism; it is the voice of the state, the state existing ideally as the embodiment of the people and their will. As the aims of a Communist government are, as a matter of political dogma, correct and therefore certain to succeed, music must express not only natural individual experience— happy or sad—great intensities of individual emotion are not in the Communist sense 'natural'—but also the society in which the composer lives, its historical tragedies, its struggles and the inevitable final triumph to which it will lead. Obviously in the works of Shostakovich, often regarded as a dangerously subjective individualist by Soviet authorities whose attitude the composer (with what inner reservations we do not know) shared, and in that of Prokofiev, Communist doctrine no more precludes the writing of masterpieces than does any other dogma religious or political.

Nevertheless, the philosophy of Socialist Realism which orders the official life of Russian music is by nature restrictive, though it can be applied with varying degrees of rigour. The offences of Shostakovitch and Prokofiev were condemned at various times since the 1930s as 'formalism' and 'subjectivism'; that is to say, they treated music as an end in itself and not as an instrument of social development. The way to avoid 'formalism' and 'subjectivism', notoriously bourgeois faults growing from the bourgeoisie's misuse of the leisure it unjustly appropriates to itself, is to use traditional, comprehended forms and to fill them with materials which are somehow related to national or regional folk song, rooted in the music of the people. The fact that in the 1970s the dogma is used with more enlightenment (so far as the evidence of Shostakovitch's poignant Fourteenth or enigmatic Fifteenth Symphonies, which have not been condemned, can take us), does not alter the fact that freedom to explore not only techniques but states of mind is only given to composers of Shostakovich's genius and persistence. In the same way, Soviet Russia is prepared to be more open to other music than it was, so that a composer like Benjamin Britten can find not only popularity within Communist Russia but an honorary status as a 'realist' composer based on the fact that he expresses himself melodically and in terms traditional enough to make his originality acceptable. But pop music, apparently popular with Soviet youth which accepts it as the international style of youth rejecting old and imperfect societies, is still condemned though it is not actually forbidden; the difficulty of governments in the second half of the twentieth century in actually banning anything which can be heard on radio, bought on records or collected on tape are all but insuperable.

> Ideology and politics [writes Nicolas Slonimsky] are integral parts of Russian musical life. . . . The gigantic experiment of directing the language of music according to a set of philosophically formulated principals is unprecedented in history.[9]

In reality, of course, the doctrine has changed little since Plato first propounded the necessity of having the poet bound to the service of the state, and it is not intellectually disreputable. It was the doctrine of the catholic and Calvinist churches at different times in their history. The unacceptable and essentially restrictive elements in it are that it contains a doctrine of what is socially relevant to the needs of the world, and such a doctrine is no less subjective than any other, and music is capable of transcending the doctrines which it is set to serve; it can create its own relevance to individual life and to society, at least in those countries which have developed away from the classic Platonic view of social necessity. Music deliberately set to limit its appeal ultimately becomes catch-penny and boring even if it comes to life in a society where the necessity of catching pennies is not a pressing preoccupation. The Western music of a fragmented society is a result of the situation created by the nineteenth century, which divorced entertainment music from serious music and promulgated the doctrine of the artist as a personality innately superior to the rest of the race and therefore under no social compulsion to discipline his work to communicate with the widest possible audience. The greatest composers are those who communicated in this way, but since the nineteenth century they have been held in some suspicion; the acceptance of Elgar by the world at large is proceeding more than forty years after his death, at a time when advanced thinkers are developing their suspicions of Britten in spite of the demonstrable fact that whatever Britten communicates is stated with facinating originality, musical intelligence and certainty of effect.

It is possible now to win intellectual acceptance for works which have abandoned the notion that music is a discipline, that it has, in a not painfully strained analogy, a grammar and a syntax. Simplifications of the language of music until only a single element remains—rhythm or texture more often than melody or harmony have become confused with originality, as though Britten's *The Turn of the Screw*, making new sounds in

---

[9] Nicolas Slonimsky: Foreword to *Prokofiev*, by Israel V. Nestyev. Stanford and Oxford University Press, 1961. p. vii.

traditional ways, is somehow more old-fashioned than the attempts of Stock-hausen to make electronic music out of the unco-ordinated improvisations of a group of players who individually produce little of any moment. The pessimist, sadly conscious of music dissipating its power, its capacity to mould societies, may feel that as Western society is either crumbling away or moulding itself into something new and probably inimical, can comfort himself with the historical knowledge that there have been earlier ages of musical disruption which have eventually synthesised themselves into musical styles broadly based enough to contain the explorations of a J. S. Bach and the cheerful prattle of a Telemann at his least exciting, to hold together Wagner and Brahms and Bruckner. Any new synthesis will belong to the society in which it is formed, to be a reflection of its character and purpose. A reflection, after all, is not the most flattering of possible images, and music in society reflects—with all a reflection's power of candid criticism—the real face of the society to which it belongs.

A Note on Currencies
referred to in this book

In 1850 the £1 sterling had the following equivalents among the various European currencies:[1]

In France: 25.2 francs.

In Germany: Berlin: 6.85 thalers. 1 thaler = 30 silver groschen. 1 groschen = 12 pfennigs.

Frankfurt am Main: 6.49 Reich dollars (thalers). 1 Reich dollar = 90 kreuzer. 1 kreuzer = 4 pfennigs.

Hamburg: 13.4 marks banco. 1 mark = 16 schillings. 1 schilling = 12 pfennigs.

Leipzig: 6.5 Reich dollars. 1 dollar (thaler) = 24 bon-gros. 1 bon-gros = 12 pfennigs.

Lübeck: 16.4 marks. 1 mark = 16 schillings. 1 schilling = 12 pfennigs.

Munich: 11.7 florins (gulden). 1 florin = 60 kreuzer. 1 kreuzer = 4 pfennigs.

In Austria: Vienna: 9.7 florins (gulden). 1 florin = 60 kreuzer. 1 kreuzer = 4 pfennigs.

In Switzerland: Zürich: 10 florins. 1 florin = 60 kreuzer. 1 kreuzer = 6 keller.

In Holland: Amsterdam: 11.9 florins. 1 florin = 100 cents.

In Italy: Milan: 28.9 Austrian francs. 1 franc = 100 cents.

Naples: 5.9 new ducats. 1 ducat = 10 carbini.

Rome: 4.7 scudi. 1 scudo = 10 paoli.

Russia: St. Petersburg: 6.3 roubles. 1 rouble = 100 kopeks.

Subject to the normal fluctuations of value, these figures provide the most reasonable indication of such salaries, costs, etc., earned or faced by musicians.

Other information of value in considering the status and earning power of the nineteenth-century musician:

1813: Weber's salary in Prague: 2000 gulden.

1821: Weber's salary in Dresden: 1500 thalers (c. £220, says Grove).

1823: Weber was offered 2500 thalers to become *Kapellmeister* at Cassel.

1826: Weber's fee for the production of *Oberon* at Covent Garden, £1000.

[1] Isaac Slater: *Universal Money Table and Commercial Exchange Standard.*

1826: Weber's dinner for two in London: 6s. 0d. = 21 groschen
4 pfennigs.

1822: Spohr's salary at Cassel: 2000 thalers; after 1829, 2500.

1836: Berlioz's commission for the *Requiem*, 3000 francs, out of which
he was responsible for the payment of copyists and all costs of
rehearsal and performance.

1838: Paganini's present to Berlioz: 20,000 francs.

1840: Berlioz's commission for the *Symphonie Funèbre et Triomphale*,
10,000 francs, out of which he was responsible for payment of copyists
and all costs of rehearsal and performance (four additional performances sponsored by the managers of the Salle Vivienne made the work
unusually profitable to the composer).

1844: Festival of Industrial Products: Receipts: 32,000 francs. Tax:
4000 francs. Berlioz's net profit: 800 francs.

1832: Wagner's salary at Würzburg: 10 gulden per month. At Riga: 800
roubles. At Dresden: 1500 thalers.

1842: Nicolai's salary as *Kapellmeister* of the Vienna Imperial Opera:
2000 gulden.

1847: Nicolai's salary as *Kapellmeister* of the Royal Opera, Berlin:
2000 thaler.

1883: Mahler's salary as Second Conductor of the Opera at Cassel:
1000 marks and living expenses.

1888: Mahler's salary as Director of the Royal Opera, Budapest:
10,000 florins and various subsidiary benefits.

1897: Mahler's salary as Director of the Imperial Opera, Vienna:
6000 florins + 2000 florins for conducting + 2000 for expenses.

Bibliography

W. J. Argent: *Philharmonic Jubilee: Half a Century of Music in Liverpool.* Liverpool, 1889.
Richard Batka: *Die Musik in Böhmen.* Bard, Marquardt, Berlin, 1906.
Frantisek Bartos: *Bedrich Smetana; Letters and Reminiscences,* translated by Daphne Rustridge, Artis, Prague, 1955.
Jacques Barzun: *Berlioz and his Century.* Meridian Books, New York, 1956.
J. R. Sterndale Bennett: *The Life of William Sterndale Bennett.* Cambridge University Press, 1907.
Hector Berlioz: *Memoirs,* translated by David Cairns. Gollancz, London, 1969.
Correspondance Gènèrale, edited by Pierre Citron Vol. 1. Flammarion, Paris, 1972.
Evenings in the Orchestra, translated by C. R. Fortescue. Penguin Books, Harmondsworth, 1963.
La Musique et les Musiciens. Colman Lévy, Paris, Gregg International, New York, 1969.
On Conducting. Translated by John Broadhouse. London 1917.
Heinrich Bihrle: *Musikalisches Akademie München.* Munich, 1911.
Werner Bollert (ed.): *Singakademie zu Berlin.* Berlin, 1966.
William Boosey: *Fifty Years of Music Publishing.* Benn, London, 1931.
Wallace Brockway and Herbert Weinstock: *The World of Opera.* Methuen, London, 1963.
Maurice J. E. Brown: *Essays on Schubert.* Macmillan, London, 1966.
Hans von Bülow: *Letters,* selected and edited by Richard, Count of Moulin-Eckhart. Translated by Hannah Waller. Knopf, New York, 1931.
Adam Carse: *The Orchestra from Beethoven to Berlioz.* Heffer, Cambridge, 1948.
The Life of Julien. Heffer, Cambridge, 1951.
Algernon Cecil: *Metternich.* Eyre and Spottiswode, London, 1933.
Gilbert Chase: *America's Music.* McGraw Hill, New York, 1955.
A. E. Cherbuliez: *Die Schweiz in der deutschen Musik Geschichte.* Verlag von Huber, Frauenfeld and Leipzig, 1932.
Chopin: *Letters,* collected by H. Opienski, translated and edited by E. Voynich. Desmond Harmsworth, London, 1932.
Henry F. Chorley: *Music and Manners of France and Germany.* 3 vols. London, 1841.
John Clapham: *Antonin Dvorák.* Faber, London, 1966.
Aaron Copland: *Our New Music.* Whitlesey House, New York, 1941.
Peter Cornelius: *Ausgewählte Schriften und Briefen.* Berlin.
J. E. Cox: *Musical Reminiscences.* London, 1872.
William L. Croston: *French Grand Opera; an art and a business.* King's Crown Press, New York, 1948.
A. Dandelot: *La Société des Concerts du Conservatoire.* Paris, 1923.
Otto Erich Deutsch: *Schubert: a Documentary Biography,* translated by Erich Blom. Dent, London, 1946.
Alfred Einstein: *Schubert,* translated by David Ascoli. Cassel, London, 1951. Panther Books, London, 1971.
John Ella: *Musical Sketches.* 3 vols. London, 1878.
Carl Fuchs: *Musical and other Recollections.* Manchester, 1937.
Hans Gal: *The Composer's World.* Thames and Hudson, London, 1965.
A. W. Ganz: *Berlioz in London.* Quality Press, London, 1956.
Wilhelm Ganz: *Memories of a Musician.* John Murray, London, 1913.
William Gardiner: *Music and Friends.* 3 vols. London, 1832.
Joseph Gmelch: *Musikgeschichte Eichstätts.* Eichstätt, 1912.
Henry-Louis de la Grange: *Mahler,* vol. 1. Gollancz, London, 1974.

Susanna Grossman-Vendrey: *Felix Mendelssohn-Bartholdy und die Musik der Vergangenheit.* Gustav Bosse Verlag, Regensburg, 1969.
Donald Jay Grout: *A History of Western Music.* Dent, London, 1962.
Heinrich Habel: *Das Odeon in München.* Walter de Gruyter, Berlin, 1967.
C. E. and M. Hallé: *The Life and Letters of Sir Charles Hallé.* London, 1896.
Eduard Hanslick: *Music Criticisms, 1846–99,* translated and edited by Henry Pleasants. Penguin, Harmondsworth, 1956.
Alec Harman, Anthony Milner and Wilfred Mellers: *Man and his Music.* Barrie and Rockliff, London, 1962.
Fritz Henneberg: *The Leipzig Gewandhaus Orchestra.* Dennis Dobson, London, 1966.
J. Hennings: *Musikgeschichte Lübecks. Band 1, Weltliche Musik.* Bärenreiter, Cassel and Basel, 1951.
Ferdinand Hiller: *Aus dem Tonleben unserer Zeit.* 3 vols, Leipzig, 1868.
George Hogarth: *Musical History, Biography and Criticism.* London, 1835.
Hajo Holborn: *A History of Modern Germany.* 2 vols. Eyre and Spottiswoode, London, 1965.
Edward Holmes. *A Ramble among the Musicians of Germany.* London, 1828.
Edgar Holt: *Risorgimento.* Macmillan, London, 1970.
M. A. de Wolfe Howe: *The Boston Symphony Orchestra: a Historical Sketch.* Houghton, Miflin and Co., Boston, 1914.
Paul Ignotus: *Hungary.* Ernest Benn, London, 1972.
Charles F. James: *The Story of the Performing Rights Society.* P.R.S., London, 1951.
Harold F. Johnson: *Sibelius.* Faber and Faber, London, 1959.
Jubiläum der Hessischen Staatskapelle. Cassel, 1960.
Michael Kennedy: *The Hallé Tradition.* Manchester University Press, 1960.
Helmut Kirchmeyer: *Das Zeitgenossiche Wagnerbild.* Gustav Bosse Verlag. 3 vols. Regensburg, 1972.
Georg Knepler: *Musikgeschichte des 19 Jahrhunderts.* 2 vols. Henschelverlag, Berlin, 1961.
Karl Kobald: *Alt-Wiener Musikstätten.* Amalthea Verlag, Vienna, 1919.
Henry Krehbiel: *The Philharmonic Society of New York.* Novello, Ewer and Co. Ltd., London and New York, 1892.
Herbert Kupferberg: *The Fabulous Philadelphians.* Charles Scribner's Sons, New York, 1959.
Constant Lambert: *Music Ho!* Faber, London, 1934. Penguin Books, 1948.
Brian Large: *Smetana.* Duckworth, London, 1970.
Karl Laux: *The Dresden Staatskapelle,* translated by Lena Jaeck; Dennis Dobson, London, 1864.
Hugo Leichtentritt: *Music, History and Ideas:* Harvard University Press, 1938.
R. A. Leonard: *A History of Russian Music.* Jarrold, London, 1956.
Benjamin Lumley: *Reminiscences of the Opera.* London, 1864.
C. A. MacCartney: *The Habsburg Empire, 1790–1918.* Wiedenfeld and Nicolson, London, 1968.
E. D. Mackerness: *A Social History of English Music.* Routledge and Kegan Paul, London, 1964.
Alma Mahler: *Gustav Mahler: Memories and Letters,* translated by Basil Creighton. New edition, introduction by Donald Mitchell. John Murray, London, 1968.
Daniel Gregory Mason: *Music in my Time.* Macmillan, New York.
Tune in America. Knopf, New York, 1931.
Wilfred Mellers: *Music and Society,* Dennis Dobson, second edition, 1950.
Music in New Found Land. Barrie and Rockliff, London 1964.
Felix Mendelssohn: *Letters,* translated and edited by G. Seldengoth, Elek, London, 1947.
Erwin Mittag: *Aus dem Geschichte der Wiener Philharmoniker.* Gerlach, Wiedling, Vienna, 1950.
Stephen Mizau (editor): *Frederic Chopin, 1810–1849.* Kosciusko Foundation, Macmillan, New York, 1949.
Rena Moisienko: *Realist Music.* Meridian Books, London, 1947.
Gotbert Moro and Ambros Wilhelmer: *Aus dem Musikgeschichten Kärnterns.* Klagenfurt, 1956.
Charlotte Moscheles: *Life of Moscheles,* translated by A. D. Coleridge. 2 vols. London, 1873.

John H. Mueller: *The American Symphony Orchestra*. John Calder, London, 1958.
Israel V. Nestiev: *Prokofiev*, translated by Florence Jonas, introduction by Nicolas Slonimsky. Stanford and Oxford University Press, London, 1951.
Ernest Newman: *The Life of Richard Wagner*. 4 vols. Cassel, London, 1933–6.
Musical Studies. John Lane, the Bodley Head, London, 1905.
Joseph d'Ortigue: *Le Balcon de l'Opéra*. Paris, 1832.
Alan Peacock and Ronald Weir: *The Composer in the Market Place*. Faber Music, London, 1975.
Eberhard Preussner: *Die Bürgerliche Musikkultur*. Bärenreiter, 2 vols. Cassel, 1950.
L. Ramaan: *Franz Liszt, artist and man*, translated by E. Cordery, London, 1882.
Nikolai Rimsky-Korsakov: *My Musical Life*, translated by A. Jaffe. Knopf, New York, 1942.
Alec Robertson and Denis Stevens (editors): *The Pelican History of Music*. Penguin Books, Harmondsworth, 1968. Volume 3.
Roland-Manuel (editor): *Histoire de la Musique*. Encyclopédie de la Pleiade. 2 vols. Paris, 1960, 1963.
Ernst Roth: *The Business of Music*. Cassell, London, 1965.
John F. Russell and J. H. Elliott: *The Brass Band Movement*. Dent, London, 1936.
Walter Salmen (editor): *Der Sozialstatus der Berufmusikers von 17 bis 19 Jahrhunderts*. Bärenreiter, Cassel, 1971.
Friedrich Schmidt: *Das Musikleben des bürgerlichen Gesellschaft Leipzig. Musikalisches Magazin Heft*. Hermann Beyer und Söhne, Langenzenn, 1912.
Arnold Schoenberg: *Letters*, edited by Erwin Stein, translated Eithne Walker and Ernst Lain. Faber, London, 1964.
Harold C. Schonberg: *The Great Pianists*. Gollancz, London, 1964.
Willi Schuh: *Schweizer Musikbuch*. Atlantis Verlag, Zürich, 1939.
Georg Schunemann: *Geschichte des Dirigierens*. Breitkopf und Härtel, Leipzig, 1913.
Karl Senn: *Der Innsbrucker Musikverein*.
G. Bernard Shaw: *The Perfect Wagnerite*. London, Constable, 1898.
London Music, 1888–89 as heard by Corno di Bassetto. Constable, London, 1937.
Music in London, 1890–94. 3 vols. Constable, London, 1932.
H. Sievers: *Die Musik in Hannover*. Sponholz Druckerei, Hanover, 1961.
Otakar Sourek: *Antonin Dvořák: Letters and Reminiscences*. Translated Roberta Finlayson Samsour, Artis, Prague, 1954.
Georg Sowa: *Anfänge Institutioneller Musikerziehung in Deutschland. 1800–1843*. Gustav Bosse Verlag, Regensburg, 1973.
Louis Spohr: *Autobiography*. English translation, London, 1878.
Vladimir Stassov: *Selected Essays on Music*, translated by Florence Jonas. Cresset Press, London, 1965.
Vladimir Stepanek, Bohumil Karasek and Ladislav Sip: *Zur Geschichte der Tschechischen und Slowakischen Musik*. Orbis, Prague, 1959.
Bence Szabolski: *The Twilight of Ferenc Liszt*. Hungarian Academy of Science, Budapest, 1959.
A. J. P. Taylor: *The Habsburg Monarchy*. Hamish Hamilton, London, 1970.
Alexander Wheelock Thayer: *The Life of Ludwig van Beethoven*, edited by H. E. Krehbiel, New York, 1921–5. New edition, introduction by Alan Pryse Jones, Centaur Press, New York, 1960.
Francis Toye: *Giuseppe Verdi*. Heineman, London, 1931.
Rossini, a Study in Tragi-Comedy. Heinemann, London, 1934.
Giuseppe Verdi: *Letters*, selected, edited and translated by Charles Osborne. Gollancz, London, 1971.
Richard Wagner: *My Life*. Authorised translation. London, 1963.
Wagner writes from Paris, edited and translated by Robert L. Jacob and Geoffrey Skelton. George Allen and Unwin, London, 1973.
Letters from the Burrell Collection, translated and edited by John N. Burke. Gollancz, London, 1951.
Ernest Walker: *A History of Music in England*. Oxford University Press, 1907. Third edition, revised by J. A. Westrup, Oxford University Press, London, 1952.
Frank Walker: *The Man Verdi*. Dent, London, 1972.
John Warrack: *Weber*. Hamish Hamilton, London, 1968.

Carl Maria von Weber: *Ausgewählte Schriften*. Edited by W. Altmann, Regensburg,
      1928.
Hildergard Weber: *Das Museum; einhundertfünfzig Jahre Frankfurter Konzertleben*.
      Verlag Waldemar Kramer, Frankfurt-am-Main, 1958.
Ludwig Wegele: *Musik in der Reichstadt Augsburg*. Verlag Die Brigge, Augsburg,
      1965.
Felix Weingartner: *On Conducting*, translated by Ernest Newman. Leipzig, 1925.
Herbert Weinstock: *Donizetti*. Methuen, London, 1964.
Alexander Werth: *Musical Uproar in Moscow*. Turnstile Press, London, 1949.
Pamela Weston: *Clarinet Virtuoi of the Past*. Robert Hale, London, 1972.
David Wooldridge: *The Conductor's World*. Barrie and Rockliff, London, 1970.
Percy M. Young: *The Concert Tradition*. Routledge and Kegan Paul, London,
      1965.

Index